Lecture Notes in Computer Scie

Edited by G. Goos and J. Hartmanis

G. Rozenberg (Ed.)

Advances in Petri Nets 1992

Springer-Verlag
Berlin Heidelberg New York
London Paris Tokyo
Hong Kong Barcelona
Budapest

Series Editors

Gerhard Goos
Universität Karlsruhe
Postfach 69 80
Vincenz-Priessnitz-Straße 1
W-7500 Karlsruhe, FRG

Juris Hartmanis
Department of Computer Science
Cornell University
5149 Upson Hall
Ithaca, NY 14853, USA

Volume Editor

Grzegorz Rozenberg
Department of Computer Science, Leiden University
P. O. Box 9512, 2300 RA Leiden, The Netherlands

CR Subject Classification (1991): F.1-3, C.1-2, D.4, I.6

ISBN 3-540-55610-9 Springer-Verlag Berlin Heidelberg New York
ISBN 0-387-55610-9 Springer-Verlag New York Berlin Heidelberg

Printed in Germany

Typesetting: Camera ready by author/editor
Printing and binding: Druckhaus Beltz, Hemsbach/Bergstr.
45/3140-543210 - Printed on acid-free paper

Preface

The main aims of the series of volumes "Advances in Petri Nets" are:
(1) to present to the "outside" scientific community a fair picture of recent advances in the area of Petri nets, and
(2) to encourage those interested in the applications and the theory of concurrent systems to take a closer look at Petri nets and then join the group of researchers working in this fascinating and challenging area.

The ESPRIT Basic Research Action DEMON (DEsign Methods based On Nets) has been a focus of developments within the Petri nets community for the last three years. The research done within DEMON spans many areas of Petri nets; it has certainly helped to consolidate and unify the knowledge about Petri nets, and it has led to many new developments. Hence, it fits the aims of "Advances" to have a special volume presenting some of the achievements of DEMON.

The papers presented in this volume have been selected from 24 papers submitted to "Advances" in response to a call for papers directed to participants of DEMON. The papers went through the refereeing process, and those that were accepted appear in this volume in a revised form.

This volume contains technical contributions giving insight into a number of major achievements of the DEMON project. It also contains four survey papers covering important research areas: basic net models and modular net classes, structural techniques in performance analysis of Petri net models, recognizable languages of infinite traces, and equivalence notions for net based systems. These surveys certainly help the reader to get an overview of a broad range of research taking place in the area of Petri nets and related models of concurrent systems. The volume begins with a description of DEMON given by its coordinator E. Best.

I want to thank E. Best for his help in preparing this volume. Special thanks go to the referees of the papers in this volume who very often are responsible for considerable improvements. The referees were: L. Aceto, M. Ajmone Marsan, E. Astesiano, J. Baeten, J. Billington, W. Brauer, M. Broy, A. Corradini, F. De Cindio, Ph. Darondeau, P. Degano, J. Desel, R. Devillers, C. Diamantini, V. Diekert, H. Ehrig, J. Esparza, U. Goltz, R. Gorrieri, J. Hall, A. Heise, R. Henderson, R. Hopkins, B. Keck, A. Kiehn, E. Kindler, M. Koutny, H.J. Kreowski, M. Kwiatkowska, M. Latteux, G. Mauri, A. Mazurkiewicz, M. Nielsen, L. Petrucci, M. Pinna, A. Poigné, L. Pomello, W. Reisig, G. Reggio, B. Rozoy, C. Simone, E. Smith, P. Starke, P. Taylor, W. Thomas, W. Vogler, K. Voss, D.N. Yankelevitch, W. Zuberek. The editor is also indebted to Mrs. M. Boon-van der Nat and Dr. A. Deutz for their help in the preparation of this volume.

Leiden, April 1992

G. Rozenberg
Editor

Table of Contents

Technical Contributions

Surveys

Esprit Basic Research Action 3148 D-E-M-O-N
(Design Methods Based on Nets)
— Aims, Scope and Achievements —

Quote of the Initial Statement of DEMON (1989)

The overall aim of the Action is to lay the foundation for the eventual development of a design calculus for concurrent systems based on the principles of Petri net theory. These principles concern basic characteristics of concurrent systems, such as decentralisation, distinctions between concurrency and nondeterminism, and an integrated view of the interplay between the states and the transitions of a system. (...) As the central net theoretic foundation for the envisaged calculus, structuring and modularity techniques are to be developed which include abstraction, refinement, composition, preservation of properties both within and across levels of abstraction, appropriate notions of equivalence and implementation, and analysis techniques, addressing the spectrum of techniques needing to be covered by a design calculus. The development of these techniques will involve original research, but shall also be guided by, and have an impact on, experience with the design of concurrent systems and existing other approaches to the modelling of concurrent systems. It shall be accompanied by the evaluation of case studies. Our proposal is thus not only meant as a further development located purely within net theory, but also as a widening of its scope as well as an exploitation of its generality, since we propose to take into account insights from complementary approaches in an important way. (...) Having identified the importance of making progress in investigating and developing the above issues (in particular, modularity), the Action proposes to concentrate on the following work:

- *The development of one or more classes of structured Petri nets which feature abstraction, refinement and composition operators, along with appropriate notions of equivalence, logic / algebraic calculi and analysis techniques. Such classes of nets would form the core of an eventual design calculus, bridging the gap which presently exists between applications of Petri nets as a non-formal graphical tool in the early stages of the design process, and applications of analytical techniques used in the final stages of the design process.*
- *The careful evaluation of the relationship to various complementary approaches aimed at similar goals, such as CSP (...), COSY, CCS, trace theory and event structures, with the aim of ensuring translatability, compatibility, and the transferral of useful techniques in both directions. (...)*
- *The investigation of the Petri net semantics of existing programming languages such as Occam, along with the transferral of techniques as described above. This investigation is done with two aims in mind: (i) to make explicit the connection to the programming of large and complex systems, and (ii) to study the possible definition of a Petri net based programming notation to provide a convenient way of expressing Petri net implementations.*
- *The study of a number of test cases to support the proposed conceptual techniques.*
- *The study of a selected number of existing design methods such as abstract data types, statecharts and logic formalisms. This is done with the aim of studying what new aspects are introduced in such methods by the consideration of true concurrency semantics; how they can be related to the Petri net framework to be developed; and how the resulting methods can be applied fruitfully in actual design. (...)*
- *The study of a number of specific and important issues which are of great practical importance but not yet theoretically fully understood. These concepts include priorities (Occam, Ada), exception handling (Ada), the compositionality aspects of buffered communication and dynamic system structure. The aim of this investigation is not just to study the semantics of these concepts in terms of the structured net classes, but also, conversely, to obtain criteria by which the usefulness of these classes can be evaluated.*

The above work of the Action will be structured into two main strands of activity, covering respectively the central Petri net theory work and the work on related areas, but strongly interrelated both in time and in contents. The first strand consists of a common effort to define new classes of modular Petri nets which are provided with means for composition, abstraction and refinement, thus establishing a common framework. In the second strand, more specialised work will be done both as motivation and input for work on the first strand, or as a result and application of it.

(End of quote)

In line with this work programme, the first, so-called 'core' strand of DEMON was intended to carry out Petri net based research that would lead to the required net classes, equivalence relations and proof methods. Strand I was accordingly organised into three Working Groups, WGs 1, 2 and 3. The second, so-called 'supporting' strand was intended to carry out work that would interface with the needs of practice and with related models. Originally, this strand was organised into seven Working Groups, but it soon became apparent (and was instigated by DEMON's reviewers) that the combination of some of these WGs would be sensible. Presently, Strand II consists of three Working Groups, WGs 4, 5 and 6:

Strand I: Working Group 1: **Structured Classes of Nets.**
Working Group 2: **Equivalence and Simulation Relations.**
Working Group 3: **Algebra and Proof Methods.**

Strand II: Working Group 4: **Abstract Models.**
Working Group 5: **High Level Nets, Case Studies and Specification.**
Working Group 6: **Programming and Related Issues.**

The DEMON Consortium and its boundary conditions have had the following shape:

DEMON Partner	**Country**	**Rôle**
Gesellschaft für Mathematik und Datenverarbeitung	D	Coordinator
Université Paris-Sud	F	Partner
Groupe Bull, Paris	F	Partner
Università degli Studi di Milano	I	Partner
Technische Universität München	D	Partner
Rijksuniversiteit te Leiden	NL	Partner
Universität Passau	D	Partner
University of Newcastle upon Tyne	GB	Partner
Université Libre de Bruxelles	B	Partner
Universidad de Zaragoza	E	Partner
Universität Hildesheim	D	Subcontractor.

Start date: June 19, 1989
End date: March 18, 1992 **Budget: ECU 731 500 . -**

Result Summary

This section is organised WG-wise. Its purpose is to provide a reasonably complete picture of the results of DEMON. However, the reader will *not* find all of the topics addressed in this section to be covered by the papers contained in this volume; information or further reading is provided by the list of references in the next section.

In addition to its original tasks (and not contained in the above quotation), DEMON has intended to produce survey and tutorial papers on some of the topics that are important to its goals. This volume contains three of these survey, while two earlier surveys (on refinements in Petri nets, and on structure theory of free choice nets, respectively) can be found in the Advances in Petri Nets 1990 (Springer Lecture Notes in Computer Science Vol.483).

Working Group 1: Structured Classes of Nets

Approach

The task of WG-1 was the definition of structured classes of nets starting from 'primitive' nets. More precisely, the aim of the group was to obtain an algebra in the mathematical sense, i.e., a carrier set (of nets) together with a set of operations (on nets). The pursuit of this goal has been constrained from two sides. The requirement to provide compositional semantics on the elementary Petri net level has tended to restrain the operators under consideration. The requirement that DEMON's net classes should form a domain for the semantics of languages with data, data sharing, communication etc. has tended to demand more, and more powerful, operators.

The WG has solved this problem by adopting a two–level approach. On the lower level, a small set of primitive operators indigenous to Petri nets have been defined: adding a place or a transition, and removing a place or a transition. On the higher level, more complex operations have been defined which, on the one hand, are based on the primitive operations of the lower level, but, on the other hand, are distinctly oriented towards the requirements of Strand II. This algebra has been christened the 'Petri Box Calculus' (PBC). WG-6 has built a finite model based on a class of high level nets.

Important cooperation has been with Working Groups 2, 3, 4 and 6. WGs 2 and 4 have provided motivation and basic work on equivalences; for instance, these WGs have paved the way for the notion of transition refinement that is presently adopted in the Box algebra. Both WGs presently continue to provide the ground work for two important further developments: the adoption of a weaker notion of equality between Boxes, and the definition of a compositional partial order semantics. WG-6 has strongly influenced the particular shape of our operators which are, partly, novel. In particular, multi-label communication, recursion and iteration have been influenced by WG-6. Conversely, WG-6 has profitted from the Box algebra by being able to define a small programming notation (with more expressiveness than occam) and its compositional Petri net semantics. Moreover, WGs 4 and 6 have done three nontrivial case studies specifically based on the notation. WGs 3 and 6 have provided the structured operational semantics for the Box algebra which is the main vehicle used so far in proofs of case studies.

Main achievements

- A survey of existing notions of net classes.
- Categorical setting at the lower level.
- A powerful algebra at the higher level, in particular as regards communication.
- A wealth of structural algebraic laws.
- Fixpoint semantics for general recursion.
- Indigenous operational semantics (in cooperation with WGs 3 and 6).

Working Group 2: Equivalence and Simulation Relations

Approach

The task of Working Group 2 was the definition of equivalence and simulation notions for models of concurrency with special emphasis on Petri nets. Important questions to be addressed were the study of equivalences based on partial orders, as well as the study of the practical relevance of the defined notions. The Working Group has approached its task by sampling existing equivalence notions (from the large existing set) and producing two surveys. Moreover, the WG has investigated the principles which underly the fact that certain ways of strengthening non-congruences (or non-behaviour preserving equivalences) would yield congruences (or behaviour-preserving congruences), while others would not, and has found a number of generally applicable methods to create one's favourite behaviour-preservation equivalence. Moreover, the WG has selected a few candidate congruences which are ready to be transported to the Box algebra framework. The transportation appears to be possible in a smooth way for two reasons: First, both WGs have based their investigations on labelled (rather than unlabelled) nets. Second, some preconditions of WG-2 theorems are actually theorems of WG-1.

In proving the desired congruence and behaviour-preservation results, WG-2 encountered (and overcame) severe technical difficulties. Apart from this work, WG-2 has also examined questions of decidability and state-based equivalences. Cooperation has been mainly with WGs 1 and 4.

Main achievements

- Categorisation and evaluation of equivalences.
- New results on congruences (for instance, for the first time taking into account systems with silent actions).
- Development of principles to define 'good' equivalences.
- New results on decidability.
- Ground work for research on state refinement and state-based equivalences.

Working Group 3: Algebra and Proof Methods

Approach

The task of Working Group 3 was the development of verification and synthesis techniques for structured nets. Classical Petri net techniques had to be adapted and extended, and their application to the verification of concurrent programs (through the net semantics defined by Working Group 6) investigated. The approach of Working Group 3 has been strongly centered upon efficiency: fast algorithms applicable only under certain constraints have been given more consideration than inefficient algorithms of wide applicability.

One line of approach has been to find very fast algorithms (polynomial time in the size of the *net*) for the checking of various important properties such as deadlock freeness. In accordance with known negative complexity results, this was expected to be possible only for subclasses of nets. The class of free choice nets has been the favoured choice for this WG, because a number of beautiful results could be found which establish strong links between the structure and the behaviour of a net, in all cases leading to the desired PTIME algorithms for a number of properties. WG-3 has developed this theory to the extent that a monograp on the subject is being currently written. WG-3 has also used and applied this theory to the problem of performance analysis of free choice systems (and their subclasses).

However, this theory, nontrivial though it is, has left WG-3 dissatisfied for several reasons. First, it is geared to unlabelled free choice nets and is thus at the same level as what has been called 'primitive' operations above (i.e. removing and adding of places and transitions – although these are obviously not the only structural operations employed in free choice theory). It seems very hard to adapt the theory to labelled nets in general, and to the operations of the PBC in particular. Indeed, WG-3 has also produced several 'impossibility' results of the nature that certain simple Box expressions cannot be simulated by free choice nets. A second reason for dissatisfaction was that only specific properties could be checked, rather than a class of properties.

WG-3 has sought and found two ways to overcome these limitations. Firstly, the WG has investigated the generalisation of its decision algorithms to semidecision algorithms which are applicable to more general classes of systems. Secondly, the generalisation from specific properties to classes of properties involves the definition of a logic and the consideration of model checking. WG-3 has approached model checking from two different angles.

(1) One of the developments has been to investigate under which circumstances model checking is feasible in polynomial time in the size of the *net* (rather than the transition system). Two recent results indicate that PTIME model checking is possible for a nontrivial class of nets (safe conflict free nets) and that the approach can be used to obtain fast model checking for persistent nets. This approach is beneficial not only by its generality, but also because persistency is a property that can be transferred immediately to labelled nets and to the PBC (as opposed to the free choice property which is much more indigenous to nets). In these results, the use of partial orders as defined in net theory (i.e. as alternations of local states and local transitions) plays a vital rôle, vindicating one of the presumptions of the project that concerns the exploitation of the strong points of Petri nets.

(2) A second development has concerned model checking in general. WG-3 has produced the notion of 'optimal simulation' which concerns the minimum amount of simulations that have to be carried out such that one still gets a correct model checker. This work is also based on concurrency semantics, albeit on the step sequences rather than on the processes of a system.

Almost all fast algorithms – be they decision algorithms, performance analysis algorithms, semidecision algorithms or algorithms for model checking of persistent nets – are based on linear algebraic and Linear Programming methods. This means that when the methods are eventually transferred to the Box expression level, they will rely on the latter's Petri Box semantics.

Main achievements

- Well–rounded structure theory of free choice nets.
- Application of structure theory to performance analysis.
- Judicious application of linear algebraic and Linear Programming methods to obtain fast algorithms.
- Various generalisations and extensions: semidecision algorithms; model checking.

Working Group 4: Abstract Models

The task of Working Group 4 was the study and extension of abstract models for concurrency – in particular Mazurkiewicz's traces – and the study of the relationships between these models and more 'concrete' models – several classes of Petri nets and process algebras.

The Working Group has obtained results on a wide spectrum of abstract models. Not only trace theory has been studied, also models such as asynchronous automata, event structures, vector synchronized systems and transition systems have been considered. Trace theory has been very thoroughly studied; several extensions – context-sensitive traces, comtraces, infinite traces – have been considered, which bring traces closer to distributed languages and extend the range of phenomena that can be modelled by the theory.

There has been interaction with WG-6 and WG-1 on action refinement and on implementations of the handshake synchronisation. Some of the work items have been carried out in cooperation with other groups (in particular, connections between free choice nets and process algebras with WG-3, research on CCS/CSP-like structuring operations with WG-1 and WG-6).

Main achievements

- Detailed study of several extensions of trace theory.
- Characterisation of processes formalised through dependency graphs.

- Advances in the recognizability problem for classical and infinite traces.
- Research on the trace languages of net classes.
- Strong relationships between elementary nets, transition systems and event structures.
- Study of action refinement in event structures.
- Study of vector synchronisation mechanisms and their effects.

Working Group 5: High Level Nets, Case Studies and Specifications

Working Group 5 was dealing with two tasks:

- Case studies. Test cases should be studied as motivation for the development of proper structuring techniques.
- Development of Specification and Requirements Engineering Techniques. Techniques for expressing formal specifications, for deriving formal specifications from semi-formal requirements and for relating specifications to each other had to be developed. Work on statecharts and logical formalisms was planned.

The Working Group has focussed its efforts on the first two phases of software development, namely the specification of requirements and the design of an operational model (the third being the actual production of code). The Group has studied logical formalisms for the requirement specification and Petri net based formalisms for the operational design. In particular, since the latter had to support data structures, high-level nets have been considered. The work on case studies has partly been done in cooperation with WGs 4 and 6.

Main achievements

- Design and study of new partial order logics.
- Design and development of the specification languages OBJSA and CO-OPN.
- Connections between high level nets and functional approaches.

Working Group 6: Programming and Related Issues

Approach

Working Groups 6 has addressed its tasks extremely pragmatically, one by one as mentioned in the DEMON work programme. In addition, WG-6 has also developed (in cooperation with WGs 1 and 3) the operational semantics for the Box calculus, and WG-6 has carried out two case studies using the calculus. Furthermore, WG-6 has defined a class of high level nets with compositionality properties and has given a semantics for the full calculus in it (the only restriction being that recursive calls must be surrounded by call/return actions).

Main achievements

- Operational semantics for the Box calculus.
- Two nontrivial case studies using the calculus. One of them includes the sematics of unbounded buffer communication by basic means (i.e. in terms of elementary Petri nets).

- Petri net semantics of occam using a version of the PBC, including all semantically significant features.
- Definition of a basic Petri net based programming notation and its denotational Petri Box semantics. This includes the semantics of handshake and bounded buffer communication.
- The development of an alternative semantic model in terms of FIFO nets for unbounded buffer communication.
- Petri net semantics of static and dynamic priorities, and development of a theory generalising causal partial orders which captures the concurrency in prioritised systems better than is otherwise possible.
- Compositional high level net semantics of general recursion.
- Investigations on dynamic structure, including the semantics of dynamic processor allocation and net modelling.

All Working Groups have made considerable progress in their respective tasks. This progress has shown a decisive tendency to converge; strong links can already be discerned. Combining their results into a single framework is within reach. The combination can have the form of a unified theory, and of a tool that implements the algebra and its semantics together with the analysis algorithms.

Acknowledgements

All DEMON-s have expended very considerable work on behalf of the project's goals.
May future readers appreciate their work.

Grzegorz Rozenberg, in his rôles both as a DEMON member and as the Editor of the Advances, has provided enormous support.

The reviewers of DEMON, Jaco de Bakker, Robin Milner, Joseph Sifakis and Glynn Winskel, have spent much effort in exerting a beneficial influence on the course of the project.

The Hildesheim Group consisting of Javier Esparza, Sabine Karmrodt, Hans-Günther Linde, Holger Schirnick and Thomas Thielke have helped in many ways, not least in preparing this overview.

Last and closing a cycle, Esprit Basic Research Management – in particular, Georges Metakides and Michel Bosco – are acknowledged for their financial support and unfailing encouragement.

Eike Best, Hildesheim, March 1992.

DEMON Literature List

[1] Eike Best, Fiorella De Cindio and Richard Hopkins: *DEMON – an ESPRIT Basic Research Action (No.3148)*. EATCS Bulletin No.41, 87–103 (June 1990).

[2] Eike Best: *Design Methods Based on Nets.* Advances in Petri Nets 1989 (ed. G.Rozenberg), Springer Lecture Notes in Computer Science Vol.424, 487–506 (1990).

[3] Volker Diekert: *Combinatorics on Traces.* Habilitation (München 1989), Springer Lecture Notes in Computer Science Vol.454 (1990). (with ASMICS)

[4] Javier Esparza: *Structure Theory of Free Choice Petri Nets.* Dissertation (Zaragoza, June 90).

[5] Younes Souissi: *Property Preservation by Composition of Petri Nets; Extension to FIFO Nets and Application to Communication Protocols.* Dissertation (Paris, 1990).

[6] Elisabeth Pelz: *Réseaux et Logique.* These d'État (Paris, 1990).

[7] Luca Bernardinello and Fiorella De Cindio: *A Survey of Basic Net Models and Modular Net Classes.* Revised version (1991). This volume.

[8] Wilfried Brauer: *Graphs, Automata, Petri Nets.* Advanced Information Processing, Springer Verlag (ed. H. Schwärtzel, I. Mizin (1990)).

[9] Einar Smith: *On Net Systems Generated by Process Foldings.* Draft Paper (June 1990). In: Advances in Petri Nets, Springer LNCS (1991), pp.253–276.

[10] Wilfried Brauer, Robert Gold and Walter Vogler: *A Survey of Behaviour and Equivalence Preserving Refinements of Petri Nets.* In: Advances in Petri Nets 1990, Springer LNCS Vol.483, 1–46 (1990).

[11] Rob J. van Glabbeek and Ursula Goltz: *Refinement of Actions in Causality Based Models.* Arbeitspapiere der GMD Nr. 428 (Jan. 1990), in: Proc. of REX Workshop on Stepwise Refinement of Distributed Systems, Springer Lecture Notes in Computer Science (1989), 267–300.

[12] Jörg Desel: *On Abstractions of Nets.* Report TUM, SFB–Bericht Nr. 342/2/90 B (April 1990). In: Advances in Petri Nets 91, Springer LNCS, pp.78–92.

[13] Walter Vogler: *Failures Semantics of Petri Nets and the Refinement of Places and Transitions.* Report TUM-I9003 (January 1990), published [27,99].

[14] Robert Gold and Walter Vogler: *Quality Criteria for Partial Order Semantics of Place/Transition Systems.* Report TUM-I9004, (January 1990), Extended Abstract in: Proc. of MFCS'90 (ed. B.Rovan), LNCS Vol.452, 306–312 (1990).

[15] Elisabeth Pelz: *Normalisation of Place/Transition Systems Preserves Net Behaviour.* Rapport LRI (1990), to appear in RAIRO.

[16] Elisabeth Pelz: *Place/Transition Systems: Concurrent Behaviour and Logic.* Rapport LRI No. 571 (1990), in: Journées Mathématiques–Informatiques du CIRM, Marseille, 5.–7-Nov 1990. Modified version accepted at the European Joint Conference on Engineering System Design and Analysis, under the changed title *A Problem in System Design: From Behaviour Oriented Specifications to Net Models* (June 1991).

[17] Lucia Pomello: *Refinement of Concurrent Systems Based on Local State Transformation.* Proc. of REX Workshop on Stepwise Refinement of Distr. Systems: Models, Formalism, Correctness, Lecture Notes in Computer Science, Springer Verlag (1989), 641–668.

[18] Lucia Pomello and Carla Simone: *Concurrent Systems as Local State Transformation Algebras: the Case of Elementary Net Systems.* Proc. of the 3rd Italian Conf. on Th. Comp. Sci, Nov. 89 (eds. A. Bertoni, C. Böhm, P. Miglioli).

[19] Lucia Pomello and Carla Simone: *A Preorder of Concurrent Systems.* DEMON Deliverable (1990).

[20] Lucia Pomello and Carla Simone: *A State Transformation Preorder over a Class of EN Systems.* In: Advances in Petri Nets (1990), pp.436–454.

[21] Giorgio De Michelis: *Domains of EN Systems.* 2nd Workshop on Concurrency and Compositionality, San Miniato (Feb./March 1990), Ext. Abstr.

[22] Eike Best, Raymond Devillers, Astrid Kiehn and Lucia Pomello: *Fully Concurrent Bisimulation.* Technical Report LIT-202, Univ. Bruxelles (July 1989). Appeared in Acta Informatica Vol.28 with the changed title: *Concurrent Bisimulation in Petri Nets,* 231–264 (1991). (with CEDISYS)

[23] Raymond Devillers: *Maximality Preserving Bisimulation.* Technical Report LIT-214, ULB (March 90), to appear in TCS.

[24] H. J. Hoogeboom and G. Rozenberg: *Diamond Properties of State Spaces of Elementary Net Systems.* Report 89-18, Univ. of Leiden (December 1989). Fundamenta Informaticae XIV, 287–300 (1991).

[25] Mogens Nielsen, Grzegorz Rozenberg and P. S. Thiagarajan: *Behavioural Notions for Elementary Net Systems.* Distributed Computing 4: 45-57 (90). (with CEDISYS)

[26] Mogens Nielsen, Grzegorz Rozenberg and P. S. Thiagarajan: *Elementary Transition Systems.* Technical Report, Univ. Leiden 90 - 13 (May 1990), to appear in TCS (Proc. of San Miniato) (1992). (with CEDISYS)

[27] W. Vogler: *Failures Semantics Based on Interval Semiwords is a Congruence for Refinement.* Extended abstract in Proc. of STACS'90, Springer LNCS Vol.415, 285–297 (1990). Full paper in Distributed Computing 4: 139–162 (1991).

[28] J. M. Colom and M. Silva: *Convex Geometry and Semiflows in P/T- Nets.* In: Advances in Petri Nets (1990), pp.79–112.

[29] J. M. Colom and M. Silva: *Improving the Linearly Based Characterisation of P/T-Nets.* In: Advances in Petri Nets (1990), pp.113–145.

[30] J. M. Couvreur and J. Martínez: *Linear Invariants in Commutative High Level Nets.* In: Advances in Petri Nets (1990), pp.146–164.

[31] J. Esparza and M. Silva: *Circuits, Handles, Bridges and Nets.* In: Advances in Petri Nets (1990), pp.210–242.

[32] Eike Best and Jörg Desel: *Partial Order Behaviour and Structure of Petri Nets.* Formal Aspects of Computing Vol. 2(2), 123–138 (1990).

[33] Ryszard Janicki and Maciej Koutny: *Net Implementation of Optimal Simulation.* Proc. of 11th PN Conference, 295–314, Paris (1990). Also TR 90–08, Dept. of Computer Science and Systems, McMaster University (1990). Also in Advances in Petri Nets (1991) with the changed title: *Optimal Simulations, Nets and Reachability Graphs*, pp.205–226.

[34] Ryszard Janicki and Maciej Koutny: *Optimal Simulation for the Verification of Concurrent Systems.* Technical Report 89–05, McMaster (1989), submitted.

[35] Younes Souissi: *Deterministic Systems of Sequential Processes.* Proc. of 11th PN Conference, Paris (1990).

[36] Alain Finkel and Laure Petrucci: *Propriétés de la composition/decomposition de réseaux de Petri et leurs graphes de couvertures.* Rapport de recherches, MASI 90 - 24 (May 90), Submitted paper. English version: *Verification of Net Properties by Composition / Decomposition.* Rapport de Recherche CEDRIC No.91–06 (1991).

[37] Laure Petrucci: *Comparing Finkel's and Jensen's Reduction Techniques to Build Covering Trees for Coloured Nets.* Petri Net Newsletter 36 (August 1990). Also: Research Report CEDRIC with the title: *Smaller Covering Trees for Coloured Nets and Semi-covering Trees for Algebraic Nets* (January 1991).

[38] Gérard Berthelot, Alain Finkel, Colette Johnen and Laure Petrucci: *A Generic Example for Testing Performance of Reachability and Covering Graph Construction Algorithms.* PN Newsletter 35 (April 1990).

[39] Jörg Desel: *Reduction and Design of Well-Behaved Concurrent Systems.* Proc. of CONCUR'90, Springer Lecture Notes in Computer Science Vol.458, 166–181 (1990).

[40] J. M. Colom and M. Silva: *On Liveness Analysis Through Linear Algebraic Techniques.* Draft Paper (1990).

[41] J. Esparza and M. Silva: *On the Analysis and Synthesis of Free Choice Systems.* In: Advances of Petri Nets'90, Springer LNCS (1990), pp.243–286.

[42] J. Esparza, E. Best and M. Silva: *Minimal Deadlocks in Free Choice Nets.* Hildesheimer Informatik-Berichte 1/89 (June 1989).

[43] J. Esparza and M. Silva: *Compositional Synthesis of Live and Bounded Free Choice Nets.* Report GISI 90.06, Univ. of Zaragoza (March 1990). To appear in Proc. of CONCUR'91, Springer LNCS (August 1991).

[44] J. Esparza and M. Silva: *Top-Down Synthesis of Free Choice Nets.* 11th Petri Net Conference, Paris (June 1990), also in: Advances in Petri Nets 1991, Springer LNCS (1991), pp.118–139. An extended and revised version of this paper is [197].

[45] J. Esparza and M. Silva: *A Polynomial-time Algorithm to Decide Liveness of Bounded Free Choice Nets.* Hildesheimer Informatik–Berichte 12/90 (December 1990). To appear in TCS (1992).

[46] J. Esparza: *Synthesis Rules for Petri Nets, and How they Lead to New Results.* Proc. of CONCUR'90, Springer LNCS Vol.458, 182–198 (1990).

[47] Eike Best, Ludmila Cherkasova, Jörg Desel and Javier Esparza: *Characterisation of Home States in Free Choice Nets.* Hildesheimer Informatik-Berichte Nr. 9 (September 90), Ext. Abstr. in Semantics of Concurrency, Springer Workshops in Computer Science Series (eds. M.Z.Kwiatkowska, M.W.Shields and R.Thomas), 16–20 (1990). Published in [96] and [97].

[48] Ursula Goltz: *CCS and Petri Nets.* Proc. of the Spring School on Semantics of Concurrency, Springer Lecture Notes in Computer Science Vol.469 (ed. I. Guessarien), 334–357 (1990).

[49] Rob J. van Glabbeek and Ursula Goltz: *A Deadlock-sensitive Congruence for Action Refinement.* SFB-Bericht Nr.342/23/90A, Technische Universität München (1990). Also: Invited contribution to the 3rd Workshop on Concurrency and Compositionality, Goslar, March 5–8 (1991). Extended abstract in [160].

[50] R. Janicki and M. Koutny: *On some Implementations of Optimal Simulation.* TR 90–07, Dept. of Computer Science and Systems, McMaster Univ. (1990). To appear in Proc. of Computer-Aided Verification Workshop, Rutgers Univ. (June 1990) (ed. R.Kurshan).
A short version of this paper will appear in the Abridged Proceedings of CAV with the changed title: *Using Optimal Simulations to Reduce Reachability Graphs* (also: TR 90–13, McMaster (1990)).

[51] N. W. Keesmaat and H. C. M. Kleijn: *Net- Based Control vs. Rational Control in Vector Controlled Concurrent Systems.* TR 89–21, Univ. Leiden (December 1989), submitted paper.

[52] Walter Vogler: *A Generalisation of Trace Theory.* Report TUM I 9018 (April 90), to appear in RAIRO.

[53] Brigitte Rozoy: *On Traces, Partial Order Sets and Recognizability.* Rapport de Recherche, LRI No. 558 (March 90). Proceedings ISCIS V, Cappadocia (1990). (with ASMICS)

[54] Brigitte Rozoy and P. S. Thiagarajan: *Event Structure and Trace Monoids.* To appear in TCS. (with ASMICS)

[55] Brigitte Rozoy: *On Distributed Languages and Models for Distributed Computation.* Rapport de Recherche, LRI 563-90. École de Printemps On the Semantics of Parallelism, Springer LNCS Vol.4669, 434–456 (April 1990). (with ASMICS)

[56] Paul Gastin and Brigitte Rozoy: *The Poset of Infinitary Traces.* Rapport de Recherche, LRI 559-90. Also: TR LITP 91.07 (1991). Accepted for TCS. (with ASMICS)

[57] Paola Bonizzoni, Giancarlo Mauri and Giovanni Pighizzini: *On Infinite Traces.* DSI-Internal Report 72/90; also: Proc. Workshop on Partially Commutative Monoids, TUM Report I9002 (January 1990). (With ASMICS.)

[58] Stefania Jesi, Nicoletta Sabadini and Giovanni Pighizzini: *Probabilistic Finite State Asynchronous Automata.* Proc. Workshop on Partially Commutative Monoids, TUM Report I9002 (January 1990). (With ASMICS.)

[59] Volker Diekert: *Combinatorial Rewriting of Traces.* Proc. of STACS'90, LNCS Vol.415, 138–151 (1990). (with ASMICS)

[60] Rolf Walter: *Specification of the Distributed Termination Problem.* Memorandum of DEMON WG 6 (October 1989).

[61] Dominik Gomm and Rolf Walter: *The Distributed Termination Problem: Formal Solution and Correctness Based on Petri Nets.* To appear in Proc. IMYCS'90 (Aspects and Prospects of TCS), Springer Lecture Notes in Computer Science Vol.464 (ed. Dassow Kelemen), 159–168 (1990).

[62] Eike Best: *Specification of a Flexible Telephone Exchange System.* Memorandum of DEMON WG6 (October 89).

[63] Luca Bernardinello and Lucia Pomello: *A Petri Net Model of a Flexible Telephone Exchange Network.* DEMON Deliverable (June 1990).

[64] Luca Bernardinello, Fiorella De Cindio and Lucia Pomello: *The Lift Example (Specification).* Memorandum of DEMON WG6 (June 1990).

[65] Javier Martínez and Joaquin Ezpeleta: *The Lift Example (Solution).* Memorandum of DEMON WG6 (May 1990).

[66] J. M. Colom, J. Esparza, J. Martínez and M. Silva: *Specification of a Flexible Manufacturing System.* Memorandum of DEMON WG6 (October 1989).

[67] Javier Martiínez and Joaquin Ezpeleta: *The Flexible Manufacturing System (Solution).* Memorandum of DEMON WG6 (May 1990).

[68] Thomas Belzner: *Collected Case Studies.* Memorandum of DEMON WG6 (1989).

[69] Jörg Desel, Wofgang Reisig and Rolf Walter: *The Alternating Bit Protocol.* Petri Net Newsletters 35 (April 1990).

[70] Raymond Devillers: *The Bankers Problem.* Memorandum of DEMON WG6 (1989).

[71] Wofgang Reisig: *Petri Nets and Algebraic Specifications.* SFB-Bericht 342/1/90/B (March 90). Theoretical Computer Science Vol.80, 1–34 (1991)

[72] Wolfgang Reisig: *On a Compositional Semantics for Hierarchies in Petri Nets and Statecharts.* Ext. Abstract, Proc. of the 2nd Workshop on Concurrency and Compositionality, San Miniato.

[73] Antonia Sinachopoulos: *Partial Order Logics for Elementary Net Systems: State and Event Approaches.* Proc. of CONCUR'90, Springer LNCS Vol.458, 442–455 (1990).

[74] Antonia Sinachopoulos and Raymond Devillers: *Partial Order for Axiomatising Concurrent Systems.* Draft paper, submitted.

[75] C. Dimitrovici, U. Hummert and Laure Petrucci: *The Properties of Algebraic Net Schemes in some Semantics.* Rapport de Recherche, LRI 5 (1990), 11th Petri Net Conference, Paris (1990). Also in Advances in Petri Nets (1991) with the title: *Semantics, composition and net properties of algebraic high level nets*, pp93–117.

[76] Eugenio Battiston, Fiorella De Cindio and Giancarlo Mauri: *OBJSA Nets: OBJ and Petri Nets for Specifying Concurrent Systems.* CNR–Progretto Finalizzato Sistemi Informatici e Calcolo Parallelo, TR 4/51(e) (October 1990). To appear in 'Case Studies with OBJ' (ed. D.Coleman, R. Gallimore and J. Goguen), Cambridge University.

[77] Eugenio Battiston: *Definitions for OBJSA Nets.* Draft paper (May 1990). CNR–Progretto Finalizzato Sistemi Informatici e Calcolo Parallelo, Tech. Rep. i.4.21 (October 1990).

[78] Eike Best: *Petri Nets Semantics of* occam *(some thoughts).* Memorandum of DEMON WG8 (November 1989).

[79] Eike Best: *Report of WG8 Meeting of December 7/8, 1989.* Memorandum of DEMON WG8 (December 1989).

[80] Oliver Botti, Fiorella De Cindio, Jon Hall and Richard Hopkins: *A Petri Net Semantics of* occam 2. WG8 Technical Report (June 1990). Technical Report, Computing Laboratory, University of Newcastle upon Tyne (1990).

[81] Oliver Botti and Fiorella De Cindio: *Some Remarks about a Petri Net Model of* occam *using* τ*–transitions.* Technical Report of DEMON WG8 (June 1990).

[82] Eike Best and Maciej Koutny: *Partial Order Semantics of Priority Systems.* Hildesheimer Informatik-Berichte Nr. 6/90 (June 90), to appear in a special volume of TCS (Proc. of San Miniato) under the title *Petri Net Semantics of Priority Systems* (1991).

[83] Richard Hopkins and Jon Hall: *PN^3-Preliminary Notions for a Petri Net Programming Notation: Generalised Communication.* DEMON Technical Report (June 1990 / January 1991).

[84] Axel Poigné: *Towards a Uniform Presentation of Nets.* Arbeitspapiere der GMD Nr.548 (August 1991).

[85] Raymond Devillers: *Interrupts and Exceptions: a Short Introduction and some Clarification.* DEMON WG9 Memorandum (February 1990).

[86] Richard Hopkins: *A Classification of Message Communication in Terms of their Petri Net Representation.* TR of DEMON WG9 (June 1990).

[87] Fiorella De Cindio and Carla Simone: *Petri Nets for Modelling Fault Tolerant Distributed Systems in a Modular and Incremental Way.* Position paper for the 4th ACM SIGOPS European Workshop on Fault Tolerance in Distributed Systems, Bologna (September 1990).

[88] R. Janicki and M. Koutny: *Is there Life Beyond Partial Order Semantics?* TR 90–06, Dept. of Computer Science and Systems, McMaster Univ. (1989).

[89] Ryszard Janicki and Maciej Koutny: *Observing Concurrent Histories.* In: Real–Time Systems, Theory and Applications, H.M.S. Zedan (ed.), Elsevier Publishers B.V. (North Holland), 133–142 (1990). Also: TR-89-06, McMaster Univ. (1989).

[90] R. Janicki and M. Koutny: *Generalised Invariant Semantics of Concurrent Systems.* TR 90–05, McMaster University, Hamilton, Canada (1990).

[91] Ryszard Janicki and Maciej Koutny: *A Bottom–Top Approach to Concurrency Theory. Part I: Observations, Invariants and Paradigms.* Technical Report 90–04, McMaster University, Hamilton, Canada. A short version will appear in the Proc. of AMAST-91 Conference, Iowa City (1991), with the changed title: *Structure of Concurrency.*

[92] Richard Hopkins: *Distributable Nets.* DEMON WG9 Technical Report, also in Advances of Petri Nets 1991, Springer LNCS (1991), pp.161–187.

[93] Richard Hopkins: *A Note on Vator Nets.* DEMON WG9 Memorandum (June 1990).

[94] Marta Pietkiewicz-Koutny: *Modelling Reconfigurability by Petri Nets.* Technical Report, Computing Laboratory, University of Newcastle upon Tyne (June 1991).

[95] J.Fanchon, D.Millot: *Models for Dynamically Placed Concurrent Processes.* Proc. of PARLE-91, Springer LNCS (1991).

[96] Eike Best, Jörg Desel and Javier Esparza: *Traps Characterise Home States in Free Choice Systems*; to appear in a special volume of TCS (Proc. of Leicester Workshop on Semantics for Concurrency) (1991).

[97] Eike Best, Ludmila Cherkasova and Jörg Desel: *Compositional Generation of Home States in Free Choice Systems.* Proc. of STACS'91 (eds. G.Choffrut and M.Jantzen), Springer LNCS Vol.480, 398–409 (1991).

[98] Jörg Desel and Javier Esparza: *Reachability in Reversible Free Choice Systems.* SFB–Bericht Nr. 342/11/90 A, TUM; Shortened version in: Proc. of STACS'91 (eds. G.Choffrut and M.Jantzen), Springer LNCS Vol.480, 384–397 (1991). Extended abstract in [160].

[99] Walter Vogler: *Bisimulation and Action Refinement.* Proc. of STACS'91, Springer LNCS Vol.480 (eds. C.Choffrut, M.Jantzen), 309–321 (1991). Extended abstract in [160].

[100] Volker Diekert: *On the Concatenation of Infinite Traces.* In Proc. of STACS'91 (eds. G.Choffrut, M.Jantzen), Springer LNCS Vol.480, 105–117 (1991). (with ASMICS)

[101] F.Baude and G.Vidal–Naquet: *Actors as a Parallel Programming Model.* In Proc. of STACS'91 (eds. G.Choffrut, M.Jantzen), Springer LNCS Vol.480, 184–195 (1991).

[102] G.Vidal–Naquet and Y.Sami: *Formalisation of the Behaviour of Actors by Coloured Petri Nets, and some Applications.* LRI Report 605 10/90 (1990). To appear in PARLE'91.

[103] R.J.van Glabbeek and U.Goltz: *Equivalences and Refinement.* SFB–Bericht 342/12/90 A, TUM (1990); Proc. of the Spring School on Semantics of Concurrency, Springer Lecture Notes in Computer Science Vol.469 (ed. I. Guessarien), 309–333 (1990).

[104] Y.Souissi: *A Modular Approach for the Validation of Communication Protocols Using FIFO Nets.* Proc. of Xth Int. Symp. on Protocol Specification, Verification and Testing (June 1990).

[105] Nicholas Guelfi: *Classes de Réseaux Structurées: Études, Utilisation et Modifications.* Paris–Orsay (September 1990).

[106] Laure Petrucci: *Techniques d'Analyse des Réseaux de Petri Algébraiques.* Thèse, Paris-Orsay (January 1991).

[107] Javier Campos: *Performance Bounds for Synchronised Queueing Networks.* PhD Thesis, Zaragoza (December 1990).

[108] Javier Campos, José Maria Colom and Manuel Silva: *Improving Throughput Upper Bounds for Net Based Models of Manufacturing Systems.* In: Proc. of IMACS Symposium of Modelling and Control of Technological Systems, Lille (May 1991).

[109] Eike Best: *Partial Order Semantics of Concurrent Programs.* Invited Address at CONCUR'90. Abstract in Proc. of CONCUR'90, Springer LNCS Vol.458, p.1 (1990).

[110] Oliver Botti: *Un modello in reti di Petri per* occam-2. (*A Petri Net Model for* occam-2.) Tesi di Laurea in Computer Science, Dip. Scienze dell'Informazione, Univ. degli Studi di Milano (A.A. 1989/90). (In Italian.)

[111] Eike Best: *Structure and Behaviour of Concurrent Systems: Selected Results of the Esprit Basic Research Action DEMON.* Proc. of the Esprit Conference 1990, Kluwer Publications, 791–803.

[112] Holger Schirnick: *Implementation of a Flexible Telephone Exchange Systems on a Network of SUN Workstations.* Thesis, Hildesheim (February 1991).

[113] Manfred Broy and Thomas Streicher: *Modular Functional Modelling of Petri Nets with Individual Tokens.* This volume.

[114] M.Nielsen, G.Rozenberg and P.S.Thiagarajan: *Elementary Transition Systems and Refinements.* TR 91–04, Univ. of Leiden (1991). (with CEDISYS)

[115] A.Ehrenfeucht and G.Rozenberg: *A Characterisation of Set Representable Labelled Partial 2-Structures through Decompositions.* Acta Informatica 28, 83–94 (1990).

[116] A.Ehrenfeucht, H.J.Hoogeboom and G.Rozenberg: *Combinatorial Properties of Dependency Graphs.* TR 91–11, Univ. of Leiden (1991).

[117] N.W.Keesmaat and H.C.M.Kleijn: *The Effect of Vector Synchronisation: Residue and Loss.* This volume.

[118] L.Bernardinello, L.Pomello and C.Simone: *Categories of EN Systems and Local State Transformation Algebras.* In: [160].

[119] W.Reisig: *The Asynchronous Stack Revisited.* Petri Net Newsletters 36 (August 1990).

[120] Walter Vogler: *Partial Words Versus Processes: a Short Comparison.* This volume.

[121] W.Vogler: *Deciding History Preserving Bisimulation.* To appear in: Proc. of ICALP 1991, Springer LNCS (1990).

[122] J.Fanchon: *Fifo-net Models for Processes with Asynchronous Communication.* Proc. of 12th Int. Conf. on Applications and Theory of Petri Nets, Århus (June 1991) and this volume.

[123] J.Campos, G.Chiola and M.Silva: *Ergodicity and Throughput Bounds of Petri Nets with Unique Consistent Firing Count Vector.* IEEE Transactions on Software Engineering Vol.17 No.2 (February 1991).

[124] A.Sinachopoulos: *The Expressive Power of Partial Order Logics for Elementary Net Systems.* TR LIT–26, Lab. d'Informatique Théorique, Univ. Libre de Bruxelles. Presented at CSL'90 (Heidelberg).

[125] L.Pomello and C.Simone: *A Survey of Equivalence Notions for Net Based Systems.* To appear in Advances in Petri Nets (1991).

[126] E.Battiston: *Una Specifica del Sistema Ascensore con le Reti OBJSA (A Specification of the Lift System Using OBJSA Nets).* CNR-Progretto Finalizzato Sistemi Informatici e Calcolo Parallelo, Tech.Rep. N.4/21 (October 1990). (In Italian.)

[127] E.Battiston, F.De Cindio, G.Mauri and L.Rapanotti: *Morphisms and Minimal Models for OBJSA Net Systems.* CNR-Progretto Finalizzato Sistemi Informatici e Calcolo Parallelo, Tech.Rep. i.4.26 (January 1991). Shorter version in Proc. of 12th Int. Conf. on Applications and Theory of Petri Nets, Gjern (June 1991).

[128] A.Finkel and L.Petrucci: *Avoiding State Explosion by Composition of Minimal Covering Graphs.* Rapport de Recherche CEDRIC 91–09 (1991). In: Proc. of CAV, Aalborg (June 1991).

[129] V.Diekert, P.Gastin and A.Petit: *Recognizable Complex Trace Languages.* Rapport de Recherche No.640, LRI (Feb. 1991). To appear in: Proc. 16th Symposium on Mathematical Foundations of Computer Science, Warszawa, Springer LNCS (1991). (with ASMICS)

[130] Javier Campos and José Maria Colom: *A Reachable Throughput Upper Bound for Live and Safe Free Choice Nets.* Proc. of 12th Int. Conf. on Applications and Theory of Petri Nets. Århus (June 1991).

[131] P.Gastin, A.Petit and W.Zielonka: *A Kleene Theorem for Infinite Trace Languages.* Report LITP 90.93 (Nov. 1990). To appear in Proc. of ICALP'91, Springer LNCS (1991). (with ASMICS)

[132] Brigitte Rozoy: *Distributed Languages, a Context Dependent Extension of Traces.* In: [160]. (with ASMICS)

[133] P.Gastin: *Infinite Traces.* Report LITP 90.68 (Sep. 1990). Ecole de Printemps On the Semantics of Parallelism, Springer LNCS No.469, 277-308 (April 1990). (with ASMICS)

[134] Manfred Broy: *Formal Modelling of Networks of Time Sensitive Interactive Systems.* To appear in: Computer Networks 91 (June 1991), University of Wroclaw.

[135] R.Janicki and M.Koutny: *Invariant Semantics of Nets with Inhibitor Arcs.* To appear in Proc. of CONCUR'91, Springer LNCS (August 1991).

[136] W.Vogler: *Is Partial Order Semantics Necessary for Action Refinement?* Report TUM I9101 SFB 342/1/91/A (January 1991).

[137] M.Koutny: *Modelling Systems with Dynamic Priorities.* Draft paper (April 1991). This volume.

[138] R.Janicki and M.Koutny: *Invariants and Paradigms of Concurrency Theory.* TR 91–10, McMaster (1991). Proceedings of PARLE'91, Lecture Notes in Computer Science 506, Springer, 59-74, 1991. Also to appear in a special issue of the journal: Future Generation Computer Systems.

[139] C.Diamantini, S.Kasangian, L.Pomello and C.Simone: *Elementary Nets and 2-Categories.* CNR–Progretto Finalizzato Sistemi Informatici e Calcolo Parallelo, TR 4.29(I) (March 1991). Extended abstract in [160].

[140] L.Pomello and C.Simone: *An Algebraic Characterisation of EN System (Observable) State Space.* CNR–Progetto Finalizzato Sistemi Informatici e Calcolo Parallelo, TR 4.30(I) (March 1991); to appear in: Formal Aspects of Computing

[141] Didier Buchs and Nicolas Guelfi: *CO-OPN: A Concurrent Object Oriented Petri Net Approach.* 12th Int. Conf. on Application and Theory of Petri Nets, Århus (June 1991).

[142] Colette Johnen and Laure Petrucci: *Computation of P–invariants for Integer Nets: Application to the Analysis of Algebraic Nets.* Rapport de Recherche CEDRIC No. 91–07 (January 1991).

[143] Alain Finkel and Laure Petrucci: *Verification of Net Properties by Composition / Decomposition.* Research Report CEDRIC (January 1991).

[144] Hans-Günther Linde: *Free Choice Simulation of Petri Nets.* Hildesheimer Informatik-Berichte Nr. 4/91 (March 1991). In: Proc. of the Fourth Int. Workshop on Petri Nets and Performance Models, Melbourne (3-5 December 1991), IEEE Computer Society, pp.236–247.

[145] Maciej Koutny: *Linear Combination of Places.* DEMON Memorandum (February 1991).

[146] Thierry Massart and Raymond Devillers: *Equality of Agents Resists to an Extension of the Universe of Actions.* Technical Report LIT-232, Univ. Libre de Bruxelles (March 1991).

[147] Thierry Massart and Raymond Devillers: *Agents or Expressions: which Semantics for a Process Calculus?* Technical Report LIT-230, Univ. Libre de Bruxelles (March 1991).

[148] Javier Campos, Giovanni Chiola, José Maria Colom and Manuel Silva: *Properties and Performance Bounds for Timed Marked Graphs.* Research Report GISI-RR-90-17 (July 1990). Submitted paper.

[149] Javier Campos, Giovanni Chiola and Manuel Silva: *Properties and Performance Bounds for Closed Free Choice Synchronised Monoclass Queueing Networks.* To appear in IEEE Transactions on Automatic Control (Special Issue on Multidimensional Queueing Systems) (1991).

[150] Javier Campos, Beatriz Sánchez and Manuel Silva: *Throughput Lower Bounds for Markovian Petri Nets: Transformation Techniques.* In: Proc. of the Fourth Int. Workshop on Petri Nets and Performance Models, Melbourne (3-5 December 1991), IEEE Computer Society, pp.322–333.

[151] Javier Campos and Manuel Silva: *Throughput Upper Bounds for Markovian Petri Nets: Embedded Subnets and Queueing Networks.* In: Proc. of the Fourth Int. Workshop on Petri Nets and Performance Models, Melbourne (3-5 December 1991), IEEE Computer Society, pp.312–321.

[152] Ghassan Chehaibar: *Replacement of Open Interface Subnets and Stable State Transformation Equivalence.* Proc. of 12th Int. Conf. on Applications and Theory of Petri Nets, Århus (June 1991).

[153] Ghassan Chehaibar: *Use of Reentrant Nets in Modular Analysis of Coloured Nets.* In Advances in Petri Nets (1991), pp.58–77, and in High Level Petri Nets–Theory and Application (eds. K.Jensen and G.Rozenberg).

[154] Raymond Devillers: *Maximality Preserving Bisimulation: Simplifications and Extensions.* Technical Report LIT-231 (February / May 1991). Abstract in [160].

[155] Didier Buchs and Nicolas Guelfi: *A Semantic Description of Actor Languages by Structured Algebraic Petri Nets.* LRI Rapport de Recherche No.639 (February 1991). Accepted as extended abstract to 14th ICSE, Melbourne, 1992

[156] Didier Buchs, Nicolas Guelfi and Fabrice Mourlin: *Semantic Description of the* occam-2 *Language: CO-OPN and PN^2, two Approaches.* Draft (May 1991).

[157] Maciej Koutny, Luigi V. Mancici and Giuseppe Pappalardo: *Formalising Replicated Distributed Processing.* Proceedings of the 10th Symposium on Reliable Distributed Systems, Pisa, 108-117 (1991).

[158] Oliver Botti and Fiorella de Cindio: *From Basic to Timed Models of* occam*: an Application to Program Placement.* (May 1991). In: Proc. of the Fourth Int. Workshop on Petri Nets and Performance Models, Melbourne (3-5 December 1991), IEEE Computer Society, pp.216–223.

[159] Eike Best: *The Petri Box Calculus for Concurrent Programs.* In: [160].

[160] Eike Best and Grzegorz Rozenberg (editors): *Proceedings of the 3rd Workshop on Concurrency and Compositionality, jointly organised by DEMON and CEDISYS, Goslar, March 5–8, 1991;* GMD-Studien Nr.191 and Hildesheimer Informatik-Bericht Nr. 6/91 (May 1991).

[161] Mogens Nielsen, Grzegorz Rozenberg, P.S. Thiagarajan: *Transition Systems, Event Structures and Unfoldings.* Extended Abstract in [160].

[162] A. Ehrenfeucht, H.J. Hoogeboom, Grzegorz Rozenberg: *On the Structure of Consistent Regular Languages of Dependency Graphs.*

[163] P.S. Thiagarajan, H.C.M. Kleijn, P. Hoogers: *A Trace Semantics for Petri Nets.*

[164] Ryszard Janicki, Maciej Koutny: *Relational Structure Semantics of Concurrent Systems.* Proceedings of the 13th IMACS Congress on Computation and Applied Mathematics, 709-713, Dublin (1991).

[165] E.Best and J.Hall: *The Box Calculus: A New Causal Algebra with Multilabel Communication.* This volume.

[166] J. Ezpeleta, J.M. Couvreur: *A New Technique for Finding a Generating Family of Siphons, Traps and ST-components. Application to Colored Petri Nets.* Proc. of 12th Conf. on Application and Theory of Petri Nets, Århus (1991).

[167] E.Best, J.Esparza and M.Koutny: *Operational Semantics for the Box Algebra.* Draft paper (October 1991).

[168] J. Ezpeleta, J. Martinez: *Petri Nets as a Specification Language for Manufacturing Systems.* To appear in Proc. of 13th IMACS World Congress on Computation and Applied Mathematics, Dublin (July 1991).

[169] Manuel Silva, J.M. Colom, J. Campos: *Linear Algebraic Techniques for the Analysis of Petri Nets.* To appear in int. Symposium on the Mathematical Theory of Networks and Systems, Kobe (June 1991).

[170] Antonia Sinachopoulos: *A Completeness Proof and Decidability for Pre Order Logics.* TR LIT–227, Univ. Libre de Bruxelles (1991), submited.

[171] Antonia Sinachopoulos: *Linear and Partial Order Temporal Logics and Refinement of Actions.* Draft (June 1991).

[172] Michael Leuschel: *Concurrent Transition Systems (CTS) - True Concurrency for Labelled Transition Systems.* TR LIT–233, Univ. Libre de Bruxelles.

[173] Michael Leuschel: *Language and Refinement.* Univ. Libre de Bruxeles (1990).

[174] TH. Massart: *A Basic Agent Caclulus and Bisimulation Laws for the Design of Systems.* Univ. Libre de Bruxelles.

[175] J.Hall: *General Recursion.* Draft paper, Univ. of Newcastle upon Tyne (June 1991/January 1992).

[176] J.Esparza: *Fixpoint Semantics of Recursion in the Box Algebra.* DEMON Memorandum (December 1991).

[177] Thierry Massart: *An Agent Calculus with Simple Actions where the Enabling and Disabling are Derived Operators.* Information Processing Letters 40 (1991), pp 213-218

[178] Thierry Massart: *A Basic Agent Calculus for the LOTOS Specification Language.* Draft paper.

[179] Didier Buchs, Nicolas Guelfi: *Open Distributed Programming using the Object Oriented Specification Formalism CO-OPN.* LRI rapport no.700 (1991), submitted.

[180] Didier Buchs, Nicolas Guelfi: *System Specification using CO-OPN.* DEMON Report, LRI (May 1991). Will appear as: *System Specification using CO-OPN*, 3rd IEEE Int. Workshop on Future Trends in Distributed Computing, Taipei (1992).

[181] Colette Johnen, Fabrice Mourlin: *Analysis of the Communication Structure of OCCAM2 Programs using Petri Nets.* Rapport de Recherche No.643, LRI (1991).

[182] Giorgio De Michelis: *Constraints and Extensions in a Calculus of EN Systems.* Proc. of 12th Conf. on Applications and Theory of Petri Nets, Gjern (1991).

[183] Giorgio De Michelis: *Morphisms and Refinements for EN Systems.* DEMON Report, DSI (May 1991).

[184] Gianni Degli Antoni: *Communicating Petri Nets.* DEMON Report, DSI (April 1991).

[185] Eugenio Battiston, Laure Petrucci, Lucia Rapanotti: *Establishing a Relationship between OBJSA Nets and Algebraic Nets Schemes.* DEMON Technical Report, DSI/LRI (May 1991).

[186] L. Bernardinello, G. Nifosí, N. Sabadini: *A Comparison between Asynchronous Automata and Superposed Automata Net Systems.* Presented at the general ASMICS meeting (February 1991) (revised May 1991). (with ASMICS)

[187] P. Bonizzoni, G. Mauri, G. Pighizzini, N. Sabadini: *Recognizing Sets of Labelled Acyclic Graphs.* Technical Report, DSI (November 1990)

[188] Carla Simone, M. Ajmone Marsan, P. Donzelli: *The Application of EB-Equivalence Rules to the Structural Reduction of GSPN Models.* Technical Report, DSI (revised version, October 1991), submitted.

[189] Gabriella Nifosí: *Automi Asincroni e Reti di Automi Sovrapposti.* (*Asynchronous Automata and Superposed Automata Nets*). DSI (1990/91) (in Italian).

[190] Lucia Rapanotti: *Una caratterizzazione semantica delle reti OBJSA.* (*A Semantical Characterization of OBJSA Nets*). DSI (1990/91) (in Italian).

[191] Claudia Diamantini: *Approcci categoriali alle reti di Petri: i sistemi EN come bicategorie.* (*Categorial Approaches to Petri Nets: EN Systems as Bicategories*). DSI (1990/91) (in Italian).

[192] David Bramini: *Specifica e implementazione prototipale di una interfaccia utente per il linguaggio delle reti OBJSA.* (*Specification and Prototypal Implementation of a User Interface for OBJSA Nets Language*). DSI (1990/91) (in Italian).

[193] S. Kasangian, G. Mauri, N. Sabadini: *Traces and Pomsets: a Categorical View.* Technical Report, DSI, revised version (February 1992).

[194] J.Esparza: *Model Checking of Persistent Petri Nets Using Partial Orders.* Draft Paper (January 1992).

[195] E.Best and J.Esparza: *Model Checking of Persistent Petri Nets.* Hildesheimer Informatikbericht (September 1991); preliminary version in the Proceedings of the Båstad Workshop (May 1991); presented at Computer Science Logic'91 (Bern, October 1991).

[196] R.Hopkins: *A (prioritised) Petri Box Algebra and its Use for a Triple Modular Redundancy Case Study.* Draft paper (June 1991); submitted.

[197] J.Esparza: *Reduction and Synthesis of Live and Bounded Free Choice Petri Nets.* Hildesheimer Informatik-Berichte Nr. 7/91 (June 1991).

[198] E.Best and J.Esparza (eds.): *Second Progress Report of the Esprit Basic Research Action 3148 DEMON.* GMD-Studien Nr.198 (September 1991).

[199] E.Best: *Overview of the Results of the Esprit Basic Research Action DEMON - Design Methods Based on Nets.* In: Proc. of the Fourth Int. Workshop on Petri Nets and Performance Models, Melbourne (3-5 December 1991), IEEE Computer Society, pp.224–235. Also in the Bulletin of the EATCS No.45 (October 1991), pp.39–58.

[200] J.Desel: *The Rank Theorem for Extended Free Choice Nets.* Draft paper (January 1992).

[201] E.Battiston, F.De Cindio, L.Petrucci and L.P.Rapanotti: *OBJSA Nets and their Relationship with other Classes of Algebraic High Level Nets.* CNR, Progretto Finalizzato 'Sistemi Informatici e Calcolo Parallelo', TR i/4/ (November 1991).

[202] Carla Simone: *Net System Morphisms and Observability in System Design.* Proceeding of ISCAS 1991, Singapore (June 1990).

[203] Oliver Botti and Fiorella De Cindio: *Comparison of* occam *Program Placements by a Generalized Stochastic Petri Net Model.* Proceedings TRANSPUTERS 92, Paris, May 92 (to appear).

[204] Aldo Restelli: *Categorie Ordinate di Sistemi Concorrenti.* (*Ordered Categories of Concurrent Systems.*) Tesi di Laurea in Computer Science, Dip. Scienze dell'Informazione, Univ. degli Studi di Milano (A.A. 1990/91). (In Italian.)

[205] Stefano Beltramolli: *Il disegno di sistemi distribuiti con le Reti OBJSA.* (*Distributed System Design with OBJSA Nets.*) Tesi di Laurea in Computer Science, Dip. Scienze dell'Informazione, Univ. degli Studi di Milano (A.A. 1990/91). (In Italian.)

[206] R.Devillers: *Maximality Preservation and the ST-idea for Action Refinements.* This volume.

[207] Paul Gastin and Antoine Petit: *Asynchronous Automata for Infinite Traces.* Rapport LRI no 707, 1991.

[208] I.Czaja, R.J.van Glabbeek and U.Goltz: *Interleaving Semantics and Action Refinement with Atomic Choice.* This volume.

[209] U.Goltz and N.Götz: *Modelling a Simple Communication Protocol in a Language with Action Refinement.* Draft (November 1991).

[210] U.Goltz and A.Rensink: *Finite Petri Nets as Models for Recursive Causal Behaviour.* Arbeitspapiere der GMD Nr.604 (December 1991).

[211] J.Esparza: *A Solution to the Covering Problem for 1-Bounded Conflict-free Petri Nets using Linear Programming.* Hildesheimer Informatikbericht (September 1991). To appear in IPL.

[212] W.Vogler: *Modular Construction of Petri Nets by Merging Places and the Refinement of Transitions.* Draft paper (March 1991).

[213] Paul Gastin and Antoine Petit: *Poset Properties of Complex Traces.* Rapport LRI (1991).

[214] Y.Souissi an G.Memmi: *Composition of Nets via a Communication Medium.* In: Advances in Petri Nets 1990, pp.457–470.

[215] Y.Souissi: *On Liveness Preservation by Composition of Nets via a Set of Places.* In: Advances in Petri Nets 1991, pp.277-295.

[216] Vittorio Patera: *Reti di Petri: Equivalenze e Morfismi nel Disegno di Sistemi Distribuiti.* (*Petri Nets: Equivalences and Morphisms in Distributed System Design.*) Tesi di Laurea in Computer Science, Dip. Scienze dell'Informazione, Univ. degli Studi di Milano (A.A. 1990/91). (In Italian.)

[217] W.Reisig: *Parallel Composition of Liveness.* Draft paper (October 1991).

[218] W.Reisig: *Concurrent Temporal Logic.* Draft paper (October 1991).

[219] L.Bernardinello, G.De Michelis, C.Diamantini, L.Pomello, A.Restelli and C.Simone: *Relationships between Categories of 'Elementary' Concurrent Systems.* Submitted paper (October1991)

[220] A. Finkel, C. Johnen and L. Petrucci: *Decomposition of Petri Nets for Parallel Analysis.* Submitted paper (January 1992).

[221] S. Christensen and L. Petrucci: *Towards a Modular Analysis of Coloured Petri Nets.* Submitted paper (January 1992).

[222] U.Goltz: *Causality Based Models for the Design of Concurrent Systems.* Invited Lecture. Abstract, CONCUR-91, LNCS 527, pp.43–44 (1991).

[223] O.Botti, J.Hall and R.P.Hopkins: *A Basic Net Algebra for Program Semantics and its Application to* occam. This volume.

[224] Ryszard Janicki and Maciej Koutny: *Structure of Concurrency.* (A full version of [91] solicited for a special issue of Theoretical Computer Science).

[225] Ryszard Janicki and Maciej Koutny: *On Deadlock Detection using Partial Orders.* Submitted paper. (1991)

[226] Paolo Consolaro: *Le reti di Petri e il paradigma object-oriented.* (*Petri Nets and the Object-oriented Paradigm.*) Tesi di Laurea in Computer Science, Dip. Scienze dell'Informazione, Univ. degli Studi di Milano (A.A. 1990/91). (In Italian.)

[227] Javier Campos and Manuel Silva: *Structural Techniques in Performance Analysis of Petri Net Models.* This volume.

[228] Paul Gastin and Antoine Petit: *A Survey on Recognizable Languages of Infinite Traces.* This volume.

[229] Lucia Pomello, Grzegorz Rozenberg and Carla Simone: *A Survey of Equivalence Notions for Net Based Systems.* This volume.

[230] Brigitte Rozoy: *On Distributed Languages and Models for Concurrency.* This volume.

The Box Calculus: a New Causal Algebra with Multi-label Communication[1]

Eike Best

Institut für Informatik, Universität Hildesheim
Marienburger Platz 22, D-3200 Hildesheim, Germany

Raymond Devillers

Laboratoire d'Informatique Théorique, Université Libre de Bruxelles
Boulevard du Triomphe, B-1050 Bruxelles, Belgium

Jon G. Hall

Computing Laboratory, The University of Newcastle-upon-Tyne
Newcastle-upon-Tyne, NE1 7RU, U.K.

Abstract

A new Petri net calculus called the calculus of Petri Boxes is described. It has been designed to allow reasoning about the structure of a net and about the relationship between nets, and to facilitate the compositional semantic translation of high level constructs such as blocks, variables and atomic actions into elementary Petri nets. The calculus is located 'midway' in such a translation.

This paper first defines an algebra of Box expressions. A corresponding algebra of Boxes is then defined and used compositionally as a semantic model of Box expressions. The two algebras feature a general asynchronous communication operation extending that of CCS. Synchronisation is defined as a unary operator. The algebras also include refinement, iteration and recursion. It is shown how they can be used to describe data and blocks.

As the main results of this paper, it is proved that the Box algebra satisfies various desirable structural laws and enjoys two important behavioural properties. The paper also contains an example proof of a mutual exclusion protocol.

Keywords

Petri Nets, Process Algebras, Compositional Semantics, Multiway Synchronisation, Refinement, Recursion, Data.

Contents

---

[1]Work done within the Esprit Basic Research Action 3148 D-E-M-O-N (Design Methods Based on Nets).

1 Introduction

Petri nets [54,56] are a causal model of concurrency in that they allow one to reason about events between which there is no causal relationship. A major drawback of Petri nets is that they have very little basic structure in an algebraic sense. This may have adverse implications for the systematic construction and verification of systems. An important alternative to Petri nets are process algebras [1,43,50]. These approaches were originally based on a single observer (interleaving) model in which the occurrence of events is serialised even for independent processes[2]. A disadvantage of this approach is that causality information may be lost.

Part of the objectives of the Esprit Basic Research Action DEMON has been the search of a good way of bringing together the two models. We quote from [13]:

> 'The long term objective for which this Action lays the foundation is the development of a design calculus based on Petri net theory and supporting modular structuring, as well as specification and analysis techniques. (...) In outline this involves: Detailed analysis of existing variants of the basic model ('net classes'), and distillation of their features into a small number of tractable, well-behaved and modular net classes of wide applicability ...'

This paper describes part of the results of this endeavour. We produce a new net-based model for specifying concurrent systems called the *Box algebra*, which has as its natural semantic domain a simple but versatile form of structured Petri nets. The Box algebra has been developed,

- to serve as the semantic domain of a compositional semantics of high level concurrent programming languages such as occam [48];
- to provide a compositional semantics in terms of Petri Nets and their associated partial order (true concurrency) behaviour.

In a sense, the Box algebra is located midway between such user-friendly high-level constructs as blocks, variables, recursion, critical sections etc., and such theoretically important primitive concepts as local states and transitions. It is designed to serve as a bridge between (Petri Net) theory and (Concurrent Programming) applications. Its aim is also to build a superstructure on top of Petri nets, which allows one to reason about the relationship between nets and about the structure of a net – rather than just about a net's immediate constituents such as places, transitions and arcs – while retaining the possibility of exploiting indigenous analysis methods known from net theory. This kind of superstructure is not achieved by the High Level net model [29,45,55], since the inscriptions of a high level net provide information neither about the net's structure nor about its relation to other nets.

The Box algebra consists of two parts:

(i) A syntactic domain of *Box expressions*, and

(ii) A semantic domain which we christen the domain of *Petri Boxes.*

There exists a semantic homomorphism from Box expressions to Boxes. Boxes are equivalence classes of Petri Nets equipped with an interface. They behave like black boxes extended with a communication facility and can be combined appropriately at their interfaces. The most important technical requirement we impose on our semantics is that of strict *compositionality*, i.e., the requirement that operators on one domain and operations on another domain should match each other. This requirement, together with the requirement of being able to model data and atomic actions, has had an interesting influence on the types of events we allow. As we have moved away from an interleaving semantics we can now give a true implementation of atomic actions as single events without the use of semaphore type constructs as in [50]. For instance, an atomic action of the form

[2] As a rule, process algebra formalisms depend on the interleaving view. For instance, the well known expansion theorem holds only in the presence of interleaving; the 'head normal form of processes' which is an important proof technique depends on the expansion theorem.

$$\langle x := y + 1; c?y; x := x + 1\rangle$$

(where the brackets $\langle\ldots\rangle$ enclose 'virtually atomic' actions – see [3] and others) involves a multi-way synchronisation of the action's constituent parts, namely the variables x and y, the channel c and the process in which the action is contained. However, since the variables (and the channel c) may be declared in different blocks, the compositionality principle makes it necessary to build this multi-way synchronisation incrementally.

The stepwise construction of multi-way synchronisations is achieved by the technical device of ***multi-labels***, that is, to allow the transitions of a net to be labelled by multisets of action names. We have found the CCS approach (with conjugate matching labels) to be more conducive to compositionality than the TCSP or COSY approach. The operators we have defined on multi-labels are, therefore, extensions of those defined on the CCS single label algebra. The generalisations allow various unifying observations to be made (such as a silent action being the empty multi-label, i.e., literally the absence of any visible action, and the use of simple disjoint union for concurrent composition). SCCS and related formalisms [18,58,50] achieve a similar generalisation. However, our approach differs fundamentally from SCCS in that it is asynchronous while SCCS is synchronous[3]. It is for this reason that commutativity of synchronisation is a nontrivial issue in our approach; the commutativity result is central to the present paper.

The paper is structured as follows. Section 2 defines the Box expression algebra. Section 3 introduces the domain of the Petri Box model. Section 4 defines the Box algebra, i.e., the set of operations on the domain. In Section 5, elementary structural properties such as the commutativity of synchronisation are stated and proved. Section 6 defines the semantic homomorphism from Box expressions to Boxes, and Section 7 describes some elementary behavioural properties of the semantics. Section 8 contains miscellaneous comments. It is described how data can be translated into Box expressions; an example is given; and some discussion on literature and on further work can be found. Section 9 contains some concluding remarks and an outlook, as well as acknowledgements.

This paper gives the reader an intermediate 'snapshot' on the development of a Petri net indigenous algebra. It is not to be viewed as a self-contained finished piece of work. Indeed, several problems have been left open here. They are being taken up in other work that is in progress, which will be reported upon in future papers. We indicate such open ends throughout the text.

2 The Box Expression Algebra

2.1 Action names

Before defining the syntax of the Box expression algebra, we describe its basic constituents. Action names are defined axiomatically; in the model, they will reappear as transition labels.

Definition 2.1

We assume a countably infinite set of action names, A, to be given. On A, we assume a bijection $\hat{}$ with the following properties to be defined:

$$\hat{}: A \to A$$
$$\text{with}\quad \hat{a} \neq a \text{ and } \hat{\hat{a}} = a \text{ for all } a \in A.$$

This bijection is called conjugation, and $a, \hat{a}$ are called conjugates of each other[4]. ■ 2.1

In applications, we shall choose the elements of A freely. Whenever a name a is chosen, it must be specified what its conjugate, $\hat{a}$, looks like. For instance, the conjugate of $c!1$ ('output the value 1 on channel c') could be $c?1$ ('input the value 1 from channel c'), but not $c?2$. Or, the conjugate of $C?$ could be $C!$; or, the conjugate of $P_2!$ (in P_1) could be $P_1?$ (in P_2).

Communications are based on multisets; Appendix A gives some definitions relating to multisets.

---

[3] The difference can be seen on the example $a\|\overline{a}\|a\|\overline{a}$ which is discussed in Section 4.5.

[4] We use the symbol $\hat{}$ instead of CCS's $^-$, because we reserve the overbarring symbol for the operational semantics of Box expressions [17].

Definition 2.2

The set of communication labels is the set $\mathcal{L} = \mathcal{M}_{\mathcal{F}}(A)$ of finite multisets over A. An element of $\mathcal{L}$ will be called multi-label. ■ 2.2

The function $\hat{}$ can be extended to a function from multisets μ over A to multisets over A by element-wise application, i.e., $\hat{\mu}(a) = \mu(\hat{a})$ for $a \in A$. The extended function has the following properties, where μ_1 and μ_2 are elements of $\mathcal{M}_{\mathcal{F}}(A)$:

Lemma 2.3

$\widehat{\mu_1 \cup \mu_2} = \widehat{\mu_1} \cup \widehat{\mu_2}$, $\widehat{\mu_1 \cap \mu_2} = \widehat{\mu_1} \cap \widehat{\mu_2}$, $\widehat{\mu_1 + \mu_2} = \widehat{\mu_1} + \widehat{\mu_2}$, $\widehat{\mu_1 \backslash \mu_2} = \widehat{\mu_1} \backslash \widehat{\mu_2}$, $\hat{\emptyset} = \emptyset$ *and* $\hat{A} = A$. ■ 2.3

As in CCS, we define relabelling as a function $f: A \to A$ satisfying $\widehat{f(a)} = f(\hat{a})$ for all $a \in A$. The particular function that maps a to b, $\hat{a}$ to $\hat{b}$ and leaves all other elements of A unchanged will often be denoted by $a \to b$. If f, g are relabellings then so is $f \circ g$, since $\widehat{f \circ g(a)} = g(\widehat{f(a)}) = g(f(\hat{a})) = f \circ g(\hat{a})$. Every relabelling $f: A \to A$ can be extended to a function f from $\mathcal{L}$ to $\mathcal{L}$ by the definition

$$f(\mu)(b) = \sum \{\mu(a) \mid f(a) = b\}.$$

The extended function satisfies $\widehat{f(\mu)} = f(\hat{\mu})$.
Refinement and recursion can be viewed as hierarchical constructs. In order to be able to express them, we need 'Box variables' that differ from elements of $\mathcal{L}$. We denote them by upper case letters $X, Y, \ldots$, and the corresponding set by $\mathcal{V} = \{X, Y, Z \ldots\}$.
From now on, we shall use the generic names a, b etc. for elements of A; β for elements of $\mathcal{L}$; X for elements of $\mathcal{V}$; and f for relabelling functions.

2.2 Box expression syntax

We use E as the generic name for Box expressions. Their abstract syntax is defined in Table 1.

E ::=	{Basic Boxes}	$\beta \mid$	multi-label action
		$X \mid$	variable
	{Sequential Constructs}	$E; E \mid$	sequence
		$E \,\square\, E \mid$	choice
	{Concurrent Constructs}	$E \| E \mid$	concurrent composition
		E **sy** $a \mid$	synchronisation
	{Abstraction Constructs}	E **rs** $a \mid$	restriction
		$[a : E] \mid$	$(= (E$ **sy** a **rs** $a))$ scoping
		$E[f] \mid$	relabelling
	{Hierarchical Constructs}	$E[X \leftarrow E] \mid$	refinement
		$\mu X.E \mid$	recursion
		$[E * E * E]$	iteration.

Table 1: Box expression syntax

We use parentheses liberally in order to denote operator precedences. When β is a singleton $\{a\}$, we sometimes omit the enclosing multiset brackets if unambiguity is ensured. A Box expression E is called closed if all variables X occur in the scope of an enclosing refinement or recursion operator. For instance, the expressions X and $(\{a\}; X)[X \leftarrow (\{b\}; X)]$ are not closed. A Box expression E is called communication closed if all action names (or their conjugates) occur in (a multiset within) the scope of an enclosing restriction or scoping operator. For instance, $[a : \{a\} \| \{\hat{b}\}]$ is not communication closed, while $[a : \{\hat{a}, \hat{b}\}]$ is communication closed.

$$
\begin{array}{lcl}
E_0 & = & \emptyset \\
E_1 & = & \{a\} \,\Box\, \{\hat{a}, b, c\} \\
E_2 & = & \{a, \hat{a}\} \| X \\
E_3 & = & \{a, a, \hat{a}, c\} \\
E_4 & = & (a\|b); (\hat{a}\|c) \ \ (= \text{Abbreviation for } (\{a\}\|\{b\}); (\{\hat{a}\}\|\{c\})\,) \\
E_5 & = & (a\|b) \,\Box\, (\hat{a}\|c) \\
E_6 & = & (a\|\hat{a}) \\
E_7 & = & (\{a, a, b\} \| \{\hat{a}, b, c\}) \\
E_8 & = & (\{a, a, b\} \| \{\hat{a}, \hat{b}, c\}) \ \mathbf{sy}\ a \\
E_9 & = & (a\|\hat{a}\|a\|\hat{a}) \\
E_{10} & = & (a\|\hat{a}\|a\|\hat{a}) \ \mathbf{sy}\ a \\
E_{11} & = & \{a, a\} \| \{\hat{a}, \hat{a}\} \\
E_{12} & = & \{a, a\} \| \{\hat{a}, \hat{a}\} \ \mathbf{sy}\ a \\
E_{13} & = & (a\|\hat{a}) \ \mathbf{sy}\ a \\
E_{14} & = & (a\|\{\hat{a}, a\}\|\hat{a}) \ \mathbf{sy}\ a \\
E_{15} & = & (a\|\hat{a}) \ \mathbf{sy}\ a \ \mathbf{rs}\ a \ \ (= [\, a : (a\|\hat{a})]) \\
E_{16} & = & [\, a : a] \\
E_{17} & = & (a[\, a \rightarrow b] \| \hat{b}) \ \mathbf{sy}\ b \\
E_{18} & = & (a[\, a \rightarrow b]) \| (\hat{b} \ \mathbf{sy}\ b) \\
E_{19} & = & (((b; X)[\, X \leftarrow a]) \| \hat{a}) \ \mathbf{sy}\ a \\
E_{20} & = & (((b; X) \| \hat{a}) \ \mathbf{sy}\ a)[\, X \leftarrow a] \\
E_{21} & = & \mu X.(a; X) \\
E_{22} & = & \mu X.((X; a) \,\Box\, a) \\
E_{23} & = & \mu X.((a; X) \,\Box\, c) \\
E_{24} & = & \mu X.((a; X; b) \,\Box\, c) \\
E_{25} & = & \mu X.(a\|X) \\
E_{26} & = & \mu X.((a\|X) \,\Box\, c) \\
E_{27} & = & \mu X.((a\|b) \,\Box\, X) \\
E_{28} & = & \mu X.(X) \\
E_{29} & = & \mu X.((a\|X[\, a \rightarrow \hat{a}]) \ \mathbf{sy}\ a) \\
E_{30} & = & (\mu X.(a\|X[\, a \rightarrow \hat{a}])) \ \mathbf{sy}\ a \\
E_{31} & = & \{a, \hat{a}\} \\
E_{32} & = & \{a, \hat{a}\} \ \mathbf{sy}\ a \\
E_{33} & = & \mu X.(\, \mu Y.((X; a_0) \,\Box\, Y[\, f]) \,\|\, b\,) \\
E_{34} & = & \mu X.(\, \mu Y.(((\emptyset; X; \emptyset); a_0) \,\Box\, Y[\, f]) \,\|\, b\,)
\end{array}
$$

Table 2: Some Box expressions (most are in abbreviated form)

Table 2 shows some examples of Box expressions. In defining these expressions we are actually using, for convenience, the associativity of || that will only later be shown to hold in the semantic model of Petri Boxes.

3 The Petri Box Model

Petri Boxes – the standard model for Box expressions – are equivalence classes of Petri nets equipped with a labelling. The labelling of a Box indicates its interface, through which Petri Boxes can be composed with one another, as shown schematically (and imprecisely) in Figure 1. The name derives from this scheme.

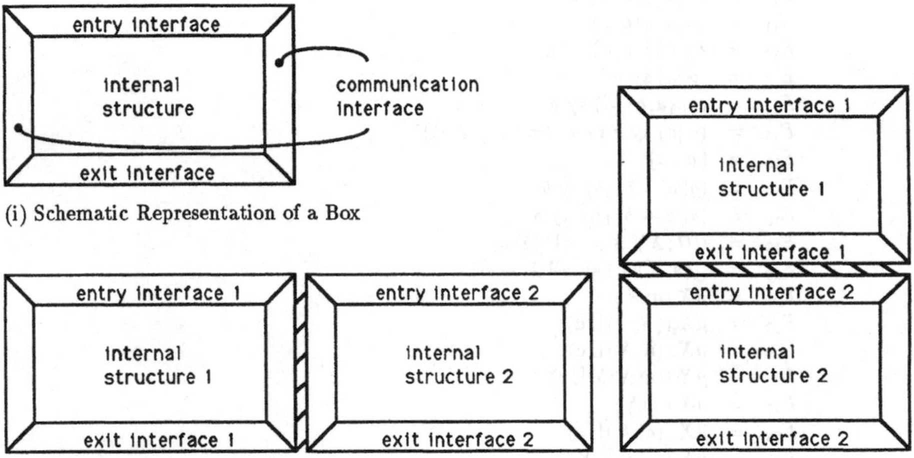

(i) Schematic Representation of a Box

(ii) Concurrent composition and synchronisation: the communication interfaces are joined

(iii) Sequential composition: the exit interface of the first Box is joined with the entry interface of the second Box

Figure 1: The Petri Box schema

We use place labels and transition labels to formalise the notion of interface. Labels for places simply state whether they are *entry places* (in which case their label is $\{e\}$ or, in abbreviated form, e), *exit places* (in which case their label is $\{x\}$ or, in abbreviated form, x) or internal places (in which case their label is $\emptyset$). Labels for transitions come in a larger variety. There may be the communication labels $\mathcal{L}$ or the variable names $\mathcal{V}$ mentioned above. A label $\emptyset$ always denotes an internal place or an internal (silent) transition. In addition, we allow the set

$$\mathcal{W} = \{f(X) \mid X \in \mathcal{V} \text{ and } f \text{ a relabelling function}\}$$

to express 'pending relabellings'; the definition of $\mathcal{W}$ is to be understood syntactically: expressions such as $f(X)$, $g(Y)$, etc. may occur as transition labels (even though they are not directly expressible in the syntax), just like variables such as X, Y etc.

Remark 3.1

We may – and will – identify the set $\mathcal{V}$ with the subset $\mathcal{V}' = \{id(X) \mid X \in \mathcal{V}\}$ of $\mathcal{W}$. ■ 3.1

3.1 Labelled Petri nets

Definition 3.2 *Labelled net*

A labelled Petri net is a quadruple $\Sigma = (S,T,W,\lambda)$, where (S,T,W) is an arc-weighted net[6], and λ is a function called the labelling of Σ such that

$$\begin{aligned} \lambda : S &\rightarrow \{\{e\},\emptyset,\{x\}\} \\ \lambda : T &\rightarrow \mathcal{L} \cup \mathcal{W} \end{aligned}$$

In the pictorial representation, for brevity, we often omit set brackets, and we usually omit the label $\emptyset$ altogether. Σ is finite iff $S \cup T$ is a finite set. ■ 3.2

The places s with $\lambda(s) = \{e\}$ are called entry places; they form the entry interface. The places with $\lambda(s) = \{x\}$ are called exit places; they form the exit interface. All other places are called internal. The transitions with $\lambda(t) \in \mathcal{L} \setminus \{\emptyset\}$ are called communication (or observable) interface transitions; they form the communication interface. The transitions with $\lambda(t) \in \mathcal{W}$ are called refinement (or hierarchical) interface transitions; they form the hierarchical interface. All other transitions, i.e., such that $\lambda(t) = \emptyset$, are called internal or silent. Some examples are shown in Figure 2.

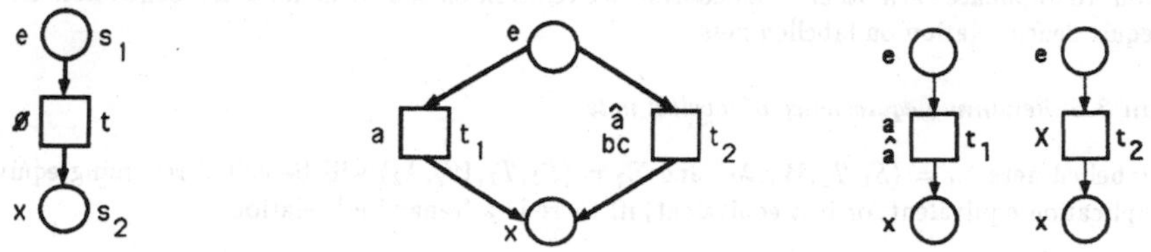

(i) Entry interface s_1, exit interface s_2. Internal transition t, no communication interface.

(ii) Communication interface t_1 and t_2.

(iii) Communication interface t_1, hierarchical interface t_2.

Figure 2: Some simple Boxes

Notation 3.3

Let $\Sigma = (S,T,W,\lambda)$ be a labelled net. We denote the set of entry places of Σ by ${}^{\bullet}\Sigma = \{s \in S \mid \lambda(s) = \{e\}\}$, and the set of exit places of Σ by $\Sigma^{\bullet} = \{s \in S \mid \lambda(s) = \{x\}\}$. ■ 3.3

3.2 Petri Boxes

Petri Boxes (or just Boxes) are equivalence classes of labelled nets. We desire a structural equivalence which allows the derivation of structural identities such as the associativity of sequential composition. A first candidate for such an equivalence is isomorphism, which abstracts from the identities of places and transitions (and hence arcs). This means, for instance, that the two labelled nets $(\{y_1,y_2\},\emptyset,\emptyset,\lambda)$ with $\lambda(y_1) = \{e\}, \lambda(y_2) = \{x\}$ and $(\{z_1,z_2\},\emptyset,\emptyset,\lambda)$ with $\lambda(z_1) = \{e\}, \lambda(z_2) = \{x\}$ are to be regarded as representatives of the same Box. This abstraction gives us freedom in choosing names for places, transitions and arcs, often with the purpose of making the underlying nets of two Boxes disjoint.
However, some of the identities which we aim to prove are not isomorphisms, but nevertheless could be called structural identities. For instance, synchronisation introduces new transitions, and in order to achieve an idempotence property, we need in some way to identify the possible duplicates introduced by

[6] I.e., S and T are sets and W is a function such that $S \cap T = \emptyset$ and $W: ((S \times T) \cup (T \times S)) \rightarrow \mathbf{N}$.

successive synchronisations. Also, it makes sense to identify the above two labelled nets with the labelled net $(\{y_1, y_1', y_2\}, \emptyset, \emptyset, \lambda)$ where $\lambda(y_1) = \lambda(y_1') = \{e\}$ and $\lambda(y_2) = \{x\}$; in our approach, all three nets denote the same Box called **stop**.

We shall define 'renaming equivalence', which caters for the two types of identifications just described, as the structural identification to be used throughout this paper. We are aware, however, that other structural identifications are possible and will in future have to be considered. Thus although we now give a precise meaning to the concept of a 'Box', we explicitly wish this concept to be understood in the less precise meaning of 'an equivalence class of labelled nets, modulo some suitable structural equivalence relation'. A reasonable requirement for the suitability of such structural equivalences might be that they encompass (are implied by) renaming equivalence. Another suitability requirement is that the operations that are defined on the algebra are independent of the representatives.

Definition 3.4 *Duplication of places and transitions*

Let $\Sigma = (S, T, W, \lambda)$ be a labelled net. Two places $s \in S$ and $s' \in S$ are said to duplicate each other in Σ if $\lambda(s) = \lambda(s')$ and for all $t \in T$, both $W(s,t) = W(s',t)$ and $W(t,s) = W(t,s')$. Similarly, two transitions $t \in T$ and $t' \in T$ are said to duplicate each other in Σ if $\lambda(t) = \lambda(t')$ and for all $s \in S$, both $W(s,t) = W(s,t')$ and $W(t,s) = W(t',s)$. ■ 3.4

The relation 'to duplicate each other' is an equivalence relation on the elements of a labelled net. On it we build an equivalence relation on labelled nets.

Definition 3.5 *Renaming equivalence of labelled nets*

Two labelled nets $\Sigma_1 = (S_1, T_1, W_1, \lambda_1)$ and $\Sigma_2 = (S_2, T_2, W_2, \lambda_2)$ will be called renaming equivalent (or duplication equivalent, or just equivalent) iff there is a 'renaming' relation

$$\rho \subseteq (S_1 \cup T_1) \times (S_2 \cup T_2)$$

such that the following holds:

(1) ρ is sort-preserving and surjective on places: $\rho(S_1) = S_2$ and $\rho^{-1}(S_2) = S_1$.

(2) ρ is sort-preserving and surjective on transitions: $\rho(T_1) = T_2$ and $\rho^{-1}(T_2) = T_1$.

(3) ρ is arc-(weight-)preserving: whenever $(s_1, s_2) \in \rho$ and $(t_1, t_2) \in \rho$ then $W_1(s_1, t_1) = W_2(s_2, t_2)$ and $W_1(t_1, s_1) = W_2(s_2, t_2)$.

(4) ρ is label-preserving: whenever $(x_1, x_2) \in \rho$ then $\lambda_1(x_1) = \lambda_2(x_2)$.

(5) ρ is bijective on hierarchical labels: if $\lambda_1(t_1) \in \mathcal{W}$ then $|\rho(t_1)| = 1$, and if $\lambda_2(t_2) \in \mathcal{W}$ then $|\rho^{-1}(t_2)| = 1$. ■ 3.5

Conditions (1)–(4) also imply that ρ is injective on equivalence classes of duplicating elements; i.e., if $(x_1, x_2) \in \rho$ and $(y_1, y_2) \in \rho$ then x_1 and y_1 duplicate each other in Σ_1 iff x_2 and y_2 duplicate each other in Σ_2. However, (1)–(5) do not imply the injectivity of ρ. If, in addition to satisfying (1)–(5), ρ is both ways injective then Σ_1 will be called *isomorphic* to Σ_2.

Lemma 3.6

Renaming equivalence is an equivalence relation on the class of labelled nets.

Proof: Symmetry and reflexivity follow immediately from the definition, while transitivity follows from an easy (and purely technical) argument. ■ 3.6

The equivalence class of Σ with respect to renaming equivalence will be denoted by $[\Sigma]$. It satisfies the following property:

Lemma 3.7

Every equivalence class of labelled nets has a canonical representative (up to isomorphism) in which no two distinct elements duplicate each other.

Proof: Removing, for each class of duplicating elements, all but one duplicate, yields a labelled net with the desired property. Alternatively, one may factor the nets by ρ. ■ 3.7

Usually, the 'minimal' representative that exists by Lemma 3.7 will be used to represent a Petri Box. We will adopt a requirement for labelled nets sometimes called T–restrictedness [9], viz. that every transition has at least one input place and at least one output place. A similar requirement for Boxes is that there is at least one entry place and at least one exit place. There is another important requirement: entry places may not have incoming arcs, and exit places may not have outgoing arcs. Finally, we shall add the requirement that $\mathcal{W}$-labelled transitions may not be contained in side conditions, and may only have bordering arcs with weights at most of size 1 (these last requirements will make the definition of refinement manageable):

Definition 3.8 *Boxes*

A Petri Box B is an equivalence class $B = [\Sigma]$, where $\Sigma = (S, T, W, \lambda)$ is a labelled net satisfying

(o) T–restrictedness: $\forall t \in T$: ${}^\bullet t \neq \emptyset \neq t^\bullet$.

(i) At least one entry place: ${}^\bullet\Sigma \neq \emptyset$.

(ii) At least one exit place: $\Sigma^\bullet \neq \emptyset$.

(iii) No arcs into entry places: $\forall s \in {}^\bullet\Sigma\ \forall t \in T: W(t,s) = 0$.

(iv) No arcs out of exit places: $\forall s \in \Sigma^\bullet\ \forall t \in T: W(s,t) = 0$.

(v) Only simple weights around hierarchical interface transitions:

$$\forall t \in T: (\lambda(t) \in \mathcal{W} \Rightarrow \forall s \in S: W(s,t) \leq 1 \wedge W(t,s) \leq 1).$$

(vi) No side conditions around hierarchical interface transitions:

$$\forall t \in T: (\lambda(t) \in \mathcal{W} \Rightarrow \forall s \in S: W(s,t) = 0 \vee W(t,s) = 0).$$

B is called finite iff there is a finite labelled net Σ such that $B = [\Sigma]$. ■ 3.8

It is easy to check that the properties (o)–(vi) are independent of the choice of representative of $[\Sigma]$. Note that a renaming equivalence class of labelled nets contains finite and infinite members at the same time. However if $[\Sigma]$ is finite then the canonical representatives are themselves finite.

Example 3.9 *Basic Boxes*

The simplest Box is the **stop** Box which is defined as follows: $\mathbf{stop} = [(\{s_1, s_2\}, \emptyset, \emptyset, \lambda)]$ with $\lambda(s_1) = \{e\}$ and $\lambda(s_2) = \{x\}$. Its canonical representative consists solely of two isolated places.

Another useful Box is the **tau** Box (**tau** in analogy to CCS's silent action), defined by

$$\mathbf{tau} = [(\{s_1, s_2\}, \{t\}, \{(s_1, t), (t, s_2)\}, \lambda)]$$

with $\lambda(s_1) = \{e\}$, $\lambda(s_2) = \{x\}$ and $\lambda(t) = \emptyset$. We will usually denote this by $Box(\emptyset)$.

More generally, let $\beta \in \mathcal{L}$. The Box $Box(\beta)$ which offers the communication possibilities of β in a single transition is defined as follows:

$$Box(\beta) = [(\{s_1, s_2\}, \{t\}, \{(s_1, t), (t, s_2)\}, \lambda)]$$

with $\lambda(s_1) = \{e\}$, $\lambda(s_2) = \{x\}$ and $\lambda(t) = \beta$.

Let $w \in \mathcal{W}$. The Box $Box(w)$ which offers the refinement (or recursion) possibility w is defined as follows:

$$Box(w) = [(\{s_1, s_2\}, \{t\}, \{(s_1, t), (t, s_2)\}, \lambda)]$$

with $\lambda(s_1) = \{e\}$, $\lambda(s_2) = \{x\}$ and $\lambda(t) = w$. ■ 3.9

Figure 3 shows examples of these basic Boxes. The identities of places and transitions are hidden; only their labels are shown. For easier cross-reference in this paper, we normally use indices which correspond to the examples of Table 2. For instance, Figure 3 depicts Boxes which correspond to the expressions of Table 2 through their indices. In relating Boxes to expressions in this way, we anticipate the correspondence that will eventually be defined in Section 6.

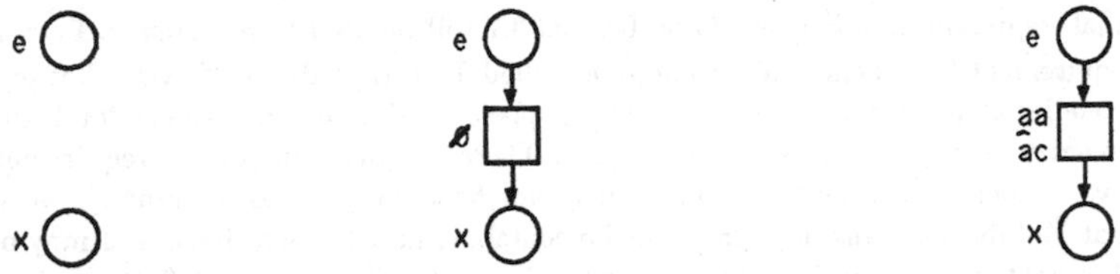

stop$= Box(E_{16})$ **tau**$= B_0 = Box(E_0)$ $B_3 = Box(E_3) = Box(\{a, a, \hat{a}, c\})$

Figure 3: Some basic Boxes

3.3 Behaviour of labelled nets and Boxes

The initial marking of a labelled net is the one which puts one token on each entry place, and zero tokens on all other places. The final marking is defined similarly on exit places.

Definition 3.10

The initial marking of a labelled net $\Sigma = (S, T, W, \lambda)$ is the function $M_e: S \to \mathbb{N}$ defined by

$$M_e(s) = \begin{cases} 1 & \text{if } \lambda(s) = \{e\} \\ 0 & \text{otherwise,} \end{cases}$$

for all $s \in S$. The final marking of Σ is the function $M_x: S \to \mathbb{N}$ defined for all $s \in S$ by

$$M_x(s) = \begin{cases} 1 & \text{if } \lambda(s) = \{x\} \\ 0 & \text{otherwise.} \end{cases}$$

$ST(\Sigma) = (S, T, W, M_e)$ is the place/transition system associated with Σ. ■ 3.10

The standard Petri net transition rule applies to yield new markings from the initial marking. In the generality defined in this section, a labelled net does not necessarily satisfy any of the pleasant behavioural properties such as safeness, boundedness or liveness. Also, the final marking may not actually be reachable from M_e.

As a guide to intuition, the reader may safely understand all of the constructions that follow in such a way that the various Boxes (more precisely, one of their representatives) are to be provided with their initial marking; their behaviours are then supposed to match the intended behaviours of the Box expression to which they are associated. It is only after the structural constructions have been fully described that we will be able to state some of the elementary behavioural properties of the semantics of Box expressions.

Here, we quote two results from [8], which are not hard to prove. The first one states that, when restricted to causal nets (i.e., acyclic place-unbranched nets), conditions (1)–(3) of Definition 3.5 imply (completed) pomset equivalence [34].

Theorem 3.11

Let two causal nets be related by a relation ρ satisfying (1), (2) *and* (3) *of Definition* 3.5. *Then there is an order-isomorphism between their events, and a corresponding bijection between their reachable cuts.* ■ 3.11

As a consequence, the two causal nets then also have the same sets of linearisations. The second result states that ρ-related systems have similarly related processes.

Theorem 3.12

Let B be a Box and $\Sigma_1, \Sigma_2 \in B$ be two ρ-related representatives of B. Then every process (in the sense of [9]*) of Σ_1, starting from its initial marking, is ρ'-related to some process of Σ_2, starting from the initial marking of Σ_2, where ρ' satisfies* (1)–(5) *of Definition* 3.5, *with the labellings inherited from the respective systems.* ■ 3.12

Together, these two theorems allow us to identify the behaviours of two renaming equivalent labelled nets, and hence define a unique behaviour of a Box. In particular, two representatives of the same Box have exactly (modulo the renaming relation) the same occurrence sequences, viz. interleavings. Moreover, some standard notions such as boundedness can be transferred.

4 The Box Algebra

We distinguish auxiliary basic Petri net operations such as adding or removing places or transitions, from operations on Boxes. There are essentially four auxiliary operations that we need: (disjoint) union $\sqcup$, adding new places or transitions $\oplus$, removing places or transitions $\ominus$, and set multiplication $\otimes$ (applied to sets of places); these operations are of a technical nature and are defined in Appendix B.

We define first the basic Boxes, and then ways of deriving more complicated Boxes from simpler ones. In particular, we define sequential composition, choice (alternative) composition, concurrent composition and other operations that correspond to the Box expression syntax. We claim no particular novelty for the operators for sequence and choice; in fact, these operators have been defined almost identically in the literature (e.g., [19,21,30,61]). We claim some novelty for the concurrent composition in combination with synchronisation.

4.1 Basic Boxes

The basic Boxes of our algebra are the Boxes $Box(\beta)$, for $\beta \in \mathcal{L}$, and the Boxes $Box(w)$, for $w \in \mathcal{W}$, as defined in Example 3.9. The **stop** Box is not basic, since it is derivable; see, for instance, Section 4.7.

4.2 Sequence

Using the 'set multiplication' operator $\otimes$ defined in Appendix B, the sequential composition of two Boxes can be defined on a pair of disjoint representatives. The exit places of the first net are 'place multiplied' with the entry places of the second. This has the effect of requiring the termination of the first net before any behaviour is allowed in the second.

Definition 4.1 *Sequential composition of Boxes*

Let $B_1 = [\Sigma_1]$ and $B_2 = [\Sigma_2]$ be such that Σ_1 and Σ_2 are sufficiently disjoint[7]. First, define

$$\begin{aligned}\Sigma_1;\Sigma_2 \;=\; (\Sigma_1 \sqcup \Sigma_2) \;&\oplus\; (\Sigma_1^{\bullet} \otimes {}^{\bullet}\Sigma_2, \emptyset)\\ &\ominus\; (\Sigma_1^{\bullet} \cup {}^{\bullet}\Sigma_2),\end{aligned}$$

where $l = \emptyset$ denotes the constant function assigning $\emptyset$ to every element of $\Sigma_1^{\bullet} \otimes {}^{\bullet}\Sigma_2$.
Define $B_1; B_2 = [\Sigma_1; \Sigma_2]$. ■ 4.1

This definition is independent of the representatives of B_1 and B_2, because if $s_1, s_1' \in \Sigma_1^{\bullet}$ duplicate each other in Σ_1, and $s_2, s_2' \in {}^{\bullet}\Sigma_2$ duplicate each other in Σ_2, then the pairs $\{s_1, s_2\}$ and $\{s_1', s_2'\}$ formed in the set $\Sigma_1^{\bullet} \otimes {}^{\bullet}\Sigma_2$ also duplicate each other in $\Sigma_1; \Sigma_2$. Furthermore, it is easy to see that $B_1; B_2$ inherits the Box properties (o)–(vi) of Definition 3.8 from the corresponding properties of B_1 and B_2. Also, we have:

[7] Here and in the following, this means that not only S_1 and S_2, but also their respective sets of sub-multisets, and the sets of transitions, are pairwise disjoint.

Lemma 4.2 *Associativity of sequential composition*

$(B_1; B_2); B_3 = B_1; (B_2; B_3)$.

Proof: Let $B_i = [\Sigma_i]$ for $i = 1,2,3$, where the Σ_i are mutually sufficiently disjoint. Let $B_1; B_2 = [\Sigma_{12}]$ and $B_2; B_3 = [\Sigma_{23}]$. By construction, (i) Σ_{12} and Σ_3, and similarly Σ_1 and Σ_{23}, are sufficiently disjoint. Furthermore, by construction, (ii) $\Sigma_{12}^\bullet = \Sigma_2^\bullet$ and ${}^\bullet\Sigma_{23} = {}^\bullet\Sigma_2$. Moreover, (iii) $\Sigma_1^\bullet \cup {}^\bullet\Sigma_2$ is disjoint from $\Sigma_2^\bullet \cup {}^\bullet\Sigma_3$.

$$
\begin{array}{rcll}
(\Sigma_1;\Sigma_2);\Sigma_3 & = & (\Sigma_{12} \sqcup \Sigma_3) \oplus (\Sigma_{12}^\bullet \otimes {}^\bullet\Sigma_3, \emptyset) \ominus (\Sigma_{12}^\bullet \cup {}^\bullet\Sigma_3) & \text{by def.} \\
& = & (\Sigma_{12} \sqcup \Sigma_3) \oplus (\Sigma_2^\bullet \otimes {}^\bullet\Sigma_3, \emptyset) \ominus (\Sigma_2^\bullet \cup {}^\bullet\Sigma_3) & \text{by (ii)} \\
& = & (\Sigma_1 \sqcup \Sigma_2 \sqcup \Sigma_3) \oplus (\Sigma_1^\bullet \otimes {}^\bullet\Sigma_2, \emptyset) \ominus (\Sigma_1^\bullet \cup {}^\bullet\Sigma_2) & \\
& & \oplus (\Sigma_2^\bullet \otimes {}^\bullet\Sigma_3, \emptyset) \ominus (\Sigma_2^\bullet \cup {}^\bullet\Sigma_3) & \text{by (i) and def.} \\
& = & (\Sigma_1 \sqcup \Sigma_2 \sqcup \Sigma_3) \oplus (\Sigma_2^\bullet \otimes {}^\bullet\Sigma_3, \emptyset) \ominus (\Sigma_2^\bullet \cup {}^\bullet\Sigma_3) & \\
& & \oplus (\Sigma_1^\bullet \otimes {}^\bullet\Sigma_2, \emptyset) \ominus (\Sigma_1^\bullet \cup {}^\bullet\Sigma_2) & \text{by (iii)} \\
& & & \text{and Lemma B.5} \\
& = & \Sigma_1; (\Sigma_2; \Sigma_3) & \\
& & \text{by a similar argument in the other direction.} &
\end{array}
$$

■ 4.2

We omit an example, as the construction should be clear.

4.3 Choice

For choice composition, the entry places of both nets are multiplied in a similar way to the above. The exit places of both nets are also multiplied, so that their flows of control rejoin after the choice.

Definition 4.3 *Choice composition of Boxes*

Let $B_1 = [\Sigma_1]$ and $B_2 = [\Sigma_2]$ be such that Σ_1 and Σ_2 are sufficiently disjoint. First, define

$$
\begin{array}{rcll}
\Sigma_1 \,\square\, \Sigma_2 & = & (\Sigma_1 \sqcup \Sigma_2) & \oplus \; ({}^\bullet\Sigma_1 \otimes {}^\bullet\Sigma_2, \mathbf{e}) \\
& & & \oplus \; (\Sigma_1^\bullet \otimes \Sigma_2^\bullet, \mathbf{x}) \\
& & & \ominus \; ({}^\bullet\Sigma_1 \cup {}^\bullet\Sigma_2 \cup \Sigma_1^\bullet \cup \Sigma_2^\bullet),
\end{array}
$$

where $\mathbf{e}$ is the constant function assigning $\{e\}$ to every element of ${}^\bullet\Sigma_1 \otimes {}^\bullet\Sigma_2$, and $\mathbf{x}$ is the constant function assigning $\{x\}$ to every element of $\Sigma_1^\bullet \otimes \Sigma_2^\bullet$.
Define $B_1 \,\square\, B_2 = [\Sigma_1 \,\square\, \Sigma_2]$. ■ 4.3

Figure 4 shows an example. Again, this definition is independent of the representatives. Furthermore, $B_1 \,\square\, B_2$ satisfies the Box properties of Definition 3.8. Also, we have:

Lemma 4.4 *Unit for choice; commutativity and associativity of choice*

$$
\begin{array}{rlcl}
\text{(i)} & B \,\square\, \mathbf{stop} & = & B \;=\; \mathbf{stop} \,\square\, B \\
\text{(ii)} & B_1 \,\square\, B_2 & = & B_2 \,\square\, B_1 \\
\text{(iii)} & (B_1 \,\square\, B_2) \,\square\, B_3 & = & B_1 \,\square\, (B_2 \,\square\, B_3).
\end{array}
$$

Proof: (i) Follows immediately from the definition.

(ii) Commutativity follows directly from the commutativity of the set multiplication operator $\otimes$.

(iii) The proof of associativity is similar to the associativity of sequence. ■ 4.4

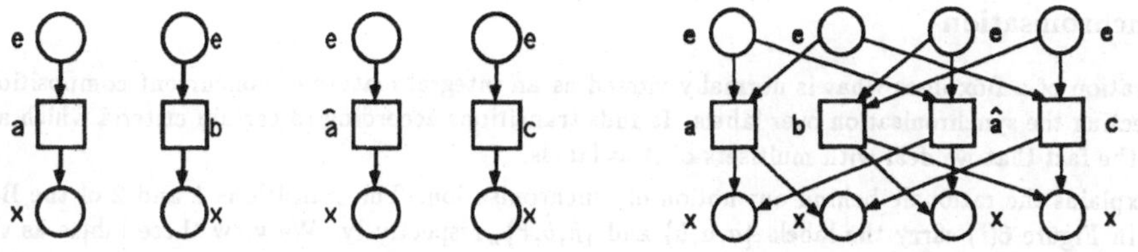

Box(*a*)‖*Box*(*b*) *Box*(*â*)‖*Box*(*c*) (*Box*(*a*)‖*Box*(*b*)) □ (*Box*(*â*)‖*Box*(*c*))

Figure 4: An example of the alternative composition of Boxes

Open Point 4.5 *Idempotence of choice*

In the present setting, we do not have that $B \,\square\, B = B$ in all generality, while this would certainly be a desirable structural identity of Boxes. To obtain it, it would probably be necessary to extend the equivalence relation which defines the Boxes. ■ 4.5

4.4 Concurrent composition

For concurrent composition we simply juxtapose Boxes, i.e., take their (disjoint) union.

Definition 4.6 *Concurrent composition of Boxes*

Let $B_1 = [\Sigma_1]$ and $B_2 = [\Sigma_2]$ such that Σ_1 and Σ_2 are disjoint.
Define $B_1 \| B_2 = [\Sigma_1 \sqcup \Sigma_2]$. ■ 4.6

Figure 5 shows an example. This definition is independent of the representatives. Also, $B_1 \| B_2$ satisfies the Box properties (o)–(vi) of 3.8. Furthermore, we have:

Lemma 4.7 *Commutativity and associativity of concurrent composition*

$$\begin{array}{lrcl} \text{(i)} & B_1 \| B_2 & = & B_2 \| B_1 \\ \text{(ii)} & (B_1 \| B_2) \| B_3 & = & B_1 \| (B_2 \| B_3). \end{array}$$

■ 4.7

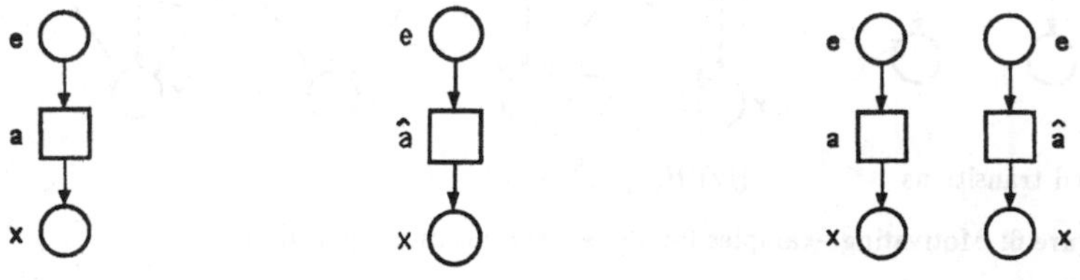

(i) *Box*(*a*) (ii) *Box*(*â*) (iii) $B_6 = Box(a) \| Box(\hat{a})$

Figure 5: An example of the concurrent composition of Boxes

4.5 Synchronisation

Synchronisation of a Box does what is normally viewed as an integral feature of concurrent composition, that of effecting the synchronisation over labels. It adds transitions according to certain criteria which are related to the fact that we deal with multisets of A as labels.

Figure 6 explains the rationale behind our notion of synchronisation. The transitions 1 and 2 of the Box B_7 shown in Figure 6(i) carry the labels $\{a, a, b\}$ and $\{\hat{a}, \hat{b}, c\}$, respectively. We view these labels as the 'synchronisation capabilities' of the transitions. Two conjugate capabilities may lead to their transitions joining up, yielding a new transition in which the conjugate capabilities that have effected the synchronisation disappear, but which otherwise has the combined capabilities of its constituents. As in CCS, original transitions are retained until (possibly) restricted away. Thus, in Figure 6(ii), the transition named 12 arises from synchronising transitions 1 and 2 over $a, \hat{a}$. This transition can be further synchronised with transition 2, again over $a, \hat{a}$, to yield the transition named 122 with capabilities $\{b, \hat{b}, \hat{b}, c, c\}$.

The procedure of 'joining up' can be performed repeatedly, apparently needing an 'iterative' definition of synchronisation. This subsection, however, presents a non-iterative formula; in the next section, we show that the formula captures the iterative procedure.

The difference between SCCS, the synchronous variant of CCS [50], and our synchronisation operation can be seen on the example B_9 (corresponding to $E_9 = a \| \hat{a} \| a \| \hat{a}$) depicted in Figure 6(iii). Upon synchronisation over $(a, \hat{a})$, our definition would produce a set of synchronisations as shown in Figure 6(iv), but *not* the four-way $\emptyset$-labelled synchronisation that SCCS would produce. The reason lies in the idea that every time an $a, \hat{a}$-link is established, these two capabilities vanish by being internalised into the result of the synchronisation, as opposed to SCCS where the possible synchronisations correspond to the (time-) steps of the original system.

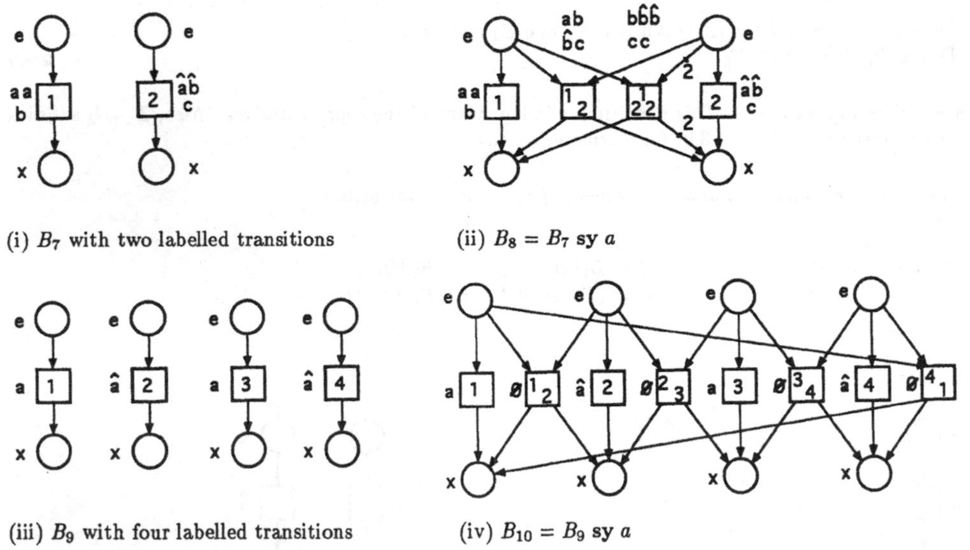

(i) B_7 with two labelled transitions (ii) $B_8 = B_7$ **sy** a

(iii) B_9 with four labelled transitions (iv) $B_{10} = B_9$ **sy** a

Figure 6: Motivating examples for the synchronisation operation

Definition 4.8 *Synchronisation of Boxes*

Let $B = [\Sigma]$ with $\Sigma = (S, T, W, \lambda)$ be a Box, and let $a \in A$ be an action name.
Let $T^a = \{t \in T \mid \{a, \hat{a}\} \cap \lambda(t) \neq \emptyset\}$ be the set of transitions of Σ that carry an a or an $\hat{a}$ in their label. Let $\tau \in \mathcal{M}_{\mathcal{F}}(T^a) \setminus \{\emptyset\}$ be a finite nonempty multiset of transitions of T^a. We define $c(\tau)$ as the

minimum of the sum of a names and the sum of $\hat{a}$ names in τ, viz.:

$$c(\tau) = \min(\sum_{t\in\tau} \lambda(t)(a)\,,\, \sum_{t\in\tau} \lambda(t)(\hat{a})\,)$$

With

$$\begin{array}{rcll} T' & = & \{\,\tau \in \mathcal{M}_{\mathcal{F}}(T^a)\backslash\{\emptyset\} \mid c(\tau) \geq |\tau| - 1\,\} & \\ \text{and } l : T' & \rightarrow & \mathcal{L}, \quad \text{defined by} & \\ l(\tau) & = & (\sum_{t\in\tau}\lambda(t)) \setminus (\,(|\tau|-1)\cdot\{a,\hat{a}\}\,) & \text{for } \tau \in T', \end{array}$$

we define Σ **sy** $a = \Sigma \oplus (T', l)$ and B **sy** $a = [\Sigma$ **sy** $a]$. ■ 4.8

For instance, in Figure 6(ii), the transition called 122 arises from the multiset $\tau = \{1,2,2\}$ for which we have $c(\tau) = 2 \geq |\tau| - 1 = 2$. Consider also Figure 6(iii); the multiset $\tau = \{1,2,3,4\}$ of transitions cannot be synchronised because we have $c(\tau) = 2 < |\tau| - 1 = 3$. Nor can the multiset $\tau = \{1,2,3\}$ be synchronised, since $c(\tau) = 1 < |\tau| - 1 = 2$. However, any of the multisets $\tau = \{1,2\}$, $\tau = \{2,3\}$, $\tau = \{3,4\}$ or $\tau = \{4,1\}$ can be synchronised, as for each of these $c(\tau) = 1 \geq |\tau| - 1 = 1$ holds true.

Definition 4.8 is independent of the representative Σ of B, because it comes to the same whether a transition $t \in T$ is viewed as occurring $m = \tau(t)$ times in τ, or whether m duplicates of t are viewed as occurring singly in τ. Furthermore, B **sy** a inherits the properties (o)–(vi) of Definition 3.8 from B; in particular, while B **sy** a may introduce arc weights greater than 1 and side conditions, it may never do so around $\mathcal{W}$-labelled transitions, since such transitions may not partake in a synchronisation. The absence of isolated transitions in Σ **sy** a follows from the exclusion of $\tau = \emptyset$.

There are two major aspects of this definition. One is the inequality $c(\tau) \geq |\tau| - 1$ which ensures that τ contains sufficiently many $a, \hat{a}$-pairs to enforce the synchronisation. If τ satisfies this condition, we will also call τ *$(a,\hat{a})$-synchronisable*. In the next section, we show that this inequality captures the incremental aspect of our intended notion of synchronisation, which can be expressed as follows:

'Repeatedly choose $a, \hat{a}$-pairs of labels and synchronise the underlying transitions.'

The other aspect is that the label of each newly created transition is defined as the sum of its constituent labels, less exactly all the capability pairs involved in the synchronisation. Figure 7 shows that another possibility – taking away $c(\tau)$ rather than $|\tau| - 1$ many pairs $\{a, \hat{a}\}$ – leads to the failure of commutativity: performing synchronisation first on a and then on b yields a 4-way synchronisation $\{\{1\},\{1,2\},\{2\}\}$ with the label $\{a,\hat{a},c,c,d,d\}$. If $c(\tau)$ many pairs are taken away, this transition cannot be created the other way round.

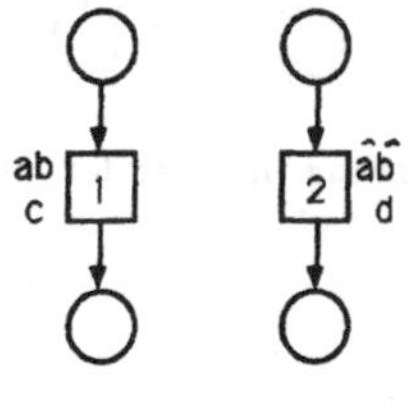

Figure 7: An example showing the need for taking away $|\tau| - 1$ many pairs $a, \hat{a}$

It may happen that $c(\tau) = 0$, in which case for synchronisation we must have $|\tau| = 1$ (say, $\tau = \{t\}$), and the label of t contains either at least one a but no $\hat{a}$, or the other way round; in this case, the transition $\{t\}$ is carried forward to Σ **sy** a without change, and hence becomes a duplicate in the synchronised net.

Normally, supposing that T itself is finite, only finitely many synchronisation transitions will be produced. Consider, for instance, the two-transition Box B_6 (cf. Figure 5(iii)) with transitions $\{1,2\}$ and labels a for transition 1 and $\hat{a}$ for transition 2. The set $\tau_1 = \{1,2\}$ describes a valid synchronisation contained in

$B_{13} = B_6$ **sy** a (cf. Figure 10(ii)), because $c(\tau_1) = 1 \geq |\tau_1| - 1 = 1$. But neither the set $\tau_2 = \{1,1,2\}$ (with $c(\tau_2) = 1 < |\tau_2| - 1 = 3 - 1 = 2$) nor the set $\tau_3 = \{1,1,2,2\}$, nor in fact any further multiset can be synchronised. However, if there are 'too many' $a, \hat{a}$-pairs in τ, the synchronisation operation may create infinitely many new transitions, as for instance in the Box $B_{32} = Box(\{a,\hat{a}\})$ **sy** a shown in Figure 8.

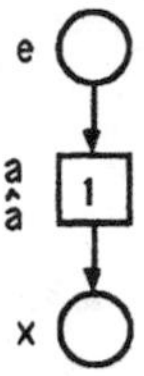

(i) B_{31} with one transition

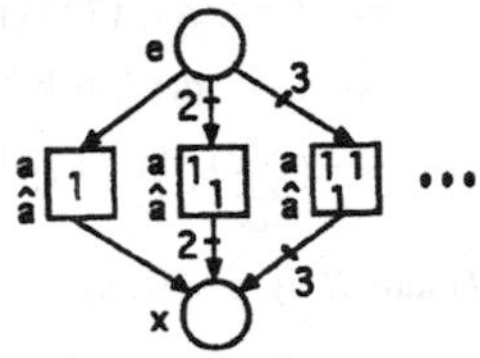

(ii) $B_{32} = B_{31}$ **sy** a with infinitely many transitions

Figure 8: Infinitely many synchronisations

Remark 4.9

There is the following, easily checkable, criterion for there to be infinitely many synchronisations: If Σ is finite then Σ **sy** a is infinite if and only if

$$\exists t \in T\colon\ \lambda(t)(a) \cdot \lambda(t)(\hat{a}) > 0$$
$$\text{or}\quad \exists t_1, t_2 \in T\colon\ \lambda(t_1)(a) > 1 < \lambda(t_2)(\hat{a}).$$

■ 4.9

The example of Figure 9 shows that multisets rather than sets are necessary in order to achieve the commutativity of synchronisation in general. When synchronisation takes place first over $(b, \hat{b})$, then both the sets $\{1,3\}$ and $\{2,4\}$ may synchronise, after which the resulting two transitions can synchronise over $(a, \hat{a})$. In order to achieve the same possibility the other way round, the label b must be duplicated in the transition $\{1,2\}$ that results when synchronisation is performed first over $(a, \hat{a})$.

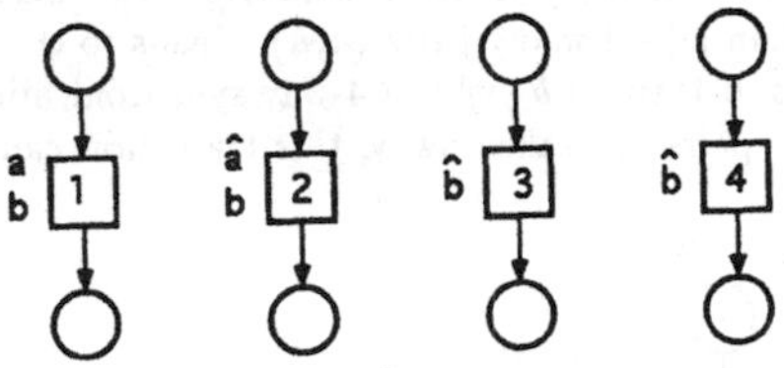

Figure 9: An example showing the need for multiset labels

4.6 Restriction

Restriction over an action name a removes those transitions of a Box whose labels contain a or $\hat{a}$.

Definition 4.10 *Restriction*

Let $B = [\Sigma]$ and $a \in A$. Define Σ **rs** $a = \Sigma \ominus T^a$, where T^a is defined as in 4.8.
Define B **rs** $a = [\Sigma$ **rs** $a]$. ■ 4.10

This definition is again independent of the representative. Also, B **rs** a satisfies the Box properties. Its equational properties will be given in the next section. Figure 10 shows an example.

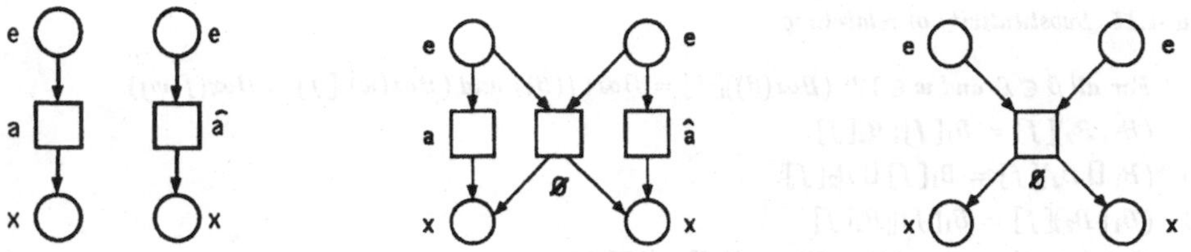

(i) $Box(a)\|Box(\hat{a})$ (ii) $B_{13} = (Box(a)\|Box(\hat{a}))$ **sy** a (iii) $B_{15} = ((Box(a)\|Box(\hat{a}))$ **sy** $a)$ **rs** a

Figure 10: An example of restriction and scoping

4.7 Scoping

Scoping is synchronisation followed by restriction. It derives its name from the fact that there is a direct translation of the block structure of, say, occam–2, into a scoping construct [16,50].

Definition 4.11 *Scoping*

Let B be a Box, and $a \in A$. Define $[\, a : B\,] = ((B$ **sy** $a)$ **rs** $a)$. ■ 4.11

The equational properties of scoping will be given in the next section. Scoping allows the **stop** Box to be derived as **stop** $= B_{16} = [\, a : Box(a)\,]$.
Figure 10 shows another example; note that $B_{15} = [\, a : Box(a)\|Box(\hat{a})\,]$.

Remark 4.12

Neither scoping, nor restriction, nor synchronisation has any effect on $\emptyset$-labelled, or $\mathcal{W}$-labelled transitions. ■ 4.12

4.8 Relabelling

Let $f: A \to A$ be a relabelling function. The relabelling of a Box B, denoted by $B[f]$ or occasionally by $f(B)$, applies f to all (non-emptyset-labelled) transitions. For a label $\beta \in \mathcal{L}$, f is simply applied to β, yielding a possibly different multiset $f(\beta) \in \mathcal{L}$. For a label $X \in \mathcal{V}$, the option of relabelling whatever the eventual refinement of the X-labelled transition may yield, is kept open by labelling the transition by $f(X) \in \mathcal{W}$ instead of $X \in \mathcal{V}$. If such relabelling is iterated, we get $g(f(X)) = (f \circ g)(X)$, not needing an extension of the set $\mathcal{W}$; and this is consistent with viewing $\mathcal{V}$ as a subset of $\mathcal{W}$, cf. Remark 3.1.

Definition 4.13 *Relabelling*

Let $B = [\Sigma]$ be a Box with $\Sigma = (S,T,W,\lambda)$.
Define $\Sigma[f] = f(\Sigma) = (S,T,W,\lambda')$ with $\lambda'|_S = \lambda|_S$ and $\forall t \in T: \lambda'(t) = f(\lambda(t))$.
Finally, $B[f] = f(B) = [f(\Sigma)]$. ■ 4.13

This definition is independent of the representative. The Box properties of $B[f]$ are inherited from B.

Remark 4.14

Like all other operations on Boxes, relabelling can be viewed as affecting only the Box's interface elements, since any relabelling function f (or rather, its extension to $\mathcal{L}$) satisfies $f(\emptyset) = \emptyset$. ■ 4.14

Call f $(a,\hat{a})$-detached iff $z \in \{a,\hat{a}\} \iff f(z) \in \{a,\hat{a}\}$. Relabelling satisfies the following equational properties.

Lemma 4.15 *Substitutivity of relabelling*

(i) *For all* $\beta \in \mathcal{L}$ *and* $w \in \mathcal{W}$: $(Box(\beta))[f] = Box(f(\beta))$ *and* $(Box(w))[f] = Box(f(w))$.

(ii) $(B_1; B_2)[f] = B_1[f]; B_2[f]$.

(iii) $(B_1 \,\square\, B_2)[f] = B_1[f] \,\square\, B_2[f]$.

(iv) $(B_1 \| B_2)[f] = B_1[f] \| B_2[f]$.

(v) *If* f *is* $(a, \hat{a})$*-detached then* $(B \textbf{ sy } a)[f] = (B[f] \textbf{ sy } a)$.

(vi) *If* f *is* $(a, \hat{a})$*-detached then* $(B \textbf{ rs } a)[f] = (B[f] \textbf{ rs } a)$.

(vii) *If* f *is* $(a, \hat{a})$*-detached then* $[a : B][f] = [a : B[f]]$.

(viii) $(B[f])[g] = B[f \circ g]$.

(ix) $B[id] = B$.

Proof: (i) follows immediately from the definition.

(ii)–(iv): f affects only transition labels. The set of transitions of (representatives of) $B_1; B_2$, $B_1 \,\square\, B_2$ and $B_1 \| B_2$ is the disjoint union of the respective sets of transitions of (representatives of) B_1, B_2. Hence the property.

(v): By ($\Rightarrow$) of $(a, \hat{a})$-detachedness, f does not impinge on $a, \hat{a}$-synchronisability. Moreover the label of any transition of B **sy** a can at most have some $(a, \hat{a})$-pairs less than the sum of the labels of the underlying transitions. Hence the application of f commutes with the computation of the new label of a transitions created by **sy** a. By ($\Leftarrow$) of $(a, \hat{a})$-detachedness, $(B[f] \textbf{ sy } a)$ does not contain more $(a, \hat{a})$-synchronisations than $(B \textbf{ sy } a)[f]$.

(vi): Similar.

(vii): From (v) and (vi).

(viii): Immediate.

(ix): By virtue of the identification of the set $\mathcal{V}$ and the set $\{id(X) \mid X \in \mathcal{V}\} \subseteq \mathcal{W}$. ∎ 4.15

Figure 11 shows two examples corresponding to E_{17} and E_{18}, respectively.

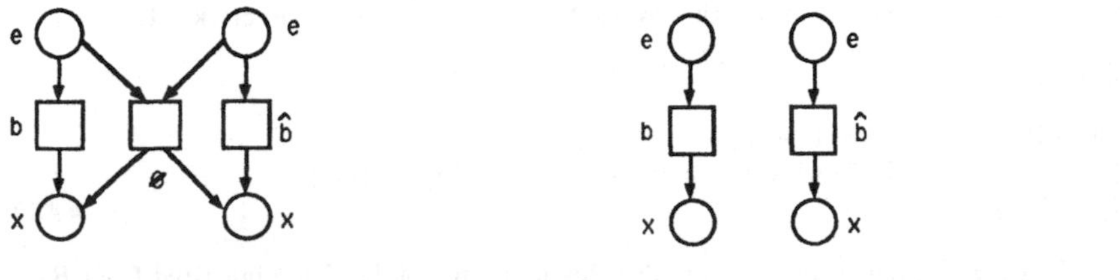

(i) $B_{17} = (Box(a)[a \to b] \| Box(\hat{b})) \textbf{ sy } b$ (ii) $B_{18} = (Box(a)[a \to b] \| (Box(\hat{b}) \textbf{ sy } b))$

Figure 11: Two examples of relabelling

4.9 Refinement

We closely follow the definition in [32]. Refinement of the form $B_1[X \leftarrow B_2]$ is defined as the replacement of every transition t labelled X in a representative of the Box B_1 by a (fresh, i.e., sufficiently disjoint) representative of the Box B_2. B_2 may contain further transitions labelled X. The replacement is done by multiplying the pre-places of t in the representative of B_1 with the entry places of the representative of B_2, and doing the same with the post-places of t and the exit places of the representative of B_2. This guarantees that the representative of B_2 that is inserted in place of t 'behaves like a transition'. The replacement of a transition t by a net is known to create problems in case t is contained in a side condition (i.e., ${}^\bullet t \cap t^\bullet \neq \emptyset$) [10]. The Box model excludes that case.

Definition 4.16 *Refinement - the finite case*

Let $B_i = [\Sigma_i]$ with $\Sigma_i = (S_i, T_i, W_i, \lambda_i)$ $(i = 1,2)$ be two Boxes. We exploit Remark 3.1, allowing the identification of X-labels and $id(X)$-labels. Let

$$T_1^X = \{t \in T_1 \mid \exists f: \lambda_1(t) = f(X)\}$$

denote the set of all transitions of Σ_1 that carry either an X-label or an $f(X)$-label, for any relabelling function f. Assume that the set T_1^X is finite. Select a transition $t \in T_1^X$.
By the properties (v,vi) of Boxes, t has bordering arcs with weights at most 1 and is free of side conditions. Therefore, with

$$\begin{aligned} {}^\bullet t &= \{s \in S_1 \mid W_1(s,t) = 1\} \\ t^\bullet &= \{s \in S_1 \mid W_1(t,s) = 1\} \end{aligned}$$

we have ${}^\bullet t \cap t^\bullet = \emptyset$ and $W(s,t) = 0 = W(t,s)$ for all $s \notin ({}^\bullet t \cup t^\bullet)$. If $f(X)$ is t's label, let $\Sigma_2^{(t)}$ denote a fresh copy[7] of $f(\Sigma_2)$. First, define

$$\begin{aligned} \Sigma_1[t \leftarrow \Sigma_2^{(t)}] &= (\Sigma_1 \sqcup \Sigma_2^{(t)}) \\ &\oplus ({}^\bullet t \otimes {}^\bullet\Sigma_2^{(t)}, l_1) \oplus (t^\bullet \otimes \Sigma_2^{(t)\bullet}, l_2) \\ &\ominus ({}^\bullet t \cup {}^\bullet\Sigma_2^{(t)}) \ominus (t^\bullet \cup \Sigma_2^{(t)\bullet}), \end{aligned}$$

where l_1 is the labelling function inherited from ${}^\bullet t$ and l_2 is the labelling function inherited from $t^\bullet$. Let $\Sigma_1[X \leftarrow \Sigma_2]$ be the result of exhaustively applying the above procedure for all $t \in T_1^X$, each time starting with the result of the previous iteration (without recalculating T_1^X).
Finally, $B_1[X \leftarrow B_2] = [\,\Sigma_1[X \leftarrow \Sigma_2] \ominus T_1^X]$. ■ 4.16

Definition 4.16 is independent of the representatives, and the Box properties are preserved at each stage.

Remark 4.17 *Independence of the representative*

This property depends on the restriction (5) of Definition 3.5. For instance, the two Boxes $Box(X)[X \leftarrow Box(a)\|Box(b)]$ and $(Box(X)\,\square\,Box(X))[X \leftarrow Box(a)\|Box(b)]$ are not renaming equivalent. ■ 4.17

Remark 4.18 *Commutativity of refinement*

We claim that Definition 4.16 does not depend on the order in which the transitions of T_1^X are chosen. The proof is, however, not immediate and is not contained in this paper. The reader is referred to [14], where it is shown that the commutativity of refinement follows from a general definition of (simultaneous) refinement. ■ 4.18

---

[7] At this point we may exploit the freedom of giving names to the places and transitions in order to utilise refinement for recursion – see citeespa and Section 4.10.

Open Point 4.19 *The infinite case*

If the set T_1^X is not finite then the iterative procedure of Definition 4.16 does not terminate. The generalisation of this definition necessarily creates a problem of cardinality. For instance, let B_{large} denote the Box shown in Figure 12. Then the Box $B_{\text{large}}[X \leftarrow (Box(a)\|Box(b))]$ generates an uncountably infinite set of places.

Because of this, we define refinement in this paper only under the restriction of the finiteness of the set T_1^X. [27] contains a definition which works even if the set T_1^X is infinite, but constrains transitions t in T_1^X to appear between two transitions labelled $\emptyset$, the 'call' and the 'return' transitions corresponding to t. If X-labels always occur in this context then refinement does not lead out of the set of finite or countably infinite labelled nets. More recent work [14] generalises the definition to avoid all restrictions, and moreover, also deals with simultaneous refinement and refinement within side conditions (lifting restriction (vi) of Definition 3.8 and consequently, the corresponding restriction on iteration).

■ 4.19

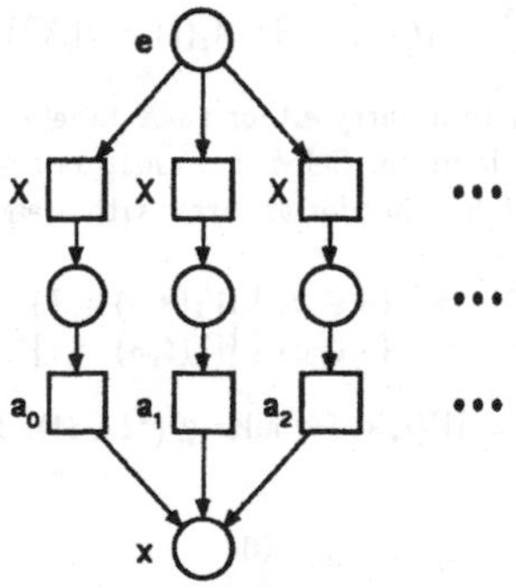

Figure 12: A countably infinite Box B_{large}

Call two Boxes B and B' (X,a)-detached iff whenever B contains a label $f(X)$ then B' contains no label containing b such that $f(b) \in \{a, \hat{a}\}$[10]. Refinement satisfies the following equational properties:

Lemma 4.20 *Substitutivity of refinement*

(i) *If B contains no label $f(X)$ then* $B[X \leftarrow B'] = B$.

(ii) $(B_1; B_2)[X \leftarrow B] = B_1[X \leftarrow B]; B_2[X \leftarrow B]$.

(iii) $(B_1 \,\square\, B_2)[X \leftarrow B] = B_1[X \leftarrow B] \,\square\, B_2[X \leftarrow B]$.

(iv) $(B_1 \| B_2)[X \leftarrow B] = B_1[X \leftarrow B] \| B_2[X \leftarrow B]$.

(v) *If B and B' are (X,a)-detached then* $(B \;\mathbf{sy}\; a)[X \leftarrow B'] = B[X \leftarrow B'] \;\mathbf{sy}\; a$.

(vi) *If B and B' are (X,a)-detached then* $(B \;\mathbf{rs}\; a)[X \leftarrow B'] = B[X \leftarrow B'] \;\mathbf{rs}\; a$.

(vii) *If B and B' are (X,a)-detached then* $[a : B][X \leftarrow B'] = [a : B[X \leftarrow B']]$.

(viii) $(B[X \leftarrow B'])[f] = (B[f])[X \leftarrow B']$.

(ix) $B[X \leftarrow B'][X \leftarrow B''] = B[X \leftarrow B'[X \leftarrow B'']]$.

(x) *If B' contains no label $f(Y)$ and B'' contains no label $f(X)$ then*
$B[X \leftarrow B'][Y \leftarrow B''] = B[Y \leftarrow B''][X \leftarrow B']$.

[10] By virtue of the identification of X-labels and $id(X)$-labels, this means, in particular, that whenever B contains a label X then B' contains no label with a or $\hat{a}$.

Proof: (i): Immediate.

(ii),(iii): From the independence of the ordering of refining transitions.

(iv): Immediate.

(v): B **sy** a has the same set of places as B, and the same set of $f(X)$-labelled transitions with the same interconnections. Therefore it comes to the same whether these transitions are refined in B or in B **sy** a, and since B' has no unsuitably labelled transitions, $B[X \leftarrow B']$ **sy** a cannot differ from $(B \textbf{ sy } a)[X \leftarrow B']$.

(vi): Similar.

(vii): From (v) and (vi).

(viii): From the definition, bearing in mind the fact that an X- or $g(X)$-labelled transition of B becomes an $f(X)$- or $(g \circ f)(X)$-labelled transition in $B[f]$, respectively.

(ix) and (x): From the definition. (But notice that $B[X \leftarrow B'][Y \leftarrow B'']$ does not equal $B[X \leftarrow B'[Y \leftarrow B'']]$ in general, e.g. if $B = Box(Y)$ and $B' = B'' = Box(\emptyset)$.) ■ 4.20

Open Point 4.21

With the definitions given thus far, refinement does not fully satisfy the axioms of 'syntactic substitution' for which, for instance, the equation

$$(B \textbf{ sy } a)[X \leftarrow B'] = B[X \leftarrow B'] \textbf{ sy } a$$

would be required. In order to see the difference, consider the examples

$$\begin{array}{rcl} B_{19} & = & (((Box(b); Box(X))\|Box(\hat{a}))[X \leftarrow Box(a)] \textbf{ sy } a) \\ B_{20} & = & (((Box(b); Box(X))\|Box(\hat{a})) \textbf{ sy } a)[X \leftarrow Box(a)] \end{array}$$

depicted in Figure 13. In B_{19}, synchronisation has been enforced while in B_{20}, there is no synchronisation due to the fact that refinement takes place after synchronisation and the latter does not affect the X-labelled transition (see Remark 4.12). This interplay between synchronisation and refinement is not the only possible solution. What we gain by adopting it is increased compositionality: an X-labelled unrefined transition needs not be taken care of in the definition of synchronisation. What we lose is a direct correspondence to calculi such as CCS which base recursion on substitution rather than refinement. This will be discussed more fully below. ■ 4.21

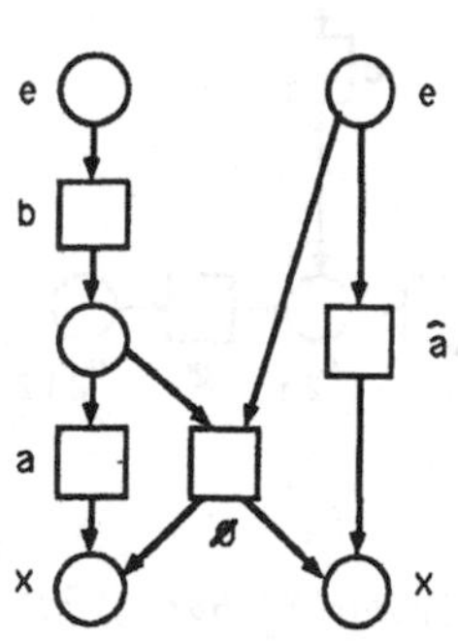

(i) B_{19}, with $E_{19} = (((b; X)\|\hat{a})[X \leftarrow a] \textbf{ sy } a)$

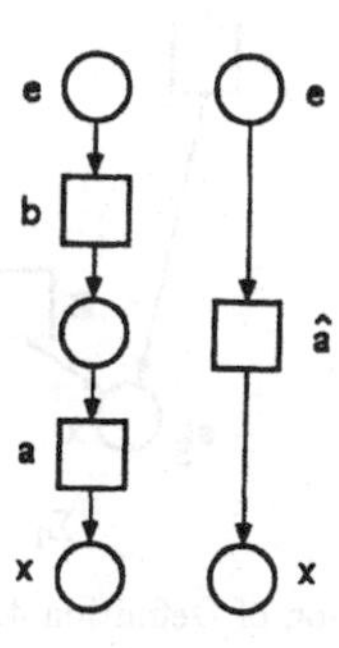

(ii) B_{20}, with $E_{20} = (((b; X)\|\hat{a}) \textbf{ sy } a)[X \leftarrow a])$

Figure 13: Illustration of the non-commutativity between synchronisation and refinement

4.10 Recursion

The Box algebra offers two approaches to the description of recursion: the high level road and the low level road. Both are nontrivial, due to the very general form of the recursion operator. We aim to associate a unique Box to every recursive expression, with none of the restrictions of [23,31,51,59] save guarding [1,50]. The High Level Box approach is developed in [38]. Every recursive expression is translated into a high level Box, which belongs to a restricted class of labelled high level Petri nets. In practically relevant cases [12] this high level Box is finite. We will not go into the details of this approach in the present paper.

The Low Level approach bases recursion on a succession of refinements. This may create infinite, but elementary, nets. The theory of this approach is the subject of other papers [17,27]. This paper only sketches the definition and gives some examples.

Definition 4.22 *Recursion*

Let $B = [\Sigma]$, with $\Sigma = (S, T, W, \lambda)$, be a Box.
Define a sequence of labelled nets $\Sigma_0, \Sigma_1, \Sigma_2, \ldots$ inductively as follows:

$$\begin{aligned} \Sigma_0 &= ({}^\bullet\Sigma \cup \Sigma^\bullet, \emptyset, \emptyset, \lambda|_{{}^\bullet\Sigma\cup\Sigma^\bullet}) \\ \Sigma_{i+1} &= \Sigma[X \leftarrow \Sigma_i]. \end{aligned}$$

(Notice that $[\Sigma_0] = \mathbf{stop}$.) By an elaborate discipline for giving new names to the places and transitions of Σ_{i+1}, coming from the definition of refinement, it can be ensured that $\Sigma_i \sqsubseteq \Sigma_{i+1}$ holds, where $\sqsubseteq$ denotes componentwise inclusion of labelled nets[11]. This construction is too sophisticated to be described in the present paper; the reader is referred to [27].
The sequence $\Sigma_0, \Sigma_1, \ldots$ successively approximates the labelled net $\mu X.\Sigma$ which is defined as the (non-disjoint) union $\bigsqcup_{i\geq 0} \Sigma_i$. Define $\mu X.B = [\mu X.\Sigma]$. ■ 4.22

Again, this definition is representative independent; and $\mu X.B$ is a Box according to Definition 3.8.

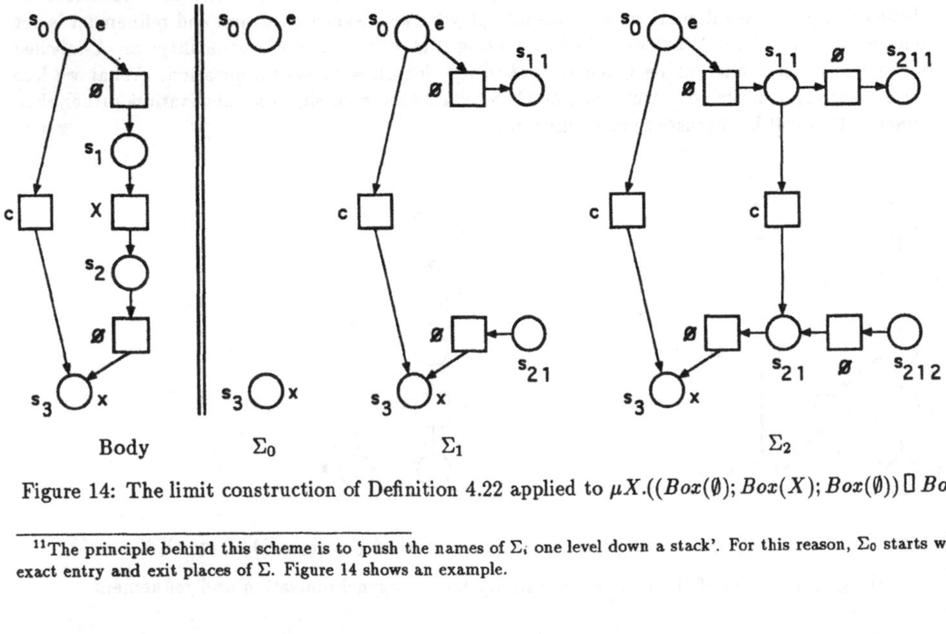

Figure 14: The limit construction of Definition 4.22 applied to $\mu X.((Box(\emptyset); Box(X); Box(\emptyset)) \,\square\, Box(c))$

[11]The principle behind this scheme is to 'push the names of Σ_i one level down a stack'. For this reason, Σ_0 starts with the exact entry and exit places of Σ. Figure 14 shows an example.

Open Point 4.23

The construction of Definition 4.22 can be defined in case Σ contains a finite set T^X of $f(X)$-labelled transitions. Otherwise, the limitation referred to in Open Point 4.19 has consequences for the semantics of a Box expression $\mu X.E$. If $Box(E)$ has an infinite set T^X, then E first needs to be transformed into a guarded expression E' by replacing every free occurrence of X in E by the subexpression $(\emptyset; X; \emptyset)$. We conjecture that there is a strong behavioural equivalence between the Boxes of E and E', and $\mu X.E$ and $\mu X.E'$, in cases where both are defined. Any attempt to lift the guardedness restriction while allowing infinite sets T^X, however, encounters the cardinality problem mentioned in 4.19. ■ 4.23

Recursion offers a different way of deriving the **stop** Box, namely as **stop** $= B_{28} = \mu X.Box(X)$. The 'internally divergent' Box is derivable as **div** $= \mu X.(Box(\emptyset); Box(X))$. Figure 16 shows some other examples which satisfy the condition that the body of the recursion is finite. An example that violates this condition is the nested recursive expression

$$E_{33} = \mu X.(\ \mu Y.((X; a_0) \,\square\, Y[f]) \,\|\, b\ )\ ,$$

where f maps a_i to a_{i+1}. The body of E_{33} creates the Box B_{large} of Figure 12. Before translating E_{33} into a Box, therefore, it must be subjected to the transformation mentioned in 4.23, yielding the expression

$$E_{34} = \mu X.(\ \mu Y.(((\emptyset; X; \emptyset); a_0) \,\square\, Y[f]) \,\|\, b\ )\ .$$

The procedure given in Definition 4.22 can be applied to E_{34}, but the result is not included in this paper. Recursion satisfies the following structural property:

Lemma 4.24 *Substitutivity of recursion*

$\mu X.B = B[X \leftarrow \mu X.B]$.

Proof: *Sketch* (cf. [27]).

Componentwise set inclusion defines a complete partial order on the class of labelled nets, with respect to which the function

$$f_\Sigma(\Pi) = \Sigma[X \leftarrow \Pi]$$

(where $\Sigma \in B$, and Π is an arbitrary labelled net such that $[\Pi]$ is some Box) is continuous. Hence its least fixoint $\mu X.\Sigma$ exists and is approximated by the sequence $\Sigma_0, \Sigma_1, \ldots$ The equation

$$\mu X.\Sigma = \Sigma[X \leftarrow \mu X.\Sigma]$$

results as the fixpoint equation $\mu X.\Sigma = f_\Sigma(\mu X.\Sigma)$. The claim follows from this equation and the representative-independence of the Box of a refinement. ■ 4.24

Open Point 4.25

We have not yet lifted the complete partial order defined for labelled nets to the level of Boxes. The advantage could be to replace the technically expensive naming scheme that achieves $\Sigma_i \subseteq \Sigma_{i+1}$ by an argument based either on injections from Σ_i to Σ_{i+1}, or on surjections from Σ_{i+1} to Σ_i or both. Figure 15 shows that antisymmetry is hard to achieve if the underlying nets are infinite: there is a structure-preserving (i.e., arc-preserving and label-preserving) injective homomorphism from each of the two nets to the other one (shown by the non-horizontal arrows in the figure); however, they are not renaming equivalent. ■ 4.25

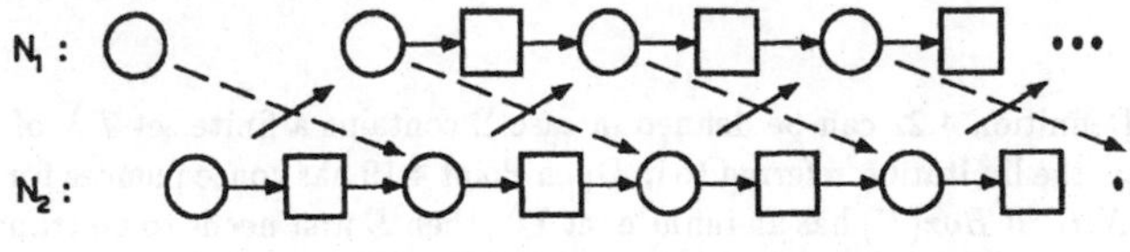

Figure 15: Two non-isomorphic infinite nets

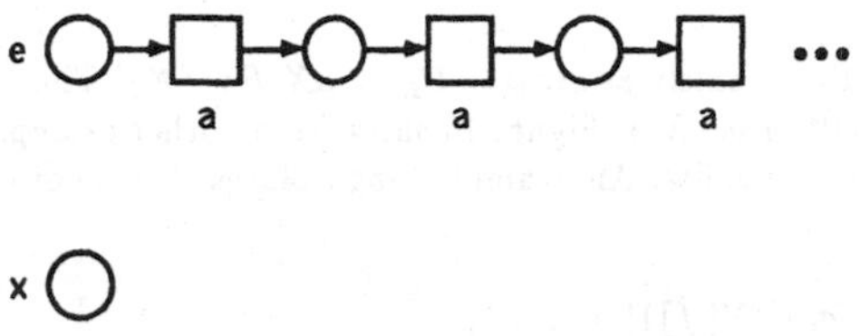

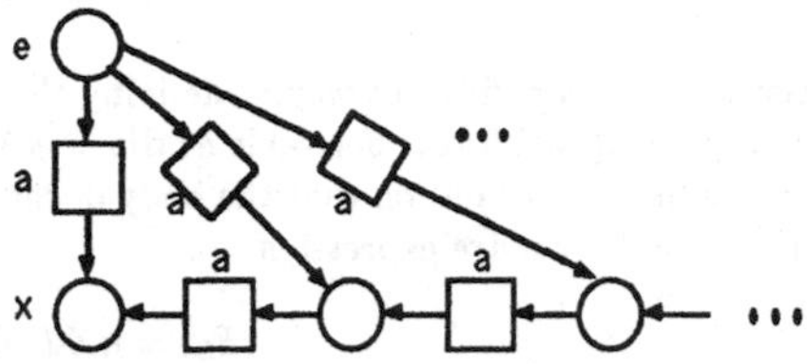

B_{21}, with $E_{21} = \mu X.(a; X)$ B_{22}, with $E_{22} = \mu X.((X; a) \,\square\, a)$

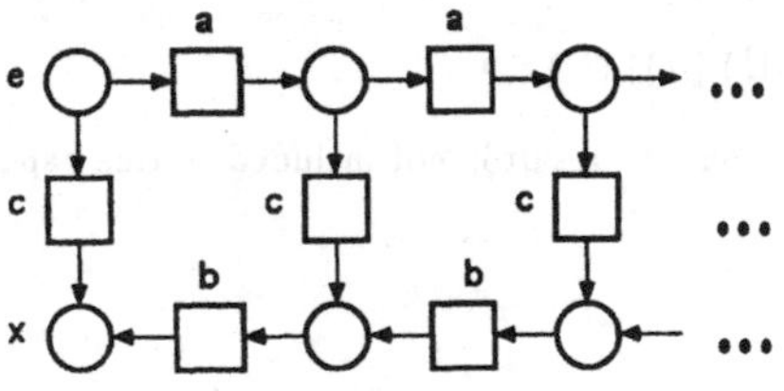

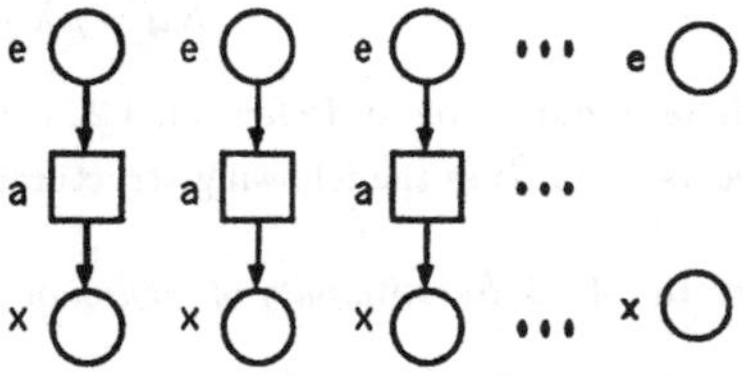

B_{24}, with $E_{24} = \mu X.((a; X; b) \,\square\, c)$ B_{25}, with $E_{25} = \mu X.(a \| X)$

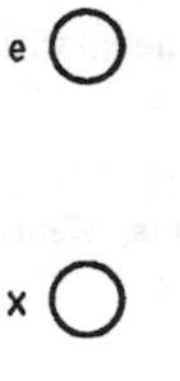

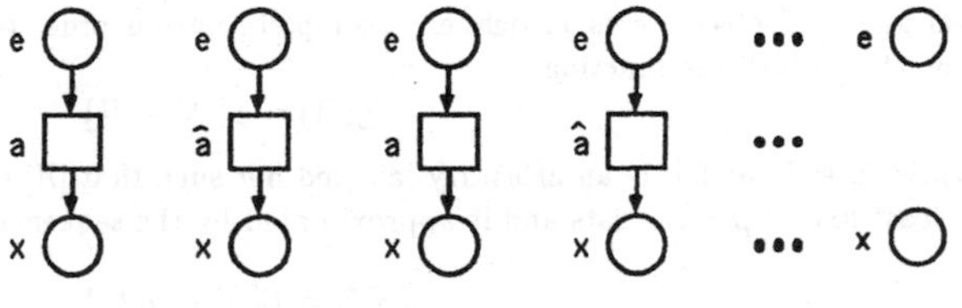

B_{28}, with $E_{28} = \mu X.(X)$ B_{29}, with $E_{29} = \mu X.((a \| X[\,a \rightarrow \hat{a}\,])$ sy $a)$

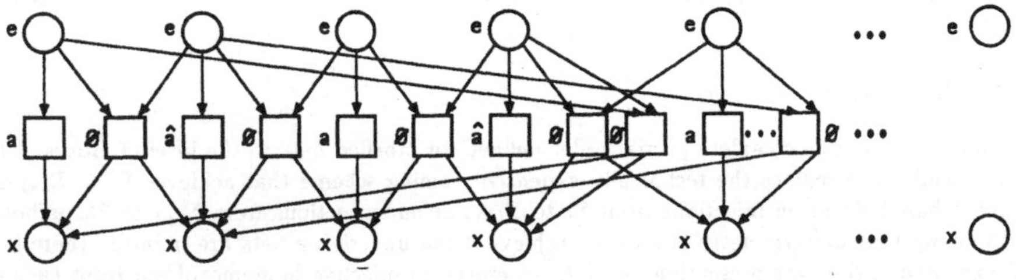

B_{30}, with $E_{30} = (\mu X.(a \| X[\,a \rightarrow \hat{a}\,]))$ sy a

Figure 16: Some examples of recursion

4.11 Iteration

Recursion creates an infinite basic net even in very simple cases such as that of Figure 16 (B_{21}) where a side condition loop with a transition labelled a would also be an acceptable translation. In the interest of enabling a finite semantics where appropriate, the Box algebra also contains an iterative construct although, in theory, this would not be necessary. Because of various caveats to do with respecting the Box properties 3.8, we have designed this construct to have the general form

$$[\,B_1 * B_2 * B_3]$$

with the meaning that B_1 is an entry Box that may be executed once, after which zero or more repetitions of the body B_2 may occur, after which exactly one execution of B_3, the exit Box, is possible to complete the execution of the entire Box. Thus we avoid involving the entry places and the exit places of the construct in violations of the Box properties 3.8(iii,iv). We require that B_2 contains no labels $f(X)$ which could belong to some 'outer' recursion. By this property, the iterative construct does not lead to any violation of the requirement 3.8(vi) of Boxes.

Definition 4.26 *Iteration*

Let $B_1 = [\Sigma_1]$, $B_2 = [\Sigma_2]$ and $B_3 = [\Sigma_3]$ be Boxes such that Σ_2 does not contain any free interface labels. We give the construction of the Box for the iterative construct in analogy with the constructions given earlier, but using a set of temporary place labels $\{i_1, i_2\}$ that are different from $\{e\}$ and $\{x\}$. The construction is in three steps: first, Σ_1 is composed sequentially with Σ_2 to yield Σ'; then the result, i.e., Σ', is sequentially composed with Σ_3 to yield Σ''; finally, the two new sets of internal places (temporarily labelled i_1 and i_2) are combined together, to yield the end result Σ.

$$\text{Step 1:}\quad \Sigma' = (\Sigma_1 \sqcup \Sigma_2) \oplus (\Sigma_1^\bullet \otimes {}^\bullet\Sigma_2, \mathrm{i}_1) \ominus (\Sigma_1^\bullet \cup {}^\bullet\Sigma_2),$$

where i_1 denotes the constant function that assigns i_1 to every element of $\Sigma_1^\bullet \otimes {}^\bullet\Sigma_2$.

$$\text{Step 2:}\quad \Sigma'' = (\Sigma' \sqcup \Sigma_3) \oplus (\Sigma'^\bullet \otimes {}^\bullet\Sigma_3, \mathrm{i}_2) \ominus (\Sigma'^\bullet \cup {}^\bullet\Sigma_3),$$

where i_2 denotes the constant function that assigns i_2 to every element of $\Sigma'^\bullet \otimes {}^\bullet\Sigma_3$.

$$\text{Step 3:}\quad \Sigma = \Sigma'' \oplus (S_1 \otimes S_2, \emptyset) \ominus (S_1 \cup S_2),$$

where S_1 denotes the set of places of Σ'' with label i_1, and S_2 denotes the set of places of Σ'' with label i_2. Define $[\,B_1 * B_2 * B_3] = [\Sigma]$. ∎ 4.26

In general, this construct does *not* guarantee safeness under the initial marking. For instance, the loop

$$[\,B_{31} * B_6 * B_0] = [\,Box(\{a,\hat{a}\}) * (Box(a) \| Box(\hat{a})) * Box(\emptyset)]$$

has a 2-bounded, but not 1-bounded, marked S/T-net as marked representative. However, 2-boundedness and the absence of auto-concurrency are always guaranteed; and if a further restriction is imposed on B_2:

> there is a representative of B_2 that has exactly one entry place or exactly one exit place,

then safeness is guaranteed as well. We call iterative constructs that satisfy this latter constraint *safe iterations.*

5 Structural Properties

In subsection 5.1 we prove a graph theoretical lemma which underlies the commutativity of synchronisation and describes the 'iterative' motivation of Definition 4.8. In subsection 5.2 we state and prove our main results concerning equational properties of synchronisation, restriction and scoping. In subsection 5.3 we discuss a CCS-like composition operator and its properties.

5.1 A graph lemma

The purpose of this section is to cast the min-formula that appears in the definition of Σ sy a (Definition 4.8) in graph theoretical terms. It can also be viewed as an 'iterative' justification of the synchronisation operation, in the sense that it shows that the min-formula is equivalent to the procedure: 'repeatedly choose pairs $\{a, \hat{a}\}$ and synchronise over these pairs in such a way that the graph obtained is minimally connected'.

Lemma 5.1

Let $G = (V, E)$ be a finite undirected graph with $V \neq \emptyset$, $E \subseteq \{\{v, v'\} \mid v \in V, v' \in V\}$, and with a labelling

$$\beta: V \to \mathcal{M}_{\mathcal{F}}(\{a, \hat{a}\}) \backslash \{\emptyset\}$$

such that** $\{v, v'\} \in E$ **iff** $v \neq v'$ **and** $a \in \beta(v)$ **and** $\hat{a} \in \beta(v')$ **(i.e.,** β **generates** E **through** $a, \hat{a}$**-pairs). Then the following are equivalent:

(i) $\min\left(\sum_{v \in V} \beta(v)(a), \sum_{v \in V} \beta(v)(\hat{a})\right) \geq |V| - 1.$

(ii) ***G is connected, and there is a set of edges** $E' \subseteq E$ **and a mapping***

$$\varepsilon: \{(v, \{v, v'\}) \mid \{v, v'\} \in E'\} \to \{a, \hat{a}\}$$

such that:

(ii1) *E' generates a spanning tree of G.*

(ii2) $\varepsilon(v, \{v, v'\}) = \varepsilon(v', \widehat{\{v, v'\}})$.

(ii3) *For all* $v \in V$: $\beta(v)(a) \geq |\{\{v, v'\} \in E' \mid \varepsilon(v, \{v, v'\}) = a\}|$
$\wedge\ \beta(v)(\hat{a}) \geq |\{\{v, v'\} \in E' \mid \varepsilon(v, \{v, v'\}) = \hat{a}\}|$.

In case $|V| = 1$, we allow (V, E') with $E' = \emptyset$ to be a 'degenerate' spanning tree of (V, E). Figure 17 shows a (non-degenerate) example.

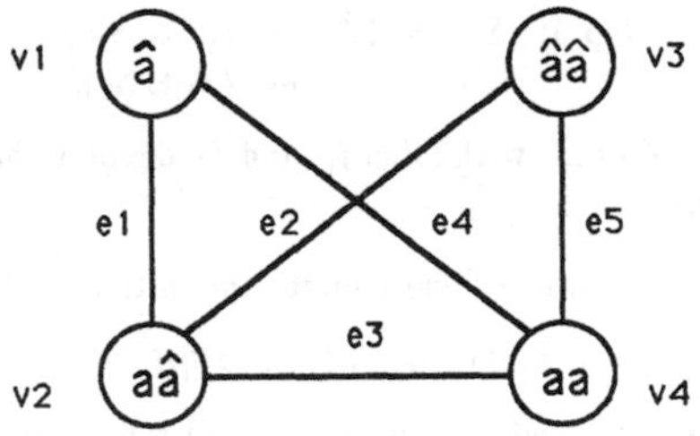

Condition (i) is satisfied, and a suitable spanning tree is generated by $E' = \{e_2, e_3, e_4\}$ with $\varepsilon(v_1, e_4) = \hat{a}$, $\varepsilon(v_4, e_4) = a$, $\varepsilon(v_4, e_3) = a$, $\varepsilon(v_2, e_3) = \hat{a}$, $\varepsilon(v_2, e_2) = a$, $\varepsilon(v_3, e_2) = \hat{a}$.

Figure 17: Illustration of the graph lemma

Proof: **(i)⇒(ii):**

It is easy to see that G is connected.

Abbreviate $\sigma_a = \sum_{v \in V} \beta(v)(a)$ and $\sigma_{\hat{a}} = \sum_{v \in V} \beta(v)(\hat{a})$.

We distinguish a special case and the general case and reduce the latter to the former.

Special case: $\sigma_a = \sigma_{\hat{a}} = |V| - 1$.

The proof is by induction on $|V|$. Note that the conditions on β and $\sigma_a, \sigma_{\hat{a}}$ exclude the case $|V| = 1$.

Base: $|V| = 2$, say $V = \{v_1, v_2\}$.

By the definition of β, $\beta(v_1) \neq \emptyset \neq \beta(v_2)$. Without loss of generality, $a \in \beta(v_1)$. Then, since $\sigma_a = \sigma_{\hat{a}} = 1$ we have $a \notin \beta(v_2)$ and $\hat{a} \in \beta(v_2)$; then (V, E') with $E' = \{\{v_1, v_2\}\}$ is a suitable spanning tree and ε may be defined as desired.

Induction step: $|V| > 2$.

Since $\sum_v |\beta(v)| = \sigma_a + \sigma_{\hat{a}} = 2 \cdot (|V| - 1)$, then by the pigeon hole principle, V contains a node v with $|\beta(v)| = 1$. Assume, without loss of generality, that $\beta(v) = \{a\}$. Consider $V' = V \backslash \{v\}$. By the choice of v, the set V' has $|V| - 2$ labels a and $|V| - 1$ labels $\hat{a}$. Hence, there is some node $v' \in V'$ with $\hat{a} \in \beta(v')$ and $|\beta(v')| > 1$.

Change β on V' into β' by taking away one $\hat{a}$ at the node v'; then there remain exactly $|V| - 2$ labels $\hat{a}$ in V'. Hence the induction hypothesis applies to the graph induced by V' and β', and we can find a suitable spanning tree on V'. The surplus label $\hat{a}$ at node v' can be used to extend this spanning tree into V, by linking v' with v. The function ε can be extended using this link.

General case: $\sigma_a \geq |V| - 1$ and $\sigma_{\hat{a}} \geq |V| - 1$.

If $|V| = 1$ then (V, E') with $E' = \emptyset$ is a suitable spanning tree. Hence we may consider $|V| > 1$ from now on.

The proof is by induction on $\sigma_a + \sigma_{\hat{a}} - 2 \cdot (|V| - 1)$ (which is ≥ 0 by the hypothesis).

Base: $\sigma_a + \sigma_{\hat{a}} = 2 \cdot (|V| - 1)$; the special case applies.

Induction step: $\sigma_a + \sigma_{\hat{a}} > 2 \cdot (|V| - 1)$.

Without loss of generality, we may assume $\sigma_a > |V| - 1$. Then there is at least one node v with $|\beta(v)| > 1$ and $a \in \beta(v)$. Change β into β' by taking away one label a at node v, thereby still keeping $\beta(v) \neq \emptyset$ for all nodes, but decreasing the number $\sigma_a + \sigma_{\hat{a}}$ by 1. By the induction hypothesis, we find a suitable spanning tree in the graph with β' instead of β. This same spanning tree is also suitable for the graph in which the a at v is included, i.e., G. The function ε can be inherited without change.

(ii)⇒(i):

The spanning tree has exactly $|V| - 1$ edges, and each edge fixes a unique action name a as well as a unique action name $\hat{a}$ in the range of β. Hence, from (ii3), there must be at least $|V| - 1$ names a and at least $|V| - 1$ names $\hat{a}$ in the range of β. The inequality of part (i) of the lemma follows immediately. ■ 5.1

In later applications of this lemma, V corresponds to the multiset of transitions that are to be $(a, \hat{a})$-synchronised. By the special properties of the function ε, the spanning tree E' serves to achieve this synchronisation incrementally. The edges of E' can be chosen in some arbitrary order; by the property that ε associates a unique pair of action names $\{a, \hat{a}\}$ to each edge $\{v, v'\}$ – one each for v and v' – taking away the pairs corresponding to $\{v, v'\}$ does not affect the synchronisation possibilities of any of the other edges of E'.

Remark 5.2 *A different interpretation of Lemma* 5.1

The function ε can also be visualised by fixing an arbitrary direction for the arcs of the spanning tree. For instance, the ordered pair $e = (v, v')$ could mean that $\{v, v'\}$ is an arc of the tree which 'leads from $\hat{a}$ to a', that is, $\varepsilon(v, \{v, v'\}) = \hat{a}$ and $\varepsilon(v', \{v, v'\}) = a$. For later use, we associate the colour $\gamma(e) = a$ to every directed edge. Part (ii2)–(ii3) of the lemma can then be reformulated as follows:

$$\begin{aligned} \beta(v)(a) &\geq |\text{ incoming arcs to } v \text{ with colour } a\,| \\ \beta(v)(\hat{a}) &\geq |\text{ outgoing arcs from } v \text{ with colour } a\,|, \end{aligned}$$

for every node $v \in V$. ■ 5.2

5.2 Commutativity of synchronisation, and other equations

We are now ready to state the main result of this section.

Theorem 5.3

(i) *The application of synchronisation is commutative (B **sy** a **sy** $b = B$ **sy** b **sy** a), conjugate-symmetric (B **sy** $a = B$ **sy** $\hat{a}$), idempotent (B **sy** a **sy** $a = B$ **sy** a) and strongly label-sensitive (if either a or $\hat{a}$ do not appear in the interface of B then B **sy** $a = B$).*

(ii) *The application of restriction is commutative, conjugate-symmetric, idempotent and label-sensitive (if neither a nor $\hat{a}$ appear in the interface of B then B **rs** $a = B$).*

(iii) *The application of scoping is commutative, conjugate-symmetric, idempotent and label-sensitive.*

(iv) *Synchronisation and restriction can be interchanged if they are applied on different action names ($\{a, \hat{a}\} \cap \{b, \hat{b}\} = \emptyset$ implies B **rs** b **sy** $a = B$ **sy** a **rs** b).*

For all cases except the ones that will be treated in the remainder of this section, the proofs are straightforward.

5.2.1 Commutativity of synchronisation.

Let $\Sigma = (S, T, W, \lambda)$ and $a, b \in A$. We prove that Σ **sy** a **sy** b and Σ **sy** b **sy** a are duplication equivalent; the commutativity of synchronisation follows directly from this.

Proof: Without loss of generality we may assume $\{a, \hat{a}\} \cap \{b, \hat{b}\} = \emptyset$, since otherwise the claim follows either trivially or directly from conjugate-symmetry.

Let t be a transition of Σ **sy** a **sy** b. We need to prove that there is a transition t' of Σ **sy** b **sy** a with the same label and the same connections as t.

If t is a transition of Σ then t clearly also belongs to Σ **sy** b **sy** a, since existing transitions are not deleted by the **sy** operator.

If t is a transition of Σ **sy** a (but not of Σ) then $t = \tau$, where τ is an $(a, \hat{a})$-synchronisable multiset of transitions of T. This same multiset also occurs in Σ **sy** b (again because existing transitions remain present after an application of **sy**). Hence t is also a transition of Σ **sy** b **sy** a.

Hence we may now consider the case in which none of the above is true, and t is a transition of Σ **sy** a **sy** b, but not of Σ **sy** a. Then t is a multiset

$$t = \tau = \{\tau_1, \ldots, \tau_n\},$$

where each τ_i is either a transition of T with at least one b- or $\hat{b}$-label, or a multiset over T also containing at least one b-label[12]. Since single transitions may be assembled in singletons (modulo duplication), we may reason in terms of multisets only. It could be true that some of the transitions of τ_i do not carry an a-label; in that case, τ_i must be a singleton set. Otherwise, τ_i is the result of an $a, \hat{a}$-synchronisation, and hence all transitions of τ_i carry an a-label. We may assume $n > 1$, because otherwise t duplicates τ_1, a transition of Σ **sy** a.

Our task is to show that t could also be constructed as an $a, \hat{a}$-synchronisation of some singleton sets or $b, \hat{b}$-synchronisations. To this end, we shall show that the multiset

$$base(t) = \tau_1 + \ldots + \tau_n \in \mathcal{M}_{\mathcal{F}}(T)$$

can be partitioned in a different way, namely as

$$base(t) = \kappa_1 + \ldots + \kappa_m,$$

[12] Here and in the following, this is to be taken as an abbreviation for: τ_i contains at least one transition with a b-label or a $\hat{b}$-label.

such that the κ_j play the same rôle as the τ_i, only with the rôles of $a, \hat{a}$ and $b, \hat{b}$ reversed. In order to find suitable multisets $\kappa_1, \ldots, \kappa_m$, we use Lemma 5.1 several times over.

Because every τ_i contains b or $\hat{b}$ (or both), the graph G_τ whose vertices are copies of $\tau_1, \ldots, \tau_n$ and whose labelling is $\lambda'(\tau_i)$ restricted to $\{b, \hat{b}\}$ (λ' being the labelling of Σ **sy** a) satisfies the preconditions of Lemma 5.1. By the definition of **sy** b, G_τ also satisfies the condition (i) of Lemma 5.1. Hence there is a (connected) spanning tree with the properties (ii1)–(ii3) of the lemma, called the 'big' spanning tree in the sequel. (The vertices of G_τ will similarly be called the 'big' vertices.) In line with Remark 5.2, we view the arcs e of the big spanning tree as directed, leading from $\hat{b}$ to b and carrying the colour $\gamma(e) = b$.

Next we employ the property that every non-singleton multiset vertex τ_i in G_τ is an $a, \hat{a}$-synchronisation, and hence, if viewed as a 'small' graph (with copies of transitions of Σ as vertices, occurring as many times as specified by the multiset τ_i), satisfies item (ii) of Lemma 5.1. This yields a set of 'small' spanning trees, one for each non-singleton multiset τ_i. Every singleton multiset has the empty spanning tree and can be viewed as both a 'big' vertex and a 'small' vertex. (It corresponds to a transition, belonging both to Σ and to Σ **sy** a, that has at least one b- or $\hat{b}$-label.) Employing Remark 5.2 again, we view the edges f of the small spanning trees (if any) as directed from $\hat{a}$ to a and carrying the colour $\gamma(f) = a$.

As a consequence of the properties (ii2) and (ii3), restated in terms of directed edges in Remark 5.2, it is possible to 'prolong' the b-coloured edges of G_τ into its nodes τ_i in such a way that the following properties are true:

(a) The undirected global graph formed both from a-coloured edges and from b-coloured edges is a connected tree.

(b) Every 'small' node v and every colour $c \in \{a, b\}$ satisfies the following:

$$\begin{array}{rcl} \lambda(v)(c) & \geq & |\text{ incoming arcs to } v \text{ with colour } c\,| \\ \lambda(v)(\hat{c}) & \geq & |\text{ outgoing arcs from } v \text{ with colour } c\,|. \end{array}$$

(a) follows from the fact that refining the nodes of a spanning tree (without duplicating edges) by trees yields another tree. (b) results from the fact that by the definition of synchronisation, there are enough labels of the adequate type.

Note that the order of synchronisation has already disappeared. We may now neglect the arcs with colour a (if any) and consider the maximal connected subgraphs built from the remaining, b-labelled, edges. Every such graph corresponds to a transition (multiset or singleton) of Σ **sy** b, since the condition of Remark 5.2 on colours remains true, every maximal connected subgraph is a tree by virtue of being part of a tree, and Lemma 5.1 may be applied in the reverse direction. Let $\kappa_1, \ldots, \kappa_m$ denote the multisets which are formed from the nodes of these subgraphs, and call G_κ the graph whose nodes are $\kappa_1, \ldots, \kappa_m$ and whose edges are defined by the colours a.

It remains to be shown that the transition t' corresponding to $\{\kappa_1, \ldots, \kappa_m\}$ of Σ **sy** b **sy** a so constructed carries the same label and has the same connections as t which corresponds to $\{\tau_1, \ldots, \tau_n\}$. The latter follows directly from the equality

$$\tau_1 + \ldots + \tau_n = base(t) = base(t') = \kappa_1 + \ldots + \kappa_m.$$

The fact that t and t' carry the same label also follows from this equality. In the computation of the label of t from the labels in $base(t)$, we first take away as many $a, \hat{a}$-pairs as there are edges in the spanning trees of the multisets τ_i $(1 \leq i \leq n)$, and thereafter as many $b, \hat{b}$-pairs as there are edges in the spanning tree of G_τ. According to the construction of the proof, the edges of the 'small' spanning trees of τ_i become edges of the 'large' spanning tree of G_κ, while the 'big' spanning tree of G_τ is fragmented into various 'small' spanning trees of the multisets κ_j $(1 \leq j \leq m)$. Nevertheless, the 'small' and the 'large' edges uniquely correspond to each other.

Therefore, and since at each synchronisation step exactly $|\tau| - 1$, i.e., exactly the number of edges of a spanning tree, many pairs of the synchronising action are taken away, exactly the same number of $a, \hat{a}$-pairs and $b, \hat{b}$-pairs get taken away in the computation of the label of t' as in the computation of the label of t. Hence the two labels are equal. ■ 5.3(i), first claim

We give an example of the construction (see Figure 18). The first part of the figure shows how six base transitions of Σ are synchronised first over $(a, \hat{a})$ and then over $(b, \hat{b})$ (using the second transition twice). The second part of the figure shows the resulting graphs G_τ, G_κ, and their common refinement.

5.2.2 Idempotence of synchronisation

Proof: This follows as a corollary to the main proof, since the expanded graph of any transition of Σ **sy** a **sy** a has all the properties for corresponding to a transition of Σ **sy** a.

■ 5.3(i), third claim

Remark 5.4 *Extension of the definition*

The commutativity and the idempotence of synchronisation allow an extension of the definition to finite sets of action names; inductively, for instance, as follows: B **sy** $\emptyset = B$ and B **sy** $(A_0 + \{a\}) = (B$ **sy** $A_0)$ **sy** a.

The main result which justifies Definition 4.8 in terms of spanning trees can also serve to extend the definition to any (possibly infinite) set of action names: a multiset τ is the synchronisation of its constituents iff it corresponds to a directed graph whose nodes satisfy the two colour inequalities as before, and which is a connected tree when considered as undirected and uncoloured. However, the compact (non-iterative) characterisation of such multisets by means of the inequality $c(\tau) \geq |\tau| - 1$ cannot immediately be generalised. ■ 5.4

5.2.3 Exchangeability of synchronisation and restriction

Let $B = [\Sigma]$ with $\Sigma = (S, T, W, \lambda)$ and $a, b \in A$.
We prove that for $\{a, \hat{a}\} \cap \{b, \hat{b}\} = \emptyset$, Σ **rs** b **sy** a $=$ Σ **sy** a **rs** b.

Proof: Let Σ **rs** $b = (S_1, T_1, W_1, \lambda_1)$ and Σ **sy** a **rs** $b = (S_2, T_2, W_2, \lambda_2)$.
By the definition of **rs** , $T_1^a = T^a \cap (T \backslash T^b) = T^a \backslash T^b$.

(1) Every transition of Σ **rs** b **sy** a duplicates a transition of Σ **sy** a **rs** b:
Every transition that results from a synchronisation not involving b's or $\hat{b}$'s may also be constructed in Σ **sy** a, and moreover, such transitions are not affected by **sy** b.

(2) Every transition of Σ **sy** a **rs** b duplicates a transition of Σ **rs** b **sy** a:
Let $t \in T_2$. By the definition of **rs** b, $\lambda_2(t) \cap \{b, \hat{b}\} = \emptyset$, and by the definition of **sy** a, t is either a multiset $\tau \in \mathcal{M}_\mathcal{F}(T^a) \backslash \{\emptyset\}$ with $c(\tau) \geq |\tau| - 1$ (as τ synchronises), or a transition in $T \backslash T^a$; hence t is also a transition of Σ **sy** b **sy** a.

$$\begin{aligned} \lambda_2(t) \cap \{b, \hat{b}\} = \emptyset \;&\Rightarrow\; (\textstyle\sum_{t' \in \tau} \lambda(t') \backslash (|\tau| - 1) \cdot \{a, \hat{a}\}) \cap \{b, \hat{b}\} = \emptyset \\ &\Rightarrow\; \forall t' \in \tau : \lambda(t') \cap \{b, \hat{b}\} = \emptyset \quad \text{as } \{a, \hat{a}\} \cap \{b, \hat{b}\} = \emptyset. \end{aligned}$$

Hence $\tau \in \mathcal{M}_\mathcal{F}(T^a \backslash T^b) = \mathcal{M}_\mathcal{F}(T_1^a)$, so that t is a transition of Σ **rs** b **sy** a. ■ 5.3(iv)

5.2.4 Commutativity of scoping

Proof: The cases $a = b$ or $a = \hat{b}$ are trivial. Hence we may assume that $\{a, \hat{a}\} \cap \{b, \hat{b}\} = \emptyset$. Then

$[a : [b : \Sigma]]$	$=$	Σ **sy** b **rs** b **sy** a **rs** a	(by definition)
	$=$	Σ **sy** b **sy** a **rs** b **rs** a	(using the exchangeability of **sy** and **rs**)
	$=$	Σ **sy** a **sy** b **rs** a **rs** b	(using the commutativity of synchronisation and restriction)
	$=$	Σ **sy** a **rs** a **sy** b **rs** b	(using the exchangeability of **sy** and **rs**)
	$=$	$[b : [a : \Sigma]]$	(by definition).

■ 5.3(iii), first claim

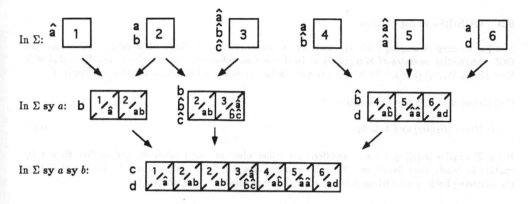

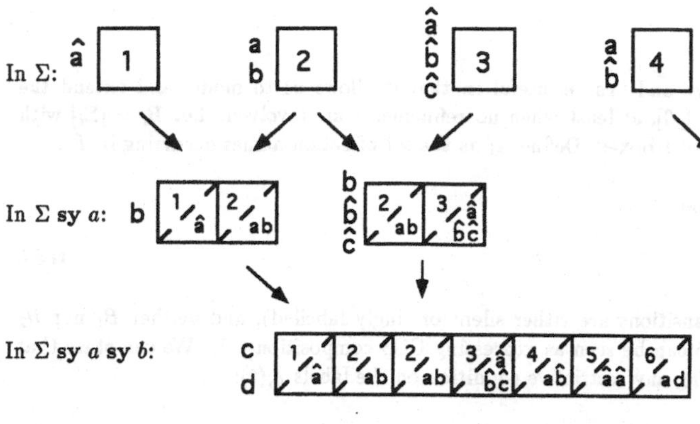

We have $\tau_1 = \{1,2\}$, $\tau_2 = \{2,3\}$ and $\tau_3 = \{4,5,6\}$, and a suitable spanning tree in G_τ is generated by the set of edges $E' = \{e_1, e_2\}$, where e_1 leads from τ_2 to τ_1 and e_2 leads from τ_3 to τ_2. The τ_i are individually synchronised by means of spanning trees with edges f_1 (for τ_1), f_2 (for τ_2) and f_3, f_4 (for τ_3). Together, the following graph results:

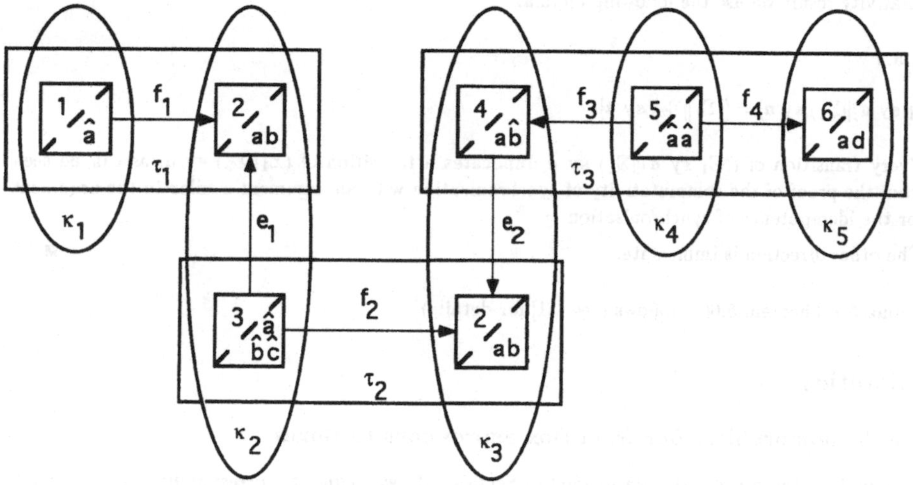

Collecting the maximal connected components (with respect to the edges e_i) on the base graph, we obtain $\kappa_1 = \{1\}$ (singleton), $\kappa_2 = \{2,3\}$ (from e_1), $\kappa_3 = \{2,4\}$ (from e_2), $\kappa_4 = \{5\}$ (singleton) and $\kappa_5 = \{6\}$ (singleton); hence $m = 5$.

Note: Both the spanning tree and the fixing of the transitions for the edges of the tree happen to be unique. In general, this need not be the case, as the reader will find out when applying the construction in the reverse direction (from κ to τ) in the same example.

Figure 18: Illustration of the construction of $\kappa_1, \ldots, \kappa_m$

5.3 CCS-like composition

The partitioning of scoping into **sy** and **rs** is useful in that it allows us to model and extend the CCS composition operator of Milner [50], at least when no refinements are involved. Let $B_i = [\Sigma_i]$ with $\Sigma_i = (S_i, T_i, W_i, \lambda_i)$ $(i = 1,2,3)$, be Petri Boxes. Define A_i as the set of action names occurring in B_i.

Definition 5.5 *CCS-like Composition*

$B_1|B_2 = (B_1\|B_2)$ **sy** $(A_1 \cup A_2)$. ■ 5.5

If $t \in T_i$ implies $|\lambda_i(t)| \leq 1$ (i.e., transitions are either silent or singly labelled), and neither B_1 nor B_2 contain $\mathcal{W}$-labels, then Definition 5.5 can be seen as expressing CCS composition [17]. We can state that the following holds, even without using any restrictive condition on the labels $\lambda_i(t)$:

Theorem 5.6 *Commutativity and Associativity*

(i) *CCS-like composition is commutative.*

(ii) *CCS-like composition is associative, i.e.,* $(B_1|B_2)|B_3 = B_1|(B_2|B_3)$.

The proof that CCS-like composition is commutative follows from the commutativity of $\|$ and $\cup$. To prove the associativity result we use the following lemma.

Lemma 5.7

$[((\Sigma_1$ **sy** $a)\|\Sigma_2)$ **sy** $a] = [(\Sigma_1\|\Sigma_2)$ **sy** $a]$.

Proof: Every transition of $((\Sigma_1$ **sy** $a)\|\Sigma_2)$ **sy** a duplicates a transition of $(\Sigma_1\|\Sigma_2)$ **sy** a, as can be seen from the proof of the commutativity of synchronisation with an argument similar to the argument for the idempotence of synchronisation.

The other direction is immediate. ■ 5.7

With Lemma 5.7 Theorem 5.6(ii) follows (see [11] for details).

6 Semantics

6.1 The homomorphism *Box* from Box expressions to Boxes

For each term E of the process algebra defined in Section 2.2, we define its corresponding Box, $Box(E)$. We recall that there are two restrictions, one for recursion and one for iteration:

(1) In any recursive expression $\mu X.E$, if (the set T^X corresponding to) $Box(E)$ is not finite then E must first be transformed into guarded form by substituting every free occurrence of X into $(\emptyset; X; \emptyset)$.

(2) In any iterative expression $[\,E_1 * E_2 * E_3]$, $Box(E_2)$ may not contain any label $f(X)$.

For elementary Box expressions β and X, the Boxes $Box(\beta)$ and $Box(X)$ have already been defined in Example 3.9. Table 3 specifies the function for non-elementary Box expressions. In all of our examples, the Box B_i equals $Box(E_i)$, where E_i $(0 \leq i \leq 34)$ is from Table 2.

$$
\begin{array}{lcl}
Box(E_1;E_2) & = & Box(E_1);Box(E_2)\\
Box(E_1 \,\square\, E_2) & = & Box(E_1) \,\square\, Box(E_2)\\
Box(E_1 \| E_2) & = & Box(E_1) \| Box(E_2)\\
Box(E \text{ sy } A_0) & = & Box(E) \text{ sy } A_0\\
Box(E \text{ rs } A_0) & = & Box(E) \text{ rs } A_0\\
Box([\, A_0 : E]) & = & [\, A_0 : Box(E)]\\
Box(E[\, f]) & = & (Box(E))[\, f]\\
Box(E[X \leftarrow E']) & = & (Box(E))[X \leftarrow Box(E')]\\
Box(\mu X.E) & = & \mu X.Box(E)\\
Box([\, E_1 * E_2 * E_3]) & = & [\, Box(E_1) * Box(E_2) * Box(E_3)],
\end{array}
$$

where the naming conventions are as in Section 2, and $A_0 \subseteq A$.

Table 3: Semantics of Box expressions

6.2 Some simple properties of the semantics

None of the operators except synchronisation and recursion introduces infinities. Hence all Boxes constructible from the operators except synchronisation and recursion are finite; note also that Remark 4.9 gives a criterion for synchronisation not to lead out of the class of finite nets. Because of the restriction on iteration, this operator does not introduce any side condition loop around X- or $f(X)$-labelled transitions. Furthermore, the T-restrictedness property 3.8(o) is preserved over all operators and is satisfied by the elementary Boxes. So are the other Box properties defined in 3.8.

If a Box expression is closed (contains no X freely) then, in the construction of its corresponding Box, any Box variable X (or its relabelled variant $f(X)$) leads to a correspondingly labelled transition at most during the construction; but such transitions disappear once the translation of the enclosing refinement or recursion operator has been completed.

For a communication closed Box expression (not containing an action name a or $\hat{a}$ outside the scope of a restriction or scoping operator), the corresponding Box contains no communication interface transitions with labels from $\mathcal{M}_{\mathcal{F}}(A)\backslash\{\emptyset\}$. In particular, if E is both closed and communication closed then $Box(E)$ has only $\emptyset$-labelled unobservable transitions.

7 Behavioural Properties

Having examined the structural aspects of the Box calculus, we now discuss the behaviour of Boxes, in particular, those of the Boxes associated via Table 3 in Section 6 to Box expressions. We state two basic behavioural properties: safeness and cleanness.

Definition 7.1 *Safeness*

A Box $B = [\Sigma]$ is safe iff Σ is safe. Σ is safe iff $ST(\Sigma)$ is safe as a Petri net, i.e., if $M: S \rightarrow \mathbf{N}$ is a marking reachable from M_e then for all $s \in S$, $M(s) \leq 1$. ■ 7.1

Definition 7.2 *Cleanness*

A Box $B = [\Sigma]$ is clean iff Σ is clean. Σ is clean iff whenever $M: S \rightarrow \mathbf{N}$ is a marking reachable from M_e in $ST(\Sigma)$ such that $\forall s \in \Sigma^{\bullet}: M(s) > 0$, then $M = M_x$. ■ 7.2

A Box is clean if whenever all of its exit places are covered by tokens then there are no tokens except on the exit places, and for each exit place, there is exactly one token. This property has also been called emptiness [10,25]; we follow the terminology of [37].

As a consequence of Theorems 3.11 and 3.12, both definitions are independent of the representative of B.

Theorem 7.3

Let B be a Box derived from a term in the Box expression syntax consisting of multi-label actions, variables, sequence, choice, concurrent composition, synchronisation, restriction, scoping and relabelling, refinement, (restricted) recursion and safe iteration.
Then B is safe and clean.

The proof can be done in two ways, both by structural induction. The first uses the interleaving semantics of Boxes. The second proves that representatives of Boxes are covered by S-components, from which both safeness and cleanness follow directly[13]. For the first proof, the reader is referred to the full version of this paper [11]. The second proof will be published in a future report.

8 Extensions and Discussion

8.1 Data and blocks

For the description of data, too (as for recursion), we provide two approaches: the high level approach and the low level approach. We sketch both of them, but for details the reader is referred to [12].
Consider a variable q with a value set V. We may define a Data Box $D(q, V)$ which, in the low level translation, consists of an e-labelled place s^0 (the initial undefined place), an x-labelled place s^1 (the terminal undefined place) and in between the two, a set of $\emptyset$-labelled places called $q = v$, one for each value $v \in V$. These places are connected via transitions in the following way[14]: a $\emptyset$-labelled transition leads from s^0 to each place $q = v$ (corresponding to a spurious initialisation which can be avoided if the variable is declared with an initial value); a transition with label $\widehat{q_{v'v}}$ from the place $q = v'$ to the place $q = v$, for each pair $v', v \in V$ (including $v' = v$), corresponding to the assignment $q := v$ when initially $q = v'$; and a non-emptyset labelled transition from each place $q = v$ to the terminal place s^1, corresponding to the loss of value of q (for use on block exit).
In the high level translation, $D(q, V)$ can be defined as a finite net with three places: s^0 and s^1 as before; and an intermediate place s^q which may contain individual tokens, one for each possible value of q. Three transitions are needed in this case: from s^0 to s^q, from s^q to s^1 and a side transition to s^q.
Using the Data Box and scoping, it is possible to give a compositional semantics of data, atomic actions (critical sections) and blocks. The translation is a modification of the one already given in [49,50]. It works as follows [12,39,40]:

- Every block is translated into a scoped expression. The scoping is done over the variables declared in the block.
- A variable declaration is translated into a Data Box which is composed concurrently with the body of the block in which the variable is declared. If there is explicit initialisation, then the translation can be simplified. Upon block exit, the variable loses its value (gets de-initialised) by means of a special synchronisation action just before block exit; this is important if the block is nested inside a loop.
- Channel declarations are translated into special Boxes, depending on the channel discipline (unbounded; buffered with finite capacity; or handshake).
- Data accesses are translated into suitable action names which get synchronised with conjugate action names of the Data Box by means of the enclosing scoping (and hence, implicit synchronisation) construct. The separation of synchronisation and concurrent composition has the effect of binding the enforcement of synchronisation to the enclosing block of a parallel construct, rather than to the parallel construct itself.
- Multiple data accesses within a single atomic action are translated into a set, β, of action names.

[13] In fact, coveredness by S-components also holds for non-safe iteration, explaining 2-boundedness. Due to cross-wise place multiplication, there may be places which are only covered by S-components that carry 2 tokens in the initial marking.
[14] We refer the reader to Section 8.2 for an example and to [12] for a discussion which shows that other kinds of Data Boxes are also feasible.

8.2 An example: Peterson's algorithm

This section contains a worked example, viz. Peterson's algorithm for the mutual exclusion of two processes [52]. We give the example at various levels of detail, from the high level expression of the algorithm down to the level of elementary Petri Boxes. Figure 19(i) shows the expression of the algorithm in a shared variable notation with atomic actions delineated by the brackets $\langle\ldots\rangle$. We are using the **if** command as an **await** (see [3] for the precise semantics). Figure 19(ii) shows the algorithm in $B(PN)^2$ [12], a language geared towards a Box calculus semantics; in $B(PN)^2$ basic commands are expressed by binary predicates, with primed and unprimed versions of variables denoting their initial and final values, respectively. Figure 19(iii) shows the Box expression of the algorithm; we use the translation of data and blocks given in [12,39] and sketched in section 8.1. Notice that this expression satisfies the criterion for the finiteness of synchronisation given in Remark 4.9, since the Data Boxes $D(.,.)$ contain only the conjugates of the action names. This property is generally true for $B(PN)^2$. Figure 19(iv) shows the basic Box associated to the expression of Figure 19(iii) via the translation of Table 3 and the standard translation of Data Boxes, together with its initial marking[15].

We use elementary structure theory of Petri nets in order to add one proof of the mutual exclusion property to the many already existing ones. In the terminology of [15], we wish to prove the modal logical formula

$$\Box(\neg s_4 \vee \neg r_4),$$

which states that no reachable marking puts tokens both on s_4 and on r_4. Let M_e denote the initial marking shown in Figure 19(iv). We use special sets of places, namely S-invariants $I \subseteq S$ and traps $Q \subseteq S$ (where S is the set of places shown in Figure 19(iv)). As 'behavioural' arguments, we use only the following well known basic properties of S-invariants and traps:

S-invariant I: If M is reachable from M_e then the number of tokens on I under M is the same as the number of tokens on I under M_e ('the token count on S-invariants remains constant').

Trap Q: If M is reachable from M_e and the number of tokens on Q under M_e is nonzero, then the number of tokens on Q under M is also nonzero ('traps cannot be emptied of tokens').

We list three S-invariants of the example:

$$\begin{aligned} I_t &= \{t^0, t=1, t=2\} \\ I_{s1} &= \{i^1=0, s_2, s_3, s_4, s_5\} \\ I_{r2} &= \{i^2=0, r_2, r_3, r_4, r_5\}. \end{aligned}$$

Note that I_t stems from a Data Box, and is therefore syntactically derivable from the structure of the Box (the same is true for other S-invariants not listed here). I_{s1} and I_{r2} are 'local' in the sense that each of them comprises a sequential process together with its local variable; this corresponds to what is otherwise known as a 'local assertion'. Note also that the S-invariants of the net alone cannot yield the proof of the desired property. This is because if one omits the side condition arcs from the net then the set of S-invariants does not change, but the property of mutual exclusion is no longer true (to see this, let the second process enter its section first; then the first process can also enter). The necessary 'global' reasoning is achieved by means of two traps:

$$\begin{aligned} Q_1 &= \{i^1=0, s_2, t=2, r_3\} \\ Q_2 &= \{i^2=0, r_2, t=1, s_3\}. \end{aligned}$$

[15] This net is actually – insignificantly – simplified, namely (a) by neglecting the initialisation of the two variables i^1 and i^2, (b) by neglecting the termination action of all variables, and (c) by omitting four dead transitions corresponding to the assignments to i^1 and i^2, respectively. We may do (a) without loss of generality because the two variables in question have an initialisation. We may do (b) without restriction of generality because the program is not contained in an outer loop. We may do (c) without loss of generality because the inclusion of the four transition would not affect the principle of our proof. The simplification has been done for no other purpose than simplifying the figure. The full Box would have 5 places and 14 transitions more than the net shown in Figure 19(iv). In total, therefore, the Box has $5+21=26$ places and $14+20=34$ transitions. We have done an experiment using first Milner's semantics of [50], Chapter 8, and then a generic approach which would give a similar semantics as that of Olderog [51] or Taubner [59], obtaining a count of 107 places and 55 transitions.

(i) A shared variable program for Peterson's mutual exclusion algorithm:

begin var $i^1, i^2 : \{0,1\}$ **init** 0; $t : \{1,2\}$;

while true do
begin $\langle i^1 := 1 \rangle$; $\langle t := 2 \rangle$;
if $\langle i^2 = 0 \vee t = 1 \rangle \rightarrow$
CS_1 (critical section 1)
fi ;
$\langle i^1 := 0 \rangle$
end while

||

while true do
begin $\langle i^2 := 1 \rangle$; $\langle t := 1 \rangle$;
if $\langle i^1 = 0 \vee t = 2 \rangle \rightarrow$
CS_2 (critical section 2)
fi ;
$\langle i^2 := 0 \rangle$
end while

end

(ii) A $B(PN)^2$ program of the same algorithm:

begin var $i^1, i^2 : \{0,1\}$ **init** 0; $t : \{1,2\}$;

do $\langle i^1 = 1 \rangle$; $\langle t = 2 \rangle$;
do $\langle i^{2\prime} = 0 \vee t' = 1 \rangle$;
CS_1; **exit**
od;
$\langle i^1 = 0 \rangle$; **repeat**
od

||

do $\langle i^2 = 1 \rangle$; $\langle t = 1 \rangle$;
do $\langle i^{1\prime} = 0 \vee t' = 2 \rangle$;
CS_2; **exit**
od;
$\langle i^2 = 0 \rangle$; **repeat**
od

end

(iii) A Box expression of the algorithm:

$$
\begin{array}{l}
[\ i^1_{00}, i^1_{01}, i^1_{10}, i^1_{11}, i^2_{00}, i^2_{01}, i^2_{10}, i^2_{11}, t_{11}, t_{12}, t_{21}, t_{22} : \\
\quad D(i^1, \{0,1\}) \parallel D(i^2, \{0,1\}) \parallel D(t, \{1,2\}) \parallel \\
\quad [\ \emptyset * (i^1_{01} \,\square\, i^1_{11}) \,;\, (t_{22} \,\square\, t_{12}) \,;\, (\{i^2_{00}, t_{22}\} \,\square\, \{i^2_{00}, t_{11}\} \,\square\, \{i^2_{11}, t_{11}\}) \,;\, CS_1 \,;\, (i^1_{00} \,\square\, i^1_{10}) * \mathbf{stop}\ ] \parallel \\
\quad [\ \emptyset * (i^2_{01} \,\square\, i^2_{11}) \,;\, (t_{11} \,\square\, t_{21}) \,;\, (\{i^1_{11}, t_{22}\} \,\square\, \{i^1_{00}, t_{11}\} \,\square\, \{i^1_{00}, t_{22}\}) \,;\, CS_2 \,;\, (i^2_{00} \,\square\, i^2_{10}) * \mathbf{stop}\ ] \\
]
\end{array}
$$

(iv) A (simplified) marked Box of the algorithm:

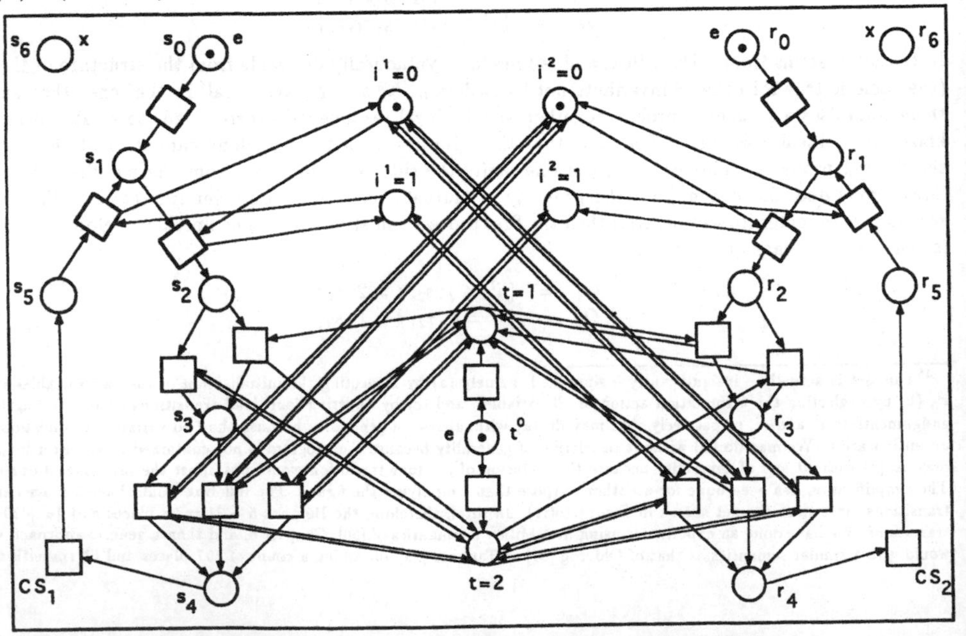

Figure 19: Peterson's algorithm in different levels of detail

Proof: (of the mutual exclusion property) *By contradiction.*
Suppose M is reachable from M_e and $M(s_4) = 1 = M(r_4)$.
By the S-invariants I_{s1} and I_{r2}, by the fact that both have exactly one token under M_e and by the S-invariant property, it follows that $M(i^1 = 0) = 0 = M(i^2 = 0)$.
The S-invariant I_t tells us that either $M(t = 1) = 0$ or $M(t = 2) = 0$ (or both). In the first case, the trap Q_2 is unmarked under M, and in the second case, the trap Q_1 is unmarked under M.
Using the trap property, this contradicts the fact that none of the two traps is unmarked under M_e.
■ (mutual exclusion property)

This example has been included for two reasons:

(1) To show the flexibility of the multi-label device, which we claim to give the 'right' Petri net semantics without any additional complications. Multi-labels occur in the entry conditions for the critical sections. Without multi-labels, one has to introduce additional semaphores which are not actually present in the program, yielding much larger translations.

(2) To show how the Box semantics can easily lend itself to the utilisation of Petri net indigenous proof techniques. In particular, we prove anew the correctness of the algorithm using simple arguments from the structure theory of Petri nets. But even if one does not intend to use Petri net techniques, the translation may be of help: it may be noticed that the places s_i and r_j correspond exactly to the values of the auxiliary variables that need to be introduced in an assertional proof [26]; and this observation is true in general.

Disclaimer: The example has *not* been included because we find the net corresponding to the algorithm particularly beautiful. In fact, one of the main points of our efforts in building an algebraic superstructure on top of a class of nets, is to make it unnecessary to visualise such nets and to be able to deal with them in a non-pictorial way instead (while still being able to exploit their potential usefulness in terms of the analysis techniques and the partial order semantics of net theory). *End of disclaimer*

Although the S-invariants and the traps of the net can be derived automatically, the proof uses them judiciously, just as an assertional style proof would use its assertions [26]. However, there is also hope that the proof can be done automatically by an extension of the fast model checking technique of [15]. The program is 'almost persistent' in the sense that its maximal partial orders are concatenations of only two essential periods (while strong persistence implies that there is a unique maximal process). In future work, we wish to explore an extension of the results of [15] to systems which have 'essentially finitely many' maximal processes.

8.3 Other extensions

It is tempting to allow the empty Box

$$\mathbf{null} = [(\emptyset, \emptyset, \emptyset, \emptyset)]$$

to play a part in the calculus, because this Box is a structural unit of concurrent composition:

$$B \| \mathbf{null} \;=\; B \;=\; \mathbf{null} \| B.$$

However, the empty Box destroys the properties (i) and (ii) of Boxes (cf. Definition 3.8). For instance, define $\delta_1 = \mathbf{null}; Box(\emptyset)$ and $\delta_2 = Box(\emptyset); \mathbf{null}$; then δ_1 has no $\{e\}$-labelled place and δ_2 has no $\{x\}$-labelled place. Moreover, the properties proved in Section 7 are also destroyed; for instance, δ_1 is neither safe nor clean.

It is also tempting to allow places to be labelled both by e and by x, as for instance in

$$\epsilon = [(\{s\}, \emptyset, \emptyset, \{(s, \{e, x\})\})].$$

With the obvious generalisation of the definition of sequential composition, this Box would be a unit for sequence:

$$\epsilon; B = B = B; \epsilon.$$

Also, we have found this Box useful in the process semantics of iteration [8] because it corresponds to the 'zero'th' complete execution of a loop.

Notice that the Box operators, and in particular synchronisation, make sense for arbitrary markings, not just for safe ones. Hence, at some later stage in the investigations, one might wish (and be able) to include the unit Boxes mentioned in this section.

8.4 Discussion and relation to other work

Historical remarks

COSY is clearly the historical root of the work presented in this paper. Long before the invention of that name, Peter Lauer was probably the first to bring together an abstract programming notation (the path expressions of Campbell and Habermann [20]) and Petri nets [46]. COSY has been developed both theoretically and in the direction of a specification language, culminating in two books on the verge of publication [44,57].

The first author's interest has gone more towards the application of the techniques of COSY to richer programming languages with data, giving a partial COSY / Petri net semantics of a shared variable language in [3,4,6]; of Hoare's original CSP in [4,5,6]; and a full Petri net semantics of both languages in [7]. This interest has been kept alive by a belief that net theory can play a similarly beneficial rôle for concurrent programming as set theory plays for sequential programming.

These translations suffered from two inter-related deficiencies. First, there was no general notion of nested parallelism (except for a restricted form of nesting within atomic actions in [3]). Secondly, the semantics was only partially compositional. These problems were to do with data, value passing and atomic actions which do not yield easily to a compositional approach.

The usual way of overcoming this problem is to ignore it at first, to treat atomic actions as 'un-interpreted' entities, and to add data on top of that. Two convincing early examples of this approach are Chapter 9 of [49] and the approach by de Bakker / Zucker [2]. However, we have chosen to explore the more integrative approach of incorporating the treatment of data from the outset. This approach has eventually led to the multi-label technique described in this paper.

A second root of the work presented here comes from a certain dissatisfaction with the lack of algebraic structure of Petri nets. Knowledge about the 'syntactic' structure of a net, i.e., the way it is built from its components, is normally, at least in an informal way, very useful in reasoning about its properties. Such information is however not offered by any of the existing high level net models. Olderog [51] makes this point very clearly:

> 'The disadvantage of analysing nets as a whole is of course that one has to redo the analysis whenever a part of the net changes. Overcoming this problem is the essence of compositionality.'

Making nets compositional means employing an algebra. This aspect of our work builds upon, and compares with, an ever growing number of recent papers and books, of which we mention [19,21,23,28,30,31,51,59]. In the sequel we will discuss some of the most salient differences and similarities.

On the choice of the algebra

First, we have restricted the basic elements to a minimum. In particular, we have no equivalent[16] of CCS's **nil**, thus potentially avoiding some of the problems encountered in [31]. Due to the modelling of termination by tokens on exit places, we do not need a variety of termination actions such as for instance ACP [1] does. Olderog's basic processes 'deadlock' and 'divergence' [51] can be derived as $\mathbf{stop} = a \ \mathbf{rs}\ a = [a : a] = \mu X.X$ and $\mathbf{div} = \mu X.(\emptyset; X)$, respectively.

With net theory as background, we have always felt that no more than one choice operator should be necessary. We have used a different symbol $\Box$ to denote what is essentially CCS's +, both in order to emphasise the connection to guarded commands and Hoare's original CSP [42], and because we slightly dislike the overloading of operators (choice + and multiset + do not correlate).

[16] Not even in the operational semantics [17].

We felt the need to keep CCS's restriction operator[17], because of the ingenious way of using it to describe blocks, pioneered by Milner in [49] (Chapter 9). The case for relabelling, we feel, is also strong; in examples and in the modelling of procedure calls [12], we found this operator to be indispensible. So we decided to include it at the expense of some technical complication (that of needing the set $\mathcal{W}$ instead of just the set $\mathcal{V}$).

Our choice to include sequencing instead of CCS's prefix operator was dictated by the needs of programming languages where one cannot really afford to derive sequential composition in a complicated way from other constructs. At any rate, refinement together with prefixing (of variables) automatically yields sequence by means of $(X; E_2)[X \leftarrow E_1] = E_1; E_2$. The decision to include refinement in the algebra was motivated not so much because this operator is interesting in its own right (which it is), but by the wish to base recursion on it.

There were two reasons for including recursion instead of (or rather, in addition to) iteration. Firstly, we wished to be able to model dynamically growing parallelism, and thus, a form of process creation – as is possible in CCS. The second reason is that we encountered a problem with non-safeness in expressions such as $[\emptyset * (a\|b) * \emptyset]$. We are aware that this problem can also be dealt with by means of a variant of the 'root unwinding' technique described, for instance, in [1,30,51]. Nevertheless, we tried to avoid this technique, particularly in view of the fact that with the guarding restriction 4.23 on recursive calls, it becomes unnecessary for recursive expressions.

We have been at some pains not to introduce any restrictions for recursion in combination with other operators. In particular, we do not require that the branches of a choice start sequentially, as [31,59] do, or that the body of a recursion start sequentially, as [59] does. We have not incorporated in the paper the way to lift the guardedness restriction; this is left to another work in progress [14] whose first results are very promising, even if we agree with Taubner when he says that guardedness is

> '... useful and harmless' [59],

moreover, we recall Remark 4.18 which demonstrates what seems to be, principally, a cardinality problem. Notice that this cardinality problem seems to be unrelated to the non-uniqueness problem usually discussed (e.g. in [1]) in connection with unguarded recursion[18].

At the time of writing this paper, there seem to exist three ways of translating recursive expressions into nets: the technique of labelling places by variables (and adding back-loops) introduced by Goltz in [31], the structured operational semantic approach initiated by Degano, De Nicola and Montanari [23] and Olderog [51], and the syntax driven approach pioneered by Taubner [59]. In his book, Taubner shows that the last two approaches are very closely related to each other.

We add to this set of techniques a further one, by which recursion is based on a succession of refinements. We do this for two reasons. First, we believe that this approach is closely consistent with our model which treats entry and exit places on an equal footing. Secondly, we have attempted to separate the structure from the behaviour of the net semantics. For instance, in $\mu X.(a; X; b)$ the refinement based approach generates a set of a-labelled transitions and a set of b-labelled transitions in a symmetrical way. It is only in terms of behaviour that we may determine that b-labelled transitions can never be enabled and executed. By contrast, the structured operational semantics approach [51] uses the behaviour of the expression (manifested in the μ-expansion law) in order to derive the net semantics. Rather than using this law in the construction, we derive it as a property of the constructed object.

It would be nice if syntactical substitution on the expression level would have refinement as its exact equivalent in the model. Unfortunately, we encounter a tradeoff, for which the balance is not yet clearly delineated: either the solution explored in this paper is adopted, by which refinement does not fully satisfy all equations of syntactical substitution; in which case the operational semantics [17] becomes more complicated than otherwise necessary. Or refinement is redefined to correspond to syntactical substitution; however this would introduce a large technical overhead in the compositional semantics[19].

---

[17] Using a different symbol with less justification.

[18] Indeed, $\mu X.X$, or $X = X$ in equation form, has a unique solution in our model, namely the **stop** Box.

[19] Essentially, one would have to allow subexpressions as transition labels.

An example taken from Figure 16 shows what distinctions between the Box calculus and CCS are implied by our provisional decision of letting refinement and syntactical substitution differ: the Box B_{29} corresponding to the expression $E_{29} = \mu X.((a\|X[a \rightarrow \hat{a}])\ \mathbf{sy}\ a)$ yields no synchronisation across levels of recursion, as opposed to the 'syntactically corresponding' CCS expression $X = (a|X[a \rightarrow \hat{a}])$. In order to achieve a similar across-the-levels synchronisation in the Box calculus, the **sy** operator would have to be moved out of the body of the recursion, as in $E_{30} = (\mu X.(a\|X[a \rightarrow \hat{a}]))\ \mathbf{sy}\ a$. Fortunately, it seems that these differences are none too serious; however, they have to be explored further.

One possible solution of this issue, advocated by Richard Hopkins[20], could be to elevate the scoping operator (in contrast to its separate parts **sy** and **rs**) to become a 'first class' operator of the Box algebra. It is possible – and perhaps reasonable – to view the brackets $[a : \ldots]$ as a name-binding scope for a, essentially disallowing the use of a outside the brackets if it (or its conjugate) is already used inside the brackets. Some extended Barendregt convention could be used to disallow expressions such as $[a : (\hat{a}\|X)][X \leftarrow a]$ where the issue is whether or not a and $\hat{a}$ can synchronise. Instead, such an expression would need to be rewritten by consistent relabelling, for instance as $[b : (\hat{b}\|X)][X \leftarrow a]$; note that the last expression does *not* imply any synchronisation. This point of view would, firstly, vindicate our semantics of synchronisation in connection with hierarchical interface labels. If one interprets the relabelling functions consistently as relabellings within scoping constructs, then, secondly, the set $\mathcal{W}$ would be unnecessary; simply using the set $\mathcal{V}$ would then be sufficient.

The most difficult decision regarding our choice of operators was related to synchronisation and concurrent composition. In the end, for an intuitive reason and a technical reason, we decided to separate the two. The intuitive reason is that in a concurrent language, synchronisation occurs when two concurrent components are brought together to communicate, be it through shared variables or through channels (which are also shared data structures). Therefore it seems logical to connect the point of synchronisation with the block of the declaration of these shared data structures. Thus we started to think of synchronisation to be connected more with restriction than with concurrent composition[21]. The technical reason for separating synchronisation and concurrent composition is that the associativity of $\|$ in the asynchronous multi-label setup was not easy to achieve, and so we preferred to argue in terms of synchronising one action at a time, rather than all of them together at once. However, we retrieve the general associativity in Theorem 5.6.

The following example explains why we have favoured the CCS approach (using conjugate labels) rather than the COSY/TCSP approach (where synchronisation is over common action names). The former appeared to us more flexible when dealing with the kind of situation shown in Figure 20 (here taking $c!$ and $c?$, etc, as conjugates). The intention is that this would produce two 3-way communications as shown in Figure 21 but not, of course, a synchronisation between the leftmost $c!$ and the rightmost $d?$ However, in order to avoid the latter in the naming discipline of COSY/TCSP, one would have to split the transition labelled $x!$ into as many alternative copies as there are processes using x in the environment, introducing a degree of non–compositionality which can be avoided in the CCS approach. It may also be noticed that multi-labels allow us to model the synchronisation of COSY/TCSP by introducing sufficiently many intermediate action names. Also, a possibly interesting variant of COSY/TCSP results if the present setup is changed simply by requiring (or allowing) $a = \hat{a}$ instead of $a \neq \hat{a}$ in Definition 2.1.

Our synchronisation operator has been criticised because the price to pay for its flexibility is the fact that the proof of its associativity is not immediate. However, we argue that 'flexibility' is a permanent property while 'the complexity of a proof' is only temporary; once this proof is done, one may forget about it and use the operator in the usual way, continuing to enjoy (hopefully) its flexibility. Moreover, an immediate idea to unify our setup would be to transfer the synchronisation operation to places. This could eventually lead to a framework in which the *only* net-building operation is synchronisation. We have refrained from pursuing this idea in consequence, because we encountered a series of small (solvable but annoying) problems, such as the following incomplete list: (a) if x is defined as the conjugate of e then there is a nice definition of sequence, but the definition of choice would be unsymmetric and hence not so nice; (b) some of the Box properties on which we now rely are no longer true.

[20] Personal communication.

[21] In fact, the only reason why we retained **sy** and **rs** as separate operators was to keep a minimum of comparability with CCS.

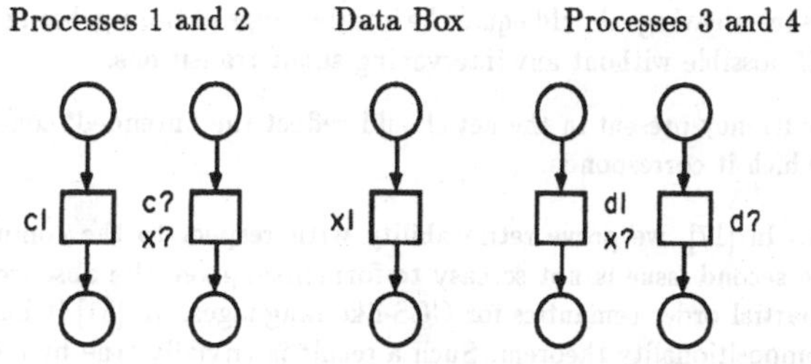

Figure 20: An example illustrating the use of conjugate labels

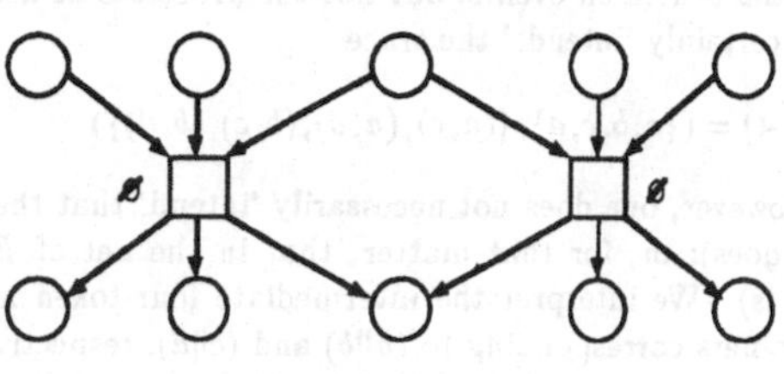

Figure 21: A synchronisation of the previous example

On the design of the Box model

The symmetry between entry places and exit places has been stressed in order to capture the 'static' aspects of composition properly. The absence of incoming arcs into entry places (and the corresponding, but less important, property for exit places) has been required to avoid compositionality problems (for instance when composing a loop at the beginning of the branch of a choice). The requirement on $\mathcal{W}$-labelled transitions is to avoid refinement problems.

When designing the operations on nets, it soon becomes clear that one needs a way of abstracting from the names of at least the underlying places. Such an abstraction is implicit in [31] and explicit in [51]. We desire a strong abstraction equivalence here, since the structural results hold only with respect to it. Isomorphism has turned out a little too strong for our purposes, whence we propose renaming equivalence as a weaker equivalence. There is a relation in [51] which serves the same purpose, called strong bisimilarity. Strong bisimilarity and renaming equivalence are incomparable notions. For instance, two nets, one with a single isolated place (and a token), and one with two isolated places (each with a token) are renaming equivalent but not strongly bisimilar. Conversely, consider the infinite representation of $\mu X.(a;X)$ with an (obvious) finite representation of the same expression; they are strongly bisimilar but not renaming equivalent. This may appear as a disadvantage of renaming equivalence, but on the other hand, we propose this equivalence as a structural rather than a behavioural one. Despite their incomparability, renaming equivalence and strong bisimilarity serve the same purposes, namely to imply 'equal concurrent behaviour'. We show this in Theorems 3.11 and 3.12 while [51] shows that strongly bisimilar nets have equal processes. We may also note that part of what we call renaming equivalence (namely, the part which concerns transitions) is already in-built in [51]'s definition of a net.

The place multiplication technique we employ is quite standard. In fact, transition multiplication of which our notion of synchronisation is a generalisation[22] already occurs in COSY [47]. G.Winskel was probably the first to introduce an analogous technique for places explicitly [61]. What we have done here is to apply the technique systematically in a symmetric way for entry and exit places. In particular, we let the branches of a choice re-join after the choice, in contradistinction to most other authors.

What is a good net semantics?

In [51], relating back to a paper by Degano, De Nicola and Montanari [24], two criteria for a 'good' net semantics are described:

[22]In order to see this, just restrict β to $|\beta| \leq 1$; the spanning trees of Section 5 then have only zero or one arcs.

Retrievability: The net's interleavings should equal the interleavings of the algebra as defined independently of nets, if possible without any intervening silent transitions.

Concurrency: The concurrency present in the net should reflect the 'intended' concurrency of the expression to which it corresponds.

We address both issues. In [17], we prove retrievability with respect to the common subset of Box expressions and CCS. The second issue is not so easy to formalise, given the absence of a generally agreed upon net-independent partial order semantics for CCS-like languages. In [51] it has, somewhat arguably, been addressed via a compositionality theorem. Such a result is trivially true by definition in our setting. Nevertheless, we find here a reason why our notion of 'equal concurrency' expressed by means of Theorems 3.11 and 3.12 covers only the partial orders on events, but not the processes as a whole. For consider the expression $E = (a\|b);(c\|d)$. One certainly 'intends' the trace

$$(A_0, \prec) = (\{a,b,c,d\}, \{(a,c),(a,d),(b,c),(b,d)\})$$

to describe an execution of E. However, one does not necessarily 'intend' that the corresponding process has a cut of size four (which it does); or, for that matter, that in the net of E, a marking with four tokens is reachable (which there is). We interpret the intermediate four-token marking as arising from duplication equivalence in the sub-nets corresponding to $(a\|b)$ and $(c\|d)$, respectively, but not as relating to the intended concurrency of the system as a whole, which is of 'size 2' and not of 'size 4'.

What good is a net semantics?

We answer merely by quoting Robin Milner from [50]:

> 'A tractable algebraic theory (...) has yet to be found if causation is to be treated.'

On compositionality

Following [51], we classify a net semantics as

compositional: if the syntactic operations have well-defined corresponding semantic operations, and as

denotational: if, in addition, fixpoint techniques are used to describe recursion.

Of the Petri net semantics for a reasonably rich process algebra considered in the literature, we claim that our approach is the only one that is compositional and goes some way towards being denotational. One deficiency could be the fact that we have not yet turned the domain of Petri Boxes – rather that the set of labelled nets – into a complete partial order: as Remark 4.25 indicates, there are difficulties in the infinite case. On the other hand, one might also argue that the approximation construction of Definitions 4.16 and 4.22 should be viewed on the same level as the set theoretical operations $\sqcup, \oplus, \ominus, \otimes$, and that therefore, turning labelled nets into a complete partial order is sufficient.

On structural versus behavioural equality, and on finite representations

Our approach is model-oriented rather than axiomatical. This implies that we wish to prove, rather than to postulate, our equalities. It is interesting to know which equalities are 'strong' structural ones and which ones are 'weaker' behavioural ones. As the main contribution of the present paper, but without claiming to be complete, we have explored a set of equalities based on a strong structural equivalence. The fact that there are so many of them has delayed the introduction of a behavioural equivalence such as bisimilarity into the calculus.

There are also two further reasons why we have been reluctant to introduce a notion of behavioural equivalence too early in the game. For one thing, the literature is presently full of various, widely or narrowly differing, notions which makes it hard to choose from, leave alone to modify them for our purposes. Before transferring a suitable behavioural equivalence notion to the Box calculus, therefore, we first intend to collect a number of criteria such a notion should satisfy. One reasonable criterion is certainly that it should be a congruence with respect to the operations, in particular with respect to refinement. However – and this is the third reason why a notion of behavioural equivalence is missing at the present time –

congruence results with respect to refinement are only a relatively recent achievement ([10,25,33,36,60] and others). Moreover, these results tend to be true only under certain caveats and restrictive preconditions such as 'no silent transitions' [33], a premise we cannot guarantee to hold. Actually, the results expressed in Theorem 7.3 already go some steps in the direction of establishing a behavioural notion of equivalence for the Box algebra, since the properties of safeness and cleanness happen to be the preconditions of the congruence results proved for the notion of MP-bisimulation [25] which is a derivative of the history preserving bisimulation of A.Rabinovich and B.Trakhtenbrot [53] (which in turn is related to the NMS-equivalence defined in [22]); this suggests MP-bisimulation as a possible candidate for transferral to our framework.

There is a tradeoff, clearly delineated in Olderog's book [51] (pages 95-96), between the strength of the equality on the one hand and the finiteness of the net representation on the other hand. In particular, wishing – as we do – to obtain the *structural* equation

$$\mu X.E \;=\; E[X \leftarrow \mu X.E]$$

necessarily implies that simple expressions such as $\mu X.(a;X)$ obtain an infinite net as their semantics. We view this not as a drawback, but as part of exploring the possibilities. Meanwhile, in other work, the finiteness issue is addressed from three different angles.

Angle 1: High level Boxes [38]. This work starts from a similar expression algebra but builds a different model based on high level nets. Of course, finite representations are obtained in most of the cases. This angle also extends Taubner's seminal work [59], first by introducing compositionality[23], and secondly also by modifying and simplifying some of the constructions.

Angle 2: After choosing a suitable behavioural equivalence relation $\cong$ on the Box model, we of course expect that, say, the (obvious) finite and the infinite representations of $\mu X.(a;X)$ are $\cong$-related. More generally, we expect that for what Olderog calls 'regular terms' ([51], page 62) – a restriction that is, not surprisingly, very similar to that defined in Taubner's finiteness results ([59], pages 112-113) – $\cong$ yields finite representatives[24], yielding a second criterion for $\cong$. And we expect iteration and recursion to be provably related as follows (this, amongst other desired equations such as $(B \,\square\, B) \cong B$, denotes a third criterion for $\cong$):

$$[E_1 * E_2 * E_3] \;\cong\; E_1; \mu X.((E_2;X) \,\square\, E_3).$$

However, whether the finite representation of, say, $\mu X.(a;X)$ can be made the fixpoint of some suitable function is a question that remains widely open; the answer depends on whether it is possible to turn the set of equivalence classes induced by $\cong$ into a complete partially ordered set (yielding yet another criterion for $\cong$).

Angle 3: Sub-syntax. U.Goltz has given a place transition net semantics to RCCS, a subset of CCS [31], for instance being able to describe by a finite net the expression $\mu X.((a;X)\|b)$, which is outside the class of regular expressions of Olderog / Taubner. Recent work including [34,35] indicates that expressions such as $\mu X(((a;X)\|b) \,\square\, c)$ can *not* be given a satisfactory semantics in terms of finite PT-nets. On the other hand, Olderog's regular terms contain non-RCCS expressions, so that the two classes are incomparable. It may be possible, then, to find a sub-syntax of the Box expression algebra which comprises, modulo comparability, the two classes of regular terms and 'representable' subset of RCCS.

Finally, we mention that the behavioural results 3.11 and 3.12 induce four behavioural equivalences, namely pomset equivalence either with or without terminating executions, and either with or without τ-labelled (unobservable) events. These equivalences are known not to be congruences in general, and so do not fulfill all of our criteria. Nevertheless, their relationship to the desired notion of behavioural equivalence must, of course, be studied.

[23]Taubner's constructions are modular in the sense that a semantical object is associated to every (sub-) expression, but not really compositional; witness pages 134-135 of [59] which show that in the definition of choice, one potentially needs to know all the elements of the constituent components, not just their entry and exit places.

[24]Excluding another source of possible infinities stemming from synchronisations; cf. Remark 4.9.

9 Conclusion and Outlook

We have defined a causal algebra whose essential new feature is multi-label communication, and presented its compositional and partly denotational semantics in terms of Petri Boxes. The main results are a set of structural equations and two simple but important behavioural properties.

A companion paper [17] defines an indigenous operational semantics and shows the relationship to CCS and to the transition rule semantics of Petri nets. Another companion paper [27] describes the details of the definition of refinement and, based on that, recursion. A third companion paper [8] defines a compositional partial order semantics. A fourth companion paper [38] defines a variant of the calculus which allows the generation of high level, instead of elementary, nets. A fifth companion paper [12] defines a higher level programming notation on top on the Box algebra. A sixth companion paper [41] applies the operational semantics on the proof of a case study. A seventh companion paper, to be found in this volume [40], uses a version of the algebra to describe a substantial subset of **occam**–2[25].

In future work, we plan to equip the algebra with an equational theory, and (more into the future) with extended Hoare-style logics.

Acknowledgements

The Box model has been conceived at a meeting of the DEMON subgroup on programming in November 1989, in which the following persons participated: E.Best, O.Botti, W.Brauer, F.De Cindio, J.Fanchon, R.Gold, J.Hall, R.Hopkins, A.Poigné. Multi-label communication in the Box setting has been proposed by R.Hopkins and J.Hall in [39].

Particularly important contributions have been made by Richard Hopkins who spent countless hours inventing and discussing examples which showed the difficulty of achieving commutativity of synchronisation in the Box algebra setting. He has also influenced this work in many other ways.

Furthermore, Javier Esparza has contributed essential aspects to the theory. Javier Esparza has participated in the proof of Lemma 5.1, in the example of Section 8.2, and in detailing the general definition of refinement and the partial order construction on which recursion is based. The remark on the cardinality problem is also due to Javier Esparza. Glynn Winskel is acknowledged for encouraging the definition of a set theoretical solution (rather than search for a partial order on Boxes), on the basis of some unpublished work of his.

The characterisation 4.9 of finite synchronisations has also been found independently by Holger Schirnick. Last but not least, we would like to thank Maciej Koutny for carefully checking the proofs; some of them have been left out of this version of the paper, so that some of his remarks will be incorporated only in the full version. All remaining mistakes are the authors' sole responsibility.

We are indebted to an anonymous referee for finding some small mistakes and making some useful suggestions on improving the presentation.

References

[1] J.C.M.Baeten and W.P.Weijland: *Process Algebra.* Cambridge Tracts in Theoretical Computer Science (1990).

[2] J.W.de Bakker and J.Zucker: Processes and the Denotational Semantics of Concurrency. Information and Control 54, 70-120 (1984).

[3] E.Best: Relational Semantics of Concurrent Programs (with some Applications). Formal Description of Programming Concepts II (ed. D.Bjørner), North Holland, pp.431-452 (1982).

[4] E.Best: Concurrent Behaviour: Sequences, Processes and Axioms. Seminar on Concurrency, Carnegie-Mellon University, Pittsburgh, PA, July 9–11, 1984 (eds. S.D.Brookes; A.W.Roscoe; G.Winskel) Springer-Verlag Lecture Notes in Computer Science Vol. 197, 221–245 (1985).

[25] The model used in [40] is based on a prior version of the algebra and differs from the one advocated here in some aspects, including the treatment of data.

[5] E.Best: COSY and its Relationship to CSP. Second Advanced Course on Petri Nets, Bad Honnef, Springer-Verlag Lecture Notes in Computer Science Vol. 255, 416-440 (1986).

[6] E.Best: Weighted Basic Petri Nets. Concurrency'88, Springer-Verlag Lecture Notes in Computer Science Vol. 335, 257-276 (1988).

[7] E.Best: *Kausale Semantik nichtsequentieller Programme.* (In German.) R.Oldenbourg-Verlag, GMD-Bericht Nr.174 (1989).

[8] E.Best, L.Cherkasova and H.G.Linde: Compositional Process Semantics of the Box Algebra. To appear.

[9] E.Best and R.Devillers: Sequential and Concurrent Behaviour in Petri Net Theory. Theoretical Computer Science Vol. 55, 87–136 (1987).

[10] E.Best, R.Devillers, A.Kiehn and L.Pomello: Fully Concurrent Bisimulation. Technical Report LIT-202, Univ. Bruxelles (July 1989). Appeared in Acta Informatica Vol.28 with the changed title: *Concurrent Bisimulation in Petri Nets*, 231–264 (1991).

[11] E.Best, R.Devillers and J.Hall: The Box Calculus: a New Causal Algebra with Multi-label Communication. Technical Report, Computing Laboratory, University of Newcastle-upon-Tyne (1992).

[12] E.Best and R.P.Hopkins: A Basic Petri Net Programming Notation. To appear.

[13] E.Best (ed.): Technical Annex of the Esprit Basic Research Action No. 3148 DEMON. GMD-Arbeitsbericht Nr.435 (1990).

[14] E.Best, R.Devillers and J.Esparza: General Refinement and Recursion in the Box Calculus. Forthcoming Report (1992).

[15] E.Best and J.Esparza: Model Checking of Persistent Petri Nets. Hildesheimer Informatikbericht 11/91. Proc. of Computer Science Logic 91, to appear in Springer-Verlag Lecture Notes in Computer Science (1992).

[16] E.Best and J.Esparza (eds.): *Second Progress Report of DEMON.* Studien der Gesellschaft für Mathematik und Datenverarbeitung Nr.198, Sankt Augustin (August 1991).

[17] E.Best, J.Esparza and M.Koutny: Operational Semantics of the Box Algebra. Forthcoming Technical Report.

[18] G.Boudol: Notes on Algebraic Calculi of Processes. In: Logics and Models of Concurrent Systems (ed. K.R.Apt), 261-304 (1985).

[19] G.Boudol and I.Castellani: Flow Models of Distributed Computations: Event Structures and Nets. Rapport de Recherche, INRIA, Sophia Antipolis (July 1991).

[20] R.H.Campbell and N.A.Habermann: The specification of Process Synchronisation by Path Expressions. Springer-Verlag Lecture Notes in Computer Science Vol. 16, 89-102 (1974).

[21] L.Cherkasova and V.Kotov: Descriptive and Analytical Process Algebras. Advances in Petri Nets 89 (ed. G.Rozenberg), Springer-Verlag Lecture Notes in Computer Science Vol. 424, 77-104 (1989).

[22] P.Degano, R. De Nicola and U.Montanari: Observational equivalences for Concurrency Models. In: Formal Description of Programming Concepts III (ed. M.Wirsing), North Holland, 105-129 (1986).

[23] P.Degano, R. De Nicola and U.Montanari: A Distributed Operational Semantics for CCS Based on C/E Systems. Acta Informatica 26 (1988).

[24] P.Degano, R. De Nicola and U.Montanari: On the Consistency of 'Truly Concurrent' Operational and Denotational Semantics. Proc. 3rd Ann. Symp. on Logics in Computer Science 88, 133-141 (1988).

[25] R.Devillers: Maximality Preservation and the ST-idea for Action Refinement. Technical Report LIT–242, Laboratoire d'Informatique Théorique, Université Libre de Bruxelles (August 1991). Also: In this Volume.

[26] E.W.Dijkstra: An Assertional Proof of a Program by G.L.Peterson. EWD-779 (1981).

[27] J.Esparza: Fixpoint Definition of Recursion in the Box Algebra. Memorandum, Universität Hildesheim (December 1991).

[28] J.Fanchon: FIFO-net Model for Processes with Asynchronous Communication. Proc. 12th Int. Conference on Applications and Theory of Petri Nets, Gjern (June 1991). Also: in this volume.

[29] H.J.Genrich and K.Lautenbach: System Modelling with High Level Petri Nets. Theoretical Computer Science 13, 109-136 (1981).

[30] R.J. van Glabbeek and F.V.Vaandrager: Petri Net Models for Algebraic Theories of Concurrency. Proc. PARLE 89, Springer-Verlag Lecture Notes in Computer Science Vol.259, 224–242 (1987).

[31] U.Goltz: *Über die Darstellung von CCS-Programmen durch Petrinetze.* (In German.) R.Oldenbourg Verlag, GMD-Bericht Nr.172 (1988). See also: U.Goltz: On Representing CCS Programs by Finite Petri Nets. Proc. MFCS-88, Springer-Verlag Lecture Notes in Computer Science Vol.324, 339–350 (1988).

[32] U.Goltz and R.J.van Glabbeek: Refinement of Actions in Causality Based Models. Proc. of REX Workshop on Stepwise Refinement of Distributed Systems, Springer-Verlag Lecture Notes in Computer Science (1989), 267–300.

[33] U.Goltz and R.J.van Glabbeek: Equivalences and Refinement. 18ème École de Printemps Semantique du Parallelisme, Springer-Verlag Lecture Notes in Computer Science Vol. 469, 309-333 (1990).

[34] U.Goltz and A.Rensink: Finite Petri Nets as Models for Recursive Behaviour. Arbeitspapiere der GMD 604 (December 1991).

[35] R.Gorrieri and U.Montanari: SCONE: a Simple Calculus of Nets. Proc. of CONCUR-90 (ed. J.Baeten and J.W.Klop), Springer-Verlag Lecture Notes in Computer Science Vol.458, 2-30 (1990).

[36] R.J.van Glabbeek: The Refinement Theorem for ST-bisimulation Semantics. Proc. IFIP Working Conference on Programming Concepts and Methods. North Holland (1990).

[37] M.Hack: Petri Net Languages. Technical Report 159, MIT, Laboratory of Computer Science (1976).

[38] J.Hall: Petri Boxes and General Recursion. DEMON Technical Report, Computing Laboratory, University of Newcastle-upon-Tyne (June 1991).

[39] J.Hall and R.P.Hopkins: PN^3–Preliminary Notions for a Petri Net Based Programming Notation: Generalised Communication. DEMON Technical Report, Computing Laboratory, University of Newcastle-upon-Tyne (June 1990 / January 1991).

[40] R.P.Hopkins, O.Botti, J.Hall: A Basic-Net Algebra for Program Semantics and its Application to **occam**. In this volume.

[41] R.P.Hopkins: A (prioritised) Petri Box Algebra and its Use for a Triple Modular Redundancy Case Study. DEMON Technical Report (July 1991).

[42] C.A.R.Hoare: Communicating Sequential Processes. CACM 21(8), 666-677 (1978).

[43] C.A.R.Hoare: *Communicating Sequential Processes.* Prentice Hall (1985).

[44] R.Janicki and P.E.Lauer: *Specification and Analysis of Concurrent Systems: the COSY Approach.* To appear in Springer-Verlag Monographs on Theoretical Computer Science.

[45] K.Jensen: Coloured Petri Nets. Springer-Verlag Lecture Notes in Computer Science Vol.254, 248-299 (1986).

[46] P.E.Lauer: Path Expressions as Petri Nets, or Petri Nets with Fewer Tears. Memorandum MRM/70, Computing Laboratory, University of Newcastle-upon-Tyne (1974).

[47] P.E.Lauer, E.Best and M.W.Shields: Formal Theory of the Basic COSY Notation. Technical Report 143, Computing Laboratory, University of Newcastle-upon-Tyne (1979).

[48] D.May: **occam**. SIGPLAN Notices, Vol.18(4), pp.69-79 (April 1983).

[49] R.Milner: *A Calculus of Communicating Systems.* Springer-Verlag Lecture Notes in Computer Science Vol.84 (1980).

[50] R.Milner: *Communication and Concurrency.* Prentice Hall (1989).

[51] E.R.Olderog: *Nets, Terms and Formulas.* Habilitation (1989). Cambridge Tracts in Theoretical Computer Science (1991).

[52] G.L.Peterson: Myths about the Mutual Exclusion Problem. IPL Vol. 12/3, 115-116 (1981).

[53] A.Rabinovich and B.Trakhtenbrot: Behaviour Structure and Nets. Fundamenta Informaticae Vol. XI/4, 357-404 (1988).

[54] W.Reisig: *Petri Nets: An Introduction.* EATCS Monographs on Theoretical Computer Science Vol.4, Springer-Verlag (1988).

[55] W.Reisig: Petri Nets and Algebraic Specifications. Theoretical Computer Science Vol.80, 1–34 (1991).

[56] G.Rozenberg and P.S.Thiagarajan: Petri Nets: Basic Notions, Structure and Behaviour. Springer-Verlag Lecture Notes in Computer Science Vol. 224, 585-8 (1986).

[57] M.W.Shields: *Concurrency.* To appear in MIT Press.

[58] R. de Simone: Higher-level Synchronising Devices in MEIJE-SCCS. Theoretical Computer Science Vol.37, 245-267 (1985).

[59] D.Taubner: *Finite Representation of CCS and TCSP Programs by Automata and Petri Nets.* Springer-Verlag Lecture Notes in Computer Science Vol. 369 (1989).

[60] W.Vogler: Failure Semantics Based on Interval Semiwords is a Congruence for Refinement. Distributed Computing 4, 139-162 (1991).

[61] G.Winskel: A New Definition of Morphism on Petri Nets. Proc. STACS'84, Springer-Verlag Lecture Notes in Computer Science Vol.166, 140–150 (1984).

A Multiset Notation

Let Z be a set. The set of multisets over Z, denoted by $\mathcal{M}(Z)$, is defined as $\mathcal{M}(Z) = \{\mu \mid \mu: Z \to \mathbf{N}\}$. Special multisets are $\emptyset$ (defined by $\emptyset(a) = 0$ for every $a \in Z$) and Z (defined by $Z(a) = 1$ for every $a \in Z$). The usual set enumeration notation can readily be extended. For instance, $\{a, a, b, c, c, c\}$ denotes the multiset μ with $\mu(a) = 2$, $\mu(b) = 1$ and $\mu(c) = 3$. A multiset μ is a set (a subset of Z) iff $\mu(a) \leq 1$ for all $a \in Z$. The set theoretical operations are extended as follows:

$$\begin{array}{lrcl}
\text{Union:} & (\mu_1 \cup \mu_2)(a) & = & \max(\mu_1(a), \mu_2(a)) \\
\text{Intersection:} & (\mu_1 \cap \mu_2)(a) & = & \min(\mu_1(a), \mu_2(a)) \\
\text{Sum:} & (\mu_1 + \mu_2)(a) & = & \mu_1(a) + \mu_2(a) \\
\text{Difference:} & (\mu_1 \backslash \mu_2)(a) & = & \begin{cases} \mu_1(a) - \mu_2(a) & \text{if } \mu_1(a) \geq \mu_2(a) \\ 0 & \text{otherwise.} \end{cases}
\end{array}$$

Multiset inclusion is defined as $\mu_1 \subseteq \mu_2$ iff $\forall a \in Z: \mu_1(a) \leq \mu_2(a)$. For $k \in \mathbf{N}$, the k-multiple of μ is defined as $k \cdot \mu$, such that $(k \cdot \mu)(a) = k \cdot (\mu(a))$ for all $a \in Z$. A multiset is finite iff its support, i.e., the set $\{a \in Z \mid \mu(a) > 0\}$ is finite; its cardinality is then defined as $|\mu| = \sum_{a \in Z} \mu(a)$. The set of finite multisets over Z is denoted by $\mathcal{M}_{\mathcal{F}}(Z)$. A finite multiset μ is called a singleton iff $|\mu| = 1$.

Let $h: Z \to \mathbf{Z}$ be an integer-valued function on Z. When summing h over a finite multiset $\mu \in \mathcal{M}_{\mathcal{F}}(Z)$, this is to be understood as counting the multiplicities of μ properly, that is:

$$\sum_{a \in \mu} h(a) = \sum_{a \in Z} \mu(a) \cdot h(a).$$

B Operations on Labelled Nets

Let $\Sigma_1 = (S_1, T_1, W_1, \lambda_1)$ and $\Sigma_2 = (S_2, T_2, W_2, \lambda_2)$ be two labelled nets. We assume $S_1 \cap T_2 = T_1 \cap S_2 = \emptyset$ and the other obvious disjointness conditions.

Σ_1 and Σ_2 are said to match each other if the labels and connectivities on common places and transitions agree with each other:

$$\forall (x, y) \in ((S_1 \times T_1) \cup (T_1 \times S_1)) \cap ((S_2 \times T_2) \cup (T_2 \times S_2)): W_1(x, y) = W_2(x, y)$$
$$\forall x \in (S_1 \cup T_1) \cap (S_2 \cup T_2): \lambda_1(x) = \lambda_2(x).$$

They are called disjoint if

$$(S_1 \cup T_1) \cap (S_2 \cup T_2) = \emptyset.$$

If Σ_1 and Σ_2 are disjoint then they match each other, but not necessarily the other way round. The first operation (net union) will be defined for matching nets.

Definition B.1 *Net union*

Let Σ_1 and Σ_2 match each other.
For $x, y \in ((S_1 \cup S_2) \times (T_1 \cup T_2)) \cup ((T_1 \cup T_2) \times (S_1 \cup S_2))$, define

$$W(x,y) = \begin{cases} W_1(x,y) & \text{if } (x,y) \in (S_1 \times T_1) \cup (T_1 \times S_1) \\ W_2(x,y) & \text{if } (x,y) \in (S_2 \times T_2) \cup (T_2 \times S_2) \\ 0 & \text{otherwise.} \end{cases}$$

W is well defined because Σ_1 and Σ_2 match.
Then define $\Sigma_1 \sqcup \Sigma_2 = (S_1 \cup S_2, T_1 \cup T_2, W, \lambda_1 \cup \lambda_2)$. ■ B.1

Lemma B.2 *Commutativity and associativity of union*

(i) $\Sigma_1 \sqcup \Sigma_2 = \Sigma_2 \sqcup \Sigma_1$.
(ii) *If* Σ_1, Σ_2 *and* Σ_3 *match each other pairwise then* $\Sigma_1 \sqcup (\Sigma_2 \sqcup \Sigma_3) = (\Sigma_1 \sqcup \Sigma_2) \sqcup \Sigma_3$. ■ B.2

When adding new places or transitions to a labelled net $\Sigma = (S, T, W, \lambda)$ in Section 4, the identities of the new elements are (multi)sets of already existing elements. We again assume[26] that the sets are sufficiently disjoint. For instance, we assume that $S \cap Y = T \cap Y = \emptyset$ where Y is the new set of elements that is to be added; in the sequel, l denotes the labelling of these new elements.

Definition B.3 *Addition of new places*

Let $Y \subseteq \mathcal{M}_\mathcal{F}(S)$ and $l: Y \to \{\{e\}, \emptyset, \{x\}\}$.
Define $\Sigma \oplus (Y, l) = (S \cup Y, T, W \cup W_Y, \lambda \cup l)$, where for $y \in Y$, W_Y is defined as follows:

- for all $t \in T$: $W_Y(y,t) = \sum_{s \in y} W(s,t)$ and $W_Y(t,y) = \sum_{s \in y} W(t,s)$. ■ B.3

The addition of transitions is defined similarly, with Z denoting the new set of transitions and $T \cap Z = S \cap Z = \emptyset$:

Definition B.4 *Addition of new transitions*

Let $Z \subseteq \mathcal{M}_\mathcal{F}(T)$ and $l: Z \to \mathcal{L} \cup \mathcal{W}$.
Define $\Sigma \oplus (Z, l) = (S, T \cup Z, W \cup W_Z, \lambda \cup l)$, where for $z \in Z$, W_Z is defined as follows:

- for all $s \in S$: $W_Z(s,z) = \sum_{t \in z} W(s,t)$ and $W_Z(z,s) = \sum_{t \in z} W(t,s)$. ■ B.4

Lemma B.5

Let $Y, Z \subseteq \mathcal{M}_\mathcal{F}(S)$ *or* $Y, Z \subseteq \mathcal{M}_\mathcal{F}(T)$ *with* $Y \cap Z = \emptyset$. *Then*

$$(\Sigma \oplus (Y, l^Y)) \oplus (Z, l^Z) \quad = \quad \Sigma \oplus (Y \cup Z, l^Y \cup l^Z) \quad = \quad (\Sigma \oplus (Z, l^Z)) \oplus (Y, l^Y).$$

■ B.5

Definition B.6 *Removal of places or transitions*

Let R be a set.
Define $\Sigma \ominus R = (\ S \backslash R\ ,\ T \backslash R\ ,\ W|_{((S \backslash R) \times (T \backslash R)) \cup ((T \backslash R) \times (S \backslash R))}\ ,\ \lambda|_{(S \backslash R) \cup (T \backslash R)}\ )$. ■ B.6

In the preceding definition, $f|_Z$ denotes the restriction of a function f to the set Z.

[26] If necessary, this can be ensured by suitable renaming through renaming equivalence.

Lemma B.7

$$\begin{array}{lllll}(\Sigma \ominus R_1) \ominus R_2 & = & \Sigma \ominus (R_1 \cup R_2) & = & (\Sigma \ominus R_2) \ominus R_1 \\ (\Sigma \ominus R) \ominus R & = & \Sigma \ominus R. & & \end{array}$$

■ B.7

We also need a multiplication operator whose use is specific only to places.

Definition B.8

Let A and B be any two sets with $A \cap B = \emptyset$. We define $A \otimes B = \{\{a, b\} \mid a \in A, b \in B\}$. ■ B.8

This operation satisfies $A \otimes B = B \otimes A$ (and also an associativity property which we do not need). It can be viewed as a symmetric Cartesian product.

Modular Functional Modelling of Petri Nets with Individual Tokens[1]

Manfred Broy
Institut für Informatik, Technische Universität München, D-8000 München 2, Germany

Thomas Streicher
Fakultät für Mathematik und Informatik, Universität Passau, D-8390 Passau, Germany

Abstract

A functional semantic modelling of Petri nets with individual tokens also called high level Petri nets is outlined. A denotational semantics for so-called high level Petri net components, i.e. nets that may contain ingoing and outgoing arcs, is given. An abstraction of the semantics is provided in terms of a predicative semantics. This semantics is modular in the sense that high level Petri net components can be composed by parallel composition and feedback in a way that the semantics of the composed net can be derived from the semantics of the net components.

1. Introduction

Petri nets are among the first attempts to provide formalizations of distributed concurrent systems. They allow an intuitively suggestive graphical representation of systems with a simple operational "firing-rule" semantics (see e.g. [Reisig 82]). Being more or less the concept of a concurrent automaton they support several kinds of state-based reasoning.

However, when trying to use Petri nets as system models in larger, more sophisticated applications the simplicity of the elementary so-called place/transition nets becomes more and more a drawback. The reasons are as follows:

(a) the involved Petri nets may get unmanageably large,

(b) notions of more refined data structures and data dependencies are missing,

(c) Petri nets in most formulations (one remarkable exception is [Winkowski 90]) describe "closed" systems such that interaction with some (loosely specified) environment cannot be expressed adequately.

---

[1] This work was supported by the ESPRIT BASIC RESEARCH ACTION Demon and by the Sonderforschungsbereich 342 Werkzeuge und Methoden für die Nutzung paralleler Architekturen

One answer to the problem mentioned in (b) has been given by the concept of so-called high level Petri nets (cf. [Reisig 85], [Reisig 90]) where instead of unstructured tokens individual data elements are sent around by the places and transitions in a net. This is closely related to data flow ideas (cf. [Dennis 74]) which evolved from the concept of single assignment languages (cf. for instance [Tesler, Enea 68]) and Petri net concepts.

The problem (a) is - as generally agreed - mainly a problem of modularity. If it is possible to compose larger nets from smaller nets such that the semantics of the larger net can be deduced from the semantics of the smaller nets, then there is hope that we do not have to consider the larger nets with all their details, but only compositional forms on nets and behavioural abstractions of nets. This idea of compositionality does help, however, only if the semantic model provides a considerable amount of abstraction from details in the Petri net. This corresponds to the possibility of hiding internal arcs, transitions or places and having a notion of refinement.

To obtain a satisfactory compositional semantics for Petri nets, in full generality, is a hard problem. One crucial question concerns the chosen forms of composition. Moreover, it is not clear, whether a straight compositional theory for proper Petri nets is the best direction to take. Another possibility is to generalize the notion of Petri net and to develop a notion of a Petri net component, where special net fragments are considered together with restricted ways of composing such fragments. This leads to the concept of Petri net components which has a number of methodological advantages for system design by specification and stepwise refinement of nets. In particular, then the semantics of net fragments and the specification of their behaviour has to be studied.

From this point of view the problems mentioned in (a) and (c) are closely related. If one is able to work with fragments of nets (that provide connections to some unspecified environment and thus can communicate with the outside world) and appropriate behavioural abstractions of net fragments then one can compose them and derive the specification of the behaviour of the composed net from the specifications of the behaviours of the net fragments. The crucial notions in such an approach to modular composition of nets are those of net fragments and those of forms of composition.

An adequate compositional theory of Petri nets is an important open problem since a long time. In order to describe or develop large distributed systems the methodology and the underlying semantic model should supply a set of forms of composition which respect semantical equivalence in order to build systems in a modular way. There have been attempts to restrict the approach to subclasses of nets for which several forms of composition respect semantic equivalence. Our approach aims at giving a compositional semantics for a class of nets containing most of the net classes studied up to now.

In the sequel instead of trying to give modular semantics for closed Petri nets we study fragments of high level Petri nets which we call "net components" where a net may include arcs without internal sources or without internal targets. These arcs are understood to come from or go to the environment of the net fragment such that they can be freely connected to the arcs of other nets or connected with other arcs of the same net (leading to feedback). Generalized high level Petri nets and also fragments of high level Petri nets are considered as data flow networks. Then a computation of a net is modelled by associating a stream with every arc (cf. [FiMe 82]) and a specific, possibly nondeterministic stream processing agent represented by a set of stream processing functions with every node, i.e. every place and every transition. Following Broy's approach to nondeterministic data flow (cf. [Broy 90]) we describe the behaviour of a nondeterministic net by a set of stream processing functions. The forms of composition correspond to forms of sequential functional and parallel composition and feedback by taking fixpoints.

However, care has to be taken about the specific forms of nondeterminism in Petri nets. There the nondeterministic choices cannot be understood fully locally w.r.t. single places or transitions. For doing choices we have to consider larger areas of a net in cases of conflicts. This specific form of "angelic" nondeterminism in Petri nets is reflected in the functional modelling by additional constraints. Here by "angelic" nondeterminism we mean the following progress property usually assumed for Petri nets: whenever transitions have the choice between doing something and doing nothing at least one of them chooses to do something.

The paper is organized as follows. We start by introducing the basic notions of functional system models and high level net components, then give a functional meaning to them and finally show how to abstract from the internal structure of nets by deriving an abstract functional behaviour. Then we study forms of composition for nets by specifying the abstract behaviour of composed nets in terms of the abstract behaviours of the constituent net components. Finally we prove the modularity, i. e. the compositionality of the semantic model w.r.t. parallel composition and feedback.

2. Basic Structures

Given a set M of messages a stream over M is a finite or infinite sequence of elements from M. By M^* we denote the finite sequences over the set M. We denote the finite sequence consisting of the elements $x_1, ..., x_n$ by $\langle x_1 ... x_n \rangle$ or by $\langle x_{i+1}: i < n \rangle$. M^* includes the empty sequence which is denoted by $\langle\rangle$.

By M^∞ we denote the infinite sequences over the set M. M^∞ can be understood to be represented by the total mappings from the natural numbers $\mathbb{N}$ to M. We denote the infinite sequence consisting of the elements $x_1, x_2, ...$ by $\langle x_{i+1}: i < \infty \rangle$.

We denote the set of streams over the set M by M^ω. Formally we have

$$M^\omega = M^* \cup M^\infty.$$

For simplicity we write also a^n for $\langle x_{i+1}: i < n \rangle$ with $x_{i+1} = a$ for all i, $0 \le i < n$. Similarly, we write S^n for the set of all streams $\langle x_{i+1}: i < n \rangle$ with $x_i \in S$ for all i, $0 \le i < n$.

Streams can be understood to represent the history of communications (on channels) between components of interactive systems. We introduce a number of functions on streams that are useful in system descriptions.

For every stream s we may define its *length*. The length of a stream is infinite or a natural number. It will be denoted by #s. Formally we have

$$\#: M^\omega \to \mathbb{N} \cup \{\infty\}$$

with

$$\#\langle x_{i+1}: i < n \rangle = n.$$

A classical operation on sequences is the *concatenation* which we denote by ˆ. The concatenation is a function that takes two sequences (say s and t) and produces a sequence as result starting with s and continuing with t . If s is infinite then the result of concatenating s with t yields s again. Formally we have for the concatenation the following functionality:

$$\hat{}: M^\omega \times M^\omega \to M^\omega$$

Concatenation is written in infix notation. Its precise meaning is defined for streams $s = \langle s_{i+1}: i < n \rangle$ and $t = \langle t_{i+1}: i < m \rangle$ by

$$s\hat{}t = \langle \textbf{ if } i < n \textbf{ then } s_{i+1} \textbf{ else } t_{i-n+1} \textbf{ fi}: i < n+m \rangle .$$

On the set M^ω of streams we define a *prefix ordering* $\sqsubseteq$. We write $s \sqsubseteq t$ for streams s and t if s is a *prefix* of t. Formally we have for streams s and t:

$$s \sqsubseteq t \text{ iff } \exists r \in M^\omega: s\hat{\ }r = t.$$

The prefix ordering defines a partial ordering on the set M^ω of streams. If $s \sqsubseteq t$, then we also say that s is an *approximation* of t. The set of streams ordered by $\sqsubseteq$ is even complete in the sense that every directed set $S \subseteq M^\omega$ of streams has a *least upper bound* denoted by lub S. A set S which is subset of a partially ordered set is called *directed*, iff S is nonempty and

$$\forall x, y \in S: \exists z \in S: x \sqsubseteq z \wedge y \sqsubseteq z.$$

Actually, directed sets of streams are linearly ordered.

Infinite streams are obtained as least upper bounds of directed sets of *finite* streams. Infinite streams are in particular of interest as (and can also be described by) fixpoints of prefix monotonic functions. Note that the streams associated with feedback loops in interactive systems correspond to such fixpoints.

A *stream processing function* is a function

$$f: M^\omega \to N^\omega$$

that is *prefix monotonic* and *continuous*. The function f is called *(prefix) monotonic*, if for all streams s and t we have

$$s \sqsubseteq t \Rightarrow f.s \sqsubseteq f.t.$$

For better readability we often write for the function application f.x instead of f(x). We assume that the function application associates to the right, i. e. f.g.x stands for f(g(x)). The function f is called *continuous*, if for all directed sets $S \subseteq M^\omega$ of streams we have

$$\text{lub } \{f.s: s \in S\} = f.\text{lub } S.$$

If a function is continuous, then its results for infinite input can be already predicted from its results on all finite approximations of the input.

By $\perp$ we denote the pseudo element which represents the result of diverging computations. We write $M^\perp$ for $M \cup \{\perp\}$. Here we assume that $\perp$ is not an element of M. On $M^\perp$ we define also a simple partial ordering by:

$$x \sqsubseteq y \quad \text{iff} \quad x = y \vee x = \perp.$$

We use the following functions on streams

$$ft: M^\omega \to M^\perp,$$

$$rt: M^\omega \to M^\omega,$$

$$.\&.: M^\perp \times M^\omega \to M^\omega.$$

They are defined as follows: the function ft selects the first element of a stream, if the stream is not empty (otherwise it returns $\perp$):

$$ft.\langle s_{i+1}: i < n \rangle = \begin{cases} \perp & \text{if } n = 0 \\ s_1 & \text{if } n > 0. \end{cases}$$

The function rt deletes the first element of a stream, if the stream is not empty:

$$\text{rt}.\langle s_{i+1}: i < n \rangle = \begin{cases} \langle\rangle & \text{if } n = 0 \\ \langle s_{i+2}: i < n-1 \rangle & \text{if } n > 0 . \end{cases}$$

We sometimes use iterated applications of the function rt. Accordingly we define:

$$\text{rt}^0.s = s,$$

$$\text{rt}^{k+1}.s = \text{rt}^k(\text{rt}.s),$$

$$\text{rt}^\infty.s = \langle\rangle.$$

The function & appends an element to a stream (as first element), if the element is defined (i.e. $\neq \bot$):

$$x \,\&\, \langle s_{i+1}: i < n \rangle = \begin{cases} \langle\rangle & \text{if } x = \bot \\ \langle s_i: i < n+1 \rangle & \text{if } x \neq \bot \text{ with } s_0 = x . \end{cases}$$

The definition of this function has been chosen carefully to keep it monotonic and continuous w.r.t. the prefix ordering. However, there are also non-formal reasons for taking this definition that have to do with an appropriate modelling of communication: the computation of a value must have been finished before subsequent values can be transmitted, therefore if the computation of the first value does not terminate then nothing at all will ever be transmitted. The properties of the functions can be expressed in an axiomatic style by the following equations:

$\bot \,\&\, s = \langle\rangle$,	$\text{rt}.\langle\rangle = \langle\rangle$,
$\text{ft}(x \,\&\, s) = x$,	$x \neq \bot \Rightarrow \text{rt}(x \,\&\, s) = s$,
$\langle\rangle\hat{\ }s = s = s\hat{\ }\langle\rangle$,	$x \neq \bot \Rightarrow (x \,\&\, s)\hat{\ }r = x \,\&\, (s\hat{\ }r)$,
$\#\langle\rangle = 0$,	$x \neq \bot \Rightarrow \#(x \,\&\, s) = 1 + \#s$.

Sometimes it is useful to work with a filter function on streams. Given a set $Q \subseteq M$ and a stream $s \in M^\omega$ we write Q©s for the stream obtained from s by eliminating elements not contained in Q. Formally we define

$$Q©\langle\rangle = \langle\rangle,$$

$$Q©(d \,\&\, s) = d \,\&\, (Q©s) \qquad \text{if } d \in Q,$$

$$Q©(d \,\&\, s) = Q©s \qquad \text{if } (d \notin Q).$$

We denote the function space of (n,m)-ary prefix continuous stream processing functions by:

$$[(M^\omega)^n \to (M^\omega)^m]$$

The prefix ordering $\sqsubseteq$ induces an ordering on tuples of streams and on this function space by extending the order componentwise.

Note that the operations ft, rt, and & are prefix monotonic and continuous, but the concatenation ^ as defined above is not prefix monotonic (in its first argument).

Prefix monotonicity reflects a characteristic property of interactive systems: communicated data cannot be changed after having appeared as output. If f.s is the stream that results as output from the input stream s then if we continue with the input r, i.e. consider the input s^r, then we get some additional output $f_s(r)$, i.e. obtain after all the output $(f.s)\hat{\ }f_s(r)$. Furthermore monotonicity gives the formal basis for handling communication in feedback loops: feedback is translated to fixpoint equations, which are known to have solutions, provided the involved functions are monotonic.

3. High Level Petri Net Components

We shall define a generalized notion of *high level net component*. For this purpose we assume a set M of data that will be used as tokens.

An *uninterpreted Petri net component* is a tuple

$$N = (P, T, I, O, R)$$

where P, T, I, O are pairwise disjoint sets of nodes called *places*, *transitions*, *input ports* and *output ports*, respectively, and R, called the *flow relation*, is a subset of

$$(I \times (P \cup T)) \cup (P \times (T \cup O)) \cup (T \times (P \cup O))$$

where each element from $I \cup O$ occurs in exactly one pair of R. For every node $n \in P \cup T \cup I \cup O$ we define its set of ingoing arcs as

$$^{\rightarrow}n = \{ (x, n) : (x, n) \in R \}$$

and its set of outgoing arcs as

$$n^{\rightarrow} = \{ (n, x) : (n, x) \in R \}.$$

The set

$$^{\rightarrow}R = R \cap (I \times (P \cup T))$$

is called the set of *input arcs* and

$$R^{\rightarrow} = R \cap ((P \cup T) \times O)$$

is called the set of *output arcs* of the net.

We may explain our basic idea about the functional modelling of high level Petri nets by a picture showing an net component:

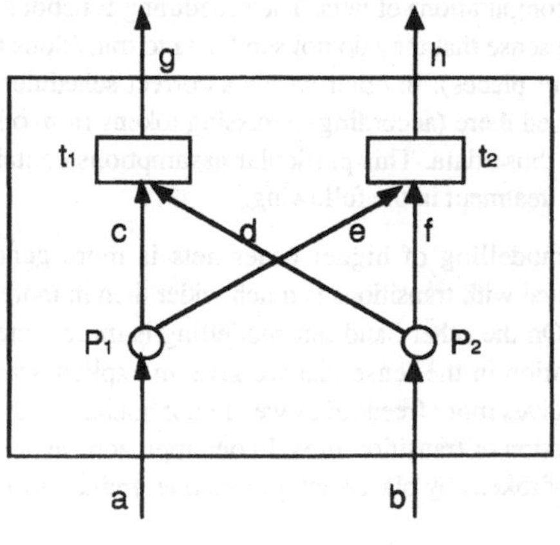

In a functional representation of a computation of a net we associate

- with each arc a *stream*, representing the sequence of data sent from the arc's source to the arcs's target
- with each place a *scheduler function* that determines which and in which ordering the ingoing tokens are distributed to the successor transitions, and
- with each transition a *(set of) stream processing function(s)* which models the transformations of the streams of incoming tokens into streams of outgoing tokens.

In the given example we may for instance associate with both transitions stream processing functions representing elementwise addition (we assume that all data elements are natural numbers) of their input streams. For a correct ("safe" and "live") computation we require that for given streams a, b the streams c, d, e, f, g, h are the least fixpoint of the following system of equations

$$g = \text{stream\_add}(c, d),$$

$$h = \text{stream\_add}(e, f),$$

$$(c, e) = \text{schedule}_1(a),$$

$$(d, f) = \text{schedule}_2(b),$$

and the schedule functions schedule_1 and schedule_2 associated with the places p_1 and p_2 have to fulfil certain conditions in order to guarantee that the computation is in accordance with the special liveness requirements of the computations of a Petri net. Of course, in our specific example there is only one fixpoint due to lack of circularity, but in general the assumption of least fixpoints is essential.

The essential difference of our approach of modelling a high level Petri net to other approaches found in the literature can be seen in our treatment of the places and the arcs. Traditionally, in Petri net models places are treated as passive components and no specific meaning is given to arcs. Places just store tokens and arcs just connect places and transitions. In our approach places are stream processing functions which play an active role in distributing tokens and arcs are connected with streams in computations. Similarly we associate individual semantic notions to transitions in the form of specific classes of stream processing functions. In this respect our modelling of computations is more concrete than in the traditional approach to Petri nets where computations are mainly described by firing rules.

In Petri nets the simple classical data flow model of nondeterministic computation (cf. for instance [Broy 90]) by choosing freely a function for every node from a set of specified functions cannot be applied naively due to a particular property assumed for computations of nets. The scheduling functions associated with the places have to be "angelic oracles" in the sense that they do not send data to transitions that cannot fire (due to lack of input on other arcs from other places). In other words a correct scheduler in a place never sends data to a transition that is not consumed there (according to missing tokens from other places) although another transition is ready to consume those data. This particular assumptions contained in the firing rules for Petri nets need a specific semantic treatment in the following.

Thus one can say that in one aspect our modelling of higher order nets is more general as the nondeterministic functions we allow to be associated with transitions is much wider then in more traditional approaches to the semantics of high level nets. On the other hand our modelling is more concrete as the runs of nets in our approach carry more information in the sense that we give an explicit account of the scheduling of tokens in places. This latter aspect gives more freedom as we are not bound to a systolic view of computation where in each step a certain collection of transition fires. In our approach we do not assume linear discrete time and therefore the scheduling of tokens by places has a more fine-grained structure.

For being able to talk about the fact that some token is actually consumed by a stream processing function associated with a transition we introduce the notion of *stable function*. Roughly speaking a stable function on tuples of streams has the property that for every tuple of input streams we can determine a least prefix of the input tuple of the input streams on which the function produces exactly the same output as on the given tuple. If this least prefix coincides with the given input, then we say that all the input is fully consumed by the computation under consideration.

Next we technically define the notion of *stable continuous stream processing function*. Let D_1 and D_2 be Scott domains, i.e. bounded complete countably algebraic cpos (see e.g. [Scott 82]), then we call a function

$$f : D_1 \to D_2$$

stable iff it is continuous and

$$f(d_1 \sqcap d_2) = f.d_1 \sqcap f.d_2$$

for all compatible objects $d_1, d_2 \in D_1$, i.e. for all objects d_1 and d_2 that have a common upper bound. Here $d_1 \sqcap d_2$ denotes the *greatest lower bound* of the elements d_1 and d_2. In case D_1 is *finitary*, i.e. any finite element in D_1 dominates only finitely many elements as e.g. in cartesian products of stream domains, it is guaranteed that for any finite approximation e to output f.d there exists a unique finite approximation d' to d such that f.d' extends e and for all d" approximating d with f.d" extending e it holds that d' approximates d". As a consequence we get that for any d in D_1 there exists a least d' approximating d and f.d = f.d'. We say then that d' is the *minimal sufficient input for* f *at* d iff d' approximates d and f.d = f.d' and for any d" approximating d' with f.d" = f.d' it already holds that d" = d'.

An *interpreted high level Petri net component* (also called *open interpreted high level Petri net*) is a tuple

$$N = (P, T, I, O, R, \varphi)$$

where (P, T, I, O, R) is an net component and φ is a function associating with each transition $t \in T$ a set $\varphi.t$ of stable continuous stream processing functions from the function space

$$[{}^{\to}t \to M^{\omega}] \to [t^{\to} \to M^{\omega}].$$

Note that $[{}^{\to}t \to M^{\omega}]$ and similarly $[t^{\to} \to M^{\omega}]$ denote families of streams indexed by the input and output arcs resp. of the transition t. The notion above comprises more general behaviours of transitions than usually considered for high level Petri nets since instead of a particular often very restricted class of sets of transition functions we allow arbitrary sets of stable continuous functions. The case of a deterministic transition function is trivially included if we choose a one-element set of functions.

For describing computations of a generalized high level Petri net component we introduce the notions of *arc valuation* and *node valuation*. An *arc valuation* γ associates with every arc of a net a stream of data elements, i.e. γ is a mapping

$$\gamma : R \to M^{\omega}.$$

A *node valuation* w.r.t. to the net interpretation φ is a mapping η defined on the set of nodes $T \cup P$ assigning to every node x a stream processing function

$$\eta.x : [{}^{\to}x \to M^{\omega}] \to [x^{\to} \to M^{\omega}]$$

where for every transition $t \in T$ we have

$$\eta.t \in \varphi.t$$

and with every place $p \in P$ a *stable scheduling function*

$$\eta.p : [{}^{\rightarrow}p \rightarrow M^{\omega}] \rightarrow [p^{\rightarrow} \rightarrow M^{\omega}]$$

is associated such that for any y in $[{}^{\rightarrow}p \rightarrow M^{\omega}]$ and $m \in M$ we have

$$\sum_{a \in p^{\rightarrow}} \#\{m\}©((\eta.p).y).a \quad \leq \sum_{a \in {}^{\rightarrow}p} \#\{m\}©(y.a) \ .$$

Intuitively, this formula expresses that the function $\eta.p$ associated with a place p in a node valuation just distributes and maybe reorders the elements of the streams of messages received on its input arcs. This condition on the scheduling functions in the places is sufficient for making sure that a place does not "invent" new messages. So it is a fundamental safety property for the behaviour of places. Liveness requirements for the behaviour of places, however, are not covered at all by the condition above. Note, if a place never sends a token the above condition is fulfilled. Note, moreover, here the words *safety* and *liveness* are not used in the usual way of Petri net theory but in the sense of *partial* versus *total correctness*.

In a liveness requirement for the behaviour of an net component we make sure that a transition gets a message needed by it if not consumed by other transitions. For an net component therefore it is important to introduce a notion of available message for output on arcs from places to the environment and the notion of ineffective messages for input arcs leading to transitions. This concept will allow us to study the behaviour of net components in contexts where output arcs having places as their source are connected to transitions.

For a net component an input is given by a valuation of the arcs leading into the net. Accordingly an *input* is given by valuation for the input arcs, i.e. by a function

$$\alpha : {}^{\rightarrow}R \rightarrow M^{\omega}$$

that associates with every input arc a stream of data elements.

Since we are in the framework of domain and fixpoint theory we are able to define computations for a given node valuation simply by the least fixpoint associated with a set of mutually recursive equations for the streams attached to the arcs. For a node valuation η and some input

$$\alpha : {}^{\rightarrow}R \rightarrow M^{\omega}$$

an arc valuation γ is called *the arc valuation generated by* η *on input* α iff γ is the least arc valuation (least fixpoint) satisfying the following equations

$$\gamma.a = \alpha.a \qquad \text{for } a \in {}^{\rightarrow}R,$$

$$\gamma.a = ((\eta.x).\gamma|_{\rightarrow x}).a \qquad \text{for } a \in x^{\rightarrow} \text{ where } x \in P \cup T\ .$$

There $\gamma|_{\rightarrow x}$ denotes the restriction of the function γ to the arguments in ${}^{\rightarrow}x$. Since the arc valuation γ is defined in terms of a least fixpoint of a continuous function, it is uniquely determined given η and α. Therefore it is correct to speak of *the* arc valuation generated by η on input α. It will be denoted by arc_val(η, α).

The arc valuation γ' is called the *minimal* arc valuation for η on input α if for the arc valuation γ generated by η on input α we have $\gamma' \sqsubseteq \gamma$ and γ' satisfies the following conditions:

- for arcs $a \in R \setminus ((I \cup P) \times T)$ we have $\gamma'.a = \gamma.a$ and
- for transitions $t \in T$ the family of streams $\gamma'|_{\rightarrow t}$ is the minimal sufficient input for $\eta.t$ with input $\gamma|_{\rightarrow t}$.

Again the minimal arc valuation γ is uniquely determined by η and α, which is denoted by min_arc_val(η, α). The input $\gamma|_{\rightarrow R}$ is called *the minimal sufficient* input for η with input α. An input α is called *minimal sufficient* for η iff α coincides with its minimal sufficient input.

The minimal arc valuation shows the input to the net to transitions and output of places that is correctly scheduled w.r.t. the demands of the transitions. This reflects the firing rule in Petri nets where the scheduling of the places i.e. the firing of the transitions is driven by the readiness (enabledness) of transitions to fire.

The idea of a minimal arc valuation can also be carried over to node valuations. Accordingly we may choose the scheduling functions as small as possible. Intuitively speaking this means that a scheduling function is chosen that does not anticipate any scheduling of data tokens not arrived so far on the input streams of a place. Accordingly a node valuation η' is called a *minimal scheduling w.r.t.* η and input α if it is the node valuation where

$\eta'.p.x = (\eta.p)(x \sqcap \gamma|_{\rightarrow p}) \sqcap \gamma|_{p\rightarrow}$, for all $p \in P$, where γ = min_arc_val(η, α),

$\eta'.t = \eta.t$ for all $t \in T$.

By definition we then have $\eta' \sqsubseteq \eta$ and the minimal arc valuation for η on α coincides with the arc valuation generated by η' on α. The minimal node valuation η' for a given node valuation η and some input α is denoted by min_sched(η, α).

For the scheduling strategy of a high level net it is generally assumed that the scheduling of tokens is done in a way that all tokens transmitted from a place to a transition are actually used by the transition, which can be seen as a safety condition for the schedulers, and that tokens that can be used by some transition are eventually sent, which is essentially the liveness condition for the schedulers connected with the places. We are now going to formalize this liveness requirement.

A node valuation η' is called a *rescheduling of* η *w.r.t.* α iff it rearranges the scheduling of unconsumed tokens only, i.e. iff

- min_sched(η, α) $\sqsubseteq \eta'$ and
- $\eta.\tau = \eta'.t$ for all $t \in T$.

Of course, minimal arc valuations may correspond to incomplete ("not liveness correct") computations due to a scheduling of the messages by places where certain tokens are not send to transitions although they could be consumed. This is the case, in general, if one chooses e.g. for every place the scheduling function with the empty streams as output. For avoiding this we define the notion of a *liveness correct arc valuation for a node valuation* η *and input* α. Intuitively, a correct scheduling means that all messages sent to some place are forwarded to transitions as much as needed, i.e. any rescheduling of unused tokens is not sufficient for advancing the computation in some transition inside the net. By this notion also liveness properties are considered. Formally this can be expressed in the following way.

A node valuation η is called a *liveness correct scheduling w.r.t. input* α iff all tokens are sent from places to transitions if they can be consumed or if at least one place sends infinitely many tokens to some transition or some output port, i.e. iff

- η = min_sched(η, α) and
- min_arc_val(η, α) = min_arc_val(η', α) for all reschedulings η' of η w.r.t. α

or

- there exists $a \in R \cap (P \times (O \cup T))$ where min_arc_val(η, α).a is infinite.

According to this definition a node valuation η is called liveness correct (w.r.t. some input α), if it is minimal and a rescheduling of unconsumed tokens to transitions cannot increase the minimal sufficient input for the transitions. In Petri net terms this means that no further firing is possible. This requirement does not apply to schedulings with some infinite output streams for places. A computation for which one transition fires infinitely often is - according to the definition above - always considered liveness correct. The distinction of the case of finite and infinite output streams for places is motivated by a classical rule semantics of Petri nets where a computation is liveness correct, if at least one node fires infinitely often. Here, of course, modified definitions might be considered.

The arc valuation generated by a correct scheduler for input α corresponds to a computation that follows the firing rules of Petri nets. It provides a semantic modelling of computations including explicit concurrency, since the basic events in the computations (the firing of transitions or places) can be represented by the tokens in the streams and partial ordering modelling causality on these elements can be deduced from the stability of the functions in the arc valuation.

4. Abstract Behaviours of Nets Components

So far we have given a meaning to Petri nets by associating streams with arcs and functions with nodes. In particular, we have considered the net component with all its internal structure consisting of nodes and internal arcs. Next we abstract from the internal arcs and nodes of a net and only restrict our consideration to ingoing and outgoing arcs by associating a function with the net component mapping valuations of the input arcs to valuations of the output arcs. Roughly speaking we consider an high level net component as an atomic node.

Given a high level Petri net and a node valuation η we define the *abstraction for* η by the function

$$f: [^{\rightarrow}R \rightarrow M^{\omega}] \rightarrow [R^{\rightarrow} \rightarrow M^{\omega}]$$

just mapping valuations of input arcs on valuations of output arcs by the following rule:

$$f.\alpha = \text{arc\_val}(\eta, \alpha)|_{R^{\rightarrow}}$$

However, for obtaining a compositional abstraction we need more information about a net than just abstractions of node valuations, since we need information about demands of tokens on the input arcs and availability of tokens on the output arcs to determine the behaviour of high level net components when composed with other net components.

Let η be a node valuation for which α is a minimal sufficient input and which is a liveness correct scheduler. We are interested to ask to which extend we can increase input α on those input arcs leading to transitions such that the node valuation η is still a liveness correct scheduler for the increased input. This can be done by associating with any arc in $R \cap (I \times T)$ a multiset which tells how much the minimal sufficient input α may be increased such that for the increased input α still is the minimal sufficient input.

For the formal definition of this concept we introduce the mathematical structure of multisets. A *multiset* b over a given set M is given by a function

$$b: M \rightarrow \mathbb{N} \cup \{\infty\}.$$

For multisets b and b' we write

$$b \subseteq b'$$

in analogy to the inclusion relation on sets iff for all $m \in M$.

$$b.m \leq b'.m.$$

The *set of multisets* over a given set M is denoted by

$$MS(M).$$

In contrast to sets multisets do not only carry the information whether an element is a member of the set but also how often it is a member. Note that every stream can be abstracted to a multiset.

We use the concept of multisets to associate with input arcs leading to transitions multisets of *ineffective* tokens. Intuitively speaking (a valuation of) multisets of data elements for input arcs leading to transitions are called *ineffective* for some input α if increasing the input by elements from the multisets does not lead to increased minimal sufficient input for the net and its scheduling. Let η be a liveness correct scheduler for some minimal sufficient input α. An assignment

$$\upsilon: R \cap (I \times T) \rightarrow MS(M)$$

of multisets to the input arcs of a net leading to transitions is called *ineffective* iff for any valuations of streams to those input arcs

$$s: R \cap (I \times T) \rightarrow M^{\omega}$$

which contain only elements from the multisets in υ, i.e. where for all messages $m \in M$ we have

$$\#\{m\}©s.a \leq (\upsilon.a).m \qquad \text{for all } a \in R \cap (I \times T)$$

and for the input arc valuation

$$\alpha': {\rightarrow}R \rightarrow M^{\omega}$$

with

$$\alpha'.a = \alpha.a\hat{\ }s.a \qquad \text{for } a \in R \cap (I \times T),$$

$$\alpha'.a = \alpha.a \qquad \text{for } a \in R \cap (I \times P).$$

η is also a liveness correct scheduler for α', i.e. in particular α' is minimal sufficient input. This means that in whichever way we add elements from the multisets in υ to the resp. input streams, these elements do not lead to increased output for the associated transitions.

Given a node valuation η, a minimal sufficient input α w.r.t. η, an output arc o with a place $p \in P$ as source, i.e. $(p, o) \in R$, a multiset S of tokens is called *available*, iff the place p has the messages in S available, i.e. for the minimal arc valuation $\gamma = \text{min\_arc\_val}(\eta, \alpha)$ for all $a \in p^{\rightarrow}$ the stream $\gamma.a$ is finite and for all $m \in M$:

$$\sum_{a \in p^{\rightarrow}} \#\{m\}©\gamma.a = S(m) + \sum_{a \in {}^{\rightarrow}p} \#\{m\}©\gamma.a .$$

or the multiset S is empty. The distinction between the case of finite and infinite output streams for places is necessary according to the firing rule semantics of Petri nets where a computation is liveness correct, if at least one node fires infinitely often.

Given a minimal arc valuation γ with correct scheduler η for a minimal sufficient input α a valuation of multisets for output arcs from

$$\rho: R \cap (P \times O) \rightarrow MS(M)$$

is called *available*, if for every arc a in $R \cap (P \times O)$ the multiset $\rho.a$ is available (cf. readiness sets in [HrBrRo 81]).

The notions of available and ineffective multisets of tokens are used in the definition of the abstract ("observable") behaviour of a Petri net. With any high level Petri net component we associate a predicate

$$C(f, \alpha, \upsilon, \rho)$$

which expresses the fact that the function f is a stable mapping from valuations of the input arcs by streams to valuations of the output arcs by streams that corresponds to a computation of the Petri net arising from a liveness correct scheduling w.r.t. the input α which is minimal sufficient and υ as ineffective and ρ is available.

The predicate C is called the *predicative semantics* of a net. The information contained in the predicative semantics of a net is sufficient to guarantee compositionality as shown in the next section.

If we consider net components where all output arcs have transitions as sources then ρ is trivial and can be omitted. If all input arcs have targets being places then υ can be omitted. The behaviour of net fragments restricted in such a way can obviously be described in a much simpler style. This restriction leads to an interesting net class of net components that will be studied for methodological reasons in a forthcoming paper.

5. Composition of Net Components

For net components there are basic two forms of composition: *parallel composition* and *feedback*. Sequential composition can be obtained by composing the two net components under consideration in parallel and then feeding back the output of the first net to the input of the second net. We shall define composition not only "syntactically" on the level of interpreted high level Petri net components but also on the level of predicative semantics. Of course, we have to show that the given predicative semantics is compositional w.r.t. parallel composition and feedback.

The *parallel composition* of two nets is a rather simple operation as long as we assume that all the nodes of the two nets are pairwise distinct. Let the nets N_1 and N_2 be given by

$$N_i = (P_i, T_i, I_i, O_i, R_i, \varphi_i) \qquad \text{for } i = 1, 2$$

and the sets of nodes of the two nets be pairwise distinct, i.e.

$$(P_1 \cup T_1 \cup I_1 \cup O_1) \cap (P_2 \cup T_2 \cup I_2 \cup O_2) = \varnothing$$

For nets for which this requirement is not fulfilled it can be established quite easily by renaming.

For the net obtained by the parallel composition of the given nets N_1 and N_2 we write $N_1 \| N_2$. This stands for the net

$$(P_1 \cup P_2, T_1 \cup T_2, I_1 \cup I_2, O_1 \cup O_2, R_1 \cup R_2, \varphi_1 \cup \varphi_2).$$

Note that for functions

$$f_i: A_i \to B \qquad \text{for } i = 1, 2$$

with disjoint domains, i. e. $A_1 \cap A_2 = \varnothing$, we denote by $f_1 \cup f_2$ the function

$$(f_1 \cup f_2): A_1 \cup A_2 \to B$$

where

$$(f_1 \cup f_2).x = \begin{cases} f_1.x & \text{if } x \in A_1 \\ f_2.x & \text{if } x \in A_2 \end{cases}$$

If C_1, C_2 represent the predicative semantics for nets N_1 and N_2, i.e. specify the behaviours of N_1 and N_2, respectively, then the predicate C describing the predicative semantics of $N_1 \parallel N_2$ is defined as follows:

$$C(f, \alpha, \upsilon, \rho)$$

holds, iff there exist $f_1, f_2, \alpha_1, \alpha_2, \upsilon_1, \upsilon_2, \rho_1, \rho_2$ of appropriate type such that

$$C_1(f_1, \alpha_1, \upsilon_1, \rho_1),$$

$$C_2(f_2, \alpha_2, \upsilon_2, \rho_2),$$

and

$$f = f_1 \cup f_2,$$

$$\alpha = \alpha_1 \cup \alpha_2,$$

$$\upsilon = \upsilon_1 \cup \upsilon_2,$$

$$\rho = \rho_1 \cup \rho_2 .$$

This shows that the predicative semantics of a net obtained by parallel composition of two nets can be obtained fairly simple by pointwise union of the resp. components.

Next we study the feedback of messages for an high level net component. This is a more complicated operation on nets. Let

$$N = (P, T, I, O, R, \varphi)$$

be an interpreted high level Petri net component and let $i \in I$ and $o \in O$ such that the introduction of an additional arc leading from the source i to the target o is feasible (i.e. i is leading to a place and o is coming from a transition or vice versa). More formally for the nodes $x, y \in P \cup T$ with $(i, x), (y, o) \in R$ we assume $x \in P$ iff $y \in T$.

We are interested in the predicative semantics of the net arising from N by connecting the source y of o and the target x of i by an arc (y, x) deleting i from the set of input nodes and o from the set of output nodes. First we define the feedback operation on the level of net components. Accordingly the *feedback of the output on* o *to the input on* i *in net* N leads to the net

$$fb(N, i, o) = (P, T, I\backslash\{i\}, O\backslash\{o\}, R', \varphi)$$

where the flow relation R' of the arising net is given by

$$R' = (R\backslash\{(i, x), (y, o)\}) \cup \{(y, x)\}.$$

Next we define the feedback operation on the level stream processing functions mapping the streams associating with the input arcs to streams associated with output arcs. For a continuous function

$$f : [^{\rightarrow}R \rightarrow M^{\omega}] \rightarrow [R^{\rightarrow} \rightarrow M^{\omega}]$$

the continuous function (let R' be defined as above)

$$fb(f, i, o) : [^{\rightarrow}R' \rightarrow M^{\omega}] \rightarrow [R^{\rightarrow} \rightarrow M^{\omega}]$$

is defined as follows. For all valuations of the input streams of the net under feedback

$$\alpha': {}^{\rightarrow}R' \rightarrow M^{\omega}$$

define

$$fb(f, i, o).\alpha' = f.\alpha$$

where α is the least element in $[{}^{\rightarrow}R \rightarrow M^{\omega}]$ satisfying the equations

$$\alpha.(i, x) = (f.\alpha).(y, o),$$

$$\alpha|_{\rightarrow R'} = \alpha'.$$

Note that this is again a definition based on the concept of a least fixpoint the existence of which is well-known from domain theory.

Next we define the predicative specification C' of the net with the feedback loop in terms of the predicative specification C of the original net. We specify that

$$C'(f, \alpha, \upsilon, \rho)$$

holds iff there exist functions $f_1, \alpha_1, \upsilon_1, \rho_1$ of appropriate types such that the following propositions hold:

$$C(f_1, \alpha_1, \upsilon_1, \rho_1),$$

$$f.x = (fb(f_1, i, o).x)|_{R'\rightarrow} \qquad \text{for all } x \in [{}^{\rightarrow}R' \rightarrow M^{\omega}],$$

$$\alpha_1((i, x)) = (fb(f_1, i, o).\alpha).(y, o),$$

$$\alpha_1|_{\rightarrow R'} = \alpha,$$

$$\upsilon_1|_{\rightarrow R'} = \upsilon,$$

$$\rho_1|_{R'\rightarrow} = \rho,$$

$$\rho_1((y, o)) \subseteq \upsilon_1((i, x)) \qquad \text{if } y \in P.$$

All the requirements listed above are fairly obvious except the last one. It expresses that if we consider feedback on an output line from a place all the tokens available on that output line cannot be consumed by the transition to which the input line leads.

The predicate C' describes the behaviour of the net obtained by identifying i and o as indicated by the following fundamental theorem.

Theorem: Compositionality on feedback

The predicate C' is equivalent to the predicative semantics of the net fb(N, i, o).

Proof: Considering only partially correct computations the theorem is simple: the same node valuations are partially correct for N and fb(N, i, o). The difficult aspect is liveness in case y is a place.

Let $f_1, \alpha_1, \upsilon_1, \rho_1$ satisfy the conditions in the scope of the existential quantifier in the definition of C'. Let η be the corresponding node valuation for the net N at α_1. We have to check that η is a liveness correct node valuation for the net fb(N, i, o) at $\alpha = \alpha_1|_{\rightarrow R'}$. This is guaranteed by the claim that the multiset $\rho_1((y, o))$ of available tokens is a submultiset of the multiset $\upsilon_1((i, x))$ of available tokens. Whenever we increase the output on (y, o) then when feeding it back to (i, x) it does not force the transition x to produce more output (as η by assumption is liveness correct for N at α_1). If min_arc_val(η, α_1)((y, o)) is infinite then min_arc_val(η, α)((y, x)) is infinite. Since x is a transition η is liveness correct for α.

For the inverse direction assume that η is a liveness correct node valuation for minimal sufficient input α in the net fb(N, i, o) with υ and ρ describing ineffective input on arcs leading to transitions and available output on arcs coming from places, respectively. We show that η is liveness correct at α_1 for the net N where

$$\alpha_1 |_{\to R'} = \alpha$$

and

$$\alpha_1((i, x)) = arc\_val_{fb(N, i, o)}(\eta, \alpha)((y, x)).$$

If we increase η to η' leaving it unchanged on T such that the output of the places to the environment is not increased, i.e.

$$arc\_val_N(\eta, \alpha_1) | _{R \cap (P \times O)} = arc\_val_N(\eta', \alpha_1) | _{R \cap (P \times O)}$$

then

$$min\_arc\_val_N(\eta', \alpha_1) = min\_arc\_val_{fb(N, i, o)}(\eta', \alpha)$$

as otherwise

$$min\_arc\_val_{fb(N, i, o)}(\eta', \alpha)$$

were strictly greater than

$$min\_arc\_val_{fb(N, i, o)}(\eta, \alpha)$$

which cannot be the case by the assumption that η is a liveness correct scheduler at α_1. For

$$\rho_1((y, o)) = \upsilon_1((i, x))$$

we choose the multiset of messages which have been sent to the place y, but not yet sent from y to o by the scheduler η. If $min\_arc\_val_{fb(N, i, o)}(\eta, \alpha)((y, x))$ is infinite then put $\rho_1((y, o)) = \emptyset$ since in this case η is already a liveness correct scheduler for the net N w.r.t. input α and the set of available tokens is empty by definition. □

The compositionality of our predicative semantics w.r.t. parallel composition is straightforward. So the theorem in particular indicates that we have a compositional semantics for high level Petri nets under parallel composition and feedback. Note that every high level net can be constructed from atomic nets consisting only of one transition or one place by parallel composition and feedback.

6. An Extended Example

Let us illustrate our approach with a simple example taken from [Poigne 90]. We consider the following high level net which models the decomposition of trees into subtrees and the computation of a function f on these subtrees:

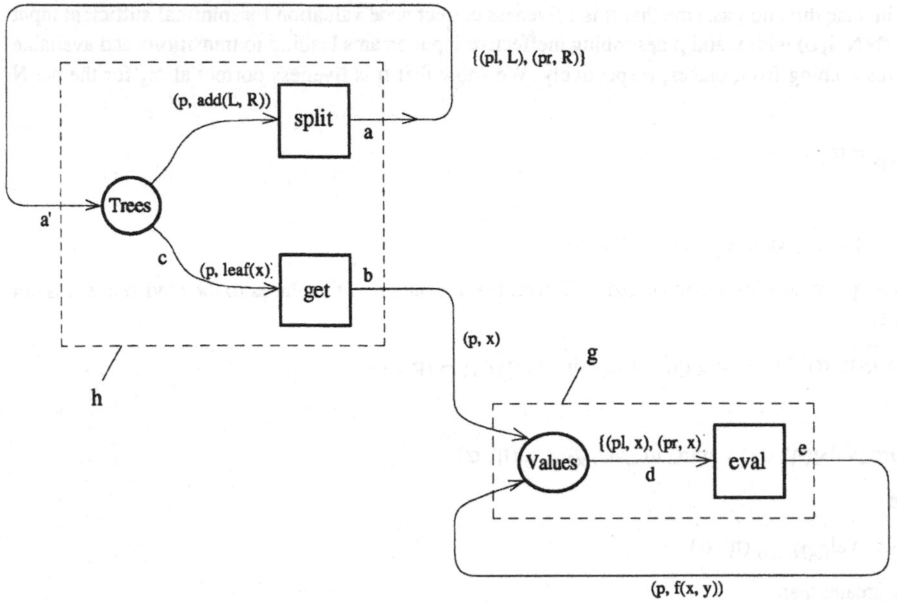

In this Petri net we identify two net components indicated by dotted lines. In the following we demonstrate how the behaviour of these two components can be described along the lines of the semantics given above.

We model the transitions by the continuous stream-processing functions that fulfil the following equations:

split((p, add(L, R)) & s) = (pl, L) & (pr, R) & split.s,

get((p, leaf.x) & s) = (p,x) & get.s,

eval((pl, x) & (pr, y) & s) = (p, f(x, y)) & eval.s.

Since we have chosen our components such that input arcs always lead to places and ouput arcs always have transitions as sources we do not have to talk about available and ineffective multisets. The behaviour of the components therefore can be expressed by a predicate

C(h, α)

If we put together the net component consisting of the place Trees, and the transitions split and get (without the arc a as feedback) we obtain the functions (with appropriate M):

h: (a' $\rightarrow M^{\omega}$) $\rightarrow$ ({a, b} $\rightarrow M^{\omega}$)

with the axioms:

#{(p, add(L, R))}©α.a' = #{(pl, L}©(h.α).a = #{(pr, R)}©(h.α).a,

#{(p, leaf.x}©α.a' = #{(p, x)}©(h.α).b.

For every input stream input arc valuation α: a' $\rightarrow M^{\omega}$, a function h that fulfils these axioms models a behaviour of the component.

The function g can be specified in analogy. The complete net then is obtained by parallel composition of f and g and the appropriate feedbacks. We obtain the system of recursive equations a' = a,

(a, b) = f.a',

e = g(b, e).

Note the freedom in decomposing and composing the nets into/from subnets.

7. Conclusions

The work presented above is rooted in a number of complementing motivations. First of all it is an attempt to unify and combine different models and techniques for distributed systems such as Petri nets and functional models of parallel systems. Second it provides concepts for components of Petri nets, a framework for the modular construction of Petri nets and a modular semantic model for it.

By slightly generalizing the notion of high level Petri net (essentially only the behaviour of transition nodes is generalized) we have arrived at a compositional semantics for high level Petri nets. However, we have not only given a modular semantics to high level nets. Additionally we have linked high level nets to data flow nets and thus to all results available from the research on functional modelling of communicating systems. This applies to the techniques for the specification and implementation of systems by functional techniques.

The link between functional system models and Petri nets leads to a lot of interesting questions and directions of further research. We mention just a few of them.

First of all our restriction to stable functions is rather technical and only motivated by the attempt to keep the modelling as close as possible to the notion of high level nets. In a more general approach we may model the behaviour of transitions (and of course also of places) immediately by predicative specifications. Another interesting direction lies in linking the functional model closer to the classical semantic models used for high level nets. In our functional model we have as part of our liveness requirement a very special "fairness" assumption which essentially corresponds to a global progress property: some transition fires as long as some transition is enabled and hence as long as one transition fires infinitely often the computation is accepted. Again this was motivated by the attempt to keep the modelling as close as possible to the notion of high level nets. An alternative concept would be weak fairness: if a transition is continuously enabled it eventually fires. To investigate this alternative and related aspects in more detail is certainly an interesting possibility of further research.

For functional system models powerful logical systems for their specification are available. It will be the task of future work to exploit the presented approach from a methodological point of view maybe leading to a more abstract specification technique for high level nets.

References

[Broy 90]
M. Broy: *Functional Specification of Time Sensitive Communicating Systems*. In: J.W. de Bakker, W.-P. de Roever, G. Rozenberg (eds.): Stepwise Refinement of Distributed Systems. Lecture Notes in Computer Science 430, Springer 1990, 153-179

[Dennis 74]
J. Dennis: *First Version of a Data Flow Procedure Language*. In: B. Robinet (ed.): Colloque sur le Programmation. Lecture Notes in Computer Science 19, Springer 1974, 35-45

[FiMe 82]
A.Finkel, G.Memmi: *FIFO Nets: A New Model of Parallel Computation*. Lecture Notes in Computer Science 145 (1982).

[HoBrRo 81]
C.A.R. Hoare, S.D. Brookes, A.W. Roscoe: *A Theory of Communicating Sequential Processes*. Oxford University Computing Laboratory Programming Research Group, Technical Monograph PRG-21, Oxford 1981

[Poigne 90]
A. Poigne: *High Level Net Semantics*. Presentation at Demon Annual General Meeting, Paris 1990.

[Reisig 82]
W. Reisig: *Petrinetze*. Springer 1982 (English version : EATCS Monograph *Petri Nets* Springer, 1985).

[Reisig 85]
W. Reisig: *Petri Nets with Individual Tokens*. TCS 41, (1985) 185-213.

[Reisig 90]
W. Reisig: *Petri Nets and Algebraic Specifications*. Technische Universität München, Institut für Informatik, Sonderforschungsbereich 342, Bericht 1/90 B, March 1990.

[Scott 82]
D. Scott: *Domains for Denotational Semantics*. LNCS 140 (1982).

[Tesler, Enea 68]
L.G. Tesler, H.J. Enea: *A Language Design for Concurrent Processes*. Spring Joint Computer Conference 1968, 403-408.

[Winkowski 90]
J. Winkowski: *A Generalisation of Petri Nets by Equipping them with Inputs and Outputs*. ICS PAS Report 686 (1990).

Interleaving Semantics and Action Refinement with Atomic Choice

Ingo Czaja
Gesellschaft für Mathematik und Datenverarbeitung
Postfach 1316, D-5205 Sankt Augustin, Germany

Rob J. van Glabbeek
Computer Science Department, Stanford University
Stanford, CA 94305, USA
rvg@cs.stanford.edu

Ursula Goltz
Gesellschaft für Mathematik und Datenverarbeitung
Postfach 1316, D-5205 Sankt Augustin, Germany
goltz@gmdzi.gmd.de

We investigate how to restrict the concept of *action refinement* such that established interleaving equivalences for concurrent systems are preserved under these restricted refinements. We show that *interleaving bisimulation* is preserved under refinement if we do not allow to refine action occurrences deciding choices and action occurrences involved in autoconcurrency. On the other hand, *interleaving trace equivalence* is still not preserved under these restricted refinements.

Keywords Concurrency, action refinement, atomicity, flow event structures, semantic equivalences, interleaving vs. partial orders, bisimulation.

Note The work presented here has partly been carried out within the Esprit Basic Research Action 3148 (DEMON) and the Sonderforschungsbereich 182 of the University of Erlangen-Nürnberg.

Contents

1 Introduction

For the design of concurrent systems, it can be useful to consider a hierarchy of representations, which allows refinement of unstructured entities on a more abstract design level by complex structures on a lower level. One approach which is being investigated is *action refinement* where the entities being refined are the actions which a system may perform. A single action in an abstract view may correspond to a process consisting of many actions in a more concrete representation. Action refinement is being investigated in process algebras [Aceto, AH, NEL] and in semantic models of concurrent systems [GG a/b/c, Vogler a/b, BDKP, Devillers, DD a/b, BGV].

Action refinement can be modelled as an operator, taking a system description P on a given level of abstraction as well as a refinement function *ref* associating processes with actions, and yielding a system description $ref(P)$ on a lower level, obtained by replacing action occurrences by occurrences of the associated processes. It differs from many other operators that are considered for concurrent systems in that applying it on a representation of a system does not yield a representation of a different system, but a different representation of the same system.

An important question being considered is the following: Which equivalence notions for concurrent systems are *preserved under refinement*? Taking two system representations, P, Q, which are equivalent for some equivalence notion $\sim$, we would expect that $ref(P) \sim ref(Q)$ for any refinement function *ref*. This expectation indicates a big difference between action refinement and many other approaches for moving to a lower level of abstraction, in which adding more information about the precise implementation of systems makes it more likely that systems turn out to be different that were indistinguishable on the higher level of abstraction. Our expectation is based on the idea that in the original system representations P and Q it is not known how the actions will be implemented. However, it is decided that different occurrences of the same action will be implemented in the same way, so that any difference between P and Q that could arise after refinement is already visible in the abstract representations, namely through the use of different action names for corresponding events.

The preservation question has been addressed in the papers mentioned above. The usual approach to this problem is: Take some well-established equivalence notion. If it is not preserved under refinement, try to find the coarsest equivalence notion contained in it which has this property (see e.g. [Vogler a/b]).

What has not been considered so far is the following question. Given a well-established equivalence notion which is not preserved under refinement, is there a way of restricting either the allowed refinements or the class of system representations under consideration such that preservation of this equivalence in the restricted setting is obtained? This question is addressed in the present paper for two of the most basic equivalences.

We consider system descriptions in which the basic building blocks are the actions which may occur in a system. In our approach an action can be any activity which is considered as a conceptual entity on a chosen level of abstraction. Now we distinguish *atomic* actions that cannot be refined, and compound ones that can. One can think of atomic actions as being instantaneous and of compound actions as durational. Many approaches to concurrency in which actions are not supposed to be refined, in particular the *interleaving* approaches, in which parallelism is equated with arbitrary interleaving of action occurrences, can be thought of as dealing exclusively with the subclass of system representations were all actions in a system are atomic. On the other hand the action refinement approaches cited above take the possibility into account that *any* action can be refined. In this paper we look at systems in which some actions are atomic, and others can be refined. In particular we consider systems in which all action occurrences deciding choices, as well as all actions that can occur concurrently with themselves are atomic. These restrictions turn out to be sufficient to apply action refinement in certain interleaving semantics, while preserving semantic equivalence. Although the distinction between atomic and compound actions may be useful for motivating this research, technically one may just as well drop this distinction and restrict the class of allowed refinement functions to a class of what we call *safe* refinements. Those refinements do not refine action occurrences deciding choices and actions involved in autoconcurrency.

It turns out that the *branching structure* (i.e. the relative order of action occurrences and choices between different courses of action) of concurrent systems plays a rôle in our results. We show that *interleaving bisimulation*, where the branching structure between alternative executions is taken into account, is preserved under safe refinements. On the other hand, we show that *interleaving trace equivalence* (where the branching structure is fully neglected) is still not preserved under these restricted refinements. To investigate safe refinements for equivalence notions between these two extremes in the linear time – branching time spectrum has to be left for future research.

2 Basic Notions

We consider systems which are capable of performing actions from a given set *Act* of action names. By an action we understand here any activity which is considered as an conceptual entity on a chosen level of abstraction. We will not distinguish external and internal actions; we do not consider abstraction by hiding of actions in this paper.

We will sometimes give process algebra terms for examples to make them easier to understand: + will denote choice (as in CCS), | will denote parallel composition (without communication), $a, b, \ldots \in Act$ denote actions, and ; denotes a general sequential composition operator (like the one of ACP). The semicolon will sometimes be omitted and we use the usual precedence rule that ; binds stronger than the other operators. However this notation is only used for intuition; formally our results are established for *event structures*.

We will describe a concurrent system by a set of events where each event corresponds to an occurrence of some action. Therefore, events are labelled by action names.

The simplest form of event structures has been introduced in [NPW] and is usually referred to as *prime event structures* with binary conflicts. A labelled prime event structure is a tuple $(E, <, \#, l)$ where E is the set of events, $< \subseteq E \times E$ is an (irreflexive) partial order (the *causality relation*), $\# \subseteq E \times E$ is the so-called *conflict relation*, and $l : E \rightarrow Act$ specifies the labelling of events by action names. As usual, we require $<$ to satisfy the *axiom of finite causes*; that is, any event may have only finitely many predecessors. Furthermore, $\#$ is required to be irreflexive and symmetric and to respect the axiom of conflict heredity: $\forall d, e, f \in E : d \# e \wedge d < f \Longrightarrow e \# f$.

A prime event structure represents a concurrent system in the following way: action names $a \in Act$ represent actions the system may perform, an event $e \in E$ labelled with a represents an occurrence of a during a possible run of the system, $d < e$ means that d is a prerequisite for e and $d \# e$ means that d and e cannot happen both in the same run.

The behaviour of a prime event structure is described by explaining which subsets of events constitute possible runs of the represented system. These subsets are called *configurations*. They have to be conflict-free and they must be left-closed with respect to $<$ (all prerequisites for any event occurring in the run must also occur).

As shown in [GG a], prime event structures are well suited to define a notion of action refinement, as long as actions are not refined by behaviours containing conflicts.

But as a consequence of the axioms explained above, it is cumbersome to define a more general notion of refinement directly for prime event structures. Whenever a given event occurs, it has to be "enabled" by a unique set of events that is independent of the particular run of the system, namely by all its predecessors according to the causality relation. However, when refining a by $a_1 + a_2$ in $a\,; b$, b should occur alternatively caused by a_1 or by a_2. In prime event structures, this may only be modelled by duplicating the b-event, leading to complicated definitions and proofs. Hence more expressive event structure representations are being used for refinement. *Free event structures* as defined in [DD a] seem to be weakest extension of prime event structures to allow refinements with conflicts in a straightforward way. However, difficulties with the interpretation of the notion of causality in this model lead in [DD b] to a restriction such that prime event structures are no longer a subclass. In [GG a, GG b], *flow event structures* [BC] have been used which are also a convenient model for CCS. This is the model we have chosen here as well, in order to establish our results also for refinements with conflicts.

We will now introduce the main concepts of flow event structures following closely [Boudol].

Definition 2.1

A *(labelled) flow event structure (over an alphabet Act)* is a 4-tuple $\mathcal{E} = (E, \prec, \#, l)$, where

- E is a set of *events*,
- $\prec \subseteq E \times E$ is an irreflexive relation, the *flow relation*,
- $\# \subseteq E \times E$ is a symmetric relation, the *conflict relation*,
- $l : E \longrightarrow Act$ is the *labelling function*.

Let $\mathbb{E}$ denote the domain of flow event structures labelled over *Act*. The components of $\mathcal{E} \in \mathbb{E}$ will be denoted by $E_{\mathcal{E}}, \prec_{\mathcal{E}}, \#_{\mathcal{E}}$ and $l_{\mathcal{E}}$. The index $\mathcal{E}$ will be omitted if clear from the context.

Two flow event structures $\mathcal{E}$ and $\mathcal{F}$ are *isomorphic* ($\mathcal{E} \cong \mathcal{F}$) iff there exists a bijection between their sets of events preserving $\prec$, $\#$ and labelling. Often, we will not distinguish isomorphic event structures; the names of events are not important for us.

The interpretation of the conflict and the flow relation is formalised by defining configurations of flow event structures. Configurations must be conflict free; in particular, self-conflicting events will never occur in any configuration. $d \prec e$ will mean that d is a *possible immediate cause* for e. For an event to occur it is necessary that a *complete* non-conflicting set of its causes has occurred. Here a set of causes is complete if for any cause which is not contained there is a conflicting event which is contained. Finally, no cycles with respect to causal dependence may occur.

We will only consider finite configurations here. As usual, we assume that in a finite period of time only finitely many actions may be performed. Now the requirement says that we only consider runs which are executable in a finite period of time. This is no restriction since the infinite configurations which are usually considered are completely determined by the finite ones (see e.g. [Boudol]).

Definition 2.2 Let $\mathcal{E} \in \mathbb{E}$.

(i) $X \subseteq E$ is *left-closed up to conflicts* iff $\forall d, e \in E$: if $e \in X, d \prec e$ and $d \notin X$ then there exists an $f \in X$ with $f \prec e$ and $d \# f$.
$X \subseteq E$ is *conflict-free* iff $\#_{\mathcal{E}} \lceil X = \emptyset$.

(ii) $X \subseteq E$ is a *(finite) configuration* of $\mathcal{E}$ iff X is finite, left-closed up to conflicts and conflict-free and does not contain a causality cycle: $<_X := (\prec \cap (X \times X))^+$ is irreflexive. $Conf(\mathcal{E})$ denotes the set of all (finite) configurations of $\mathcal{E}$.

(iii) A configuration $X \in Conf(\mathcal{E})$ is called *maximal* iff $X \subseteq Y \in Conf(\mathcal{E})$ implies $X = Y$. It is *complete* iff $\forall d \in E : d \notin X \Rightarrow \exists e \in X$ with $d \# e$.

The relation $<_X$ expresses causal dependence in the configuration X. Note that prime event structures are special flow event structures defining $d \prec e$ iff $d < e$. In prime event structures, the requirement of left-closedness up to conflicts for configurations reduces to left-closedness: $\forall d, e \in E$: if $e \in X \wedge d < e$ then $d \in X$; furthermore, in each configuration X, the relation $<_X$ coincides with $<$. However in prime event structures every maximal configuration is complete, whereas in flow event structures this need not be the case (although every complete configuration must be maximal). In [GG c] the difference between complete and maximal configurations is used to model deadlock behaviour: complete configurations indicate successful termination, whereas incomplete maximal configurations model deadlocks.

The following observations may offer some additional motivation for the definition of configurations above.

Definition 2.3 Let $\mathcal{E} \in \mathbb{E}$, $X \in Conf(\mathcal{E})$.

(i) X *enables* $e \in E$ iff $e \notin X$ and $X \cup \{e\} \in Conf(\mathcal{E})$.

(ii) A subset $Y \subseteq X$ is a *prefix* of X iff $\forall d \in X,\ e \in Y:\ d <_X e \Rightarrow d \in Y$ (i.e. Y is left-closed in X w.r.t. $<_X$).

Proposition 2.1 Let $\mathcal{E} \in \mathbb{E}$, $X \in Conf(\mathcal{E})$.

(i) X enables e iff $e \notin X, \neg(\exists d \in X$ with $d \# e)$ and $\forall d \prec e$ we have $d \in X \vee \exists f \in X$ with $f \prec e$ and $d \# f$.

(ii) X can be written as $X = \{e_1, \ldots, e_n\}$ such that for $k < n : \{e_1, \ldots, e_k\}$ enables e_{k+1}.

(iii) For $Y \subseteq X$, $Y \in Conf(\mathcal{E})$ iff Y is a prefix of X.

Proof See [Boudol]. □

We now define transition relations between configurations, describing which event or which action may occur in a configuration and which configuration may then be obtained.

Definition 2.4 Let $\mathcal{E} \in \mathbb{E}$.

$X \xrightarrow{e}_{\mathcal{E}} X'$ iff X enables e and $X' = X \cup \{e\}$.
$X \xrightarrow{a}_{\mathcal{E}} X'$ iff $X \xrightarrow{e}_{\mathcal{E}} X'$ and $l(e) = a \in Act$.

The index $\mathcal{E}$ is omitted if clear from the context.

Next we introduce a relation co_X expressing when two events are *concurrent* (independent) within a configuration X, as well as a global relation co, expressing *possible concurrency*, and show that the relations correspond. Furthermore we define when there is a *choice* between two events.

Definition 2.5 Let $\mathcal{E} \in \mathbb{E}$.

(i) For $X \in Conf(\mathcal{E})$, let $co_X \subseteq X \times X$ be defined by
$d\ co_X\ e$ iff $\neg(d <_X e \vee e <_X d)$.

(ii) $co \subseteq E \times E$ is defined by
$d\ co\ e$ iff $\exists X \in Conf(\mathcal{E})$, X enables both d and e and $X \cup \{d, e\} \in Conf(\mathcal{E})$.

(iii) $ch \subseteq E \times E$ is defined by
$d\ ch\ e$ iff $\exists X \in Conf(\mathcal{E})$, X enables both d and e and $X \cup \{d, e\} \notin Conf(\mathcal{E})$.

Proposition 2.2 Let $\mathcal{E} \in \mathbb{E}$, $d, e \in E$.

(i) $d\ co\ e \Leftrightarrow \exists X \in Conf(\mathcal{E})$ with $d\ co_X\ e$.

(ii) $d\ ch\ e \Rightarrow d \# e$.

Proof

(i):
"$\Rightarrow$": Let $d\ co\ e$. Then there exists $X \in Conf(\mathcal{E})$ with d, e both enabled by X.
Let $Y := X \cup \{d, e\}$. We show that $d\ co_Y\ e$.
Assume $d <_Y e$. Then $X \cup \{e\}$ would not be a prefix of Y, hence $X \cup \{e\}$ would not be a configuration and e not enabled by X. Thus $\neg(d <_Y e)$ and by symmetry $\neg(e <_Y d)$.
"$\Leftarrow$": Let $X \in Conf(\mathcal{E})$ with $d\ co_X\ e$. Let $X' = X - \{f \in X \mid d <_X f \vee e <_X f\}$.
$d, e \in X'$, since $d, e \in X$ and d and e are not in $<_X$-relation.
Moreover d and e are maximal in X' w.r.t. $<_X$.
Let $X_1 := X' - \{d\}$, $X_2 := X' - \{e\}$, $X'' := X' - \{d, e\}$.
Then $X', X_1, X_2, X'' \in Conf(\mathcal{E})$ with proposition 2.1(iii) and $d\ co\ e$.

(ii):
Suppose $d\ ch\ e$, but $\neg(d \# e)$. We show that for each configuration X enabling d and e, also $X' := X \cup \{d, e\}$ is a configuration.
Let $X \in Conf(\mathcal{E})$, with $X \xrightarrow{d} X_1$ and $X \xrightarrow{e} X_2$. Let $X' := X \cup \{d, e\}$.

X' is finite, since $X \in Conf(\mathcal{E})$.

X' is conflict-free, since $X_1, X_2 \in Conf(\mathcal{E})$ and $\neg(d \# e)$.

X' is left-closed up to conflicts:
Suppose $f \in X'$, $g \in E - X'$ and $g \prec f$. Then $f \in X_i$ for $i = 1$ or $i = 2$ and $g \notin X_i$, so $\exists h \in X_i \subseteq X'$ with $h \prec f$ and $g \# h$, since $X_i \in Conf(\mathcal{E})$.

X' contains no cycles w.r.t. $\prec$:
Suppose X' contains a causality cycle. Since $X_2 \in Conf(\mathcal{E})$ this cycle must contain d. However, we will show that there is no $c \in X'$ with $d \prec c$. Since $X, X_1 \in Conf(\mathcal{E})$, X must be a prefix of X_1 by proposition 2.1(iii), implying that d is maximal in X_1. Thus the only candidate for c is e. So suppose $d \prec e$. Since $d \notin X_2$ and $e \in X_2 \in Conf(\mathcal{E})$ there must be an $f \in X_2 \subseteq X'$ with $f \prec e$ and $d \# f$, contradicting the conflict-freeness of X'.

Thus $X' \in Conf(\mathcal{E})$. □

For prime event structures, the choice relation coincides with the non-inherited conflicts.

Definition 2.6 Let $\mathcal{E} \in \mathbb{E}$ be a prime event structure.

$\#^1 \subseteq E \times E$ (*immediate conflict*) is defined by
$d \#^1 e$ iff $d \# e$, $f < d \Rightarrow \neg(f \# e)$ and $f < e \Rightarrow \neg(f \# d)$.

Proposition 2.3 Let $\mathcal{E} \in \mathbb{E}$ be a prime event structure, $d, e \in E$.

Then $d \; ch \; e \;\Leftrightarrow\; d \#^1 e$.

Proof
"$\Rightarrow$": Let $d \; ch \; e$. Then there exists $X \in Conf(\mathcal{E})$ enabling both d and e.
$d \# e$ by proposition 2.2.
Assume there is an f with $f < d$. Then $f \in X$, since $X \cup \{d\}$ is left-closed. Since $f \in X \cup \{e\} \in Conf(\mathcal{E})$, we have $\neg(f \# e)$.
Similarly $f < e \Rightarrow \neg(f \# d)$.
"$\Leftarrow$": Let $d \#^1 e$. Let $X := \{f \in E \mid f < d \vee f < e\}$.
Since $d \# e$ it cannot be the case that $d < e$ or $e < d$ by the axiom of conflict heredity and the irreflexivity of $\#$. Thus $d, e \notin X$.
Let $X_1 = X \cup \{d\}$ and $X_2 := X \cup \{e\}$.
Since $d \# e$ we have $X \cup \{d, e\} \notin Conf(\mathcal{E})$, so it suffices to prove that X, X_1 and X_2 are configurations.
X, X_1 and X_2 are finite (axiom of finite causes).
X, X_1 and X_2 are left-closed (transitivity of $<$).
X, X_1 and X_2 are conflict-free:
It suffices to prove that X_1 is conflict-free, since this implies that X is conflict-free, and the conflict-freeness of X_2 follows by symmetry.
Suppose $d', e' \in X_1$ and $d' \# e'$. We may assume $d' \leq d$ and $e' < e$, since the cases that d' and e' are both predecessors of d or of e are excluded by the axiom of conflict heredity and the irreflexivity of $\#$. But then $d \# e'$ by conflict heredity, violating the definition of $\#^1$. □

Note that for prime event structures the conflict relation is fully determined by the immediate conflicts, and hence by the choice relation. On the other hand, in flow event structures the choice relation does not determine the conflict relation. Moreover, the part of the conflict relation that is not determined by the choice relation influences the set of configurations (as well as the deadlock behaviour [GG c]).

Example 2.1

Consider the following two flow event structures, where the labelling is the identity. Here and later we represent the flow relation by arrows of the form ⟶.

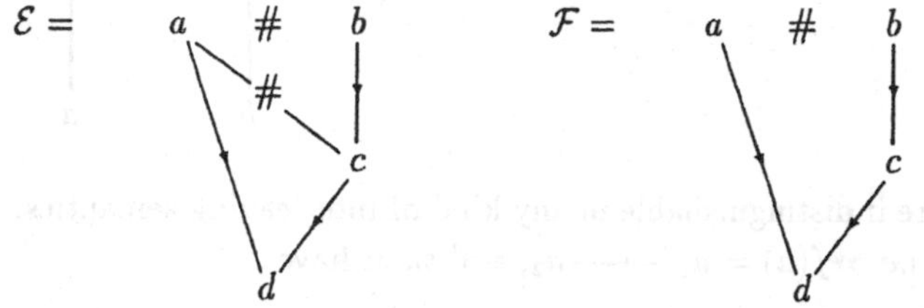

In both event structures the events a and c are in *semantic conflict*, in the sense that they cannot occur in the same configuration. However, in $\mathcal{F}$ they are not in *syntactic conflict*: $\neg(a \#_{\mathcal{F}} c)$.
We have $E_{\mathcal{E}} = E_{\mathcal{F}}$, $\prec_{\mathcal{E}} = \prec_{\mathcal{F}}$ and $l_{\mathcal{E}} = l_{\mathcal{F}}$. Moreover the choice relations of $\mathcal{E}$ and $\mathcal{F}$ agree: only a *ch* b. Nevertheless $\mathcal{E}$ has a configuration $\{a, d\}$ which $\mathcal{F}$ has not.

Refinement of actions in flow event structures may now be defined as follows. We assume a refinement function $ref : Act \longrightarrow \mathbb{E}-\{O\}$ (where O denotes the empty flow event structure) and replace each event labelled by a by a disjoint copy of $ref(a)$. The conflict and causality structure will be inherited. Refinements in which some actions are replaced by the empty process can drastically change the behaviour of concurrent systems and can not be explained by a change in the level of abstraction at which these systems are regarded [GG a]. Therefore they are not considered here.

Definition 2.7

(i) A function $ref : Act \longrightarrow \mathbb{E}-\{O\}$ is called a *refinement function* .

(ii) Let $\mathcal{E} \in \mathbb{E}$ and let ref be a refinement function.
Then the *refinement of $\mathcal{E}$ by ref*, $ref(\mathcal{E})$, is the flow event structure defined by

- $E_{ref(\mathcal{E})} = \{(e, e') \mid e \in E_{\mathcal{E}}, e' \in E_{ref(l_{\mathcal{E}}(e))}\}$,
- $(d, d') \prec_{ref(\mathcal{E})} (e, e')$ iff $d \prec_{\mathcal{E}} e$ or $(d = e \wedge d' \prec_{ref(l_{\mathcal{E}}(d))} e')$,
- $(d, d') \#_{ref(\mathcal{E})} (e, e')$ iff $d \#_{\mathcal{E}} e$ or $(d = e \wedge d' \#_{ref(l_{\mathcal{E}}(d))} e')$,
- $l_{ref(\mathcal{E})}(e, e') = l_{ref(l_{\mathcal{E}}(e))}(e')$.

The following examples illustrate that the usual interleaving equivalences are not preserved under this refinement operation.

The event structures we consider in examples from now on will always be prime; hence we will only draw immediate conflicts and omit arcs for the elements of the flow relation obtainable by transitivity.

Example 2.2

Consider the event structures $\mathcal{E}$ and $\mathcal{F}$ below, corresponding to $a|b$ and $ab + ba$.

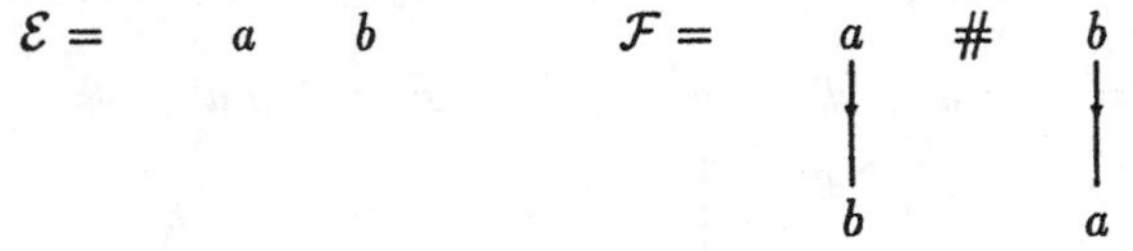

$\mathcal{E}$ and $\mathcal{F}$ are indistinguishable in any kind of interleaving semantics. We refine action a by a_1a_2, i.e. $ref(a) = a_1 \longrightarrow a_2$, and then have

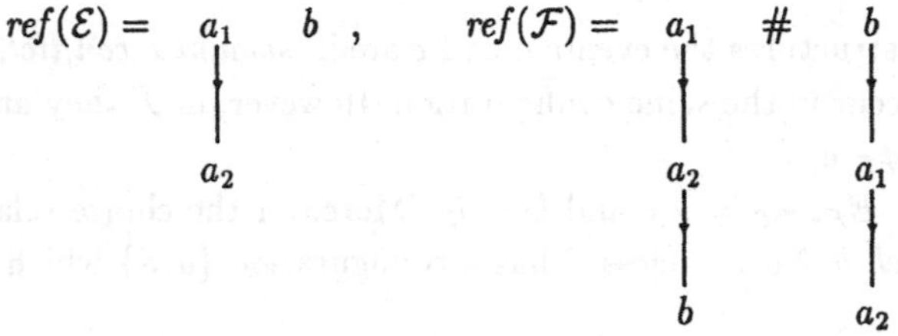

$ref(\mathcal{E})$ and $ref(\mathcal{F})$ are not interleaving equivalent, since $a_1 b\, a_2$ is a possible execution of $ref(\mathcal{E})$ but not of $ref(\mathcal{F})$.

Example 2.3

Consider the event structures $\mathcal{E}$ and $\mathcal{F}$ below, corresponding to $a|a$ and aa.

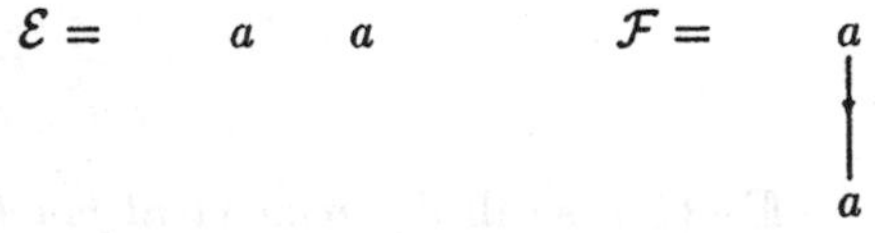

$\mathcal{E}$ and $\mathcal{F}$ are indistinguishable in common interleaving semantics. We refine a by a_1a_2 and then have

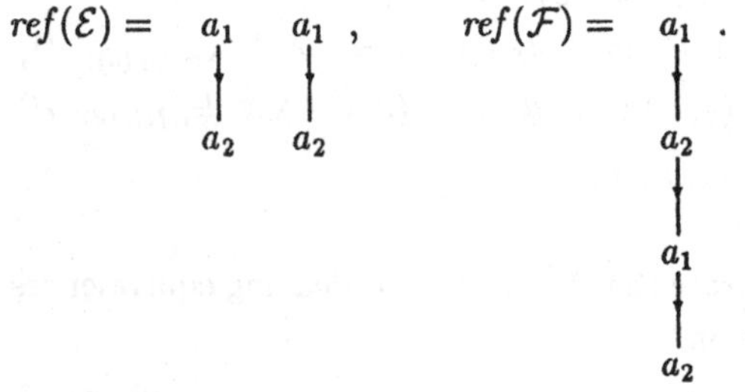

Now $ref(\mathcal{E})$ and $ref(\mathcal{F})$ are not interleaving equivalent, since only in $ref(\mathcal{E})$ it is possible to start with two occurrences of a_1.

We observe that in example 2.2 an event of $\mathcal{F}$ is refined which decides a choice. In example 2.3, an action is refined which may occur concurrently with itself. Hence we have identified two classes of events which will definitely cause problems for interleaving semantics if they are refined. We will now call actions labelling such events *critical* (with respect to a particular event structure $\mathcal{E}$) and consider the subclass of flow event structures where all critical actions are atomic, in the sense that they cannot really be refined. We could restrict the allowed refinement functions such that atomic actions may only be 'refined' by themselves. However, our refinement theorem will hold even in a slightly more general setting. First of all we may allow *renaming* of atomic actions, obtained by refining them by conflict-free event structures containing exactly one event, as well as *restriction* of certain (atomic) actions, obtained by refining them by event structures consisting of one self-conflicting event. In this way the relabelling and restriction operators of CCS can still be understood as instances of the refinement operator. Moreover we allow *generalised renamings*, replacing (atomic) actions by (possibly infinite) choices $a_1 + a_2 + \ldots$. The crucial restriction is that the execution of any event of a refined atomic action a leads to its immediate termination, thereby preserving atomicity for these actions. Formally this is ensured if and only if every non-empty configuration of $ref(a)$ is complete. This can be obtained by requiring that all events of $ref(a)$ are mutually in conflict.

Definition 2.8 Let $\mathcal{E} \in \mathbb{E}$.

(i) An action $a \in Act$ is *critical* in $\mathcal{E}$ iff
$\exists d, e \in E$ with $d \; ch \; e$ and $l(d) = a$ or
$\exists d, e \in E$, $d \neq e$ with $d \; co \; e$ and $l(d) = l(e) = a$.
$Crit_{\mathcal{E}} := \{a \in Act \mid a \text{ is critical in } \mathcal{E}\}$ is the set of all critical actions in $\mathcal{E}$.

(ii) A refinement function ref is called *safe* w.r.t. $\mathcal{E}$ iff
$\forall a \in Crit_{\mathcal{E}} \; \forall d, e \in E_{ref(a)}, \; d \neq e : \; d \#_{ref(a)} e$.

Proposition 2.4 Let $\mathcal{E} \in \mathbb{E}$, $a \in Crit_{\mathcal{E}}$, and ref a safe refinement w.r.t. $\mathcal{E}$.

Then every non-empty configuration of $ref(a)$ is complete.

Proof Trivial. □

In flow event structures it may be difficult to find out which actions are critical and should therefore be atomic. A safe strategy is to avoid autoconcurrency altogether and make every event which is in conflict with another event atomic. The result of this strategy depends on the particular flow event structure representation of a system by the choice of a syntactic conflict relation $\#$ (recall that semantic and syntactic conflict do not coincide for flow event structures). The most liberal possibilities for refinement are obtained by choosing a minimal conflict relation to model the intended behaviour.

3 Interleaving trace semantics

We now investigate whether interleaving equivalences are preserved by safe refinements. We start by considering the simplest notion, the usual *interleaving trace equivalence* where the possible sequences of actions are compared.

Definition 3.1

$w = a_1 \dots a_n \in Act^*$ is a *(sequential) trace* of $\mathcal{E} \in \mathbb{E}$ iff
$\exists X_0, \dots, X_n \in Conf(\mathcal{E}) : X_0 = \emptyset$ and $X_{i-1} \xrightarrow{a_i} X_i$, $i = 1, \dots, n$.

$SeqTraces(\mathcal{E})$ denotes the set of all sequential traces of $\mathcal{E}$.

$\mathcal{E}, \mathcal{F} \in \mathbb{E}$ are called *interleaving trace equivalent* ($\mathcal{E} \approx_{it} \mathcal{F}$) iff
$SeqTraces(\mathcal{E}) = SeqTraces(\mathcal{F})$.

The following example shows that this equivalence is not preserved by safe refinements.

Example 3.1

Consider the event structures $\mathcal{E}$ and $\mathcal{F}$ below, corresponding to $a(b|c)$ and $abc + acb$.

$\mathcal{E} =$

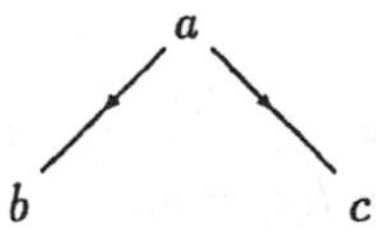

$\mathcal{F} =$

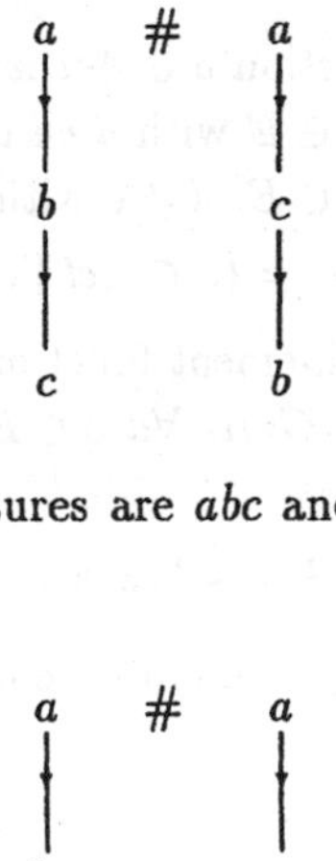

$\mathcal{E} \approx_{it} \mathcal{F}$, since the only traces for both event structures are abc and acb (and the prefixes). Action b is not critical. We refine b by $b_1 b_2$.

$ref(\mathcal{E}) =$

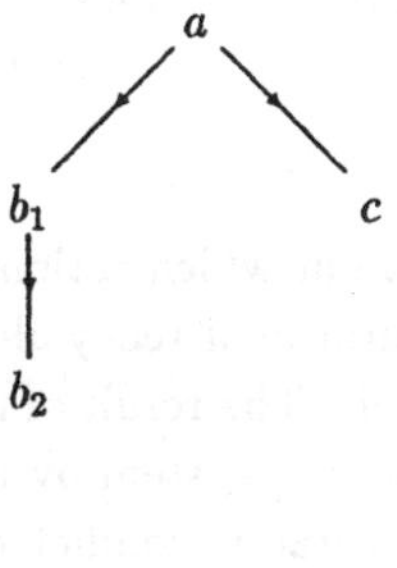

$ref(\mathcal{F}) =$

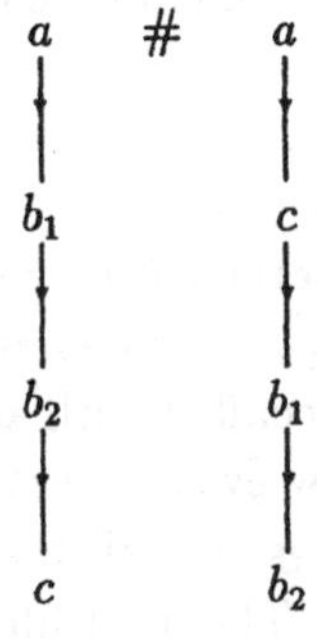

We have $ref(\mathcal{E}) \not\approx_{it} ref(\mathcal{F})$, since $ab_1c \in SeqTraces(ref(\mathcal{E}))$,
but $ab_1c \notin SeqTraces(ref(\mathcal{F}))$.

One can now ask if it is possible to strengthen the requirement of safe refinements, say into *trace-safe* refinements, by requiring more actions to be atomic, in such a way that interleaving trace equivalence is preserved under trace-safe refinements. Requiring all actions that can occur concurrently with another action to be atomic would work, but this constraint is very restrictive. It seems not easy to find a less restrictive one.

4 Interleaving bisimulation semantics

In this section we will show that interleaving bisimulation equivalence [Park, Milner] is preserved under safe refinements.

Definition 4.1 Let $\mathcal{E}, \mathcal{F} \in \mathbb{E}$.

A relation $R \subseteq Conf(\mathcal{E}) \times Conf(\mathcal{F})$ is called an *interleaving bisimulation between $\mathcal{E}$ and $\mathcal{F}$* iff $(\emptyset, \emptyset) \in R$, and if $(X, Y) \in R$ then

- $X \xrightarrow{a} X' \Rightarrow \exists Y'$ with $Y \xrightarrow{a} Y'$ and $(X', Y') \in R$,
- $Y \xrightarrow{a} Y' \Rightarrow \exists X'$ with $X \xrightarrow{a} X'$ and $(X', Y') \in R$.

$\mathcal{E}$ and $\mathcal{F}$ are *interleaving bisimulation equivalent* ($\mathcal{E} \approx_{ib} \mathcal{F}$) iff there exists an interleaving bisimulation between $\mathcal{E}$ and $\mathcal{F}$.

In [GG a] it has been shown that the configurations of a refined event structure may be deduced compositionally from the configurations of the original event structure and those of the refinements of actions. We will use this result and the following lemmas in the proof of the refinement theorem.

Definition 4.2 Let $\mathcal{E} \in \mathbb{E}$, let *ref* be a refinement function.

(i) We call $\tilde{X}$ a *refinement of a configuration* $X \in Conf(\mathcal{E})$ *by ref* iff

- $\tilde{X} = \bigcup_{e \in X} (\{e\} \times X_e)$ where $\forall e \in X : X_e \in Conf(ref(l_{\mathcal{E}}(e))) - \{\emptyset\}$,
- $busy(\tilde{X}) \subseteq max(X)$ where
  - $max(X)$ denotes the set of all maximal events in X w.r.t. $<_X$,
  - $busy(\tilde{X}) := X - compl(\tilde{X})$ and
  - $compl(\tilde{X}) := \{e \in X \mid X_e \text{ is a complete configuration}\}$.

(ii) $ref(X)$ denotes the set of refinements of $X \in Conf(\mathcal{E})$ by *ref* and for $S \subseteq Conf(\mathcal{E})$, $ref(S) = \bigcup_{X \in S} ref(X)$.

Clearly, if $\tilde{X} \in ref(X)$ then $X = pr(\tilde{X}) := \{e \in E_{\mathcal{E}} \mid \exists e' \in E_{ref(l(e))} : (e, e') \in \tilde{X}\}$ and we have $compl(\tilde{X}) \subseteq pr(\tilde{X})$, $pr(\tilde{X}) - max(pr(\tilde{X})) \subseteq compl(\tilde{X})$.

Proposition 4.1 [GG a] Let $\mathcal{E} \in \mathbb{E}$, let *ref* be a refinement function.

Then $Conf(ref(\mathcal{E})) = ref(Conf(\mathcal{E}))$.

Lemma 4.1 Let $\mathcal{E} \in \mathbb{E}$, *ref* a refinement function and $\tilde{X} \in Conf(ref(\mathcal{E}))$.

If $compl(\tilde{X}) \subseteq Y \subseteq pr(\tilde{X})$ then $Y \in Conf(\mathcal{E})$.

Proof Immediate from proposition 2.1(iii), since $pr(\tilde{X}) - max(pr(\tilde{X})) \subseteq Y \subseteq pr(\tilde{X})$. □

With lemma 4.1 we have in particular $compl(\tilde{X}) \in Conf(\mathcal{E})$.

Lemma 4.2 Let $\mathcal{E} \in \mathbb{E}$, $X \in Conf(\mathcal{E})$ and $a \notin Crit_{\mathcal{E}}$.

$X \xrightarrow{a} X_1,\ X \xrightarrow{a} X_2 \Rightarrow X_1 = X_2$.

Proof Immediate from the definitions. □

Lemma 4.3 Let $\mathcal{E} \in \mathbb{E}$, *ref* a safe refinement function w.r.t. $\mathcal{E}$ and $\tilde{X} \in Conf(ref(\mathcal{E}))$.

If $e \in pr(\tilde{X}) - compl(\tilde{X})$ then $l_{\mathcal{E}}(e) \notin Crit_{\mathcal{E}}$.

Proof With proposition 4.1 we have $X_e \in Conf(ref(l_{\mathcal{E}}(e))) - \{\emptyset\}$.
If $l_{\mathcal{E}}(e) \in Crit_{\mathcal{E}}$ than X_e is complete by proposition 2.4.
However, since $e \in pr(\tilde{X}) - compl(\tilde{X})$, X_e is not complete. □

Lemma 4.4 Let $\mathcal{E} \in \mathbb{E}$, *ref* a safe refinement function w.r.t. $\mathcal{E}$ and $\tilde{X} \in Conf(ref(\mathcal{E}))$.

If $compl(\tilde{X}) \cup \{e\} \in Conf(\mathcal{E})$ then $pr(\tilde{X}) \cup \{e\} \in Conf(\mathcal{E})$.

Proof W.l.o.g. we assume that $e \notin pr(\tilde{X})$.
With proposition 2.1(i) we prove that $pr(\tilde{X})$ enables e.

Suppose $\exists d \in pr(\tilde{X})$ with $d\#e$. Since $compl(\tilde{X}) \cup \{e\}$ is conflict-free, it follows that $d \in pr(\tilde{X}) - compl(\tilde{X})$. Thus $compl(\tilde{X})$ enables d (with lemma 4.1) as well as e, so $d\ ch\ e$. However, with lemma 4.3 we have $l(d) \notin Crit_{\mathcal{E}}$, contradicting $d\ ch\ e$.

Now suppose $d \prec e$ and $d \notin pr(\tilde{X}) \supseteq compl(\tilde{X})$. Since $compl(\tilde{X}) \cup \{e\} \in Conf(\mathcal{E})$ there is an $f \in compl(\tilde{X}) \subseteq pr(\tilde{X})$ with $f \prec e$ and $d\#f$. □

With these lemmas we can prove the theorem.

Theorem 4.1 Let $\mathcal{E}, \mathcal{F} \in \mathbb{E}$, let *ref* be a safe refinement function w.r.t. $\mathcal{E}$ and $\mathcal{F}$.

Then $\mathcal{E} \approx_{ib} \mathcal{F} \quad \Rightarrow \quad ref(\mathcal{E}) \approx_{ib} ref(\mathcal{F})$.

Proof Let R be a bisimulation between $\mathcal{E}$ and $\mathcal{F}$.
Let $\tilde{R} = \{(\tilde{X},\tilde{Y}) \in Conf(ref(\mathcal{E})) \times Conf(ref(\mathcal{F})) \mid$
$(compl(\tilde{X}), compl(\tilde{Y})) \in R$,
there exist bijections $f : pr(\tilde{X}) \longrightarrow pr(\tilde{Y})$ with $l_{\mathcal{F}}(f(e)) = l_{\mathcal{E}}(e)$
and $\tilde{f} : \tilde{X} \longrightarrow \tilde{Y}$ with $\tilde{f}(e,e') = (f(e),e')\}$

We show that $\tilde{R}$ is a bisimulation between $ref(\mathcal{E})$ and $ref(\mathcal{F})$.

i. Obviously $(\emptyset,\emptyset) \in \tilde{R}$.

ii. Let $(\tilde{X},\tilde{Y}) \in \tilde{R}$. Then $(compl(\tilde{X}), compl(\tilde{Y})) \in R$ and there are bijections f and $\tilde{f}$ as required in the definition of $\tilde{R}$. We have to show the bisimulation properties. It suffices to check one of them, the other follows by symmetry.

Let $\tilde{X} \xrightarrow{a} \tilde{X}'$. Let $\tilde{X}' - \tilde{X} = \{(e^\circ, e^*)\}$, $l_{\mathcal{E}}(e^\circ) = b$. Then $l_{ref(\mathcal{E})}((e^\circ,e^*)) = l_{ref(b)}(e^*) = a$.
Now we have to show : $\exists \tilde{Y}' \in Conf(ref(\mathcal{F}))$ with $\tilde{Y} \xrightarrow{a} \tilde{Y}'$ and $(\tilde{X}',\tilde{Y}') \in \tilde{R}$.
For the construction of $\tilde{Y}'$, we distinguish two cases.

1. $pr(\tilde{X}') = pr(\tilde{X})$.

In this case we can use the bijection f to define $\tilde{Y}'$, since its domain is not affected by adding the new event.

Let $\tilde{Y}' := \{(f(e),e') \mid (e,e') \in \tilde{X}'\}$.
With $\tilde{Y} = \{(f(e),e') \mid (e,e') \in \tilde{X}\}$ we have $\tilde{Y}' = \tilde{Y} \cup \{(f(e^\circ),e^*)\}$.

First we show that $\tilde{Y}'$ is a configuration with $\tilde{Y} \xrightarrow{a} \tilde{Y}'$.
Then we define the new functions f' and $\tilde{f}'$ and check their properties.
Finally we prove $(compl(\tilde{X}'), compl(\tilde{Y}')) \in R$.

With proposition 4.1 we show $\tilde{Y}' \in Conf(ref(\mathcal{F}))$:

- $pr(\tilde{Y}') = f(pr(\tilde{X}')) = f(pr(\tilde{X})) = pr(\tilde{Y}) \in Conf(\mathcal{F})$, since $\tilde{Y} \in Conf(ref(\mathcal{F}))$;
- $\forall d \in pr(\tilde{Y}')$: $Y'_d = X'_{f^{-1}(d)} \in Conf(ref(l_{\mathcal{E}}(f^{-1}(d)))) - \{\emptyset\} = Conf(ref(l_{\mathcal{F}}(d))) - \{\emptyset\}$, since $\tilde{X}' \in Conf(ref(\mathcal{E}))$;
- $busy(\tilde{Y}') = pr(\tilde{Y}') - compl(\tilde{Y}') \subseteq pr(\tilde{Y}) - compl(\tilde{Y}) \subseteq max(pr(\tilde{Y})) = max(pr(\tilde{Y}'))$, since $pr(\tilde{Y}) = pr(\tilde{Y}')$ and $compl(\tilde{Y}) \subseteq compl(\tilde{Y}')$.

Thus $\tilde{Y}'$ is a configuration of $ref(\mathcal{F})$.
Since $l_{ref(\mathcal{F})}((f(e^\circ),e^*)) = l_{ref(b)}(e^*) = a$ we have $\tilde{Y} \xrightarrow{a} \tilde{Y}'$.

Let $f' := f$ and $\tilde{f}' := \tilde{f} \cup \{((e^\circ,e^*),(f(e^\circ),e^*))\}$. The new function $\tilde{f}'$ is bijective, since the events (e°,e^*) and $(f(e^\circ),e^*)$ do not occur in the domain and the range of $\tilde{f}$, respectively. By construction f' and $\tilde{f}'$ have the required properties.

In order to establish $(\tilde{X}',\tilde{Y}') \in \tilde{R}$ we still have to show $(compl(\tilde{X}'), compl(\tilde{Y}')) \in R$.
Again we have two cases:

1.1. $compl(\tilde{X}') = compl(\tilde{X})$.

Using the properties of $\tilde{f}'$, $compl(\tilde{Y}') = f'(compl(\tilde{X}')) = f(compl(\tilde{X})) = compl(\tilde{Y})$, hence $(compl(\tilde{X}'), compl(\tilde{Y}')) \in R$.

1.2. $compl(\tilde{X}') \neq compl(\tilde{X})$.

Then $compl(\tilde{X}') = compl(\tilde{X}) \cup \{e^\circ\}$ and $compl(\tilde{X}) \xrightarrow{b} compl(\tilde{X}')$.

Since $(compl(\tilde{X}), compl(\tilde{Y})) \in R$ there is a $Y' \in Conf(\mathcal{F})$ with $compl(\tilde{Y}) \xrightarrow{b} Y'$ and $(compl(\tilde{X}'), Y') \in R$.

Using the properties of $\tilde{f}'$, $compl(\tilde{Y}') = f'(compl(\tilde{X}')) = f(compl(\tilde{X}) \cup \{e^\circ\}) = compl(\tilde{Y}) \cup \{f(e^\circ)\}$, hence $compl(\tilde{Y}) \xrightarrow{b} compl(\tilde{Y}')$.

Since $e^\circ \in compl(\tilde{X}') \subseteq pr(\tilde{X}') = pr(\tilde{X})$, it follows that $e^\circ \in pr(\tilde{X}) - compl(\tilde{X})$ and with lemma 4.3 $b = l_\mathcal{E}(e^\circ) \notin Crit_\mathcal{E}$. Hence $Y' = compl(\tilde{Y}')$ with lemma 4.2.

Thus $(compl(\tilde{X}'), compl(\tilde{Y}')) \in R$, which had to be proved.

2. $pr(\tilde{X}') \neq pr(\tilde{X})$.

The proof of the second case is similar to that of the first case. However the construction of $\tilde{Y}'$ is more complicated since we cannot just use the function f. We need to describe the events by which f is extended.

$pr(\tilde{X}') = pr(\tilde{X}) \cup \{e^\circ\}$ and $l_\mathcal{E}(e^\circ) = b$.

$$compl(\tilde{X}') = \begin{cases} compl(\tilde{X}) \cup \{e^\circ\} & \text{if } \{e^*\} \text{ is a complete configuration of } ref(b) \\ compl(\tilde{X}) & \text{otherwise} \end{cases}$$

Thus $compl(\tilde{X}') \subseteq compl(\tilde{X}) \cup \{e^\circ\} \subseteq pr(\tilde{X}) \cup \{e^\circ\} = pr(\tilde{X}')$.
With lemma 4.1 it follows that $compl(\tilde{X}) \cup \{e^\circ\} \in Conf(\mathcal{E})$.
Hence $compl(\tilde{X}) \xrightarrow{b} compl(\tilde{X}) \cup \{e^\circ\}$.
Since $(compl(\tilde{X}), compl(\tilde{Y})) \in R$, there is a $d^\circ \in E_\mathcal{F}$ with $compl(\tilde{Y}) \xrightarrow{b} compl(\tilde{Y}) \cup \{d^\circ\}$, $l_\mathcal{F}(d^\circ) = b$ and $(compl(\tilde{X}) \cup \{e^\circ\}, compl(\tilde{Y}) \cup \{d^\circ\}) \in R$.

We now extend the bijection f by (e°, d°).
For this we verify that d° is not in the range of f:
Suppose $d^\circ \in pr(\tilde{Y})$. Since $d^\circ \notin compl(\tilde{Y})$, $f^{-1}(d^\circ) \in pr(\tilde{X}) - compl(\tilde{X})$. Thus $compl(\tilde{X}) \cup \{f^{-1}(d^\circ)\} \in Conf(\mathcal{E})$ with lemma 4.1 and $compl(\tilde{X}) \xrightarrow{b} compl(\tilde{X}) \cup \{f^{-1}(d^\circ)\}$.
Hence $b \notin Crit_\mathcal{E}$ with lemma 4.3 and then $e^\circ = f^{-1}(d^\circ)$ with lemma 4.2.
Thus $e^\circ \in pr(\tilde{X})$ which contradicts $pr(\tilde{X}') \neq pr(\tilde{X})$. So $d^\circ \notin pr(\tilde{Y})$.

Now we can define $\tilde{Y}'$, f' and $\tilde{f}'$.
Let $f' := f \cup (e^\circ, d^\circ)$ and $\tilde{Y}' := \{(f'(e), e') \mid (e, e') \in \tilde{X}'\} = \tilde{Y} \cup \{(d^\circ, e^*)\}$.

Using proposition 4.1 we proof $\tilde{Y}' \in Conf(ref(\mathcal{F}))$:

- $pr(\tilde{Y}') = pr(\tilde{Y}) \cup \{d^\circ\} \in Conf(\mathcal{F})$ with lemma 4.4;
- $\forall d \in pr(\tilde{Y}')$: $Y'_d = X'_{f'^{-1}(d)} \in Conf(ref(l_\mathcal{E}(f'^{-1}(d)))) - \{\emptyset\} = Conf(ref(l_\mathcal{F}(d))) - \{\emptyset\}$;

- $busy(\tilde{Y}') = pr(\tilde{Y}') - compl(\tilde{Y}') = pr(\tilde{Y}) \cup \{d^o\} - compl(\tilde{Y}') \subseteq pr(\tilde{Y}) \cup \{d^o\} - compl(\tilde{Y})$, since $compl(\tilde{Y}) \subseteq compl(\tilde{Y}')$.
  It remains to show that $pr(\tilde{Y}) \cup \{d^o\} - compl(\tilde{Y}) \subseteq max(pr(\tilde{Y}) \cup \{d^o\})$.
  By proposition 2.1(iii) $pr(\tilde{Y})$ is a prefix of $pr(\tilde{Y}) \cup \{d^o\}$, so $d^o \in max(pr(\tilde{Y}) \cup \{d^o\})$.
  Now suppose $d \in pr(\tilde{Y}) - compl(\tilde{Y})$, but $d \notin max(pr(\tilde{Y}) \cup \{d^o\})$.
  Then $d \in max(pr(\tilde{Y}))$ by proposition 4.1, so $d <_{pr(\tilde{Y}) \cup \{d^o\}} d^o$. Since $compl(\tilde{Y}) \cup \{d^o\}$ is a prefix of $pr(\tilde{Y}) \cup \{d^o\}$ by proposition 2.1(iii), we have $d \in compl(\tilde{Y})$, which yields a contradiction.

Thus $\tilde{Y}'$ is a configuration of $ref(\mathcal{F})$ and with $l_{ref(\mathcal{F})}(d^o, e^*) = a$ we have $\tilde{Y} \xrightarrow{a} \tilde{Y}'$.

The new function f' is bijective, as shown above. The same for $\tilde{f}' := \tilde{f} \cup \{((e^o, e^*), (d^o, d^*))\}$. By construction f' and $\tilde{f}'$ have the required properties.

Now we show $(\tilde{X}', \tilde{Y}') \in \tilde{R}$ by proving $(compl(\tilde{X}'), compl(\tilde{Y}')) \in R$.
There are again two cases:

2.1. $compl(\tilde{X}') = compl(\tilde{X})$.
By construction of $\tilde{Y}'$ (as in part 1.1 of the proof) $compl(\tilde{Y}') = compl(\tilde{Y})$ and hence $(compl(\tilde{X}'), compl(\tilde{Y}')) \in R$.

2.2. $compl(\tilde{X}') \neq compl(\tilde{X})$.
Then $compl(\tilde{X}') = compl(\tilde{X}) \cup \{e^o\}$ and by construction of $\tilde{Y}'$, $compl(\tilde{Y}') = compl(\tilde{Y}) \cup \{d^o\}$. We had already that $(compl(\tilde{X}) \cup \{e^o\}, compl(\tilde{Y})) \cup \{d^o\}) \in R$, hence $(compl(\tilde{X}'), compl(\tilde{Y}')) \in R$.

Thus $\tilde{R}$ is a bisimulation between $ref(\mathcal{E})$ and $ref(\mathcal{F})$. □

Conclusion

We have investigated here how two well-established interleaving equivalences behave with respect to a restricted notion of action refinement. We have considered a class of refinements where events deciding choices are considered atomic. It turned out that interleaving trace semantics — neglecting the branching structure — is then still not preserved under refinements whereas interleaving bisimulation yields the desired preservation result.

It remains to be investigated what happens for other interleaving equivalences in the linear time – branching time spectrum, e.g. for failure semantics. Another interesting question is what happens for step semantics (where several actions happening simultaneously are considered). The example $a(bc|d)$ versus $ab(c|d) + a(b|d)c$ with $ref(d) = d_1 d_2$ may be used to show that *step trace equivalence* is not preserved under safe refinements as considered here. For *step bisimulation equivalence* we conjecture that we do have preservation under safe refinements.

Acknowledgements
The idea to investigate refinements with atomic choice was suggested by Manfred Broy. Three anonymous referees helped with their comments to improve the paper.

References

[Aceto] L. Aceto: *Action Refinement in Process Algebras*, PhD-Thesis, University of Sussex, 1990, Report No. 3/91, University of Sussex, Computer Science, February 1991

[AH] L. Aceto, M. Hennessy: *Adding Action Refinement to a Finite Process Algebra*, Report No. 6/90, University of Sussex, Computer Science, November 1990, extended abstract in: Proc. ICALP 91, LNCS 510, Springer-Verlag, pp 506–519, 1991

[BDKP] E. Best, R. Devillers, A. Kiehn, L. Pomello: *Concurrent Bisimulation in Petri Nets*, Acta Informatica, Vol. 28, pp 231–264, 1991

[Boudol] G. Boudol: *Flow Event Structures and Flow Nets*, in I. Guessarian (ed.): Semantics of Systems of Concurrent Processes, LNCS 469, Springer-Verlag, pp 62–95, 1990

[BC] G. Boudol, I. Castellani: *Permutation of Transitions: An Event Structure Semantics for CCS and SCCS*, in J.W. de Bakker, W.-P. de Roever & G. Rozenberg (eds.): Linear Time, Branching Time and Partial Order in Logics and Models for Concurrency, LNCS 354, Springer-Verlag, pp 411–427, 1989

[BGV] W. Brauer, R. Gold, W. Vogler: *A Survey of Behaviour and Equivalence Preserving Refinements of Petri Nets*, in: Advances in Petri Nets 1990, LNCS 483, Springer-Verlag, pp 1–46, 1990

[DD a] Ph. Darondeau, P. Degano: *Event structures, Causal trees, and Refinements*, in: Proc. MFCS 90, LNCS 452, Springer-Verlag, pp 239–245, 1990

[DD b] Ph. Darondeau, P. Degano: *Refinement of Actions in Event Structures and Causal Trees*, manuscript, 1991

[Devillers] R. Devillers: *Maximality Preserving Bisimulation*, Technical Report LIT-1214, Université Libre de Bruxelles, March 1990, to appear in TCS

[GG a] R.J. van Glabbeek, U. Goltz: *Refinement of Actions in Causality Based Models*, in J.W. de Bakker, W.-P. de Roever & G. Rozenberg (eds.): Stepwise Refinement of Distributed Systems: Models, Formalism, Correctness, LNCS 430, Springer-Verlag, pp 267–300, 1990

[GG b] R.J. van Glabbeek, U. Goltz: *Equivalences and Refinement*, in: I. Guessarian (ed.): Semantics of Systems of Concurrent Processes, LNCS 469, Springer-Verlag, pp 309–333, 1990

[GG c] R.J. van Glabbeek, U. Goltz: *A Deadlock-sensitive Congruence for Action Refinement*, SFB-Bericht Nr. 342/23/90 A, TUM-19044, Technische Universität München, November 1990

[Milner] R. Milner: *A Calculus of Communicating Systems*, LNCS 92, Springer-Verlag, 1980

[NEL] M. Nielsen, U. Engberg, K. S. Larsen: *Fully Abstract Models for a Process Language with Refinement*, in J.W. de Bakker, W.-P. de Roever & G. Rozenberg (eds.): Linear Time, Branching Time and Partial Order in Logics and Models for Concurrency, LNCS 354, Springer-Verlag, pp 523–548, 1989

[NPW] M. Nielsen, G.D. Plotkin, G. Winskel: *Petri Nets, Event Structures and Domains, Part I*, Theoretical Computer Science, Vol. 13, No. 1, pp 85–108, 1981

[Park] D. Park: *Concurrency and Automata on Infinite Sequences*, in P. Deussen (ed.): Proc. 5th GI-Conference on Theoretical Computer Science, LNCS 104, Springer-Verlag, pp 167–183, 1981

[Vogler a] W. Vogler: *Failures Semantics Based on Interval Semiwords is a Congruence for Refinement*, Distributed Computing, Vol. 4, pp 139–162, 1991

[Vogler b] W. Vogler: *Bisimulation and Action Refinement*, in: Proc. STACS 91, LNCS 480, Springer-Verlag, pp 309–321, 1991

Maximality Preservation and the ST-idea for Action Refinements

Raymond Devillers
Laboratoire d'Informatique Théorique, Université Libre de Bruxelles
Boulevard du Triomphe, B-1050 Bruxelles

(Research supported by ESPRIT Basic Research Action, project 3148: DEMON)

ABSTRACT

The paper shows, in the framework of labelled P/T nets, that strengthening classical bisimulations through a maximality preservation property or through the introduction of ST-configurations leads to equivalent bisimulation notions, that they are preserved by a large class of action refinements, that they may be characterized through specific refinements and that they are the coarsest equivalences preserved by refinements and implying the original bisimulations.

Keywords

Bisimulation, Concurrency, Action refinement, Petri nets.

CONTENTS

1 Introduction

Since a current practice in software engineering is to consider various levels of abstraction, especially for top-down designs, and since various system descriptions may often correspond to similar behaviours, it is rather natural to search for equivalence relations between system descriptions which are preserved at the various abstraction levels.

We will essentially consider concurrent systems described by labelled P/T nets with silent moves (but we are confident that most of our results may be translated to other popular system models; in fact, some of them were initially developed for prime event structures, for instance). The top-down design will be modelled by the refinement of some visible actions, and we will be interested in bisimilarities, i.e. equivalences which respect the branching structure of the system descriptions.

Our aim in this paper will be to present in a synthetic and selfcontained way some of the main results obtained in this field during the DEMON project (BRA 3148). Consequently, many developments will not be completely new; some are consolidations and (mild) improvements of previous papers and reports; some are translations in net terms (with extensions and variations) of results obtained first in other models. This will be made clear in the text.

In order not to lengthen uselessly the presentation, and to burden the reader, some proofs will be omitted when they are similar to previous ones; they may be found in the report [10]. Moreover, in order not to disrupt the flow of the presentation, we shall gather in an appendix all the proofs which are a little bit long and technical; we preferred to keep them in the paper in order to allow the interested reader to see how they work, and where the possible preconditions are used.

A first result in this direction was obtained in [8] where we have defined an equivalence relation based on the process semantics of labelled P/T nets, called maximality preserving (MP, for short) bisimilarity, which is preserved by the simple but nevertheless interesting class of empty in/out refinements, even in the presence of internal actions. This notion is a strengthening of the fully concurrent bisimilarity [2], which is the equivalent for the net framework of the history preserving bisimilarity [12] and of the behaviour structure bisimilarity [23] (see also [7] and [6]), for which preservation results were already obtained for systems without silent moves (or with restricted silent moves).
Slightly later, but independently, a similar result was obtained by W.Vogler in [25] in the context of prime event structures with conflict-free refinements (see also [5]). From this study, it occurred that there seemed to be a strong relationship between the maximality preservation property and the usage of ST-configurations, that the same idea may be applied to strengthen various bisimulation notions and that this has to do with the behaviour of refined systems.
This led us to translate, and sometimes improve, Vogler's ideas in the context of labelled P/T nets in order to insert MP-bisimilarity in a more general setup. As a consequence, we will show that strengthening the fully concurrent bisimilarity, or the usual interleaving bisimilarity, through a maximality preservation property or through the introduction of ST-configurations leads to equivalent bisimulation notions; these bisimulations are preserved by the refinement of visible actions through SM-refinements and of selfconcurrency-free actions through memoryless refinements; they may be characterized through specific refinements and are the coarsest equivalences preserved by refinements and implying the bisimulation notion we started with; for most practical systems (i.e. for the safe or bounded ones), they may be characterized from the reachable markings and are decidable.

After recalling some basic net notions we shall use throughout the paper in section 2, and presenting the general ideas of bisimulations, refinements, maximality preservation and ST-configurations in section 3, we will develop the theory obtained by strenghtening the fully concurrent bisimilarity in section 4 and the interleaving bisimilarity in section 5. Section 6 will then summarize the main results obtained thus far in a synoptic table. Section 7 will then consider the full refinement problem, where the refinement systems as well as the systems to be refined are related by some bisimulation notion to be preserved, and section 8 will recall some open problems.

2 Basic Definitions

2.1 Unlabelled Systems

We briefly recall the definitions of some basic concepts, referring e.g. to [3,1].

- A net with arc weights is a triple $N = (S, T, W)$ with $S \cap T = \emptyset$ and

  $$W: ((S \times T) \cup (T \times S)) \rightarrow \mathbf{N} = \{0, 1, 2, \ldots\}.$$

  T is a set of transitions and S is a set of places.
  We assume all nets to be finite, i.e. $|S \cup T| \in \mathbf{N}$.
  A net $N = (S, T, W)$ is ordinary iff for all $(x, y) \in ((S \times T) \cup (T \times S))$: $W(x, y) \leq 1$.
  In an ordinary net, the weight function can (and will) be replaced by a flow relation $F \subseteq ((S \times T) \cup (T \times S))$, following the rule that $(x, y) \in F \Longleftrightarrow W(x, y) \neq 0$.
  For $x \in S \cup T$, the pre-set ${}^\bullet x$ is defined as ${}^\bullet x = \{y \in S \cup T \mid W(y, x) \neq 0\}$ and the post-set $x^\bullet$ is defined as $x^\bullet = \{y \in S \cup T \mid W(x, y) \neq 0\}$. For $X \subseteq S \cup T$, ${}^\bullet X = \bigcup_{x \in X} {}^\bullet x$ and $X^\bullet = \bigcup_{x \in X} x^\bullet$.
  Two transitions t_1, t_2 are independent if $({}^\bullet t_1 \cup t_1^\bullet) \cap ({}^\bullet t_2 \cup t_2^\bullet) = \emptyset$.

- A marking of a net (S,T,W) is defined as a function $M: S \to \mathbf{N}$, giving the number of tokens contained in each place. The transition rule states that a transition t is enabled by M iff $M(s) \geq W(s,t)$ for all $s \in S$, and that an enabled transition t may occur, producing a successor marking M' by the rule $M'(s) = M(s) - W(s,t) + W(t,s)$ for all $s \in S$. The occurrence of t is denoted by $M[t\rangle M'$.

- Two transitions t_1, t_2 (not necessarily distinct) are concurrently enabled by a marking M iff $M(s) \geq W(s,t_1) + W(s,t_2)$ for all $s \in S$; this will be denoted by $M[t_1, t_2\rangle$.
This may be extended to sets and bags (or multisets) of transitions.

- A system net (or a marked P/T net) (S,T,W,M_0) is a net (S,T,W) with an initial marking M_0.

- A sequence $\sigma = M_0 t_1 M_1 t_2 \ldots$ is an occurrence sequence iff $M_{i-1}[t_i\rangle M_i$ for $1 \leq i$.
A sequence $t_1 t_2 \ldots$ is a transition sequence (starting with M) iff there is an occurrence sequence $M t_1 M_1 t_2 \ldots$. If the finite sequence $t_1 t_2 \ldots t_n$ leads from M to M', then we write $M[t_1 t_2 \ldots t_n\rangle M'$.
The set of reachable markings of a marked net (S,T,W,M_0) is defined as
$[M_0\rangle = \{M \mid \exists t_1 t_2 \ldots t_n : M_0[t_1 t_2 \ldots t_n\rangle M\}$.
A marked net (S,T,W,M_0) is (1-)safe iff $\forall M \in [M_0\rangle\ \forall s \in S: M(s) \leq 1$.
It is bounded iff $\exists n\ :\ \forall M \in [M_0\rangle\ \forall s \in S: M(s) \leq n$.

- An occurrence net $N = (B,E,F)$ is an acyclic ordinary net without branched places, i.e., $\forall x,y \in B \cup E: (x,y) \in F^+ \Rightarrow (y,x) \notin F^+$ (acyclicity) and $\forall b \in B: |{}^\bullet b| \leq 1 \wedge |b^\bullet| \leq 1$ (no branching of places). For an occurrence net (B,E,F), the pair $(X, \prec)$ with $X = B \cup E$ and $\prec = F^+$ is a strict partial order. Often, elements of E are called events and elements of B are called conditions.

- A B-cut $c \subseteq B$ of an occurrence net (B,E,F) is a maximal unordered set of B-elements (taking F^+ as the ordering).
$\downarrow c = \{x \in B \cup E \mid \exists y \in c: (x,y) \in F^*\}$ denotes the set of elements below or on c, and
$\uparrow c = \{x \in B \cup E \mid \exists y \in c: (y,x) \in F^*\}$ denotes the set of elements after or on c.

- In order to avoid minor but annoying technical difficulties, we will suppose from now on that all our nets are T-restricted, i.e. : $\forall t \in T : {}^\bullet t \neq \emptyset \neq t^\bullet$.

- $Min(N)$ and $Max(N)$ are the B-cuts defined by the sets $\{x \in B \cup E \mid {}^\bullet x = \emptyset\}$ and $\{x \in B \cup E \mid x^\bullet = \emptyset\}$, respectively.

- A process $\pi = (N,p) = (B,E,F,p)$ of a system $\Sigma = (S,T,W,M_0)$ consists of an occurrence net $N = (B,E,F)$ together with a labelling $p: B \cup E \to S \cup T$ which satisfy appropriate properties such that π can be interpreted as a concurrent run of Σ, i.e. :

  $p(B) \subseteq S, p(E) \subseteq T$ (conditions are instances of place holdings, events are occurrences of transitions);

  $Min(N)$ is a B-cut which corresponds to the initial marking M_0, that is,
  $\forall s \in S: M_0(s) = |p^{-1}(s) \cap Min(N)|$;

  $\forall e \in E\ \forall s \in S$: $W(s,p(e)) = |p^{-1}(s) \cap {}^\bullet e|$ and $W(p(e),s) = |p^{-1}(s) \cap e^\bullet|$ (transition environments are respected)[1].

  The initial process of Σ is the one for which $E = \emptyset$; it will generally be denoted as π°.

- If a marking M of Σ and a B-cut c of a process π of Σ satisfy $\forall s \in S: M(s) = |p^{-1}(s) \cap c|$, then M is said to correspond to c.

- If c is a B-cut of a process $\pi = (B,E,F,p)$, then $\Downarrow(\pi,c)$ denotes the process $(B \cap \downarrow c, E \cap \downarrow c, F \cap (\downarrow c \times \downarrow c), p|_{\downarrow c})$, i.e. the prefix of π up to (and including) c; similarly, $\Uparrow(\pi,c)$ denotes the structure $(B \cap \uparrow c, E \cap \uparrow c, F \cap (\uparrow c \times \uparrow c), p|_{\uparrow c})$, i.e. the suffix of π

[1] For infinite processes there needs to be an additional requirement, but we will not be interested in infinite processes here; the interested reader may find an extensive discussion on this subject in [1].

from (and including) c, which is a process for the system (S,T,W,M) where M is the marking corresponding to c.

- A process π of a system Σ is an extension of another process π' of the same system if there is a B-cut c of π such that $\pi' = \Downarrow(\pi,c)$; it may be observed that, in this case, $c = Max(N')$ is uniquely defined and that the extension part is $\pi'' = \Uparrow(\pi,c)$. This will sometimes be represented by the notation $\pi' \longrightarrow \pi$, or $\pi' \xrightarrow{\pi''} \pi$, or $\pi - \pi' = \pi''$; π' is also called a prefix of π; let us notice that any process is a prefix of itself, and that the initial process is a prefix of any other one.

- The set $Lin(\pi)$, for a process π of Σ, is the set of all occurrence sequences of Σ which are linearizations (of the events and their separating B-cuts) of π. It is known that if Σ is finite then each finite process has a non-empty Lin-set. $Lin(\Sigma)$ will denote the set of all the occurrence sequences of Σ.

- For an occurrence sequence σ of Σ, $\Pi(\sigma)$ denotes the set of all the processes π of Σ (up to isomorphism) such that σ linearizes π; Π is thus the inverse of Lin. $\Pi(\Sigma)$ will denote the set of all the processes of Σ (up to isomorphism, again).

2.2 Labelled Systems

- An alphabet A is a set of visible actions; we assume that $\tau \notin A$ (τ will denote the internal or silent action).

- A labelling of a net $N = (S,T,W)$ is a function $\lambda: T \to A \cup \{\tau\}$. If $\lambda(t) \in A$ then t is called visible; otherwise, t is called silent or invisible.
  $\bar{\lambda}$ will denote the classical extension of λ to sequences ($\bar{\lambda} : T^* \to A^*$), recursively defined by $\bar{\lambda}(\epsilon) = \epsilon$, $\bar{\lambda}(t) = \lambda(t)$ if t is visible, $\bar{\lambda}(t) = \epsilon$ if t is silent and $\bar{\lambda}(t\sigma) = \bar{\lambda}(t)\bar{\lambda}(\sigma)$.

- $\Sigma = (S,T,W,M_0,\lambda)$ is a labelled system, or a labelled P/T net, iff (S,T,W,M_0) is a system net and λ is a labelling of (S,T,W). In the following, we will suppose that all our systems have their labels in the same alphabet A, and we will denote by $A(\Sigma)$ the subset of A which is actually used by a system Σ, i.e. if $\Sigma = (S,T,W,M_0,\lambda) : A(\Sigma) = \lambda(T) \setminus \{\tau\}$.

- An action $a \in A$ in a labelled system $\Sigma = (S,T,W,M_0,\lambda)$ is said to be auto-concurrent at a marking M iff M concurrently enables two observable transitions t_1, t_2 (not necessarily distinct) such that $\lambda(t_1) = \lambda(t_2) = a$. Σ is free of auto-concurrency iff for all $M \in [M_0\rangle$: no observable action is auto-concurrent at M. Absence of auto-concurrency may be viewed as a kind of safeness, it has also been termed the disjoint labelling condition in [22,21].

- An observable transition t of a labelled system $\Sigma = (S,T,W,M_0,\lambda)$ is said to be self-concurrent at a marking M iff M concurrently enables t twice. Σ is free of self-concurrency iff for all $M \in [M_0\rangle$: no observable transition is self-concurrent at M.

- Let $\Sigma = (S,T,W,M_0,\lambda)$ be a labelled system. Let $\pi = (B,E,F,p)$ be a process of it. Then the abstraction of π with respect to λ is denoted by $\alpha_\lambda(\pi) = (E',\prec,\lambda')$ and is defined by

$$E' = \{e \in E \mid \lambda(p(e)) \neq \tau\} \ (= p^{-1}(\lambda^{-1}(A)) \ ),$$
$$\prec = \{(e_1,e_2) \in E' \times E' \mid (e_1,e_2) \in F^+\} \ (= F^+ \cap E' \times E' \ ),$$
$$\lambda' = \lambda \circ p|_{E'}, \text{ i.e. } \forall e \in E' : \lambda'(e) = \lambda(p(e)).$$

  $(E',\prec)$ is a partial order, and $\alpha_\lambda(\pi) = (E',\prec,\lambda')$ is thus a labelled poset (with labels in A).
  If e is an event of π, its final label is $\lambda(p(e))$.

- Let $\alpha_{\lambda_1} = (E_1',\prec_1,\lambda_1')$ and $\alpha_{\lambda_2} = (E_2',\prec_2,\lambda_2')$ be two abstractions (of two processes π_1 and π_2, possibly arising from two different systems Σ_1 and Σ_2) as in the previous definition, both with labels in A. Then $\alpha_{\lambda_1} \cong \alpha_{\lambda_2}$ iff there is a bijection $\beta: E_1' \to E_2'$ such that:

  (i) $\forall e \in E_1'$: $\lambda_1'(e) = \lambda_2'(\beta(e))$.

(ii) $\forall e_1, e_2 \in E_1' : e_1 \prec_1 e_2 \iff \beta(e_1) \prec_2 \beta(e_2)$.

i.e. these abstractions are (labelled) order-isomorphic.

- If $\pi = (B, E, F, p)$ is a process of some labelled system $\Sigma = (S, T, W, M_0, \lambda)$ and $\mathcal{A} \subseteq A$ is a subset of visible labels, $Maxevents(\pi, \mathcal{A}) = (E \setminus {}^{\bullet\bullet}E) \cap p^{-1}(\lambda^{-1}(\mathcal{A}))$ is the set of the maximal events of π which are finally labelled by $\mathcal{A}$.

3 Bisimulations, Refinements, Maximality Preservation and ST-Configurations

In this chapter, we will not in general give full definitions for the above notions; this will be done later, when the need will arise. Instead, our aim here is simply to sketch them in order to allow the reader to build some intuition and to get a general idea about the subjects that will be technically developed in the next chapters.
Intuitively, two systems are bisimilar if there is a bisimulation between them, i.e. a relation between their "evolutions" such that for each evolution of one of the systems there is a corresponding evolution of the other system such that the evolutions are observationally "equivalent" and lead to systems which are again bisimilar ([19,18,20,2]).
The semantics of the concurrent systems we are considering will be captured by their processes, and their extension relation. Consequently, we will use them to model the "evolutions" of the systems; sometimes however, when feasible, it will be preferable to characterize the relation from the reachable markings only (and the occurrence rule), which constitute a much smaller set.
The variety of possible bisimulations arises from the various ways we may define equivalences between processes and between process extensions.
In general, thus, two labelled systems Σ_1 and Σ_2 will be said bisimilar iff there is a set $\mathcal{B} \subseteq \{(\pi_1, \pi_2, \beta) \mid \pi_1 \in \Pi(\Sigma_1), \pi_2 \in \Pi(\Sigma_2), \beta$ is a relation between the visible events of π_1 and $\pi_2\}$ with the following properties:

(i) $(\pi_1^\circ, \pi_2^\circ, \emptyset) \in \mathcal{B}$, where π_1° and π_2° are the initial processes of Σ_1 and Σ_2, respectively.

(ii) $(\pi_1, \pi_2, \beta) \in \mathcal{B} \Longrightarrow \beta$ fulfills some properties characterizing the fact that the evolutions π_1 and π_2 are equivalent.

(iii) $\forall (\pi_1, \pi_2, \beta) \in \mathcal{B}$

  (a) if π_1' is an extension of π_1,
  there is some $(\pi_1', \pi_2', \beta') \in \mathcal{B}$ where π_2' is an extension of π_2 and $\beta \subseteq \beta'$;
  moreover, β' will possibly have to fulfill some additional properties with respect to $(\pi_1' - \pi_1)$ and $(\pi_2' - \pi_2)$.

  (b) Vice versa.

Such a triple set $\mathcal{B}$ is a bisimulation between Σ_1 and Σ_2.

Intuitively again, a refinement $ref(\Sigma, a, D)$ of some labelled system Σ will be obtained by replacing in Σ each transition with a visible label a by a separate copy of some refinement system D; of course, care will have to be taken on the way each copy will be connected to the surrounding of the replaced transition and on the definition of the initial marking (see also [13] for this problem).
It is also possible to define refinements for the processes of Σ, by replacing each event with a final label a by some process of D. Some processes of D will be said to be complete, when they correspond to a terminating evolution of D; clearly, an event which is not maximal in its Σ-process, i.e. which is followed by other (succeeding) events, corresponds to a terminated action and may thus be refined by a complete D-process only; on the contrary, a maximal event in a Σ-process may be refined by any thus possibly non-complete) D-process.

Finally, we may refine a whole set $\mathcal{A}$ of visible labels, instead of only one of them, each label $a \in \mathcal{A}$ being associated to a separate refinement system D_a. In order to be slightly more general, we shall specify a subset $\mathcal{A}$ of visible labels which may be refined; taking $\mathcal{A} = \emptyset$ will then lead to refinementless theories, $\mathcal{A} = A$ will lead to fully refined theories, and intermediate cases will correspond to situations where some actions have already been fully refined before, while other ones may still be (further) refined (they thus correspond to higher abstraction levels).

The maximality preservation property (for a label subset $\mathcal{A}$) expresses the fact that [8], in a bisimulation, the maximality of $\mathcal{A}$-finally labelled events may be preserved: if a new event with final label in $\mathcal{A}$ is added on one side and it is maximal, it is possible to extend the other side in such a way that the corresponding event (with the same final label in general) is also maximal - and if an event finally labelled in $\mathcal{A}$ is maximal on one side before and after the extension while on the other side the corresponding event is also maximal before the extension, then this event remains maximal after the extension too.
More formally, in terms of the condition (iii) above, this may be written

(iii) $\forall(\pi_1, \pi_2, \beta) \in \mathcal{B}$

(a) if π_1' is an extension of π_1,
there is some $(\pi_1', \pi_2', \beta') \in \mathcal{B}$ where π_2' is an extension of π_2 and $\beta \subseteq \beta'$;
moreover, β' will possibly have to fulfill some additional properties with respect to $(\pi_1' - \pi_1)$ and $(\pi_2' - \pi_2)$, and in particular

- e_1' is added, maximal and $\mathcal{A}$-finally labelled $\Longrightarrow$ so is $\beta'(e_1')$,
- e_1 is still maximal and is $\mathcal{A}$-finally labelled $\Longrightarrow$ so is $\beta(e_1)$.

(b) Vice versa.

The connection with refinements arises from the observation that in the refinement of a process a maximal event may be refined by any evolution (process) of the refinement system, while a non-maximal event may only be refined by a complete evolution (process).
It may be observed that, from a strict observational point of view, the maximality of an event in a process π may be considered as irrelevant: only the maximality in the abstraction $\alpha(\pi)$ may be observed and the subsequent occurrence of silent events (corresponding to internal transitions) in π is by definition unobservable. However, our intention is not to stick to a strict observational approach and (as it will be seen later) this type of condition is exactly the one we need to add to usual bisimulation notions to get congruences; moreover, such a maximal event in a process may be seen as an engaged one, i.e. an event corresponding to a visible transition which has started its work but not terminated it (which may be considered as observable). This thus leads to the next idea, which will be proved equivalent to the maximality preserving one.

The ST-idea [14] consists in considering that some actions (those of $\mathcal{A}$) are not truly instantaneous (as it is usually done in the occurrence rule); they last for some time and have a start and an end; again, this has obvious connections with refinements, since the refinement of a high level action exhibits its non-instantaneous nature.
As a consequence, in an evolution represented by some process, some events may be considered as engaged and not yet terminated; this may only be the case for ($\mathcal{A}$-finally labelled) maximal events since the other ones, having successors, must have completed their work previously (or may be considered as instantaneous), hence an intuitive connection with the maximality preservation property since maximal $\mathcal{A}$-finally labelled events play a special rôle.
This may be captured by the introduction of $\mathcal{A}$ST-configurations, and their usage as a model for the system evolution instead of the processes :

Definition 3.1 *AST-configurations.*

Let Σ be a labelled system and $\mathcal{A} \subseteq A$ be a subset of visible actions;
an AST-configuration of Σ is a pair $(\pi, \mathcal{E})$ where
π is a process of Σ
$\mathcal{E}$ is a set of maximal $\mathcal{A}$-finally labelled events of π (the engaged events);
an evolution rule may be defined on them, which extends the process evolution rule :

$$(\pi, \mathcal{E}) \longrightarrow (\pi', \mathcal{E}') \text{ iff } \pi \longrightarrow \pi' \text{ and } E \setminus \mathcal{E} \subseteq E' \setminus \mathcal{E}',$$

meaning that terminated events must obviously remain terminated (notice that it may happen that $\pi = \pi'$, the only difference being that some engaged events get terminated).
When $\mathcal{A} = A$, we will simply speak about ST-configurations, and we may observe that $\emptyset$ST-configurations may be identified with simple processes since then $\mathcal{E}$ is always empty and does not afford any additional information. ■ 3.1

Such configurations may of course replace processes in bisimulation definitions, if we adapt them accordingly.
This will be detailed in the next chapters.

4 Strengthening Fully Concurrent Bisimilarity.

We already know that the fully concurrent bisimilarity is preserved by a large class of refinements when there are no silent moves, or when the refinements are slightly restricted [2]; consequently, this bisimilarity seems to be a natural candidate to start with when applying the general ideas introduced in the previous section in order to obtain more general results.

4.1 Equivalent Strengthenings.

Let us first recall the definition of the fully concurrent bisimilarity

Definition 4.1 *Fully concurrent bisimilarity*

If Σ_1 and Σ_2 are two labelled systems, $\Sigma_1 \approx_{FC} \Sigma_2$ iff there is a set $\mathcal{B} \subseteq \{(\pi_1, \pi_2, \beta) \mid \pi_1 \in \Pi(\Sigma_1), \pi_2 \in \Pi(\Sigma_2), \beta$ is a relation between the visible events of π_1 and $\pi_2\}$ with the following properties:

(i) $(\pi_1^\circ, \pi_2^\circ, \emptyset) \in \mathcal{B}$ *, where π_1° and π_2° are the initial processes of Σ_1 and Σ_2, respectively.*

(ii) $(\pi_1, \pi_2, \beta) \in \mathcal{B} \Longrightarrow \beta$ *is an order-isomorphism between $\alpha_{\lambda^1}(\pi_1)$ and $\alpha_{\lambda^2}(\pi_2)$*

(iii) $\forall (\pi_1, \pi_2, \beta) \in \mathcal{B}$

- *(a) if π_1' is an extension of π_1,*
  there is some $(\pi_1', \pi_2', \beta') \in \mathcal{B}$ where π_2' is an extension of π_2 and $\beta \subseteq \beta'$.
- *(b) Vice versa.*

Σ_1 and Σ_2 are then said to be fully concurrent (FC) bisimilar and $\mathcal{B}$ is an FC-bisimulation between them. ■ 4.1

As noticed in [2] (Prop 5.5), checking the definition may be considerably simplified by only considering in (iii) extensions with only one event more in the premises.

The maximality preserving bisimilarity, as defined in [8], is then obtained by adding the maximality preservation property to the fully concurrent bisimilarity :

Definition 4.2 *AMP-bisimilarity.*

If Σ_1 and Σ_2 are two labelled systems and $\mathcal{A} \subseteq A$ is a subset of visible actions, $\Sigma_1 \approx_{\mathcal{A}MP} \Sigma_2$ iff there is a set $\mathcal{B} \subseteq \{(\pi_1, \pi_2, \beta) \mid \pi_1 \in \Pi(\Sigma_1), \pi_2 \in \Pi(\Sigma_2), \beta$ is a relation between the visible events of π_1 and $\pi_2\}$ with the following properties :

(i) $(\pi_1^\circ, \pi_2^\circ, \emptyset) \in \mathcal{B}$ *, where π_1° and π_2° are the initial processes of Σ_1 and Σ_2, respectively*

(ii) $(\pi_1, \pi_2, \beta) \in \mathcal{B} \Longrightarrow \beta$ *is an order-isomorphism between $\alpha_{\lambda^1}(\pi_1)$ and $\alpha_{\lambda^2}(\pi_2)$*

(iii) $\forall (\pi_1, \pi_2, \beta) \in \mathcal{B}$

(a) if π_1' is an extension of π_1,
then there is some $(\pi_1', \pi_2', \beta') \in \mathcal{B}$ where π_2' is an extension of π_2 and $\beta \subseteq \beta'$;
moreover,

- *if $e_1' \in E_1' \setminus E_1$, $\lambda_1(p_1'(e_1')) \in \mathcal{A}$ and e_1' is a maximal event in π_1', then $\beta'(e_1')$ is a maximal event of π_2'*
- *for any event e_1 of π_1, if $\lambda_1(p_1(e_1)) \in \mathcal{A}$ and if e_1 and $\beta(e_1)$ are maximal events in π_1' and π_2, respectively, then $\beta(e_1)$ is still a maximal event in π_2'.*

(b) Vice versa.

Σ_1 and Σ_2 will then be said $\mathcal{A}$MP-bisimilar, and $\mathcal{B}$ is an $\mathcal{A}$MP-bisimulation between them. ■ 4.2

We sticked here to the terminology "MP-bisimilarity" for historical reasons, but we now know that a better (but a little bit lengthy) denomination would have been $\mathcal{A}$FCMP-bisimilarity in order to recall that we started from fully concurrent bisimilarity.
We may observe that $\approx_{FC} = \approx_{\emptyset MP}$.
Two systems will be called MP-bisimilar if they are maximality preserving bisimilar for all visible actions, i.e. $\approx_{MP} = \approx_{AMP}$.
If $\mathcal{A} = \{a\}$, we will simply write $\approx_{aMP}$ instead of $\approx_{\{a\}MP}$, and say that two systems are maximality preserving bisimilar with respect to a, instead of $\{a\}$.
If $\mathcal{A}' \subset \mathcal{A} \subseteq A$, then $\approx_{\mathcal{A}MP}$ is stronger than $\approx_{\mathcal{A}'MP}$, and in particular MP-bisimilarity is stronger than FC-bisimilarity.

We may also observe that the very same relation may be obtained by starting from the simplified version of the definition of FC-bisimilarity, i.e. by using single event extensions in the premisses; this leads to a characterization which may be easier to check :

Proposition 4.3 *AMP-bisimilarity and single extensions.*

If Σ_1 and Σ_2 are two labelled systems and $\mathcal{A} \subseteq A$ is a subset of visible actions, $\Sigma_1 \approx_{\mathcal{A}MP} \Sigma_2$ iff there is a set $\mathcal{B} \subseteq \{(\pi_1, \pi_2, \beta) \mid \pi_1 \in \Pi(\Sigma_1), \pi_2 \in \Pi(\Sigma_2), \beta$ is a relation between the visible events of π_1 and $\pi_2\}$ with the following properties :

(i) $(\pi_1^\circ, \pi_2^\circ, \emptyset) \in \mathcal{B}$ *, where π_1° and π_2° are the initial processes of Σ_1 and Σ_2, respectively*

(ii) $(\pi_1, \pi_2, \beta) \in \mathcal{B} \Longrightarrow \beta$ *is an order-isomorphism between $\alpha_{\lambda^1}(\pi_1)$ and $\alpha_{\lambda^2}(\pi_2)$*

(iii) $\forall (\pi_1, \pi_2, \beta) \in \mathcal{B}$

(a) if π_1' is an extension of π_1 with only one event e_1' more,
there is some $(\pi_1', \pi_2', \beta') \in \mathcal{B}$ where π_2' is an extension of π_2 and $\beta \subseteq \beta'$;
moreover,

- *if $\lambda_1(p_1'(e_1')) \in \mathcal{A}$, then $\beta'(e_1')$ is a maximal event of π_2'*
- *for any event e_1 of π_1, if $\lambda_1(p_1(e_1)) \in \mathcal{A}$ and if e_1 and $\beta(e_1)$ are maximal events in π_1' and π_2, respectively, then $\beta(e_1)$ is still a maximal event in π_2'.*

(b) Vice versa.

Proof: Clearly, 4.2 implies the characterization with single event extensions.
Conversely, since single event extensions generate any (finite) extension, an iterative use of them immediately leads to the characterization with general extensions. ■ 4.3

This proof, like many other ones which will follow may also be found in [9], which may be considered as an earlier version of the present paper.
It may be checked for instance that the systems Σ_1 and Σ_2 on Figure 1(i) are FC-bisimilar but not MP-bisimilar (this example was used in [2] to show that FC-bisimilarity is not always preserved by refinements), while the systems Σ_1' and Σ_2' on Figure 1(ii) are MP-bisimilar (this example was used to show that MP-bisimilarity is weaker than branching-bisimilarity, another kind of bisimilarity which was introduced in [16] and is preserved by refinements for sequential systems).

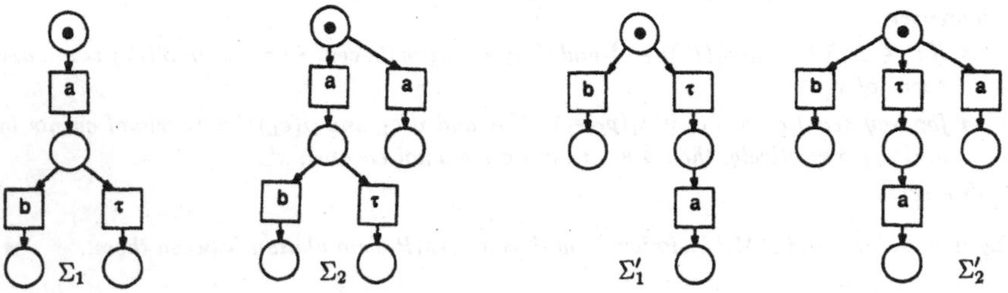

(i) two FC-bisimilar systems (ii) two MP-bisimilar systems

Figure 1: FC-bisimilarity and MP-bisimilarity

Now, let us apply the ST-idea to the fully concurrent bisimilarity :

Definition 4.4 *AST-bisimilarity.*

If Σ_1 and Σ_2 are two labelled systems and $\mathcal{A} \subseteq A$ is a subset of visible actions, $\Sigma_1 \approx_{AST} \Sigma_2$ iff there is a set $\mathcal{B} \subseteq \{((\pi_1, \mathcal{E}_1), (\pi_2, \mathcal{E}_2), \beta) \mid (\pi_1, \mathcal{E}_1)$ is an AST-configuration of Σ_1, $(\pi_2, \mathcal{E}_2)$ is an AST-configuration of Σ_2, β is a relation between the visible events of π_1 and $\pi_2\}$ with the following properties:

(i) $((\pi_1^\circ, \emptyset), (\pi_2^\circ, \emptyset), \emptyset) \in \mathcal{B}$ *, where π_1° and π_2° are the initial processes of Σ_1 and Σ_2, respectively.*

(ii) $((\pi_1, \mathcal{E}_1), (\pi_2, \mathcal{E}_2), \beta) \in \mathcal{B} \Longrightarrow \beta$ *is an order-isomorphism between $\alpha_{\lambda^1}(\pi_1)$ and $\alpha_{\lambda^2}(\pi_2)$, and* $\beta(\mathcal{E}_1) = \mathcal{E}_2$.

(iii) $\forall((\pi_1, \mathcal{E}_1), (\pi_2, \mathcal{E}_2), \beta) \in \mathcal{B}$

(a) if $(\pi_1, \mathcal{E}_1) \longrightarrow (\pi_1', \mathcal{E}_1')$,
there is some $((\pi_1', \mathcal{E}_1'), (\pi_2', \mathcal{E}_2'), \beta') \in \mathcal{B}$ *where* $(\pi_2, \mathcal{E}_2) \longrightarrow (\pi_2', \mathcal{E}_2')$ *and* $\beta \subseteq \beta'$.

(b) Vice versa.

Σ_1 and Σ_2 are then said to be AST-bisimilar (or AFCST-bisimilar to be more specific, or AhST-bisimilar to follow Vogler's terminology for prime event structures), and $\mathcal{B}$ is an AST-bisimulation between them. ■ 4.4

The same argument as above may be used to show that starting from the simplified version of the fully concurrent bisimilarity characterization would lead to the same equivalence notion; the resulting formulation is a little bit longer than the general one, but it is generally more efficient to practically check the relation :

Proposition 4.5 *AST-bisimilarity and simple extensions.*

If Σ_1 and Σ_2 are two labelled systems and $\mathcal{A} \subseteq A$ is a subset of visible actions, $\Sigma_1 \approx_{\mathcal{A}ST} \Sigma_2$ iff there is a set $\mathcal{B} \subseteq \{((\pi_1,\mathcal{E}_1),(\pi_2,\mathcal{E}_2),\beta) \mid (\pi_1,\mathcal{E}_1)$ is an $\mathcal{A}ST$-configuration of Σ_1, $(\pi_2,\mathcal{E}_2)$ is an $\mathcal{A}ST$-configuration of Σ_2, β is a relation between the visible events of π_1 and $\pi_2\}$ with the following properties:

(i) $((\pi_1^\circ,\emptyset),(\pi_2^\circ,\emptyset),\emptyset) \in \mathcal{B}$, *where π_1° and π_2° are the initial processes of Σ_1 and Σ_2, respectively.*

(ii) $((\pi_1,\mathcal{E}_1),(\pi_2,\mathcal{E}_2),\beta) \in \mathcal{B} \Longrightarrow \beta$ *is an order-isomorphism between $\alpha_{\lambda^1}(\pi_1)$ and $\alpha_{\lambda^2}(\pi_2)$, and* $\beta(\mathcal{E}_1) = \mathcal{E}_2$.

(iii) $\forall((\pi_1,\mathcal{E}_1),(\pi_2,\mathcal{E}_2),\beta) \in \mathcal{B}$

(a) if $(\pi_1,\mathcal{E}_1) \longrightarrow (\pi_1',\mathcal{E}_1')$ with either $\pi_1 = \pi_1'$ and $\mathcal{E}_1'$ exhibits only one event less than $\mathcal{E}_1$
or π_1' exhibits only one event more than π_1,
it is not finally labelled in $\mathcal{A}$ and $\mathcal{E}_1 = \mathcal{E}_1'$
or π_1' exhibits only one event more than π_1, it is finally labelled in $\mathcal{A}$ and $\mathcal{E}_1'$ is $\mathcal{E}_1$ augmented by this single event,
there is some $((\pi_1',\mathcal{E}_1'),(\pi_2',\mathcal{E}_2'),\beta') \in \mathcal{B}$ where $(\pi_2,\mathcal{E}_2) \longrightarrow (\pi_2',\mathcal{E}_2')$ and $\beta \subseteq \beta'$.

(b) Vice versa.

Proof: Clearly, 4.4 implies the characterization with simple extensions in the premises.
Conversely, it may be checked that such simple extensions generate any (finite) extension, so that an iterative use of 4.5 immediately leads to the general extensions used in the original definition.
■ 4.5

The main property of this section (slightly extending a similar result in [25], where only the case $\mathcal{A} = A$ is considered) is then :

Proposition 4.6 *Equivalence of MP and ST strengthenings.*

$\forall \mathcal{A} \subseteq A \, : \approx_{\mathcal{A}MP} = \approx_{\mathcal{A}ST}$

Proof: see Appendix A.1. ■ 4.6

4.2 Preservation through Refinements.

We have already shown in [8] that $\mathcal{A}$MP-bisimilarity (and thus, from 4.6, $\mathcal{A}$ST-bisimilarity) is preserved by refinements; this is not true in all generality, however, and we need to constrain slightly the refinement systems and the labels to be refined, or to constrain more severely the refinement systems alone. Let us first summarize the main definitions and results of [8] in this respect.

Definition 4.7 *Empty in/out systems.*

A labelled system $D = (S^D,T^D,W^D,M_0^D,\lambda^D)$ will be called an empty in/out system iff

(i) there is a unique (input) place s_{in} without predecessor and a (different) unique (output) place s_{out} without successor: $\forall t \in T^D : W^D(t,s_{in}) = 0 = W^D(s_{out},t)$ and $s_{in} \neq s_{out}$

(ii) initially there is a unique token in s_{in} and at the end there is a unique token in s_{out} :
$M_0^D(s_{in}) = 1$ *and* $\forall s \neq s_{in} : M_0^D(s) = 0;$
$\forall M \in [M_0^D\rangle : M(s_{out}) > 0 \Rightarrow [M(s_{out}) = 1 \wedge \forall s \neq s_{out} : M(s) = 0]$

(iii) s_{in} and s_{out} only have ordinary arcs :
$\forall t \in T^D : W^D(s_{in},t) \leq 1 \geq W^D(t,s_{out})$. ■ 4.7

The adjective "empty" used in this definition recalls the fact that, initially and at the end (if it is reachable), there are no tokens inside the system (i.e. but in s_{in} and s_{out}).
Refinements of an action a correspond to replacing each transition labelled with a by a separate copy of the considered refinement system, and to connect it to the surrounding of the replaced transition accordingly :

Definition 4.8 *Refinement by an empty in/out system.*

Let $\Sigma = (S,T,W,M_0,\lambda)$ be a labelled system, let $a \in A(\Sigma)$ and let $D = (S^D,T^D,W^D,M_0^D,\lambda^D)$ be an empty in/out system. The refinement $ref(\Sigma,a,D)$ is the labelled system obtained from Σ by applying the following construction for each $t \in \lambda^{-1}(a)$ (the order does not matter, but the λ used here is the one of Σ and not the one constructed for $ref(\Sigma,a,D)$ below):

(i) drop t (and restrict W and λ accordingly)

(ii) create a copy of D without s_{in} and s_{out};
the new nodes will be called $< x,t >$ for $x \in S^D \cup T^D$;
W, M_0 and λ will be modified accordingly, i.e.
$\forall x,y \in S^D \cup T^D : W(< x,t >,< y,t >) = W^D(x,y), \forall x \in T^D : \lambda(< x,t >) = \lambda^D(x)$
and $\forall x \in S^D \backslash \{s_{in}, s_{out}\} : M_0(< x,t >) = 0$

(iii) connect the successors of s_{in} to the predecessors of t and the predecessors of s_{out} to the successors of t:
$\forall x \in s_{in}^{\bullet}, \forall y \in {}^{\bullet}t : W(y,< x,t >) = W(y,t)$
$\forall x \in {}^{\bullet}s_{out}, \forall y \in t^{\bullet} : W(< x,t >,y) = W(t,y)$

It may be noticed that, at the end, $\Sigma' = ref(\Sigma,a,D)$ will be a labelled system with $A(\Sigma') = A(\Sigma) \setminus \{a\} \cup A(D)$. ■ 4.8

The refinement notion may also be extended to processes of a system, by replacing each event with a final label a by a (non initial) process of D (with the restriction that non maximal events may only be replaced by complete processes).

Definition 4.9 *Empty refinement of a process.*

Let $\pi = (B,E,F,p)$ be a process of a labelled system $\Sigma = (S,T,W,M_0,\lambda)$; let $a \in A(\Sigma)$ be a visible action and let D be an empty in/out system;
let ζ be a function: $p^{-1}(\lambda^{-1}(a)) \longrightarrow \Pi(D)$ such that if $e \in p^{-1}(\lambda^{-1}(a))$ is not a maximal event in π, then $\zeta(e)$ is a complete process of D, i.e. with a (unique) maximal condition corresponding to s_{out}; we will also suppose that $\zeta(e)$ is never the initial process of D.
Then the refinement $ref(\pi,a,\zeta)$ is obtained from π by applying the following construction for each $e \in p^{-1}(\lambda^{-1}(a))$ (the order does not matter):

(i) drop e (and modify F,p accordingly)

(ii) if $\zeta(e)$ is a complete process of D,
create a copy of $\zeta(e)$, drop the Min and Max of it (corresponding to s_{in} and s_{out}),
replace the labelling $p^{\zeta(e)}$ of this copy by $p^e : x \longrightarrow < p^{\zeta(e)}(x), p(e) >$,
and connect the (unique) minimal event of the copy to the predecessor conditions of e and the (unique) maximal event of the copy to the successor conditions of e

(iii) if $\zeta(e)$ is not complete, create a copy of $\zeta(e)$, drop the Min of it (corresponding to s_{in}) and the successor conditions of e,
replace the labelling $p^{\zeta(e)}$ of this copy by $p^e : x \longrightarrow < p^{\zeta(e)}(x), p(e) >$,
and connect the (unique) minimal event of the copy to the predecessor conditions of e. ■ 4.9

Refined processes are processes of the refined system but the reverse is not true in general, as exhibited in Figure 2.

We will say that $ref(\Sigma,a,D)$ has refined processes iff $\forall \tilde{\pi} \in \Pi(ref(\Sigma,a,D)), \exists \pi \in \Pi(\Sigma)\ \exists \zeta$ such that $\tilde{\pi} = ref(\pi,a,\zeta)$ (up to isomorphism). In that case there is a kind of commutativity between the refinement operation and the operation of capturing the semantics through processes.

The central result about MP-bisimilarity is then :

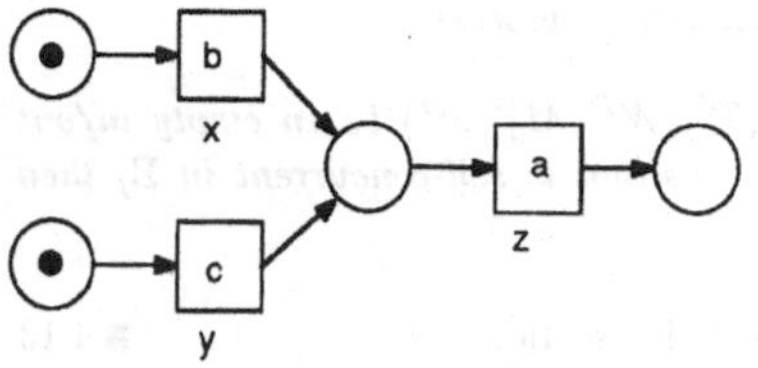

Σ

(i) a system to be refined

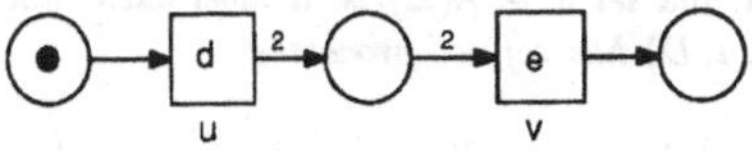

D

(ii) an in/out system

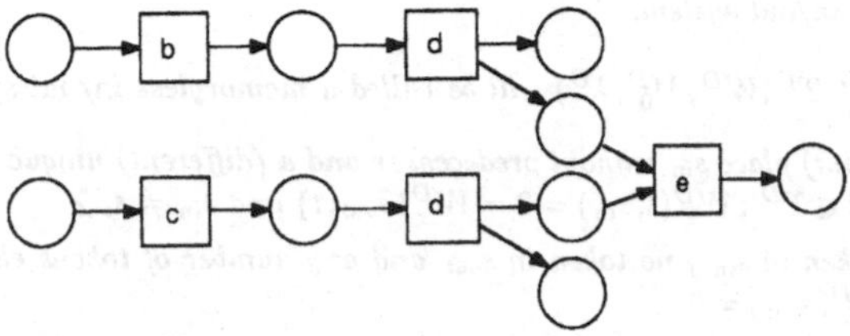

(iii) a process of $ref(\Sigma, a, D)$ which is not a refined process of Σ

Figure 2: Processes of a refined system are not always refined processes

Proposition 4.10 *Refinements with refined processes preserve MP-bisimilarity.*

If Σ_1 and Σ_2 are two labelled systems, $a \in \mathcal{A} \subseteq A$ and D is an empty in/out system such that $ref(\Sigma_1, a, D)$ and $ref(\Sigma_2, a, D)$ have refined processes, then

$$\Sigma_1 \approx_{\mathcal{A}MP} \Sigma_2 \Longrightarrow ref(\Sigma_1, a, D) \approx_{\mathcal{A}'MP} ref(\Sigma_1, a, D)$$

with $\mathcal{A}' = \mathcal{A} \setminus [A(\Sigma_1) \cap A(\Sigma_2)] \cup A$.
In particular, with $\mathcal{A} = A = \mathcal{A}'$, refinements with refined processes preserve MP-bisimilarity.

Proof: see [8]; look also at property 4.22 in the present paper. ■ 4.10

Definition 4.11 *SM-systems and refinements.*

An SM-system is an empty in/out system D such that
$\forall t \in T^D : |^\bullet t| = 1 = |t^\bullet|$ and $W^D(^\bullet t, t) = 1 = W^D(t, t^\bullet)$
i.e. D is essentially a state machine net.
An SM-refinement is a refinement through an SM-system. ■ 4.11

The main interest of SM-refinements for our concern here (besides the fact that relabellings, transition splittings and choices correspond to special cases of SM-refinements) is that :

Proposition 4.12 *SM-refinements have refined processes.*

If Σ_1 and Σ_2 are two labelled systems, $a \in \mathcal{A} \subseteq A$ and D is an SM-system, then $ref(\Sigma_1, a, D)$ and $ref(\Sigma_2, a, D)$ have refined processes, so that

$$\Sigma_1 \approx_{\mathcal{A}MP} \Sigma_2 \Longrightarrow ref(\Sigma_1, a, D) \approx_{\mathcal{A}'MP} ref(\Sigma_2, a, D)$$

with $\mathcal{A}' = \mathcal{A} \setminus [A(\Sigma_1) \cap A(\Sigma_2)] \cup A$.
In particular, with $\mathcal{A} = A = \mathcal{A}'$, SM-refinements preserve MP-bisimilarity.

Proof: see [8]. ■ 4.12

Another way to obtain refinements with refined processes is through self-concurrency freeness.

Proposition 4.13 *Empty refinements without selfconcurrency have refined processes.*

Let $\Sigma = (S, T, W, M_0, \lambda)$ be a labelled system , let $D = (S^D, T^D, W^D, M_0^D, \lambda^D)$ be an empty in/out system and let $a \in A(\Sigma)$ be a label such that no a-labelled transition is self-concurrent in Σ, then $ref(\Sigma, a, D)$ has refined processes

Proof: see [8], but we shall prove a more general result in the rest of this section. ■ 4.13

As mentioned in [8], the theory may be extended to a larger class of refinements. The theory is then technically slightly more complicated, but we shall do it explicitly here.

Definition 4.14 *Memoryless in/out system.*

A labelled system $D = (S^D, T^D, W^D, M_0^D, \lambda^D)$ will be called a memoryless in/out system iff

(i) there is a unique (input) place s_{in} without predecessor and a (different) unique (output) place s_{out} without successor: $\forall t \in T^D : W^D(t, s_{in}) = 0 = W^D(s_{out}, t)$ and $s_{in} \neq s_{out}$

(ii) initially there is a token in s_{in} , no token in s_{out} and any number of tokens elsewhere: $M_0^D(s_{in}) = 1$ and $M_0^D(s_{out}) = 0$.

(iii) any initial transition needs a token from s_{in} : $M_0^D[t\rangle \Longrightarrow s_{in} \in {}^\bullet t$

(iv) at the end, the initial marking is reproduced, except in s_{in} and s_{out} : $\forall M \in [M_0^D\rangle$, $M(s_{out}) \geq 1 \Longrightarrow M(s_{out}) = 1, M(s_{in}) = 0, \forall s \in S^D \setminus \{s_{in}, s_{out}\} : M(s) = M_0^D(s)$ ■ 4.14

Definition 4.15 *Memoryless refinement.*

Let $\Sigma = (S, T, W, M_0, \lambda)$ be a labelled system, let $a \in A(\Sigma)$ and let $D = (S^D, T^D, W^D, M_0^D, \lambda^D)$ be a memoryless in/out system. The refinement $ref(\Sigma, a, D)$ is the labelled system obtained from Σ by applying the following construction for each $t \in \lambda^{-1}(a)$ (the order does not matter, but the λ used here is the one of Σ and not the one constructed for $ref(\Sigma, a, D)$ below):

(i) drop t (and restrict W and λ accordingly)

(ii) create a copy of D without s_{in} and s_{out};
the new nodes will be called $< x, t >$ for $x \in S^D \cup T^D$;
W, M_0 and λ will be modified accordingly, i.e.
$\forall x, y \in S^D \cup T^D : W(< x, t >, < y, t >) = W^D(x, y)$, $\forall x \in T^D : \lambda(< x, t >) = \lambda^D(x)$
and $\forall x \in S^D \setminus \{s_{in}, s_{out}\} : M_0(< x, t >) = M_0^D(x)$

(iii) connect the successors of s_{in} to the predecessors of t and the predecessors of s_{out} to the successors of t:
$\forall x \in s_{in}^\bullet, \forall y \in {}^\bullet t : W(y, < x, t >) = W(y, t) \cdot W^D(s_{in}, x)$
$\forall x \in {}^\bullet s_{out}, \forall y \in t^\bullet : W(< x, t >, y) = W(t, y) \cdot W^D(x, s_{out})$

It may be noticed that, at the end, $\Sigma' = ref(\Sigma, a, D)$ will be a labelled system with $A(\Sigma') = A(\Sigma) \setminus \{a\} \cup A(D)$. ■ 4.15

We may notice that condition 4.14(iii) is essential in order to avoid the type of problem exhibited on Figure 3 (this example has also been analyzed in [4], for instance).

The memorylessness condition 4.14(iv) is also crucial, as shown in Figure 4 (this example was also considered in [24]).

We may also observe that, with respect to the definition of an empty in/out system and of an empty refinement, the extended definitions 4.14-4.15 relax another constraint since we no longer require that the arcs from s_{in} and to s_{out} have weight 1, and this is reflected in the weights of the connecting arcs in the refined system. However, this extension of the theory will not be really effective. Indeed, as memoryless

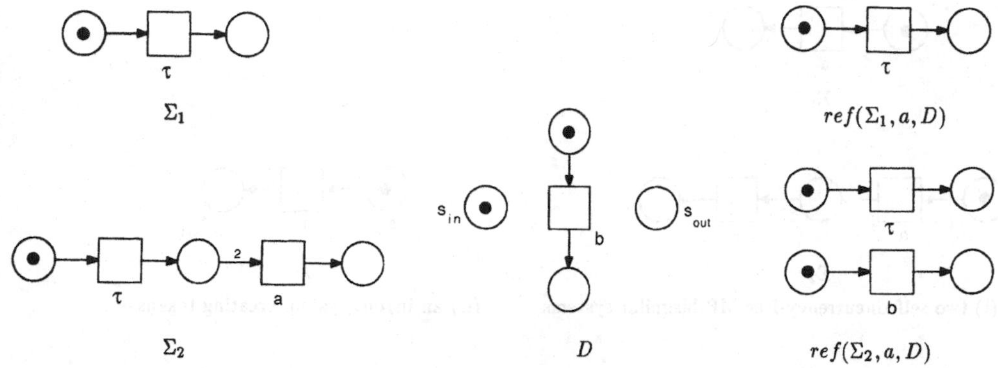

(i) two selfconcurrency-free MP-bisimilar systems

(ii) an in/out system without 4.14(iii)

(iii) the refinements are not even language equivalent

Figure 3: Trouble without condition 4.1(iii)

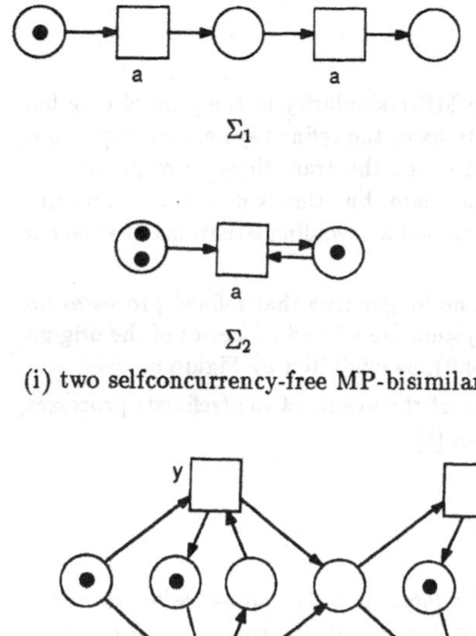

(i) two selfconcurrency-free MP-bisimilar systems

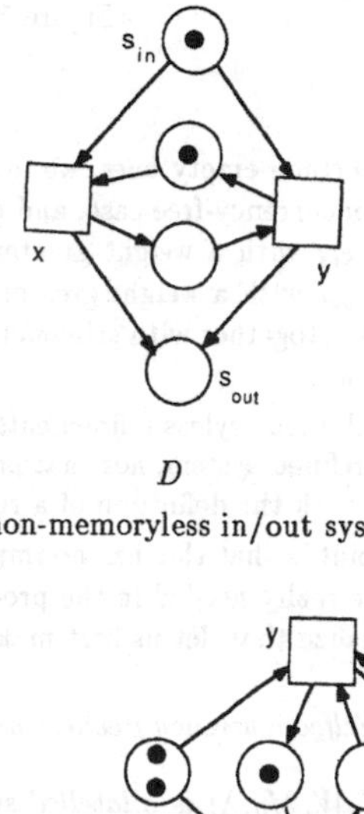

(ii) a non-memoryless in/out system

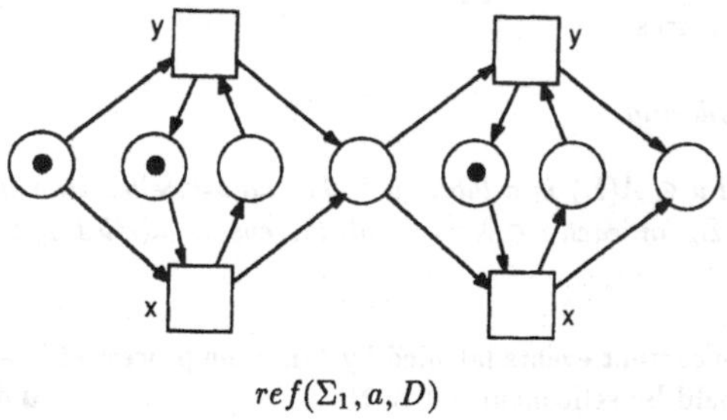

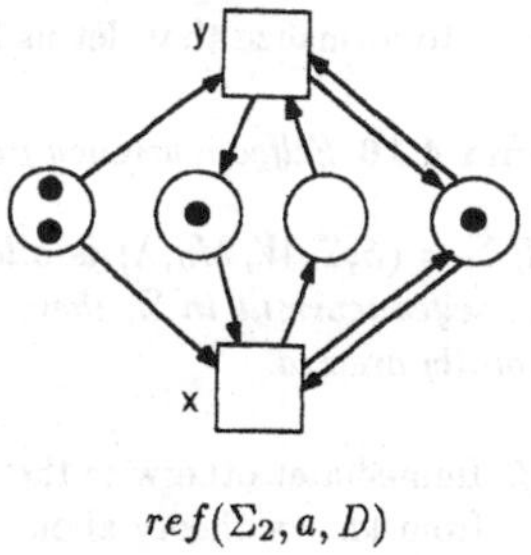

(iii) the refinements are not even language equivalent

Figure 4: Trouble without condition 4.1(iv)

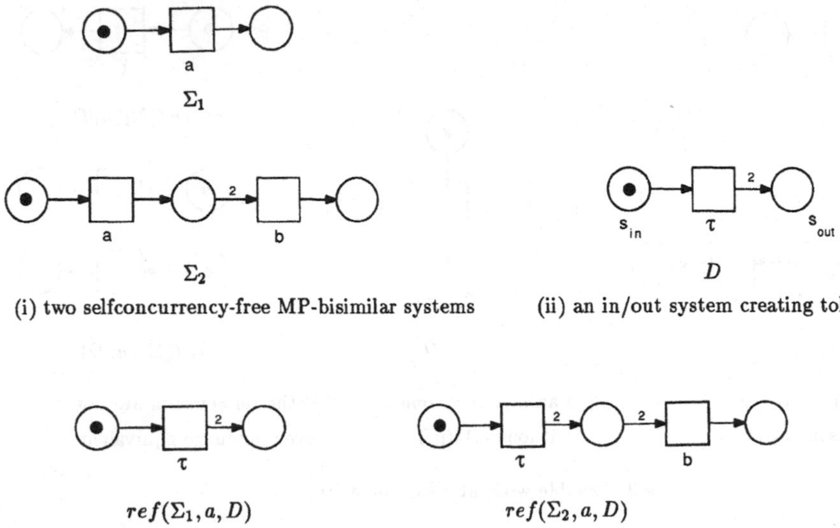

(i) two selfconcurrency-free MP-bisimilar systems

(ii) an in/out system creating tokens

$ref(\Sigma_1, a, D)$

$ref(\Sigma_2, a, D)$

(iii) the refinements are not even language equivalent

Figure 5: Trouble with token creation

in/out systems include empty ones, we may not hope to preserve MP-bisimilarity in the general case but only in the selfconcurrency-free case, and consequently the transitions in the refined system corresponding to successors of s_{in} with a weight greater than 1 will always be dead; the transitions corresponding to predecessors of s_{out} with a weight greater than 1 will also be dead here, but this is due to the condition on s_{out} in 4.14(iv) (together with selfconcurrency-freeness) and is aimed at avoiding situations like the one shown in Figure 5.
The problem with memoryless refinements is that, for them, it is no longer true that refined processes are processes of the refined system, nor that processes of the refined system are refined processes of the original system (at least with the definition of a refined process given in 4.9), as exhibited by Figure 6.
But the main point is that this has no impact on the partial order of the events of the (refined) processes, which is what we really needed in the proof of the central result of [8].
In order to formalize that, let us first make some remarks.

Lemma 4.16 *Selfconcurrency freeness and total ordering.*

If $\Sigma = (S, T, W, M_0, \lambda)$ is a labelled system and $a \in A(\Sigma)$ is a label such that no a-labelled transition is selfconcurrent in Σ, then, in any process of Σ, for each $t \in \lambda^{-1}(a)$, all the events labelled by t are totally ordered.

Proof: Immediate: otherwise there would be two concurrent events labelled by t in some process of Σ and, from known theory about processes [1], t would be selfconcurrent in Σ. ■ 4.16

Lemma 4.17 *Processes of a memoryless system.*

If $D = (S^D, T^D, W^D, M_0^D, \lambda^D)$ is a memoryless in/out system, then

(a) if π is a non initial process of D, there is a unique minimal event e, preceded by a unique condition c labelled by s_{in}, and they precede any other event in π;

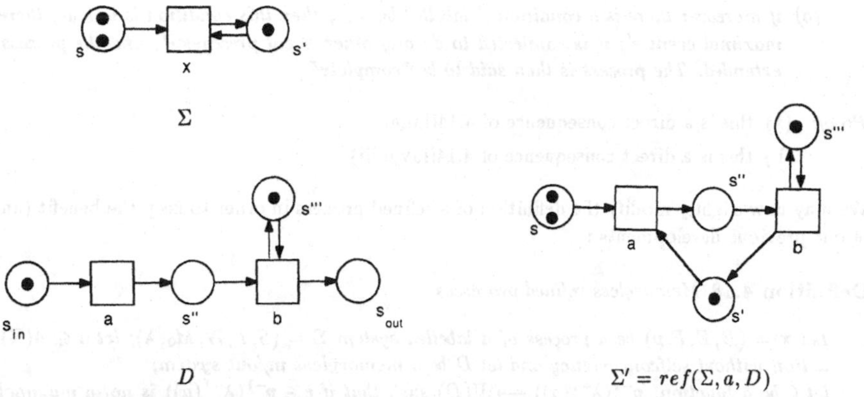

(i) a selfconcurrency-free system and a memoryless in/out system

(ii) the refined system

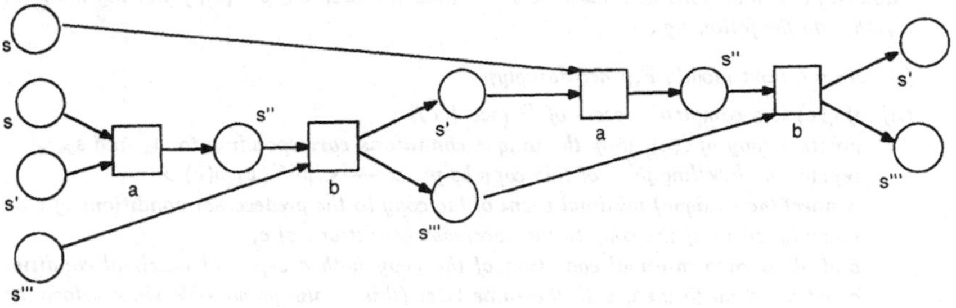

(iii) a process of Σ'

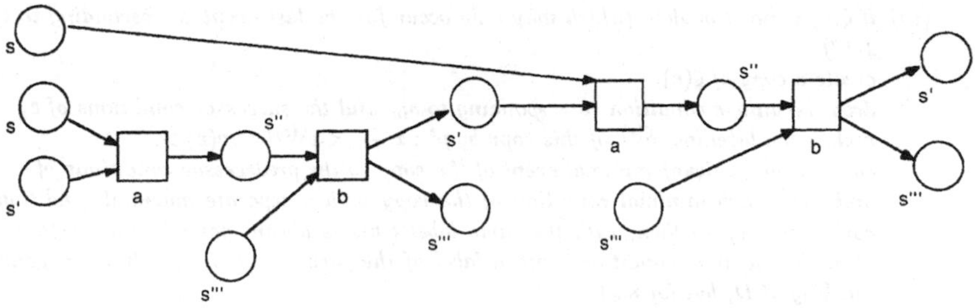

(iv) a refined process of Σ

Figure 6: Memoryless refinements and processes

(b) if moreover there is a condition c' labelled by s_{out}, then this condition is unique; there is a unique maximal event e'; it is connected to c'; any other event precedes e'; and the process may not be extended. The process is then said to be "complete".

Proof: (a) this is a direct consequence of 4.14(i,ii,iii)
(b) this is a direct consequence of 4.14(i,iv,ii,iii) ∎ 4.17

We may now slightly modify the definition of a refined process in order to keep the benefit (and the spirit) of our previous developments :

Definition 4.18 *Memoryless refined processes.*

Let $\pi = (B, E, F, p)$ be a process of a labelled system $\Sigma = (S, T, W, M_0, \lambda)$; let $a \in A(\Sigma)$ be a visible action without selfconcurrency and let D be a memoryless in/out system;
let ζ be a function: $p^{-1}(\lambda^{-1}(a)) \longrightarrow \Pi(D)$ such that if $e \in p^{-1}(\lambda^{-1}(a))$ is not a maximal event in π, then $\zeta(e)$ is a complete process of D; we will also suppose that $\zeta(e)$ is never the initial process of D.
Then $ref(\pi, a, \zeta)$ is the set of objects obtained from π by applying the following construction:
for each transition $t \in \lambda^{-1}(a)$ in Σ (the order does not matter) and for each $s \in S^D$,
add $M_0^D(s)$ conditions with labels $< s, t >$ and, for each $e \in p^{-1}(t)$, following their total order (see 4.16), do the following :

(i) drop e (and modify F,p accordingly)

(ii) if $\zeta(e)$ is a complete process of D (see 4.17) :
create a copy of $\zeta(e)$, drop the unique conditions corresponding to s_{in} and s_{out},
replace the labelling $p^{\zeta(e)}$ of this copy by $p^e : x \longrightarrow < p^{\zeta(e)}(x), p(e) >$,
connect the (unique) minimal event of the copy to the predecessor conditions of e and the (unique) maximal event of the copy to the successor conditions of e,
and blend each minimal condition of the copy with a separate maximal condition of the object constructed up to then, with the same label (this is always possible since before the refinement of each such e, the maximal conditions with a label of the form $< ., t >$ exactly correspond to the initial marking of D, but for s_{in});

(iii) if $\zeta(e)$ is not complete (which may only occur for the last event corresponding to t, see 4.16 and 4.17) :
create a copy of $\zeta(e)$,
drop the unique condition corresponding to s_{in} and the successor conditions of e,
replace the labelling $p^{\zeta(e)}$ of this copy by $p^e : x \longrightarrow < p^{\zeta(e)}(x), p(e) >$,
connect the (unique) minimal event of the copy to the predecessor conditions of e
and blend each minimal condition of the copy with a separate maximal condition of the object constructed up to then, with the same label (this is always possible since before the refinement of e, the maximal conditions with a label of the form $< ., t >$ exactly correspond to the initial marking of D, but for s_{in}) ∎ 4.18

It should be clear that any object in $ref(\pi, a, \zeta)$, which we shall call a refined process, is a process of the refined system $ref(\Sigma, a, D)$; it is not unique in general (since there may be various ways to realize the condition blending, except when M_0^D is 1-safe, i.e. if $M_0^D(s) \leq 1$ for each place s) but they all have the same associated partial order on their events as the one associated to the unique object (which is not a process of $ref(\Sigma, a, D)$, but of a system with the same structure and a larger initial marking) obtained by the following expansion procedure:

Definition 4.19 *Expanded process.*

Under the same assumptions as in definition 4.18, $exp(\pi, a, \zeta)$ is the object obtained by the same construction without the condition blending. ∎ 4.19

Proposition 4.20 *Refined processes of a same refinement have the same event partial order as the associated expanded process.*

Under the same assumptions as in 4.18, if $\tilde{\pi} \in ref(\pi, a, \zeta)$, then $\tilde{\pi}$ defines the same partial order on its events as $\tilde{\pi}' = exp(\pi, a, \zeta)$.

Proof: The property results from the following observation:
The differences concerning the partial orders on the events in $\tilde{\pi}$ and $\tilde{\pi}'$ arise from the fact that due to the condition blendings extra connections may be created between an event $\tilde{e}_2$ in the refinement of an event with a label $t \in \lambda^{-1}(a)$ in the original process π and an event $\tilde{e}_1$ in the refinement of a previous event with the same label t in π through some terminal condition, as shown schematically in Figure 7.

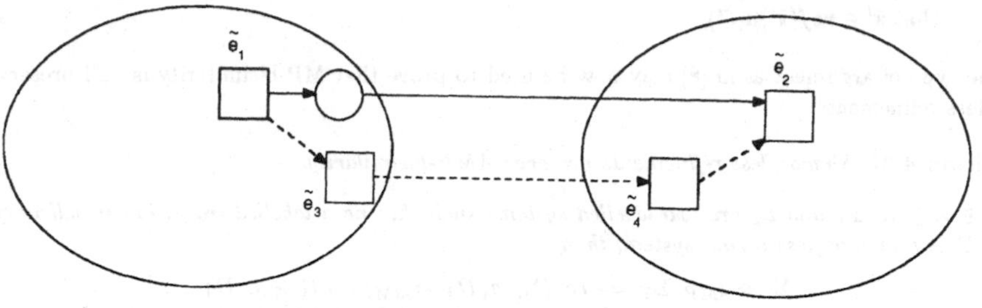

Figure 7: An extra connection in $\tilde{\pi}$

One may see that

- from 4.17(b), $\tilde{e}_1 \prec \tilde{e}_3$ where $\tilde{e}_3$ is the last event of the same sub-component as for $\tilde{e}_1$,
- from 4.17(a), $\tilde{e}_4 \prec \tilde{e}_2$ where $\tilde{e}_4$ is the first event of the same sub-component as for $\tilde{e}_2$,
- and, as the original system does not exhibit any selfconcurrency for a, $\tilde{e}_3 \prec \tilde{e}_4$ since this was the case for the corresponding events in π.

Consequently, the extra connection does not add anything to the partial ordering on the events associated with the non blended object, i.e. $\tilde{\pi}'$. ■ 4.20

Also, all the processes of the refined system are refined processes of the original net :

Proposition 4.21 *Processes of a refined system are refined processes.*

Let $\Sigma = (S, T, W, M_0, \lambda)$ be a labelled system, let $a \in A(\Sigma)$ be a visible action without selfconcurrency and let D be a memoryless in/out system;

$$\forall \tilde{\pi} \in \Pi(ref(\Sigma, a, D))\ \exists \pi \in \Pi(\Sigma)\ \exists \zeta : p^{-1}(\lambda^{-1}(a)) \longrightarrow \Pi(D) \text{ such that } \tilde{\pi} \in ref(\pi, a, \zeta).$$

Proof: Let us proceed by induction on the number of events in $\tilde{\pi}$.
The property is trivially true if $\tilde{\pi}$ is the initial process, i.e. if there is no event in $\tilde{\pi}$.
Let us assume that the property is true up to n events and let us add one more ($\tilde{\pi} \xrightarrow{\tilde{e}} \tilde{\pi}'$); various cases are possible:

- if the label of $\tilde{e}$ is not of the form $< t', t >$ with $t \in \lambda^{-1}(a)$ and $t' \in T^D$, then the same event may be connected the same way to π ($\pi \xrightarrow{\tilde{e}} \pi'$, since $\tilde{e}$ may not be connected to an incomplete subcomponent of $\tilde{\pi}$) and one clearly has that $\tilde{\pi}' \in ref(\pi', a, \zeta)$;

- if the label of $\tilde{e}$ is of the form $< t', t >$ with $t \in \lambda^{-1}(a)$ and $t' \in s_{in}^{\bullet}$, then $\tilde{e}$ needs $W(s_{in}, t')$ times the same tokens as t, plus as many other tokens from S^D as t' does; but then, the last process of D corresponding to t (if any) must be complete (otherwise in π it would be possible to add a t-labelled event in parallel to the last one, which would contradict the selfconcurrency freeness for a), $W(s_{in}, t') = 1$ (otherwise after π it would be possible to fire t twice, which would again contradict the selfconcurrency freeness for a) and all the available internal tokens exactly correspond to M_0^D (from the memoryless property) so that t' is a possible initial transition for D; a t-labelled event e may thus be connected to π (giving π') in a way similar to $\tilde{e}$ for $\tilde{\pi}$, one may extend ζ with an association $e \to \pi_{t'}$ (where $\pi_{t'}$ is the process of D with only one event labelled by t') giving a ζ' and we clearly have $\tilde{\pi}' \in ref(\tilde{\pi}', a, \zeta')$;
- if the label of $\tilde{e}$ is of the form $< t', t >$ with $t \in \lambda^{-1}(a)$ and $t' \in T^D \setminus s_{in}^{\bullet}$, since at the beginning of the last D-process corresponding in $\tilde{\pi}$ to the last t-labelled event e in π, there was exactly a set of maximal conditions with labels of the form $< ., t >$ corresponding to M_0^D, then $\tilde{e}$ simply extends this last D-process and that we may modify $\zeta(e)$ accordingly (giving ζ') so that $\tilde{\pi}' \in ref(\tilde{\pi}', a, \zeta')$. ■ 4.21

The same type of argument as in [8] may now be used to prove that MP-bisimilarity is still preserved by memoryless refinements.

Proposition 4.22 *Memoryless refinements preserve AMP-bisimilarity.*

If $a \in \mathcal{A} \subseteq A$, Σ_1 and Σ_2 are two labelled systems such that no a-labelled transition is selfconcurrent and D is a memoryless in/out system, then

$$\Sigma_1 \approx_{\mathcal{A}MP} \Sigma_2 \Longrightarrow ref(\Sigma_1, a, D) \approx_{\mathcal{A}'MP} ref(\Sigma_2, a, D)$$
$$\text{with } \mathcal{A}' = A \setminus [A(\Sigma_1) \cap A(\Sigma_2)] \cup \mathcal{A}$$

$$\Longrightarrow ref(\Sigma_1, a, D) \approx_{\mathcal{A}MP} ref(\Sigma_2, a, D).$$

Proof: see Appendix A.2. ■ 4.22

Corollary 4.23 *Memoryless refinements preserve MP-bisimilarity.*

If $a \in A$, Σ_1 and Σ_2 are two labelled systems such that no a-labelled transition is selfconcurrent and D is a memoryless in/out system, then

$$\Sigma_1 \approx_{MP} \Sigma_2 \Longrightarrow ref(\Sigma_1, a, D) \approx_{MP} ref(\Sigma_2, a, D).$$

Proof: Immediate from 4.22, with $\mathcal{A} = A = \mathcal{A}'$. ■ 4.23

One may also define refinements simultaneously for a set of visible actions:

Definition 4.24 *Simultaneous refinements.*

let $\Sigma = (S, T, W, M_0, \lambda)$ be a labelled system, let $\mathcal{R} \subseteq A$ be a set of visible actions, and let D be a function associating a memoryless in/out system D_a to each action $a \in \mathcal{R}$. The refinement $ref(\Sigma, \mathcal{R}, D)$ is the labelled system obtained from Σ by applying the refinement construction for each $a \in \mathcal{R}$ and each $t \in \lambda^{-1}(a)$. ■ 4.24

Clearly, $ref(\Sigma, a, D_a) = ref(\Sigma, \{a\}, D)$, but $ref(\Sigma, \mathcal{R}, D)$ may not always be obtained by an iterative use of single action refinements since, if $\mathcal{R} = \{a, b, ...\}$, it may happen that new b-labelled transitions are added in $ref(\Sigma, a, D_a)$ through D_a.
However, the same result may be obtained by relabelling first each D_a in such a way that $\forall a \in \mathcal{R}$: $A(D_a) \cap \mathcal{A} = \emptyset = A(D_a) \cap A(\Sigma)$ and $\forall b \in \mathcal{R} : b \neq a \Longrightarrow A(D_a) \cap A(D_b) = \emptyset$, then using successive single action refinements (in any order) and finally going back to the original labels.
Consequently we have :

Corollary 4.25 *MP-bisimilarity is preserved by simultaneous refinements.*

If Σ_1 and Σ_2 are two labelled systems, $\mathcal{R} \subseteq \mathcal{A} \subseteq A$ and D is a function mapping $\mathcal{R}$ to a family of memoryless in/out systems, then
if for any $a \in \mathcal{R}$ either $D(a)$ is an SM-system or no a-labelled transition in Σ_1 or Σ_2 is self-concurrent:

(a) $\Sigma_1 \approx_{\mathcal{A}MP} \Sigma_2 \Longrightarrow ref(\Sigma_1, \mathcal{R}, D) \approx_{\mathcal{A}'MP} ref(\Sigma_2, \mathcal{R}, D)$ *with* $\mathcal{A}' = A \setminus [A(\Sigma_1) \cap A(\Sigma_2)] \cup \mathcal{A}$
$\Longrightarrow ref(\Sigma_1, \mathcal{R}, D) \approx_{\mathcal{A}MP} ref(\Sigma_2, \mathcal{R}, D)$

(b) $\Sigma_1 \approx_{MP} \Sigma_2 \Longrightarrow ref(\Sigma_1, \mathcal{R}, D) \approx_{MP} ref(\Sigma_2, \mathcal{R}, D)$

(c) $\Sigma_1 \approx_{\mathcal{R}MP} \Sigma_2 \Longrightarrow ref(\Sigma_1, \mathcal{R}, D) \approx_{FC} ref(\Sigma_2, \mathcal{R}, D)$

Proof: Immediate from the above remark, the fact that relabellings are special cases of SM-refinements (for which MP-bisimilarity is always preserved), the fact that memoryless refinements do not modify selfconcurrency freeness of non-refined transitions (from 4.20 and 4.21), and the previous results. ■ 4.25

Corollary 4.26 *MP-bisimilarity is preserved for 1-safe systems.*

For 1-safe systems, $\mathcal{A}$MP-bisimilarity is preserved by simultaneous memoryless refinements, i.e., if Σ_1 and Σ_2 are two 1-safe labelled systems, $\mathcal{R} \subseteq \mathcal{A} \subseteq A$ and D is a function mapping $\mathcal{R}$ to a family of memoryless in/out systems, then
$\Sigma_1 \approx_{\mathcal{A}MP} \Sigma_2 \Longrightarrow ref(\Sigma_1, \mathcal{R}, D) \approx_{\mathcal{A}'MP} ref(\Sigma_2, \mathcal{R}, D)$ *with* $\mathcal{A}' = A \setminus [A(\Sigma_1) \cap A(\Sigma_2)] \cup \mathcal{A}$
$\Longrightarrow ref(\Sigma_1, \mathcal{R}, D) \approx_{\mathcal{A}MP} ref(\Sigma_2, \mathcal{R}, D)$.

Proof: Immediate from 4.25, since there is no selfconcurrency in 1-safe systems. ■ 4.26

4.3 A Simpler Characterization and the Optimality Result

Checking MP-bisimilarity through 4.3 or 4.5 may be a huge task, still more intricate than checking FC-bisimilarity. Fortunately, it is possible to simplify considerably the problem by using a very simple characteristic SM-refinement :

Proposition 4.27 *Split characterization of MP-bisimilarity.*

Let $\mathcal{A} \subseteq A$ be a subset of visible actions and for any $a \in \mathcal{A}$ let

$split(a) =$ 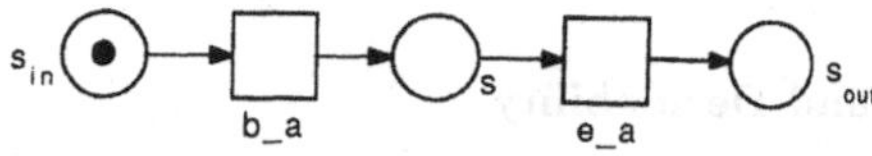

Let Σ_1 and Σ_2 be two labelled systems such that $\cup_{a \in \mathcal{A}}\{b\_a, e\_a\} \subseteq A \setminus [A(\Sigma_1) \cup A(\Sigma_2)]$, then

$$\Sigma_1 \approx_{\mathcal{A}MP} \Sigma_2 \Longleftrightarrow ref(\Sigma_1, \mathcal{A}, split) \approx_{FC} ref(\Sigma_2, \mathcal{A}, split)$$

i.e. one simply has to split each a-labelled transition, for $a \in \mathcal{A}$, and check fully concurrent bisimilarity.

Proof: see Appendix A.3. ■ 4.27

Corollary 4.28 *Optimality result.*

$\mathcal{A}MP$-bisimilarity is the coarsest equivalence relation on the class of labelled P/T systems which is preserved by SM-refinements of $\mathcal{A}$-labelled transitions (and memoryless in/out refinements of non-selfconcurrent $\mathcal{A}$-labelled transitions) which implies FC-bisimilarity.

Proof: We already know from 4.25 that

$$\begin{aligned}\Sigma_1 \approx_{\mathcal{A}MP} \Sigma_2 &\Longrightarrow ref(\Sigma_1,\mathcal{A},D) \approx_{\mathcal{A}'MP} ref(\Sigma_2,\mathcal{A},D) \text{ for some } \mathcal{A}' \supseteq \mathcal{A}\\ &\quad\text{and for any family } D \text{ of refinements as specified}\\ &\Longrightarrow ref(\Sigma_1,\mathcal{A},D) \approx_{\mathcal{A}MP} ref(\Sigma_2,\mathcal{A},D)\end{aligned}$$

Conversely, if $\sim$ is a congruence as specified, then

$$\begin{aligned}\Sigma_1 \sim \Sigma_2 &\Longrightarrow ref(\Sigma_1,\mathcal{A},split) \sim ref(\Sigma_2,\mathcal{A},split) && \text{since } \sim \text{ is preserved by refinements}\\ &\Longrightarrow ref(\Sigma_1,\mathcal{A},split) \approx_{FC} ref(\Sigma_2,\mathcal{A},split) && \text{since } \sim \text{ implies } \approx_{FC}\\ &\Longrightarrow \Sigma_1 \approx_{\mathcal{A}MP} \Sigma_2 && \text{from 4.27.}\end{aligned}$$

■ 4.28

This generalizes a result obtained by W.Vogler in [25], for labelled prime event structures and under an image finiteness constraint.
As another consequence of our result, we get

Corollary 4.29 *Split in two implies split in n.*

If two systems are FC-bisimilar after splitting each $\mathcal{A}$-labelled transition into two parts, then they will still be FC-bisimilar after splitting them into any number of parts.

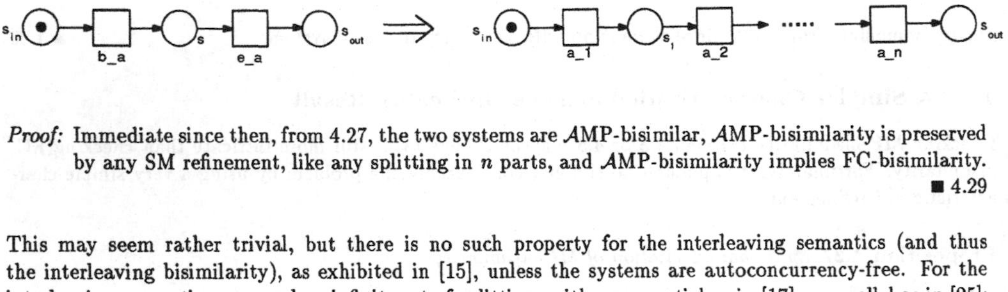

Proof: Immediate since then, from 4.27, the two systems are $\mathcal{A}$MP-bisimilar, $\mathcal{A}$MP-bisimilarity is preserved by any SM refinement, like any splitting in n parts, and $\mathcal{A}$MP-bisimilarity implies FC-bisimilarity.

■ 4.29

This may seem rather trivial, but there is no such property for the interleaving semantics (and thus the interleaving bisimilarity), as exhibited in [15], unless the systems are autoconcurrency-free. For the interleaving semantics, we need an infinite set of splittings, either sequential as in [17] or parallel as in [25]; this will be addressed in section 5.4.

4.4 Ordered Markings and Decidability

Property 4.27 reduces the problem of checking $\mathcal{A}$MP-bisimilarity to the one for fully concurrent bisimilarity. However, the definition of the latter relies on the processes of the system, and for live or reactive systems they constitute an infinite set, often with a complex structure.
A common way to overcome this type of difficulty is to (try to) find a characterization of the involved notion in terms of reachable markings, since most of the nets which actually occur in real systems are bounded, or even 1-safe.
W.Vogler devised such a characterization in [27] for the practically important class of 1-safe systems (improving an earlier result already presented in [25] for 1-safe systems without silent moves). Let us summarize these results here (with some reformulations).

Definition 4.30 *Generalized ordered markings.*

If $\Sigma = (S,T,W,M_0,\lambda)$ is a 1-safe labelled system, a generalized ordered marking of Σ is a labelled acyclic graph $G = (X,F,l)$,
where X is the node set,
$F \subseteq X \times X$ is the arc set,
$l : X \longrightarrow S \cup T$ is the labelling function
such that
(i) $l \mid_{Max(X)}$ is injective into S
(ii) $\forall c \in Max(X) : l \mid_{^\bullet c}$ is injective into $\lambda^{-1}(A)$
(iii) $X = Max(X) \cup {}^\bullet Max(X)$. ■ 4.30

As usual, $\forall Y \subseteq X, {}^\bullet Y = \{z \in X \mid \exists y \in Y : (z,y) \in F\}$, so that ${}^\bullet X$ is the subset of all the non-maximal nodes, and $Max(X) = X \setminus {}^\bullet X$ denotes the set of maximal elements of X.
Intuitively, a generalized ordered marking will correspond to a part of the labelled partial order defined by a process π of Σ : $\max(X) = Max(\pi)$ will correspond to the 1-safe marking reached after π and $\forall c \in Max(X)$, ${}^\bullet c$ will correspond to the visible events of π which are predecessors of c and which are maximal for this criterion. Figure 8 illustrates this remark.

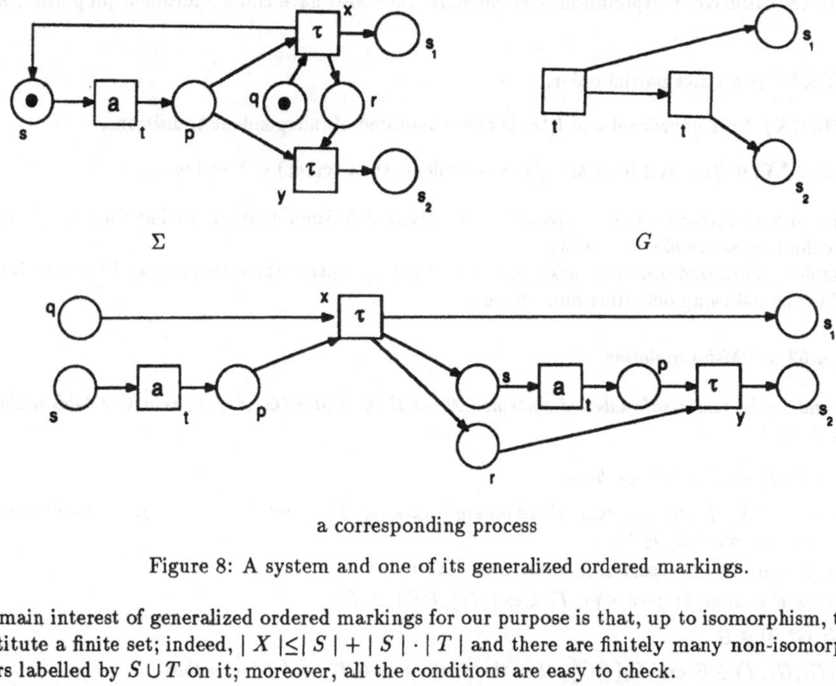

Figure 8: A system and one of its generalized ordered markings.

The main interest of generalized ordered markings for our purpose is that, up to isomorphism, they always constitute a finite set; indeed, $\mid X \mid \leq \mid S \mid + \mid S \mid \cdot \mid T \mid$ and there are finitely many non-isomorphic partial orders labelled by $S \cup T$ on it; moreover, all the conditions are easy to check.
In fact, we are not really interested in all the generalized ordered markings we defined, but only in the "reachable ones" , i.e. the ones exactly corresponding to the intuitive interpretation given above; this depends on the (often infinite set of) processes, but it is possible to define equivalently the reachability notion in another (feasible) way :

Definition 4.31 *Reachable generalized ordered markings.*

(i) $G^o = (M_0, \emptyset, id)$ is the initial generalized ordered marking
where we identified as usual the 1-safe marking M_0 with its supporting places;
id is the identity function.

(ii) *if G is a generalized ordered marking of Σ and $t \in T$ is any transition, we will write $G \xrightarrow{t} G'$ or $G[t\rangle G'$, and say that G' is reached from G through the occurrence of t, iff* [2]

- $^\bullet t \subseteq Max(X)$
- $X' = M' \cup \bigcup_{x \in M'} pred(x)$ *with* $M' = (Max(X) \setminus {}^\bullet t) \cup t^\bullet$ *and*
  $\forall c \in Max(X) \setminus {}^\bullet t : pred(c) = {}^\bullet c$
  $\forall c \in t^\bullet$, *if* $\lambda(t) = \tau$ *then* $pred(c) = Max({}^\bullet C)$ *with* $C = {}^\bullet t$
  otherwise $pred(c) = \{e\}$ *where e is a newly created node*
- $\forall x \in X'$, $l'(x) = x$ *if* $x \in t^\bullet$
  $l(x)$ *if* $x \in X$
  t *if* $x = e$ *(thus if* $\lambda(t) \in A$*)*
- *if* $\lambda(t) = \tau$, *then* $F' = \bigcup_{x \in M'} \bigcup_{y \in pred(x)} \{(y,x)\} \cup [F \cap (X' \setminus M') \times (X' \setminus M')]$
  otherwise $F' = \bigcup_{x \in M'} \bigcup_{y \in pred(x)} \{(y,x)\} \cup [\tilde{F} \cap (X' \setminus M') \times (X' \setminus M')]$
  where $\tilde{F} = F \cup \{(e', e) \mid e' \in X$ *and* $\exists s \in {}^\bullet t : (e', s) \in F^*\}$

(iii) *as usual, G is a reachable generalized ordered marking iff there is some $\sigma \in T^*$ such that $G^\circ \xrightarrow{\sigma} G$*

■ 4.31

It may be checked that the reachable generalized ordered markings are exactly the ones which indeed correspond to the intuitive interpretation; consequently, they also have some additional properties, such as:

- $F \cap {}^\bullet X \times {}^\bullet X$ is a strict partial order,
- $\forall c \in Max(X)$, ${}^\bullet c$ is unordered and $l({}^\bullet c)$ is only composed of independent transitions,
- $\forall e_1 \neq e_2 \in {}^\bullet X$, if $l(e_1)$ and $l(e_2)$ are not independent, then $(e_1, e_2) \in F$ or $(e_2, e_1) \in F$.

In fact, we could have introduced these properties directly in definition 4.30 but we left them out in order to keep the definition as simple as possible.
Now, (reachable) generalized ordered markings may be used to capture the essence of an FC-bisimulation, as exhibited in the following definition and property.

Definition 4.32 *GOM-bisimulation.*

Let Σ_1 and Σ_2 be two 1-safe labelled systems. A set $\mathcal{B}$ of triples (G_1, G_2, f) is a GOM-bisimulation between them if :

(i) *for all $(G_1, G_2, f) \in \mathcal{B}$, we have*
- *$G_1 = (X_1, F_1, l_1)$ is a generalized ordered marking of Σ_1 and $G_2 = (X_2, F_2, l_2)$ is a generalized ordered marking of Σ_2,*
- *f is an injective partial function from ${}^\bullet X_1$ to ${}^\bullet X_2$,*
- $\forall e, e' \in dom(f) : (e, e') \in F_1 \iff (f(e), f(e')) \in F_2$.

(ii) $(G_1^\circ, G_2^\circ, \emptyset) \in \mathcal{B}$

(iii) *if $(G_1, G_2, f) \in \mathcal{B}$ and $G_1[t\rangle G_1'$, then there exists $\sigma_2 \in T_2^*$ and f' such that*
   (a) $\bar{\lambda}_1(t) = \bar{\lambda}_2(\sigma_2)$,
   (b) $G_2[\sigma_2\rangle G_2'$ *and* $(G_1', G_2', f') \in \mathcal{B}$,
   (c) *if* $\lambda_1(t) = \tau$, *then* $f' = f \cap (X_1' \times X_2')$,
   (d) *if* $\lambda_1(t) = \lambda_2(t') \in A$ *and* $\sigma_2 = \sigma' t' \sigma''$ *with* $G_2[\sigma'\rangle G'[t'\sigma''\rangle G_2'$, *then*
   - *if* $Q = \bigcup_{s \in {}^\bullet t} l_1^{-1}(s)$ *in* G_1 *and* $Q' = \bigcup_{s \in {}^\bullet t'} l'^{-1}(s)$ *in* G',
     f is defined on $P = Max({}^\bullet Q)$ *and* $f(P) = Max({}^\bullet Q')$,

[2] in the rest of the section, $^\bullet$ will refer to the structure of Σ when applied to t, and to the graph G otherwise.

- *if e is the new event labelled by t in G_1' and e' is the new event labelled by t' in G_2', $f' = \{(e,e')\} \cup (f \cap X_1' \times X_2')$.*

(iv) Vice versa.

■ 4.32

It may be observed that, in the previous definition, we may also avoid any redundant evolution, i.e. if $\lambda_1(t) = \tau$ we may constrain σ_2 in such a way that it never produces twice the same generalized ordered marking, and if $\lambda(t) \in A$ the same is true separately for σ' and σ''.

Proposition 4.33 *Fully concurrent bisimilarity and GOM-bisimulation.*

Two 1-safe labelled systems are FC-bisimilar iff there is a GOM-bisimulation between them.

Proof: See [27]. ■ 4.33

And as a consequence

Corollary 4.34 *Decidability of AMP-bisimilarity.*

For finite 1-safe systems, FC-bisimilarity and AMP-bisimilarity are decidable.

Proof: See [27] and the above remarks. ■ 4.34

5 Strengthening Interleaving Bisimilarity

As noticed by W.Vogler, it is not necessary to start from a strong bisimilarity notion (like the fully concurrent one) to get interesting results, and in particular to get preservation properties through refinements. At the other end (W.Vogler also considered intermediate cases in [25], like the pomset bisimilarity and the partial word bisimilarity, which lead to interesting but, up to now, slightly less extended results, and the step bisimilarity which leads to the same ST-strengthening as the interleaving bisimilarity; consequently, and in order not to make the presentation uselessly lengthy, we shall not develop these cases here), we may start from the most permissive one, i.e. the usual (interleaving) bisimilarity, which is defined in net theory as (see [20]) :

Definition 5.1 *Interleaving bisimilarity.*

If $\Sigma_1 = (S_1, T_1, W_1, M_1^0, \lambda_1)$ and $\Sigma_2 = (S_2, T_2, W_2, M_2^0, \lambda_2)$ are two labelled systems, $\Sigma_1 \approx_i \Sigma_2$ iff there is a relation $\mu \subseteq [\,M_1^0\rangle \times [\,M_2^0\rangle$ with the following properties:

(i) $(M_1^0, M_2^0) \in \mu$

(ii) $\forall (M_1, M_2) \in \mu$

(a) if $M_1[\sigma_1\rangle M_1'$, there is $M_2[\sigma_2\rangle M_2'$ such that $\bar{\lambda}_1(\sigma_1) = \bar{\lambda}_2(\sigma_2)$ and $(M_1', M_2') \in \mu$

(b) Vice versa.

The two systems are then said to be (sequentially or interleaving) bisimilar, and μ is an interleaving bisimulation between them. ■ 5.1

This definition is based on the reachable markings of the systems, but in order to apply the strengthenings we introduced in Chapter 3 we need to use a process-oriented one. Fortunately, interleaving bisimilarity may also be characterized from processes instead of from markings (see also [25]).

Proposition 5.2 *Process characterization of interleaving bisimilarity.*

If Σ_1 and Σ_2 are two labelled systems, $\Sigma_1 \approx_i \Sigma_2$ iff there is a set $\mathcal{B} \subseteq \{(\pi_1, \pi_2, \beta) \mid \pi_1 \in \Pi(\Sigma_1), \pi_2 \in \Pi(\Sigma_2), \beta$ is a relation between the visible events of π_1 and $\pi_2\}$ with the following properties :

(i) $(\pi_1^\circ, \pi_2^\circ, \emptyset) \in \mathcal{B}$, *where π_1° and π_2° are the initial processes of Σ_1 and Σ_2, respectively*

(ii) $(\pi_1, \pi_2, \beta) \in \mathcal{B} \Longrightarrow \beta$ *is a label preserving bijection*

(iii) $\forall (\pi_1, \pi_2, \beta) \in \mathcal{B}$

(a) if π_1' is an extension of π_1 ,
there is some $(\pi_1', \pi_2', \beta') \in \mathcal{B}$ where π_2' is an extension of π_2 and $\beta \subseteq \beta'$;

(b) Vice versa.

Proof: $\Longrightarrow$

if $\Sigma_1 \approx_i \Sigma_2$ and μ is an interleaving bisimulation between them, let $\mathcal{B} = \{(\pi_1, \pi_2, \beta) \mid \beta$ is a label preserving bijection between the visible events of π_1 and π_2, π_1 leads to a marking M_1, π_2 leads to a marking M_2 and $(M_1, M_2) \in \mu\}$;
it is now rather easy to check that $\mathcal{B}$ fullfills all the conditions of the theorem;

$\Longleftarrow$

if $\mathcal{B}$ fulfills all the above properties, let $\mu = \{(M_1, M_2) \mid \exists (\pi_1, \pi_2, \beta) \in \mathcal{B}$ such that π_1 leads to M_1 and π_2 leads to $M_2\}$;
it is now rather easy to check that μ is an interleaving bisimulation. ■ 5.2

Again, it may be observed that slightly simpler characterizations may be obtained by only considering extensions with one transition or one event on the left hand side of conditions (iii)(a) in 5.1 and 5.2. Again also, it may be argued that such a characterization is not acceptable from a strict (interleaving) observational point of view but, besides the fact that (as we already said) we never advertised that we shall stick to such an approach, we will come back to it in section 5.3.

5.1 Equivalent Strengthenings

Following the same manner of proceeding as in section 4.1, we may define

Definition 5.3 *AiMP-bisimilarity.*

If Σ_1 and Σ_2 are two labelled systems and $\mathcal{A} \subseteq A$ is a subset of visible actions, $\Sigma_1 \approx_{\mathcal{A}iMP} \Sigma_2$ iff there is a set $\mathcal{B} \subseteq \{(\pi_1, \pi_2, \beta) \mid \pi_1 \in \Pi(\Sigma_1), \pi_2 \in \Pi(\Sigma_2), \beta$ is a relation between the visible events of π_1 and $\pi_2\}$ with the following properties :

(i) $(\pi_1^\circ, \pi_2^\circ, \emptyset) \in \mathcal{B}$, *where π_1° and π_2° are the initial processes of Σ_1 and Σ_2, respectively.*

(ii) $(\pi_1, \pi_2, \beta) \in \mathcal{B} \Longrightarrow \beta$ *is a label preserving bijection.*

(iii) $\forall (\pi_1, \pi_2, \beta) \in \mathcal{B}$

(a) if π_1' is an extension of π_1,
then there is some $(\pi_1', \pi_2', \beta') \in \mathcal{B}$ where π_2' is an extension of π_2 and $\beta \subseteq \beta'$;
moreover,

- *if $e_1' \in E_1' \setminus E_1$, $\lambda_1(p_1'(e_1')) \in \mathcal{A}$ and e_1' is a maximal event in π_1', then $\beta'(e_1')$ is also a maximal event, of π_2'*
- *for any event e_1 of π_1, if $\lambda_1(p_1(e_1)) \in \mathcal{A}$ and if e_1 and $\beta(e_1)$ are maximal events in π_1' and π_2, respectively, then $\beta(e_1)$ is still a maximal event in π_2'.*

(b) Vice versa.

Σ_1 and Σ_2 will then be said $\mathcal{A}$iMP-bisimilar, and $\mathcal{B}$ is an $\mathcal{A}$iMP-bisimulation between them.
As usual, if $\mathcal{A} = A$ they will simply be said iMP-bisimilar. ■ 5.3

Or, equivalently,

Proposition 5.4 *AiMP-bisimilarity and single extensions.*

If Σ_1 and Σ_2 are two labelled systems and $\mathcal{A} \subseteq A$ is a subset of visible actions, $\Sigma_1 \approx_{\mathcal{A}iMP} \Sigma_2$ iff there is a set $\mathcal{B} \subseteq \{(\pi_1, \pi_2, \beta) \mid \pi_1 \in \Pi(\Sigma_1), \pi_2 \in \Pi(\Sigma_2), \beta$ is a relation between the visible events of π_1 and $\pi_2\}$ with the following properties :

(i) $(\pi_1^\circ, \pi_2^\circ, \emptyset) \in \mathcal{B}$, *where π_1° and π_2° are the initial processes of Σ_1 and Σ_2, respectively.*

(ii) $(\pi_1, \pi_2, \beta) \in \mathcal{B} \Longrightarrow \beta$ *is a label preserving bijection.*

(iii) $\forall (\pi_1, \pi_2, \beta) \in \mathcal{B}$

(a) if π_1' is an extension of π_1 with only one event e_1' more, there is some $(\pi_1', \pi_2', \beta') \in \mathcal{B}$ where π_2' is an extension of π_2 and $\beta \subseteq \beta'$; moreover,

- *if $\lambda_1(p_1'(e_1')) \in \mathcal{A}$, then $\beta'(e_1')$ is a maximal event of π_2',*
- *for any event e_1 of π_1, if $\lambda_1(p_1(e_1)) \in \mathcal{A}$ and if e_1 and $\beta(e_1)$ are maximal events in π_1' and π_2, respectively, then $\beta(e_1)$ is still a maximal event in π_2'.*

(b) Vice versa.

Proof: Same argument as for 4.3. ■ 5.4

Again, we may observe that

- $\approx_i = \approx_{\emptyset iMP}$
- if $\mathcal{A}' \subset \mathcal{A} \subseteq A$, then $\approx_{\mathcal{A}iMP}$ is stronger than $\approx_{\mathcal{A}'iMP}$
- and, in particular, $\mathcal{A}$iMP-bisimilarity is stronger than interleaving bisimilarity.

A comparison of the definitions 5.3 and 4.2 shows that $\mathcal{A}$iMP-bisimilarity is weaker than $\mathcal{A}$MP-bisimilarity; the fact that it is strictly weaker results, for instance, from the example depicted in Figure 9.

Figure 9: Two $\mathcal{A}$iMP-bisimilar systems which are not $\mathcal{A}$MP-bisimilar

Now, let us apply the ST-idea to the interleaving bisimilarity :

Definition 5.5 *AiST-bisimilarity*

If Σ_1 and Σ_2 are two labelled systems and $\mathcal{A} \subseteq A$ is a subset of visible actions, $\Sigma_1 \approx_{\mathcal{A}iST} \Sigma_2$ iff there is a set $\mathcal{B} \subseteq \{((\pi_1, \mathcal{E}_1), (\pi_2, \mathcal{E}_2), \beta) \mid (\pi_1, \mathcal{E}_1)$ is an $\mathcal{A}ST$-configuration of Σ_1, $(\pi_2, \mathcal{E}_2)$ is an $\mathcal{A}ST$-configuration of Σ_2, β is a relation between the visible events of π_1 and $\pi_2\}$ with the following properties:

(i) $((\pi_1^\circ, \emptyset), (\pi_2^\circ, \emptyset), \emptyset) \in \mathcal{B}$, *where π_1° and π_2° are the initial processes of Σ_1 and Σ_2, respectively.*

(ii) $((\pi_1, \mathcal{E}_1), (\pi_2, \mathcal{E}_2), \beta) \in \mathcal{B} \Longrightarrow \beta$ *is a label preserving bijection and* $\beta(\mathcal{E}_1) = \mathcal{E}_2$.

(iii) $\forall ((\pi_1, \mathcal{E}_1), (\pi_2, \mathcal{E}_2), \beta) \in \mathcal{B}$

(a) *if* $(\pi_1, \mathcal{E}_1) \longrightarrow (\pi_1', \mathcal{E}_1')$,
there is some $((\pi_1', \mathcal{E}_1'), (\pi_2', \mathcal{E}_2'), \beta') \in \mathcal{B}$ *where* $(\pi_2, \mathcal{E}_2) \longrightarrow (\pi_2', \mathcal{E}_2')$ *and* $\beta \subseteq \beta'$.

(b) *Vice versa.*

Σ_1 *and* Σ_2 *are then said to be AiST-bisimilar, and* $\mathcal{B}$ *is an AiST-bisimulation between them.* ■ 5.5

The same argument as above may be used to show that the use of simple extensions would lead to the same equivalence notion, with a characterization slightly longer but easier to be checked :

Proposition 5.6 *AiST bisimilarity and simple extensions.*

If Σ_1 *and* Σ_2 *are two labelled systems and* $\mathcal{A} \subseteq A$ *is a subset of visible actions,* $\Sigma_1 \approx_{\mathcal{A}iST} \Sigma_2$ *iff there is a set* $\mathcal{B} \subseteq \{((\pi_1, \mathcal{E}_1), (\pi_2, \mathcal{E}_2), \beta) \mid (\pi_1, \mathcal{E}_1)$ *is an AST-configuration of* Σ_1, $(\pi_2, \mathcal{E}_2)$ *is an AST-configuration of* Σ_2, β *is a relation between the visible events of* π_1 *and* $\pi_2\}$ *with the following properties:*

(i) $((\pi_1^\circ, \emptyset), (\pi_2^\circ, \emptyset), \emptyset) \in \mathcal{B}$, *where* π_1° *and* π_2° *are the initial processes of* Σ_1 *and* Σ_2, *respectively.*

(ii) $((\pi_1, \mathcal{E}_1), (\pi_2, \mathcal{E}_2), \beta) \in \mathcal{B} \Longrightarrow \beta$ *is a label preserving bijection and* $\beta(\mathcal{E}_1) = \mathcal{E}_2$.

(iii) $\forall ((\pi_1, \mathcal{E}_1), (\pi_2, \mathcal{E}_2), \beta) \in \mathcal{B}$

(a) *if* $(\pi_1, \mathcal{E}_1) \longrightarrow (\pi_1', \mathcal{E}_1')$ *with either* $\pi_1 = \pi_1'$ *and* $\mathcal{E}_1'$ *exhibits only one event less than* $\mathcal{E}_1$
or π_1' *exhibits only one event more than* π_1,
it is not finally labelled in $\mathcal{A}$ *and* $\mathcal{E}_1 = \mathcal{E}_1'$
or π_1' *exhibits only one event more than* π_1, *it is finally labelled in* $\mathcal{A}$ *and* $\mathcal{E}_1'$ *is* $\mathcal{E}_1$ *augmented by this single event,*
there is some $((\pi_1', \mathcal{E}_1'), (\pi_2', \mathcal{E}_2'), \beta') \in \mathcal{B}$ *where* $(\pi_2, \mathcal{E}_2) \longrightarrow (\pi_2', \mathcal{E}_2')$ *and* $\beta \subseteq \beta'$.

(b) *Vice versa.*

Proof: Same argument as for 4.5. ■ 5.6

Now, the main property of this section (slightly extending a similar result in [25]) is :

Proposition 5.7 *Equivalence of iMP and iST strengthenings*

$\forall \mathcal{A} \subseteq A \ : \approx_{\mathcal{A}iMP} = \approx_{\mathcal{A}iST}$

Proof: The proof is very similar to the one for 4.6: see [10]. ■ 5.7

5.2 Preservation through Refinements

We may now extend the bisimilarity preservation property to our framework. The preservation of iST-bisimilarity under refinements was first exhibited in [25] for prime event structures, generalizing a similar result without silent moves in [11]. An immediate translation (and a slight extension) then leads to :

Proposition 5.8 *Memoryless refinements preserve AiMP-bisimilarity.*

If $a \in \mathcal{A} \subseteq A$, Σ_1 *and* Σ_2 *are two labelled systems such that no a-labelled transition is selfconcurrent and D is a memoryless in/out system, then*

$$\Sigma_1 \approx_{\mathcal{A}iMP} \Sigma_2 \Longrightarrow ref(\Sigma_1, a, D) \approx_{\mathcal{A}'iMP} ref(\Sigma_2, a, D)$$
$$\text{with } \mathcal{A}' = A \setminus [A(\Sigma_1) \cap A(\Sigma_2)] \cup \mathcal{A}$$
$$\Longrightarrow ref(\Sigma_1, a, D) \approx_{\mathcal{A}iMP} ref(\Sigma_2, a, D).$$

Proof: The proof is very similar to the one for 4.22; the main difference is that here β and $\tilde{\beta}$ are only label preserving bijections, and not necessarily order isomorphisms: see [10]. ■ 5.8

Proposition 5.9 *SM refinements preserve AiMP-bisimilarity.*

If $a \in \mathcal{A} \subseteq A$, Σ_1 and Σ_2 are two labelled systems and D is an SM-system, then

$$\Sigma_1 \approx_{\mathcal{A}iMP} \Sigma_2 \Longrightarrow ref(\Sigma_1, a, D) \approx_{\mathcal{A}'iMP} ref(\Sigma_2, a, D)$$
$$\text{with } \mathcal{A}' = A \setminus [A(\Sigma_1) \cap A(\Sigma_2)] \cup \mathcal{A}$$
$$\Longrightarrow ref(\Sigma_1, a, D) \approx_{\mathcal{A}iMP} ref(\Sigma_2, a, D).$$

Proof: The only difference with 5.8 is that here $\tilde{\pi}_1 = ref(\pi_1, a, \zeta_1)$ and $\tilde{\pi}_2 = ref(\pi_2, a, \zeta_2)$, there is no condition blending, and instead of 4.22 we may adapt here the corresponding result for $\mathcal{A}$MP-bisimilarity in [8]. ■ 5.9

And then we have

Corollary 5.10 *AiMP-bisimilarity is preserved by simultaneous refinements.*

If Σ_1 and Σ_2 are two labelled systems, $\mathcal{R} \subseteq \mathcal{A} \subseteq A$ and D is a function applying $\mathcal{R}$ to a family of memoryless in/out systems, then
if for any $a \in \mathcal{R}$ either D(a) is an SM-system or no a-labelled transition in Σ_1 or Σ_2 is self-concurrent:

(a) $\Sigma_1 \approx_{\mathcal{A}iMP} \Sigma_2 \Longrightarrow ref(\Sigma_1, \mathcal{R}, D) \approx_{\mathcal{A}'iMP} ref(\Sigma_2, \mathcal{R}, D)$ *with* $\mathcal{A}' = A \setminus [A(\Sigma_1) \cap A(\Sigma_2)] \cup \mathcal{A}$
$\Longrightarrow ref(\Sigma_1, \mathcal{R}, D) \approx_{\mathcal{A}iMP} ref(\Sigma_2, \mathcal{R}, D)$

(b) $\Sigma_1 \approx_{iMP} \Sigma_2 \Longrightarrow ref(\Sigma_1, \mathcal{R}, D) \approx_{iMP} ref(\Sigma_2, \mathcal{R}, D)$

(c) $\Sigma_1 \approx_{\mathcal{R}iMP} \Sigma_2 \Longrightarrow ref(\Sigma_1, \mathcal{R}, D) \approx_{i} ref(\Sigma_2, \mathcal{R}, D)$

Proof: From 5.8 and 5.9, the argument is the same as for 4.25. ■ 5.10

Corollary 5.11 *AiMP-bisimilarity is preserved for 1-safe systems.*

If Σ_1 and Σ_2 are two 1-safe labelled systems, $\mathcal{R} \subseteq \mathcal{A} \subseteq A$ and D is a function applying $\mathcal{R}$ to a family of memoryless in/out systems, then

$\Sigma_1 \approx_{\mathcal{A}iMP} \Sigma_2 \Longrightarrow ref(\Sigma_1, \mathcal{R}, D) \approx_{\mathcal{A}'iMP} ref(\Sigma_2, \mathcal{R}, D)$ *with* $\mathcal{A}' = A \setminus [A(\Sigma_1) \cap A(\Sigma_2)] \cup \mathcal{A}$
$\Longrightarrow ref(\Sigma_1, \mathcal{R}, D) \approx_{\mathcal{A}iMP} ref(\Sigma_2, \mathcal{R}, D)$

Proof: Immediate from 5.10, since there is no selfconcurrency in 1-safe systems. ■ 4.26

5.3 ST-Markings and Decidability

The definitions 5.3 and 5.5 are based on the processes of Σ_1 and Σ_2 and thus, even for very simple systems like 1-safe ones, they generally relate to an infinite set of possible evolutions; moreover, they depend on the partial order semantics of the systems, while this chapter concerns interleaving semantics; the point is that we may give another characterization based on the reachable markings and on the definition of concurrent bags (and thus on the interleaving step semantics); this characterization will lead to finite sets for finite bounded systems.

To do this, let us first introduce a slight extension (and variation) of a notion already proposed in [14] and [26]:

Definition 5.12 *AST-markings.*

Let $\Sigma = (S, T, W, M_0, \lambda)$ be a labelled system and $\mathcal{A} \subseteq A$ be a subset of visible actions;

(a) an $\mathcal{A}ST$-marking of Σ is a pair $(M, \beta^{\mathcal{A}})$ where $M \in [M_0\rangle$ is a reachable marking and $\beta^{\mathcal{A}}$ is a bag of $\mathcal{A}$-labelled transitions (i.e. $\beta^{\mathcal{A}} : \lambda^{-1}(\mathcal{A}) \longrightarrow \mathbf{N}$, which may be represented by an integer vector indexed by the $\mathcal{A}$-labelled transitions) concurrently enabled by M;
as usual, $\emptyset$ will be used to denote the empty bag and the set operators will be used to denote the corresponding operations on bags (f.i. $t \in \beta^{\mathcal{A}}$ iff $\beta^{\mathcal{A}}(t) > 0$, $\beta'^{\mathcal{A}} = \beta^{\mathcal{A}} \backslash \{t\}$ iff $\beta'^{\mathcal{A}}(t') = \beta^{\mathcal{A}}(t') - \delta_{tt'}$, ... where, as usual, $\delta_{xy} = 1$ if $x = y$ and 0 otherwise);

(b) the transitions between $\mathcal{A}ST$-markings are defined as follows:
if $t \in \beta^{\mathcal{A}}$ and $\forall s \in S : M'(s) = M(s) - W(s,t) + W(t,s)$, then $(M, \beta^{\mathcal{A}}) \xrightarrow{-t} (M', \beta^{\mathcal{A}} \setminus \{t\})$;
if $t \in \lambda^{-1}(\mathcal{A})$ and $M[\beta^{\mathcal{A}} \cup \{t\}\rangle$, i.e. t may occur concurrently with $\beta^{\mathcal{A}}$ from M,
then $(M, \beta^{\mathcal{A}}) \xrightarrow{t} (M, \beta^{\mathcal{A}} \cup \{t\})$;
if $t \notin \lambda^{-1}(\mathcal{A})$, $M[\beta^{\mathcal{A}} \cup \{t\}\rangle$ and $\forall s \in S : M'(s) = M(s) - W(s,t) + W(t,s)$,
then $(M, \beta^{\mathcal{A}}) \xrightarrow{t} (M', \beta^{\mathcal{A}}\})$. ■ 5.12

The mentioned extension consists in the introduction of a designated action subset $\mathcal{A}$, and of bags instead of sets of transitions; the variation consists in using the marking M before the occurrence of the concurrent bag instead of after it.
In some sense, an $\mathcal{A}$ST-marking $(M, \beta^{\mathcal{A}})$ represents the end part of an $\mathcal{A}$ST-configuration $(\pi, \mathcal{E})$, in much the same way a generalized ordered marking represented the significative part of a process for $\mathcal{A}$MP-bisimulations : $\beta^{\mathcal{A}}$ corresponds to the engaged set $\mathcal{E}$, M corresponds to the marking reached by π just before $\mathcal{E}$, and this is enough to capture the essence of an $\mathcal{A}$iMP-bisimulation, as shown by the following :

Proposition 5.13 *Interleaving characterization of $\mathcal{A}iMP$-bisimilarity.*

If Σ_1 and Σ_2 are two labelled systems and $\mathcal{A} \subseteq A$ is a subset of visible actions, $\Sigma_1 \approx_{\mathcal{A}iMP} \Sigma_2$ iff there is a set C of triples $((M_1, \beta_1^{\mathcal{A}}), (M_2, \beta_2^{\mathcal{A}}), \beta_{12})$ where $(M_1, \beta_1^{\mathcal{A}})$ is an $\mathcal{A}ST$-marking of Σ_1, $(M_2, \beta_2^{\mathcal{A}})$ is an $\mathcal{A}ST$-marking of Σ_2 and β_{12} is a label preserving bijection between $\beta_1^{\mathcal{A}}$ and $\beta_2^{\mathcal{A}}$,
i.e. $\forall a \in \mathcal{A} : \beta_{12}(a) : \lambda_1^{-1}(a) \times \lambda_2^{-1}(a) \longrightarrow \mathbf{N}$ such that $\sum_{t_1 \in \lambda_1^{-1}(a)} \beta_{12}(a)(t_1, t_2) = \beta_2^{\mathcal{A}}(t_2)$ and $\sum_{t_2 \in \lambda_2^{-1}(a)} \beta_{12}(a)(t_1, t_2) = \beta_1^{\mathcal{A}}(t_1)$, with the following properties :

(i) $((M_1^0, \emptyset), (M_2^0, \emptyset), \mathbf{0}) \in C$ where $\mathbf{0}$ denotes the constant function zero

(ii) $\forall ((M_1, \beta_1^{\mathcal{A}}), (M_2, \beta_2^{\mathcal{A}}), \beta_{12}) \in C$

(a)
- *if $(M_1, \beta_1^{\mathcal{A}}) \xrightarrow{-t_1} (M_1', \beta_1^{\mathcal{A}} \setminus \{t_1\})$ with $\lambda_1(t_1) = a \in \mathcal{A}$, then for each $t_2 \in \lambda_2^{-1}(a)$ such that $\beta_{12}(a)(t_1, t_2) > 0$, $(M_2, \beta_2^{\mathcal{A}}) \xrightarrow{-t_2} (M_2', \beta_2^{\mathcal{A}} \setminus \{t_2\})$ and $((M_1', \beta_1^{\mathcal{A}} \setminus \{t_1\}), (M_2', \beta_2^{\mathcal{A}} \setminus \{t_2\}, \beta_{12}') \in C$ with $\beta_{12}'(a)(t, t') = \beta_{12}(a)(t, t') - \delta_{tt_1}\delta_{t't_2}$*
- *if $(M_1, \beta_1^{\mathcal{A}}) \xrightarrow{t_1} (M_1, \beta_1^{\mathcal{A}} \cup \{t_1\})$ with $\lambda_1(t_1) \in \mathcal{A}$, then for some transition sequence $\sigma_2 \in \lambda_2^{-1}(\tau)^*$ and for some $t_2 \in \lambda_2^{-1}(\lambda_1(t_1))$, we have $(M_2, \beta_2^{\mathcal{A}}) \xrightarrow{\sigma_2 t_2} (M_2', \beta_2^{\mathcal{A}} \cup \{t_2\})$ and $((M_1, \beta_1^{\mathcal{A}} \cup \{t_1\}), (M_2', \beta_2^{\mathcal{A}} \cup \{t_2\}), \beta_{12}') \in C$ with $\beta_{12}'(a)(t, t') = \beta_{12}(a)(t, t') + \delta_{tt_1}\delta_{t't_2}$;*
- *if $(M_1, \beta_1^{\mathcal{A}}) \xrightarrow{t_1} (M_1', \beta_1^{\mathcal{A}})$ with $\lambda_1(t_1) \notin \mathcal{A}$, then for some transition sequence $\sigma_2 \in T_2^*$ with $\bar{\lambda}_2(\sigma_2) = \bar{\lambda}_1(t_1)$, we have $(M_2, \beta_2^{\mathcal{A}}) \xrightarrow{\sigma_2} (M_2', \beta_2^{\mathcal{A}})$ and $((M_1', \beta_1^{\mathcal{A}}), (M_2', \beta_2^{\mathcal{A}}), \beta_{12}) \in C$.*

(b) Vice versa.

C is an alternate (with respect to definition 5.4) $\mathcal{A}iMP$-bisimulation (we could also say $\mathcal{A}iST$-bisimulation) between Σ_1 and Σ_2.

Proof: see Appendix A.4. ■ 5.13

The interest of $\mathcal{A}$ST-markings for our concern here is that, while most systems have an infinite process set, there is a finite number of $\mathcal{A}$STP-markings iff the system is bounded (which is a rather common constraint in system design). Indeed, the number of reachable markings is by definition finite (only) for a bounded system and, for each marking M, since our nets are always finite and T-restricted, the number of possible concurrent bags is also finite (it is bounded by $\prod_{t\in T}(1 + \min_{s\in {}^{\bullet}t} \lfloor M(s)/W(s,t) \rfloor)$).
Moreover, we may again drop any redundant evolutions in 5.13; we may thus always constrain σ_2 in such a way that it never contains any silent loop :
if $\sigma_2 = \sigma'\sigma''\sigma'''$, $\bar{\lambda}(\sigma'') = \epsilon$, $\sigma'' \neq \epsilon$ and $(M_2, \beta_2^{\mathcal{A}}) \xrightarrow{\sigma'} (M', \beta_2^{\mathcal{A}}) \xrightarrow{\sigma''} (M'', \beta_2^{\mathcal{A}})$, then $M' \neq M''$.
As a consequence,

Corollary 5.14 *Decidability of $\mathcal{A}$iMP-bisimilarity.*

For bounded systems, $\mathcal{A}$iMP-bisimilarity is decidable.

Proof: Immediate from 5.13 and the above remarks. ■ 5.14

5.4 Characteristic Refinements and the Optimality Result

Now, in order to get a characterization of $\mathcal{A}$iMP-bisimilarity through characteristic refinements and to deduce the optimality of this equivalence notion, in a way similar to the one developed in section 4.3, we need a constraint on the class of nets we handle; it may happen that the property is much more general but the proof would probably also be much more complicated than the one we shall use (inspired from the one of W.Vogler in [25]).

Definition 5.15 *τ-boundedness.*

A system Σ is τ-bounded iff $\forall M \in [M_0\rangle : |\{M'$ such that $\exists M \xrightarrow{\sigma} M'$ with $\bar{\lambda}(\sigma) = \epsilon\}| < \infty$
i.e., from any reachable marking the set of markings reachable by silent transitions is finite. ■ 5.15

This property is not very strong since every bounded system is τ-bounded, and unbounded systems will also be τ-bounded if their unboundedness only arises from visible transitions; thus, the only case which is excluded concerns a form of divergence, where silent moves may by themselves generate unbounded markings.

Proposition 5.16 *Characteristic refinements for $\mathcal{A}$iMP-bisimilarity.*

For each $a \in \mathcal{A} \subseteq A$, let us consider the infinite family [3] of SM-systems (for $k \geq 1$)

$D^k(a)$ =

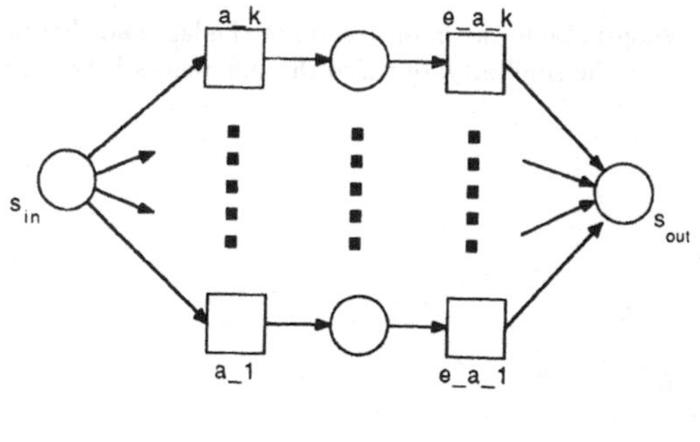

If Σ_1 and Σ_2 are two τ-bounded systems such that $\bigcup_{a\in\mathcal{A}}\{a\_k, e\_a\_k \mid k \geq 1\} \subseteq A \setminus [A(\Sigma_1) \cap A(\Sigma_2)]$,

$$\Sigma_1 \approx_{\mathcal{A}iMP} \Sigma_2 \iff \forall k \geq 1 \ : \ ref(\Sigma_1, \mathcal{A}, D^k) \approx_i ref(\Sigma_2, \mathcal{A}, D^k)$$

[3] this family has also been considered in [24] for similar purposes.

Proof: see Appendix A.5. ■ 5.16

In this theorem, we needed an infinite family of split refinements, instead of a single one as for $\mathcal{A}$MP-bisimilarity, and the results of [15] indicate that this is necessary, at least in the general case (i.e. possibly with unbounded auto-concurrency); consequently, we may not use it to effectively reduce the checking of $\mathcal{A}$iMP-bisimilarity to the checking of interleaving bisimilarity, but this is not very important since we solved the problem differently in the previous section.
In fact, a careful examination of the proof shows that we need such an infinite family in order to be able to distinguish the various (maximal) events with a same final label in $\mathcal{A}$; consequently, for systems with a bounded level of autoconcurrency (for the labels in $\mathcal{A}$), we could have used a single refinement system (with enough "choices") and dropped the τ-boundedness condition; in particular, this will always be the case for bounded systems. We could also have used a single refinement system with an infinite number of choices (and dropped the τ-boundedness condition), but this would not respect our decision to stick to finite systems, and would not solve our algorithmic problems.
The true importance of the obtained result is not of an algorithmic nature; it arises from the following corollary :

Corollary 5.17 *Optimality result.*

AiMP-bisimilarity is the coarsest equivalence relation on the class of labelled P/T systems which is preserved by SM-refinements of A-labelled transitions (and memoryless in/out refinements of non-selfconcurrent A-labelled transitions) which implies interleaving bisimilarity.

Proof: We already know that

$$\Sigma_1 \approx_{\mathcal{A}iMP} \Sigma_2 \implies ref(\Sigma_1,\mathcal{A},D) \approx_{\mathcal{A}'MP} ref(\Sigma_2,\mathcal{A},D) \text{ for some } \mathcal{A}' \supseteq \mathcal{A}$$
and for any family D of refinements as specified
$$\implies ref(\Sigma_1,\mathcal{A},D) \approx_i ref(\Sigma_2,\mathcal{A},D)$$
since $\mathcal{A}'$iMP-bisimilarity implies interleaving bisimilarity

Conversely, if $\sim$ is a congruence as specified, then

$$\Sigma_1 \sim \Sigma_2 \implies ref(\Sigma_1,\mathcal{A},D^k) \sim ref(\Sigma_2,\mathcal{A},D^k)\ \forall k \geq 1 \quad \text{since } \sim \text{ is preserved by refinements}$$
$$\implies ref(\Sigma_1,\mathcal{A},D^k) \approx_i ref(\Sigma_2,\mathcal{A},D^k)\ \forall k \geq 1 \quad \text{since } \sim \text{ implies } \approx_i$$
$$\implies \Sigma_1 \approx_{\mathcal{A}iMP} \Sigma_2 \quad \text{from 5.16.}$$

■ 5.17

6 Synoptic Summary

Let us summarize in a synoptic table the main results of the last two chapters.
We will so better appreciate the similarity, but also the differences between the two theories.

from fully concurrent bisimilarity	**from interleaving bisimilarity**
$\approx_{AMP} = \approx_{AST}$	$\approx_{AiMP} = \approx_{AiST}$
$\Sigma_1 \approx_{AMP} \Sigma_2 \Longrightarrow$ $ref(\Sigma_1,\mathcal{A},\mathcal{D}) \approx_{AMP} ref(\Sigma_2,\mathcal{A},\mathcal{D})$	$\Sigma_1 \approx_{AiMP} \Sigma_2 \Longrightarrow$ $ref(\Sigma_1,\mathcal{A},\mathcal{D}) \approx_{AiMP} ref(\Sigma_2,\mathcal{A},\mathcal{D})$
if, $\forall a \in \mathcal{A}$, either $\mathcal{D}(a)$ is an SM-refinement or a is selfconcurrency-free and $\mathcal{D}(a)$ is a memoryless in/out system	
$\approx_{AMP}$ reduces to $\approx_{FC}$ through a *single* split refinement	*for τ-bounded systems,* $\approx_{AiMP}$ reduces to $\approx_i$ through an *infinite family* of split refinements
$\approx_{AMP}$ is the coarsest equivalence preserved by refinements of $\mathcal{A}$-labelled transitions which implies FC-bisimilarity	*for τ-bounded systems,* $\approx_{AiMP}$ is the coarsest equivalence preserved by refinements of $\mathcal{A}$-labelled transitions which implies interleaving bisimilarity
for 1-safe systems, $\approx_{AMP}$ may be characterized in terms of *generalized ordered markings*	$\approx_{AiMP}$ may be characterized in terms of *ST-markings*
for 1-safe systems, $\approx_{AMP}$ is decidable	*for bounded systems,* $\approx_{AiMP}$ is decidable

7 The Full Refinement Problem

The problem considered up to now is only a part of the full refinement problem, which may be formulated as follows:

> What are the equivalence relations ($\sim$) such that, for a large class of systems and a large class of refinements,
> if $\Sigma_1 \sim \Sigma_2$ and $\forall a \in \mathcal{A} \subseteq A : D_1(a) \sim D_2(a)$, then $ref(\Sigma_1,\mathcal{A},D_1) \sim ref(\Sigma_2,\mathcal{A},D_2)$

In fact, we may consider that we have solved the first half of the problem, i.e. when $D_1 = D_2$, but as we shall see, this is the hard part: the other half is more classical.

More precisely, we have developed two solutions, but we mentioned that there may be other ones; the $\mathcal{A}$MP- and the $\mathcal{A}$iMP-bisimilarities are thus good candidates for such equivalence relations. In order to shorten the presentation, we shall only consider the first one here, but a similar theory may be developed for the other one.

We now have to look at the second half of the problem, i.e. the dual problem when $\Sigma_1 = \Sigma_2$, and then to combine both parts.

Unfortunately, $\mathcal{A}$MP-bisimilarity is not strong enough in order to cope with the dual problem: we need two additional (and classical) conditions in order to avoid situations like the ones exhibited on Figures 10 and 11 (the emergence of these two conditions is not very surprising since they occur in process algebras to get congruences with respect to binary choice and sequence operators, and refinements may be used to synthesize these operators from the simple choice and the simple split systems with two visible actions).

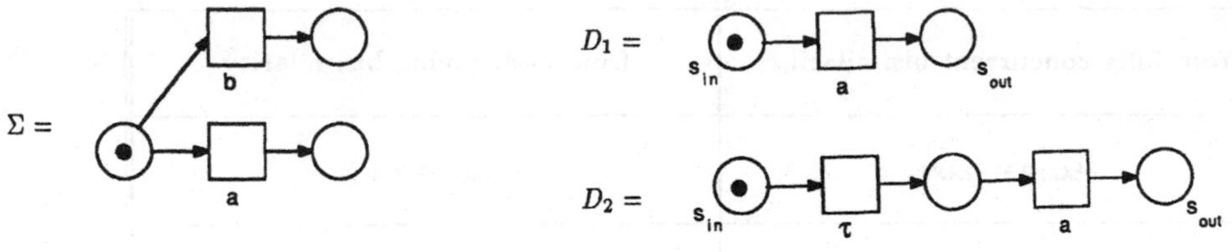

(i) a selfconcurrency-free system (ii) two MP-bisimilar SM-systems

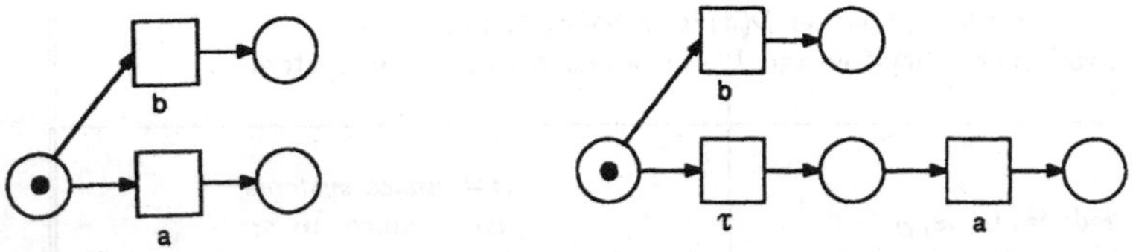

$\Sigma_1' = ref(\Sigma, a, D_1)$ $\Sigma_2' = ref(\Sigma, a, D_2)$

(iii) the refined systems are not bisimilar since a τ in Σ_2' may only correspond to an empty evolution in Σ_1', which may then be followed by a b

Figure 10: The stability problem

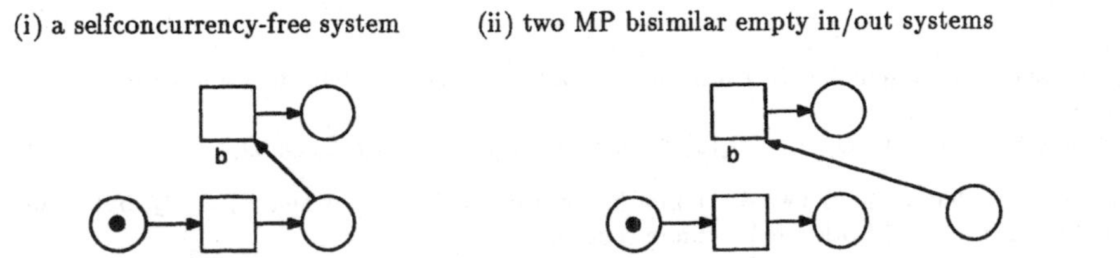

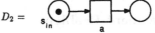

(i) a selfconcurrency-free system (ii) two MP bisimilar empty in/out systems

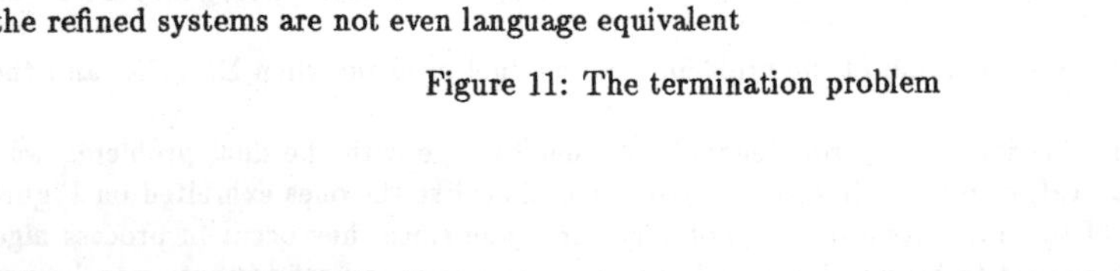

$\Sigma_1' = ref(\Sigma, a, D_1)$ $\Sigma_2' = ref(\Sigma, a, D_2)$

(iii) the refined systems are not even language equivalent

Figure 11: The termination problem

The stability problem illustrated by Figure 10 arises when an evolution of one of the systems may only correspond to the initial state of the other one (it remains stable when the first one progresses); this may be avoided by adding a condition saying that in a bisimulation an initial process may only correspond to another initial process.

The termination problem illustrated by Figure 11 may be viewed as a kind of dual of the previous one: it arises when an evolution to a complete process on one side may only correspond to evolutions to uncomplete processes on the other side; this may be avoided with an additional condition saying that this is not possible, or equivalently by saying that the two systems remain equivalent when we extend them by a transition with a unique visible label.
Combining these two observations then leads to

Lemma 7.1 *Congruence condition.*

Let D_1, D_2 be two memoryless in/out systems; the following three conditions are equivalent:

(1) there is a set $B \subseteq \{(\pi_1, \pi_2, \beta) \mid \pi_1 \in \Pi(D_1), \pi_2 \in \Pi(D_2), \beta$ is a relation between the visible events of π_1 and $\pi_2\}$ with the following properties:

(i) $(\pi_1^\circ, \pi_2^\circ, \emptyset) \in B$, where π_1° and π_2° are the initial processes of D_1 and D_2, respectively; moreover, if $(\pi_1^\circ, \pi_2, \emptyset) \in B$ then $\pi_2 = \pi_2^\circ$, and if $(\pi_1, \pi_2^\circ, \emptyset) \in B$ then $\pi_1 = \pi_1^\circ$;

(ii) $(\pi_1, \pi_2, \beta) \in B \Longrightarrow \beta$ is an order-isomorphism between $\alpha_{\lambda^1}(\pi_1)$ and $\alpha_{\lambda^2}(\pi_2)$;

(iii) $\forall(\pi_1, \pi_2, \beta) \in B$, with $\pi_1 = (B_1, E_1, F_1, p_1)$ and $\pi_2 = (B_2, E_2, F_2, p_2)$,

(a) if $\pi_1' = (B_1', E_1', F_1', p_1')$ is an extension of π_1, there is some $(\pi_1', \pi_2', \beta') \in B$ where $\pi_2' = (B_2', E_2', F_2', p_2')$ is an extension of π_2 and $\beta \subseteq \beta'$; moreover,

- *if $e_1' \in E_1' \setminus E_1$, $\lambda_1(p_1'(e_1')) \in A$ and e_1' is a maximal event in π_1', then $\beta'(e_1')$ is also a maximal event of π_2',*
- *for any $e_1 \in E_1$, if $\lambda_1(p_1(e_1)) \in A$ and if e_1 and $\beta(e_1)$ are maximal events in π_1' and π_2, respectively, then $\beta(e_1)$ is still a maximal event in π_2',*

(b) Vice versa.

(iv) if $(\pi_1, \pi_2, \beta) \in B$ and π_1 is a complete process of D_1, then there is some $(\pi_1, \pi_2', \beta) \in B$ where π_2' is a complete extension of π_2; conversely, if $(\pi_1, \pi_2, \beta) \in B$ and π_2 is a complete process of D_2, then there is some $(\pi_1', \pi_2, \beta) \in B$ where π_1' is a complete extension of π_1.

(2) if D_1' and D_2' are defined as follows

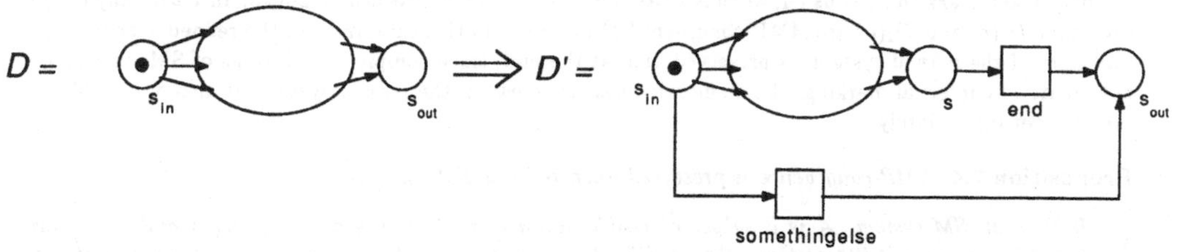

with somethingelse, end $\in A \setminus [A(D_1) \cup A(D_2)]$, then $D_1' \approx_{AMP} D_2'$.

(3) if Σ is the following labelled system

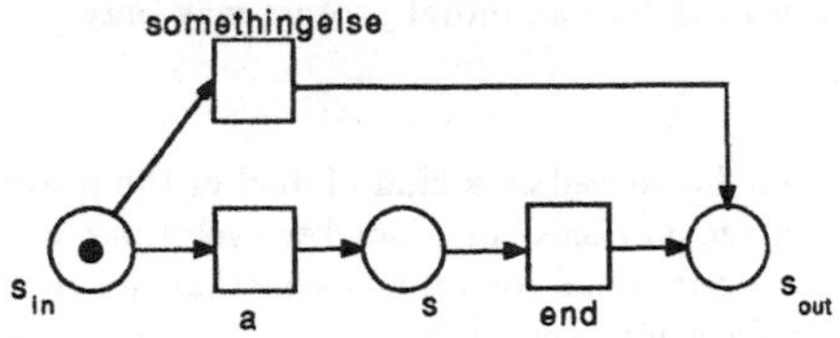

with somethingelse, end $\in A \setminus [A(D_1) \cup A(D_2)]$,
then $ref(\Sigma, a, D_1) \approx_{AMP} ref(\Sigma, a, D_2)$.

The two systems D_1 and D_2 are then said to be AMP-congruent, which is denoted $D_1 \cong_{AMP} D_2$, and $\mathcal{B}$ is an AMP-congruence between them.

Proof: see [10]. ■ 7.1

Now the second part of the refinement problem may be solved

Proposition 7.2 *AMP-congruence is preserved when refining memoryless systems.*

If Σ is a memoryless in/out system, $\mathcal{A}$ is a subset of visible actions without selfconcurrency in Σ and, for any $a \in \mathcal{A}$, $D_1(a)$ and $D_2(a)$ are two AMP-congruent memoryless in/out systems, then $ref(\Sigma, \mathcal{A}, D_1)$ and $ref(\Sigma, \mathcal{A}, D_2)$ are also AMP-congruent memoryless in/out systems;
more precisely, they are at least $\mathcal{A}'MP$ congruent, for $\mathcal{A}' = (A \setminus [A(D_1) \cap A(D_2)]) \cup \mathcal{A}$.

Proof: One simply has to adapt the proof for 4.22, see [10]. ■ 7.2

We also have an optimality result

Proposition 7.3 *Optimal congruence preserved when refining memoryless systems.*

AMP-congruence is the coarsest equivalence notion implying AMP-bisimilarity which is preserved when refining $\mathcal{A}$-actions in memoryless in/out systems without selfconcurrency for them.

Proof: This is an immediate consequence of 7.2 and 7.1, since the system Σ in 7.1(3) is a memoryless in/out system without any concurrency. ■ 7.3

We may also remark that, as usual, we may relax the selfconcurrency-freeness condition in 7.2 for any $a \in \mathcal{A}$ such that $D_1(a)$ and $D_2(a)$ are AMP-congruent SM-systems. In this case, indeed, the refined aspect of the processes of the refined systems is preserved and, at the end, since complete evolutions of SM-systems do not create any internal marking, the memorylessness property of the refined systems is also preserved.
We also get immediately

Proposition 7.4 *AMP-congruence is preserved when refining SM-systems.*

If Σ is an SM-system, $\mathcal{A}$ is a subset of visible actions and, for any $a \in \mathcal{A}$, $D_1(a)$ and $D_2(a)$ are two AMP-congruent SM-systems, then $ref(\Sigma, \mathcal{A}, D_1)$ and $ref(\Sigma, \mathcal{A}, D_2)$ are also AMP-congruent SM-systems;
more precisely, they are at least $\mathcal{A}'MP$-congruent, for $\mathcal{A}' = (A \setminus [A(D_1) \cap A(D_2)]) \cup \mathcal{A}$.

Proof: This is an immediate consequence of 7.2 since SM-systems are automatically (self)concurrency-free memoryless in/out systems and it is easy to check that an SM-refinement of an SM-system is still an SM-system. ■ 7.4

And finally, we get a solution for the full refinement problem

Proposition 7.5 *The full refinement problem.*

(i) if Σ_1 and Σ_2 are $\mathcal{A}$MP-congruent memoryless in/out systems, $\mathcal{A}$ is a subset of visible actions and, for any $a \in \mathcal{A}$, either $D_1(a)$ and $D_2(a)$ are two $\mathcal{A}$MP-congruent SM-systems or a is not selfconcurrent in Σ_1 and Σ_2 and D_1 and D_2 are two $\mathcal{A}$MP-congruent memoryless in/out systems, then $ref(\Sigma_1, \mathcal{A}, D_1)$ and $ref(\Sigma_2, \mathcal{A}, D_2)$ are also $\mathcal{A}$MP-congruent memoryless in/out systems.

(ii) if Σ_1 and Σ_2 are $\mathcal{A}$MP congruent SM-systems, $\mathcal{A}$ is a subset of visible actions and, for any $a \in \mathcal{A}$, $D_1(a)$ and $D_2(a)$ are two $\mathcal{A}$MP-congruent SM-systems , then $ref(\Sigma_1, \mathcal{A}, D_1)$ and $ref(\Sigma_2, \mathcal{A}, D_2)$ are also $\mathcal{A}$MP-congruent SM-systems.

(iii) $\mathcal{A}$MP-congruence is the coarsest equivalence relation implying FC-bisimilarity which is preserved by full refinements as exhibited in (i) or (ii).

Proof: (i) from 7.2 (and the remark after 7.3) we know that $ref(\Sigma_1, \mathcal{A}, D_1) \cong_{\mathcal{A}MP} ref(\Sigma_1, \mathcal{A}, D_2)$, and from 4.22 we have $ref(\Sigma_1, \mathcal{A}, D_2) \approx_{\mathcal{A}MP} ref(\Sigma_2, \mathcal{A}, D_2)$; moreover, from the way the $\mathcal{A}$MP-bisimulation is constructed for the refined systems in 4.22 and from the fact that Σ_1 and Σ_2 are not only $\mathcal{A}$MP-bisimilar but also $\mathcal{A}$MP-congruent, we may see that their refinements are also $\mathcal{A}$MP-congruent: a refined process corresponding to the initial one may only be initial and a refined process corresponding to a complete one (which thus only has complete subcomponents) may be extended to a complete process (by only adding invisible events);

(ii) this is an immediate consequence of point (i) since we already know that SM-systems are selfconcurrency-free memoryless in/out ones and that the refinement of an SM-system through SM-systems is still an SM-system;

(iii) this is an immediate consequence of 4.28 and 7.3. ■ 7.5

8 Open problems

Except for the non-SM-refinements of selfconcurrent actions, the theory developed up to now may be considered quite satisfactory since we know when bisimilarities are preserved by (full) refinements, how to characterize them and when they are decidable. However, some important open problems have still to be tackled, for instance:

- Develop the theory for the non-SM-refinements in presence of selfconcurrency (a first approach of this problem may be found in [10]).
- Develop the theory from other (intermediate) bisimilarities.
- Do we have that $\Sigma_1 \approx_{\mathcal{A}MP} \Sigma_2 \iff \forall a \in \mathcal{A} : \Sigma_1 \approx_{\{a\}MP} \Sigma_2$?
  and similarly for $\mathcal{A}$iMP-bisimilarity;
- Are there efficient algorithms to check $\mathcal{A}$MP- or $\mathcal{A}$iMP-bisimilarity ?
  Otherwise, find system subclasses for which this is the case.
- Is it possible to weaken, or drop, the τ-boundedness condition in theorem 5.16, the 1-safeness condition in theorem 4.33, ... ?

A Technical Proofs

A.1 Proof of 4.6.

Proof: Let us first show that, for any labelled systems Σ_1 and Σ_2,
if $\Sigma_1 \approx_{\mathcal{A}MP} \Sigma_2$, then $\Sigma_1 \approx_{\mathcal{A}ST} \Sigma_2$;
let $\mathcal{B}$ be an $\mathcal{A}$MP-bisimulation between Σ_1 and Σ_2, and let us define
$\mathcal{B}' = \{((\pi_1, \mathcal{E}_1), (\pi_2, \mathcal{E}_2), \beta) \mid (\pi_1, \pi_2, \beta) \in \mathcal{B}$, $\mathcal{E}_1$ is a set of $\mathcal{A}$-finally labelled maximal events of π_1, $\mathcal{E}_2$ is a set of $\mathcal{A}$-finally labelled maximal events of π_2 and $\beta(\mathcal{E}_1) = \mathcal{E}_2\}$;
we simply have to check that $\mathcal{B}'$ is an $\mathcal{A}$ST-bisimulation between Σ_1 and Σ_2 :

(i) $((\pi_1^\circ,\emptyset),(\pi_2^\circ,\emptyset),\emptyset) \in \mathcal{B}'$ since $(\pi_1^\circ,\pi_1^\circ,\beta) \in \mathcal{B}$,

(ii) if $((\pi_1,\mathcal{E}_1),(\pi_2,\mathcal{E}_2),\beta) \in \mathcal{B}'$, since $(\pi_1,\pi_2,\beta) \in \mathcal{B}$, β is an order-isomorphism between $\alpha_{\lambda^1}(\pi_1)$ and $\alpha_{\lambda^2}(\pi_2)$, and by definition $\beta(\mathcal{E}_1) = \mathcal{E}_2$,

(iii)(a) if $((\pi_1,\mathcal{E}_1),(\pi_2,\mathcal{E}_2),\beta) \in \mathcal{B}'$ and $(\pi_1,\mathcal{E}_1) \longrightarrow (\pi_1',\mathcal{E}_1')$, since $(\pi_1,\pi_2,\beta) \in \mathcal{B}$, we know that there is $\pi_2 \longrightarrow \pi_2'$ and $\beta \subseteq \beta'$ such that $(\pi_1',\pi_2',\beta') \in \mathcal{B}$, and moreover

- $\forall e_1 \in \mathcal{E}_1' \cap \mathcal{E}_1$: e_1 and $\beta(e_1)$ are $\mathcal{A}$-finally labelled, $\beta'(e_1) = \beta(e_1) \in \mathcal{E}_2$ is maximal in π_2, e_1 is still maximal in π_1' and thus $\beta(e_1)$ is also still maximal in π_2',
- $\forall e_1' \in \mathcal{E}_1' \backslash \mathcal{E}_1$: e_1' is added, maximal in π_1', $\mathcal{A}$-finally labelled and thus $\beta'(e_1')$ is also maximal in π_2',

consequently, $(\pi_2',\beta'(\mathcal{E}_1'))$ is an $\mathcal{A}$ST-configuration of Σ_2
and $(\pi_2,\mathcal{E}_2) \longrightarrow (\pi_2',\beta'(\mathcal{E}_1'))$ since $\beta'(\mathcal{E}_1')$ only contains events which were already in $\mathcal{E}_2$ or which have been added;
hence the desired property.

(iii)(b) vice versa.

Let us now show that, for any labelled systems Σ_1 and Σ_2,
if $\Sigma_1 \approx_{\mathcal{A}ST} \Sigma_2$, then $\Sigma_1 \approx_{\mathcal{A}MP} \Sigma_2$;
let $\mathcal{B}$ be an $\mathcal{A}$ST-bisimulation between Σ_1 and Σ_2, and let us define
$\mathcal{B}' = \{(\pi_1,\pi_2,\beta) \mid \exists((\pi_1,\mathcal{E}_1),(\pi_2,\mathcal{E}_2),\beta) \in \mathcal{B}$ with $\mathcal{E}_1 = Maxevents(\pi_1,\mathcal{A}) \cap \beta^{-1}(Maxevents(\pi_2,\mathcal{A}))$
and
$\mathcal{E}_2 = Maxevents(\pi_2,\mathcal{A}) \cap \beta(Maxevents(\pi_1,\mathcal{A}))\ \}$;
we simply have to check that $\mathcal{B}'$ is an $\mathcal{A}$MP-bisimulation between Σ_1 and Σ_2 :

(i) $(\pi_1^\circ,\pi_1^\circ,\beta) \in \mathcal{B}'$ since $((\pi_1^\circ,\emptyset),(\pi_2^\circ,\emptyset),\emptyset) \in \mathcal{B}$,

(ii) if $(\pi_1,\pi_2,\beta) \in \mathcal{B}'$, since there is a $((\pi_1,\mathcal{E}_1),(\pi_2,\mathcal{E}_2),\beta) \in \mathcal{B}$, β is an order-isomorphism between $\alpha_{\lambda^1}(\pi_1)$ and $\alpha_{\lambda^2}(\pi_2)$,

(iii)(a) if $(\pi_1,\pi_2,\beta) \in \mathcal{B}'$ and $\pi_1 \longrightarrow \pi_1'$, we know that there is some $((\pi_1,\mathcal{E}_1),(\pi_2,\mathcal{E}_2),\beta) \in \mathcal{B}$ with $\mathcal{E}_1 = Maxevents(\pi_1,\mathcal{A}) \cap \beta^{-1}(Maxevents(\pi_2,\mathcal{A}))$
and $\mathcal{E}_2 = Maxevents(\pi_2,\mathcal{A}) \cap \beta(Maxevents(\pi_1,\mathcal{A}))$; moreover,
$(\pi_1,\mathcal{E}_1) \longrightarrow (\pi_1',\mathcal{E}_1')$ with $\mathcal{E}_1' = [Maxevents(\pi_1',\mathcal{A}) \cap \mathcal{E}_1] \cup [Maxevents(\pi_1',\mathcal{A}) \backslash E_1]$, so that, from 4.4(iii)(a), there is some $(\pi_2,\mathcal{E}_2) \longrightarrow (\pi_2',\mathcal{E}_2')$ and $\beta \subseteq \beta'$ such that $((\pi_1',\mathcal{E}_1'),(\pi_2',\mathcal{E}_2'),\beta') \in \mathcal{B}$, and $\beta'(\mathcal{E}_1') = \mathcal{E}_2'$; consequently

- if e_1 is $\mathcal{A}$-finally labelled, maximal in π_1 and in π_1', and if $\beta(e_1)$ is maximal in π_2, we have : $e_1 \in \mathcal{E}_1 \cap Maxevents(\pi_1',\mathcal{A})$, $\beta(e_1) \in \mathcal{E}_2$, $e_1 \in \mathcal{E}_1'$ and $\beta'(e_1) = \beta(e_1) \in \mathcal{E}_2'$ is thus still maximal in π_2',
- if e_1' is $\mathcal{A}$-finally labelled, added to π_1 and maximal in π_1', we have :
$e_1' \in Maxevents(\pi_1',\mathcal{A}) \setminus E_1 \subseteq \mathcal{E}_1'$ and $\beta'(e_1') \in \mathcal{E}_2'$ is also maximal in π_2';

hence the desired property.

(iii)(b) vice versa. ■ 4.6

A.2 Proof of 4.22.

Proof: Let $\mathcal{B}$ an $\mathcal{A}$MP-bisimulation between Σ_1 and Σ_2, and let us define $\tilde{\mathcal{B}}$ as the set of triples $(\tilde{\pi}_1,\tilde{\pi}_2,\tilde{\beta})$ such that there is a triple $(\pi_1,\pi_2,\beta) \in \mathcal{B}$ and ζ,ζ' with the following properties :

$\tilde{\pi}_1 \in ref(\pi_1,a,\zeta)$, $\tilde{\pi}_2 \in ref(\pi_2,a,\zeta')$,

$\zeta' = \zeta \circ \beta^{-1}$, i.e. ζ' is the image of ζ through β,

$\tilde{\beta}$ is identical to β on the visible events common to $\tilde{\pi}_1$ and π_1 on one side and to $\tilde{\pi}_2$ and π_2 on the other side, and is the identity relation (restricted to visible events) for the corresponding identical copies (due to the definition of ζ') of the processes of D refining the corresponding a-finally labelled events of π_1 and π_2.

It should be clear that

- $(\tilde{\pi}_1^\circ, \tilde{\pi}_2^\circ, \emptyset) \in \tilde{\mathcal{B}}$, if $\tilde{\pi}_1^\circ$ and $\tilde{\pi}_2^\circ$ are the initial processes of $ref(\Sigma_1, a, \zeta)$ and $ref(\Sigma_2, a, \zeta)$
- if $(\tilde{\pi}_1, \tilde{\pi}_2, \tilde{\beta}) \in \tilde{\mathcal{B}}$, then $\tilde{\beta}$ is an order-isomorphism between the abstractions of $\tilde{\pi}_1$ and $\tilde{\pi}_2$, since it is constructed from β which is itself an order-isomorphism and from identity relations
- if $(\tilde{\pi}_1, \tilde{\pi}_2, \tilde{\beta}) \in \tilde{\mathcal{B}}$ and $\tilde{\pi}_1$ is extended into $\tilde{\pi}_1'$ by an event $\tilde{e}_1'$, three cases are possible
  (a) either $\tilde{e}_1'$ extends a D-process refining some a-finally labelled event e_1 in π_1 and the same prolongation may be applied to the identical process refining $\beta(e_1)$ in π_2; $\tilde{\beta}$ may be extended accordingly and it should be clear that we will obtain an extension triple which is still in $\tilde{\mathcal{B}}$ (since we know from property 4.20 that no "parasit" ordering may be added by the special way the new event is connected to previous subcomponents) and which preserves the maximality for all the visible actions (for the same reason);
  (b) either $\tilde{e}_1'$ does not belong to any D-process refining some a-finally labelled event in π_1; then $\tilde{e}_1'$ also extends π_1 into π_1' ($\tilde{e}_1'$ may not be connected to an incomplete subcomponent of $\tilde{\pi}_1$) and $\tilde{\pi}_1' \in ref(\pi_1', a, \zeta)$; from the $\mathcal{A}$MP-bisimulation definition, there are π_2' and β' extending π_2 and β such that $(\pi_1', \pi_2', \beta') \in \mathcal{B}$ and maximality of $\mathcal{A}$-finally labelled events is preserved;
  it should be clear that $\tilde{\pi}_1'$, $\tilde{\pi}_2' \in ref(\pi_2', a, \zeta \circ \beta^{-1})$ with the same condition blendings as in $\tilde{\pi}_2$ and the $\tilde{\beta}'$ corresponding to β' will give a triple belonging to $\tilde{\mathcal{B}}$ with the good properties; indeed, the only possible problem is that an additional event in π_2' would have to be connected in $\tilde{\pi}_2'$ to an incomplete refining process of D (which would be impossible), but then there is the same incomplete process in $\tilde{\pi}_1'$ and they both correspond to maximal β-corresponding a-finally labelled events e_1'' and e_2'' in π_1' and π_2' respectively; in π_1', e_1 may not be connected to e_1'' (otherwise the D-process corresponding to the latter would be complete), thus e_1'' remains maximal but then so must be e_2'' and nothing new may be connected to its (incomplete) corresponding process, hence the contradiction;
  the only visible events the maximality of which could be destroyed are clearly the ones with that property in Σ_1 and Σ_2;
  (c) either $\tilde{e}_1'$ is the beginning of a new D-process refining some new a-finally labelled event e_1' extending π_1 into π_1';
  by extending ζ into ζ' with the pair (e_1',D-process corresponding to $\tilde{e}_1'$), we have $\tilde{\pi}_1' \in ref(\pi_1', a, \zeta')$; from the $\mathcal{A}$MP-bisimulation definition, there are π_2' and β' extending π_2 and β such that $(\pi_1', \pi_2', \beta') \in \mathcal{B}$ and maximality of $\mathcal{A}$-finally labelled events is preserved;
  it should be clear that $\tilde{\pi}_1'$, any $\tilde{\pi}_2' \in ref(\pi_2', a, \zeta' \circ \beta'^{-1})$ with the same condition blendings as in $\tilde{\pi}_2$ and the $\tilde{\beta}'$ corresponding to β' will give a triple belonging to $\tilde{\mathcal{B}}$ with the good properties (since we know from property 4.20 that no "parasit" ordering may be added by the special way the new event is connected to previous subcomponents) ; the same reasoning as in (b) may be resumed, with the additional remark that, $\beta'(e_1')$ being also maximal, there is no problem in refining it.

  and symmetrically for the vice versa part.
  Consequently the maximality is preserved for any visible action but the ones for which this is not the case in Σ_1 and Σ_2, hence the formula for $\mathcal{A}'$.

Finally, since $\mathcal{A} \subseteq \mathcal{A}'$, we know that $\mathcal{A}'$MP-bisimilarity is stronger than $\mathcal{A}$MP-bisimilarity.

■ 4.22

A.3 Proof of 4.27.

Proof: $\Longrightarrow$

results from the observation that, $\forall a \in \mathcal{A}$, $split(a)$ is an SM-system, that SM-refinements preserve any $\mathcal{A}$MP-bisimilarity and that $\mathcal{A}$MP-bisimilarity implies FC-bisimilarity.

$\Longleftarrow$

in [8], we already showed that, for any system Σ, all the processes of $ref(\Sigma, \mathcal{A}, split)$ are refinements of processes of Σ; more precisely, for any process $\tilde{\pi}$ of $ref(\Sigma, \mathcal{A}, split)$, there is a unique process

$\pi = squeeze(\tilde{\pi})$ of Σ, obtained by replacing each $< b\_a, t >$-labelled event ($a \in \mathcal{A}$), together with its following $< e\_a, t >$-labelled event if any, by a t-labelled one, and each isolated b_a in $\tilde{\pi}$ corresponds to a maximal a in π; this also defines a unique bijection $\beta squeeze(\tilde{\pi})$ between the visible events of $\tilde{\pi}$, but the e_a ones, and the visible events of π, with the label correspondance $x \rightarrow x$ if $x \notin \mathcal{A}$ and $b\_a \rightarrow a$ if $a \in \mathcal{A}$; *squeeze* is trivially monotonic w.r.t. process extension and, if we define the label transformation

$$\lambda_{\mathcal{A}} : \begin{cases} b\_a & \longrightarrow & a & \forall a \in \mathcal{A} \\ e\_a & \longrightarrow & \tau & \forall a \in \mathcal{A} \\ x & \longrightarrow & x & \forall x \notin \mathcal{A} \end{cases}$$

we may see that $\forall \tilde{\pi} : \alpha_{\lambda_{\mathcal{A}} \circ \tilde{\lambda}}(\tilde{\pi}) \cong \alpha_{\lambda}(squeeze(\tilde{\pi}))$, the isomorphism being $\beta squeeze(\tilde{\pi})$, i.e. squeeze preserves the partial order abstraction through $\lambda_{\mathcal{A}}$.
Also, if $\tilde{\mathcal{B}}$ is an FC-bisimulation between $ref(\Sigma_1, \mathcal{A}, split)$ and $ref(\Sigma_2, \mathcal{A}, split)$, and if $(\tilde{\pi}_1, \tilde{\pi}_2, \tilde{\beta}) \in \tilde{\mathcal{B}}$, we have $\alpha_{\lambda_{\mathcal{A}} \circ \tilde{\lambda}_1}(\tilde{\pi}_1) \cong \alpha_{\lambda_{\mathcal{A}} \circ \tilde{\lambda}_2}(\tilde{\pi}_2)$, the isomorphism being the restriction of $\tilde{\beta}$ to the events remaining visible through $\lambda_{\mathcal{A}}$.
Now, let $\mathcal{B} = \{(\pi_1, \pi_2, \beta) \mid$ for some $(\tilde{\pi}_1, \tilde{\pi}_2, \tilde{\beta}) \in \tilde{\mathcal{B}}, \pi_1 = squeeze(\tilde{\pi}_1), \pi_2 = squeeze(\tilde{\pi}_2)$, $\beta = \beta squeeze(\tilde{\pi}_2) \circ \tilde{\beta} \circ \beta squeeze(\tilde{\pi}_1)^{-1}$ and there is no maximal event $\tilde{e}$ in $\tilde{\pi}_1$ with a final label e_a for some $a \in \mathcal{A}$ such that $\tilde{\beta}(\tilde{e})$ is also maximal in $\tilde{\pi}_2$ $\}$;
we may check that $\mathcal{B}$ fulfills all the conditions characterizing an $\mathcal{A}$MP-bisimulation :

(i) $(\pi_1^\circ, \pi_2^\circ, \emptyset) \in \mathcal{B}$ since $\pi_i^\circ = squeeze(\tilde{\pi}_i^\circ)$ for $i = 1, 2$;

(ii) if $(\pi_1, \pi_2, \beta) \in \mathcal{B}$, from the above remarks, β is an order isomorphism between the abstractions of π_1 and π_2;

(iii) (a) if $(\pi_1, \pi_2, \beta) \in \mathcal{B}$ and π_1 is extended to π_1' by a single event e_1', then there is a corresponding extension $\tilde{\pi}_1'$ of $\tilde{\pi}_1$, obtained by adding an event with the same label if it does not belong to $\lambda_1^{-1}(\mathcal{A})$ and with a label $< b\_a, t_1 >$ if it has a label $t_1 \in \lambda_1^{-1}(a)$ for $a \in \mathcal{A}$, plus possibly some $< e\_a, t >$ labelled events if needed, i.e. if e_1' is connected to maximal events of π_1 with final labels in $\mathcal{A}$ such that their $\beta squeeze(\tilde{\pi}_1)$ correspondents are also maximal in $\tilde{\pi}_1$; let $\tilde{\pi}_2'$ be a corresponding extension of $\tilde{\pi}_2$ and $\tilde{\beta}'$ the corresponding extension of $\tilde{\beta}$, and let $\pi_2' = squeeze(\tilde{\pi}_2')$ with $\beta' = \beta squeeze(\tilde{\pi}_2') \circ \tilde{\beta}' \circ \beta squeeze(\tilde{\pi}_1')^{-1}$;
it should be clear that $\beta \subseteq \beta'$ and π_2' is an extension of π_2;
moreover,

- if e_1' has a final label in $\mathcal{A}$, $\beta'(e_1')$ is maximal in π_2' (its corresponding event in $\tilde{\pi}_2'$ has no event finally labelled by e_a following it, since this is also the case for the event corresponding to e_1' in $\tilde{\pi}_1'$)
- if e_1 and $\beta(e_1)$ are maximal events in π_1 and π_2, with a final label a in $\mathcal{A}$, their corresponding events in $\tilde{\pi}_1$ and $\tilde{\pi}_2$ have no final labels e_a; consequently, if e_1' is not connected to e_1, no e_a-finally labelled events will be added to them, neither in $\tilde{\pi}_1'$ nor in $\tilde{\pi}_2'$, and $\beta(e_1)$ remains maximal in π_2'.

(b) Symmetrically. ■ 4.27

A.4 Proof of 5.13.

Proof: $\Longrightarrow$: if $\mathcal{B}$ is an $\mathcal{A}$iMP bisimulation between Σ_1 and Σ_2,
let $\mathcal{C}$ be the set of triples $((M_1, \beta_1^{\mathcal{A}}), (M_2, \beta_2^{\mathcal{A}}), \beta_{12})$ such that there is $(\pi_1, \pi_2, \beta) \in \mathcal{B}$ and $\hat{\beta} \subseteq \beta \cap$ (maximal events of π_1 finally labelled by $\mathcal{A}$ $\times$ maximal events of π_2 finally labelled by $\mathcal{A}$), $\beta_1^{\mathcal{A}}$ being the bag corresponding to the domain of $\hat{\beta}$, $\beta_2^{\mathcal{A}}$ being the bag corresponding to the range (or codomain) of $\hat{\beta}$, β_{12} being the correspondence between $\beta_1^{\mathcal{A}}$ and $\beta_2^{\mathcal{A}}$ associated to $\hat{\beta}$, M_1 being the marking to which π_1 leads before $dom(\hat{\beta})$ and M_2 being the marking to which π_2 leads before $ran(\hat{\beta})$; more precisely,
$\forall t_1 \in \lambda_1^{-1}(\mathcal{A}) \; : \; \beta_1^{\mathcal{A}}(t_1) = \mid \{e_1 \text{ such that } p_1(e_1) = t_1 \text{ and } \exists (e_1, e_2) \in \hat{\beta}\} \mid$,
$\forall t_2 \in \lambda_2^{-1}(\mathcal{A}) \; : \; \beta_2^{\mathcal{A}}(t_2) = \mid \{e_2 \text{ such that } p_2(e_2) = t_2 \text{ and } \exists (e_1, e_2) \in \hat{\beta}\} \mid$,
$\forall a \in \mathcal{A} \, \forall t_1 \in \lambda_1^{-1}(a) \, \forall t_2 \in \lambda_2^{-1}(a) \; : \; \beta_{12}(a)(t_1, t_2) = \mid \{(e_1, e_2) \in \hat{\beta} \cap p_1^{-1}(t_1) \times p_2^{-1}(t_2)\} \mid$,

if π_1' is the prefix of π_1 such that $E_1 \setminus E_1' = \{e_1$ such that $\exists(e_1,e_2) \in \hat{\beta}\}$, π_1' leads to M_1, and if π_2' is the prefix of π_2 such that $E_2 \setminus E_2' = \{e_2$ such that $\exists(e_1,e_2) \in \hat{\beta}\}$, π_2' leads to M_2.

We may now check that $\mathcal{C}$ fulfills all the conditions of the theorem:

(i) $((M_1^0,\emptyset),(M_2^0,\emptyset),0) \in \mathcal{C}$ since $(\pi_1^0,\pi_2^0,\emptyset) \in \mathcal{B}$

(ii) (a)
- if $(M_1,\beta_1^{\mathcal{A}}) \xrightarrow{-t_1} (M_1',\beta_1^{\mathcal{A}} \setminus \{t_1\})$, we may drop from $\hat{\beta}$ any pair (e_1,e_2) such that $p_1(e_1) = t_1$ and we then get the property, with $t_2 = p_2(e_2)$;
- if $(M_1,\beta_1^{\mathcal{A}}) \xrightarrow{t_1} (M_1,\beta_1^{\mathcal{A}} \cup \{t_1\})$,we may extend π_1 by adding an event e_1 with the label t_1 without using the output conditions of the events of $dom(\hat{\beta})$ since t_1 may occur concurrently with $\beta_1^{\mathcal{A}}$ from M_1; then, π_2 may also be extended correspondingly by some silent events plus a maximal event e_2 with a label $t_2 \in \lambda_2^{-1}(\lambda_1(t_1))$, without destroying the maximality of $ran(\hat{\beta})$, hence the property;
- if $(M_1,\beta_1^{\mathcal{A}}) \xrightarrow{t_1} (M_1',\beta_1^{\mathcal{A}})$, we may extend π_1 by adding an event labelled by t_1 without using the output conditions of the events of $dom(\hat{\beta})$ since t_1 may occur concurrently with $\beta_1^{\mathcal{A}}$ from M_1; then, π_2 may also be extended correspondingly by some silent events, plus an event with $\lambda_1(t_1)$ as final label if it is visible and again some silent events, without destroying the maximality of $ran(\hat{\beta})$, hence the property.

(b) The vice versa case is symmetrical

$\Longleftarrow$: if $\mathcal{C}$ is as above,
let $\mathcal{B}$ be the set of triples (π_1,π_2,β) such that there is $((M_1,\beta_1^{\mathcal{A}}),(M_2,\beta_2^{\mathcal{A}}),\beta_{12}) \in \mathcal{C}$, $\pi_1^< \in \Pi(\Sigma_1), \pi_2^< \in \Pi(\Sigma_2)$ with the following properties:
$\pi_1^<$ leads to M_1, $\pi_2^<$ leads to M_2, $\pi_1^<$ is a prefix of π_1, $\pi_2^<$ is a prefix of π_2, $E_1 \setminus E_1^<$ is an unordered set of events finally labelled by $\mathcal{A}$ corresponding to the bag $\beta_1^{\mathcal{A}}$, $E_2 \setminus E_2^<$ is an unordered set of events finally labelled by $\mathcal{A}$ corresponding to the bag $\beta_1^{\mathcal{A}}$ and $\beta = \beta' \cup \beta''$ where β' is any label preserving bijection between the visible events of $\pi_1^<$ and $\pi_2^<$, and β'' is any label preserving bijection between $E_1 \setminus E_1^<$ and $E_2 \setminus E_2^<$ compatible with β_{12} ; more precisely $\forall t_1 \in \lambda_1^{-1}(\mathcal{A}) \; : \; \beta_1^{\mathcal{A}}(t_1) = \mid (E_1 \setminus E_1^<) \cap p_1^{-1}(t_1) \mid$, $\forall t_2 \in \lambda_2^{-1}(\mathcal{A}) \; : \; \beta_2^{\mathcal{A}}(t_2) = \mid (E_1 \setminus E_1^<) \cap p_2^{-1}(t_2) \mid$ and $\forall a \in \mathcal{A} \; \forall t_1 \in \lambda_1^{-1}(a) \; \forall t_2 \in \lambda_2^{-1}(a) \; : \; \beta_{12}(a)(t_1,t_2) = \mid \beta'' \cap (p_1^{-1}(t_1) \times p_2^{-1}(t_2)) \mid$;

We may now check that $\mathcal{B}$ is an $\mathcal{A}$iMP bisimulation between Σ_1 and Σ_2 :

(i) $(\pi_1^0,\pi_2^0,\emptyset) \in \mathcal{B}$ since $((M_1^0,\emptyset),(M_2^0,\emptyset),0) \in \mathcal{C}$;

(ii) by definition, β is a label preserving bijection between the visible events of π_1 (which are those of $\pi_1^<$, plus $E_1 \setminus E_1^<$) and those of π_2;

(iii) (a) if π_1 is extended into π_1' with a single event e_1, then
- either e_1 does not use any output condition of $E_1 \setminus E_1^<$ and has a label $t_1 \in \lambda_1^{-1}(a)$, with $a \in \mathcal{A}$;
then $(M_1,\beta_1^{\mathcal{A}}) \xrightarrow{t_1} (M_1,\beta_1^{\mathcal{A}} \cup \{t_1\})$ and, from the definition of $\mathcal{C}$, there is some $(M_2,\beta_2^{\mathcal{A}}) \xrightarrow{\sigma_2 t_2} (M_2',\beta_2^{\mathcal{A}} \cup \{t_2\})$ with $\hat{\lambda}_2(\sigma_2) = \epsilon$ and $\lambda_2(t_2) = a$; but this means that it is possible to extend π_2 into a process π_2' by silent events corresponding to σ_2 without using the output conditions of $E_2 \setminus E_2^<$, and by a maximal t_2-labelled event e_2 without using again the output conditions of $E_2 \setminus E_2^<$; by taking $\beta' = \beta \cup \{(e_1,e_2)\}$, and by adding e_1 to $E_1 \setminus E_1^<$ and e_2 to $E_2 \setminus E_2^<$, we will then get the desired extension property;
- either e_1 does not use any output condition of $E_1 \setminus E_1^<$ and has a label $t_1 \in \lambda_1^{-1}(\tau) \cup \lambda_1^{-1}(A \setminus \mathcal{A})$, i.e. such that $\lambda_1(t_1) \notin \mathcal{A}$;
then $(M_1,\beta_1^{\mathcal{A}}) \xrightarrow{t_1} (M_1',\beta_1^{\mathcal{A}})$ and, from the definition of $\mathcal{C}$, $(M_2,\beta_2^{\mathcal{A}}) \xrightarrow{\sigma_2} (M_2',\beta_2^{\mathcal{A}})$ with $\hat{\lambda}_2(\sigma_2) = \hat{\lambda}_1(t_1)$; but this means that it is possible to extend π_2 into a process π_2' by events corresponding to σ_2 (one of them, e_2, being visible if $\lambda_1(t_1) \neq \tau$, none otherwise) without using the output conditions of $E_1 \setminus E_1^<$; by taking $\beta' = \beta \cup \{(e_1,e_2)\}$ or β, we will then get the desired extension property

- either e_1 uses output conditions of $\{e_1^1,...,e_1^n\} \subseteq (E_1 \setminus E_1^<)$;
  if we may drop $\{e_1^1,...,e_1^n\}$ from $(E_1 \setminus E_1^<)$ and add them to $\pi_1^<$, we will come back to one of the first two cases; this corresponds to the $\mathcal{A}$ST-marking evolution $(M_1, \beta_1^{\mathcal{A}}) \xrightarrow{-\sigma_1} (M_1', \beta_1^{\mathcal{A}} \setminus \{e_1^1,...,e_1^n\})$ with $\sigma_1 = p_1(e_1^1...e_1^n)$; let $e_2^i = \beta(e_1^i)$ for $i = 1,...,n$; from the definition of C (and in particular from the fact that any t_2 corresponding to some t_1 may be used in a negative transition), we will have $(M_2, \beta_2^{\mathcal{A}}) \xrightarrow{-\sigma_2} (M_2', \beta_2^{\mathcal{A}} \setminus \{e_2^1,...,e_2^n\})$ with $\sigma_2 = p_2(e_2^1...e_2^n)$ and the same triple (π_1, π_2, β) corresponds to a triple $((M_1', \beta_1^{\mathcal{A}} \setminus \{e_1^1,...,e_1^n\}), (M_2', \beta_2^{\mathcal{A}} \setminus \{e_2^1,...,e_2^n\}), \beta_{12}') \in C$ with an adequate β_{12}'; hence the desired property.

(b) The vice versa case is symmetrical. ■ 5.13

A.5 Proof of 5.16.

Proof: $\Longrightarrow$

immediate from 5.10(c)

$\Longleftarrow$

From the hypothesis, $\forall k \geq 1 : ref(\Sigma_1, \mathcal{A}, D^k) \approx_i ref(\Sigma_2, \mathcal{A}, D^k)$, so that from 5.2 there is a set $\mathcal{B}^k$ of triples $(\tilde{\pi}_1^k, \tilde{\pi}_2^k, \tilde{\beta}^k)$ with the aforementioned properties. We may notice that if $\mathcal{B}_1^k$ and $\mathcal{B}_2^k$ are such sets, then $\mathcal{B}_1^k \cup \mathcal{B}_2^k$ also has the needed properties, so that there is a unique maximal triple set with them (which is the union of all those sets); we shall always choose this particular set $\mathcal{B}^k$.
One may see that each reachable marking of Σ_1 is also reachable in $ref(\Sigma_1, \mathcal{A}, D^k)$, if we extend this marking with zero values for all the places which are not in Σ_1; the same is true for Σ_2, of course.
Let C be the set of triples $((M_1, \beta_1^{\mathcal{A}}), (M_2, \beta_2^{\mathcal{A}}), \beta_{12})$ such that, for an infinite number of k values, there is a triple $(\tilde{\pi}_1^k, \tilde{\pi}_2^k, \tilde{\beta}^k) \in \mathcal{B}^k$ with the following properties :

- there is a prefix $\tilde{\pi}_1^{<k}$ of $\tilde{\pi}_1^k$ such that $\tilde{\pi}_1^{<k}$ leads to the marking M_1 of Σ_1 and the events of $\tilde{E}_1^k \setminus \tilde{E}_1^{<k}$ are unordered, have labels of the form $< a\_j, t_1 >$ where all the j's are different and correspond to $\beta_1^{\mathcal{A}}$ (i.e. $\forall t_1 \in \lambda_1^{-1}(\mathcal{A}) : \beta_1^{\mathcal{A}}(t_1) = | \{< a\_j, t_1 > \in \tilde{p}_1^k(\tilde{E}_1^k \setminus \tilde{E}_1^{<k})\} |$); we will then say that $(M_1, \beta_1^{\mathcal{A}})$ corresponds to $\tilde{\pi}_1^k$;
- similarly for $(M_2, \beta_2^{\mathcal{A}})$;
- $\tilde{\beta}^k(\tilde{E}_1^k \setminus \tilde{E}_1^{<k}) = \tilde{E}_2^k \setminus \tilde{E}_2^{<k}$;
- $\forall a \in \mathcal{A}\, \forall t_1 \in \lambda_1^{-1}(a)\, \forall t_2 \in \lambda_2^{-1}(a)$:
  $\beta_{12}(a)(t_1, t_2)$ is the number of pairs $(\tilde{e}_1^k, \tilde{e}_2^k) \in \tilde{\beta}^k \cap (\tilde{E}_1^k \setminus \tilde{E}_1^{<k}) \times (\tilde{E}_2^k \setminus \tilde{E}_2^{<k})$ such that $\tilde{e}_1^k$ has a label of the form $< a\_j, t_1 >$ for some j and $\tilde{e}_2^k$ has a label of the form $< a\_j, t_2 >$ (for the same j).

Let us first notice that in $\tilde{\pi}_1^{<k}$, no maximal event may have a label of the form $< a\_j, t_1 >$, otherwise the final marking would not also be a marking of Σ_1; consequently, the events in $\tilde{E}_1^k \setminus \tilde{E}_1^{<k}$ are the only maximal events of $\tilde{\pi}_1^k$ with such labels (and similarly for Σ_2), so that $\tilde{\pi}_1^{<k}$ and $\tilde{\pi}_2^{<k}$ are unique; the condition that all the j's are different only needs that $k \geq | \beta_1^{\mathcal{A}} | = \sum_{t_1} \beta_1^{\mathcal{A}}(t_1)$ $(= | \beta_2^{\mathcal{A}} |)$ and implies that there is no freedom in the choice of $\tilde{\beta}^k$ on $E_1^k \setminus E_1^{<k}$ (the j's are the same for Σ_1 and Σ_2).

We shall now check that C is an alternate $\mathcal{A}$iMP-bisimulation (in the sense of 5.13) between Σ_1 and Σ_2 :

(i) $((M_1^0, \emptyset), (M_2^0, \emptyset), 0) \in C$ since $\forall k \geq 1$ $(\pi_1^o, \pi_2^o, \emptyset) = (\tilde{\pi}_1^{ko}, \tilde{\pi}_2^{ko}, \emptyset) \in \mathcal{B}^k$

(ii) • if $(M_1, \beta_1^{\mathcal{A}}) \xrightarrow{-t_1} (M_1', \beta_1^{\mathcal{A}} \setminus \{t_1\})$, with $\lambda_1(t_1) = a \in \mathcal{A}$,
then for each k and $(\tilde{\pi}_1^k, \tilde{\pi}_2^k, \tilde{\beta}^k)$ with the mentioned properties, we have that, for each t_2 such that $\beta_{12}(a)(t_1, t_2) > 0$, there is $(\tilde{e}_1^k, \tilde{e}_2^k) \in \tilde{\beta}^k \cap (\tilde{E}_1^k \setminus \tilde{E}_1^{<k}) \times (\tilde{E}_2^k \setminus \tilde{E}_2^{<k})$ where $\tilde{e}_1^k$ has a label of the form $< a\_j, t_1 >$ for some j and $\tilde{e}_2^k$ has a label of the form $< a\_j, t_2 >$ for the same j.

The $\mathcal{A}$ST-marking $(M_1', \beta_1^{\mathcal{A}} \setminus \{t_1\})$ corresponds to the process $\bar{\pi}_1'^k$ obtained from $\bar{\pi}_1^k$ by adding an $< e\_a\_j, t_1 >$-labelled event $\tilde{e}_1'^k$ after $\tilde{e}_1^k$ (if one adds $\tilde{e}_1^k$ and $\tilde{e}_1'^k$ to $\bar{\pi}_1^{<k}$); let $\bar{\pi}_2'^k$ be the process obtained similarly by adding to $\bar{\pi}_2^k$ an $< e\_a\_j, t_2 >$-labelled event $\tilde{e}_2'^k$ after $\tilde{e}_2^k$: for the same reason, it corresponds to an $\mathcal{A}$ST- marking $(M_2', \beta_2^{\mathcal{A}} \setminus \{t_2\})$ and $(M_2, \beta_2^{\mathcal{A}}) \xrightarrow{-t_2} (M_2', \beta_2^{\mathcal{A}} \setminus \{t_2\})$.

With $\bar{\beta}'^k = \bar{\beta}^k \cup \{(\tilde{e}_1'^k, \tilde{e}_2'^k)\}$, $(\bar{\pi}_1'^k, \bar{\pi}_2'^k, \bar{\beta}'^k) \in \mathcal{B}^k$ since $\mathcal{B}^k$ is maximal. Indeed, if this were not the case, let $\mathcal{B}'^k = \mathcal{B}^k \cup \{(\bar{\pi}_1'^k, \bar{\pi}_2'^k, \bar{\beta}'^k)\}$: $\mathcal{B}'^k$ still has all the required properties since if $\bar{\pi}_1^k$ is an extension of $\bar{\pi}_1'^k$, it is also an extension of $\bar{\pi}_1^k$, there is $(\bar{\pi}_1^k, \bar{\pi}_2^k, \bar{\beta}) \in \mathcal{B}^k \subset \mathcal{B}'^k$ where $\bar{\pi}_2^k$ is an extension of $\bar{\pi}_2^k$ and $\bar{\beta}^k \subset \bar{\beta}$, but $\bar{\pi}_2^k$ is also an extension of $\bar{\pi}_2'^k$ and $(\tilde{e}_1', \tilde{e}_2') \in \bar{\beta}$ since there is only one way to add a first $< e\_a\_j, . >$-labelled event to $\bar{\pi}_2^k$, hence the contradiction. Notice that if $\mathcal{B}^k$ were not maximal, it could impose to add some more silent events at the end of $\bar{\pi}_2'^k$.

Thus $((M_1', \beta_1^{\mathcal{A}} \setminus \{t_1\}), (M_2', \beta_2^{\mathcal{A}} \setminus \{t_2\}), \beta_{12}') \in \mathcal{C}$
with $\beta_{12}'(x)(t, t') = \beta_{12}(x)(t, t') - \delta_{xa}\delta_{tt_1}\delta_{t't_2}$, as required.

- if $(M_1, \beta_1^{\mathcal{A}}) \xrightarrow{t_1} (M_1, \beta_1^{\mathcal{A}} \cup \{t_1\})$, with $\lambda_1(t_1) = a \in \mathcal{A}$,
then for each $k > \mid \beta_1^{\mathcal{A}} \mid +1$ (there is still an infinity of them since we may only lose one k) and $(\bar{\pi}_1^k, \bar{\pi}_2^k, \bar{\beta}^k)$ with the mentioned properties, since t_1 may occur concurrently with $\beta_1^{\mathcal{A}}$ from M_1, we may extend $\bar{\pi}_1^k$ with an event $\tilde{e}_1^k$ labelled by $< a\_j, t_1 >$, without using the output conditions of $\tilde{E}_1^k \setminus \tilde{E}_1^{<k}$ and with a j different from all the other ones already in the labels of $\tilde{E}_1^k \setminus \tilde{E}_1^{<k}$, giving a process $\bar{\pi}_1'^k$ which corresponds to the $\mathcal{A}$ST-marking $(M_1, \beta_1^{\mathcal{A}} \cup \{t_1\})$.
There is thus a triple $(\bar{\pi}_1'^k, \bar{\pi}_2'^k, \beta') \in \mathcal{B}^k$, where $\bar{\pi}_2'^k$ is an extension of $\bar{\pi}_2^k$ and $\beta' \supset \beta$ is a label preserving bijection; the events of $(\tilde{E}_2^k \setminus \tilde{E}_2^{<k}) \cup \{\beta'(e_1'^k)\}$ are maximal in $\bar{\pi}_2'^k$ since no (visible) event finally labelled by some e_a_x has been added, and no other event finally labelled by some a_x has been added, so that there is an $\mathcal{A}$ST-marking $(M_2'^k, \beta_2^{\mathcal{A}} \cup \{t_2\})$ corresponding to $\bar{\pi}_2'^k$ and $(M_2, \beta_2^{\mathcal{A}}) \xrightarrow{\sigma_2^k t_2^k} (M_2'^k, \beta_2^{\mathcal{A}} \cup \{t_2^k\})$ for some sequence σ_2^k such that $\bar{\lambda}_2(\sigma_2^k) = \epsilon$ and some $t_2^k \in \lambda_2^{-1}(a)$.
It may happen that σ_2^k and t_2^k effectively depend on k but, from the τ-boundedness hypothesis, we know that from $(M_2, \beta_2^{\mathcal{A}})$ there is only a finite number of $\mathcal{A}$ST-markings reachable with silent sequences, and from each of them there is a finite number of $\mathcal{A}$ST-markings obtained by adding a transition labelled by a to $\beta_2^{\mathcal{A}}$; thus there is still an infinity of values k for which those $\mathcal{A}$ST-markings are the same $(M_2', \beta_2^{\mathcal{A}} \cup \{t_2\})$, so that
$(M_2, \beta_2^{\mathcal{A}}) \xrightarrow{\sigma_2 t_2} (M_2', \beta_2^{\mathcal{A}} \cup \{t_2\})$ for some sequence σ_2 such that $\bar{\lambda}_2(\sigma_2) = \epsilon$ and some $t_2 \in \lambda_2^{-1}(a)$, and $((M_1, \beta_1^{\mathcal{A}} \cup \{t_1\}), (M_2', \beta_2^{\mathcal{A}} \cup \{t_2\}), \beta_{12}) \in \mathcal{C}$
with $\beta_{12}'(x)(t, t') = \beta_{12}(x)(t, t') + \delta_{xa}\delta_{tt_1}\delta_{t't_2}$, as required.

- if $(M_1, \beta_1^{\mathcal{A}}) \xrightarrow{t_1} (M_1', \beta_1^{\mathcal{A}})$, with $\lambda_1(t_1) = \tau$ or $b \notin \mathcal{A}$,
then for each k and $(\bar{\pi}_1^k, \bar{\pi}_2^k, \bar{\beta}^k)$ with the mentioned properties, since t_1 may occur concurrently with $\beta_1^{\mathcal{A}}$ from M_1, we may extend $\bar{\pi}_1^k$ with an event $\tilde{e}_1^k$ labelled by t_1, without using the output conditions of $\tilde{E}_1^k \setminus \tilde{E}_1^{<k}$, giving a process $\bar{\pi}_1'^k$ which corresponds to the $\mathcal{A}$ST-marking $(M_1', \beta_1^{\mathcal{A}})$.
There is thus a triple $(\bar{\pi}_1'^k, \bar{\pi}_2'^k, \beta') \in \mathcal{B}^k$, where $\bar{\pi}_2'^k$ is an extension of $\bar{\pi}_2^k$ and $\beta' \supseteq \beta$ is a label preserving bijection; the events of $(\tilde{E}_2^k \setminus \tilde{E}_2^{<k})$ are still maximal in $\bar{\pi}_2'^k$ since no (visible) event finally labelled by some e_a_x has been added, and no event finally labelled by some a_x has been added either, so that there is an $\mathcal{A}$ST-marking $(M_2'^k, \beta_2^{\mathcal{A}})$ corresponding to $\bar{\pi}_2'^k$ and $(M_2, \beta_2^{\mathcal{A}}) \xrightarrow{\sigma_2^k} (M_2'^k, \beta_2^{\mathcal{A}})$ for some sequence σ_2^k such that $\bar{\lambda}_2(\sigma_2^k) = \bar{\lambda}_1(t_1)$.
It may happen that σ_2^k effectively depends on k but, from the τ-boundedness hypothesis, we know again that from $(M_2, \beta_2^{\mathcal{A}})$ there is only a finite number of $\mathcal{A}$ST-markings reachable with silent sequences, or with a silent sequence followed by a transition with the same label as t_1 and followed again by a silent sequence; thus there is still an infinity of values i for which those $\mathcal{A}$ST-markings are the same $(M_2', \beta_2^{\mathcal{A}})$, so that $(M_2, \beta_2^{\mathcal{A}}) \xrightarrow{\sigma_2} (M_2', \beta_2^{\mathcal{A}})$

for some sequence σ_2 such that $\bar{\lambda}_2(\sigma_2) = \bar{\lambda}_1(t_1)$, and $((M_1', \beta_1^A), (M_2', \beta_2^A), \beta_{12}) \in \mathcal{C}$, as required.

The vice versa case is symmetrical. ■ 5.16

Acknowledgements

I am very indebted to W.Vogler for many encouragements and fruitful ideas, and to three anonymous referees whose deep comments greatly helped in preparing this paper.

References

[1] E.Best and R.Devillers: Sequential and Concurrent Behaviour in Petri Net Theory. TCS 55, pp.87-136 (1987).

[2] E.Best , R.Devillers, A.Kiehn and L.Pomello: Concurrent Bisimulations in Petri Nets, Acta Informatica 28, pp.231-264 (1991).

[3] E.Best and C.Fernández: Notation and Terminology on Petri Net Theory. Arbeitspapiere der GMD Nr.195 (February 1987).

[4] W.Brauer, R.Gold and W.Vogler: Behaviour and Equivalences Preserving Refinements of Petri Nets. In: Advances in Petri Nets 1990 (ed. G.Rozenberg), LNCS 483, pp.1-46 (1991).

[5] F.Cherief and P.Schnoebelen: τ-Bisimulations and Full Abstraction for Refinement of Actions. Technical report LIFIA-Imag (Grenoble, France), (1990).

[6] Ph.Darondeau and P.Degano: Causal Trees. In Proc. 11th Int. Coll. on Automata and Languages - ICALP89, LNCS 372, pp.234-248 (1989).

[7] P.Degano, R.De Nicola and U.Montanari: Partial Ordering Description of Nondeterministic Concurrent Systems. In Proc. REX School on Linear Time, Branching Time and Partial Order in Logics and Models for Concurrency, LNCS 354, pp.438-466 (1989).

[8] R.Devillers: Maximality Preserving Bisimulation . Technical report LIT-214, Université Libre de Bruxelles (March 1990). To appear in TCS.

[9] R.Devillers: Maximality Preserving Bisimilarity : Simplifications and Extensions . Technical report LIT-231, Université Libre de Bruxelles (May 1991).
Abstract in the Proceedings of the Third Workshop on Concurrency and Compositionality (ed. E.Best and G.Rozenberg), Goslar (FRG). GMD-Studien 191, pp.80-82 (1991).

[10] R.Devillers: Maximality Preservation and the ST-idea for Action Refinement (Full Report). Technical report LIT-242, Université Libre de Bruxelles (August 1991).

[11] R.van Glabbeek: The Refinement Theorem for ST-Bisimulation semantics. Proc. IFIP Working Conference on Programming Concepts and Methods (ed. M.Broy and C.B.Jones), See of Galilee (1990).

[12] R.van Glabbeek and U.Goltz: Equivalence Notions for Concurrent Systems and Refinement of Actions. Arbeitspapiere der GMD 366 (1989).
Extended abstract in Proc. MFCS 89, LNCS 379, pp.237-248 (1989).

[13] R.van Glabbeek and U.Goltz: Refinement of Actions in Causality Based Models. Proc. REX Workshop on Stepwise Refinement of Distributed Systems: Models, Formalism, Correctness, LNCS 430, pp.267-300 (1990).

[14] R.van Glabbeek and F.Vaandrager: Petri Net Models for Algebraic Theories of Concurrency. Proc. PARLE, vol.II (ed. J.W.de Bakker et al.), LNCS 259, pp.224-242 (1987).

[15] R.van Glabbeek and F.Vaandrager: The Difference between Splitting in n and $n+1$. Abstract in the Proceedings of the Third Workshop on Concurrency and Compositionality (ed. E.Best and G.Rozenberg), Goslar (FRG). GMD-Studien 191, pp.117-121 (1991).

[16] R.van Glabbeek and W.Weijland: Refinement in Branching Time Semantics. Proceedings of the International Conference on Algebraic Methodology and Software Technology - Iowa City (USA), pp.197-201 (1989).

[17] R. Gorrieri and C.Laneve: Split and ST-semantics for CCS. Proceedings MFCS 91. Abstract in the Proceedings of the Third Workshop on Concurrency and Compositionality (ed. E.Best and G.Rozenberg), Goslar (FRG). GMD-Studien 191, pp.122-124 (1991).

[18] R.Milner: Calculi for Synchrony and Asynchrony. TCS 25, pp.267-310 (1983).

[19] D.Park: Concurrency and Automata on Infinite Sequences. Proc. 5th GI Conference on Theoretical Computer Science (ed. P.Deussen), LNCS 104, pp.167-183 (1981)

[20] L.Pomello: Some Equivalence Notions for Concurrent Systems. An Overview. In: Advances in Petri Nets 1985 (ed. G.Rozenberg), LNCS 222, pp.381-400 (1986).

[21] L.Pomello: Observing Net Behaviour. In: Concurrency and Nets (ed. K.Voss et al.), Springer Verlag, pp.403-421 (1987).

[22] G.Rozenberg and R.Verraedt: Subset Languages of Petri Nets. TCS 26, pp.301-323 (1983).

[23] A.Rabinovitch and B.A.Trakhtenbrot: Behavior Structures and Nets. Fundamenta Informaticae XI, pp.357-404 (1988).

[24] W.Vogler: Failures Semantics Based on Interval Semiwords is a Congruence for Refinement. Distributed Computing 4, pp.139-162 (1991). Extended abstract in Proc. STACS'90, LNCS 415, pp.285-297 (1990).

[25] W.Vogler: Bisimulation and Action Refinement. Technical report SFB-Bericht 342/10/90A, Technische Universität München (May 1990). An extended abstract of the first part may also be found in the Proceedings STACS 91, LNCS 480, pp.309-321 (1991). The second part has also been presented as "Deciding History Preserving Bisimilarity" at ICALP 91.

[26] W.Vogler: Is Partial Order Semantics Necessary for Action Refinement? Technical report SFB-Bericht 342/1/91A, Technische Universität München (January 1991).

[27] W.Vogler: Generalized OM-Bisimulation. Technical report SFB-Bericht 342/8/91A, Technische Universität München (May 1991).

A Fifo-net model for processes with asynchronous communication

J. FANCHON

Laboratoire de Recherche en Informatique
CNRS UA 410
Bat. 490, Université Paris-Sud
91405 Orsay Cedex. FRANCE

Telephone : (+33) 1.69.41.64.32
Telefax : (+33) 1.64.46.19.92
E-mail : fanchon@lri.lri.fr

Abstract: *We define net-based formal models for concurrent processes communicating by asynchronous message passing. Programs specified in an abstract language are modelled by fifo-nets with composition operators, and for the first time extended compositionality and partial order semantics are considered in the fifo-net context. This leads to an algebra of fifo-nets, together with different congruences, which extends to the asynchronous communication part of the work on CCS, TCSP and ACP.*

Keywords: *Concurrent processes, asynchronous communication, fifo-nets algebra, partial order semantics.*

CONTENTS

Introduction

We intend to contribute to fill the existing gap between the distributed algorithms field, where processes have asynchronous communications, and net-based semantics for abstract languages with synchronous communications, CCS, TCSP, ACP, COSY ([GlVa],[Gol],[DDM],[Bes2]). Different models for asynchronous communication have been defined: finite state machines communicating through fifos [GoRo], fifo-nets [FiMe], which can be simulated by high-level nets. None is defined as a compositional model for an abstract language, although some of them may have some composition features.
We want to specify and model distributed algorithms with point to point communication, where the messages are neither duplicated nor lost, and, for each channel, received in the order they were emitted. For such programs an abstract language and a purely equational model have been defined in [BKT], giving an interleaving semantics to terms, with both bag-like and fifo-like behaviours of the channels.

Starting from a similar language, we define a compositional fifo-net model of terms, called Algebra of Fifo-Nets denoted AFN, leading to various semantics, in particular partial order semantics (see [Gra],[Bes1],[DDM],[BoCa]..).

Terms are constructed from atomic actions, by sequencing, choice and parallel operator. We distinguish actions which specify a channel and a message (sent or received), and internal actions (i.e. changing local state of variables etc..) denoted by a special symbol. An iteration operator is defined in the last section, we do not introduce it at first for simplicity's sake .

Principally two problems appear : How to define nets representing terms in such a way they can be composed; how to define semantics on these nets and in particular concurrent semantics, noting that the current semantics of fifo-nets are always interleaving ones.

In distributed algorithms , two types of causal dependency between events can be defined:
a) local (structural) causality which orders totally events in the execution of a sequential subprocess.
b) communication causality : on each channel the receipt of a message has to follow its emission.
The first dependency is related to the structure of the term, events from p precede events from q in the sequential composition p;q. The communication dependency expresses the asynchronous semantics of the actions. The net representation of terms and the different semantics reflect this distinction: on one side there is the semantics of the operators on terms (the structural aspect), on the other side the semantics of atomic actions (the communication view). [Ki]
In nets, events (i.e. fired transitions) causally depend on each other w.r.t. the flow relation, where places are involved. We distinguish two types of places:
a) state places model local dependency between their input and ouput transitions. The input and output edges of state places model the control flow of the program, and carry anonymous tokens. Thus on transition firing, state places behave like bags. The subnet generated by state places is a 1-safe labelled Petri net, which reflects the structure of the term, and called the control subnet.
State places without input arcs are called initial places and are the only marked places at initial marking. Places without output arcs are called final places, and final markings are those where all such places hold a token. The set of initial and final places of a net are used as an interface by which it can be composed with another one.
b) channel places model communication dependency. They behave like fifos, and their markings are finite words on the alphabet of messages. The channels through which a component (term) can communicate form its communication alphabet and are divided in three classes:
- local channels are the ones used for both sending and receiving messages by some concurrent components.
- input channels are used only for receipt.
- output channels are used only for emission.

Only local channels of a term are represented by channel places in its net representation.

To overcome the possible concurrent emissions of different messages in a channel, we impose a restriction on terms being modeled: two concurrent components may not have a common ouput channel or a common input channel. When composing two terms in parallel, the channels which are both input for one and output for the other become local for the resulting term. This is the only way channels may be local for a term : two sequential (or choice) components may not communicate together through a channel (they may share local memory), thus sequential subterms may not have local channels.
To describe communication dependency, we use the fact that all emissions (resp. receipts) in a channel are totally ordered by local dependency, due to the restrictions on terms. The order on communications along a channel c can then be defined as a prefix of the product of two total orders :

send mess 1 → send mess 2 → . . → send mess n

receive mess 1 → receive mess 2 → . . → receive mess n

A partially ordered behaviour which respects communication constraints on a channel "contains" such a prefix, and we say it is "balanced" for that channel. We show that the (partial) language of a net in AFN is the intersection of the (partial) language of its control subnet with the set of behaviours respecting communication constraints on all local channels (i.e. balanced for all local channels).

We define two semantics on terms based on sets of behaviours: the sequential semantics is based on the set of sequential behaviours of the net, the partial order semantics on the set of its partially ordered behaviours. We say "based on" because one can add more information, like distinguishing terminating behaviours, or deadlocking ones, etc. We use termination information, but other observations like deadlocks, failure sets or ready sets should be investigated too.

The partial order semantics is a weakly concurrent semantics in the sense of [Gra] : it does not express the maximal concurrency of executions, as for example any (totally ordered) firing sequence fulfills the weak firing pomset conditions. To represent a term by all its weakly firable pomsets, or only by those expressing the maximal concurrency, do not induce the same equalities on terms: in the first case (a||b + a;b) and a||b are identified, not in the second. This approach is due to the use of a "weak" parallel operator on balanced pomsets which allows a compositional definition of the partially ordered behaviours of fifo-nets. Maximally concurrent behaviours can be retreived from firing sequences as in [Bes1] [Maz] and [GlVa].

In the section V of the paper we introduce an iteration operator on sequential processes, extending the net algebra by nets with infinite sets of behaviours. The sequential and partial order semantics extend to the new algebra. The nets which model a process without inner parallelism, i.e. which is the parallel composition of sequential processes, and whose channels correspond to pairs of concurrent communicating (sequential) components, are Communicating Finite State Machines [BZ] . Any CFSM can be denoted by such a process, due to the fact that any finite state machine can be simulated by a sequential process and that the conditions on communications to compose FSM's are more restrictive.

We finally mention two developments:
- In/Out semantics , which abstracts from local activity, and identify processes which have the same activity on their Input and Output channels.
- The asynchronous exchange of anonymous messages (tokens), yielding a Petri Net model.

I. Asynchronous terms and the algebra of fifo-nets

I.a. Syntax for asynchronously communicating processes

Processes are finite terms constructed from a set A of elementary actions (emissions, receipts and internal action) by operators specifying sequencing (;), choice (+) and concurrent (||) composition of two processes. Due to restrictions mentioned in introduction, these operators are conditional: the composition of two terms is allowed depending on the channels occuring in their actions.

We distinguish in the set Ch(p) of channels used by a term p, the input ones, noted In(p), the output ones, Out(p), and the local ones, Loc(p).

The set $D(p,q) = (In(p) \cap Out(q)) \cup (Out(p) \cap In(q))$ is used to simplify the definitions, in particular it denotes the new local channels added by the parallel composition to the sets of local channels of p and q.Thus the operators Ch(), In(), Out(), Loc() and D() are introduced in the signature, and defined recursively by equations.

Definitions:

Ch is the set of channels names, Mes the set of messages, $A = Ch^{+}xMes \cup Ch^{-}xMes \cup \{\tau\}$ is the set of actions, where $Ch^{+} = \{c^{+}, c \in Ch\}$, $Ch^{-} = \{c^{-}, c \in Ch\}$, τ is the internal action, $Ch^{+}xMes$ the set of emissions, $Ch^{-}xMes$ the set of receipts. The emission and the receipt of a message m in a channel c are then specified by $c^{+}m$ and $c^{-}m$.

The signature Σ :

Sorts:

message, channel, set of channels, action, process.

Operators:

$\_^{-}\_$, $\_^{+}\_$: channel x message -> action
$\_$: action -> process
$\_;\_$, $\_+\_$, $\_||\_$: process x process -> process
In (_), Out(_), Loc(_), Ch(_) : process -> set of channels
D(_,_): process x process -> set of channels

Constants:

Ch : channel, Mes : message, τ : action.

Equations :

$Ch(p)=In(p) \cup Out(p) \cup Loc(p)$
$D(p,q)=(In(p) \cap Out(q)) \cup (Out(p) \cap In(q))$
$In(x^{-}m) = \{x\} = Out(x^{+}m)$
$In(x^{+}m) = Out(x^{-}m) = \emptyset = Loc(x^{+}m) = Loc(x^{-}m)$

p;q and p+q are defined iff $Loc(p) \cap Ch(q) = Loc(q) \cap Ch(p) = D(p,q) = \emptyset$.

$In(p;q) = In(p+q) = In(p) \cup In(q)$
$Out(p;q) = Out(p+q) = Out(p) \cup Out(q)$
$Loc(p;q) = Loc(p+q) = Loc(p) \cup Loc(q)$

p||q is defined iff $In(p) \cap In(q) = Out(p) \cap Out(q) = Loc(p) \cap Ch(q) = Loc(q) \cap Ch(p) = \emptyset$.

$Loc(p||q) = Loc(p) \cup Loc(q) \cup D(p,q)$
$In(p||q) = In(p) \cup In(q) - Loc(p||q)$
$Out(p||q) = Out(p) \cup Out(q) - Loc(p||q)$

x is a channel variable, m a message variable, p and q are process variables.

Note: the condition $Loc(p) \cap Ch(q) = Loc(q) \cap Ch(p) = \emptyset$ has to hold to compose p and q with any operator, a channel local to a subterm may not be accessed from others. To compose p and q in sequence or choice, D(p,q) has to be empty, and we put the condition $In(p) \cap In(q) = Out(p) \cap Out(q) = \emptyset$ for the || operator, as discussed in introduction. We only define finite terms without recursion, thus the recursive calculus of In, Out, and Loc on a term always terminates.

We note P the set of process terms on Σ. As P is a partial algebra, equations in P only apply to closed substitutions of their variables such that both sides are defined.

Notation: , p,q, p_i range over P, c ranges over Ch , m over Mes.We note N the set of integers.

I.b. The fifo-net model

The net domain for the representation of terms is a class of fifo-nets we call Fifo-Nets with Control subnet noted FNC, with two types of places, state and channel places. We define recursively how we model terms by such nets, starting from the model of actions, then modeling operators. The model of a term is defined up to nets isomorphism, and the Algebra of Fifo-Nets AFN is the subset of isomorphism classes of FNC which model the terms P through the representation function noted N . We show some basic properties of the nets in AFN, in particular of the subnet generated by state places, which is a 1-safe labelled Petri-net.

I.b.1. The net domain FNC

Definitions:

A net FNC is a 5-uple $N= (S \cup C,T,F \cup W,l,M_{in})$, such that $E(N)= (S,T,F,l,M_{in}/S)$ is a labelled Petri-net:

S is the set of **state places,** disjoint from Ch, the set of channels.

T is the set of **transitions** disjoint from $S \cup Ch$.

F is the **(control) flow relation,** $F: SxT \cup TxS \text{ -> } \{0,1\}$.

l is the **labelling function,** l : T-> A .

C is the set of **channel places** and it is a subset of Ch .

W is the **communication weight function,** $W : CxT \cup TxC \text{ --> } Mes \cup \{\lambda\}$,

where λ is the empty word in the monoid Mes*.

M_{in} and M_{in}/S are the **initial markings** and are defined below,

The **preset** (resp. **postset**) of x in $S \cup C \cup T$ is defined as $°x = \{y \in S \cup C \cup T \mid F(y,x) \neq 0$ or $W(y,x) \neq \lambda\}$, (resp. $x° = \{y \in S \cup C \cup T \mid F(x,y) \neq 0$ or $W(x,y) \neq \lambda \}$).

Notation: we use t , t', t_i to range over T , s to range over S .

We have to ensure the consistency of the weight function w.r.t.the transition labels : a transition is in the preset (resp. postset) of a channel place iff it is labelled by an emission (resp. receipt) through that channel. Furthermore that edge has to be labelled by the message occuring in the label. Thus we require that the weight function W, the set of channel places C and the labelling l satisfy the following consistency rules :

r1 : $c \in C \Rightarrow [(t \in °c \Leftrightarrow l(t) \in c^+Mes)$ and $(t \in c° \Leftrightarrow l(t) \in c^-Mes)]$.

r2 : $W(t,c) = m \Leftrightarrow (c \in C$ and $l(t) = c^+m)$, $W(c,t) = m \Leftrightarrow (c \in C$ and $l(t) = c^-m)$.

Two nets $N= (S \cup C,T,F \cup W,l,M_{in})$ and $N'= (S' \cup C',T',F' \cup W',l',M_{in}')$ are **isomorphic** iff

a) E(N) and E(N') are isomorphic as labelled Petri-nets , i.e. there is a bijection f: $S \cup T \text{ -->} S' \cup T'$ such that $f(S)= S'$, $f(T)= T$, $F(f(x),f(y)) = F(x,y)$ and $l'(f(t)) = l(t)$.

b) C = C', two isomorphic nets have the same set of channel places.

Note that $W'(c,f(t)) = W(c,t)$ and $W'(f(t),c) = W(t,c)$ (this is a consequence of the consistency rules and of the definition.).

Among the state places, we distinguish initial places as places without input transition, and final places, those without output transitions:

Initial places : $°N = \{ s \in S \mid °s = \emptyset \}$.

Final places : $N° = \{ s \in S \mid s° = \emptyset \}$.

A marking of N is a pair $M = (M_S,M_C)$, M_S:S-->$\mathcal{N}$ $\in \mathcal{N}^S$, M_C:C-->Mes* $\in$ Mes*^{C} : the first component is a Petri-net marking from state places to integers, the second a Fifo-net marking fom channel places to words of messages. State places have adjacent arcs weighted by 1, thus hold sets of anonymous tokens. Channel places have adjacent arcs weighted by letters in Mes, they hold words on Mes. We abbreviate and note M(x) when there is no confusion possible on x (i.e. between $M_S(x)$ and $M_C(x)$). A marking of E(N) is an element of $\mathcal{N}^S$ (also called S-marking). The **restriction to S** of a marking (M_S,M_C) of N, noted $(M_S,M_C)/S$ is the marking M_S of E(N) (see the initial marking of E(N)). At the **initial marking** M_{in}, only the initial places contain one token, other state places and channel places are empty : M_{in}= $(°N,\{\lambda\}^C)$. A **final marking** is such that final places hold a token, the other state places are empty, and the channels contain any marking.
We note $M_f = N° \times Mes*^C$ the set of final markings. E(N) has a single final marking, N°.

Two transitions t and t' are said to be **colocated** iff for some channel c in Ch, (l(t) and l(t') $\in$ c^+Mes) or (l(t) and l(t') $\in$ c^-Mes). A transition t **directly precedes** a transition t', noted t ->t', iff $t° \cap °t' \cap S \neq \emptyset$ (A state place has to be in both the postset of t and the preset of t'). We take -*> as the reflexive transitive closure of ->, t **precedes** t' iff t -*>t'.

I.b.2.The representation of terms

The model N(p) of a term p is an isomorphism class of FNC. We first define N for elementary actions, then define N(p1*p2) from N(p1) and N(p2), for any operator * such that p1*p2 is defined, using representatives of N(p1) and N(p2) which have disjoint sets of state places and transitions. Recall that to compose two terms by any operator, they must have disjoint sets of local channels.
To simplify notations, we write $N = (S \cup C,T,F \cup W,l,M_{in})$ = N(p) when we use a particular representative N of N(p).

The set C of channel places in N(p) is the set of local channels of p, C = Loc(p). Once we have defined $(S \cup C,T,F,l)$ for a representative of N(p), the weight function W is deduced from the labelling l on transitions by rules r1 and r2 defined above. The only operator for which channel places are added to the ones of components is ||, and it is also the only one where rules r1 and r2 have to be applied to retrieve the weight function of the corresponding adjacent edges in the resulting net.

In a similar way °N and N° are determined by the components S,T and F of N, and the initial and final markings by the definitions M_{in}= $(°N,\{\lambda\}^C)$ and $M_f = N° \times Mes*^C$. Thus we do not repeat these definition for each case.

a) Single actions

The net model N(a) of the single action term a of A has two state places (one initial, one final place), one transition labelled by the action name, and no channel place :

a ——>

Operators

Let $N_1 = N(p_1)$ and $N_2 = N(p_2)$, with $N_i = (S_i \cup C_i, T_i, F_i \cup W_i, l_i, M_{in_i})$, be two disjoint representatives. Then $N(p_1 * p_2)$ is the class of the net $N = (S \cup C, T, F \cup W, l, M_{in}) = N_1 * N_2$, defined below, depending on operator $*$.
We benefit from previous works (see [Gol] [GlVa]) to define the sequencing and choice operators, using cartesian products of initial and/or final places of the components.
We use the operation symbol $\cup$ on mappings in an obvious meaning, when domains are disjoint.

b) Sequencing

ex:

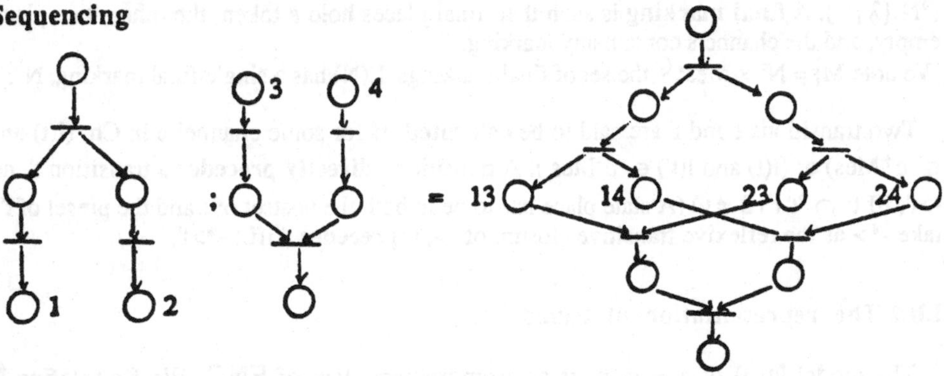

The net $N = N_1;N_2$ is defined by: $S = S_1 \cup S_2 - (N_1^\circ \cup {}^\circ N_2) \cup N_1^\circ \times {}^\circ N_2$, i.e. we replace, in the union of the state places, the final places of the first operand and the initial places of the second by their cartesian product, $C = C_1 \cup C_2$, $T = T_1 \cup T_2$, $(l/T_1 = l_1$ and $l/T_2 = l_2)$, $W = W_1 \cup W_2$ and
$F = ((F_1 \cup F_2) \cap (S \times T \cup T \times S)) \cup \{((s,s'),t), (s',t) \in F_2\} \cup \{(t,(s,s')), (t,s) \in F_1\}$.
We can deduce that ${}^\circ N = {}^\circ N_1$ and $N^\circ = N_2^\circ$.

c) Choice

ex:

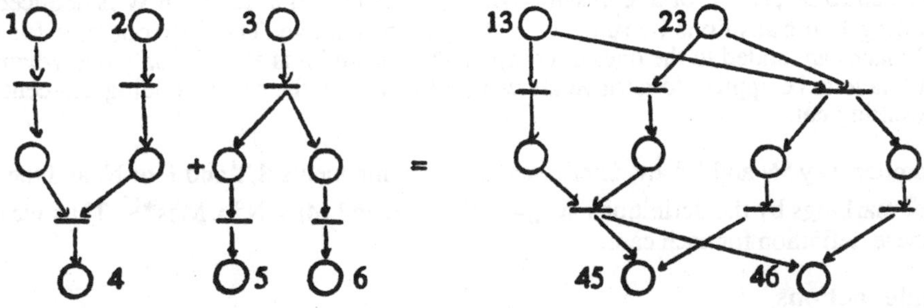

The net $N = N_1+N_2$ is defined by: $S= S_1 \cup S_2 - (°N_1 \cup °N_2 \cup N_1° \cup N_2°) \cup (°N_1 \times °N_2) \cup (N_1° \times N_2°)$, i.e. we replace the initial and final places of both nets by the cartesian products of the corresponding sets in the two nets, $C = C_1 \cup C_2$, $T = T_1 \cup T_2$, $(l/T_1 = l_1$ and $l/T_2 = l_2)$, $W = W_1 \cup W_2$ and

$F = ((F_1 \cup F_2) \cap (S \times T \cup T \times S)) \cup \{((s,s'),t),\ (s,t) \in F_1 \text{ or } (s',t) \in F_2\} \cup \{(t,(s,s')),\ (t,s) \in F_1 \text{ or } (t,s') \in F_2\}$.

In this case $°N = °N_1 \times °N_2$ and $N° = N_1° \times N_2°$.

d) Parallel composition

The net $N = N_1 \parallel N_2$ is defined by: $S= S_1 \cup S_2$, $C = C_1 \cup C_2 \cup D(p_1,p_2)$, $T = T_1 \cup T_2$, $(l/T_1 = l_1$ and $l/T_2 = l_2)$, $F = F_1 \cup F_2$, $W = W_1 \cup W_2 \cup W_d$ with

$W_d : D(p_1,p_2) \times T \cup T \times D(p_1,p_2) \to Mes \cup \{\lambda\}$ satisfying conditions r1 and r2.

We deduce $°N = °N_1 \cup °N_2$ and $N° = N_1° \cup N_2°$.

Ex:

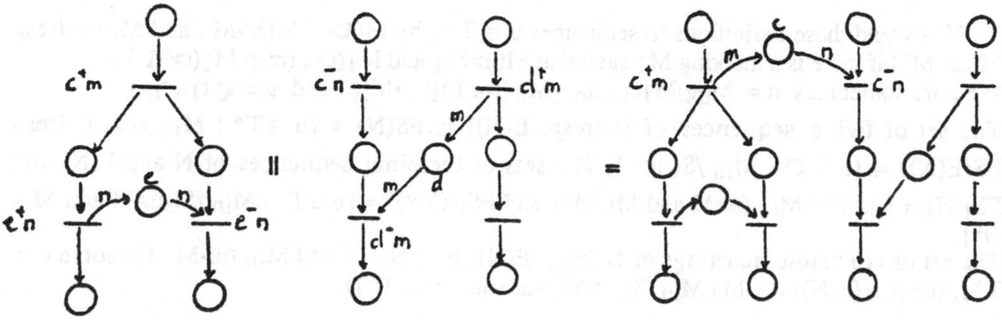

The construction of N(a) and $N(p_1{*}p_2)$ ensures that the sets of initial and final places of any net in AFN are not empty. Furthermore if a transition is in the postset of an initial place (resp. in the preset of a final place) then any place in its preset is an initial place (resp. any place in its postset is a final place).

Note : the equivalence relation noted $=_{\mathcal{N}}$, induced on terms by the identity of their corresponding net classes, i.e. $p =_{\mathcal{N}} q \iff N(p) = N(q)$, is a congruence for the operators on terms and some equations satisfied in the quotient algebra $P/{=_{\mathcal{N}}}$ can be checked easily with the net constructions : the choice and parallel operators are associative and commutative, te sequencing operator is associative.

I.c. Firing rules and general properties of AFN

From now on we always consider nets in AFN, i.e. representing some term of P.

Let $N = N(p) = (S \cup C, T, F \cup W, l, M_{in})$ be such a net.

The firing rules reflect the double aspect of the net : a transition t is enabled at a marking M in N iff:
1) it is enabled in E(N) for M/S (i.e. if any state place of its preset contains a token).
2) a channel place c of its preset contain a word whose first letter is equal to the weight W(c,t) .

Definition :
A transition t is **S-enabled** for a S-marking $M \in \mathcal{N}^S$, noted $M(_st>$, iff

$$M(s) \geq F(s,t) \text{ for all } s \text{ in } S.$$

If t is S-enabled at M then t can fire and yields a new marking M', noted $M(_st>M'$, with

$$M'(s)=M(s) - F(s,t) + F(t,s), \text{ for } s\in S.$$

Definition :
A transition t is **enabled** at marking $M = (M_S,M_C)$, noted $M(t>$, iff t is S-enabled for M_S , and

$$c \in C \Rightarrow M(c)\in W(c,t).Mes^*.$$

If t is enabled at M then t can fire and yields a new marking M', noted $M(t>M'$, with

$$M'(s)=M(s) - F(s,t) + F(t,s) \quad \text{for } s\in S, \text{ and}$$

$$M(c).W(t,c)= W(c,t).M'(c) \quad \text{for } c \in C.$$

We extend these definitions to sequences $u \in T^*$, by $M(\lambda>$, $M(\lambda>M$, and $M(ut>$ (resp $M(ut>M'$) if there is a marking M_1 such that $M(u>M_1$ and $M_1(t>$, (resp $M_1(t>M'$) .
We note sometimes $u = M_0t_0M_1t_1....t_{n-1}M_n$ for $M_i(t_i>M_{i+1}$ and $u = t_0.t_1...t_{n-1}$.
The set of **firing sequences** of N (resp. E(N)) is $FS(N) = \{u \in T^* \mid M_{in} (u> \}$, (resp $FS(E(N)) = \{u \in T^* \mid M_{in} /S(_su> \})$.The sets of **terminal sequences** of N and E(N) are: $FS_t(N) = \{u\in T^* \mid M_{in} (u>M \text{ and } M\in M_f\}$ and $FS_t(E(N)) = \{u \in T^* \mid M_{in} /S(_su>M \text{ and } M = N°\}$.
The set of **reachable markings** of N (resp. E(N)) is $R(N) = \{ M \mid M_{in} (u>M$, for some u in $T^*\}$, (resp. $R(E(N)) = \{ M \mid M_{in} /S(_su>M$, for some u in $T^*\}$).

The following lemma is a direct consequence of the definitions and states that the (terminal) firing sequences of N are (terminal) firing sequences of E(N) and that the restriction to S of a reachable marking in N is reachable in E(N):

Lemma 1:
$FS(N) \subset FS(E(N))$, $FS_t(N) \subset FS_t(E(N))$.
$(M_S,M_C)\in R(N) \Rightarrow M_S \in R(E(N))$.

The following proposition establishes the main properties of E(N) needed in the following. The operator ||| on languages is the shuffle and is defined in chapter II.a.

Proposition 1:
For any term p, let N = N(p), we have :
a) E(N) is 1-safe .
b) $M \in R(E(N))$ and $N° \subset M \Rightarrow M= N°$. If a reachable marking contains the output places , then it is the final marking of E(N).
c)For any terms p_1, p_2 such that p_1*p_2 is defined, let $N_i = N(p_i)$, $E(N_i) = (S_i,T_i,F_i,l_i,M_{ini}/S_i)$ for i = 1, 2, be two disjoint representatives, we have depending on * :

$FS(E(N_1;N_2))=FS(E(N_1))\cup FS_t(E(N_1)).FS(E(N_2))$ and
$FS_t(E(N_1;N_2))=FS_t(E(N_1)).FS_t(E(N_2))$.
$FS(E(N_1+N_2))= FS(E(N_1)) \cup FS(E(N_2))$ and $FS_t(E(N_1+N_2)) = FS_t(E(N_1)) \cup FS_t(E(N_2))$.
$FS(E(N_1 \parallel N_2))= FS(E(N_1)) \mathbin{|||} FS(E(N_2))$ and $FS_t(E(N_1 \parallel N_2)) = FS_t(E(N_1)) \mathbin{|||} FS_t(E(N_2))\}$.

Proof(hint):
by induction on p.
(a) and (b) are obvious for single transition nets. One proves that if (a) and (b) are valid for $N_1 = N(p_1)$ and $N_2 = N(p_2)$, then (c) holds for p_1*p_2 when defined, and (a),(b) follow for $N = N(p_1*p_2)$ .We prove that $FS(E(N_1; N_2)) \subset FS(E(N_1)) \cup FS_t(E(N_1)).FS(E(N_2))$, the other cases of (c) being simpler.
Let $N = N_1; N_2$ and $u \in FS(E(N))$, $u = M_{in}t_0M_0t_1..t_nM_n$. If all t_j are in T_1, then u is in $FS(E(N_1))$. Else let $i = Inf(\{j, t_j \in T_2\})$, then $v= t_0.t_1...t_{i-1} \in FS(E(N_1))$. The marking M_{i-1} enables the transition t_i of T_2 after a sequence of T_1*. Due to the construction of $N_1;N_2$, the preset of t_i in N must be included in $N_1°x °N_2$, and $M_{i-1}(s,s')\neq 0$ for any pair (s,s') in $N_1°x °N_2$ such that s' is in the preset of t_i in N_2 . To achieve this, if M' is the marking of $R(N_1)$ such that $M_{in1}(t_0.t_1...t_{i-1}>M'$, we must have $N_1° \subset M'$. From (b) we have $M' = N_1°$ and then $M_{i-1}=N_1°x °N_2$. For all j>i , $t_j \in T_2$ and u = vw where $v \in FS_t(N_1)$ and $w \in FS(N_2)$.
The 1-safeness of $E(N_1; N_2)$ is implied by the fact that any of its reachable markings is reachable also in one of the components.

II. Pomsets, balanced words and balanced pomsets

First we recall the framework on partial words or pomsets (see [Gra], [Pra]). Then we define the framework for balanced words and pomsets of transitions. We define in particular a new operation called balanced parallel composition (or balanced shuffle on words) which is an asynchronous version of the merge operation on words extended to pomsets.

II.a. Partial words, pomsets

Given an alphabet X, we call a **X-labelled poset**, X-LP in short, a triplet $s = (E, \leq, l)$ where E is a finite set of elements also called events, $\leq$ is a partial order on E, $l : E \longrightarrow X$ is a labelling function.
An **isomorphism** between two X-LPs is a one-to-one mapping of their events sets preserving order and labelling . The **set of partial words on X** [Gra] noted PW(X), is the set of isomorphism classes of X-LPs, also called pomsets on X [Pra]. Unless specified, we only work on partial words and we use the same notation $(E,\leq,l)$. A partial language on X is a subset PL of PW(X) .
We can view X as a subset of PW(X) , by identifying an element a in X with $(\{\varepsilon\}, =, l)$ where $l(\varepsilon) = a$. We note 1 the empty partial word : $1= (\emptyset, \emptyset, \emptyset)$.

We recall the classical operations of **concatenation, parallel and product composition** on partial words noted ";" , "||" and "x". Let $s_i = (E_i, \leq_i, l_i)$ with $l_i: E_i\text{-}> X_i$, for i = 1, 2, such that $E_1 \cap E_2 = \emptyset$:

$s_1;s_2 = (E_1 \cup E_2, \leq, l)$ where $\leq$ is the order generated on $E_1 \cup E_2$ by $\leq_1 \cup \leq_2 \cup E_1 x E_2$, and $l: E_1 \cup E_2 \to X_1 \cup X_2$ s.t. $l/E_i = l_i$.

$s_1 \| s_2 = (E_1 \cup E_2, \leq, l)$ where $\leq$ is the order generated on $E_1 \cup E_2$ by $\leq_1 \cup \leq_2$, and l defined as above.

$s_1 \, x \, s_2 = (E_1 x E_2, \leq, l)$ where $l(a,b) = (l_1(a), l_2(b))$, and $\leq = \leq_1 x \leq_2$, i.e $(a,b) \leq (c,d) \iff a \leq_1 c$ and $b \leq_2 d$. In this last case the labels alphabet of the product is the set product $X_1 x X_2$.

These operations can be extended to partial languages in an obvious way.

Let s be a poset $(E, \leq)$, $F \subset E$, the preset of F is $\downarrow F = \{ y \in E \mid \exists x \in F, y \leq x \}$.

A partial word s_1 is a **prefix** of s_2, noted $s_1 \leq s_2$, if and only if for some representatives $(E_1, \leq_1, l_1)$ and $(E_2, \leq_2, l_2)$ of s_1 and s_2 we have : $E_1 \subset E_2$, $\leq_1 = \leq_2 / E_1$, $E_1 = \downarrow E_1$ for $\leq_2$ and $l_1 = l_2 / E_1$. The residue $s_2 - s_1$ is the pomset represented by $(E_2 - E_1, \leq_2 / E_2 - E_1, l_2 / E_2 - E_1)$. We note $Pref(s) = \{s', s' \leq s\}$.

A partial word s_1 is **less sequential** than s_2, noted $s_1 \ll s_2$, if and only if for some representatives $(E_1, \leq_1, l_1)$ and $(E_2, \leq_2, l_2)$ of s_1 and s_2 we have : $E_1 = E_2$, $\leq_1 \subset \leq_2$ and $l_1 = l_2$. Pratt says s_2 is an augment of s_1, Grabowski calls it a weakening. The **set of augments** of s is $Aug(s) = \{s' \mid s \ll s'\}$. The **set of linearisations** of s, Lin(s) , is the subset of totally ordered elements of Aug(s) :

$$Lin(s) = Aug(s) \cap X^*.$$

These operations can be defined on partial languages in the usual way. A partial language PL is **closed for augment** (weak language in [Gra]) iff PL = Aug(PL). The **projection** of $s = (E, \leq, h)$ on a subset X' of X is the partial word $s|X' = (E', \leq', h')$ with $E' = \{e \in E \mid h(e) \in X'\}$, $\leq' = \leq / E'xE'$ and $l' = l / E'$.

The following are standart results([Gra], [Pra]):
Pref(Aug(s)) = Aug(Pref(s)), in particular we get : Pref(Lin(s)) = Lin(Pref(s)).
Aug(PL * PL') = Aug(PL) * Aug(PL'), where * may be the partial language concatenation or union . The same holds for Lin in place of Aug.

Words on an alphabet X can be viewed as totally ordered pomsets on X: the partial order is an initial segment [1..n] of positive integers with the usual total order .

$$\text{Ex: } v = v_1 \ldots v_n = ([1..n], \leq, l), \text{ with } l(i) = v_i, \text{ and } \leq \text{ the order on integers.}$$

We note λ the empty word, neutral for concatenation. The pomset parallel composition of two words is not a word. We use the **shuffle** operation on words noted $|||$: $u \, ||| \, v = Lin(u \| v)$, which yields a subset of X^*.

II.b. Balanced words and pomsets on A

Recall that A, the alphabet of actions, is $A = Ch^+ x Mes \cup Ch^- x Mes \cup \{\tau\}$, A^* and PW(A) are the sets of words and pomsets on A. Words and pomsets on A which respect the communication constraint on a channel c, i.e. the emission of a message in c precedes its receipt, are called balanced for c. For pomsets, we require the additional property that all emissions (receipts) through c are totally ordered.

Definitions:
Let c a channel in Ch, $A(c) = \{c^+, c^-\} x$ Mes, is the set of **actions on c.**

If C is a subset of Ch, then $A(C) = \cup_{c\in C} A(c)$.
Let $\alpha = (E,\leq, h)$ a pomset on A, the **projection of α on C** is the partial word $\alpha|C = (E',\leq',h')$ with $E' = \{e \in E \mid h(e) \in A(C)\}$, $\leq' = \leq/E'xE'$, $l' = l/E'$.

The set of **complete communication pomsets** on a channel c of Ch, denoted CP(c), is the partial language whose elements are products of the (totally ordered) word $c^+.c^-$ and any (totally ordered) word of Mes*:

$$CP(c) = c^+.c^- \times Mes^* .$$

Ex: the pomset $c^+.c^- \times m_1...m_n$ is the following:

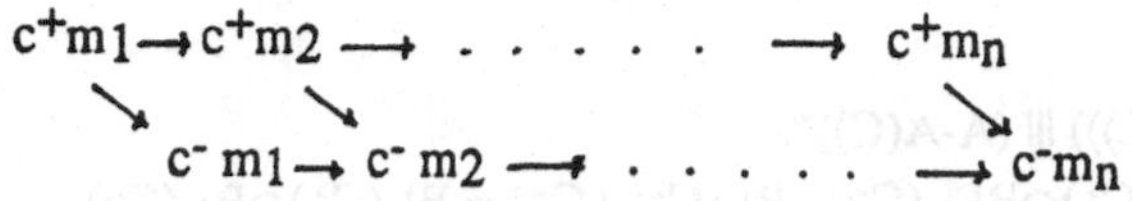

The set of complete communication pomsets on a subset C of Ch is $CP(C)= ||_{c\in C}\ CP(c)$. We define $CP(\emptyset) = \{1\}$.

A pomset α on A is balanced for C iff its projection on C is an (augmented) prefix of some complete communication pomset :

α **is balanced for C** $\Leftrightarrow$ $\alpha|C \in Aug(Pref(CP(C))$.

Ex: the following pomset is balanced for {c}, but not for {d} or {c,d}:

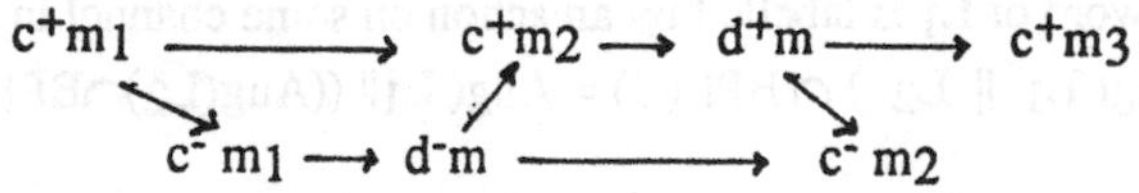

A word u on A is **balanced for C** $\Leftrightarrow$ $u|C\in Lin(Pref(CP(C)))$.

The set of balanced pomsets for C is the **balanced partial language** $BPL(C) =\{ \alpha\in PW(A), \alpha|C \in Aug(Pref(CP(C))\} = Aug(Pref(CP(C)) \parallel PW(A-A(C)))$.
The set $BL(C) = Lin(BPL(C))$, is the **balanced language** for C.

Note that BPL(C) (and BL(C)) is prefix closed: BPL(C) = Pref(BPL(C))

The **balanced parallel composition** of two pomsets α ,β, **w.r.t a set C of channels**, is the set

$$\alpha \parallel_C \beta = Aug(\alpha \parallel \beta) \cap BPL(C) .$$

Note that BPL(C) and $\alpha \parallel_C \beta$ are closed for augment .

Ex: the pomset in the previous example belongs to $\alpha \parallel_{\{c\}} \beta$ but not to $\alpha \parallel_{\{c,d\}} \beta$, if α and β are the pomsets

$$c^+m_1 \rightarrow c^+m_2 \rightarrow d^+m \longrightarrow c^+m$$

and

$$c^-m_1 \longrightarrow d^-m \longrightarrow c^-m_2$$

The balanced shuffle of two words u, v, w.r.t . a set C of channels is the set :

$$u \mid\mid\mid_C v = u \mid\mid\mid v \cap BL(C).$$

We define $\alpha \mid\mid_\emptyset \beta = Aug(\alpha \mid\mid \beta)$ and $u \mid\mid\mid_\emptyset v = u \mid\mid\mid v$.

Properties

The first following properties are easy to check:

Lemma 2 :

a) $BL(C) = Pref(Lin(CP(C))) \mid\mid\mid (A-A(C))^*$.

b) $BPL(C_1 \cup C_2) = BPL(C_1) \cap BPL(C_2)$, $BL(C_1 \cup C_2) = BL(C_1) \cap BL(C_2)$.

c) $u \mid\mid\mid_C v = Lin(u \mid\mid_C v)$. [$= Lin(Pref(Aug(u \mid\mid v)) \cap BPL(C)) = Pref(Lin(u \mid\mid v)) \cap BL(C)$].

d)Let $\alpha \in PW(A)$ and a subset C of Ch such that all events of α labelled by an emission (resp. receipt) on the same channel of C are totally ordered, then $Lin(\alpha) \subset BL(C) \Rightarrow \alpha \in BPL(C)$.

Note that $Lin(\alpha) \subset BL(C) \not\Rightarrow \alpha \in BPL(C)$, see $\alpha = c^+m \mid\mid c^+n$.

The following lemmas are used in propositions 3 and 6 :

Lemma 3:

Let be L_1 and $L_2 \subset PW(A)$ two partial languages, and $C \subset Ch$ such that $L_1 \subset PW(A-A(C))$, i.e no event in any partial word of L_1 is labelled by an action on some channel in C, then:

$$L_1 \mid\mid_C L_2 =_{def} Aug(L_1 \mid\mid L_2) \cap BPL(C) = Aug(L_1 \mid\mid ((Aug(L_2) \cap BPL(C))).$$

Proof:

Let $\alpha \in Aug(L_1 \mid\mid L_2) \cap BPL(C)$

For some $\alpha_i = (E_i, \leq_i, h_i) \in L_i$, $i = 1, 2$, we have $\alpha = (E_1 \cup E_2, \leq, h_1 \cup h_2) \in Aug(\alpha_1 \mid\mid \alpha_2)$, with $\leq_i \subset \leq/E_i x E_i$. Let $\alpha_2' = (E_2, \leq/E_2 x E_2, h_2)$, then $\alpha|C = \alpha_2'|C$, and $\alpha \in BPL(C) \Leftrightarrow \alpha_2' \in BPL(C)$. Thus $\alpha \in Aug(\alpha_1 \mid\mid \alpha_2')$ such that $\alpha_1 \in L_1$, $\alpha_2' \in Aug(L_2)$ and $\alpha_2' \in BPL(C)$.

We conclude that $\alpha \in Aug(L_1 \mid\mid (Aug(L_2) \cap BPL(C)))$. The reverse inclusion's proof is alike.

If we restrict to words , the lemma 3 can be formulated as follows:

Lemma 3w(ords):

Let be L_1 and $L_2 \subset A^*$, and $C \subset Ch$ such that $L_1 \subset (A-A(C))^*$ then:

$$L_1 \mid\mid\mid_C L_2 =_{def} L_1 \mid\mid\mid L_2 \cap BL(C) = L_1 \mid\mid\mid (L_2 \cap BL(C)).$$

Let $N = (S \cup C, T, F \cup W, l, Min)$ be a net in $\mathcal{AFN}$, we consider now elements of T^* and PW(T), the sets of words and partial words on T. Recall that l is a labelling function from T to A . A partial word $s = (E, \leq, h)$ on T, $s \in PW(T)$, is naturally mapped through l in a partial word on A : $l(s) = (E, \leq, l.h)$, $l(s) \in PW(A)$. A word on T can be viewed as a word on A by the same mean. Thus in the following, we extend the notion of balanced words and partial words to elements of T* and PW(T): a pomset α on T is balanced for C iff $l(\alpha)$ is balanced for C. As far as there is no confusion, BL(C) and BPL(C) will denote the subsets of T* and PW(T) consisting of words and partial words balanced for C.

III. Sequential semantics

Both sequential and pomset semantics of a term are derived from the net model in two steps: we first work out the behaviours of E(N), and retreive those of N restricting to the ones satisfying communication constraints. In the transition firing rule of N, the condition on channels restricts the firing sequences (resp. firing pomsets) to the balanced language BL(C) (resp. the balanced partial language BPL(C)).

We need two lemmas and the definition of the numbered labelling of events in a sequence, which indicates the range of an event, among events of same type (emission or receipt on the same channel).

Definition :
Let $u = t_1 \ldots t_n$ in T*, l the labelling function, the **numbered labelling** of u is the function $ln : [1..n] \dashrightarrow A \times N$, where

$$ln(i) = (l(t_i), |u[i]|_{c+}) \text{ if } l(t_i) \in c^+Mes,$$

$$ln(i) = (l(t_i), |u[i]|_{c-}) \text{ if } l(t_i) \in c^-Mes,$$

$$ln(i) = (\tau, 0) \text{ if } l(t_i) = \tau.$$

where $|u[i]|_{c+} = |\{j \leq i, l(t_j) \in c^+Mes\}|$ and $|u[i]|_{c-} = |\{j \leq i, l(t_j) \in c^-Mes\}|$.

The following lemma is a characterization of balanced words on T by a property of their numbered labelling:

Lemma 4:
Let be $u = t_1 \ldots t_n$ and ln the numbered labelling of u, then:
$u \in BL(\{c\}) \Leftrightarrow$ for any $i \in [1..n]$, $(ln(i) = (c^-m, k) \Rightarrow \exists\, j < i$ such that $ln(j) = (c^+m, k))$.

Definition:
Let c a channel in C, we define two functions from T to Mes : $I_c(t) = W(t,c)$, $O_c(t) = W(c,t)$, which we extend in a morphism from T* to Mes*. Let u a word on T, $I_c(u)$, (resp. $O_c(u)$), is the input (resp. ouput) word of c along u.

Lemma 5 :
Let $u = t_1 \ldots t_n$ such that M(u>M' and ln the numbered labelling of u, then for any $c \in C$:

a) $I_c(u) = m_1 \ldots m_q \Leftrightarrow u|(c^+Mes) = t_{i_1} \ldots t_{i_q}$ and $ln(i_j) = (c^+m_j, j)$, for $j \in [1..q]$.

b) $O_c(u) = m_1 \ldots m_q \Leftrightarrow u|(c^-Mes) = t_{i_1} \ldots t_{i_q}$ and $ln(i_j) = (c^-m_j, j)$, for $j \in [1..q]$.

c) $M(c).I_c(u) = O_c(u).M'(c)$.

Proof:
(a) and (b) are a direct consequence of the definitions. For (c), if $u = M_0 t_1 M_1 t_2 .. t_n M_n$ and $M_{i-1}(c).W(t_i,c) = W(c,t_i).M_i(c)$, for $i = 1,n$, $M_0=M$, $M_n=M'$, then $M_0(c).I_c(t_1..t_i) = O_c(t_1..t_i).M_i(c)$ for $i = 1,n$

The sequential behaviours FS(N) of N, are the ones in FS(E(N)) which are balanced for the local channels of N.

Proposition 2 :
$FS(N) = FS(E(N)) \cap BL(C)$.

Proof:
Step 1) $FS(N) \subset FS(E(N)) \cap BL(C)$.
We know that $FS(N) \subset FS(E(N))$, we need to prove that $FS(N) \subset BL(\{c\})$ for any $c \in C$.
Let be $u = t_1 ... t_n \in FS(N)$, $c \in C$, let $i \in [1..n]$ such that $ln(i) = (c^-m, k)$, and let be $v = t_1 ... t_{i-1}$ and M_{in} (v>M . We know that $m = W(c,t_i)$, that $M(c) \in W(c,t_i).Mes^*$ (definition of $M(t_i>)$ and that $I_c(v) = O_c(v).M(c)$ (Lemma 5) .Then $I_c(v) = m_1 ... m_{k-1}.W(c,t_i).m_{k+1} ... m_q$.
We conclude that $\exists\, j \le i-1$ such that $ln(j) = (c^+m, k)$ (Lemma 5), thus $u \in BL(\{c\})$ (Lemma 4).

Step 2) $FS(E(N)) \cap BL(C) \subset FS(N)$.
Let $u = t_1 ... t_n \in FS(E(N)) \cap BL(C)$, and $i = Sup\{j \in [1..n] \mid t_1 ... t_j \in FS(N)\}$ which is defined because $t_1 \in FS(N)$). If $i \neq n$ then let $v = t_1 ... t_i$ and M_{in} (v>M . We know that $M(_s t_{i+1}>$ and if $W(c,t_{i+1}) = \lambda$ for any $c \in C$, then $M(t_{i+1}>$, which contradicts the definition of i.
Suppose that $W(c,t_{i+1}) = m \neq \lambda$, let ln the numbered labelling of u. By hypothesis $v.t_{i+1} \in BL(\{c\})$, then $ln(i+1) = (c^-m, k) \Rightarrow \exists\, j \le i$ such that $ln(j) = (c^+m, k)$, where $k = |O_c(v)| + 1$.
We can write $I_c(v) = m_1 ... m_{k-1} m_k ... m_q$ with $m_k = m$.
Using $I_c(v) = O_c(v).M(c) = m_1 ... m_{k-1}.M(c)$, we conclude that $M(c) = m.m_{k+1} ... m_q \in W(c,t_{i+1}).Mes^*$. Thus $M(t_{i+1}>$ which contradicts the definition of i.

The following proposition describes the sequential behaviours of AFN nets and yields the compositionality of the sequential semantics expressed by the proposition 4.

Proposition 3 :
For any terms p_1, p_2, s.t. $p_1 * p_2$ is defined, let $N_i = N(p_i) = (S_i \cup C_i, T_i, F_i \cup W_i, l_i, M_{ini})$ two disjoint representatives, we have, depending on *:

1)$FS(N_1;N_2)) = FS(N_1) \cup FS_t(N_1).FS(N_2)$ and $FS_t(N_1;N_2)) = FS_t(N_1).FS_t(N_2)$.

2)$FS(N_1+N_2)) = FS(N_1) \cup FS(N_2)$ and $FS_t(N_1+N_2)) = FS_t(N_1) \cup FS_t(N_2)$.

3)$FS(N_1 \| N_2)) = FS(N_1) \,|||_{D(p_1,p_2)}\, FS(N_2)$ and $FS_t(N_1 \| N_2)) = FS_t(N_1) \,|||_{D(p_1,p_2)}\, FS_t(N_2)$

Proof(hint):
Only use propositions 1 and 2, taking in account the conditions on channels for the operators.
We show 3): $FS(N(p_1 \| p_2)) = FS(E(N(p_1 \| p_2))) \cap BL(C)$.

$$= (FS(E(N_1)) \,|||\, FS(E(N_2))) \cap BL(C_1 \cup C_2 \cup D(p_1,p_2))$$

$$= (FS(E(N_1)) \mid\mid\mid FS(E(N_2))) \cap BL(C_1) \cap BL(C_2) \cap BL(D(p_1,p_2))$$

(1) $$= ((FS(E(N_1)) \cap BL(C_1)) \mid\mid\mid (FS(E(N_2)) \cap BL(C_2))) \cap BL(D(p_1,p_2))$$

$$= (FS(N_1) \mid\mid\mid FS(N_2)) \cap BL(D(p_1,p_2))$$

$$= FS(N_1) \mid\mid\mid_{D(p1,p2)} FS(N_2) .$$

To deduce (1), use $C_1 \cap Ch(p_2) = \emptyset$ (because $C_1 = Loc(p_1)$) and then by the lemma 3w: $(FS(E(N_1)) \mid\mid\mid FS(E(N_2))) \cap BL(C_1) = (FS(E(N_1)) \cap BL(C_1)) \mid\mid\mid FS(E(N_2))$.

The sequential semantics on terms is now defined considering words on actions A instead of words on transitions through the labelling function l:

Definitions :
Let l the labelling function of a net N , l is extended to a function from T* to A* .
The language of a net N is the set $L(N) = \{l(u) , u \in FS(N)\}$, its **terminal language** is $L_t(N) = \{l(u) \mid u \in FS_t(N)\}$.
Two isomorphic nets have the same language, thus we can define the **language of a term** p (with termination information) as the pair $L(p) = (L(N(p)), L_t(N(p)))$.
The **sequential equivalence** $=_s$ on P is defined by $p1 =_s p2 \iff L(p1) = L(p2)$.

Proposition 4 :
The equivalence $=_s$ is a congruence for the operators of the signature and $=_{\mathcal{N}} \subset =_s$.

Equations .

The quotient algebra $P/=_s$ satisfies some expected equations. The choice and parallel operator are associative and commutative, the choice operator is idempotent.
Furthermore this semantics does not respect causality or branching time, and this is expressed by the following relations :
for all a, b in A, p, q and r in P such that both sides are defined:
$a|||b =_s a;b + b;a$, $\quad p;(q+r) =_s p;q + p;r$, $\quad (p+q);r =_s p;r + q;r$.

IV. Partial order semantics

As for sequential semantics, we first study the partially ordered behaviours of E(N) which express the structural causality between events. When composing two terms in parallel, they may not have common input channels, or common output channels, and it induces that for any reachable marking in E(N), two emissions or two receipts in the same channel may not be concurrently enabled. This property allows to define a step and pomset firing rules for a fifo-net N in AFN, using the ones for E(N). As mentionned in introduction, we define a weakly concurrent compositional semantics. In the last section we retrieve the causal order between events in a maximally concurrent behaviour, from any of its linearized representations (firing sequence). The map Pom (resp.Spom) associates to each firing sequence of N (resp. E(N)) the corresponding most concurrent firing pomset. [GlVa].

The whole process can be described by the following diagram, where FP(N) denotes the weak firing pomsets of N, and MFP(N) its maximally concurrent ones.

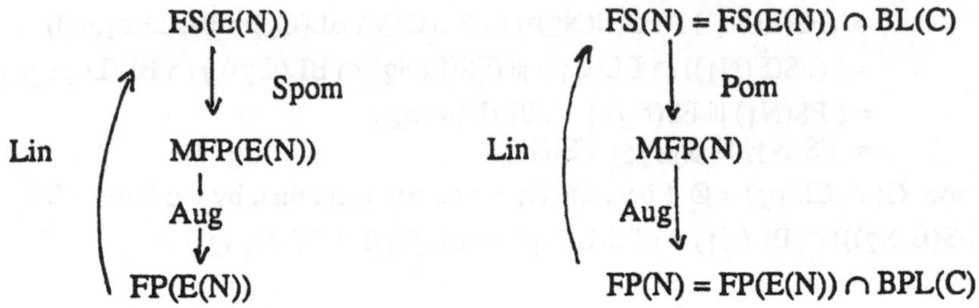

IV.a. Step and pomset firing rules

We consider $N = N(p) = (S \cup C, T, F \cup W, l, M_{in})$ for a term p of P.

We first define the step firing rule in E(N), and work out some properties of concurrently enabled transitions in E(N). A step μ is a multiset on T , i.e. a function from T to the set of integers. It can be viewed as a pomset on T with an empty order. The support of μ is the set $[\mu] = T - \mu^{-1}(0)$.

Definition (step firing rule in E(N):
Let M in R(E(N)) , a **multiset** μ of transitions is **S-enabled** at the S-marking M, noted $M({}_S\mu>$, iff

$$M(s) \geq \Sigma_{t \in T}\, \mu(t)F(s,t) \quad \text{for all s in S.}$$

If μ is S-enabled at M then μ can fire and yields a new marking M', noted $M({}_S\mu>M'$, where

$$M'(s)=M(s) - \Sigma_{t \in T}\, \mu(t)F(s,t) + \Sigma_{t \in T}\, \mu(t)F(t,s).$$

Note: If μ is S-enabled at M, then all linearizations of μ are S-enabled at M and yield the same marking.

The following lemma states that if μ is S-enabled at M, then all linearizations of μ are S-enabled at M and yield the same marking (obvious from definition):

Lemma 6 :
$M({}_S\mu>M'$ and $u \in Lin(\mu) \Rightarrow M({}_Su>M'$.

To define the step firing rule in N, we need to be sure that if some emissions and receipts in the same channel are concurrently enabled, at most one of each type is, so that the new marking of channels can be deterministically defined.The properties of E(N), and the restrictions on operators forbid concurrent firings of the same transition, or concurrent firings of colocated transitions.

Lemma 7 :
$M \in R(E(N))$ and $M({}_S\mu> \Rightarrow$ i) $\mu(t) \leq 1$
ii) $t \neq t'$, t and t' are colocated $\Rightarrow \mu(t).\mu(t') = 0$.

Proof:
i) is due to the 1-safeness of E(N).
ii) by induction on p. The property is obvious if p is an action.
Let $N = N(p) = N(p_1 * p_2)$ with $N_i = N(p_i) = (S_i \cup C_i, T_i, F_i \cup W_i, l_i, M_{in_i})$.
1) If $p = p_1;p_2$ or $p = p_1+p_2$, then
$\mu(t).\mu(t') \neq 0 \Rightarrow M({}_St.t'>$ and $M({}_St'.t>$
$\Rightarrow$ (t and $t' \in T_1$) or (t and $t' \in T_2$) (proposition 1c).

The multiset μ is enabled either in N_1 or in N_2 and by the induction hypothesis , t and t' cannot be colocated.
2) If p =p1|| p2 and $\mu(t).\mu(t')\neq 0$ then either t and t' belong to the same set T_i, and are not colocated by the induction hypothesis, otherwise they cannot be colocated due to the condition $In(p1) \cap In(p2) = Out(p1) \cap Out(p2) = \emptyset$ for the || operator.

A consequence of this lemma is that any channel c has at most one input and one output transition in any S-enabled multiset:

$$c \in {}^{\circ}[\mu] \Rightarrow |c^{\circ} \cap [\mu]| = 1 \text{ and } c \in [\mu]^{\circ} \Rightarrow |{}^{\circ}c \cap [\mu]| = 1.$$

Hence for such a multiset μ , we can define for any channel c an input word and an output word:

if $c \in [\mu]^{\circ}$ and $t = {}^{\circ}c \cap [\mu]$, then $I_c(\mu) = W(t,c)$, else $I_c(\mu) = \lambda$

if $c \in {}^{\circ}[\mu]$ and $t = c^{\circ} \cap [\mu]$, then $O_c(\mu) = W(c,t)$, else $O_c(\mu) = \lambda$

We can define the step firing rule in N:

Definition (step firing rule in N):
Let M in R(N) , a multiset μ of transitions is **enabled** at marking M , noted $M(\mu>$, iff
μ is S-enabled for M/S and
$t \in [\mu] \Rightarrow M(c) \in W(c,t).Mes^*$
If μ is enabled at M then μ can fire and yields a new marking M', noted $M(\mu>M'$, where

$M'(s)=M(s) - \Sigma_{t \in T}\,\mu(t)F(s,t) + \Sigma_{t \in T}\,\mu(t)F(t,s)$ for $s \in S$, and

$M(c).I_c(\mu) = O_c(\mu).M'(c)$ for $c \in C$.

From the definitions we see that any linearization of an enabled multiset is a enabled sequence:

Lemma 8 :
$M(\mu>M'$ and u in $Lin(\mu) \Rightarrow M(u>M'$.

Pomset firing rules

Definition (pomset firing rule in E(N)):
Let $\alpha = [(E, \leq, h)]$ in PW(T), α is (weakly) **S-enabled** at marking $M \in R(E(N))$, noted $M({}_s\alpha>$, iff for any prefix β of α, $\beta = (F,\leq,h)$:

i) $u \in Lin(\beta) \Rightarrow M({}_s u> M'$ for some M',

ii) for any subset G of E such that $x \in G \Rightarrow (x \notin F$ and $\downarrow x \subset F \cup \{x\})$, then $M'({}_s h(G)>$, where h(G) is the multiset on T of the labels of G (in particular G is a set of pairwise unordered events called a cut of α).

Note: for any pomset α, if u, $v \in Lin(\alpha)$ then $M({}_s u>M'$ and $M({}_s v>M'' \Rightarrow M' = M''$ because $M'(s) = M''(s) = M(s) - \Sigma_{t \in T}\,\alpha(t)F(s,t) + \Sigma_{t \in T}\,\alpha(t)F(t,s)$ for all s in S , where $\alpha(t)$ is the number of events labelled by t in α, u and v.

The following lemma states that firings of colocated transitions are totally ordered in firing pomsets of E(N):

Lemma 9 :
let M in R(E(N)), $\alpha = [(E, \leq, h)] \in PW(T)$ such that $M({}_s\alpha >$, and let $e, e' \in E$, then:
h(e) and h(e') are colocated => $e \geq e'$ or $e' \leq e$.

Proof:
If neither $e \leq e'$ nor $e' \geq e$, then $F = \downarrow\{e,e'\} - \{e,e'\}$ is a prefix of E and from the definition of the pomset firing rule, it can fire, leading to a marking for which the step {h(e), h(e')} is S-enabled. With the lemma 7 we conclude that h(e) and h(e') may not be colocated.

We can now define firable pomsets in N:

Definition (pomset firing rule in N):
Let $\alpha = [(E, \leq, h)]$ in PW(T), α is (weakly) **enabled** at marking $M \in R(N)$, noted $M(\alpha>$, iff for any prefix β of α, $\beta = (F, \leq, h)$:

i) $u \in Lin(\beta) \Rightarrow M(u>M'$ for some M',

ii) for any subset G of E such that $x \in G \Rightarrow (x \notin F$ and $\downarrow x \subset F \cup \{x\})$, then

M'(h(G)> (G is a cut of α).

From that definition we see that to be enabled at the marking M a pomset has to be S-enabled at the marking M/S. Also all prefixes of an enabled (S-enabled) pomset are enabled.
If a pomset is enabled (resp. S-enabled) for a marking M (resp. M/S), then all its augments are enabled (resp.S-enabled): if $\beta \in Aug(\alpha)$, a cut of β is a cut of α, and if α fulfills the firing conditions, then β does too.

If all colocated transitions are totally ordered in a pomset α, we have for any words u, v $\in Lin(\alpha)$: $I_c(u)=I_c(v)$ and $O_c(u)=O_c(v)$. In that case we define the **input and ouput words for c along** α as $I_c(\alpha) = I_c(u)$ and $O_c(\alpha) = O_c(u)$ for any $u \in Lin(\alpha)$. This applies to any S-enabled pomset to define the obtained marking in the following way:

Definition :
If α is enabled at a marking M then it can fire, yielding a new marking M', noted $M(\alpha>M'$, where

$$M'(s)=M(s) - \Sigma_{t \in T}\, \alpha(t)F(s,t) + \Sigma_{t \in T}\, \alpha(t)F(t,s), \text{ for } s \in S, \text{ and}$$
$$M(c).I_c(\alpha) = O_c(\alpha).M'(c), \text{ for } c \in C.$$

The marking M' does not changes when we increase the order of events in α, i.e. considering augments (and linearizations) of α. This property together with the ones mentionned above are summarized in the following lemma:

Lemma 10:
$M({}_s\alpha>M'$ and $\beta \in Aug(\alpha) \Rightarrow M({}_s\beta > M'$.
$M(\alpha> M' \Rightarrow M({}_s\alpha>$ and $(\beta \in Aug(\alpha) \Rightarrow M(\beta >M'$).

IV.b. Weak Partial order behaviours

Definition :
The set of firing pomsets of E(N) is $FP(E(N)) = \{\alpha \in PW(T) \mid M_{in}/S({}_S\alpha >\}$, the set of terminal firing pomsets is $FP_t(E(N))= \{\alpha \in PW(T) \mid M_{in}/S({}_S\alpha > N^\circ\}$.

The following proposition describes the firing pomsets of $E(N_1*N_2)$ as particular compositions of those of $E(N_1)$ and $E(N_2)$, yielding the compositionality of the pomsets semantics.

Proposition 5 :
For any terms p_1, p_2 such that $p_1 * p_2$ is defined, let $N_i = N(p_i)$ for i= 1,2, be two disjoint representatives, we have depending on $*$:
$FP(E(N_1;N_2))=FP(E(N_1)) \cup FP_t(E(N_1));FP(E(N_2))$ and
$FP_t(E(N_1;N_2))=FP_t(E(N_1));FP_t(E(N_2))$.
$FP(E(N_1+ N_2)) =FP(E(N_1)) \cup FP(E(N_2))$ and $FP_t(E(N_1+N_2)) = FP_t(E(N_1)) \cup FP_t(E(N_2))$.
$FP(E(N_1 \| N_2))= FP(E(N_1)) \|_\emptyset FP(E(N_2))$ and $FP_t(E(N_1 \| N_2))= FP_t(E(N_1)) \|_\emptyset FP_t(E(N_2))$

Proof(hint):
We prove $FP(E(N_1; N_2)) \subset FP(E(N_1)) \cup FP_t(E(N_1));FP(E(N_2))$. Let be $N = N_1; N_2$ and $\alpha = (E, \leq, h) \in FP(E(N))$. If E is not empty, then the set $F = \{e \in E \mid h(\downarrow e) \subset T_1\}$ is not empty, because it contains at least an element e such that $^\circ h(e) \subset {}^\circ N = {}^\circ N_1$.The partial word $\beta = (F, \leq/FxF, h/F)$ is a prefix of α:
If E = F then $\alpha = \beta \in FP(E(N_1))$, which is what we want.
Else let M be the marking such $M_{in}(\beta >M$, and $G = \{ e \in E\text{-}F \mid e'<e \Rightarrow e' \in F\}$. We have $e \in E \Rightarrow h(e) \in T_2$ and $M(h(G)) >$. The only marking of R(N) enabling a transition of T_2 after firing transitions of T_1 is $M= N_1{}^\circ x\, {}^\circ N_2$. We have then $\beta \in FP_t(E(N_1))$ and $\gamma = (E\text{-}F, \leq/(E\text{-}F)x(E\text{-}F), h/(E\text{-}F)) \in FP(E(N_1))$.
We conclude that $\alpha = \beta;\gamma$, due to the fact that $\leq = \leq/FxF \cup \leq/(E\text{-}F)x(E\text{-}F) \cup (F \times (E\text{-}F))$:
The inclusion from left to right is obvious,
The right to left inclusion is due to the inclusion $(F \times (E\text{-}F)) \subset \leq$: if $e \in F$, $e' \in E\text{-}F$ and $e \leq e'$ does not hold , then for some linearisation $(E, \leq', h)$ of , we have $e' \leq' e$, with $h(e) \in T_1$ and $h(e') \in T_2$, which contradicts the proposition 1c .

As we did for sequential semantics, we show that the partial order behaviours of N are the ones of E(N) which are balanced for local channels of N. The compositionality of the (weak) pomset semantics will follow from this property and the proposition 5.

Definition :
The set of firing pomsets of N is $FP(N) = \{\alpha \in PW(T) \mid M_{in}(\alpha >\}$, the set of terminal firing pomsets is $FP_t(N)= \{\alpha \in PW(T) \mid M_{in}(\alpha >M'$ and $M' \in M_f \}$.

Proposition 6 :
$FP(N) = FP(E(N)) \cap BPL(C)$

Proof :

1)$FP(N) \subset FP(E(N)) \cap BPL(C)$. We have to prove that $FP(N) \subset BPL(C)$:

let $\alpha \in FP(N)$, the property follows from the fact that all linearizations of α are in FS(N), thus they belong to BL(C) by proposition 2. Then α is in BPL(C) due to lemma 2d.

2) $FP(E(N)) \cap BPL(C) \subset FP(N)$. Let $\alpha = (E, \leq, h) \in FP(E(N)) \cap BPL(C)$, and a prefix β of α, $\beta = (F,\leq,h)$ (β is also in $FP(E(N)) \cap BPL(C)$) :

i) the linearizations of β are firable :

$Lin(\beta) \subset Lin(FP(E(N)) \cap BPL(C)) = FS(E(N)) \cap BL(C) = FS(N)$.

Let $u \in Lin(\beta)$ and $M_{in}(u>M$,

ii) Let G a subset of E such that $x \in G \Rightarrow (x \notin F$ and $\downarrow x \subset F \cup \{x\})$. The multiset h(G) has to be enabled for M:

a) It is S-enabled , $\alpha \in FP(E(N)) \Rightarrow M({}_s h(G)>$.

b)To show that $t \in [h(G)] \Rightarrow M(c) \in W(c,t).Mes^*$, let be $x \in G$ and $c \in C$ such that $t = h(x)$ and $W(c,t)=m \neq \lambda$ ($\Leftrightarrow l(t) = (c^-m)$).Then $\gamma = (F= F\cup\{x\}, \leq/F'xF', l/F')$ is a prefix of α and we have: $\gamma \in BPL(\{c\})$, $u.t \in Lin(\gamma)$ (by definition of G) and thus $u.t \in BL(\{c\})$. We have also $(u.t \mid c^+Mes) = c^+xI_c(u)$, $(u.t \mid c^-Mes) = (c^-xO_c(u)).(c^-m)$, and $u.t \in BL(\{c\}) \Rightarrow I_c(u) \in O_c(u).m.Mes^*$. From $I_c(u)= O_c(u).M(c)$, we conclude that $M(c) \in m.Mes^* = W(c,t).Mes^*$.

The following proposition on (weak) firing pomsets of AFN, is the basis to prove the compositionality of the pomset semantics stated in proposition 8.

Proposition 7 :

For any terms p1, p2, such that p1*p2 is defined, let $N_i= N(p_i) = (S_i\cup C_i,T_i,F_i\cup W_i,l_i,M_{ini})$ for i= 1,2, be two disjoint representatives, we have, depending on *:

1)$FP(N_1;N_2)) = FP(N_1) \cup FP_t(N_1);FP(N_2)$ and $FP_t(N_1;N_2)) = FP_t(N_1);FP_t(N_2)$.

2)$FP(N_1+N_2)) = FP(N_1) \cup FP(N_2)$ and $FP_t(N_1+N_2)) = FP_t(N_1) \cup FP_t(N_2)$.

3)$FP(N_1 \| N_2)) = FP(N_1) \|_{D(p1,p2)} FP(N_2)$ and
$FP_t(N_1 \| N_2)) = FP_t(N_1) \|_{D(p1,p2)} FP_t(N_2)$.

Proof. We show 3):

$FP(N(p_1 \| p_2)) = FP(E(N(p_1 \| p_2))) \cap BPL(C).$

$= Aug((FP(E(N_1)) \| FP(E(N_2))) \cap BPL(C_1\cup C_2 \cup D(p_1,p_2))$

$= Aug(FP(E(N_1)) \| FP(E(N_2))) \cap BPL(C_1) \cap BPL(C_2) \cap BPL(D(p_1,p_2))$

(1) $= Aug(Aug(FP(E(N_1)) \cap BPL(C_1)) \| Aug(FP(E(N_2)) \cap BPL(C_2))) \cap BPL(D(p_1,p_2))$

$= Aug (FP(N_1) \| FP(N_2)) \cap BPL(D(p_1,p_2))$

$= FP(N_1) \|_{D(p1,p2)} FP(N_2)$.

For (1), we have $C_1 \cap Ch(p_2) =Loc(p_1) \cap Ch(p_2)= \emptyset$ and due to lemma 3:

$Aug(FP(E(N_1)) \| FP(E(N_2))) \cap BPL(C_1) = Aug(Aug(FP(E(N_1)) \cap BPL(C_1)) \| FP(E(N_2)))$.

The pomset semantics on terms is now defined considering pomsets of actions A instead of pomsets on transitions, through the labelling function l :

Definitions :
The (weak) **partial language of a net** N is the set $PL(N) = \{l(\alpha)\ ,\ \alpha \in FP(N)\}$, its **terminal partial language** is $PL_t(N) = \{l(\alpha)\ ,\ \alpha \in FP_t(N)\ \}$.
Two isomorphic nets have the same partial language, we can then define the (weak) **partial language of a term** p (with termination information) as the pair:

$$PL(p) = (PL(N(p)), PL_t(N(p))).$$

The (weak) **pomset equivalence** $=_p$ on P is defined by $p1 =_p p2 \Leftrightarrow PL(p1) = PL(p2)$.

The following proposition derives directly from the proposition 7 .

Proposition 8:
The equivalence $=_p$ is a congruence for the operators of the signature and $=_{\mathcal{N}} \subset =_p \subset =_s$.

Equations

As for the sequential semantics, we point out some equations valid in the quotient algebra $\mathcal{P}/=_p$. The choice and parallel operator are associative and commutative, the choice is idempotent. This semantics respects causality but not branching time:
for all terms p,q, r such that both sides are defined , we have

$$p;(q+r) =_p p;q + p;r \qquad (p+q);r =_p p;r+q;r.$$

IV.c. Maximally concurrent behaviours

Informally the maximally concurrent partially ordered behaviours of a net are the concurrent behaviours $(E,\leq,h)$ such that if $(E,\leq',h)$ is also a concurrent behaviour, then $\leq'$ cannot be stricly contained in $\leq$. The order $\leq$ is the causality order on events, and not any augment of it.

Definition:
The set of maximal firing partial words of a net N (resp. E(N)) is the set

$$MFP(N) =\{\ (E,\leq,h) \in FP(N)\ |\ \leq' \subsetneq \leq\ \Rightarrow (E,\leq',h) \notin FP(N)\ \}\ ,$$

$$(\text{resp. } MFP(E(N)) =\{\ (E,\leq,h) \in FP(E(N))\ |\ \leq' \subsetneq \leq\ \Rightarrow (E,\leq',h) \notin FP(E(N))\ \}\ ).$$

For nets in AFN as for 1-safe nets, maximally concurrent behaviours can be retreived from firing sequences . In E(N), the causality does not depend on communications but on the precedence relation which reflects the structure of the net, and for that reason we call structure-pomset of u, Spom(u), the maximally concurrent pomset associated to the sequence u . In the full net N, the causality is due to communication and to the precedence relation. The causality due to communication between events on a channel depends of the marking of that channel when the sequence begins to fire, its the reason why the pomset induced by a firing sequence u is defined w.r.t. a marking M, and noted Pom(M)(u). When all channels are empty at M, and for the initial marking in particular, we note Pom(u).

Definition :
Let u a sequence on T, $u = t_1 \ldots t_n$, we define on [1..n] a labelling $h : h(i) = t_i$, and a partial order $<_s = \{(i,j)\ |\ i<j$ for the order on integers, and $h(i) \xrightarrow{*} h(j)\}$. The partial word $Spom(u) = ([1..n], <_s, h)$ is the **S-pomset** of u. We note $\equiv_s$ the equivalence relation on T* defined by $u \equiv_s v \Leftrightarrow Spom(u)= Spom(v)$.

The following properties are similar to standart results on more general 1-safe nets [Bes1] : if u is S-enabled at the marking M then Spom(u) is too. The S-pomsets of the firing sequences are the maximally concurrent firing pomsets of E(N). This is summarized by the lemma:

Lemma 11 :
MFP(E(N)) = {Spom(u) | u ∈ FS(E(N)) }.

Definition :
Let u a sequence on T, u = $t_1...t_n$, such that M(u>M', we define on [1..n] a labelling h, h(i) =t_i, and the following partial orders :
$<_S$ = {(i,j) | i<j for the order on integers , and h(i) -*>h(j) }, and for any channel c in C,
$<_c$ = {(i,j) | for some integer k , messages m and m': ln(i) = (c^+m , k + |M(c)|) and ln(j) = (c^-m' , k))}, where ln is the numbered labelling of events in u (see definition in chapter III).
The partial word Pom(M)(u) =([1..n] , ≤, h), where ≤ is the least order containing $\cup_{c\in C}<_c \cup <_S$, is the **pomset of u w.r.t. the marking M**. We denote Pom(M)(u) by Pom(u)when M = M_{in}.
We denote by ≡ the equivalence relation on T* defined by u ≡ v <=> Pom(u)= Pom(v).

Comparing this definition with the one of Spom(u), we can see that Pom(u) is an augment of Spom(u), thus Pom(u)∈ FP(E(N)). Furthermore it is balanced for C (lemma 2d), thus Pom(u)∈ FP(N) by the proposition 6. The pomsets associated in that way to firing sequences are exactly the maximally concurrent firing pomsets of N.

Lemma 12 :
MFP(N) = {Pom(u) | u ∈ FS(N) }.

V. An iteration operator on sequential processes

We introduce terms with infinite behaviours using a COSY-like iteration operator [Bes2] which applies only to sequential processes : the process [s/a], where a is an atomic action and s a sequential process, loops on s, and may chose before each iteration to terminate after an execution of the action a. The properties worked out all along the paper apply to the derived nets.

V.a.Syntax

The specification has a new sort, sequential process, and terms are terminal strings in the following grammar, where a is any action in A:

S:= a | S;S | S+S | [S/a] for sequential processes.
P:= S | P;P | P+P | P||P for processes .

The equations in the section I.b, involving In(), Out() and Loc(), apply to both sorts. There are some conditions and equations for the iteration operator :
s' = [s/a] is defined iff s;a is defined (see conditions on sequencing).
In(s') = In(s;a) Out(s')= Out(s;a) Loc(s') = Loc(s;a) = Ø.
The conditions on operators imply that sequential terms have no local channels.

V.b. The net model

The net model of a sequential term has always a single initial and a single final place and its control subnet is a finite state machine.
When we model [s/a] by a net, the possibility for the term to be placed in a choice context, i.e. [s/a] + s', or in a loop context, i.e. [[s/a]/b], imposes to unfold the first iteration of the loop.

Formally N([s/a]) is defined in the following way:
Let N_1 and N_2, with $N_i = (S_i,T_i,F_i,l_i,M_{in_i})$, two disjoint representatives of N(s), where we note $\{s_i\} = {}^\circ N_i$ and $\{s_i'\} = N_i^\circ$. Let N_2' be the net obtained from N_2 replacing the arcs (t, s2') relating transitions to the final place, by arcs (t,s2) to the initial one :
$N_2' = (S_2',T_2,F_2',l_2,M_{in_2})$ where

$$S_2' = S_2 - \{s_2'\}$$

$$F_2' = (F_2 \cap (S_2' \times T_2 \cup T_2 \times S_2')) \cup \{(t,s_2) \mid (t,s_2') \in F_2)$$

Then $N = (S,T,F,l,M_{in}) = N([s/a])$ is defined by :

$S = (S_1 - \{s_i'\}) \cup S_2' \cup \{s\}$ where s is a new place

$T = T_1 \cup T_2 \cup \{t_1,t_2\}$ where t_1 and t_2 are two new transitions

$$F = (F_1 \cap (S \times T \cup T \times S)) \cup \{(t,s_2) \mid (t,s_1') \in F_1\} \cup F_2' \cup \{(s_1,t_1),(t_1,s),(s_2,t_2),(t_2,s)\}.$$

$l/T_i = l_i$, $l(t_1) = l(t_2) = a$

${}^\circ N = \{s_1\}$, $N^\circ = \{s\}$.

The term $[\, c_1^-m;(c_2^+n + c_3^+n)/c_1^-n]$ is modelled by the following net:

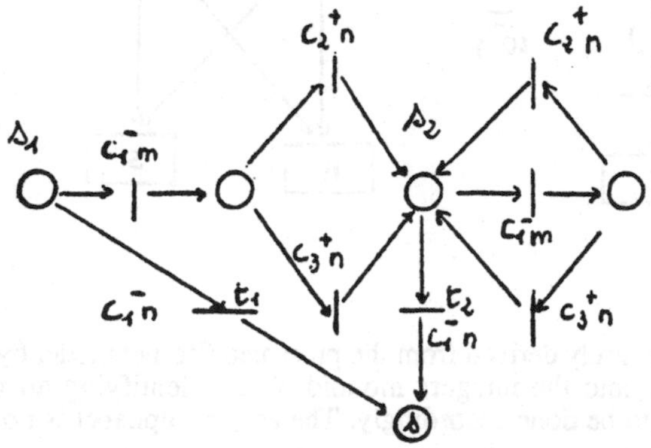

V.c.Properties

The nets modelling sequential processes are finite state machines and their markings are bounded by 1. A sequential term s (an iterative one in particular) has no local channel, and thus the behaviours of N and E(N) for N =N(s) are identical , and their sequential and partial ordered behaviours are identical.
Let N = N(p)

p is sequential $\Rightarrow$ FS(N) = FS(E(N)) = FP(N) = FP(E(N)).

The set of firing sequences of N is infinite, but still may be described compositionally using the star operator on words : $u^* = \{u^n \mid n \in N\}$. We have :
$FS(N) = \{t_1\} \cup FS(N_1) \cup FS_t(N_1).FS(N_2)^*.(\{t_2\} \cup FS(N_2))$ and
$FS_t(N) = \{t_1\} \cup FS_t(N_1).FS_t(N_2)^*.\{t_2\}$

The firing rules defined in the paper apply to the newly created nets: the proposition 1 and the lemmas 7 and 9 are still valid, taking in account that in sequential nets, only one single place is marked in any reachable marking. Both sequential and pomset semantics and equivalences can thus be defined on the new algebra, and *all* the propositions apply to it.

VI. Some features

IO-semantics

IO-semantics focus on external communications, hiding communications occuring on local channels. Both sequential and partially ordered IO-behaviours of nets are obtained by projection of their firing sequences and firing pomsets on external communications, and they still can be defined compositionally using propositions 3 and 7.
These semantics leads to some interesting identifications on terms like ($p;c^+m$) || ($c^-m;q$) and (p;q), or (p||q);(r||s) and ($p;a^+m;b^-m;r$) || ($q;a^-m;b^+m;s$) , when both sides are defined :

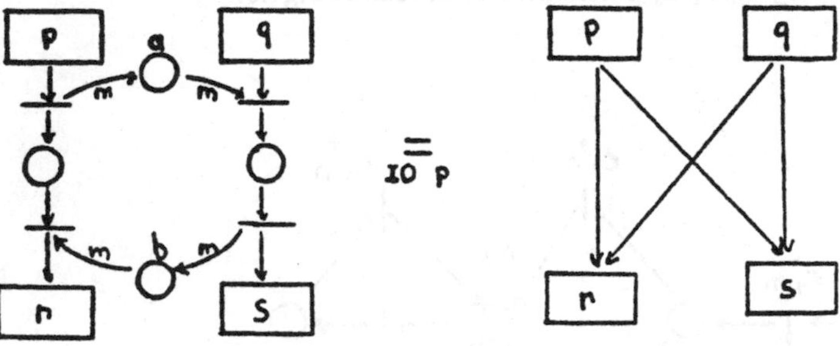

A Petri Net model

A Petri Net model can be entirely derived from the presented fifo-net model by mapping Mes*, the free monoid on Mes, onto the integers monoid *N* by identifying all messages. In all definitions, changes have to be done accordingly. The actions alphabet is now isomorphic to $Ch^+ \cup Ch^- \cup \{\tau\}$, channel places behave like usual net places, their input and output arcs being labelled by 1. Balanced behaviours are changed in consequence: the set $c^+.c^-$ x Mes* (the set of complete communication pomsets) is isomorphic to $c^+.c^-$ x *N*, whose element $c^+.c^-$ x 3 is the pomset:

c^+ --->c^+ --->c^+

c^---->c^- --->c^-

All the semantics defined for the Fifo model apply to this model which is more abstract.

These last two points, IO semantics and abstraction from messages' contents, are abstractions from different particular parts of information and suggest interesting directions for future work.

VII.Conclusion

Net-based semantics for process algebras and Nets theory benefit from each other. The present paper, with a net model for processes with asynchronous communication, contributes to the fifo-nets theory, with both compositionality and concurrent semantics. This model is related to the existing net models for processes with synchronous communication by the algebraic structures of terms, which are similar. We could profit of this similarity to develop both directions.

Asynchronous communication is widely used in distributed computation. In many distributed algorithms, processes act on local memory and exchange information by typed messages, after the receipt of a message a process acts differently depending on the type of the message. The algebra of processes presented here allows an abstract view of such programs (the types can be represented by the messages defined in the algebra), together with a fifo-net representation. The algebraic structure and the definition of congruences allows rewritings and equational calculii on programs.

Many directions for future work are opened. We can look for weaker conditions on operators, which could preserve the concurrent semantics of the fifo net model. Recursion would be a great enhancement. Deadlocks and failure semantics have to be investigated too, as quoted by the referees, as well as weak bisimulations and I/O semantics. Another aspect is the research of the decidable properties of the obtained nets, which could be used in proofs of distributed algorithms.

Acknowledgments: I am grateful to E.Pelz, R. Devillers and R.P. Hopkins for numerous efficient comments. Many improvements are (and will be in the following) due to the three anonymous referees whom I thank for their accurate reading.

References:

[BKT] J.A. Bergstra, J.W. Klop, J.V. Tucker, *Process algebra with asynchronous communication mechanism,* Seminar on concurrency, LNCS 197(1985).

[Bes1] E. Best,*Concurrent behaviours: sequences, processes and axioms,* LNCS 255 (1987).

[Bes2] E. Best,*COSY: its relationship to Nets and CSP,* LNCS 197 (1986).

[BZ] D.Brand,P.Zafiropoulos, *On Communicating Finite-state Machines,* JACM vol n°2, April 1983.

[BoCa] G. Boudol, I. Castellani, *Concurrency and Atomicity,* Theoretical Computer Science 59 (1988), pp. 25-84

[DDM] P.Degano, R.De Nicola, U.Montanari, *A distributed operational semantics for CCS based on C/E systems,* Acta Informatica, 26, 1988.

[Fan] J. Fanchon, *An Algebra of Fifo-Nets,* RR LRI, to appear.

[FiMe] A.Finkel, G.Memmi, *Fifo nets: a new model of parallel computation,* Proc. 6th conf. on Theor. Comp. Sci., LNCS 145, 1983.

[GlVa] R.van Glabeek, F.Vaandrager,*Petri nets models for algebraic theories of concurrency,* LNCS 259 (1987) 224-242.

[Gol] U. Goltz, *CCS and Petri Nets* , LNCS 469, 1990.

[GoRo] M.G.Gouda, L.E. Rosier, *Priority networks of communicating finite state machines,* SIAM J.Comput. Vol.14, n°3 (1985) .

[Gra] J. Grabowski, *On partial languages,* Fundamenta Informaticae IV.2, 1981.

[Ki] A.Kiehn,*Local and Global Causes,* TUM research report n° 342/23/91 A, August 1991.

[Maz] A. Mazurkiewicz, *Trace theory,* LNCS 255 (1986).
[Mil] R. Milner, *Lectures on a Calculus for Communicating Systems*, Proc. Seminar on Concurrency, LNCS 197, 1985, pp. 197-220
[Pom] L.Pomello, *Some equivalence notions for concurrent systems,* LNCS 222 (1986).
[Pra] V. Pratt, *Modeling Concurrency with Partial Orders*, International Journal of Parallel Programming, vol 15 (1), 1986, pp. 36-91.

A Basic-Net Algebra for Program Semantics and its Application to OCCAM*

Richard Hopkins(1), Jon Hall(1), Oliver Botti(2)

(1) The Computing Laboratory,
The University of Newcastle upon Tyne
NE1 7RU, U.K.

(2) Dipartimento di Scienze dell'Informazione
Universita degli Studi di Milano
Via Comelico, 39-20135 Milano, Italy

Abstract. We define an algebra comprising a class of basic Petri nets, enhanced with place and transition labels, together with operations of sequence, choice, parallel, iteration, prioritised choice and label hiding. An important characteristic of the algebra is that it combines transition-based composition for modelling synchronous communication, as in Petri net semantics for CCS or TCSP, with place composition for modelling shared variables. We use the algebra to give a family of net semantics for a version of OCCAM, comprising a full semantics, for which we have consistency with the Laws of OCCAM, and a range of semantics for partial data abstraction which give smaller nets (for more practical use of net tools and techniques) with a limited consistency such that safety (but not liveness) properties transfer from more-abstracted to less-abstracted semantics.

Keywords: OCCAM, Programming Language Semantics, Petri Net Algebras, Data Abstraction.

CONTENTS

* This work was supported by ESPRIT Basic Research Action 3148 - DEMON

0. Introduction

This paper is concerned with obtaining compositional Petri net semantics for programming languages, in particular addressing representation of data and practicability of the net obtained for use with Petri net tools. We use the term "net translation" when we wish to emphasize the latter aspect rather than the formal semantics definition aspect. The substance of the paper is a semantics for the fundamental constructs of OCCAM which has sufficient of a consistency with the OCCAM semantics of [ROSC85] ("Roscoe Semantics") to ensure that the algebraic laws of OCCAM in [RH86] ("The Laws") hold under a particular notion of behavioural equivalence defined on the nets which we use.

Typically (and specifically for Roscoe Semantics), a denotational semantics of a programming language involves a semantic evaluation function ξ as $\xi\{P\}\rho\sigma = B$ where B is a model for the behaviour of a program fragment (here "process") P in context ρ and with initial state σ. The ρ gives e.g. variables' types and bindings to storage locations, and σ gives bindings of variables or locations to values - we use the term "state" to mean such a data state, total "process state" combines that with control state. ξ is interpreted as yielding first a semantic object, a function from σ to B, which is the meaning of P within a program context represented by ρ. For the Roscoe Semantics, B includes possible final states, failures and divergences, drawing on both state transformation semantics for sequential programming languages and concurrency theory concepts. Compositionality of semantics requires that for any syntactic constructor *cons*, there be a corresponding semantic constructor *cons'* which is its meaning, e.g., $\xi\{cons(P,Q)\}$ = $cons'(\xi\{P\}, \xi\{Q\})$ for a constructor on two processes P and Q.

In our semantics we do not need ρ. The semantic function is from process to, as semantic object, a particular form of (labelled, unmarked) Place/Transition Net. For a consistency result with the pre-existing Roscoe semantics the state σ used there must be definable in terms of the places and markings of the nets produced - we represent each possible value of each variable by a distinct place (due to using basic nets). Also the required form of behaviour representation B must be extracted from the behaviour of a net under a standard Petri net transition rule, although the other behavioural representations native to nets can also be used.

There are two major issues addressed by the paper:

0.1 Net Algebra

Petri nets as such are without an algebraic structure. Thus it is necessary to add additional information, here a labelling of transitions and places, to give composable entities, called "(OCCAM) Boxes", on which appropriate compositions are defined to give what we term the OCCAM Box algebra. From the point of view of practicable net translations, we require modularity: that the net of a program fragment is meaningful, and analysable, independently of any context (and this motivates the absence of ρ); that to some extent the results of such separate analysis can be utilized in the analysis of a composition; that the compositions be "efficient" in the sense of operating on an interface to the net which has (generally) very much less information than the entire net.

With an appropriately defined new algebra we have the possibility of using it to give a semantics to other programming languages giving, immediately, their translation to nets and the applicability of all the existing (and future) theory, tools and techniques for the analysis and verification of nets, including treatment of true concurrency issues. At the end of the paper we will discuss an existing use of net semantics for OCCAM.

Existing work on Petri net semantics of process algebras, such as [MILN89] for CCS or [OLD91] for TCSP, effectively yield net algebras in which the net composition operators are those of the process algebra. As will be discussed at the end of the paper, our OCCAM box algebra differs from such approaches in that: we include variables explicitly as places; and net composition involves merging places for the same shared variable in the composed nets. This approach gives significant benefit in defining a simple semantics for shared variables.

The handling of variables also distinguishes between this work and that of the PBC [BH92, this volume]. Otherwise the two approaches are similar.

0.2 Partial Data Abstraction

Although the use of the basic net model is reasonable for a formal semantics, and appropriate due to its simplicity and fundamental status in Petri net theory, it gives a size of net which is impracticable as a net translation. We address this by defining a family of net semantics parameterised by a set of values to be explicitly represented, with all other values abstracted to a single representative. At one extreme we have the full semantics with all values explicitly represented, for which the consistency result holds. Towards the other more abstracted extreme we have, for example, a semantics in which only boolean variables are fully represented, by three places (including "error" value); and for every other variable there is only one place (always marked) representing any possible value. The smaller net obtained by increasing abstractness is less deterministic, in a specific sense which means that any safety property shown on an abstracted net holds also for a less abstracted net of the same program, and in particular for the actual program. We have also [HOPK92] defined an extension of the basic net semantics which includes also annotations to produce a full and practicable High Level net translation.

We include in the Box structure a priority relation on transitions, derived from PRIALT constructs of an OCCAM program. However we are mainly interested in obtaining a compositional semantics of OCCAM in a basic net class, for which purpose this priority relation has to be ignored. Also, priorities are generally considered just "configuration information" [INMOS88] of no significance to formal semantics, and are ignored in the Roscoe Semantics. Nonetheless, we have included them in the definitions of Boxes and their compositions for the practical reason that they may be a crucial aspect of program behaviour which can be captured by using the translation with tools which recognize priorities (or inhibitor arcs, to which priorities can be translated).

0.3 Layout of the Paper

Section 1 gives an extended informal treatment of Boxes and their operations together with our semantics of OCCAM. This will provide examples of their use and (to a significant extent) motivates the details of their formulation. In that, and in the subsequent definitions of the Box algebra and formulation of the consistency results, a number of issues arise concerning both the syntax used and the semantics given. These will be discussed in Section 5.

Section 2 contains the details of the denotational semantics excluding the definitions relating to Boxes themselves, which is contained in Section 3.

Section 4 gives the main results of the paper: that our semantics is consistent with that of the restricted subset of OCCAM given in [RH86]; and that we also have limited consistency between differing levels of abstraction within our semantics.

Section 5 contains a discussion of the issues raised in the rest of the paper.

Section 6 gives conclusions and pointers to related work.

1. Informal Description of OCCAM Boxes and the OCCAM Semantics

1.1. Box Structure

An OCCAM Box has the usual Petri Net structure (transitions T, places S and flow relation $\rightarrow$), enhanced with:

(i) Priority Relation, $>$ - This allows prioritisation between arbitrary transition pairs to be represented. If priorities are to be used in obtaining behaviour, (which is not the case in the definition of behaviour used here), then $t>u$ means that the ordinary enabling of t prevents the firing of u. (Self-prioritisation, $t>t$, gives a dead transition; and contradictory prioritisations, $t>u$ and $u>t$ gives that if both are enabled then neither can fire.)

(ii) Transition Labelling, λ - Each transition represents either:

(a) A communication action, labelled with a channel-value pair, $\langle c:v \rangle$. (Note that the labelling treats input and output as the same, as is necessary to obtain consistency with the Roscoe Semantics.)

(b) An internal action, with the "empty" label ε (assignment, SKIP or completed communication).

(iii) Place Labelling, λ - Each place is either:

(a) A Data Place - This is labelled by a variable-value pair, $\langle x:v \rangle$, meaning it represents x having value v, for x being a free (not-yet-declared) variable. In any composition joining two Boxes, data places with the same label are identified (or "merged"). The data place labelling is in fact injective and we will use $\langle x:v \rangle$ as synonymous with a place itself.

(b) An external control Place - There are two possibilities, distinguished by labels - entry (EN), exit (EX).

(c) An internal Place - Label ε, obtained by constructions which internalise an external control place or a data place. Declaring a variable internalises its data places. In for example sequential composition the exit places of one Box and the entry places of the other are merged and internalised.

From a Box B and a state σ, assigning values to some variables, we obtain an initial marking for B in which are marked: the entry place(s); and a subset of the data places which give values to free variables as defined by σ. When referring to an initial marking of a box we will always mean one obtained in this way. A reachable marking in which all exit places are marked is interpreted as termination.

Any Box, such as shown in Figure 2(c), has a boundary (the broken lines) which contains all internal elements (places and transitions). The interface of a Box is its non-internal places and transitions with their immediate flow relation arcs. The composition operators on Boxes only involve their interfaces, with their internal structures having no effect and being left unchanged.

(e , f are expressions; c a channel, C a set of channels; x a variable)

P ::=	STOP I act I SEQ (P_1, .. P_n) I PAR (C_1:P_1, .. C_n:P_n)
	I ALT (GP_1, .. GP_n) I IF (CP_1, .. CP_n) I PRIALT (GP_1, .. GP_n)
	I WHILE (CP)
	I CHAN c : P I t VAR x : P
GP ::=	e & $c?_t f$: P I e & SKIP : P I $c?_t f$: P
	I ALT (GP_1, .. GP_n) I PRIALT (GP_1, .. GP_n)
CP ::=	e : P
act ::=	SKIP I $x :=_t e$ I $c\,!_t e$ I $c?_t x$
t ::=	INT I BOOL I BYTE I ANY

Table A - Syntax of OCCAM, P∈PROC

We next explain the Box operators, *Base* , ;, [], | |, *, / and []>, and the definition of a semantics for OCCAM using them. Table A gives the OCCAM syntax used, and Tables B and D the semantic definitions. For the moment we will use Table C which is the special case of Table D in the following two respects (these and Table D itself will be dealt with fully later):

(i) Typing - The syntax includes type information, e.g., $x :=_{INT} e$. Table C only applies for the special case of the unrestricted type, ANY; and in examples we will write, for example, $x := e$ for $x :=_{ANY} e$ when unambiguity is ensured.

(ii) Partial Data Abstraction - The domain of values for OCCAM programs is taken as $OCC^+ = OCC \uplus \{EV\}$, where EV is taken as a special error value. The semantic functions are parameterised by a subset A of OCC^+ such that all values not in A are to be abstracted to the same representation. Table C only applies to the special case of A = OCC^+, that is the full semantics with no data abstraction.

There are three semantic functions: ξ (general command evaluation), β (basic action evaluation) and $\mathcal{E}$ (expression evaluation). The latter gives the value for an expression with respect to a state σ which assigns values to some variables. We also use *Vars* which gives the set of variables in a set of syntactic constructs. The notation $\sigma{:}\leftarrow\{(x,v)\}$ means the state which has x bound to v, and is otherwise the same as σ.

1.2. Basic Boxes, the Base Constructor and beta-expressions.

The semantics of a basic OCCAM construct (action, guard or condition) will be given via the semantics for a "beta-expression". This has syntax $e \vdash act$ for an action a conditional on a boolean expression e (which is more general than required for OCCAM). The action is assignment ($x := f$), input ($c?x$), output ($c\,!f$) or none (SKIP). (There is also a special form for assigning the value XV which concerns only variable declaration, dealt with later.) For example Figure 1(a) shows the basic Box for (NOT y) $\vdash$ $x :=$ NOT x. A basic Box has an entry place as an input place of all transitions, an exit place as an output place

(a) $\xi_A\{act\} = \beta_A\{\text{TRUE} \vdash act\}$

(b) $\xi_A\{\text{STOP}\} = \beta_A\{\text{FALSE} \vdash \text{SKIP}\}$

(c) $\xi_A\{\text{SEQ}(P_1, .. P_n)\} = \xi_A\{P_1\} ; .. ; \xi_A\{P_n\}$

(d) $\xi_A\{\text{PAR}(C_1{:}P_1, .. C_n{:}P_n)\} =$

$$(\xi_A\{P_1\} \,||_{C_1'} (\xi_A\{P_2\} \,||_{C_2'} (.. \,||_{C_{n-1}'} \xi_A\{P_n\}) ..)/C$$

where $C_i' = C_i \cap \bigcup_{j=i+1..n} C_j$ and $C = \bigcup_{i=1..n} C_i$

(e) $\xi_A\{\text{ALT}(GP_1, .. GP_n)\} = \xi_A\{GP_1\} \; [] \; .. \; [] \; \xi_A\{GP_n\}$

(f) $\xi_A\{e\&act{:}P\} = \beta_A\{e \vdash act\} ; \xi_A\{P\}$

(g) $\xi_A\{c?_t x{:}P\} = \xi_A\{\text{TRUE}\&c?_t x{:}P\}$ $\qquad \xi_A\{e{:}P\} = \xi_A\{e\&\ \text{SKIP}{:}P\}$

(h) $\xi_A\{\text{IF}(e_1{:}P_1, .. e_n{:}P_n)\} = \;\; \xi_A\{\text{ALT}\,(e_1'{:}P_1, .. e_n'{:}P_n\}$

for $e_i' = e_i$ AND (NOT(e_{i-1})) AND .. (NOT (e_1))

(i) $\xi_A\{\text{WHILE}(e{:}P)\} = \beta_A\{\text{NOT}(e) \vdash \text{SKIP}\} \; [] \; * \; \xi_A\{e{:}P\}$

(j) $\xi_A\{\text{CHAN}c{:}P\} = \xi_A\{P\}$

(k) $\xi_A\{t\,\text{VAR}x{:}P\} = (\xi_A\{P\} ; \beta_A\{TRUE \vdash x :=_t XV\})/_{rep_A(EV),XV}\{x\}$

(m) $\xi_A\{\text{PRIALT}(GP_1, .. GP_n)\} = \xi_A\{GP_1\} \; []\!> .. \; []\!> \xi_A\{GP_n\}$

Table B - Semantics of OCCAM Commands, ξ_A : *PROC* → *BOX*

beta−expr ::= $e \vdash act \mid e \vdash x{:=}XV$ for which define

$$Sig = \{\sigma{:}Vars(\{e, act\}) \to (OCC^+) \mid \mathcal{E}\{e\}\sigma{=}TRUE\}$$

$\beta\{e \vdash \text{SKIP}\} = Base(\{(\sigma,\varepsilon,\sigma) \mid \sigma \in Sig\})$

$\beta\{e \vdash x :=_{ANY} f\} = Base(\{(\sigma,\varepsilon,\sigma{:}\leftarrow\{(x,v)\}) \mid \sigma \in Sig \wedge v{=}\mathcal{E}\{f\}\sigma \neq \text{EV}\})$

$\beta\{e \vdash c\,!_{ANY} f\} = Base(\{(\sigma,\langle c{:}v\rangle,\sigma) \mid \sigma \in Sig \wedge v{=}\mathcal{E}\{f\}\sigma \neq \text{EV}\})$

$\beta\{e \vdash c?_{ANY} x\} = Base(\{(\sigma,\langle c{:}v\rangle,\sigma{:}\leftarrow\{(x,v)\}) \mid \sigma \in Sig \wedge v \in OCC\})$

$\beta\{e \vdash x :=_{ANY} XV\} = Base(\{(\sigma,\varepsilon,\sigma{:}\leftarrow\{(x,XV)\}) \mid \sigma \in Sig\})$

Table C - Syntax and Precise, un-typed Semantics for beta-expressions ($\beta = \beta_{OCC^+}$)

of all transitions, and a number of data places. (We use abbreviations in Figures: one double-headed arc for arcs in both directions, T/F for truth values, $a{:}b$ for $\langle a{:}b\rangle$; we also often omit the box boundary and ε labels.) Each transition (e.g. t_1 of Figure 1(a)) is characterized by:

(a) the labels of its input data places ($\langle y{:}F\rangle$, $\langle x{:}T\rangle$ - it depends on y being False, and x being true.);

(b) its own label (ε - internal);

(c) the labels of its output data places (‹*y* :*F* ›, ‹*x* :*F* ›- *y* remains False, *x* negated). Viewing (a) as a set of variable-value pairs, it constitutes a partial function σ from variables to values, the "pre-state"; and (c) likewise the "post-state", σ'.

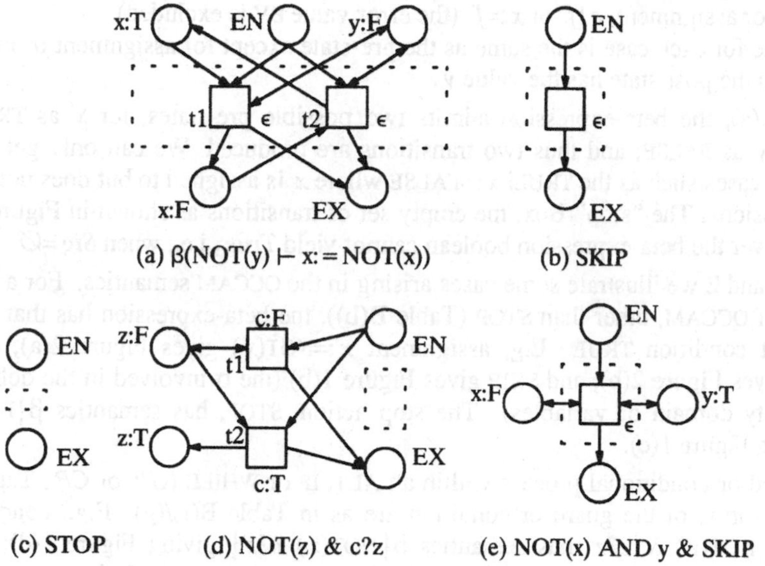

Figure 1 – Basic Boxes

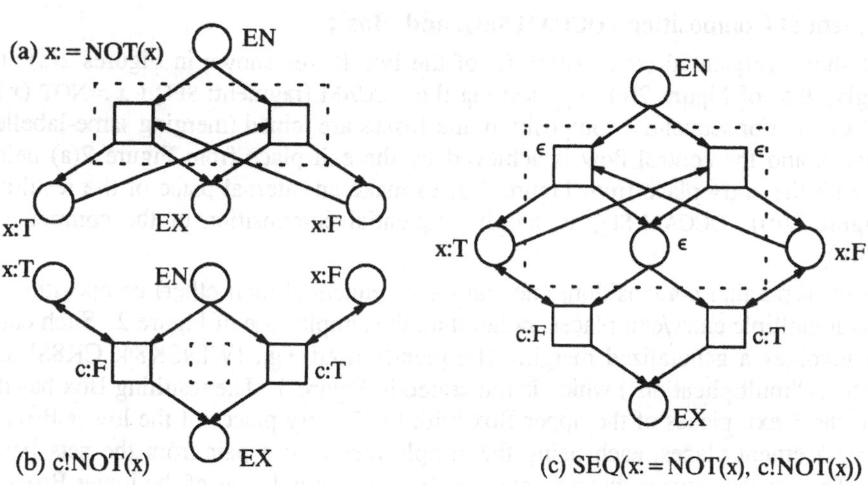

Figure 2 – Sequential Composition

The semantics (Table C) of a beta-expression uses the *Base* constructor of the algebra to give a basic Box with a set of alternative transitions quantified over:
(i) possible pre-states (*Sig*) on the variables involved, such that the boolean expression evaluates to *True*.
(ii) possible values, v, which can be: received for input, $c?x$; or yielded by evaluation of f for output or assignment, $c\,!f$ or $x:=f$ (the error value EV is excluded).
The post-state for each case is the same as the pre-state except for assignment or input to x, where x in the post-state has the value v.

For Figure 1(a), the beta-expression admits two possible pre-states, for x as TRUE or FALSE, and y as FALSE; and thus two transitions are produced. We can only get an EV data place in cases such as the TRUE⊢x:=FALSE where x is assigned to but does not occur in the expressions. The "stop" Box, the empty set of transitions as shown in Figure 1(c), arises whenever the beta-expression boolean cannot yield *True*, i.e., when $Sig = \varnothing$.

In Figures 1 and 2 we illustrate some cases arising in the OCCAM semantics. For a primitive action of OCCAM, other than STOP (Table B(b)), the beta-expression has that action and constant condition TRUE. E.g, assignment x:=NOT(x) gives Figure 2(a); output c !NOT(x) gives Figure 2(b); and SKIP gives Figure 1(b) (the σ involved in the definition has the empty domain of variables). The stop action, STOP, has semantics $\beta\{$FALSE⊢SKIP$\}$, giving Figure 1(c).

For a guarded or conditional process within an ALT, IF or WHILE (*GP* or *CP*, Table A), the possible forms of the guard or condition are as in Table B(f)/(g). E.g., conditional input guard, NOT(z) & $c?z$, has semantics $\beta\{$NOT(z)⊢$c?z\}$ giving Figure 1(d); guard NOT(x) AND y & SKIP, and condition NOT(x) AND y, will both have semantics $\beta\{$NOT(x)AND(y)⊢SKIP$\}$ giving Figure 1(e).

1.3. Sequential Composition - OCCAM SEQ, and Box ;

Figure 2 shows sequential composition (;) of the two Boxes shown in Figures 2(a) and 2(b) to give that of Figure 2(c), representing the OCCAM fragment: SEQ (x:=NOT (x) , (c !(NOT x))). For sequential composition, the Boxes are joined (merging same-labelled data places), and the control flow is achieved by the exit place from Figure 2(a) being merged with the entry place from Figure 2(b) to make an internal place of the resulting Box (Figure 2(c)). OCCAM SEQ is simply sequential composition of the components (Table B(c)).

As a result of parallel composition, one can have sequential (and other) composition of Boxes with multiple entry/exit places, rather than the simple case of Figure 2. Such composition involves a generalized merging (frequently used e.g., [WINSK84, CK88] and referred to as "multiplication") which is illustrated in Figure 3. The resulting Box has the merge of the 3 exit places of the upper Box with the 2 entry places of the lower Box, to give 6 replacement places, each being the simple merge of a pair from the sets being merged. The consequence is that no transition from the initial ones of the lower Box can fire until every transition from the final ones of the upper Box has. This is proper distributed termination since there is no single point of synchronisation between the two successive parallel processes.

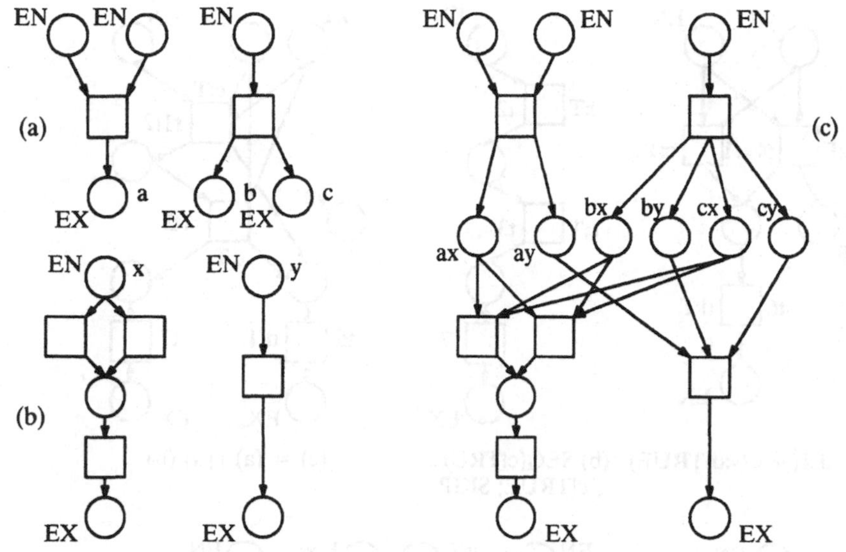

Figure 3 – General Place Merging

1.4. Parallel Composition - OCCAM PAR, and Box || (parallel), / (channel concealment)

We consider in Figure 4 an example corresponding to

PAR (*{d}* : SKIP ,
{c} : SEQ(*c* !TRUE, *c* !TRUE, SKIP) ,
{c , d} : ALT(*y* &*c* ?*y* : *d* !TRUE))

The PAR specifies for each arm a communication alphabet, comprising the set of channels on which its process is to synchronise with those of other arms. This is a feature not present in actual OCCAM programs, for which the information would be extracted from the text of the component processes (and thus in this example, the *d* alphabet for the first arm, is artificial). In examples we will often omit an empty alphabet. The semantics (Table B(d)) involves a sequence of parallel compositions on the arms of the PAR (which could be done in any order) and then a concealment of the channels used. For this example the steps are as follows:

First, $||_{\{c\}}$ joins the boxes for the second and third processes, Figures 4(a) and 4(b), and deals with synchronisation on the specified synchronisation alphabet *{c}*, the channels common to the communication alphabets of the arms being composed, to give Figure 4(c). Except where there is synchronisation, transitions on the two sides ($t6$ and $t7$) are potentially concurrent. The possibility of synchronisation is attained by adding in synchronisation transitions merging each pair of transitions from different arms which have the same label and use a channel in the synchronisation alphabet - in this case $t1t2$ and $t1t3$ which are the two possible synchronisations of $t1$ with $t2$ or $t3$. The || also deletes

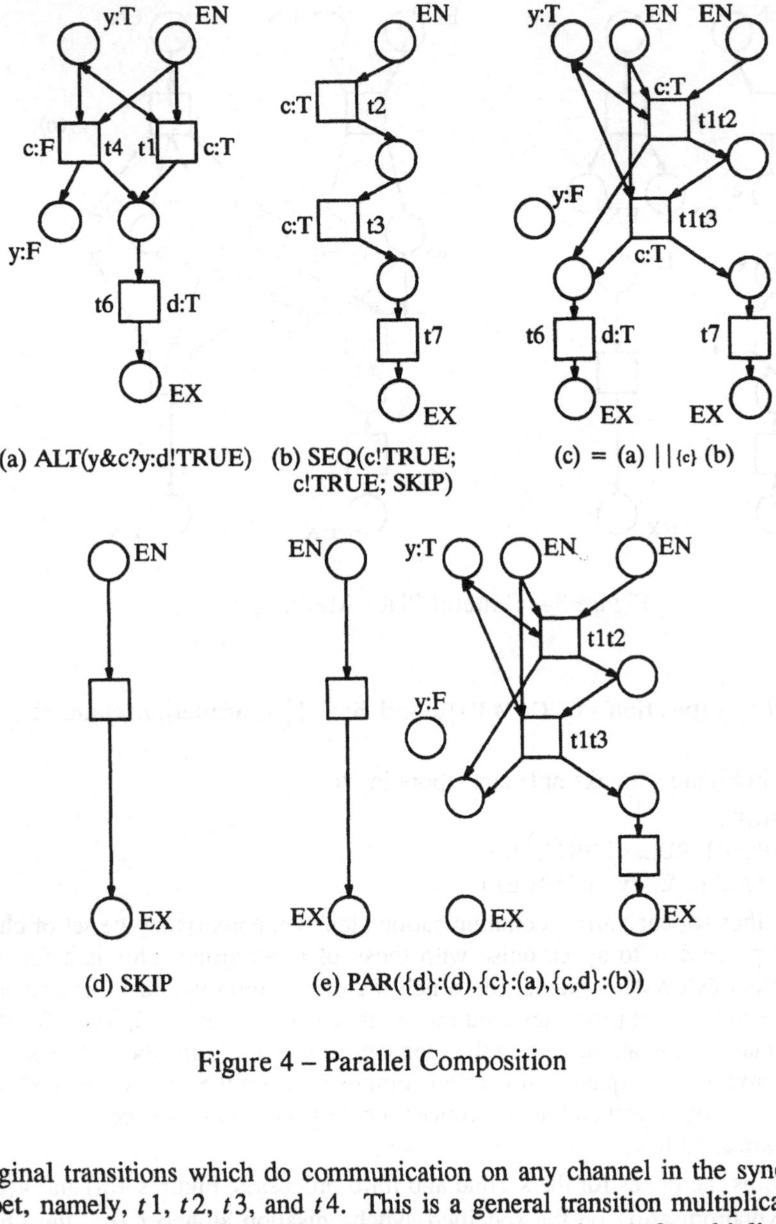

Figure 4 – Parallel Composition

all original transitions which do communication on any channel in the synchronisation alphabet, namely, $t1$, $t2$, $t3$, and $t4$. This is a general transition multiplication, analogous to the above place multiplication. In this case there is a 1×2 multiplication on the two sets of transitions labelled $c:T$; and a 0×2 on those labelled $c:F$, which gives no transitions and thus leaves $y:F$ as an isolated place.

The resulting Box (Figure 4(c)) is then composed with that for the first arm (Figure 4(d)) using $||_{\{d\}}$ with synchronisation alphabet being those channels common to this arm and any of the arms already composed. There is just a 0×1 multiplication which deletes $t6$, giving Figure 4(e) (but with the same labelling for $t1t2$ and $t1t3$ as in Figure 4(c)).

The final step for the semantics of PAR is "channel concealment", $/\{c, d\}$, to give Figure 4(e). This internalises (re-labels as ε) every transition doing communication on a channel in $\{c, d\}$ (the total communication alphabet of all arms), i.e. the synchronisation transitions which were created. (The deletion of original transitions and internalising of synchronisations is necessary for Roscoe Consistency, although alternative definitions are possible.)

1.5. Choice - OCCAM IF, ALT, PRIALT, and Box [], []>

As shown in Figure 5, choice between two Boxes is by joining them, merging their respective entry places and merging their respective exit places. The effect is that the firing of any initial transition from one arm disables every initial transition from the other arm; and that when all the final transitions from one arm have fired, all the exit places are marked.

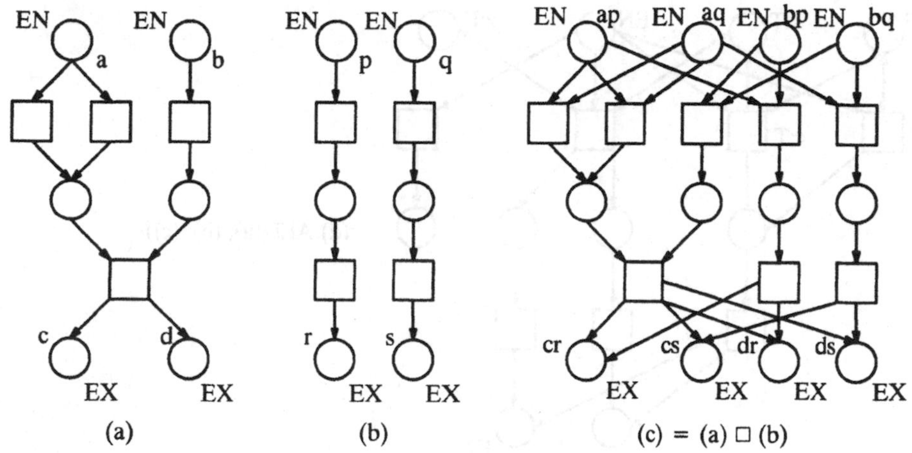

Figure 5 – General Choice

An ALT (Table B(e)) comprises a number of guarded commands (Table B(f) and B(g)) each comprising a guard followed by a process. Figure 6 illustrates the semantics for

ALT (NOT(x)&$c?x$: SKIP ,
(NOT(z)) AND x & SKIP : PAR(SKIP,SKIP) ,
TRUE & SKIP : STOP)

The result, Figure 6(d), is that of choice over the Boxes shown in Figures 6(a) - 6(c) for the three guarded processes, each of which is the sequential composition of the Box for its guard with the Box for its process. Thus we model a guard as an action, a set of alternative transitions for each possible successful guard evaluation. The initial transitions of Figure 6(d) comprise all the alternative initial transitions of all guards, and thus there is the potential for non-deterministic choice in that several of these may become

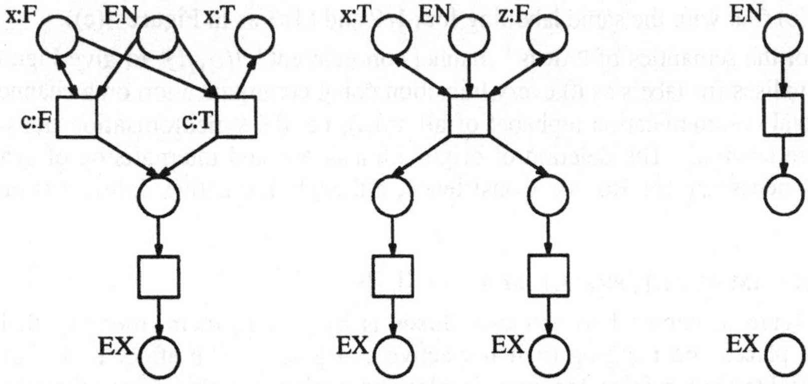

(a) NOT(x) & c?x: SKIP (b) NOT(z) AND x & SKIP: PAR({}:SKIP,{}:SKIP) (c) TRUE & SKIP:STOP

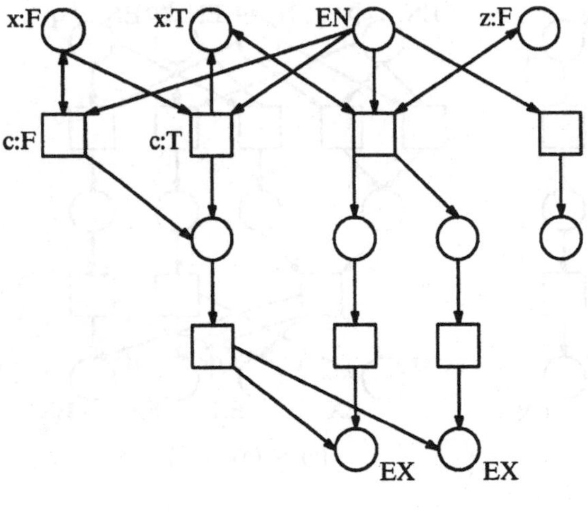

(d) ALT((a), (b), (c))

Figure 6 – ALT

simultaneously enabled. It should be noted that even if the guard is a complex expression, such as the (NOT (z)) AND x of Figure 6(b), its semantics is a single transition dependent simultaneously on all the conditions necessary for its success.

In Figure 7 we similarly illustrate semantics of IF (Table B(h)) over conditional commands each comprising a boolean guard followed by a process. This example is :

IF (x : STOP , y : SKIP , x : SKIP)

The semantics is given as being the same as for

ALT (x : STOP) (NOT(x) AND y : SKIP) (NOT(x) AND NOT(y) AND x : SKIP) which is the choice composition of Boxes represented in Figures 7(a) - 7(c) to give that of Figure 7(d). Of course IF gives a deterministic ALT. It is possible, as here, that the conjunction of the negation of previous conditions in the sequence leads to an always-*False* condition at some point, and thus by the beta-expression semantics will have an initial "stop" Box which prevents that arm from being entered. Note the difference between the leftmost branch of Figure 7(d), where the "stop" Box ($\beta\{False \vdash \text{SKIP}\}$) occurs after a non-"stop" Box ($\beta\{x \vdash \text{SKIP}\}$), and the rightmost branch where the situation is reversed - the former can start to execute, giving deadlock, whereas the latter cannot start.

The PRIALT is a special version of ALT for which there is a special version []> of []. For B []> A, the effect is as for [] with the addition of a prioritisation of any initial transition B over any initial transition of A. The possible interpretations of priorities will be discussed later.

1.6. Iteration - OCCAM WHILE, and Box *

The iteration of a Box, e.g., WHILE (x : PAR(SKIP, SKIP)) as shown in Figure 8(a), is obtained by merging its exit places with its entry places, to give the entry places of the new Box (shown in Figure 8(b)) which has also a new isolated exit place, needed for subsequent composition. An iterated Box on its own of course cannot terminate; but can be composed by [] with a Box to allow termination (for example, that shown in Figure 8(d) giving the Box shown in Figure 8(c)). After zero or more completed iterations, the entry places are marked allowing either another iteration, or entry of the terminating Box.

The semantics (Table B(i)) is choice between: the termination Box, produced as the negation of the while condition (x); and the iteration of the Box for the conditional process, which is again the sequential composition of that for the condition with that for the process.

1.7. Declaration and Concealment - OCCAM VAR, CHAN; Box /

There are two possibilities for concealment, $/\{c, .., d\}$ for channels c .. d and $/_{u,v}\{x, .., y\}$ for variables x labelled with one of those channels or variables. The former occurs as part of the semantics of PAR, as already discussed, and so the semantics of CHAN (channel declaration) is trivial (Table B(j)). The latter occurs in variable declaration, VAR, changing a free variable to a "scoped" variable. This requires some care in achieving two goals. Firstly, that the data places of a variable become internal places when it is scoped, so that, e.g., the two instances of x in PAR (VAR x : P, VAR x : Q) are not identified. Secondly, that when a Box terminates, its internal places are unmarked; this being particularly important when it is composed within an iteration - leaving residual tokens on internal places would introduce the danger of marking several data places for the same variable. These goals motivate the form of concealment operator for variables. That is $/_{u,v}$ specifying an entry value u and exit value v, such that the data places $\langle x:u \rangle$ .. $\langle y:u \rangle$ become entry places and $\langle x:v \rangle$ .. $\langle y:v \rangle$ become exit places, as shown in Figures 9(c) and 9(d) for concealing x in Figure 9(c), with entry value EV and exit value XV.

On this basic mechanism of /, the OCCAM semantics (Table B(k)) for variable declaration is as shown in Figures 9(a)-9(d) for variable x with scope a process giving the Box shown in Figure 9(a), i.e., the semantics for VAR x : SEQ(x:=TRUE, x:=x). This Box is post-fixed with the Box for x:=XV (Figure 9(b)) to ensure the required final value, as

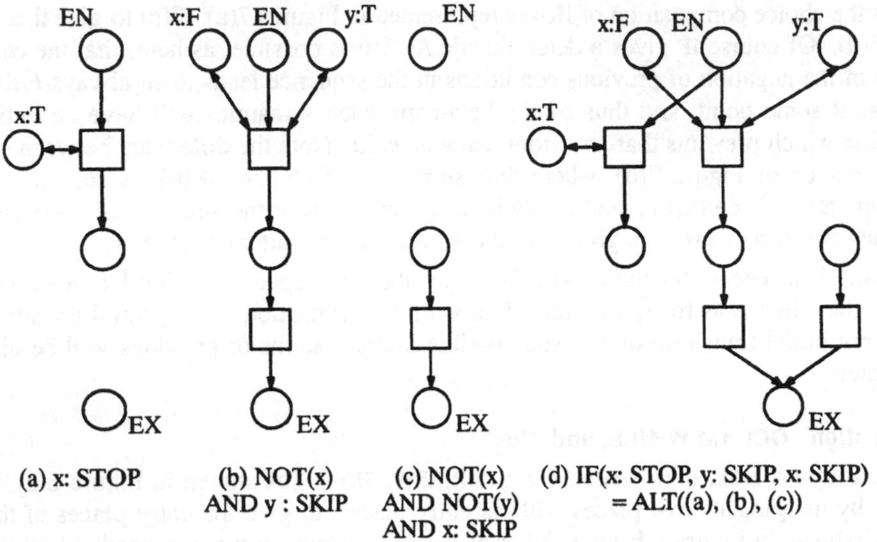

Figure 7 – IF

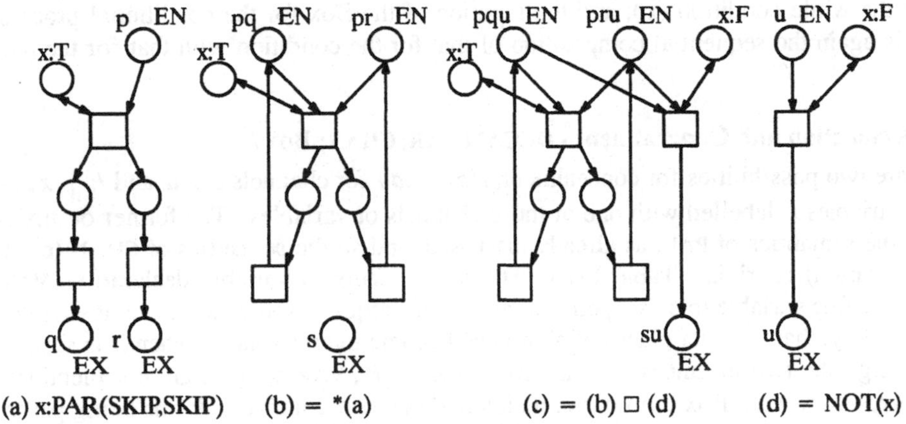

Figure 8 – Iteration

in Figure 9(c). (The $rep_{A(EV)}$ allows for the possibility that EV is one of the abstracted values (as discussed in Section 1.8); if not it gives EV.) To this is applied the / with the appropriate entry and exit values, giving Figure 9(d).

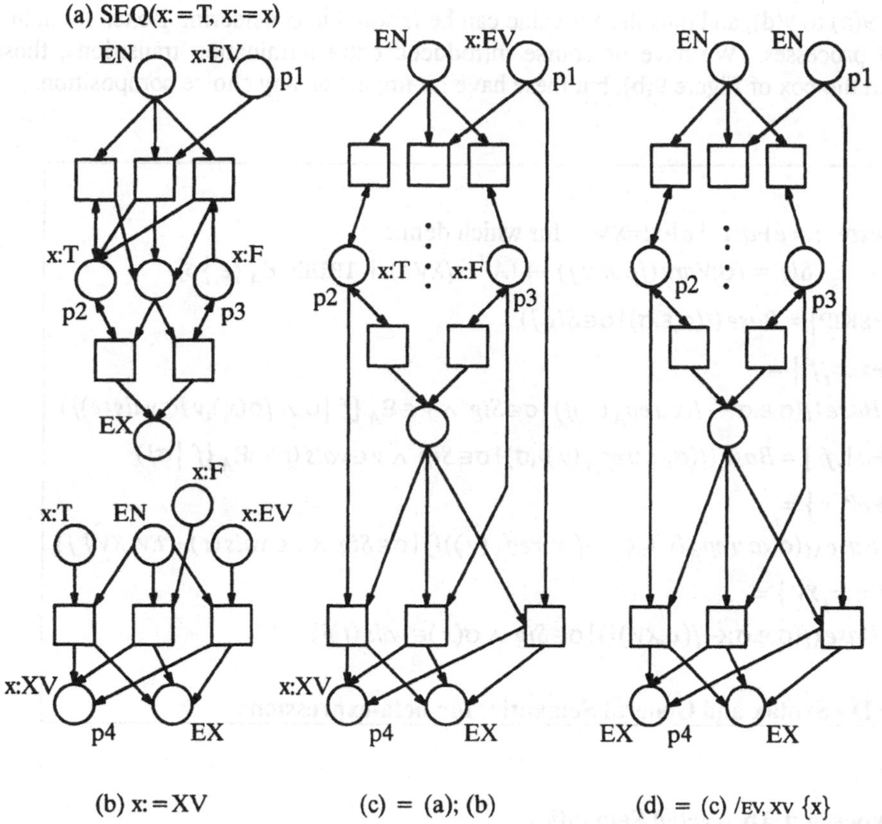

Figure 9 – Declaration

For Figure 9(a), where x is free, the initial marking can mark any one of the places $p1$–$p3$, for the three possible values of x; and at termination any of those could in principle be marked. In Figure 9(d), where x is no longer free, we have places $p1$–$p3$ corresponding to those in Figure 9(a), and $p4$ corresponding to that for the XV value of x in Figures 9(b) and 9(c). An initial marking of the Box in Figure 9(d) will mark $p1$ since that is now an entry place, and thus we have the effect that on entry to the scope of this x it has initial value EV. A sequential predecessor achieves this initialisation due to the merging of its exit places with the entry places of the Box shown in Figure 9(d). The initialisation is achieved without any additional initialisation transition, a property which would be important if there were choice composition between that shown in Figure 9(d) and another box, since it would still be the initial transitions from the Box in Figure 9(a) which govern the choice. (However such structures cannot arise in OCCAM - an arm of an ALT or IF must start with a guard, not a declaration.) Similarly, termination requires that $p4$ be marked, giving the effect of requiring x to have the final value XV. It should be noted that the data place label $x{:}XV$ occurs only as an intermediate step in going from

Figures 9(a) to 9(d), and thus the XV value can be ignored in considering Boxes for actual OCCAM processes. We have of course introduced extra termination transitions, those shown in the box of Figure 9(b), but these have no impact on any choice composition.

$$\mathit{beta\text{-}expr} ::= e \vdash \mathit{act} \mid e \vdash \mathrm{x}{:=}\mathrm{XV} \quad \text{for which define}$$

$$\mathit{Sig} = \{\sigma{:}\mathit{Vars}(\{e,\mathit{act}\}) \to (A^{+} - \{XV\}) \mid \mathrm{TRUE} \in \mathcal{E}_A \{e\} \sigma\}$$

$$\beta_A \{e \vdash \mathrm{SKIP}\} = \mathit{Base}(\{(\sigma,\varepsilon,\sigma) \mid \sigma \in \mathit{Sig}\})$$

$$\beta_A \{e \vdash x :=_t f\} =$$

$$\mathit{Base}(\{(\sigma,\varepsilon,\sigma{:}\leftarrow\{(x,\mathit{rep}_A(v))\}) \mid \sigma \in \mathit{Sig} \wedge v \in \mathcal{E}_A \{f\} \sigma \wedge \{\sigma(x),v\} \subseteq \mathit{vals}(t)\})$$

$$\beta_A \{e \vdash c\,!_t f\} = \mathit{Base}(\{(\sigma,\langle c{:}\mathit{rep}_A(v)\rangle,\sigma) \mid \sigma \in \mathit{Sig} \wedge v \in \mathit{vals}(t) \cap \mathcal{E}_A \{f\} \sigma\})$$

$$\beta_A \{e \vdash c?_t x\} =$$

$$\mathit{Base}(\{(\sigma,\langle c{:}\mathit{rep}_A(v)\rangle,\sigma{:}\leftarrow\{(x,\mathit{rep}_A(v))\}) \mid \sigma \in \mathit{Sig} \wedge v \in \mathit{vals}(t) - \{EV,XV\}\})$$

$$\beta_A \{e \vdash x :=_t XV\} =$$

$$\mathit{Base}(\{(\sigma,\varepsilon,\sigma{:}\leftarrow\{(x,XV)\}) \mid \sigma \in \mathit{Sig} \wedge \sigma(x) \in \mathit{vals}(t)\})$$

Table D - Syntax and General Semantics for beta-expressions

1.8. Types and Abstracted Semantics

We now consider the full definition of the β_A function in Table D, which addresses two (independent) aspects of reducing the size of the net produced. Firstly, we incorporate typing. For say $x{:=}y$, if we did not have any type information, then we would have to create transitions and places to cater for all possible typings of x and y. To allow that to be avoided we have type decoration t for $:=_t$, $!_t$ and $?_t$. These are used in the β_A function to constrain the possibilities considered for values assigned/communicated, and for the pre-value of the assigned variable, to be those appropriate to the type, as given by $\mathit{vals}(t)$ (with type ANY for no type constraint). We also have declarations t VAR as typed - to restrict the number of places and transitions produced for the assignment of the XV (Table B(k)); and assume that the expression syntax involves similar decorations where necessary to restrict pre-state values - for example $x =_{BOOL} y$ giving error, and thus no contribution the net, for the cases of either x or y having integer pre-value. (It should be noted that OCCAM is strongly typed and does all type conversions by explicit operators.) These devices are unnecessary from a formal semantics point of view - for a type-correct complete OCCAM program, using type ANY throughout will give the same behaviours as using the actual types - but they are important from a practical translation point of view.

The second aspect is that of obtaining partial data abstraction. For the β_A function of Table D and ξ_A of Table B, the A is those values from OCC^{+} (recall, natural values and EV) which are to be explicitly represented, as is also always XV. The remaining values are abstracted, all represented by the single generic value ¿. We use A^+ as the set of values which can actually occur within labels in the net, namely A, XV, and (in the case of A being a proper subset of OCC^+) also ¿.

In Table D we use an expression evaluation function, $\mathcal{E}_A|e|\sigma$, which takes σ as giving values in A^+. It proceeds by expanding σ to the set of all possible states which can be obtained by replacing each ¿ by some value it can represent, and yields the set of every (non-EV) value that can be obtained by normal evaluation of e in any of this set of states. In producing the transitions labels we quantify over all these possibilities, and in each case convert the yielded value to its representation, using the rep_A function which maps an abstracted value to ¿, and any other value to itself.

	y:0	y:1	y:¿
x:0	0	1	¿
x:1	1	¿	0, ¿
x:¿	¿	0, ¿	0, 1, ¿

(i) A = {TRUE, FALSE, 0, 1}

	y:0	y:¿
x:0	0	¿
x:¿	¿	0, ¿

(ii) A = {TRUE, FALSE, 0}

Table E - Transitions for $x :=_{INT} x+y$ in two partially abstracted semantics

We now give examples of two increasingly abstracted semantics. Firstly we take A = {TRUE, FALSE, 0, 1}. Each boolean variable will have three data places, for FALSE, TRUE and ¿ (representing just EV); each integer variable will have three data places, for 0, 1 and ¿; and each byte variable will have one data place, for ¿. (The explicit type conversions in OCCAM means we can take values 0 and 1 for BYTE as being distinct from 0 and 1 for INT.) For $x :=_{INT} x+y$, the semantics gives 13 transitions, as shown in Table E(i) for the set of possible post-values of x for each combination of pre-values for x and y. For example y:¿ and x:¿ include 4 and -4 for the represented values of x and y and thus 0 is a possible evaluation - one of the transitions produced will have y:¿ and x:¿ as input places, and y:¿ and x:0 as output places. The table also characterizes the values communicated in 13 alternative transitions produced for $c\,!_{INT}\,(x+y)$. For that in parallel with $c?_{INT}\,z$ there would be 3×13 synchronisations, each for one of the above with one of the possible pre-values, 0, 1 or ¿, for z.

In Table E(ii) we similarly show the case for a more abstracted semantics in which 1 also is abstracted to ¿. For two abstractions which are related in this way, the abstracted values in one being a subset of those in the other, there is for each place and transition of the less abstracted net a place or transition which represents it in the more abstracted net. For example, place x:1 of (i) is represented by x:¿ of (ii); the transition of (i) which produces 0 from x:¿ and y:1, is represented in (ii) by that which produces 0 from x:¿ and y:¿. This relationship forms the basis for a subsequently formulated consistency result which gives that any safety property established on an abstracted net holds also for a less abstracted net for the same program.

The abstraction will generally result in IF becoming non-deterministic, as in the following example, for A = {TRUE, FALSE, 0, 1}.

IF ($x =_{INT} y$ AND b : P , TRUE : P')

For the pre-state σ with x:¿, y:¿, b:TRUE, there will be a non-deterministic choice between P and P' - the set of expression evaluations under σ for $x =_{INT} y$ will include TRUE as will the set for NOT($x =_{INT} y$), and thus the semantics gives for either arm of the IF an initial transition with x:¿, y:¿ and b:TRUE as its data input places. However, for any other possible pre-state, the choice is fully determined.

It should be noted that changing abstraction level changes some behavioural equivalences; for example SEQ (x:=20 , y:=20 , z:=x−y) is equivalent to SEQ (x:=20 , y:=20 , z:=0) in the full semantics but not in the above abstracted semantics.

There is one abstracted semantics worth noting in particular, namely the control semantics, $\xi_{\emptyset}$, which captures control structure but no data computation. For each variable x, there will be one place, x:¿, which is a side condition on all transitions accessing x. This has no effect on behaviour other than in preventing concurrency between two actions in parallel which access a common variable. Every communication action on a channel c will give one transition labelled c:¿, which produces one potential synchronisation transition for every communication action on c in a parallel process. Apart from loss of concurrency due to data places, this corresponds to the natural notion of the "control net" for the program.

2. Notation, Domains and Functions

We here define the constructs used in Tables B/C/D and to be used in the next section which defines the Box algebra.

2.1. Notation for Functions and Sequences

For a function F:$Dom \rightarrow Range$, we assume its extension to $2^{Dom} \rightarrow 2^{Range}$, its inverse F^{-1}:$Range \rightarrow 2^{Dom}$ and inverse extended to $2^{Range} \rightarrow 2^{Dom}$.

For $F_1 : Dom_1 \rightarrow Range_1$ and $F_2 : Dom_2 \rightarrow Range_2$, we use $F_1 :\leftarrow F_2$ for the function $F : Dom_1 \cup Dom_2 \rightarrow Range_1 \cup Range_2$ such that if $x \in Dom_2$ then $F(x) = F_2(x)$, otherwise $F(x) = F_1(x)$.

We use $[D :\rightarrow d]$ for the unique constant function F:$D \rightarrow \{d\}$.

We freely interpret a function as a set of pairs, and vice-versa when the set has the required properties.

For a function F, we use $F \downarrow S$ for F with its domain restricted to $Dom(F) \cap S$.

2.2. Syntactic and Semantic Domains

$x, y \in X, Y \subseteq VAR$ - The countable set of OCCAM (identifiers of) variables.

$c, d \in C, D \subseteq CHAN$ - The countable set of OCCAM (identifiers of) channels. ($CHAN \cap VAR = \emptyset$.)

$t \in TYPE=\{$INT, BOOL, BYTE, ANY$\}$ - The set of identifiers for basic OCCAM types and for unspecified type.

$v, w \in V, W \subseteq Values$ where *Values* is any one of the following value domains, which are various combinations of natural OCCAM values with the previously described special values EV, XV and ¿:
OCC - Natural OCCAM values, finite.
$OCC^+ = OCC \uplus \{EV\}$ - Values that can occur in a box for an OCCAM program under full semantics.
$OCC^{++} = OCC^+ \uplus \{XV\}$ - Values that can occur during its construction.
$VAL = OCC^{++} \uplus \{¿\}$ - All values that can occur in a box.
We use $A \subseteq OCC^+$ for the set of explicitly represented (i.e., not abstracted) values, with always $A^+ = A \cup \{XV\}$ for $A = OCC^+$ and $A^+ = A \cup \{XV, ¿\}$ otherwise.

$g, h \in G, H \subseteq COMM = CHAN \times VAL$ - The communications, written $\langle c:v \rangle$.
$\delta \in BIND = VAR \times VAL$ - Bindings, written $\langle x:v \rangle$.
$\sigma \in STATE = VAR \to VAL$ $(\sigma \subseteq 2^{BIND})$ - Total data state.
$\sigma \in SSTATE = X \to VAL$ $(\sigma \subseteq 2^{BIND})$ - Partial data state (sub-state), with X finite.
(Unless explicitly mentioned a σ is a partial state.)
For any D derived from VAL, such as $D = COMM$, we use D_V for the domain similarly derived from some value domain $V \subseteq VAL$.

$e, f \in Expr$ - The syntactic domain of OCCAM expressions.
$act \in ACT$ - The syntactic domain of OCCAM actions, as given by syntax of Table A.
$P, Q, R \in PROC$ - The syntactic domain of finite OCCAM processes, as given by syntax of Table A.
$B \in BOX$ - The set of Boxes, to be defined.
$\Sigma \in MBOX$ - The set of marked Boxes, to be defined.

2.3. Functions

$Vars : Expr \cup ACT \to 2^{VAR}$ - Yields the variables occurring in an OCCAM expression or action.

$vals : TYPE \to 2^{OCC^+}$ - The value domain for each type, with $vals(\text{ANY}) = OCC^+$ and $\text{EV} \in vals(t)$ for all $t \in TYPE$.

$rep_A : OCC^{++} \to A^+$ - Defined as if $x \in A^+$ then $rep_A(x) = x$, otherwise $rep_A(x) = ¿$.

$exp_A : A^+ \to 2^{OCC^{++}}$ - Defined as rep_A^{-1} - expansion of a value to the set of values it represents. We also extend this to states (and subsequently other structures):
$exp_A(\sigma) = \{\sigma' \mid Dom(\sigma') = Dom(\sigma) = X \wedge \forall x \in X : \sigma'(x) \in exp_A(\sigma(x))\}$.

$\mathcal{E} : Exp \to SSTATE_{OCC^+} \to OCC^+$ - Basic evaluation of an OCCAM expression. We assume (e AND f), NOT (e), TRUE and FALSE all exist in Exp and that these produce the expected effect with respect to $\mathcal{E}$; and that EV as value for any variable in an expression gives EV for the result of the expression.

$\mathcal{E}_A : Exp \to SSTATE_{A^+ - \{XV\}} \to 2^{OCC^+}$ - Defined as:

$$\mathcal{E}_A | e | \sigma = \{v \in OCC \mid \exists \sigma' \in exp_A(\sigma) : v = \mathcal{E} | e | \sigma'\}$$

$\xi_A : PROC \to BOX$ - The semantics of OCCAM commands.

β_A : *beta−expr* → *BOX* - The semantics of beta-expressions.

3. The OCCAM Box Algebra

We now define the Box algebra comprising the domain *BOX* and operations ;, [] etc. We first define a pre-Box, with *BOX* being the set of pre-Boxes that satisfy certain additional requirements.

3.1. Structure

We introduce some additional domains:

NODE - A countably infinite set from which are drawn the places and transitions for basic Boxes. (Compound Boxes will also have transitions and places from the closure of *NODE* under pairing.)

We use $t, u \in T, U \subseteq NODE$ for transitions; and $s \in S \subseteq NODE$ for places.

$l \in TLAB = COMM \cup \{\varepsilon\}$ - Transition labels (we use the empty sequence, ε, for internal transitions, so that mapping a transition sequence through the labelling eliminates internals).

$l \in PLAB = BIND \cup \{\mathrm{EN}, \mathrm{EX}, \varepsilon\}$ - Place labels.

A pre-Box, B, has the form

$B = (S, T, \rightarrow, \lambda, >)$ such that -

$S \cap T = \emptyset$; T and S are both finite;

$\rightarrow \subseteq (S \times T) \cup (T \times S)$;

$\lambda :\ (S \cup T) \rightarrow (PLAB \cup TLAB)$; $\lambda(S) \subseteq PLAB$ and $\lambda(T) \subseteq TLAB$;

$> \subseteq T \times T$.

For pre-Boxes B, B', B_i etc. we use T, T', T_i etc. for their transitions, and likewise for the other components.

We define the usual • notation for the input/output places of a transition, place or set thereof. We also define:

$E(B) = \lambda^{-1}(EN)$; $X(B) = \lambda^{-1}(EX)$ - the set of entry, respectively exit, places;

$Data(B) = \lambda^{-1}(BIND)$ - the set of data places.

$Vars(B) = \{x \in VAR \mid \exists v \in VAL, s \in S : \lambda(s) = \langle x : v \rangle\}$ - The set of variables for which there are data places.

$Vals(B) = \{v \in VAL \mid \exists st \in T \cup S, cx \in CHAN \cup VAR : \lambda(st) = \langle cx : v \rangle\}$ - The set of values which occur in data place or transition labels.

Two Boxes B and B' are *disjoint* iff $(S \cup T) \cap (S' \cup T') = \emptyset$.

Before presenting the definitions of the operations, we deal with the behaviour of marked pre-Boxes and the structural and behavioural properties which characterize actual Boxes.

3.2. Marked pre-Boxes and Behaviour

A marked pre-Box is a pair, written (B, M), where B is a pre-Box, and $M \subseteq S$ is a (safe) marking. We define the function Δ which gives a Marked Box for a particular state $\sigma \in SSTATE$, by marking the entry places and appropriate data places:

$\Delta(B, \sigma) = (B, M)$ with $M = \{s \in S \mid \lambda(s) \in \sigma \cup \{EN\}\}$

For a marked Box, the set of variables having values is
$Valued(B,M) = \{x \in VAR \mid \exists v \in VAL : \langle x:v \rangle \in \lambda^{-1}(M)\}$.

The firing of a transition $t \in T$ in a marked Box (B,M), to give a marked Box (B,M'), is defined as $(B,M)\ [t> (B,M')$ iff $\bullet t \subseteq M$ and $M' = (M - \bullet t) \cup t\bullet$.

We use $(B,M_1) \Rightarrow (B,M_n)$ for $(B,M_1)[t_1>(B,M_2)..[t_{n-1}>(B,M_n)$.

Using markings as just sets of places, together with a firing rule which ignores output place marking, is justified by the safeness property below. In formally defining behaviours of a Box we here ignore prioritisation and true concurrency, since the results to be presented are based on the behaviour representation of Roscoe which addresses neither.

A pre-Box B is a Box if:

(i) $E(B) \neq \varnothing$ and $X(B) \neq \varnothing$ - composability;

And for any state $\sigma \in SSTATE$ and any marking M such that $\Delta(B,\sigma) \Rightarrow (B,M)$:

(ii) If $(B,M)[t>(B,M')$ then $(\{t\}\bullet - \bullet\{t\}) \cap M = \varnothing$
Safeness - no output place, except a side-condition, is already marked;

(iii) $\lambda(Data(B) \cap M)$ is a function $\sigma' : Valued(\Delta(B,\sigma)) \rightarrow VAL$
Data coherence - each reachable marking associates a single value to each of the same set of variables;

(iii) $E(B) \subseteq M \Rightarrow M - Data(B) = E(B)$ and $X(B) \subseteq M \Rightarrow M - Data(B) = X(B)$
Control coherence - in an initial marking (all entry places marked) or a final marking (all exit places), no internal place is marked.

3.3. Base Constructor

Following the description in section 1.2, we now define the *Base* constructor, which produces a Box for a set t_i of transitions each defined by a pre-state σ_i, transition label l_i, and a post-state σ'_i. The pre-state and post-state give the labels of, respectively, the input and output data places of t_i.

For $D = \{D_1, \ldots D_N\}$ with $D_i = (\sigma_i, l_i, \sigma'_i) \in SSTATE \times TLAB \times SSTATE$, such that $Dom(\sigma_i) = Dom(\sigma'_i) = Y_i$.

Base(D) gives a Box, B, built with: a set of transitions t_i, one for each element of D; an entry place p and an exit place q; and those places needed from the set of potential data places $d_{j,k}$ comprising one labelled $\langle y_j : v_k \rangle$ for each possible value v_k of each variable y_j in any element of D.

Let $\{y_1, \ldots, y_M\} = Y = \bigcup_{i=1..N} Y_i$ and $\{v_1, \ldots, v_L\} = VAL$

Let $T = \{t_1, \ldots, t_N\}$, $NX = \{p, q\}$ and $DP = \bigcup_{j=1..M, k=1..L} \{d_{j,k}\}$ such that:
$T \uplus NX \uplus DP \subseteq NODE$.

Then $B = (S, T, \rightarrow, \lambda{\downarrow}(S \cup T), \varnothing)$, with

$S = NX \cup \{d \in DP \mid \lambda(d) \in \bigcup_{i=1..N} \sigma_i \cup \sigma'_i\}$.

$\rightarrow\ = \bigcup_{i=1..N} (\{(p,t_i), (t_i,q)\} \cup \{(s,t_i) \mid \lambda(s) \in \sigma_i\} \cup \{(t_i,s) \mid \lambda(s) \in \sigma'_i\})$

$\lambda = \{(t_i,l_i) \mid i \in \{1..N\}\} \cup \{(p,\mathrm{EN}),(q,\mathrm{EX})\} \cup \{(d_{j,k}, \langle y_j : v_k \rangle) \mid j \in \{1..M\} \wedge k \in \{1..L\}\}$

3.4. Pre-Box Operations

We now define some primitive operations on pre-boxes, to be used in subsequently defining the actual box operations. Throughout B, B' etc. are pre-Boxes.

3.4.1. $:\leftarrow_\lambda$ - Label Modification

For $\lambda':Z \to LAB = PLAB \cup TLAB$, with $Z \subseteq S \cup T$, we define $B :\leftarrow_\lambda \lambda' = (S, T, \lambda :\leftarrow \lambda', >)$

3.4.2. $+_>$ - Prioritisation enhancement

For $>' \subseteq T^2$ we define $B +_> >' = (S, T, \lambda, > \cup >')$

3.4.3. $\odot$ - Deletion of Places and Transitions

For $Z \subseteq S \cup T$ we define

$$B \odot Z = (S - Z, T - Z, \to \cap ((T \cup S) - Z)^2, \lambda{\downarrow}((T \cup S) - Z), > \cap (T - Z)^2)$$

3.4.4. $\oplus$ - Add in place or transition pair(s)

We first define the addition of a place (or transition) which combines a pair of existing places (or transitions), and then extend this to addition of a set of such for a set of pairs.

For $z = (a, b) \in (S \times S) \cup (T \times T)$,

$B \oplus z = (S \cup (\{z\} \cap (S \times S)),\ T \cup (\{z\} \cap (T \times T)),\ \to \cup \to',\ \lambda \cup \lambda',\ > \cup >' \cup >'')$, where

$\to' = \{(r, z) \mid (r, a) \in \to \vee (r, b) \in \to\} \cup \{(z, r) \mid (a, r) \in \to \vee (b, r) \in \to\}$

$\lambda' = [\{z\} :\to l]$ with $l = \lambda(a)$ if $\lambda(a) = \lambda(b)$, and $l = \varepsilon$ otherwise.

$>' = \{(t, z) \mid t \in T \wedge ((t, a) \in > \vee (t, b) \in >)\} \cup \{(z, t) \mid t \in T \wedge ((a, t) \in > \vee (b, t) \in >)\}$

$>'' = \{(z, z)\}$ if $\{a, b\}^2 \cap > \neq \emptyset$; otherwise $>'' = \emptyset$.

The new transition or place has flow and priority from both mergees; if they have same label it inherits that, otherwise it has the ε label. Also the priority relation allows for self-prioritisation - adding in (t, u) with say $t > u$ or $t > t$ giving $(t, u) > (t, u)$.

For $Z = \{(a_1, b_1) .. (a_n, b_n)\}$, with $\{a_1, b_1 .. a_n, b_n\} \in 2^S \cup 2^T$ we use the commutativity of application of $\oplus$ to define:

$$B \oplus Z = B \oplus (a_1, b_1) \oplus .. \oplus (a_n, b_n)$$

3.4.5. $\otimes$ - Merge in a set of pairs of place or transition sets

For $ZZ = \{(A_1, B_1) .. (A_n, B_n)\}$ with $\bigcup_{i=1..n} A_i \cup B_i \in 2^S \cup 2^T$, we define

$$B \otimes ZZ = (B \oplus \bigcup_{i=1..n} A_i \times B_i) \odot \bigcup_{i=1..n} A_i \cup B_i$$

For a pair (A_1, B_1) of two sets of places, this performs the place "multiplication" as shown in Figure 3, for A_1 being the exit places of Box (a) and B_1 being the entry places for Box (b); and similarly for transitions, as in Figure 4.

3.4.6. $\oplus\oplus$ - Join a number of Boxes

For disjoint Boxes B and B' we define

$$B \oplus\oplus B' = (S \cup S', T \cup T', \lambda \cup \lambda', > \cup >') \otimes \{(\{p\}, \{q\}) \mid \lambda(p) = \lambda'(q) \in BIND\}$$

That is, disjoint union of Boxes, with merging of same-labelled data places.

3.5. The Box Operations

In the following we take B to be a Box, B_1 and B_2 to be disjoint Boxes, X to be a set of variables, C to be a set of channels, and v and w to be distinct values in VAL.

3.5.1. Sequencing, Choice and Concealment

$B_1 ; B_2 = (B_1 \oplus\oplus B_2) \otimes \{(X(B_1), E(B_2))\}$
$B_1 [] B_2 = (B_1 \oplus\oplus B_2) \otimes \{(E(B_1), E(B_2)), (X(B_1), X(B_2))\}$
$B_1 []> B_2 = (B_1 [] B_2) +_{>} (E(B_1)\bullet \times E(B_2)\bullet)$
$B /_{v,w} X = B :\leftarrow_{\lambda} [(\lambda^{-1}(X \times VAL)) :\rightarrow \varepsilon] :\leftarrow_{\lambda} [(\lambda^{-1}(X \times \{v\})) :\rightarrow EN])$
$\quad :\leftarrow_{\lambda} [(\lambda^{-1}(X \times \{w\})) :\rightarrow EX]$
$B / C = B :\leftarrow_{\lambda} [(\lambda^{-1}(C \times VAL)) :\rightarrow \varepsilon])$

The definitions of sequencing ;, choice [] and prioritised choice []> are straightforward from the previous descriptions. Their use in Table B relies on the associativity of ;, [] and []>.

Concealment first does a general relabelling: every place (or transition) which has a label involving a variable in X (or channel in C) is internalised with label ε. This is then modified to label places $\langle x : v \rangle$ as entry place and $\langle x : w \rangle$ as exit place for all x in X.

3.5.2. Parallel

$B_1 \| _C B_2 = (B_1 \oplus\oplus B_2) \otimes \{(\lambda_1^{-1}(g), \lambda_2^{-1}(g)) \mid g \in C \times VAL\} \ominus Z$ where
$Z = \{(t, u) \in T_1 \times T_2 \mid \exists x, v, w : \{\langle x : v \rangle, \langle x : w \rangle\} \subseteq \lambda_1(t\bullet) \cup \lambda_2(u\bullet) \wedge v \neq w\}\}$

For parallel, the synchronisation is over a set C of channels. The $\otimes$ construction used achieves a two-way synchronisation between any two transitions which are from different components of the parallel, and have the same communication for their label (provided this is on a channel in C). The final $\ominus$ is to ensure the data coherence property. Without it we could get a situation like that in Figure 10 where 10(a) in parallel with 10(b) would give 10(c). If $x:T$ is marked, the firing of $t1t4$ gives both $x:T$ and $x:F$ marked, violating the data coherence property. This situation could not arise in OCCAM due to restrictions on shared variables, but nonetheless has to be dealt with properly at the Box algebra level. This is by deleting any created synchronisation transitions having two distinct output places for the same variable x, giving 10(d) in this case.

3.5.3. Iteration

For $|E(B)|=1$ or $|X(B)|=1$ define
$*B = (B \otimes \{(E(B), X(B))\}) :\leftarrow_{\lambda} \lambda' ; Base(\varnothing)$ where $\lambda' = [(E(B) \times X(B)) :\rightarrow EN]$

As illustrated in Figure 8, iteration first merges the entry places and exit places, which by definition of $\oplus$ leaves no entry or exit; it then relabels the newly created places as entry places and creates an isolated exit place by sequential composition with the "stop" Box. That gives a 0×1 place merge which has the effect of deleting the entry place of the stop Box. We assume for this that sequential composition has been defined as above for pre-boxes. We insist that the iterated process not have both initial and final parallelism. This

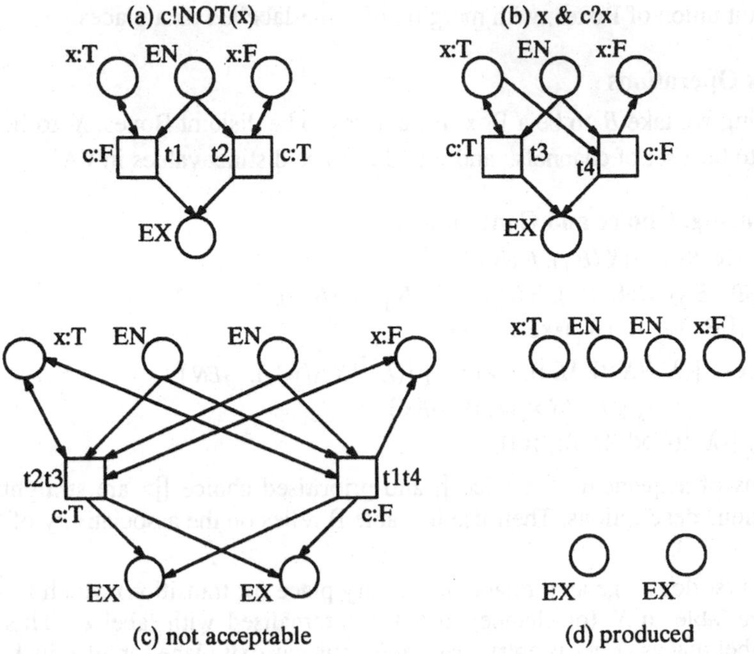

Figure 10 – Synchronisation of transitions with a common variable

restriction holds for OCCAM since a WHILE is guarded with a condition and thus cannot have initial parallelism. The * operation is in fact defined in a way that could structurally allow both initial and final parallelism. However this is behaviourally unacceptable as seen in the example of Figure 11, which is

$$*(((B\,;B)\,||_{\varnothing}\,(B\,;B)),\quad \text{with } B=\beta(\text{TRUE}\vdash\text{SKIP})$$

We see that from an initial marking of all entry places, the firing of just t_1 gives a marking which violates the safeness property at place *bp* for the firing of t_2.

4. Consistency Results

Here we formulate the main results from [HOPK92]. There is of course the requirement to show that the operations preserve Box-ness, i.e. the properties of safeness, data coherence and control coherence formulated in section 3.2; and also a number of expectable properties of associativity etc. The two more substantial results concern exact consistency of our full semantics with the Laws of OCCAM; and a less-deterministic consistency between any abstracted semantics and a less abstracted semantics. Both of these results are based on a behaviour representation motivated by that of the Roscoe Semantics (an "*ft*" structure).

The Roscoe semantics ξ_R uses a storage state L as a function from storage locations (in LOC) to values (in OCC^+), and an environment ρ giving (amongst other things) the current mapping from variables to locations. We will find it convenient to assume $|LOC|$

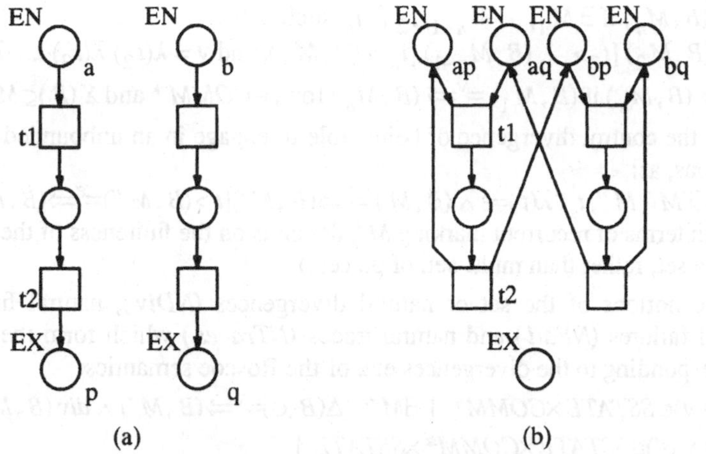

Figure 11 – Unsafe Iteration

$= |VAR|$. For a program fragment, or process, P in environment ρ and initial storage state L, the semantics $\xi_R \{P\} \rho L$ gives an *ft* structure (F, T) comprising:

(i) A set of Failures F, each failure f being a pair comprising a sequence ν of communications (each in $CHAN \times OCC$), and a set G of communications such that P can do ν and then be in a process state at which it refuses G (i.e. cannot do anything in G as a next communication). A refused set G can include $\surd$ ("tick"), which means refusal to terminate. (Actual termination is represented within (ii), rather than by $\surd$ at the end of ν).

(ii) A termination function T which maps any communication sequence ν to either:

(a) $\perp$ - It is possible that after doing ν, P diverges. Divergence is a single notion which captures all semantic errors, namely - *data error*s such as division by zero, or accessing an uninitialised variable; the *control error* which is being able to do an unbounded sequence of internal actions.

(b) A set of (location) states, $\{L_1, \ldots, L_n\}$ - for each (ν, L_i) pair it is possible for P to do ν and terminate leaving L_i as the values of locations. (If this set is empty, P cannot terminate on ν).

We first formulate how to obtain the required behaviour representations from Boxes.

4.1. Failures/Terminations Representation of Box Behaviour

For a set D, D^* is the set of finite sequences over D. The empty sequence is denoted ε. Elements of sequences are formed as $a \cdot b$, the concatenation of a and b where a or b are in $D \cup D^*$. We use ν, υ and ω for sequences in $COMM^*$ or $COMM\surd^*$ with $COMM\surd = COMM_{OCC} \uplus \{\surd\}$.

We define a communication sequence $\nu \in COMM\surd^*$ from marked Box (B, M_1) to (B, M_n) as

$(B, M_1) =^{\nu}\Rightarrow (B, M_n)$ if $\exists M_1, \dots M_{n-1}, t_2 \dots t_n$ such that
$(B, M_1)\,[t_2> (B, M_2)\,[t_3> \dots (B, M_{n-1})\,[t_n> (B, M_n)$, and $\nu = \lambda(t_2)\cdot\lambda(t_3)\cdot \dots \cdot\lambda(t_n)$.
$(B, M_1) =^{\nu\cdot\surd}\Rightarrow (B, M_n)$ if $(B, M_1) =^{\nu}\Rightarrow (B, M_n)$ for $\nu\in COMM^*$ and $X(B)\subseteq M_n$.

We define *div*, the control divergence of being able to engage in an unbounded sequence of internal actions, as:

$div(B,M)$ iff $\exists M', M'', t : \lambda(t)=\varepsilon \wedge (B,M)=^{\varepsilon}\Rightarrow(B,M')[t>(B,M'')=^{\varepsilon}\Rightarrow(B,M')$

(Defining this in terms of recurrent marking M', depends on the finiteness of the net and a marking being a set, rather than multi-set, of places.)

We now define notions of the set of natural divergences (*NDiv*), natural final states (*NFin*), natural failures (*NFail*) and natural traces (*NTraces*) which form the basis for structures corresponding to the divergences etc. of the Roscoe semantics:

$NDiv(B) = \{(\sigma,\nu)\in SSTATE\times COMM^* \mid \exists M' :\ \Delta(B,\sigma)=^{\nu}\Rightarrow(B,M') \wedge div(B,M')\}$

$NFin(B) = \{(\sigma,\nu,\sigma')\in SSTATE\times COMM^*\times SSTATE \mid$
$\exists M' :\ \Delta(B,\sigma)=^{\nu}\Rightarrow(B,M') \wedge X(B)\subseteq M' \wedge \sigma'=\lambda(Data(B)\cap M')\}$

$NFail(B) = \{(\sigma,\nu,G)\in SSTATE\times COMM^*\times 2^{COMM\surd} \mid$
$\exists M' :\ \Delta(B,\sigma)=^{\nu}\Rightarrow(B,M') \wedge \forall g\in G : \neg((B,M')=^{g\cdot\varepsilon}\Rightarrow)\}$

$NTraces(B) = \{(\sigma,\nu)\in SSTATE\times COMM^* \mid \exists M' :\ \Delta(B,\sigma)=^{\nu}\Rightarrow(B,M')\}$

That is, *NDiv* identifies conditions (initial state and communication sequence) which allow the Box to enter into an unbounded sequence of internal actions; *NFin* similarly identifies possible final states; and *NFail* possible refusal sets, including refusing termination; *NTraces* just gives every possible communication sequence from a particular initial state.

In the Roscoe Semantics, if a process P has ν as a possible divergence, it is taken that whenever that sequence has occurred the process is henceforth completely unpredictable, other than in being unable to terminate. That is, for any $\omega\in COMM_{OCC}{}^*$: the divergences should include $\nu\cdot\omega$; the failures should include $(\nu\cdot\omega, G)$ for any $G\subseteq COMM\surd$; and there should be no final states for $\nu\cdot\omega$. Thus, for comparing our full semantics with Roscoe, we now formulate an *ft* behavioural representation, *FT*, via the Box obtained as $\xi\{P\}$, which matches this extended notion of the failures etc. of a process. The *ft* structure consists of *Fail* which incorporates the necessary extensions of *NFail*; and *Term* (Terminations) which is a function incorporating the necessary extensions to *NFin* and *NDiv* (divergence being represented by $\perp$):

For a Box B we have

1. $Term\{B\} : STATE_{OCC^+} \rightarrow COMM_{OCC^+}{}^* \rightarrow TERM$ where

   $TERM = (2^{STATE_{OCC^+}} \cup \{\perp\})$

2. $Fail\{B\} : STATE_{OCC^+} \rightarrow 2^{FAIL}$ where $FAIL = COMM_{OCC}{}^* \times 2^{COMM\surd}$

   defined as follows, for $\sigma\in STATE$ and $\sigma'\in SSTATE$

$Term\{B\}\sigma\nu =$
(i) If $\exists\upsilon,\omega$: $\upsilon\cdot\omega = \nu \wedge (\sigma,\upsilon)\in NDiv(B)$ Then $\perp$
(ii) otherwise $\{\sigma{:}\leftarrow\sigma' \mid (\sigma,\nu,\sigma')\in NFin(B)\}$

$Fail\{B\}\sigma = \{(\nu,G) \mid Term\{B\}\sigma\nu=\perp \vee (\sigma,\nu,G)\in NFail(B)\}$

For a process P, we define $FT\{P\} = (Fail((\xi\{P\}), Term((\xi\{P\}))$
We define an equivalence $\approx$ on processes as $P \approx P'$ iff $FT\{P\} = FT\{P'\}$.

4.2. Consistency with the Laws of OCCAM

The Laws of OCCAM [RH86] only apply to OCCAM processes in which the only form of iteration is the canonical control error WHILE(TRUE:SKIP) (so called *finite* processes). Throughout this section we consider only finite processes P and Q. The consistency result we obtain is that the equivalence on processes, $\approx$ of Section 4.1, is the same as the equivalence, $\approx'$, induced by the laws of OCCAM [RH86]. It is known that the Roscoe Semantics give that equivalence, i.e. $P \approx' Q$ iff $\xi_R\{P\}\rho L = \xi_R\{Q\}\rho L$ for all ρ and L. Thus it suffices to show a consistency between ξ_R and our ξ and FT functions (avoiding the need to consider each law individually).

Theorem 1

Let P be a finite process, ρ an environment, and $\sigma \in STATE$ a (total) initial state. Then
$N(FT\{syn(P)\}\sigma) = \xi_R\{P\}\rho L$ with $L = N(\sigma)$ where

(i) States - N is a bijection from variables to locations with natural extension to map a variable-based state or *ft* structure to the corresponding location-based one. We require that N agree with the variable to location mapping provided by ρ, on those variables $FREE_P$ which occur free in P. We also require that for any variable x not in $FREE_P$, $\sigma(x)$=EV. This is because: if there is a declaration for y within P, the ξ_R in environment ρ will allocate it a location, l, to which some such x maps, $N(x)=l$; the initial value for y is taken to be that of l (which must therefore be EV for consistency with our semantics); on termination l is set to EV, which is consistent with our semantics not changing the value of x.

(ii) Syntax - We require that P be in the common language subset (discussed in Section 5.1), and that the finiteness condition holds for P (since otherwise the Laws do not apply to P and it is consistency with the laws which is the goal). The function *Syn* maps from the syntax used in Roscoe to that used here, the significant change being to add the type decorations of our syntax, using ANY, since Roscoe does not have such decorations and allows the possibility of any variable having any value.

(iii) Data Errors - We require P, ρ and σ to be such that no data error can occur since these are treated differently in the two semantics - Roscoe gives divergence for data errors whereas we by-pass them (e.g. for x a boolean variable and a state with it having value EV, the process ALT (x : $P1$, TRUE : $P2$) will in Roscoe give immediate divergence, whereas in our semantics we get the behaviour of $P2$). Due to the WHILE restriction in (ii), we formulate this restriction as being that: if every WHILE(TRUE:SKIP) in P is replaced by STOP, then the Roscoe semantics gives no divergences.

It should be remarked that there are several significant differences between the two semantic frameworks involved in the formulation of the consistency result making it rather complex. Once formulated, however, the proof is a straightforward application of structural induction on the OCCAM process P.

We have the following corollary:

Corollary 2
For processes satisfying (ii) and (iii) of Theorem 1 the equivalence ≈ is the same as that induced by the Laws of OCCAM.

4.3. Consistency between Abstracted Semantics

We now have to manipulate the structures *NDiv* etc. of 4.1 so as to be able to compare these when arising from semantics with different degrees of abstractness. We do this by expanding to eliminate any ¿ value. For any $struct(z_1,..,z_n)$, where *struct* may be set, sequence or tuple construction, we define

$exp_A(struct(z_1,..,z_n)) = \{struct(z_1',..,z_n') \mid \forall i \in 1..n : z_i' \in exp_A(z_i)\}$ (and $exp_A(\surd) = \{\surd\}$)

Now, with respect to sets A_1 and A_2 of explicitly represented values, we define the less-determined ordering on two Boxes B_1 and B_2 as $B_1 \leq_{A_1,A_2} B_2$ iff

$$exp_{A_2}(NDiv(B_2)) \subseteq exp_{A_1}(NDiv(B_1)) \wedge exp_{A_2}(NFin(B_2)) \subseteq exp_{A_1}(NFin(B_1)) \wedge$$
$$exp_{A_2}(NTraces(B_2)) \subseteq exp_{A_1}(NTraces(B_1))$$

The result we have is that:

Theorem 3
For all P in syntax Table A, $A_1 \subseteq A_2 \Rightarrow \xi_{A_1}\{P\} \leq_{A_1,A_2} \xi_{A_2}\{P\}$.

The result uses the idea sketched in discussing Table E. If $B_1 = \xi_{A_1}\{P\}$, the box for the more abstracted semantics, and $B_2 = \xi_{A_2}\{P\}$, the box for the less abstracted semantics, there will be a representation function, a surjection *rep*, from places and transitions of B_2 to those of B_1 such that (extending *rep* to sets, and taking *exp* as giving {ε}, {EV} and {XV} for respectively ε, EV and XV):
(i) for all $t \in T_2$: $rep(\bullet t) = \bullet(rep(t))$ and $rep(t\bullet) = (rep(t))\bullet$
(ii) for all $x \in S_2 \cup T_2$: $exp_{A_2}(\lambda_2(x)) \subseteq exp_{A_1}(\lambda_1(rep(x)))$
(iii) for all σ, if $\Delta(B_2,\sigma) \Longrightarrow (B_2,M)$ then $|M| = |rep(M)|$

The existence of such a surjection *rep* is established by the properties of the β semantic function and preserved by the the [] etc. compositions. From property (i) and (iii) of *rep* we have that if $(B_2,M)[t>(B_2,M')$ then $(B_1,rep(M))[rep(t)>(B_1,rep(M'))$. This together with property (ii) gives the above stated result.

The consequence of this result is that for certain kinds of properties, the verification of the property on the relatively small net of a more abstracted semantics implies that property for any less abstracted semantics, and particularly for the full semantics, i.e. for the actual program. The relevant properties are essentially safety properties specifying restrictions on what can occur in terms of communication sequences and final state (or divergence) produced. However there is in general no transfer of liveness properties such as lack of deadlock between different levels of abstractness. For example,

P = SEQ (x:=y , ALT ($x \neq y$: STOP , x=y : SKIP))
P' = SEQ (x:=y , ALT ($x \neq y$: SKIP))

For P the control semantics gives a deadlock possibility which is not present in the full semantics, whereas the situation is exactly reversed for P'.

The above consistency result means that the more abstracted net has in general more behaviours (in the sense of its (expanded) occurrence sequences) than the less abstracted one. However their actual representation, as say part of a reachability graph being explored by a Petri net tool, would use the unexpanded ¿ form, and thus in general will be smaller than the corresponding structure for a less abstracted net.

5. Discussion

In the following sections we discuss a variety of issues, moving from the specifics of the OCCAM syntax used and semantics obtained, to more general characteristics of the Box algebra for program semantics.

5.1. Comparison with Standard and Roscoe OCCAM

In [RH86], each arm of a PAR is decorated with "using" information on how it uses global variables (read/write/unused) and global channels (input/output/internal/unused), in order to deal with certain restrictions, namely: A channel may only be used such that it is declared as input for one component of a parallel, and as output for one other component, and actual use is consistent with that; A variable which is assigned to in one a component of a parallel may not be used in any other component. In contrast, standard OCCAM [INMOS88] has no such declarations; a violation is either detected as a syntax error, employing information from the body of each arm, or allowed to pass, which may lead to unpredictable program behaviour (divergence). The Roscoe syntax imposes these declarations in order to be able to give divergence for genuine violations and to accommodate program transformations which would otherwise introduce apparent violations. In our syntax, we have reduced the PAR decorations to the minimum necessary to be still able obtain Roscoe consistency in cases where the program does satisfy the above restrictions, and have $||_C$ as a reasonably general associative binary operator.

There are certain features of standard OCCAM which are omitted in both [RH86] and Box OCCAM, namely PRIPAR, PLACEDPAR and timers. The Box semantics includes a treatment of PRIALT which are not addressed by the Roscoe semantics. There are also a number of features included in [RH86] which are excluded here, namely: procedures and structured data; replicators which would be a considerable complication with little semantic significance; and the input/output forms $c?$ANY and $c!$ANY which present no difficulty, but are omitted for brevity.

The only substantial difference between (the $FT(P)$ derived from) our semantics and Roscoe's is that we essentially ignore errors (or give deadlock if no alternative is possible), whereas Roscoe gives divergence. It would have been possible for us to obtain the latter by say an implicit boolean variable which is set when an error occurs and is recognized as divergence by the FT function. However this would be unuseful for highly abstracted translations since there would tend to be many spurious data error possibilities. As an extreme case, in the control semantics, $\xi_\varnothing$, every access to a variable x would involve an error possibility since in that case $x:¿$ includes $x:EV$.

5.2. Language Issues

The Box algebra defined here may or may not be appropriate for Petri-net semantics of a particular programming language, and we now discuss both its limitations and generalities in this respect. For the latter we use a notation, expressing more of its generality, comprising the operations ;, [] etc., and beta-expressions $e \vdash act$ (see syntax of Table A) which we now extend by allowing *act* for TRUE$\vdash act$. (Using β as the semantic function for this notation, we extend it by $\beta\{P\ []\ Q\} = \beta\{P\}\ []\ \beta\{Q\}$ etc.)

There are a number of possibly useful language features, not found in OCCAM, which are directly expressible in the above notation, including: general sharing of variables between parallel processes and multi-way synchronisation (both discussed below); both output and input guards; assignment guards as in ($x \vdash x$:=FALSE ; P) which achieves a binary semaphore on entry to P; initial parallelism in choice (see Figure 5); initial parallelism in iteration, provided the unsafeness of Figure 8 is avoided, e.g. a language construct REPEATEDLY DO P having semantics $*(\xi\{P\}\ ;\ \beta\{\text{SKIP}\})$.

The most noticeable omission is procedures and general recursion. For OCCAM there are procedures, but without recursion. We could include such simple procedures by the semantics of the procedure definition being the Box produced in the usual way for its body, and the semantics of a procedure call being the Box for the procedure with a re-labelling of transitions and places to replace the formal parameter variables and channels with the corresponding actual parameters. This would require an additional re-labelling operation for the algebra, and an environment in the semantics to carry for each procedure name its binding to a Box and information about its parameters. A more general treatment of procedures to allow recursion requires either an infinite net or a high-level net, which we wished to avoid here. The treatment of recursion in a high-level "Box" model, is given in [HALL92].

The range of data types dealt with is very limited. The generalization to structured data types such as arrays would be straight-forward but tedious, by having data-place labels with the required structure, e.g. ‹$x.i.j$:v› labelling the data place of value v for a particular element of two-dimensional array x. Structures of channels can be dealt with by a similar approach for transition labels. The form of semantics we have given disallows the possibility of a variable retaining a value outside its syntactic scope, as occurs with "own" variables, and also disallows reference variables. To deal with these would require an environment mapping variables to locations. Although this is the more usual approach, even in the absence of own/reference variables, we prefer to avoid it since it would make the semantics more complex and translation less direct. Also it would seriously reduce modularity in that data places would be for locations rather than for variables and would never be internalised. However using locations and an environment mapping would allow structured variables without the need for the above suggested extension to the place labelling.

The particular semantics of communication given by the $||_C$ and $/C$ here uses a TCSP style of communication, as does the Roscoe Semantics. There is no inherent distinction between input and output, this being dealt with in the language semantic definitions rather than Box algebra. Also, multi-way synchronisation is possible, as in say ($c!1\ ||_{\{c\}}\ c?x\ ||_{\{c\}}\ c?y$)/$\{c\}$ where all three processes successfully synchronise on ‹c:1›. An alternative algebra and OCCAM semantics could have been given by a $||$ and / which uses a

CCS style communication, as in [HHBD90]. For that: the labels would be of form $\langle c!v \rangle$ and $\langle c?v \rangle$ for communications, with $||$ giving label ε to synchronisations; a synchronisation alphabet would not be used for $||$; and deletion of transitions which fail to synchronise would be done by / rather than $||$ (on channel declaration since it is then known that a matching communication is impossible). Although that would not be an unreasonable semantics for OCCAM, it would be inconsistent with the Roscoe semantics.

The algebra can accommodate general shared variables between parallel components, with no restrictions on updating. The only potential definitional difficulty arises when there is synchronisation between two transitions which access the same variable, x. Our rule for this case, is that for the synchronisation to succeed, both must agree on the same post-value of x. For $(c!not(x) \; ||_{\{c\}} \; c?x) \, /\{c\}$ the two processes disagree resulting in deadlock (see similar example of Figure 10), whereas for $(c!x \; ||_{\{c\}} \; c?x) \, /\{c\}$ they agree and the effect is as for SKIP.

For OCCAM, two parallel processes accessing the same variable x may not update it, and thus we could have given the semantics for this as replication of x rather than actual sharing. The PAR of two process P and Q would introduce an extra parallel process R to send copies of the global x which are received into local x variables by P and Q. The only significant difference would be increased concurrency compared with variable-sharing since in the latter each shared variable will have its data places as side-conditions to each of the transitions accessing it, enforcing interleaving of such accesses. We have taken shared-variable semantics since the alternative is more complex, requires knowledge of what variables are used by the arms of a PAR, and make no difference to the interleaving-based behaviour which provides the consistency result.

5.3. Alternative Algebras for Net Semantics of Programming Languages

As alternatives to defining the OCCAM Box Algebra (OBA) as a route to net semantics for programming languages, one could use an existing net semantics of a process algebras such as CCS or TCSP, e.g. [TAUB89], [GM84], [OLD91], [DDM87], with the language semantic function giving a term of the algebra. Such semantics would give a number of differences in the resulting nets. For example, we use sequential composition as a basic operation rather than deriving it (from action prefix, parallel composition, relabelling and restriction), as is done in much of process algebra work; and in the net for $(P\,[]\,Q);R$, we obtain one copy of the net for R whereas this often gives two copies, one following P and one following Q; for iteration we have a specific operator giving a finite cyclic net, rather than going via recursion which in many process algebra net semantics gives an infinite net.

Most significantly from the viewpoint of this paper is that the treatment of variables would be very different in any of the above process algebra net semantics, this being particularly so if one wishes to accommodate shared updatable variables. Going via (value-passing) CCS would involve the technique used in [MILN89] whereby each variable is a process which communicates with the processes using it by "get" and "set" actions. (This is necessary for communication of variable state, even for a variable whose scope is a single sequential process, because sequential composition has to be modelled using parallel composition.) An assignment such as $x:=x+y$ would involve three transitions: two concurrent get communications on x and y, followed by a set communication on x.

The consequence is that there may be interference with another such update to x in a concurrent process. The solution proposed in [MILN89] is to include in the semantic definition locking mechanisms, involving communications with "semaphore" processes to achieve the required mutual exclusion. Even without shared updatable variables, the evaluation of guards can be problematic. Consider the example ALT($c?x$:SKIP, $x=y$ & $d?z$:SKIP). If the semantics of the guard $x=y$ & $d?z$ involves several transitions in its evaluation then there will be circumstances (for example, $x=y$ but no communication is offered on d) in which the right-hand branch can be entered without it being able to complete. This gives either deadlock, incorrectly if communication is offered on c; or a divergence (again incorrect) if the semantics allows for repeated attempts to successfully evaluate the guard.

In contrast, the OBA uses the natural way in a Petri net of representing a variable by a set of places, yielding a simple semantics in which evaluating a guard or executing an assignment is the firing of a single transition; exploiting the fact that Petri nets deal equally with states and actions in a way that cannot be easily done via an action-oriented algebra. The cost of this is the additional complexity that a primitive action of the algebra (an operand for the *Base* constructor) is not just a communication, but a communication together with a data state transformation; and a certain loss of behavioural compositionality discussed below.

Somewhat intermediate between the approaches of the OBA and of process algebra net semantics, is that of the Petri Box Calculus, PBC [BH92, this volume]. The PBC and OBA have similar formulations of a "Box", as a Place/Transition net with an interface in the labelling of places and transitions, and composition operators thereon. The PBC is however more general, and algebraically more fully developed than the OBA, although in ways that are not of direct relevance to semantics for a language such as OCCAM. From such perspective they are sufficiently similar that the semantic definitions of Tables B/C/D can be used to give a PBC semantics of OCCAM ([HOPK92]) such that the resulting net has a structural correspondence to that obtained by the OBA semantics, and thus the Roscoe consistency result also holds for the PBC semantics.

There is again a significant difference in the way of handling variables - the PBC semantics represents a variable as a process with "put" and "get" communications, but by using multi-sets of communications for transition labels avoids the problems mentioned above of such an approach for a CCS semantics. The PBC potentially obtains a compositionality of behaviours which cannot be obtained in the OBA if shared updatable variables are allowed. The occurrence sequences of the net produced by the OBA semantics do not allow for the possibility that a free variable may be externally updated during its execution, and thus the occurrence sequences for the parallel composition of two process which update and use the same variable are in general not derivable from the occurrence sequences of the two processes in isolation. On the other hand, in the absence of shared updatable variables, the OBA semantics gives a more directly accurate representation of a program with free variables and an analysis/simulation of the net is more directly interpretable in terms of the original program. Also synchronisation of transitions which access the same variable, as in the example discussed above of $x=y$ & $d?z$ synchronising with $d!x+y$, is much easier to deal with by the place merging approach of the OBA.

5.4. Priorities

Although in the behaviours that we have used the prioritisations have been ignored, if they were to be recognized it would be either by expanding the prioritised net to an unprioritised net, as defined in [BK91]; or by use of a prioritised firing rule [JAN87]. These two alternatives give the same result other than differences in the extent of concurrency in some circumstances, as discussed in [BK91]. The former, expansion, semantics is important because it brings the net used into a standard well-studied net class, namely n-safe Place/Transition nets. However the general construction for the expansion is complicated and the safeness bound n is dependent on the program as a whole. An alternative approach has been proposed in [BOTTI90] which gives a simpler construction and ensures 2-safeness. This depends on a change to the semantics of parallel composition, using a $||'$, such that $B\,||'B' =$ SKIP ; $(B\,||\,B')$; SKIP. (This also has the benefit of making * a total operation). For the OCCAM semantics the use of $||'$ rather than $||$ would have made no difference to the Roscoe Consistency result. However it would make a significant difference for a parallel composition immediately within choice since the artificially introduced initial SKIP can disable other arms of the choice. Again, such a construction cannot arise in OCCAM.

It should be observed that in general it is possible to get contradictory prioritisation, e.g. in $(c!1 [\,]\!\!> d!1 \;||_{\{c,d\}}\; d?x [\,]\!\!> c?x)/\{c,d\}$, where there are two alternative synchronisation transitions each having priority over the other due to the prioritisations of the transitions which they combine. In either of the possible priority semantics, the result is that neither transition can fire. However this situation cannot arise for OCCAM because in a synchronisation of two transitions, only one (the input) can be involved in a PRIALT and thus only that one can carry a prioritisation.

It would be possible to use prioritisation to give a give a translation for PRIPAR which is distinct from that of PAR. For PRIPAR $(P_1, .. P_n)$ there would be a prioritisation of every transition of P_i having priority over every transition of every P_j with $j>i$. However to do this would introduce some difficulties. Such a construction seriously compromises the notion of modularity, in that it involves all transitions of all the processes. Also, it becomes possible to construct OCCAM programs with contradictory prioritisation. For example

PRIPAR ($\{c\}$: $c?x$, $\{c\}$: $c!FALSE$)

gives a single transition which has priority over itself and thus cannot fire - a deadlock which does not occur if PRIPAR is relaced by PAR. This means that this modelling of PRIPAR is not consistent with the view that changing a PAR to a PRIPAR is just additional implementation detail.

For both PRIPAR and PRIALT, it is claimed in [INMOS88] that these are only to do with "configuration" and make no difference to the logical behaviour of the program; and thus the Roscoe semantics is justified in ignoring these constructs, i.e. effectively mapping them to PAR or ALT. For PRIALT we find that for our translation using a prioritised firing rule we obtain a net which is more deterministic (in the full Roscoe sense) than that obtained by replacing PRIALT with ALT. (Although this only applies if all channels used in guards of prioritised choices have been declared - if there is prioritised choice involving external communication, the Roscoe semantics cannot adequately capture the behaviour). Thus any safety or liveness property found for the ALT version will also hold for the PRIALT version - i.e. the PRIALT version relates to the ALT version as does implementation to specification; and this fact justifies our translation for PRIALT. The above example shows that this would not hold for modelling PRIPAR using simple prioritisation. The alternatives are to either give PRIPAR a probabilistic interpretation (see below); or to make some special provision for synchronisation between the prioritised processes, as is suggested in [HH90].

6. Conclusions

We have defined for a basic net model a form of net algebra which is adequate for obtaining a reasonably concise formal semantics of OCCAM which conforms to the Laws of OCCAM; and is likely to be applicable to (recursion-free subsets of) other concurrent programming languages. We obtain a net semantics which is substantially different from what would be obtained via CCS or TCSP and their net semantics, particularly in the different treatment of variables. A particular contribution is the approach of defining a family of semantics exhibiting different levels of data abstraction.

There is currently application of Petri net tools for the analysis of programs, for example deadlock detection [MSS89] and [MV91] which finds this beneficial even using hand translation of program to net. The OCCAM semantics given here have been applied [BD92] to produce a stochastic timed net from an OCCAM program, for performance evaluation, and in particular for optimal placement over a set of processors of the parallel processes within a PLACEDPAR. It should also be noted that modularity can be exploited in the timing analysis of a complete program by doing timing analyses of small components and using the results to set probability parameters in a net where each of those components is treated as a single timed transition. Such work is expected to lead to semi-automatic placement optimisation of concurrent programs over multi-processor architectures and even more ambitious goals such as the optimisation of the level of parallelism for an program [BOTTI90]. A stochastic timed net approach also allows a treatment of PRIPAR (and possibly also PRIALT) as a probabilistic construct, which would avoid the PRIPAR / PAR inconsistency mentioned above.

Acknowledgements

The work reported here was within a working group of the DEMON [BDH90] project, owing particular debt to contributions from Eike Best, Fiorella De Cindio, Jean Fanchon and Axel Poigne; and is a further development of the OCCAM semantics of [HHBD90]. Thanks are due to useful suggestions and careful reading by four anonymous referees.

References

[BD92] Botti O., De Cindio F., "From Basic to Timed Models of OCCAM: an Application to Program Placement", Proc. 4th Int. Workshop on Petri Nets and Performance Models, Melbourne, IEEE Press (1992).

[BDH90] Best E., De Cindio F., Hopkins R.P., "DEMON -- Design Methods based on Nets: an ESPRIT Basic Research Action (No.3148)", EATCS Bulletin No.41 (1990).

[BH92] Best E., Hall J., "The Box Calculus: a New Causal Algebra with Multi-Label Communication", this volume.

[BK91] Best E., Koutny M., "Petri Net Semantics of Priority Systems", Theoretical Computer Science (1991).

[BOTTI90] Botti O., "Un Modello in Reti di Petri per OCCAM2", MSc Thesis, DSI, University of Milano (1990).

[CK88] Cherkasova L., Kotov V., "Descriptive and Analytic Process Algebras", Proc. 9th Europ. Workshop on Apllication and Theory of Petri Nets, Venice (1988).

[DDM87] Degano P., De Nicola R., Montanari U.," CCS is an (augmented) contact free C/E system", Math. models for the semantics of parallelism, Springer-Verlag, LNCS 280 (1987).

[GM84] Goltz U., Mycroft A., "On the relationship of CCS and Petri Nets", ICALP 84, Springer-Verlag, LNCS 172 (1984).

[HALL92] Hall J., "High Level Petri Boxes and General Recursion", DEMON Final Report (January 1992).

[HH90] Hopkins R.P., Hall J., "Towards a Petri Net Programming Notation", DEMON Research Memorandum, Computing Laboratory, University of Newcastle upon Tyne (1990).

[HHBD90] Hall J., Hopkins R.P., Botti O., De Cindio F., "A Petri Net Semantics of OCCAM 2", Technical Report, Computing Laboratory, University of Newcastle upon Tyne (1990).

[HOPK92] Hopkins R.P., "Petri Net Semantics of OCCAM - Some Results", Technical Report, Computing Laboratory, University of Newcastle upon Tyne (1992).

[INMOS88] INMOS, "OCCAM 2 Reference Manual", Prentice Hall (1988).

[JAN87] Janicki R., "A Formal Semantics for Concurrent Systems with a Priority Relation", Acta Informatica 24 (1987).

[KOT78] Kotov V.E., "An Algebra for Parallelism Based on Petri Nets", MFCS, Springer-Verlag, LNCS 64 (1978).

[MILN89] Milner R., "Communication and Concurrency", Prentice-Hall (1989).

[MSS89] Murata T., Shenker B., Shatz S.M., "Detection of ADA Static Deadlocks Using Petri Nets", IEEE Transactions on Software Engineering, Vol.15(3) (1989).

[MV91] McLendon W.W., Vidale R.F, "Analysis of an Ada System using Coloured Petri Nets and Occurrence Graphs", Technical Report, Draper Laboratory, Cambridge MA (1991).

[OLD91] Olderog E.R., "Nets, Terms and Formulae", Habilitation (1989). Cambridge Tracts in Theoretical Computer Science (1991).

[RH86] Roscoe A.W., Hoare C.A.R., "The Laws of OCCAM Programming", Technical Monograph PRG-53, Oxford University (1986).

[ROSC85] Roscoe A.W., "Denotational Semantics for OCCAM", Proc. 1984 Seminar on Concurrency, Carnegie Mellon, Springer-Verlag, LNCS 197 (1985).

[TAUB89] Taubner D., "Finite Representations of CCS and TCSP Programs by Automata and Petri Nets", Springer-Verlag, LNCS 369 (1989).

[WINSK84] Winskel G., "A New Definition of Morphism on Petri Nets", Proc. STACS'84, Springer-Verlag, LNCS 166 (1984).

THE EFFECT OF VECTOR SYNCHRONIZATION: RESIDUE AND LOSS

N.W. Keesmaat

PTT Research Neher Laboratory
P.O. Box 421, 2260 AK Leidschendam, The Netherlands

H.C.M. Kleijn

Department of Computer Science, Leiden University
P.O. Box 9512, 2300 RA Leiden, The Netherlands
All correspondence to the second author

ABSTRACT In a Vector Controlled Concurrent System (VCCS) a fixed number of sequential processes operate under the control of a vector synchronization mechanism. Thus, the original behaviour of each of the component processes is constrained by the control mechanism. This observation leads to the introduction of the notion of residue (the remaining behaviour possibilities) and the complementary notion of loss (of behaviour possibilities). For various submodels of the general VCCS model obtained by varying the classes of component processes and by varying the synchronization mechanism, we characterize in a language theoretical sense their residue families and their loss families. In addition we establish for these VCCS submodels the borderline between decidable and undecidable emptiness and finiteness problems for the corresponding families of losses and residues.

Keywords vector synchronization, Vector Controlled Concurrent Systems, residual behaviour, vector languages, formal languages.

CONTENTS

0. INTRODUCTION

In the framework of Vector Controlled Concurrent Systems (VCCS), introduced in [KeeKleRoz90], a concurrent system consists of a (finite fixed) number of sequential components together with a *vector synchronization mechanism* controlling their mutual synchronization. The behaviour of a VCCS is described by a *vector language* consisting of those combinations of computations of the components of the system that satisfy the synchronization constraints.

The VCCS model has been inspired by the synchronization mechanism as used in the theory of path expressions (COSY) and its vector firing sequence semantics. Path expressions were first introduced in [CamHab74] and later modified in [LauCam75], where they were equipped with a Petri net semantics; the idea of expressing the behaviour of the system as a vector language comes from [Shi79], where vector firing sequences are used as a semantics for path programs.

In the path expression approach (see also [Bes87]) a system is specified via a finite set of paths. Each path determines a sequential constraint on the events of the system and is given by a regular expression (with an outermost star) over the events (actions) of the system. Paths can be viewed as (cyclic) sequential components of the system. In the vector firing sequence semantics, the behaviour of the system is described in a nonsequential way by means of vector firing sequences. The i-th entry of such a vector is a firing sequence (i.e., a prefix of a word from the language) of the i-th path and all entries of the vector agree on the number and the order of occurrences of common events. In order to define this formally, one associates with each event of the system a vector, in our terminology a synchronization vector, with entries either equal to this event or empty and such that the i-th entry is non-empty if and only if the event is in the alphabet of the i-th path, meaning that the i-th component participates in this event. Then, by definition, the vector firing sequences of the system are precisely those elements of the cartesian product of the firing sequences of the paths that can be obtained by a component-wise concatenation of these synchronization vectors. Note that such a vector expresses per se the concurrency of a finite fixed number of computations; the decomposition into synchronization vectors expresses the synchronization between these computations.

While retaining the idea of modelling a concurrent system as being composed of a number of sequential components communicating by hand-shake synchronization, the VCCS model generalizes the path expression model by incorporating a more general synchronization mechanism. Synchronization of different actions in different components is allowed, as a consequence of which the alphabet of synchronization vectors has to be given explicitly. Moreover the control of the synchronization may now be dynamic, i.e. the synchronization constraints are given through a control language over the synchronization vectors, and so the current set of synchronization vectors is determined by the history of the system. In addition, there are no a priori constraints on the complexity or form of the behaviours (languages) of the sequential components; thus, e.g., prefix closedness or regularity are no prerequisites for Vector Controlled Concurrent Systems. Note that in various papers on path expressions and COSY already some of the specific technical constraints on path expressions are modified. See, e.g., [Jan85], where a vector firing sequence semantics for path expressions is defined in which the prefix closure of the firing sequences is omitted; further in [Bes87] prefix closures are used to describe partial (incomplete) computations and a COSY 'dialect' is considered in which the path expressions do not define starred regular languages; in [JanLauKouDev86] the control of the synchronization is modified to allow only maximal concurrent executions of paths.

In [BeaNiv80], [Niv82], and [Arn82] the basic model of path expressions has been extended in a way very similar to ours. This has led to models closely related to the VCCS model. For a discussion of the relationship between these models and the VCCS model the interested reader may consult [KeeKleRoz90].

We have generalized the original path expression model in order to obtain a uniform framework for the investigation of systems with a finite number of sequential components working concurrently but synchronizing on certain events. The framework provided by Vector Controlled Concurrent Systems is flexible in the sense that it allows one to specify the components and the synchronization mechanism separately. Submodels of the general VCCS model are obtained by imposing restrictions on component languages and/or control mechanisms. Various submodels are defined in [KeeKleRoz90] and further investigated in [KeeKleRoz91] in a comparison of static and dynamic synchronization mechanisms with regular or non-regular components. In particular a net-based synchronization mechanism (the Individual Token Net Controller) is introduced to formalize the idea of a distributed finite state control of the synchronization of the various components. In [KeeKle89] this mechanism is compared with the finite state control from [Arn82]. In addition various submodels, among which the path expression model and the models from [Arn82], are related to one another with respect to their expressive power in terms of vector languages.

The subject of this paper is the effect that synchronization has on the behaviour of combinations of one or more of the sequential components of a Vector Controlled Concurrent System. In the VCCS model it is relatively easy to isolate behaviours of sequential components within a concurrent system. By projection on a particular component of the vector language of a VCCS, the language is obtained which is the behaviour of that component when subject to the synchronization constraints of the system. Thus one may study the *residue* (residual behaviour) of a sequential component and, by taking its complement w.r.t. the total unrestricted behaviour of that component, the notion of *loss* of behaviour is derived. In addition to these two notions for separate components we also investigate the effect of synchronization on m-tuples of components. Thus we have, for each $m \geq 1$, *m-dimensional vector residues* which are m-dimensional vector languages obtained from the vector language of a VCCS by simultaneous projection on m of the components. The corresponding *m-dimensional vector losses* are then the vector languages resulting from complementation of these m-dimensional residues w.r.t. the corresponding m-fold cartesian product of the component languages. Since the n-dimensional residue of a concurrent system with n components is the vector language of that system, it follows that results obtained for these residues are at the same time results for the behaviours of the concurrent systems as a whole.

Our study of the effect of synchronization on the behaviour of sequential components is based on the notions of (vector) residue and (vector) loss. In particular we want to establish, for various submodels of the general VCCS model, properties of the corresponding families of (vector) residues and (vector) losses.

Our idea now is to start from a linearly ordered hierarchy of language families to define a whole range of VCCS submodels. For these submodels the synchronization effect is investigated along two different lines. The first approach determines for each submodel the resulting language family of residues and language family of losses and compares them with the families from the hierarchy. In this way one may measure the synchronization effect in terms of an increase or decrease of the language complexity.

Our second line of research is derived from the idea to use these notions for the measurement of the "tightness" of synchronization. If a residual behaviour is "small" in comparison with the unrestricted behaviour, then for this component the synchronization can be considered as "tight", whereas a "small" behavioural loss indicates the opposite, i.e. a "loosely coupled" component. Thus it is natural to investigate the "size" of (vector) residues and (vector) losses and in particular it is interesting to know whether a (vector) residue or (vector) loss is empty or finite. The decidability of these questions is determined for each of the VCCS submodels under consideration. Using, among other things, the language classification results discussed above, a complete characterization of the decidability of both the emptiness and the finiteness problem for all families of (vector) residues and (vector) losses is obtained.

The hierarchy of language families underlying our VCCS submodels is based on the classical Chomsky hierarchy. It consists in the first place of the two families **Mon** $= \{\Sigma^* | \Sigma$ is a finite set of letters$\}$, the family of freely generated monoids, and **Reg**, the family of regular languages. These two families have been used extensively in the study of VCCSs. The family of regular languages is important in the sense that it reflects the idea of an underlying finite state mechanism which is a very natural restriction both for component languages and for control languages (see [KeeKleRoz91], [KeeKle89], [Arn82]). The family **Mon**, when used to describe control languages, characterizes the phenomenon of so-called "static" control (history independent synchronization), see [KeeKleRoz90] and [KeeKle89].

At the other end of the spectrum the family **RE** of recursively enumerable languages is chosen, because it is the largest family of "computable" languages. For the intermediate steps of the hierarchy we choose the families **Lin**, **CF**, and **CS** of linear, context-free, and context-sensitive languages, respectively. Thus a linearly ordered hierarchy is obtained consisting of well-known language families with many well-known properties.

Finally, the attention is turned to the notion of *completeness.* This notion has been introduced in [KeeKleRoz90] as a structural property of Individual Token Net Controllers. Later, in [KeeKle89], completeness has been translated into a property of vector languages incorporating the idea that any combination of independent concurrent computations is again a computation. We study the effect of synchronization mechanisms with this property on (vector) residues and (vector) losses in a similar set-up as above.

The paper is organized as follows.

The first section is a preliminary one in which we provide some general technical notions, notations, and results in order to fix our notations and keep the paper self-contained. Section 2 contains the basic definitions concerning Vector Controlled Concurrent Systems, (vector) residue and (vector) loss, and a number of technical results concerning these notions, which form the basis of most of the results in the rest of the paper. In Section 3 (vector) residues are investigated in full. First of all the residue languages are identified in terms of known families of languages and then the decidability of the emptiness and finiteness problem are characterized w.r.t. the resulting language hierarchy. Section 4 concerns the properties of (vector) losses. It is divided into two subsections. In Subsection 4.1, both the language hierarchical and decidability properties of (1-dimensional) losses are given. In Subsection 4.2, the decidability properties of higher dimensional vector losses are treated. Section 5 treats the questions of Sections 3 and 4, but now for VCCSs with complete control. The results obtained are summarized and discussed in the final section. In this section also the decidability of the completeness property itself is considered.

1. PRELIMINARIES, BASIC DEFINITIONS, AND BASIC OBSERVATIONS

Throughout this paper the reader is assumed to be familiar with the basic notions, terminology and results of formal language theory (see, e.g., [HopUll79]). Familiarity with the theory of rational relations (as presented in, e.g., [Ber79]) is not assumed, though acquaintance with its basic concepts is certainly useful.

In this section we first fix some general notation and terminology that may not be familiar to all readers. In particular, the necessary terminology concerning vectors, vector languages, etc. is explained. Then we recall the results from the theory of rational relations that are needed in this paper.

For each positive integer n, $[n]$ denotes the set $\{1,\ldots,n\}$. Function composition is denoted by $\circ$. The set difference of the sets V and W is denoted by $V - W$. For a set V, the free monoid generated by V is denoted by V^*; thus V^* is the set of strings (lists) of finite length of elements of V. The concatenation of two elements v and w of V^* is simply denoted by vw. The unit of any such monoid (the empty string) is written as Λ. The identity homomorphism from V^* to V^* is written as $\mathbf{id}_V$. By V^+ we denote the set $V^* - \{\Lambda\}$.

Any element of a cartesian product of sets is a *vector*. Vectors are denoted either horizontally or vertically. In this paper a 1-dimensional vector is not identified with its only component (see [KeeKleRoz90], Section 1). For a set V, the set of 1-dimensional vectors $\{(x) \,|\, x \in V\}$ is denoted by $\times V$. For the n-dimensional vector $w = (w_1,\ldots,w_n)$, where $n \geq 1$, and for $i \in [n]$, $\mathbf{proj}_i(w)$ denotes the *projection* of w on its i-th *component*, i.e., $\mathbf{proj}_i(w) = w_i$. For $m \in [n]$, $\mathbf{proj}_{[m]}(w)$ denotes the projection of w on its first m components, i.e., $\mathbf{proj}_{[m]}(w) = (w_1,\ldots,w_m)$. Note that both $\mathbf{proj}_i$ and $\mathbf{proj}_{[m]}$ are in a sense "universal" functions: there is no reference to the domains of the functions. Further note that $\mathbf{proj}_1 \neq \mathbf{proj}_{[1]}$, because of our distinction between 1-dimensional vectors and their components.

An *alphabet* is a finite and possibly empty set. Given n alphabets, where $n \geq 1$, we define below the notion of a vector alphabet over these given alphabets. Vector alphabets are again alphabets, i.e. finite and possibly empty sets. Following the usual approach in formal language theory, we assume throughout the paper that all (vector) alphabets used are subsets of some fixed infinite set (of *letters*).

Let $n \geq 1$ and let $\Sigma_1,\ldots,\Sigma_n$ be alphabets.

Any vector $\alpha \in ((\Sigma_1 \cup \Lambda) \times \ldots \times (\Sigma_n \cup \Lambda))$ such that $\mathbf{proj}_i(\alpha) \neq \Lambda$, for some $i \in [n]$, is called an *(n-dimensional) vector letter (over* $\Sigma_1,\ldots,\Sigma_n$*)*. Any set of vector letters over $\Sigma_1,\ldots,\Sigma_n$ is called an *(n-dimensional) vector alphabet (over* $\Sigma_1,\ldots,\Sigma_n$*)*. The *total vector alphabet over* $\Sigma_1,\ldots,\Sigma_n$, denoted by $\mathbf{Tot}(\Sigma_1,\ldots,\Sigma_n)$, is the set of all vector letters over $\Sigma_1,\ldots,\Sigma_n$.

Let Δ be an alphabet. Elements of Δ^* are called *words* (*over* Δ). Any subset of Δ^* is referred to as a *language* (*over* Δ). For a language K, the set of letters occurring in K is denoted by $\mathbf{alph}(K)$.

Let $n \geq 1$ and let $\Sigma_1, \ldots, \Sigma_n$ be alphabets.

Any vector $w \in \Sigma_1^* \times \ldots \times \Sigma_n^*$ is called an (*n-dimensional*) *word vector* (*over* $\Sigma_1, \ldots, \Sigma_n$). The component-wise concatenation of two n-dimensional word vectors v and w is denoted by $v \odot w$; note that, for vector letters α and β, the word $\alpha\beta$ differs from the word vector $\alpha \odot \beta$. The (*n-dimensional*) *empty word vector* is the vector $(\Lambda, \ldots, \Lambda)$ which is usually denoted by $\bar{\Lambda}$; in general its dimension will be clear from the context. Any subset of $\Sigma_1^* \times \ldots \times \Sigma_n^*$ is called an (*n-dimensional*) *vector language* (*over* $\Sigma_1, \ldots, \Sigma_n$). For two n-dimensional vector languages V and W, we write $V \odot W$ for $\{v \odot w | v \in V, w \in W\}$. The iterated component-wise concatenation of a vector language V is the set $V^\otimes = \{w_1 \odot \ldots \odot w_m | m \geq 1, w_1, \ldots, w_m \in V\} \cup \{\bar{\Lambda}\}$.

Let Θ be an n-dimensional vector alphabet. Then $\Theta^\otimes$ is a (in general non-free) monoid generated by Θ by component-wise concatenation and with $\bar{\Lambda}$ as its unit. The canonical homomorphism from the monoid Θ^* to the monoid $\Theta^\otimes$ is called a *collapse* and is denoted by $\mathbf{coll}_\Theta$; it is defined by $\mathbf{coll}_\Theta(\alpha_1 \ldots \alpha_m) = \alpha_1 \odot \ldots \odot \alpha_m$ where $m \geq 0$ and $\alpha_1, \ldots, \alpha_m \in \Theta$. Thus $\mathbf{coll}_\Theta(\Lambda) = \bar{\Lambda}$. In general we will write $\mathbf{coll}$ instead of $\mathbf{coll}_\Theta$ if no confusion arises. Then $\mathbf{coll}$ is viewed as a "universal" function. Note that whenever the inverse is used the reference to the vector alphabet can *not* be omitted: consider, e.g., the word vector $\binom{a}{bc}$ and the two vector alphabets $\Theta = \{\binom{a}{b}, \binom{\Lambda}{c}\}$ and $\Gamma = \{\binom{a}{c}, \binom{\Lambda}{b}\}$. Then $\mathbf{coll}_\Theta^{-1}(w) = \{\binom{a}{b}\binom{\Lambda}{c}\}$ while $\mathbf{coll}_\Gamma^{-1}(w) = \{\binom{\Lambda}{b}\binom{a}{c}\}$. Thus $\mathbf{coll}_\Theta^{-1}$ will never be written $\mathbf{coll}^{-1}$.

Let, for $i \in [n]$, the projection function $\mathbf{proj}_{\Theta^*,i} : \Theta^* \to \mathbf{proj}_i(\Theta)^*$ be the homomorphism defined by: for all $\alpha \in \Theta$, $\mathbf{proj}_{\Theta^*,i}(\alpha) = \mathbf{proj}_i(\alpha)$ and let, for $m \in [n]$, $\mathbf{proj}_{\Theta^*,[m]} : \Theta^* \to \mathbf{proj}_{[m]}(\Theta)^\otimes$ be the homomorphism defined by: for all $\alpha \in \Theta$, $\mathbf{proj}_{\Theta^*,[m]}(\alpha) = \mathbf{proj}_{[m]}(\alpha)$. Note that $\mathbf{proj}_{\Theta^*,[m]}$ maps words (in Θ^*) to word vectors (in $\mathbf{proj}_{[m]}(\Theta)^\otimes$). Further note that $\mathbf{proj}_{\Theta^*,[m]} = \mathbf{proj}_{[m]} \circ \mathbf{coll}_\Theta$.

Example 1.1. Let $\Theta = \{\begin{pmatrix} a \\ b \\ \Lambda \end{pmatrix}, \begin{pmatrix} \Lambda \\ c \\ c \end{pmatrix}\}$ and let $w = \begin{pmatrix} a \\ b \\ \Lambda \end{pmatrix}\begin{pmatrix} \Lambda \\ c \\ c \end{pmatrix}\begin{pmatrix} a \\ b \\ \Lambda \end{pmatrix}$. Then $w \in \Theta^*$ and $\mathbf{coll}_\Theta(w) = \begin{pmatrix} aa \\ bcb \\ c \end{pmatrix} \in \Theta^\otimes$.

Now $\mathbf{proj}_{\Theta^*,2}(w) = \mathbf{proj}_2(\begin{pmatrix} a \\ b \\ \Lambda \end{pmatrix})\mathbf{proj}_2(\begin{pmatrix} \Lambda \\ c \\ c \end{pmatrix})\mathbf{proj}_2(\begin{pmatrix} a \\ b \\ \Lambda \end{pmatrix}) = bcb$,

whereas $\mathbf{proj}_{\Theta^*,[2]}(w) = \mathbf{proj}_{[2]}(\begin{pmatrix} a \\ b \\ \Lambda \end{pmatrix}) \odot \mathbf{proj}_{[2]}(\begin{pmatrix} \Lambda \\ c \\ c \end{pmatrix}) \odot \mathbf{proj}_{[2]}(\begin{pmatrix} a \\ b \\ \Lambda \end{pmatrix}) = \binom{a}{b} \odot \binom{\Lambda}{c} \odot \binom{a}{b} = \binom{aa}{bcb}$. □

Let Σ and Δ be alphabets. A homomorphism $\rho : \Sigma^* \to \Delta^*$ is a *weak coding* if

$\rho(\Sigma) \subseteq \Delta \cup \{\Lambda\}$. A weak coding $\rho : \Sigma^* \to \Delta^*$ is a *coding* if $\rho(\Sigma) \subseteq \Delta$.

Let $n \geq 1$, let $\Sigma, \Delta_1, \ldots, \Delta_n$ be alphabets, and let $\rho_i : \Sigma^* \to \Delta_i^*$ be a weak coding for all $i \in [n]$. The homomorphism $\rho_1 \otimes \ldots \otimes \rho_n : \Sigma^* \to \mathbf{Tot}(\Delta_1, \ldots, \Delta_n)^*$ is defined by: for all $b \in \Sigma, (\rho_1 \otimes \ldots \otimes \rho_n)(b) = \Lambda$ if $(\rho_1(b), \ldots, \rho_n(b)) = \bar{\Lambda}$, and $(\rho_1 \otimes \ldots \otimes \rho_n)(b) = (\rho_1(b), \ldots, \rho_n(b))$ otherwise. Clearly $\rho_1 \otimes \ldots \otimes \rho_n$ is a weak coding. We refer to it as the *distributed* weak coding *determined by* $\rho_1, \ldots, \rho_n$. Often these distributed weak codings are used in combination with collapses. In that case — if $n = 2$ and ρ_1 and ρ_2 are homomorphisms — we end up with Nivat's bimorphisms ([Niv68], [Ber79]): $\mathbf{coll} \circ (\rho_1 \otimes \rho_2)$ is a homomorphism from Σ^* to $\Delta_1^* \times \Delta_2^*$ satisfying $\mathbf{coll} \circ (\rho_1 \otimes \rho_2)(w) = \begin{pmatrix} \rho_1(w) \\ \rho_2(w) \end{pmatrix}$ for all $w \in \Sigma^*$.

Example 1.2. Let $\Sigma = \{A, B, C\}$, $\Delta_1 = \{a\}$, $\Delta_2 = \{b, c\}$, and $\Delta_3 = \{c\}$. Let, for $i \in \{1, 2, 3\}, \rho_i : \Sigma^* \to \Delta_i^*$ be the weak coding defined by:
$\rho_1(A) = a, \rho_1(B) = \Lambda, \rho_1(C) = \Lambda$,
$\rho_2(A) = b, \rho_2(B) = c, \rho_2(C) = \Lambda$, and
$\rho_3(A) = \Lambda, \rho_3(B) = c, \rho_3(C) = \Lambda$.
Let $\xi = \rho_1 \otimes \rho_2 \otimes \rho_3$. Then $\xi(ABCA) = \xi(A)\xi(B)\xi(C)\xi(A) = \begin{pmatrix} a \\ b \\ \Lambda \end{pmatrix} \begin{pmatrix} \Lambda \\ c \\ c \end{pmatrix} \Lambda \begin{pmatrix} a \\ b \\ \Lambda \end{pmatrix} = \begin{pmatrix} a \\ b \\ \Lambda \end{pmatrix} \begin{pmatrix} \Lambda \\ c \\ c \end{pmatrix} \begin{pmatrix} a \\ b \\ \Lambda \end{pmatrix}$. Clearly $\mathbf{coll} \circ \xi(ABCA) = \begin{pmatrix} aa \\ bcb \\ c \end{pmatrix} = \begin{pmatrix} \rho_1(ABCA) \\ \rho_2(ABCA) \\ \rho_3(ABCA) \end{pmatrix}$. □

In this paper we use the phrase "family of languages" to refer to any class of languages closed under "renaming" of symbols, indicating that all languages from that class have a structure which does not depend on the name of the letters chosen to represent a language from the class. More formally, a class $\mathbf{L}$ of languages is a *family of languages* if $\rho(L) \in \mathbf{L}$, for every injective coding $\rho : \Sigma^* \to \Delta^*$ and for all $L \in \mathbf{L}$ with $L \subseteq \Sigma^*$. All concrete classes of languages considered in this paper are families of languages. In addition we feel free to use the term "family" also for classes of vector languages, whenever they are defined in terms of families of languages without any reference to actual symbols.

For families of languages $\mathbf{K}$ and $\mathbf{L}$, the family $\{K \cap L | K \in \mathbf{K}, L \in \mathbf{L}\}$ is denoted by $\mathbf{K} \wedge \mathbf{L}$, the family $\{K \cup L | K \in \mathbf{K}, L \in \mathbf{L}\}$ is denoted by $\mathbf{K} \vee \mathbf{L}$, the family $\{K - L | K \in \mathbf{K}, L \in \mathbf{L}\}$ is denoted $\mathbf{K} \backslash \mathbf{L}$, and finally the family $\{\Sigma^* - K | K \in \mathbf{K}, K \subseteq \Sigma^*\}$ is denoted by co-$\mathbf{K}$. Let $\mathbf{WCod}$ denote the class of all weak codings. If $\mathbf{L}$ is a family of languages, then $\mathbf{WCod}(\mathbf{L})$ denotes the family $\{\Phi(L) | L \in \mathbf{L}, \Phi \in \mathbf{WCod}, L$ is a subset of the domain of $\Phi\}$. Similarly $\mathbf{WCod}^{-1}(\mathbf{L})$ denotes the family $\{\Phi^{-1}(L) | L \in \mathbf{L}, \Phi \in \mathbf{WCod}\}$.

Certain basic properties of the families from the extended Chomsky hierarchy $\mathcal{F} = \{\mathbf{Mon}, \mathbf{Reg}, \mathbf{Lin}, \mathbf{CF}, \mathbf{CS}, \mathbf{RE}\}$ will be used later in this paper without any further reference. For the sake of convenience we state them here explicitly, but each of them can be found in [HopUll79], except for some trivial properties of **Mon**.
$\mathbf{Mon} \subset \mathbf{Reg} \subset \mathbf{Lin} \subset \mathbf{CF} \subset \mathbf{CS} \subset \mathbf{RE}$;
$\mathbf{WCod}(\mathbf{F}) = \mathbf{F}$, for each $\mathbf{F} \in \mathcal{F} - \{\mathbf{CS}\}$ and $\mathbf{WCod}^{-1}(\mathbf{F}) = \mathbf{F}$, for each $\mathbf{F} \in \mathcal{F}$;
$co-\mathbf{Reg} = \mathbf{Reg}$; $\mathbf{F} \vee \mathbf{F} = \mathbf{F}$ and $\mathbf{F} \wedge \mathbf{Reg} = \mathbf{F}$ for each $\mathbf{F} \in \mathcal{F} - \{\mathbf{Mon}\}$;
$\mathbf{CS} \wedge \mathbf{CS} = \mathbf{CS}$, and $\mathbf{RE} \wedge \mathbf{RE} = \mathbf{RE}$;

The emptiness problem and the finiteness problem are both decidable for **CF**.

Now we briefly turn to the rational relations. For more details the reader is referred to [Ber79].

The family of *(n-dimensional) rational relations in* the monoid $\Theta^{\otimes}$, where Θ is an n-dimensional vector alphabet, is the smallest family of subsets of $\Theta^{\otimes}$ that contains $\emptyset$ and $\{w\}$ for all $w \in \Theta^{\otimes}$, and that is closed under union $\cup$, component-wise concatenation $\odot$, and iterated component-wise concatenation $^{\otimes}$.

The following is an easy characterization of the family of rational relations in terms of collapses of regular languages over vector alphabets (see also [KeeKle89]). It follows directly from the characterization originally presented by Nivat in [Niv68] (see also [Ber79], Theorem III.3.2).

Lemma 1.3. *Let Θ be an n-dimensional vector alphabet. Then R is a rational relation in $\Theta^{\otimes}$ if and only if there exists a regular language R' over Θ such that $R = \mathbf{coll}(R')$.* □

The following fact is frequently used in this paper: the intersection of an n-dimensional rational relation with a set of the form $\times_{i=1}^{n} R_i$, where R_i is a regular language for all $i \in [n]$, is a rational relation again. This result follows from Mezei's characterization of recognizable relations (see [Ber79], Theorem III.1.5) and the closure of rational relations under intersection with recognizable sets (see, e.g., [Ber79], Proposition III.2.6).

The following lemma states the undecidability of a number of problems concerning rational relations. The problems are the emptiness and finiteness problem of complements of rational relations and some variations thereof. A slight variation of the construction used in [Ber79] for the original problems is sufficient to conclude the undecidability of all these problems.

Lemma 1.4. *It is undecidable, for arbitrary alphabets Σ_1 and Σ_2 and arbitrary regular language R over $\mathbf{Tot}(\Sigma_1, \Sigma_2)$,*
(1) *whether or not $(\Sigma_1^* \times \Sigma_2^*) - \mathbf{coll}(R)$ is empty (finite),*
(2) *whether or not $(\Sigma_1^+ \times \Sigma_2^*) - \mathbf{coll}(R)$ is empty (finite),*
(3) *whether or not $(\Sigma_1^+ \times \Sigma_2^+) - \mathbf{coll}(R)$ is empty (finite).*

Proof. The proof is based on the same reduction from Post's Correspondence Problem (PCP) as is used in [Ber79], Theorem III.8.4. Starting from a PCP instance P consisting of two sequences of *non-empty* words, two alphabets Σ_1 and Σ_2 are obtained and a regular language R over $\mathbf{Tot}(\Sigma_1, \Sigma_2)$ such that $(\Sigma_1^* \times \Sigma_2^*) - \mathbf{coll}(R)$ is not empty (not finite) if and only if P has a solution. Thus (1) above is proved. The fact that P consists of sequences of non-empty words, which is *not* assumed in [Ber79], can now be used to conclude that $(\{\Lambda\} \times \Sigma_2^*) \cup (\Sigma_1^* \times \{\Lambda\}) \subseteq \mathbf{coll}(R)$. Thus (2) and (3) are proved. □

2. VECTOR CONTROLLED CONCURRENT SYSTEMS; RESIDUE AND LOSS

In this section we first recall the formal definition of a Vector Controlled Concurrent System together with a definition of its vector language (see [KeeKleRoz90]). In addition a characterization for the vector language of a VCCS is presented that forms the basis of the technical observations later in this section.

The notions of (vector) residues and (vector) losses of Vector Controlled Concurrent Systems are introduced followed by alternative, set-theoretic, formulations using projections and inverse projections. Further, criteria are provided for generalizing these alternative formulations using arbitrary weak codings and arbitrary inverse weak codings. Thus a language-theoretic characterization is obtained which is extensively used in the next sections. Most of the observations in this section are direct consequences of the interactions between the various vector operations and therefore need little proof.

Definition 2.1. Let $n \geq 1$. A *vector controlled concurrent system (of size n)*, an (n-)VCCS for short, is a construct $W = (K_1, \ldots, K_n; (\Theta, M))$ where
(1) for each $i \in [n]$, K_i is a language, and
(2) Θ is an n-dimensional vector alphabet and M is a language over Θ. □

The languages $K_1, \ldots, K_n$ are called the *component languages of* W, Θ is called the *synchronization alphabet of* W, and M is called the *control language of* W.

Definition 2.2. Let $n \geq 1$ and let $W = (K_1, \ldots, K_n; (\Theta, M))$ be an n-VCCS. The *vector language of* W, denoted by $V(W)$, is defined by $V(W) = (K_1 \times \ldots \times K_n) \cap \mathbf{coll}(M)$. □

Thus a concurrent computation $(w_1, \ldots, w_n) \in K_1 \times \ldots \times K_n$ is a word vector from the vector language of the VCCS $W = (K_1, \ldots, K_n; (\Theta, M))$ if and only if $w_1, \ldots, w_n$ can be synchronized as described by M, that is $(w_1, \ldots, w_n)$ has a decomposition into a word from M. In view of the fact that $\mathbf{coll}_\Theta^{-1}(\times_{i=1}^n K_i) = \bigcap_{i=1}^n \mathbf{proj}_{\Theta^*,i}^{-1}(K_i)$ this means that we have the following characterization of $V(W)$.

Lemma 2.3. *Let $n \geq 1$ and let $W = (K_1, \ldots, K_n; (\Theta, M))$ be an n-VCCS. Then $V(W)$ $= \mathbf{coll}(\mathbf{proj}_{\Theta^*,1}^{-1}(K_1) \cap \ldots \cap \mathbf{proj}_{\Theta^*,n}^{-1}(K_n) \cap M)$.* □

In the above lemma we silently used the following observation, which also plays a role in later proofs: for all functions f and all sets A and B such that B is contained in the domain of f, we have that $A \cap f(B) = f(f^{-1}(A) \cap B)$.

Let $n \geq 1$ and let $\mathbf{K}_1, \ldots, \mathbf{K}_n, \mathbf{K}$ be families of languages. An n-VCCS $W = (K_1, \ldots, K_n; (\Theta, M))$ is said to be *of type* $(\mathbf{K}_1, \ldots, \mathbf{K}_n; \mathbf{K})$ if $M \in \mathbf{K}$ and $K_i \in \mathbf{K}_i$ for all $i \in [n]$. Note that in this paper, unlike the definition in [KeeKle89], a type may be *non-uniform*, i.e. $\mathbf{K}_1, \ldots, \mathbf{K}_n$ may be distinct families of languages.

For the rest of this paper n is an arbitrary but fixed positive integer.

Now we are ready to introduce the notions of (vector) residue and (vector) loss for a VCCS. Informally speaking, the m-dimensional residue (where $m \in [n]$) of an n-VCCS $W = (K_1, \ldots, K_n; (\Theta, M))$ describes the (combined) behaviour of the first m components within W: it consists of those vector words $(w_1, \ldots, w_m)$ in $K_1 \times \ldots \times K_m$ for which there exist words $w_{m+1}, \ldots, w_n$ such that $(w_1, \ldots, w_n) \in V(W)$. Because of the synchronization constraints within the system, there will in general be a loss of behaviour for $K_1 \times \ldots \times K_m$. This leads to the notion of m-dimensional loss to describe those combinations of words from the first m components which cannot occur together in $V(W)$; this vector language consists of those $(w_1, \ldots, w_m)$ in $K_1 \times \ldots \times K_m$ for which there do *not* exist words $w_{m+1}, \ldots, w_n$ such that $(w_1, \ldots, w_n) \in V(W)$. Thus the m-dimensional residue of W and the m-dimensional loss of W complement each other within $K_1 \times \ldots \times K_m$.

In order to investigate the effect of synchronization on single individual components and to classify the resulting behaviour in terms of ("non-dimensional") language families, we also introduce the derived notions of residue and loss of a VCCS.

Definition 2.4. Let $W = (K_1, \ldots, K_n; (\Theta, M))$ be an n-VCCS. Let $m \in [n]$.
(1) The vector language $\mathbf{proj}_{[m]}(V(W))$ is called the *m-dimensional residue of* W and is denoted by m-$\mathbf{res}(W)$.
(2) The language $\mathbf{proj}_1(V(W))$ is called the *residue of* W and is denoted by $\mathbf{res}(W)$.
(3) The vector language $(K_1 \times \ldots \times K_m) - \mathbf{proj}_{[m]}(V(W))$ is called the *m-dimensional loss of* W and is denoted by m-$\mathbf{loss}(W)$.
(4) The language $K_1 - \mathbf{proj}_1(V(W))$ is called the *loss of* W and is denoted by $\mathbf{loss}(W)$.
□

Let W be an n-VCCS. Then we have n-$\mathbf{res}(W) = V(W)$ and n-$\mathbf{loss}(W) = (K_1 \times \ldots \times K_n) - V(W)$. Further, $\mathbf{res}(W) = \mathbf{proj}_1(1\text{-}\mathbf{res}(W))$ and $1\text{-}\mathbf{res}(W) = \times\, \mathbf{res}(W)$, and similarly $\mathbf{loss}(W) = \mathbf{proj}_1(1\text{-}\mathbf{loss}(W))$ and $1\text{-}\mathbf{loss}(W) = \times\, \mathbf{loss}(W)$.

To m-dimensional residues and losses, where $m \in [n]$, we also refer as *vector residues* and *vector losses*, respectively.

As defined above (m-dimensional) residues and (m-dimensional) losses concentrate at the *first* (m) component(s) of a VCCS. By a suitable permutation of components—including the entries in the control language—every choice of a component (m components) out of n components in a VCCS can be reduced to a choice of the first (m) component(s). Thus, by permuting components one may study also the (m-dimensional) residue and (m-dimensional) loss of a VCCS with respect to other components than the first one. This "invariance" of VCCSs under component permutation is used occasionally throughout the paper.

Let $\mathbf{K}_1, \ldots, \mathbf{K}_n, \mathbf{K}$ be some families of languages. Then we let $\mathbf{Res}(\mathbf{K}_1, \ldots, \mathbf{K}_n; \mathbf{K})$ denote the family $\{\mathbf{res}(W) | W$ an n-VCCS of type $(\mathbf{K}_1, \ldots, \mathbf{K}_n; \mathbf{K})\}$ and we let $\mathbf{Loss}(\mathbf{K}_1, \ldots, \mathbf{K}_n; \mathbf{K})$ denote the family $\{\mathbf{loss}(W) | W$ an n-VCCS of type $(\mathbf{K}_1, \ldots, \mathbf{K}_n; \mathbf{K})\}$. For $m \in [n]$ we use the notation m-$\mathbf{Res}(\mathbf{K}_1, \ldots, \mathbf{K}_n; \mathbf{K})$ for $\{m\text{-}\mathbf{res}(W) | W$ an n-VCCS of type $(\mathbf{K}_1, \ldots, \mathbf{K}_n; \mathbf{K})\}$ and similarly we use m-$\mathbf{Loss}(\mathbf{K}_1, \ldots, \mathbf{K}_n; \mathbf{K})$ to denote $\{m\text{-}\mathbf{loss}(W) | W$ an n-VCCS of type $(\mathbf{K}_1, \ldots, \mathbf{K}_n; \mathbf{K})\}$.

From now on we concentrate on observations concerning vector residues only. When appropriate we formulate explicitly the (derived) results for vector losses, residues, and losses.

We start out with some general auxiliary observations on interactions between projections and distributed weak codings when applied to vector languages.

Lemma 2.5. *Let $\Sigma, \Delta_1, \ldots, \Delta_n$ be alphabets and let $\rho_i : \Sigma^* \to \Delta_i^*$ be a weak coding for each $i \in [n]$. Let $\sigma = \rho_1 \otimes \ldots \otimes \rho_n$ and let $\Theta = \sigma(\Sigma) - \{\Lambda\}$. Let $m \in [n]$ and let $\pi =$*

$\mathbf{coll}_\Theta \circ (\rho_1 \otimes \ldots \otimes \rho_m)$. *Then*
(1) $\rho_i = \mathbf{proj}_{\Theta^*,i} \circ \sigma$ *for all* $i \in [n]$,
(2) $\pi = \mathbf{proj}_{\Theta^*,[m]} \circ \sigma$,
(3) $\bigcap_{i=1}^m \rho_i^{-1}(K_i) = \pi^{-1}(\bigtimes_{i=1}^m K_i)$ *for all languages* $K_1, \ldots, K_m$,
(4) $\pi(\bigcap_{i=1}^m \rho_i^{-1}(K_i) \cap B) = (\bigtimes_{i=1}^m K_i) \cap \pi(B)$ *for all languages* $K_1, \ldots, K_m$ *and for all* $B \subseteq \Sigma^*$,
(5) $\pi(\bigcap_{i=m+1}^n \rho_i^{-1}(K_i) \cap K) = \mathbf{proj}_{\Theta^*,[m]}(\bigcap_{i=m+1}^n \mathbf{proj}_{\Theta^*,i}^{-1}(K_i) \cap \sigma(K))$ *for all languages* $K_{m+1}, \ldots, K_n$ *and for all* $K \subseteq \Sigma^*$.

Proof. (1), (2), and (3) are immediate consequences of the definitions of π, σ, and Θ.
(4) follows from (3) by observing that $f(f^{-1}(A) \cap B) = A \cap f(B)$ for all functions f and all sets A and B with B a subset of the domain of f.
(5) follows from (1) and (2) by applying (repeatedly) the reasoning: $f(f^{-1}(A_1) \cap f^{-1}(A_2) \cap B) = A_1 \cap f(f^{-1}(A_2) \cap B)) = A_1 \cap A_2 \cap f(B)$ for all functions f and all sets A_1, A_2, and B with B a subset of the domain of f. □

With this lemma we can now prove:

Theorem 2.6. *Let* $W = (K_1, \ldots, K_n; (\Theta, M))$ *be an* n-VCCS *and let* $m \in [n]$. *Then*
(1) $m\text{-}\mathbf{res}(W) = \bigtimes_{i=1}^m K_i \cap \mathbf{proj}_{\Theta^*,[m]}(\bigcap_{i=m+1}^n \mathbf{proj}_{\Theta^*,i}^{-1}(K_i) \cap M)$,
(2) $\mathbf{res}(W) = K_1 \cap \mathbf{proj}_{\Theta^*,1}(\bigcap_{i=2}^n \mathbf{proj}_{\Theta^*,i}^{-1}(K_i) \cap M)$,
(3) $m - \mathbf{loss}(W) = \bigtimes_{i=1}^m K_i - \mathbf{proj}_{\Theta^*,[m]}(\bigcap_{i=m+1}^n \mathbf{proj}_{\Theta^*,i}^{-1}(K_i) \cap M)$, *and*
(4) $\mathbf{loss}(W) = K_1 - \mathbf{proj}_{\Theta^*,1}(\bigcap_{i=2}^n \mathbf{proj}_{\Theta^*,i}^{-1}(K_i) \cap M)$. □

Proof. By Definition 2.4 and Lemma 2.3, the m-dimensional residue of W can be written as m-$\mathbf{res}$(W) $= \mathbf{proj}_{[m]}(V(W)) = \mathbf{proj}_{[m]} \circ \mathbf{coll}(\bigcap_{i=1}^n \mathbf{proj}_{\Theta^*,i}^{-1}(K_i) \cap M)$. From the observation that $\mathbf{proj}_{[m]} \circ \mathbf{coll}(w) = \mathbf{proj}_{\Theta^*,[m]}(w)$ for all $w \in \Theta^*$, it follows that m-$\mathbf{res}$(W) $= \mathbf{proj}_{\Theta^*,[m]}(\bigcap_{i=1}^n \mathbf{proj}_{\Theta^*,i}^{-1}(K_i) \cap M)$.
Next we apply Lemma 2.5.(4) with $\rho_i = \mathbf{proj}_{\Theta^*,i}$ for all $i \in [n]$. Then $\pi = \mathbf{coll}_\Theta \circ (\rho_1 \otimes \ldots \otimes \rho_m) = \mathbf{proj}_{\Theta^*,[m]}$ and $\sigma = \mathbf{id}_{\Theta^*}$. And so m-$\mathbf{res}$(W) $= \mathbf{proj}_{\Theta^*,[m]}(\bigcap_{i=1}^n \mathbf{proj}_{\Theta^*,i}^{-1}(K_i) \cap M) = (\bigtimes_{i=1}^m K_i) \cap \mathbf{proj}_{\Theta^*,[m]}(\bigcap_{i=m+1}^n \mathbf{proj}_{\Theta^*,i}^{-1}(K_i) \cap M)$. □

Theorem 2.6 and its proof show how a vector residue can be constructed, using (inverse) projections, from the languages which form the component languages and the control language of the n-VCCS under consideration. Combining Lemma 2.5.(5) with Theorem 2.6 leads to the insight that this construction can be generalized: vector languages built in an analogous way using general (inverse) weak codings, instead of (inverse) projections, will be vector residues of VCCSs as well.

Corollary 2.7. *Let* $\rho_1, \ldots, \rho_n, m, \pi, \sigma, \Sigma$, *and* Θ *be as in the statement of Lemma 2.5. Let* $K_1, \ldots, K_n$, *and* K *be languages, where* $K \subseteq \Sigma^*$. *Then*

$$(\bigtimes_{i=1}^m K_i) \cap \pi(\bigcap_{i=m+1}^n \rho_i^{-1}(K_i) \cap K) = m\text{-}\mathbf{res}(W),$$

$$K_1 \cap \rho_1(\bigcap_{i=2}^n \rho_i^{-1}(K_i) \cap K) = \mathbf{res}(W),$$

$$(\bigtimes_{i=1}^{m} K_i) - \pi(\bigcap_{i=m+1}^{n} \rho_i^{-1}(K_i) \cap K) = m\textbf{-loss}(W), \textit{ and}$$

$$K_1 - \rho_1(\bigcap_{i=2}^{n} \rho_i^{-1}(K_i) \cap K) = \textbf{loss}(W),$$

where W is the n-VCCS $(K_1, \ldots, K_n; (\Theta, \sigma(K)))$. □

Note that the VCCS having a vector language as given in the statement of Corollary 2.7 as a (vector) residue or (vector) loss has the first n languages as its component languages and a *weak coding* of the $(n+1)$-st language as its control language. This distributed weak coding σ "remembers" the n given weak codings $\rho_1, \ldots, \rho_n$. By keeping one of the weak codings ρ_j connected to the corresponding component language—thus using $\rho_j^{-1}(K_j)$ rather than K_j as a component language and replacing ρ_j with an identity in the distributed weak coding—we obtain a reformulation of the above result in which the control language of the constructed VCCS is an *injective coding* of the $(n+1)$-st language.

Corollary 2.8. *Let $\rho_1, \ldots, \rho_n, m, \pi$, and Σ be as in the statement of Lemma 2.5. Let $K_1, \ldots, K_n$, and K be languages, where $K \subseteq \Sigma^*$. Let $j \in [n] - [m]$ and let $\tau = \rho_1 \otimes \ldots \otimes \rho_{j-1} \otimes \mathbf{id}_\Sigma \otimes \rho_{j+1} \otimes \ldots \otimes \rho_n$. Then*

$$(\bigtimes_{i=1}^{m} K_i) \cap \pi(\bigcap_{i=m+1}^{n} \rho_i^{-1}(K_i) \cap K) = m\textbf{-res}(W),$$

$$K_1 \cap \rho_1(\bigcap_{i=2}^{n} \rho_i^{-1}(K_i) \cap K) = \textbf{res}(W),$$

$$(\bigtimes_{i=1}^{m} K_i) - \pi(\bigcap_{i=m+1}^{n} \rho_i^{-1}(K_i) \cap K) = m\textbf{-loss}(W), \textit{ and}$$

$$K_1 - \rho_1(\bigcap_{i=2}^{n} \rho_i^{-1}(K_i) \cap K) = \textbf{loss}(W),$$

where W is the n-VCCS $(K_1, \ldots, K_{j-1}, \rho_j^{-1}(K_j), K_{j-1}, \ldots, K_n; (\tau(\Sigma), \tau(K)))$. □

Thus, from Corollary 2.7 and Corollary 2.8, we have obtained the following characterization for families of residues and losses in terms of weak codings, inverse weak codings, intersections, and differences. This characterization is the main tool for the language classification of residues and losses in the following sections.

Theorem 2.9. *Let $\mathbf{K}_1, \ldots, \mathbf{K}_n$, and $\mathbf{K}$ be families of languages. If either $\mathbf{K}$ is closed under weak codings or there is a $j \in [n] - [1]$ such that $\mathbf{K}_j$ is closed under inverse weak codings, then*
(1) $\mathbf{Res}(\mathbf{K}_1, \ldots, \mathbf{K}_n; \mathbf{K}) = \mathbf{K}_1 \wedge \mathbf{WCod}(\mathbf{WCod}^{-1}(\mathbf{K}_2) \wedge \ldots \wedge \mathbf{WCod}^{-1}(\mathbf{K}_n) \wedge \mathbf{K})$,
and
(2) $\mathbf{Loss}(\mathbf{K}_1, \ldots, \mathbf{K}_n; \mathbf{K}) = \mathbf{K}_1 \setminus \mathbf{WCod}(\mathbf{WCod}^{-1}(\mathbf{K}_2) \wedge \ldots \wedge \mathbf{WCod}^{-1}(\mathbf{K}_n) \wedge \mathbf{K})$.
Proof. The inclusions from the left hand sides in the right hand sides of (1) and (2) follow directly from Theorem 2.6.(2) and (4), respectively.

The converse inclusions follow from Corollary 2.7 and Corollary 2.8. In the two corollaries it is required that the weak codings $\rho_1, \ldots, \rho_n$ have the same domain Σ^* and that the language $K \in \mathbf{K}$ satisfies $K \subseteq \Sigma^*$. This may always be assumed without loss of generality: weak codings $\tilde{\rho}_1, \ldots, \tilde{\rho}_n$, with domains $\Sigma_1^*, \ldots, \Sigma_n^*$ respectively, may be replaced by the weak codings $\rho_1, \ldots, \rho_n$, with common domain $\Sigma = (\bigcup_{i=1}^n \Sigma_i) \cup \mathbf{alph}(K)$, if, for each $i \in [n], \rho_i$ coincides with $\tilde{\rho}_i$ on Σ_i and maps the elements of $\Sigma - \Sigma_i$ to a new symbol not in $K_1, \ldots, K_n$, and K. □

If $n = 1$ we have the following characterization which follows directly from the definitions of residue and loss and Definition 2.2.

Theorem 2.10. *For all families of languages* $\mathbf{K}_1$ *and* $\mathbf{K}$,
(1) $\mathbf{Res}(\mathbf{K}_1, \mathbf{K}) = \mathbf{K}_1 \wedge \mathbf{K}$, *and*
(2) $\mathbf{Loss}(\mathbf{K}_1, \mathbf{K}) = \mathbf{K}_1 \setminus \mathbf{K}$. □

3. RESIDUE

The previous section has provided us with general descriptions of vector languages that can be obtained as vector residues of VCCSs. This has led to a full characterization in terms of $\mathbf{K}_1, \ldots, \mathbf{K}_n$, and $\mathbf{K}$ for the language family $\mathbf{Res}(\mathbf{K}_1, \ldots, \mathbf{K}_n; \mathbf{K})$. Apart from the assumptions formulated in Theorem 2.9, each of these families $\mathbf{K}_1, \ldots, \mathbf{K}_n$, and $\mathbf{K}$ can be any family. Starting from these general observations, we investigate in this section properties of (vector) residues of VCCSs for "concrete" families of component languages and control languages. As has been argued in the Introduction these "concrete" families are chosen from the extended Chomsky hierarchy $\mathcal{F} = \{\mathbf{Mon}, \mathbf{Reg}, \mathbf{Lin}, \mathbf{CF}, \mathbf{CS}, \mathbf{RE}\}$, i.e., we study $\mathbf{Res}(\mathbf{K}_1, \ldots, \mathbf{K}_n; \mathbf{K}_{n+1})$, etc., for $\mathbf{K}_1, \ldots, \mathbf{K}_n, \mathbf{K}_{n+1} \in \mathcal{F}$.

This section is organized as follows. First, each of the families $\mathbf{Res}(\mathbf{K}_1, \ldots, \mathbf{K}_n; \mathbf{K}_{n+1})$, where $\mathbf{K}_i \in \mathcal{F}$ for all $i \in [n+1]$, is determined in a language hierarchical sense. This gives some insight in the way vector synchronization constraints influence the behaviour of individual components. Our results here are a direct application of the characterizations given in Theorem 2.9.(1) and Theorem 2.10.(1).

In the second part we concentrate on the families of vector languages m-$\mathbf{Res}(\mathbf{K}_1, \ldots, \mathbf{K}_n; \mathbf{K}_{n+1})$ where $\mathbf{K}_i \in \mathcal{F}$ for all $i \in [n+1]$. Since there seems to be no generally accepted hierarchy of families of *vector* languages, we do not provide a hierarchical classification of the families of vector residues. Instead we investigate the decidability status of their emptiness and finiteness problem. As usual when dealing with decidability we will assume that the languages from $\mathbf{K}_1, \ldots, \mathbf{K}_{n+1}$ are given effectively, e.g., by one of the standard mechanisms (automata, grammars, etc.).

Both emptiness and finiteness of residues can be viewed as indications of the amount of synchronization in a VCCS. Emptiness then reflects the situation that the synchronization is too tight: the subsystem under consideration (and thus the complete system) is not able to do anything under the given synchronization constraints. Finiteness of an m-dimensional residue indicates that the constraints may be looser but still are very tight: only a finite number of concurrent computations from the first m components is not blocked. Note that the system as a whole may still exhibit an infinite behaviour.

A main part of the above decidability problems can be settled by using the language classification given for the families $\mathbf{Res}(\mathbf{K}_1, \ldots, \mathbf{K}_n; \mathbf{K}_{n+1})$. Our investigation of these families makes use of the following corollary which is a consequence of Theorem 2.9.(1) and Theorem 2.10.(1). Each of the families **Mon, Reg, Lin, CF, CS,** and **RE** is closed under inverse weak codings, which implies that $\mathbf{WCod}^{-1}(\mathbf{K}) = \mathbf{K}$ if $\mathbf{K}$ is one of these families and so we immediately have:

Corollary 3.1. *Let* $\mathbf{K}_1, \ldots, \mathbf{K}_n, \mathbf{K}_{n+1}$ *be families of languages from* $\mathcal{F}$.
(1) $\mathbf{Res}(\mathbf{K}_1; \mathbf{K}_2) = \mathbf{K}_1 \wedge \mathbf{K}_2$.
(2) *If* $n \geq 2$ *then* $\mathbf{Res}(\mathbf{K}_1, \ldots, \mathbf{K}_n; \mathbf{K}_{n+1}) = \mathbf{K}_1 \wedge \mathbf{WCod}(\mathbf{K}_2 \wedge \ldots \wedge \mathbf{K}_n \wedge \mathbf{K}_{n+1})$. □

Based on this observation Table 3.2 below has been constructed. It provides a full overview of the language theoretical classification of the families $\mathbf{Res}(\mathbf{K}_1, \ldots, \mathbf{K}_n; \mathbf{K}_{n+1})$, depending on the language families chosen for $\mathbf{K}_1, \ldots, \mathbf{K}_{n+1}$. The results mentioned in the table are direct consequences, by applying Corollary 3.1, of known results from formal language theory for the families from $\mathcal{F}$.

In the table, the columns headed by **R** indicate the resulting families $\mathbf{Res}(\mathbf{K}_1, \ldots, \mathbf{K}_n; \mathbf{K}_{n+1})$, which, in case $n = 1$, are equal to $\mathbf{K}_1 \wedge \mathbf{K}_2$ and, in case $n \geq 2$, are equal to $\mathbf{K}_1 \wedge \mathbf{WCod}(\mathbf{K}_2 \wedge \ldots \wedge \mathbf{K}_{n+1})$. For later use some of these families are accompanied by a symbol "d". The column headed by **M** indicates the intermediate result $\mathbf{WCod}(\mathbf{K}_2 \wedge \ldots \wedge \mathbf{K}_{n+1})$ in the case that $n \geq 2$.

The possible choices for $\mathbf{K}_1, \ldots, \mathbf{K}_{n+1}$ are divided into groups depending on the largest family among $\mathbf{K}_1, \ldots, \mathbf{K}_{n+1}$, which is denoted by $\bigcup_{i=1}^{n+1} \mathbf{K}_i$ in the first column of the table. Within each group the various cases are ordered in ascending (language complexity) order of their residues. In the table we have assumed that $\mathbf{K}_2 \supseteq \ldots \supseteq \mathbf{K}_{n+1}$. This causes no loss of generality. For $\mathbf{K}_2, \ldots, \mathbf{K}_n$ this is clear from the "invariance" of VCCSs under component permutations. For $\mathbf{K}_{n+1}$ this follows from Corollary 3.1. (Note also that $\mathcal{F}$ is linearly ordered by set inclusion.) Because of the asymmetry in Corollary 3.1.(2) between $\mathbf{K}_1$ on the one hand and $\mathbf{K}_2, \ldots, \mathbf{K}_n, \mathbf{K}_{n+1}$ on the other hand we distinguish whether $\mathbf{K}_1$ or $\mathbf{K}_2 = \bigcup_{i=2}^{n+1} \mathbf{K}_i$ is the biggest family occurring in $\mathbf{K}_1, \mathbf{K}_2, \ldots, \mathbf{K}_n, \mathbf{K}_{n+1}$. In addition $\mathbf{K}_2$ and $\mathbf{K}_3 = \bigcup_{i=3}^{n+1} \mathbf{K}_i$ are separately specified in order to be able to distinguish the case of one or more occurrences in $\mathbf{K}_2, \ldots, \mathbf{K}_n, \mathbf{K}_{n+1}$ of the largest family as specified by $\mathbf{K}_2$. This is of particular importance when $\mathbf{K}_2 \in \{\mathbf{Lin}, \mathbf{CF}\}$. An entry of the form $\subseteq \mathbf{K}$ ($\supseteq \mathbf{K}$, respectively) indicates that the family specified by that entry may be any family from $\mathcal{F}$ contained in $\mathbf{K}$(containing $\mathbf{K}$).

Within each group determined by some $\mathbf{F} = \bigcup_{i=1}^{n+1} \mathbf{K}_i \in \mathcal{F}$, one can read off how the complexity of the residue language increases depending on the precise instantiation of the various VCCS types of the group, i.e. the types $(\mathbf{K}_1, \ldots, \mathbf{K}_n; \mathbf{K}_{n+1})$ with $\bigcup_{i=1}^{n+1} \mathbf{K}_i = \mathbf{F}$.

The table below is complete in the sense that, for every possible combination of $\mathbf{K}_1, \ldots, \mathbf{K}_n, \mathbf{K}_{n+1}$ from $\mathcal{F}$, the resulting $\mathbf{Res}(\mathbf{K}_1, \ldots, \mathbf{K}_n; \mathbf{K}_{n+1})$ can be read off, using permutations to obtain $\mathbf{K}_2 \supseteq \ldots \supseteq \mathbf{K}_{n+1}$ if necessary.

The table demonstrates once more the obvious fact that the complexity of the control language influences the complexity of the resulting behaviour of the individual components. For example the residue family **Res(Mon,...,Mon;K)** $\supseteq \mathbf{K}$ for every $\mathbf{K} \in \mathcal{F}$. Similarly, **Res(CF,Mon,...,Mon;CF)** $= \mathbf{CF} \wedge \mathbf{CF}$, a family strictly larger than **CF** (see [HopUll79]). In addition, we see that the residual behaviour of a single component is also determined by the other components, e.g., **Res(Reg,CF,Mon,...,Mon;Mon) = CF** in which case the regular behaviours of the first components are lifted to context-free residues as a consequence of the synchronization with context-free second components.

Table 3.2. $\mathbf{R} = \mathbf{Res}(\mathbf{K}_1,\ldots,\mathbf{K}_n;\mathbf{K}_{n+1})$, $\mathbf{M} = \mathbf{WCod}(\mathbf{K}_2 \wedge \ldots \wedge \mathbf{K}_n \wedge \mathbf{K}_{n+1})$

				$n=1$		$n \geq 2$		
$\bigcup_{i=1}^{n+1} \mathbf{K}_i$	$\mathbf{K}_1$	$\mathbf{K}_2$	$\mathbf{K}_3$	**R**		**M**	**R**	
Mon	**Mon**	**Mon**	**Mon**	**Mon**	d	**Mon**	**Mon**	d
Reg	**⊆Reg**	**⊆Reg**	**⊆Reg**	**Reg**	d	**⊆Reg**	**Reg**	d
Lin	**Lin**	**⊆Reg**	**⊆Reg**	**Lin**	d	**⊆Reg**	**Lin**	d
	⊆Reg	**Lin**	**⊆Reg**	**Lin**	d	**Lin**	**Lin**	d
	Lin	**Lin**	**⊆Reg**	**Lin∧Lin**		**Lin**	**Lin∧Lin**	
	⊆Reg	**Lin**	**Lin**	**Lin**	d	**RE** [1]	**RE**	
	Lin	**Lin**	**Lin**	**Lin∧Lin**		**RE** [1]	**RE**	
CF	**CF**	**⊆Reg**	**⊆Reg**	**CF**	d	**⊆Reg**	**CF**	d
	⊆Reg	**CF**	**⊆Reg**	**CF**	d	**CF**	**CF**	d
	CF	**Lin**	**⊆Reg**	**CF∧Lin**		**Lin**	**CF∧Lin**	
	Lin	**CF**	**⊆Reg**	**CF∧Lin**		**CF**	**CF∧Lin**	
	CF	**CF**	**⊆Reg**	**CF∧CF**		**CF**	**CF∧CF**	
	⊆Reg	**CF**	**⊇Lin**	**CF**	d	**RE** [1]	**RE**	
	Lin	**CF**	**⊇Lin**	**CF∧Lin**		**RE** [1]	**RE**	
	CF	**CF**	**⊇Lin**	**CF∧CF**		**RE** [1]	**RE**	
CS	**CS**	**⊆CF**	**⊆Reg**	**CS**		**⊆CF**	**CS**	
	CS	**⊇Lin**	**⊇Lin**	**CS**		**RE** [1]	**RE**	
	⊆CS	**CS**	**⊆CS**	**CS**		**RE**	**RE**	
RE	**⊆RE**	**⊆RE**	**⊆RE**	**RE**		**⊆RE**	**RE**	

[1]) This follows from the fact that **RE = WCod(Lin ∧ Lin)**, see, e.g., [BakBoo74]. □

Now we turn to the investigation of the emptiness and finiteness problem for (vector) residues.

For the families $\mathbf{Res}(\mathbf{K}_1,\ldots,\mathbf{K}_n;\mathbf{K}_{n+1})$ we can directly use the classification results of Table 3.2, because each member of such a family has an effective description, determined by the effective description of component and control languages. For each of the families mentioned in the table the decidability status of both the emptiness and finiteness problem is known: for language families included in **CF** these problems are decidable; whereas they are undecidable in the case of families that include **Lin ∧ Lin** (This follows from a reduction from Post's Correspondence Problem, see, e.g., in [HopUll79], the proof of Theorem 8.9, for a similar reduction; the languages L_A and L_B defined there are linear and their intersection is empty (finite) if and only if the given instance A, B of PCP has no solution). In Table 3.2 we have marked the families for which these problems are decidable with a "d". Note that $(\mathbf{Lin} \wedge \mathbf{Lin}) - \mathbf{CF} \neq \emptyset$ and that $\mathbf{Lin} \wedge \mathbf{Lin} \subseteq \mathbf{CF} \wedge \mathbf{Lin} \subseteq \mathbf{CS} \subseteq \mathbf{RE}$. Thus we have the following sharp borderline between decidable and undecidable finiteness (emptiness) problems.

Theorem 3.3. *The finiteness (emptiness) problem for* $\mathbf{Res}(\mathbf{K}_1,\ldots,\mathbf{K}_n;\mathbf{K}_{n+1})$, *where* $\mathbf{K}_1,\ldots,\mathbf{K}_n,\mathbf{K}_{n+1}\in\mathcal{F}$, *is decidable if and only if there exists a* $j\in[n+1]$ *such that* $\mathbf{K}_j\subseteq\mathbf{CF}$ *and* $\bigcup_{i=1,i\neq j}^{n+1}\mathbf{K}_i\subseteq\mathbf{Reg}$. □

Instead of the above (somewhat) indirect way via Table 3.2, one might also directly transfer the various decidability results known from formal language theory. This is based on the following observation showing that languages and intersections of languages can directly be obtained as residues of VCCSs: for languages K_1, K_2 over an alphabet Σ, we have that $K_1 = \mathbf{res}(W_1)$ and $K_1\cap K_2 = \mathbf{res}(W_2)$ where W_1 is the 1-dimensional VCCS $W_1 = (K_1;(\Theta_1,\Theta_1^*))$ with $\Theta_1 = \ \bigtimes\Sigma$ and W_2 is the 2-dimensional VCCS $W_2 = (K_1,K_2;(\Theta_2,\Theta_2^*))$ with $\Theta_2 = \{\binom{\sigma}{\sigma}\mid \sigma\in\Sigma\}$.

Note that the borderline as given in Theorem 3.3 does not depend on n: it is the same for the cases $n=1$ and $n\geq 2$.

Since 1-$\mathbf{res}(W) = \ \bigtimes(\mathbf{res}(W))$ for every VCCS W, this theorem also settles the problem for 1-dimensional vector residues. For m-dimensional vector residues, $m\geq 2$, we still have the same borderline depending on $\mathbf{K}_1,\ldots,\mathbf{K}_n,\mathbf{K}_{n+1}$ between the decidable and undecidable cases. For the emptiness problem this is an immediate consequence of the following observation.

For any n-VCCS W and any $m\in[n]$, we have: m-$\mathbf{res}(W) = \mathbf{proj}_{[m]}(V(W)) = \emptyset$ if and only if $V(W)=\emptyset$ if and only if $\mathbf{proj}_1(V(W)) = \mathbf{res}(W)=\emptyset$. Thus:

Theorem 3.4. *The emptiness problem for* m-$\mathbf{Res}(\mathbf{K}_1,\ldots,\mathbf{K}_n;\mathbf{K}_{n+1})$, *where* $m\in[n]$ *and* $\mathbf{K}_1,\ldots,\mathbf{K}_n,\mathbf{K}_{n+1}\in\mathcal{F}$, *is decidable if and only if there exists a* $j\in[n+1]$ *such that* $\mathbf{K}_j\subseteq\mathbf{CF}$ *and* $\bigcup_{i=1,i\neq j}^{n+1}\mathbf{K}_i\subseteq\mathbf{Reg}$. □

For the decidable cases of the finiteness problem we can use our earlier remark that for each n-VCCS W and for each $\ell\in[n]$, there is a "component permuted" version W_ℓ of W such that $\mathbf{proj}_\ell(V(W)) = \mathbf{proj}_1(V(W_\ell)) = \mathbf{res}(W_\ell)$. Now m-$\mathbf{res}(W)$ is finite, for an n-VCCS W and an $m\in[n]$, if and only if $\mathbf{proj}_i(V(W)) = \mathbf{res}(W_i)$ is finite for all $i\in[m]$. Thus finiteness of m-$\mathbf{res}(W)$ can be decided by considering the finiteness of $\mathbf{res}(W_i)$ for each $i\in[m]$. Note that if W is of a type satisfying the characterization given in the statement of Theorem 3.3, then also W_ℓ is of a type satisfying this characterization. Thus it follows that the finiteness problem for m-$\mathbf{Res}(\mathbf{K}_1,\ldots,\mathbf{K}_n;\mathbf{K}_{n+1})$ is decidable if, for some $j\in[n+1]$, $\mathbf{K}_j\subseteq\mathbf{CF}$ and $\bigcup_{i=1,i\neq j}^{n+1}\mathbf{K}_i\subseteq\mathbf{Reg}$.

For all remaining cases the problem turns out to be undecidable. However, a similar reasoning as has been used for the emptiness problem is not possible now, because infiniteness of m-$\mathbf{res}(W)$, for an n-VCCS W and an $m\in[n]$, does *not* imply that $\mathbf{res}(W)$ is infinite. Thus, in case of an undecidable finiteness problem for a family $\mathbf{Res}(\mathbf{K}_1,\ldots,\mathbf{K}_n;\mathbf{K}_{n+1})$, we cannot reduce this problem to the finiteness problem for m-$\mathbf{Res}(\mathbf{K}_1,\ldots,\mathbf{K}_n;\mathbf{K}_{n+1})$, by simply switching for each instance $\mathbf{res}(W)$ of the former problem to the instance m-$\mathbf{res}(W)$ of the latter problem. Therefore we use the direct approach of translating (intersections of) languages into vector residues of VCCSs, analogous to the approach which was noted earlier.

What should be proved is that the finiteness problem is undecidable for all families m-$\mathbf{Res}(\mathbf{K}_1,\ldots,\mathbf{K}_n;\mathbf{K}_{n+1})$, where $m \in [n]$, such that either $\mathbf{Lin} \subseteq \mathbf{K}_i$ for at least two $i \in [n]$ or $\mathbf{CS} \subseteq \mathbf{K}_i$ for at least one $i \in [n]$. To this aim we show how the (undecidable) finiteness problems of, respectively, $\mathbf{Lin} \wedge \mathbf{Lin}$ and $\mathbf{CS}$ can be reduced to the above two finiteness problems.

We start out by considering arbitrary languages $K_1,\ldots,K_{n+1}$ over some alphabet Σ. Let W be the n-VCCS defined by $W = (K_1,\ldots,K_n;(\sigma(\Sigma),\sigma(K_{n+1})))$ where σ is the injective coding $\sigma = \mathbf{id}_\Sigma \otimes \ldots \otimes \mathbf{id}_\Sigma$. Then clearly, for all $i \in [n]$, $\mathbf{proj}_i(V(W)) = K_1 \cap \ldots \cap K_n \cap K_{n+1}$. Thus m-$\mathbf{res}(W)$ is finite if and only if $\bigcap_{i=1}^{n+1} K_i$ is finite. The above two reductions are now obtained by choosing K_i from $\mathbf{Lin}$ for at least two $i \in [n]$ or by choosing K_i from $\mathbf{CS}$ for at least one $i \in [n]$. For all other i, K_i is to be chosen from $\mathbf{Mon}$. Note that $\sigma(K_{n+1})$ is always in the same family as K_{n+1}, because σ is an injective coding.

In summary, we have proved:

Theorem 3.5. *The finiteness problem for* m-$\mathbf{Res}(\mathbf{K}_1,\ldots,\mathbf{K}_n;\mathbf{K}_{n+1})$, *where* $m \in [n]$ *and* $\mathbf{K}_1,\ldots,\mathbf{K}_n,\mathbf{K}_{n+1} \in \mathcal{F}$, *is decidable if and only if there exists a* $j \in [n+1]$ *such that* $\mathbf{K}_j \subseteq \mathbf{CF}$ *and* $\bigcup_{i=1,i\neq j}^{n+1} \mathbf{K}_i \subseteq \mathbf{Reg}$. □

For the proof of the above theorem a somewhat indirect method has been used (via 1-dimensional residues, etc.). In the cases that $\mathbf{K}_1,\ldots,\mathbf{K}_{n+1}$ are all either $\mathbf{Mon}$ or $\mathbf{Reg}$ a more direct approach is possible using rational relations. Using Nivat's characterization of rational relations in terms of regular languages and (bi-) morphisms ([Niv68], see also Lemma 1.3), it is possible to model (2-dimensional) rational relations as 2-dimensional residues of VCCSs. There are essentially two different ways.

Let R be a regular language over an alphabet Σ and let $\varphi_i : \Sigma^* \to \Sigma_i^*$ be a coding for i = 1,2 where Σ_i is an alphabet. Then $M = \{\begin{pmatrix}\varphi_1(w)\\ \varphi_2(w)\end{pmatrix} | w \in R\}$ is a 2-dimensional rational relation.

Following the first method, let $\Theta = \{\begin{pmatrix}\varphi_1(\sigma)\\ \varphi_2(\sigma)\end{pmatrix} | \sigma \in \Sigma\} - \{\bar{\Lambda}\}$ and let $R' = (\varphi_1 \otimes \varphi_2)(R)$. Then clearly $M = 2$-$\mathbf{res}(W_1)$ where W_1 is the 2-dimensional VCCS $W_1 = (\Sigma_1^*, \Sigma_2^*; (\Theta, R'))$.

Following the second method, let $\Gamma = \{\begin{pmatrix}\varphi_1(\sigma)\\ \varphi_2(\sigma)\\ \sigma\end{pmatrix} | \sigma \in \Sigma\}$. Then $M = 2$-$\mathbf{res}(W_2)$ where W_2 is the 3-dimensional VCCS $W_2 = (\Sigma_1^*, \Sigma_2^*, R; (\Gamma, \Gamma^*))$. Note that $V(W_2) = \{\begin{pmatrix}\varphi_1(w)\\ \varphi_2(w)\\ w\end{pmatrix} | w \in R\}$.

The above methods of modelling rational relations in VCCSs will reappear in Section 4.2 in the context of higher-dimensional losses. Since losses are complements of residues the rational relations will appear complemented.

4. LOSS

Having investigated in Section 3 properties of (vector) residues of VCCSs with components and control languages from $\mathcal{F}$, we now focus on the (vector) losses of these VCCSs.

Similar to the approach followed in Section 3 we first identify each of the families $\mathbf{Loss}(\mathbf{K}_1, \ldots, \mathbf{K}_n; \mathbf{K}_{n+1})$ in a language hierarchical sense by relating them to (composites of) known language families. Again these results are based on the characterization provided by Theorem 2.9 and Theorem 2.10. Whereas residues are characterized using weak codings and intersections only, the notion of loss requires an additional complement operation. As a consequence we end up with more different families $\mathbf{Loss}(\mathbf{K}_1, \ldots, \mathbf{K}_n; \mathbf{K}_{n+1})$ than families $\mathbf{Res}(\mathbf{K}_1, \ldots, \mathbf{K}_n; \mathbf{K}_{n+1})$.

Next we turn to the emptiness and finiteness problem for (vector) losses of VCCSs of type $(\mathbf{K}_1, \ldots, \mathbf{K}_n; \mathbf{K}_{n+1})$ where $\mathbf{K}_i \in \mathcal{F}$ for all $i \in [n+1]$. As in the case of residues, the decidability status of each of these problems for the various families of losses, now related to known language families, follows from literature. Again we have for the emptiness problem and the finiteness problem a same borderline between decidable and undecidable cases. This borderline however, is slightly different from the one obtained in the previous section for residues. This difference is again a consequence of the complementation occurring in the definition of loss.

Clearly all results concerning the families of losses can directly be carried over to the families of 1-dimensional losses. The higher dimensional cases are treated separately and require more effort. For the families of m-dimensional losses, the borderline between decidable and undecidable emptiness (finiteness) problems is no longer independent of m in contrast to the situation of m-dimensional residues. For all $m \geq 2$, the borderline is of the same form, but for 1-dimensional losses it is essentially different. Once more it is the use of complementation (with respect to the first m components) that underlies these dependences on m.

4.1. LOSS AND 1-DIMENSIONAL LOSS

The families of losses of VCCSs with component languages and control languages from $\mathcal{F} = \{\mathbf{Mon}, \mathbf{Reg}, \mathbf{Lin}, \mathbf{CF}, \mathbf{CS}, \mathbf{RE}\}$ are investigated here. Analogous to Corollary 3.1 for the families of residues we obtain from Theorem 2.9.(2) and Theorem 2.10.(2) the following characterization of these families of losses.

Corollary 4.1.1. *Let* $\mathbf{K}_1, \ldots, \mathbf{K}_n, \mathbf{K}_{n+1} \in \mathcal{F}$.
(1) $\mathbf{Loss}(\mathbf{K}_1; \mathbf{K}_2) = \mathbf{K}_1 \backslash \mathbf{K}_2$.
(2) *If* $n \geq 2$, *then* $\mathbf{Loss}(\mathbf{K}_1, \ldots, \mathbf{K}_n; \mathbf{K}_{n+1}) = \mathbf{K}_1 \backslash \mathbf{WCod}(\mathbf{K}_2 \wedge \ldots \wedge \mathbf{K}_n \wedge \mathbf{K}_{n+1})$. □

Using this observation a table for the various families of losses can be constructed analogous to Table 3.2 for the residue families. In Table 4.1.2, assuming again that $\mathbf{K}_2 \supseteq \mathbf{K}_3 \supseteq \ldots \supseteq \mathbf{K}_{n+1}$, the columns headed by $\bigcup_{i=1}^{n+1} \mathbf{K}_i, \mathbf{K}_1, \mathbf{K}_2, \mathbf{K}_3$, and $\mathbf{M} = \mathbf{WCod}(\mathbf{K}_2 \wedge \ldots \wedge \mathbf{K}_n \wedge \mathbf{K}_{n+1})$ convey the same information as the corresponding columns in Table 3.2. Again we distinguish between $n = 1$ and $n \geq 2$. In the first case the column headed by $\mathbf{L}$ gives the families $\mathbf{Loss}(\mathbf{K}_1; \mathbf{K}_2)$ which are computed using the characterization $\mathbf{K}_1 \backslash \mathbf{K}_2$.

For $n \geq 2$, the column headed by **L** provides the families **Loss**($\mathbf{K}_1, \ldots, \mathbf{K}_n; \mathbf{K}_{n+1}$) = $\mathbf{K} \setminus \mathbf{M}$. In formulating the resulting families of languages we have used the equality $\mathbf{K} \setminus \mathbf{M} = \mathbf{K} \wedge$ co$-\mathbf{M}$, for any pair of language families **K** and **M**. If a loss family is given together with the symbol "d", then this family has a decidable emptiness (finiteness) problem. For a given family **K**, the family $\mathbf{K}^+ = \{K - \{\Lambda\} | K \in \mathbf{K}\}$.

Note that this table makes more case distinctions than Table 3.2. One reason for this, is the occurrence of the language families $\mathbf{K}^+$, for $\mathbf{K} \in \mathcal{F}$, whenever $\bigcup_{i=2}^{n+1} \mathbf{K}_i = \mathbf{Mon}$ and $\mathbf{K}_1 \neq \mathbf{Mon}$. These families, which are distinct—if only slightly—from the families from $\mathcal{F}$, give extra rows in almost each of the groups in the table. Another reason for the greater size of the table is the necessary case distinction in the group where $\bigcup_{i=1}^{n+1} \mathbf{K}_i = \mathbf{RE}$. In Table 3.2 in this group all cases—with $\mathbf{K}_1 \subseteq \mathbf{RE}$ and $\mathbf{M} \subseteq \mathbf{RE}$—yielded the same result: $\mathbf{R} = \mathbf{RE}$. In Table 4.1.2 the three cases (1) $\mathbf{K}_1 = \mathbf{RE}, \mathbf{M} \subseteq \mathbf{CF}$, (2)$\mathbf{K}_1 \subseteq \mathbf{CS}, \mathbf{M} = \mathbf{RE}$, and (3) $\mathbf{K}_1 = \mathbf{M} = \mathbf{RE}$, provide mutually different results: either $\mathbf{L} = \mathbf{RE}$ (or $\mathbf{L} = \mathbf{RE}^+$), $\mathbf{L} =$ co-**RE**, or $\mathbf{L} = \mathbf{RE} \wedge$co-**RE**.

On basis of Table 4.1.2 it is easy to determine which families **Loss**($\mathbf{K}_1, \ldots, \mathbf{K}_n; \mathbf{K}_{n+1}$) have a decidable emptiness (finiteness) problem and which do not. For the families included in **CF** these problems are decidable. (Note that, again, each member of such a family has an effective description provided its component languages and control language are effectively given.) The undecidability of the two problems for the remaining families follows from the undecidability of these problems for the single family co-**Lin**, because this family is included in all remaining ones. The undecidability of the emptiness problem for co-**Lin** is proved on page 215 of [HopUll79] using the approach of [BakBoo74] (Lemma 1, see also [Gre69], Theorem 4.2, which uses essentially the same proof). For the undecidability of the finiteness problem for co-**Lin** no explicit reference could be found, but it can easily be proved using the observation that the set of *invalid* computations of (deterministic) Turing machines is linear (see again page 215 of [HopUll79] and see also the remark made in the last paragraph of the proof of Lemma 1 in [BakBoo74]). For the sake of completeness, we give here a rather straightforward reduction from Post's Correspondence Problem similar to the reduction in the proof of Lemma 1 of [BakBoo74]: Given an instance $A = w_1, \ldots, w_m$ and $B = x_1, \ldots, x_m$ of PCP over some alphabet Σ, we consider the languages $L_A = \{w_{i_1} \ldots w_{i_k} a_{i_k} \ldots a_{i_1} | k \geq 1\}$ and $L_B = \{x_{i_1} \ldots x_{i_k} a_{i_k} \ldots a_{i_1} — k \geq 1\}$, where $\Delta = \{a_1, \ldots, a_m\}$ is a new alphabet disjoint with Σ. Then $L_A \cap L_B$ is infinite (not empty) if and only if the instance A, B of PCP has a solution (see also the proof of Theorem 8.9 in [HopUll79]). Now let C_A be the complement of L_A in $(\Sigma \cup \Delta)^*$ and let C_B be the complement of L_B in $(\Sigma \cup \Delta)^*$. Then C_A is linear, because it is the union of the regular set $(\Sigma \cup \Delta)^* - \{w_1, \ldots, w_m\}^+ \Delta^+$ and the linear set $\{w a_{i_k} \ldots a_{i_1} | w \in \{w_1, \ldots, w_m\}^+, k \geq 1$, and $w \neq w_{i_1} \ldots w_{i_k}\}$; similar for C_B and so $C_A \cup C_B$ is linear. Since $L_A \cap L_B = (\Sigma \cup \Delta)^* - (C_A \cup C_B)$, it follows that $(\Sigma \cup \Delta)^* - (C_A \cup C_B)$ is infinite (not empty) if and only if the instance A, B of PCP has a solution.

In Section 3 we showed a direct way of transforming (intersections of) languages to residues of VCCSs. For losses similar direct techniques can be used to replace the above indirect ones (which use Table 4.1.2, etc.). For a language K over an alphabet Σ, we

Table 4.1.2. $\mathbf{L} = \mathbf{Loss}(\mathbf{K}_1,\ldots,\mathbf{K}_n;\mathbf{K}_{n+1})$, $\mathbf{M} = \mathbf{WCod}(\mathbf{K}_2 \wedge \ldots \wedge \mathbf{K}_n \wedge \mathbf{K}_{n+1})$

				$n=1$		$n \geq 2$		
$\bigcup_{i=1}^{n+1} \mathbf{K}_i$	$\mathbf{K}_1$	$\mathbf{K}_2$	$\mathbf{K}_3$	**R**		**M**	**L**	
Mon	**Mon**	**Mon**	**Mon**	**Mon** $\setminus$ **Mon**	d	**Mon**	**Mon** $\setminus$ **Mon**	d
Reg	**Reg**	**Mon**	**Mon**	**Reg**$^+$	d	**Mon**	**Reg**$^+$	d
	$\subseteq$**Reg**	**Reg**	$\subseteq$**Reg**	**Reg**	d	**Reg**	**Reg**	d
Lin	**Lin**	**Mon**	**Mon**	**Lin**$^+$	d	**Mon**	**Lin**$^+$	d
	Lin	**Reg**	$\subseteq$**Reg**	**Lin**	d	**Reg**	**Lin**	d
	$\subseteq$**Reg**	**Lin**	$\subseteq$**Reg**	co-**Lin**		**Lin**	co-**Lin**	
	Lin	**Lin**	$\subseteq$**Reg**	**Lin**$\wedge$co-**Lin**		**Lin**	**Lin**$\wedge$co-**Lin**	
	$\subseteq$**Reg**	**Lin**	**Lin**	co-**Lin**		**RE** [1]	co-**RE** [2]	
	Lin	**Lin**	**Lin**	**Lin**$\wedge$co-**Lin**		**RE** [1]	co-**RE** [2]	
CF	**CF**	**Mon**	**Mon**	**CF**$^+$	d	**Mon**	**CF**$^+$	d
	CF	**Reg**	$\subseteq$**Reg**	**CF**	d	**Reg**	**CF**	d
	$\subseteq$**Reg**	**CF**	$\subseteq$**Reg**	co-**CF**		**CF**	co-**CF**	
	CF	**Lin**	$\subseteq$**Reg**	**CF**$\wedge$co-**Lin**		**Lin**	**CF**$\wedge$co-**Lin**	
	Lin	**CF**	$\subseteq$**Reg**	**Lin**$\wedge$co**CF**		**CF**	**Lin**$\wedge$co-**CF**	
	CF	**CF**	$\subseteq$**Reg**	**CF**$\wedge$co-**CF**		**CF**	**CF**$\wedge$co-**CF**	
	$\subseteq$**Reg**	**CF**	$\supseteq$**Lin**	co-**CF**		**RE** [1]	co-**RE** [2]	
	Lin	**CF**	$\supseteq$**Lin**	**Lin**$\wedge$co-**CF**		**RE** [1]	co-**RE** [2]	
	CF	**CF**	$\supseteq$**Lin**	**CF**$\wedge$co-**CF**		**RE** [1]	co-**RE** [2]	
CS	**CS**	**Mon**	**Mon**	**CS**$^+$		**Mon**	**CS**$^+$	
	CS	$\supseteq$**Reg**, $\subseteq$**CF**	$\subseteq$**Reg**	**CS** [3]		$\supseteq$**Reg**, $\subseteq$**CF**	**CS** [3]	
	CS	$\supseteq$**Lin**	$\supseteq$**Lin**	**CS** [3]		**RE** [1]	co-**RE** [2]	
	$\subseteq$**CS**	**CS**	$\subseteq$**CS**	**CS** [3]		**RE**	co-**RE** [2]	
RE	**RE**	**Mon**	**Mon**	**RE**$^+$		**Mon**	**RE**$^+$	
	RE	$\supseteq$**Reg**, $\subseteq$**CF**	$\subseteq$**Reg**	**RE** [4]		$\supseteq$**Reg**, $\subseteq$**CF**	**RE** [4]	
	$\subseteq$**CS**	**RE**	$\subseteq$**RE**	co-**RE** [2]		**RE**	co-**RE** [2]	
	RE	$\supseteq$**Lin**, $\subseteq$**CS**	$\supseteq$**Lin**	**RE** [4]		**RE** [1]	**RE**$\wedge$co-**RE**	
	RE	**CS**	$\subseteq$**CS**	**RE** [4]		**RE**	**RE**$\wedge$co-**RE**	
	RE	**RE**	$\subseteq$**RE**	**RE**$\wedge$co-**RE**		**RE**	**RE**$\wedge$co-**RE**	

[1]) **RE** = **WCod**(**Lin** $\wedge$ **Lin**) by [BakBoo74].
[2]) **K** $\setminus$ **RE** = **K** $\wedge$ co-**RE** = co-(co-**K** $\vee$ **RE**) = co-**RE** for all **K** $\subseteq$ **CS**.
[3]) **CS** $\setminus$ **K** = **CS** $\wedge$ co-**K** = **CS** for all **K** $\in \mathcal{F} - \{$**Mon**, **RE**$\}$.
[4]) **RE** $\setminus$ **K** = **RE** $\wedge$ co-**K** = **RE** for all **K** $\in \mathcal{F} - \{$**Mon**, **RE**$\}$.
[2]), [3]), and [4]) use closure properties of **CS** and **RE** and the equality **CS** = co-**CS** (see [Imm88] and [Sze88]), which implies that co-**K** $\subseteq$ **CS** for all **K** $\subseteq$ **CS**. □

have that $K - \{\Lambda\} = \mathbf{loss}(W_1)$ and $\Sigma^* - K = \mathbf{loss}(W_2)$, where W_1 is the 1-dimensional VCCS $W_1 = (K;(\Theta,\Theta^*))$ with $\Theta = \emptyset$, and where W_2 is the 1-dimensional VCCS $W_2 = (\Sigma^*;(\Theta, M))$ with $\Theta = \times\,\Sigma$ and $M = \mathbf{coll}_\Theta^{-1}(\times\,K)$.

By consultation of Table 4.1.2, the borderline between "decidable" families of losses (included in **CF**; in Table 4.1.2 they are marked with a "d") and "undecidable" families of losses (containing **co-Lin**) can be determined. It is formulated in the following characterization holding for both $n = 1$ and $n \geq 2$.

Theorem 4.1.3. *The finiteness (emptiness) problem for* $\mathbf{Loss}(\mathbf{K}_1,\ldots,\mathbf{K}_n;\mathbf{K}_{n+1})$, *where* $\mathbf{K}_1,\ldots,\mathbf{K}_n,\mathbf{K}_{n+1} \in \mathcal{F}$, *is decidable if and only if* $\mathbf{K}_1 \subseteq \mathbf{CF}$ *and* $\bigcup_{i=2}^{n+1} \mathbf{K}_i \subseteq \mathbf{Reg}$. □

The criterium given above to distinguish the undecidable cases from the decidable cases resembles closely the one given in Theorem 3.3 for residues. There, however, the family **CF** could occur as any one of the families $\mathbf{K}_1,\ldots,\mathbf{K}_n,\mathbf{K}_{n+1}$, whereas here it may appear as $\mathbf{K}_1$ only. Obviously, this is due to the undecidability of the finiteness and emptiness problem for **co-Lin** and **co-CF**.

All results obtained so far can directly be translated to the families of 1-dimensional losses, because 1-loss(W) = $\times$ loss(W) for all VCCS W. In particular we have:

Theorem 4.1.4. *The finiteness (emptiness) problem for* $1\text{-}\mathbf{Loss}(\mathbf{K}_1,\ldots,\mathbf{K}_n;\mathbf{K}_{n+1})$, *where* $\mathbf{K}_1,\ldots,\mathbf{K}_n;\mathbf{K}_{n+1} \in \mathcal{F}$, *is decidable if and only if* $\mathbf{K}_1 \subseteq \mathbf{CF}$ *and* $\bigcup_{i=2}^{n+1} \mathbf{K}_i \subseteq \mathbf{Reg}$. □

4.2. HIGHER DIMENSIONAL LOSS

In this subsection we establish the decidability status of the emptiness problem and the finiteness problem for families of higher dimensional loss, viz., for the families m-$\mathbf{Loss}(\mathbf{K}_1,\ldots,\mathbf{K}_n;\mathbf{K}_{n+1})$ where $m \geq 2$ and where $\mathbf{K}_i \in \mathcal{F}$, for all $i \in [n+1]$. Thus in this subsection we assume that $n \geq 2$ and we let m be an arbitrary but fixed integer from $[n]$ satisfying $m \geq 2$.

From Theorem 4.1.4 we know that the families $1\text{-}\mathbf{Loss}(\mathbf{K}_1,\ldots,\mathbf{K}_n;\mathbf{K}_{n+1})$ with $\mathbf{K}_1$, ... ,$\mathbf{K}_n$, $\mathbf{K}_{n+1} \in \mathcal{F}$, for which emptiness (finiteness) is undecidable, are precisely those which satisfy either the condition that $\mathbf{CS} \subseteq \mathbf{K}_1$, or the condition that $\mathbf{Lin} \subseteq \bigcup_{i=2}^{n+1} \mathbf{K}_i$.

For the higher dimensional case we will find similar conditions. It will turn out that the emptiness (finiteness) problem for m-$\mathbf{Loss}(\mathbf{K}_1,\ldots,\mathbf{K}_n;\mathbf{K}_{n+1})$, with $\mathbf{K}_1,\ldots,\mathbf{K}_n,\mathbf{K}_{n+1} \in \mathcal{F}$, is undecidable if either $\mathbf{CS} \subseteq \mathbf{K}_j$, for some $j \in [m]$, or $\mathbf{Reg} \subseteq \bigcup_{i=m+1}^{n+1} \mathbf{K}_i$; in the other cases both problems are decidable.

The first of these conditions refers to $\mathbf{K}_1,\ldots,\mathbf{K}_m$, corresponding to the components for which the loss is investigated, whereas the second condition considers $\mathbf{K}_{m+1},\ldots,\mathbf{K}_n,\mathbf{K}_{n+1}$, corresponding to the components which induce the loss (in $\mathbf{K}_1,\ldots,\mathbf{K}_m$). This situation resembles strongly the situation in the one-dimensional case, where we have a condition on $\mathbf{K}_1$ and a condition on $\mathbf{K}_2,\ldots,\mathbf{K}_n,\mathbf{K}_{n+1}$. Moreover the requirement $\mathbf{CS} \subseteq \mathbf{K}_1$ for undecidability in the one-dimensional case, is generalized to the similar condition $\mathbf{CS} \subseteq \mathbf{K}_j$, for a $j \in [m]$, which guarantees undecidability in the m-dimensional case.

On the other hand the undecidability border given through $\mathbf{K}_{m+1},\ldots,\mathbf{K}_n,\mathbf{K}_{n+1}$ for m-

$\mathbf{Loss}(\mathbf{K}_1,\ldots,\mathbf{K}_n;\mathbf{K}_{n+1})$ is "lower" than the border expressed through $\mathbf{K}_2,\ldots,\mathbf{K}_n,\mathbf{K}_{n+1}$ for 1-$\mathbf{Loss}(\mathbf{K}_1,\ldots,\mathbf{K}_n;\mathbf{K}_{n+1})$. Essentially, this is due to the difference in (computational) complexity between complements of 1-dimensional regular sets and higher dimensional "regular" (i.e., rational) sets: Both $\mathbf{K}_{m+1},\ldots,\mathbf{K}_n,\mathbf{K}_{n+1}$ and $\mathbf{K}_2,\ldots,\mathbf{K}_n,\mathbf{K}_{n+1}$ appear "complemented" in the definitions of m-$\mathbf{Loss}(\mathbf{K}_1,\ldots,\mathbf{K}_n;\mathbf{K}_{n+1})$ and 1-$\mathbf{Loss}(\mathbf{K}_1,\ldots,\mathbf{K}_n;\mathbf{K}_{n+1})$ respectively. In the one-dimensional case we have a decidable emptiness and finiteness problem for co-**Reg** = **Reg** (and undecidability for co-**Lin**), whereas in the higher dimensional case the occurrence of **Reg** within $\mathbf{K}_{m+1},\ldots,\mathbf{K}_n,\mathbf{K}_{n+1}$ gives rise to complements of (m-dimensional) rational relations, for which both the emptiness and finiteness problem are undecidable (see, e.g., [Ber79]).

The above is proved as follows. First we show, by a simple reduction from the one-dimensional case, that the emptiness and finiteness problem are undecidable for the families m-$\mathbf{Loss}(\mathbf{K}_1,\ldots,\mathbf{K}_n;\mathbf{K}_{n+1})$ with $\mathbf{K}_1,\ldots,\mathbf{K}_n,\mathbf{K}_{n+1}\in\mathcal{F}$ and $\mathbf{CS}\subseteq\bigcup_{i=1}^{m}\mathbf{K}_i$. Next we prove, based on properties of rational relations, that the emptiness problem and finiteness problem are also undecidable for the families m-$\mathbf{Loss}(\mathbf{K}_1,\ldots,\mathbf{K}_n;\mathbf{K}_{n+1})$ with $\mathbf{K}_1,\ldots,\mathbf{K}_n,\mathbf{K}_{n+1}\in\mathcal{F}$ and $\mathbf{Reg}\subseteq\bigcup_{i=m+1}^{n+1}\mathbf{K}_i$. Finally we prove that emptiness and finiteness are decidable problems for all remaining cases, i.e., for the families m-$\mathbf{Loss}(\mathbf{K}_1,\ldots,\mathbf{K}_n;\mathbf{K}_{n+1})$ with $\mathbf{K}_1,\ldots,\mathbf{K}_n,\mathbf{K}_{n+1}\in\mathcal{F}$ where $\bigcup_{i=1}^{m}\mathbf{K}_i\subseteq\mathbf{CF}$ and $\bigcup_{i=m+1}^{n+1}\mathbf{K}_i\subseteq\mathbf{Mon}$. This third proof constitutes a major part of this subsection.

The following transformation which is used to reduce 1-dimensional losses to higher-dimensional losses is very general. It can therefore also be used in later sections. Basically, however, these undecidability results are derived from the analogous undecidability results for languages (or complements of languages). As we have seen earlier, languages (and complements of languages) can be directly transferred into losses of VCCSs. It only remains to show how additional components can be inserted. This is done in the following transformation.

Transformation 4.2.1. Let $W=(K_1,\ldots,K_{n-m+1};(\Theta,K))$ be an $(n-m+1)$-VCCS. Define W' to be the n-VCCS given by: $W'=(K_1,O_2,\ldots,O_m,K_2,\ldots,K_{n-m+1};(\epsilon(\Theta),\epsilon(K)))$, where $O_i=\emptyset^*=\{\Lambda\}$ for all $i\in[m]-[1]$, and ϵ is the injective coding which maps each vector letter $(\alpha_1,\ldots,\alpha_{n-m+1})$ from Θ to the n-dimensional vector letter $(\alpha_1,\lambda_2,\ldots,\lambda_m,\alpha_2,\ldots,\alpha_{n-m+1})$, where $\lambda_i=\Lambda$ for all $i\in[m]-[1]$. Then m-$\mathbf{loss}(W')=(K_1\times O_2\times\ldots\times O_m)$ - $\mathbf{proj}_{[m]}(V(W'))=(K_1$ - $\mathbf{proj}_1(V(W)))\times O_2\times\ldots\times O_m$.

Consequently m-$\mathbf{loss}(W')$ is empty (finite) if and only if $\mathbf{loss}(W)=K_1$ - $\mathbf{proj}_1(V(W))$ is empty (finite). □

Lemma 4.2.2. *Let* $\mathbf{K}_1,\ldots,\mathbf{K}_n,\mathbf{K}_{n+1}\in\mathcal{F}$ *and let* $j\in[m]$ *be such that* $\mathbf{CS}\subseteq\mathbf{K}_j$. *Then the finiteness (emptiness) problem for* m-$\mathbf{Loss}(\mathbf{K}_1,\ldots,\mathbf{K}_n;\mathbf{K}_{n+1})$ *is undecidable.*

Proof. Without loss of generality we may assume that $j=1$. Given an $(n-m+1)$-VCCS W of type (**CS**,**Mon**,...,**Mon**;**Mon**) we obtain, using Transformation 4.2.1, an n-VCCS W' of type $(\mathbf{K}_1,\ldots,\mathbf{K}_n;\mathbf{K}_{n+1})$ such that m-$\mathbf{loss}(W')$ is finite (empty) if and only if $\mathbf{loss}$(W) is finite (empty). This reduction proves the lemma, because, by Theorem 4.1.3, the finiteness (emptiness) problem for **Loss**(**CS**,**Mon**,...,**Mon**;**Mon**) is undecidable. Note that in fact the undecidability of the emptiness and finiteness problem for **CS** has been used here. □

The following transformation uses generalizations (to dimension m) of the two methods for modelling rational relations in VCCSs, sketched at the end of Section 3.

Transformation 4.2.3. Let $\Sigma_1, \ldots, \Sigma_m$ be alphabets, let R be a regular language over $\Theta = \mathbf{Tot}(\Sigma_1, \ldots, \Sigma_m)$, and let $j \in [n+1] - [m]$. Define $W^{\Theta,R,j}$ to be the n-VCCS $(R_1, \ldots, R_n; (\Gamma, R_{n+1}))$ given as follows. $\Gamma = \{(\mathbf{proj}_1(\vartheta), \ldots, \mathbf{proj}_m(\vartheta), \vartheta, \ldots, \vartheta) \mid \vartheta \in \Theta\}$. $R_i = \Sigma_i^*$ for all $i \in [m]$. $R_i = \Theta^*$ for all $i \in [n] - [m] - \{j\}$. Further, if $j \in [n] - [m]$, then $R_j = R$ and $R_{n+1} = \Gamma^*$, and if $j = n+1$, then $R_{n+1} = \mathbf{proj}^{-1}_{\Gamma^*,[m]}(\mathbf{coll}(\mathrm{R}))$.

Then, in both cases $\mathbf{proj}_{\Gamma^*,[m]}(\bigcap_{i=m+1}^{n} \mathbf{proj}^{-1}_{\Gamma^*,i}(R_i) \cap R_{n+1})$ is equal to $\mathbf{coll}(\mathrm{R})$: in the first case it equals $\mathbf{proj}_{\Gamma^*,[m]}(\mathbf{proj}^{-1}_{\Gamma^*,j}(R) \cap \Gamma^*) = \mathbf{coll}(\mathrm{R})$ and in the second case it equals $\mathbf{proj}_{\Gamma^*,[m]}(\Gamma^* \cap \mathbf{proj}^{-1}_{\Gamma^*,[m]}(\mathbf{coll}(\mathrm{R}))) = \mathbf{coll}(\mathrm{R})$.

Consequently, by Theorem 2.6.(3), m-$\mathbf{loss}(W^{\Theta,R,j}) = (\times_{i=1}^{m} \Sigma_i^*)$ - $\mathbf{proj}_{\Gamma^*,[m]}(\bigcap_{i=m+1}^{n} \mathbf{proj}^{-1}_{\Gamma^*,i}(R_i) \cap R_{n+1}) = (\times_{i=1}^{m} \Sigma_i^*) - \mathbf{coll}(\mathrm{R})$. □

As an example we give a small application of Transformation 4.2.3.

Let $n = 3$ and let $m = 2$; $\Sigma_1 = \{a, c\}$ and $\Sigma_2 = \{d\}$. Then $\Theta = \mathbf{Tot}(\Sigma_1, \Sigma_2) = \{\binom{a}{\Lambda}, \binom{c}{\Lambda}, \binom{\Lambda}{d}, \binom{a}{d}, \binom{c}{d}\}$. Let $R = \{\alpha\beta\gamma\}^*$, where $\alpha = \binom{a}{\Lambda}$, $\beta = \binom{c}{d}$ and $\gamma = \binom{\Lambda}{d}$.

The 3-VCCS $W^{\Theta,R,j} = (R_1, R_2, R_3; (\Gamma, R_4))$ is now defined as follows.

$\Gamma = \{\begin{pmatrix} a \\ \Lambda \\ \alpha \end{pmatrix}, \begin{pmatrix} c \\ \Lambda \\ x \end{pmatrix}, \begin{pmatrix} \Lambda \\ d \\ \gamma \end{pmatrix}, \begin{pmatrix} a \\ d \\ y \end{pmatrix}, \begin{pmatrix} c \\ d \\ \beta \end{pmatrix}\}$, where $x = \binom{c}{\Lambda}$ and $y = \binom{a}{d}$; $R_1 = \{a, c\}^*$, $R_2 = \{d\}^*$.

If $j = 3$, then $R_3 = R = \{\alpha\beta\gamma\}^*$ and $R_4 = \Gamma^*$. In this case $V(W^{\Theta,R,3}) = \mathbf{coll}((\alpha'\beta'\gamma')^*)$, where $\alpha' = \begin{pmatrix} a \\ \Lambda \\ \alpha \end{pmatrix}$, $\beta' = \begin{pmatrix} c \\ d \\ \beta \end{pmatrix}$, and $\gamma' = \begin{pmatrix} \Lambda \\ d \\ \gamma \end{pmatrix}$. Then 2-$\mathbf{res}(W^{\Theta,R,3}) = \mathbf{coll}(\mathrm{R})$ and 2-$\mathbf{loss}(W^{\Theta,R,3}) = (\Sigma_1^* \times \Sigma_2^*) - \mathbf{coll}(R)$.

If $j = 4$, then $R_3 = \Theta^*$ and $R_4 = \{\Lambda\} \cup \alpha'(\beta'(\alpha'\gamma' \cup \gamma'\alpha'))^*\beta'\gamma'$. In this case $V(W^{\Theta,R,4}) = \mathbf{coll}(R_4)$. Hence, 2-$\mathbf{res}(W^{\Theta,R,4}) = \mathbf{proj}_{[2]}(\mathbf{coll}(R_4)) = \mathbf{coll}(\mathrm{R})$ and 2-$\mathbf{loss}(W^{\Theta,R,4}) = (\Sigma_1^* \times \Sigma_2^*) - \mathbf{coll}(R)$.

In contrast to the previous lemma in the following one the fact that $m \geq 2$ is essential.

Lemma 4.2.4. *Let* $\mathbf{K}_1, \ldots, \mathbf{K}_n, \mathbf{K}_{n+1} \in \mathcal{F}$ *and let* $j \in [n+1] - [m]$ *be such that* $\mathbf{Reg} \subseteq \mathbf{K}_j$. *Then the finiteness (emptiness) problem for* m-$\mathbf{Loss}(\mathbf{K}_1, \ldots, \mathbf{K}_n; \mathbf{K}_{n+1})$ *is undecidable.*

Proof. Given alphabets $\Sigma_1, \ldots, \Sigma_m$ and a regular language R over $\Theta = \mathbf{Tot}(\Sigma_1, \ldots, \Sigma_m)$, we obtain, using Transformation 4.2.3, an n-VCCS $W^{\Theta,R,j}$ of type $(\mathbf{K}_1, \ldots, \mathbf{K}_n; \mathbf{K}_{n+1})$ such that m-$\mathbf{loss}(W^{\Theta,R,j})$ is finite (empty) if and only if $(\times_{i=1}^{m} \Sigma_i^*) - \mathbf{coll}(R)$ is finite (empty). This reduction proves the lemma, because, by Lemma 1.4.(1), the finiteness (emptiness) problem for complements of collapses of regular languages is undecidable. Thus the well-known undecidability of the finiteness (emptiness) problem for complements of rational relations is used here. By Lemma 1.3, collapses of regular languages correspond to rational relations. □

Lemmas 4.2.2 and 4.2.4 provide us with families m-**Loss**$(\mathbf{K}_1, \ldots, \mathbf{K}_n; \mathbf{K}_{n+1})$ for which the emptiness and finiteness problem are undecidable. For all remaining families m-**Loss**$(\mathbf{K}_1, \ldots, \mathbf{K}_n; \mathbf{K}_{n+1})$ with $\mathbf{K}_1, \ldots, \mathbf{K}_n, \mathbf{K}_{n+1} \in \mathcal{F}$ these problems are decidable, as we show next. That is, we prove next that whenever $\mathbf{K}_1, \ldots, \mathbf{K}_n, \mathbf{K}_{n+1} \in \mathcal{F}$ are such that $\bigcup_{i=1}^{m} \mathbf{K}_i \subseteq \mathbf{CF}$ and $\bigcup_{i=m+1}^{n+1} \mathbf{K}_i = \mathbf{Mon}$, then the emptiness problem and the finiteness problem for m-**Loss**$(\mathbf{K}_1, \ldots, \mathbf{K}_n; \mathbf{K}_{n+1})$ are decidable.

First we reduce these problems to simpler (looking) ones.

Lemma 4.2.5. *Let W be an n-VCCS of type $(\mathbf{K}_1, \ldots, \mathbf{K}_n; \mathbf{K}_{n+1})$ with $\mathbf{K}_i \in \mathcal{F}$ for all $i \in [n+1]$ such that $\bigcup_{i=m+1}^{n+1} \mathbf{K}_i = \mathbf{Mon}$. Then m-**loss**(W) $= (\times_{i=1}^{m} K_i) - \Theta^{\otimes}$, where $K_i \in \mathbf{K}_i$, for all $i \in [m]$, and Θ is an m-dimensional vector alphabet.*

Proof. Let $W = (K_1, \ldots, K_n; (\Gamma, K_{n+1}))$. Then m-**loss**(W) $= (\times_{i=1}^{m} K_i) - \mathbf{proj}_{\Gamma^{\bullet},[m]} (\bigcap_{i=m+1}^{n} \mathbf{proj}\,_{\Gamma^{\bullet},i}^{-1}(K_i) \cap K_{n+1})$, by Theorem 2.6.(3). Since $K_i \in \mathbf{Mon}$, for all $i \in [n+1] - [m]$, and since **Mon** is closed under inverse weak codings and under intersections, it follows that $\bigcap_{i=m+1}^{n} \mathbf{proj}_{\Gamma^{\bullet},i}^{-1}(K_i) \cap K_{n+1} = \Delta^*$ for an n-dimensional vector alphabet $\Delta \subseteq \Gamma$. By letting $\Theta = \mathbf{proj}_{\Gamma^{\bullet},[m]}(\Delta) - \{\Lambda\}$, the statement follows. □

For the rest of this section we consider m fixed effectively defined context-free languages $K_1, \ldots, K_m$ and a fixed effectively defined m-dimensional vector alphabet Θ. We let $\Sigma_1, \ldots, \Sigma_m$ be alphabets such that $K_i \subseteq \Sigma_i^*$, for all $i \in [m]$, and $\Theta \subseteq \mathbf{Tot}(\Sigma_1, \ldots, \Sigma_m)$. We investigate the properties of the m-dimensional vector language $V = (\times_{i=1}^{m} K_i) - \Theta^{\otimes}$.

The algorithm deciding the emptiness and finiteness of V(for non-empty $K_1, \ldots, K_m$) is based on the following intuitive observations. In order for V to be empty (finite), $\Theta^{\otimes}$ must contain all (most) of the word vectors from $\times_{i=1}^{m} K_i$. Now, suppose b is a letter—occurring in the j-th component ($j \in [m]$) of vector letters from Θ—that always needs partners, i.e. b never occurs "free" (as j-th component) in one of the vector letters of Θ. Then, if a word vector of $\Theta^{\otimes}$ has a long j-th component with many occurrences of b, then, for this word vector, at least one of the other components must be long as well. Hence, if b occurs in K_j in unbounded amounts, then infinitely many of the word vectors of $\times_{i=1}^{m} K_i$ are not in $\Theta^{\otimes}$, namely all word vectors combining a "long" j-th component having large amounts of b's with "short" other components. Thus, for V to be empty (finite), all letters occurring in unbounded amounts in one of the K_i must occur free in Θ. For context-free languages the pumping lemma provides an effective way to determine these "unbounded" letters. After checking the freeness of the unbounded letters and subsequently removing them from the words of the K_i, only a finite "rest" check (of short, non-pumpable words) is sufficient to settle the problem of the emptiness (finiteness) of V. The precise elaboration of the above intuition (including the case of empty $K_1, \ldots, K_m$) will be given below.

We start out by checking whether or not one of the K_i is empty (this can be done effectively). If that is the case, we are done: V is empty (and thus also finite). Hence from now on we assume that none of the context-free languages $K_1, \ldots, K_m$ is empty.

Next we consider the "amount of freedom" allowed by Θ(when used to synchronize words from $K_1, \ldots, K_m$). Let $j \in [m]$ and let $b \in \mathbf{alphoproj}_j(\Theta)$. We say that b is *free in the j-th component of* Θ whenever there exists $a\beta \in \Theta$ such that $\mathbf{proj}_j(\beta) = b$ and $\mathbf{proj}_i(\beta) = \Lambda$ for all $i \in [m] - \{j\}$. By **free**(j) we denote the set of all letters which are free in the j-th component of Θ.

By definition each letter $c \in \mathbf{alphoproj}_j(\Theta) - \mathbf{free}(j)$ occurs in the j-th component of a vector letter γ from Θ only if γ provides at least one partner for c in one of its other components. Hence, for all $w \in \Theta^\otimes$, it holds that $|\mathbf{eras}_{\mathbf{free}(j)}(\mathbf{proj}_j(w))| \leq \sum_{i=1,i\neq j}^{m} |\mathbf{proj}_i(w)|$ where, for all words w, $|w|$ denotes the length of w and, for all alphabets Δ, $\mathbf{eras}_\Delta$ is the erasing homomorphism satisfying $\mathbf{eras}_\Delta(b) = \Lambda$ if $b \in \Delta$ and $\mathbf{eras}_\Delta(b) = b$ if $b \notin \Delta$.

Now, if $w_1 \in K_1, \ldots, w_m \in K_m$, then, for each $u \in K_j$ such that $|\mathbf{eras}_{\mathbf{free}(j)}(u)| > \sum_{i=1,i\neq j}^{m} |w_i|$, the word vector $v = (w_1, \ldots, w_{j-1}, u, w_{j+1}, \ldots, w_m)$ is not an element of $\Theta^\otimes$. Hence, whenever $\mathbf{eras}_{\mathbf{free}(j)}(K_j)$ is infinite, there are infinitely many word vectors $v \in K_1 \times \ldots \times K_m$ such that $v \notin \Theta^\otimes$(recall that $K_1, \ldots, K_m$ are non-empty).

In all, if, for some $j \in [m]$, $\mathbf{eras}_{\mathbf{free}(j)}(K_j)$ is infinite, then $(\times_{i=1}^{m} K_i) - \Theta^\otimes$ is infinite. For the effectively given context-free languages K_i, the languages $\mathbf{eras}_{\mathbf{free}(i)}(K_i)$ are effectively context-free (see, [HopUll79], Theorem 6.2) and thus their finiteness can be decided. In the rest of this section we therefore assume that $\mathbf{eras}_{\mathbf{free}(i)}(K_i)$ is finite for all $i \in [m]$.

Thus the algorithm has taken care of the situation where non-free letters occur in unbouded amounts in one of the K_i. It remains to check the remaining "short" words in each K_i, i.e., words obtained from longer words in K_i by erasing free letters.

Whenever a word vector is not contained in $\Theta^\otimes$, erasing free letters from its components yields word vectors which are again not contained in $\Theta^\otimes$ as the following argument shows. Let $j \in [m]$, let $u_1, \ldots, u_m, v_1, v_2$ be words, and let $b \in \mathbf{free}(j)$. Then $w = (u_1, \ldots, u_{j-1}, v_1 v_2, u_{j+1}, \ldots, u_m) \in \Theta^\otimes$ implies that $w = w_1 \odot w_2$ for some word vectors w_1 and w_2 from $\Theta^\otimes$ such that $\mathbf{proj}_j(w_1) = v_1$ and $\mathbf{proj}_j(w_2) = v_2$. Since b is free in the j-th component of Θ, it follows that $(u_1, \ldots, u_{j-1}, v_1 b v_2, u_{j+1}, \ldots, u_m) = w_1 \odot (\Lambda, \ldots, \Lambda, b, \Lambda, \ldots, \Lambda) \odot w_2 \in \Theta^\otimes$.

This observation forms the basis for our final decidability proof. It is shown that, for each of the context-free languages K_i, there exists a *finite* subset L_i such that every word from K_i can be reduced to a word from L_i by erasing some occurrences of letters from **free**(i). The decision algorithm has these finite "test" sets $L_1, \ldots, L_m$ rather than $K_1, \ldots, K_m$ as its input.

Let us now formalize this notion of erasing occurrences from a given word. Let Σ and Δ be alphabets. The partial order $\leq_\Delta$ on Σ^* is defined as follows: $v \leq_\Delta w$ if there exist $k \geq 0$, words $v_1, \ldots, v_k \in \Sigma^*$, and words $u_1, \ldots, u_{k+1} \in \Delta^*$, such that $v = v_1 \ldots v_k$ and $w = u_1 v_1 u_2 v_2 \ldots . u_k v_k u_{k+1}$. In other words, $v \leq_\Delta w$ if v can be obtained from w by erasing in w some of the occurrences of symbols from Δ.

The pumping lemma for context-free languages provides us (in an effective way) with finite test sets of the desired form.

Lemma 4.2.6. *Let $K \subseteq \Sigma^*$ be a context-free language and let Δ be an alphabet such that $\mathbf{eras}_\Delta(K)$ is finite. Let p be a pumping constant for K, and let $L = \{w \in K \mid |w| \leq p\}$. Then, for all $z \in K$, there exists a $t \in L$ such that $t \leq_\Delta$ z.*

Proof. Assume to the contrary that there exists a word $z \in K$ such that, for all $t \in L$, *not* $t \leq_\Delta z$. Let z be a shortest word with this property. Then $z \notin L$, because of the reflexivity of $\leq_\Delta$; therefore $|z| >$ p. Hence $z = uvwxy$, for some words u, v, w, x, y such that (1) $vx \neq \Lambda$, and (2) for all $i \geq 0, uv^i wx^i y \in$ K. Since $\{\mathbf{eras}_\Delta(uv^i wx^i y) | i \geq 0\} \subseteq \mathbf{eras}_\Delta(K)$ is finite, both $v \in \Delta^*$ and $x \in \Delta^*$. Hence $uwy \leq_\Delta z$ and, by transitivity of $\leq_\Delta$, there does *not* exist a $t \in L$ such that $t \leq_\Delta uwy$. Since $|uwy| < |z|$ this leads to a contradiction with the assumed minimality of $| z |$. □

Since for each context-free language, a pumping constant p and a language L as in the statement of Lemma 4.2.6 can be effectively determined ([HopUll79], Lemma 6.1), and since $\mathbf{eras}_{\mathbf{free}(i)}(K_i)$ is finite for each K_i, this leads to:

Corollary 4.2.7. *For all $i \in [m]$, there exists effectively a finite subset L_i of K_i such that, for all $z \in K_i$, there is a $t \in L_i$ with the property that $t \leq_{\mathbf{free}(i)} z$.* □

Let $L_1, \ldots, L_m$ be as in Corollary 4.2.7.
The emptiness of $V = (\times_{i=1}^{m} K_i) - \Theta^{\otimes}$ can now be decided as follows.

Lemma 4.2.8.($\times_{i=1}^{m} K_i) - \Theta^{\otimes}$ *is empty if and only if* $(\times_{i=1}^{m} L_i) - \Theta^{\otimes}$ *is empty.*
Proof. The only-if-part is trivial.
For the if-part, assume that $(w_1, \ldots, w_m) \in (\times_{i=1}^{m} K_i) - \Theta^{\otimes}$. By Corollary 4.2.7, there exists a word vector $(v_1, \ldots, v_m) \in (\times_{i=1}^{m} L_i)$ such that $v_i \leq_{\mathbf{free}(i)} w_i$ for all $i \in [m]$. The assumption that $(v_1, \ldots, v_m) \in \Theta^{\otimes}$, would imply that $(w_1, \ldots, w_m) \in \Theta^{\otimes}$, because the latter word vector can be obtained from the former by (suitably) inserting free letters to each of the components. Hence $(v_1, \ldots, v_m) \notin \Theta^{\otimes}$. □

Since $\times_{i=1}^{m} L_i$ is finite, the emptiness of $(\times_{i=1}^{m} L_i) - \Theta^{\otimes}$ is decidable and so the above lemma proves:

Corollary 4.2.9. *Let $\mathbf{K}_1, \ldots, \mathbf{K}_n, \mathbf{K}_{n+1} \in \mathcal{F}$ be such that $\bigcup_{i=1}^{m} \mathbf{K}_i \subseteq \mathbf{CF}$ and $\bigcup_{i=m+1}^{n+1} \mathbf{K}_i$ $= \mathbf{Mon}$. Then the emptiness problem for m-$\mathbf{Loss}(\mathbf{K}_1, \ldots, \mathbf{K}_n; \mathbf{K}_{n+1})$ is decidable.* □

The decidability of the finiteness of $(\times_{i=1}^{m} K_i) - \Theta^{\otimes}$ is based on the following (three-step) reduction.

Lemma 4.2.10.(1)($\times_{i=1}^{m} K_i) - \Theta^{\otimes}$ *is finite if and only if, for all $i \in [m]$, $(L_1 \times \ldots \times L_{i-1} \times K_i \times L_{i+1} \times \ldots \times L_m) - \Theta^{\otimes}$ is finite.*
(2) *Let $j \in [m]$. Then $(L_1 \times \ldots \times L_{j-1} \times K_j \times L_{j+1} \times \ldots \times L_m) - \Theta^{\otimes}$ is finite if and only if $(\{w_1\} \times \ldots \times \{w_{j-1}\} \times K_j \times \{w_{j+1}\} \times \ldots \times \{w_m\}) - \Theta^{\otimes}$ is finite, for all $(w_1, \ldots, w_m) \in (\times_{i=1}^{m} L_i)$.*
(3) *Let $j \in [m]$. Then $(\{w_1\} \times \ldots \times \{w_{j-1}\} \times K_j \times \{w_{j+1}\} \times \ldots \times \{w_m\}) - \Theta^{\otimes}$ is finite if and only if the context-free language K_j - $\mathbf{proj}_j((\{w_1\} \times \ldots \times \{w_{j-1}\} \times \Sigma_j^* \times \{w_{j+1}\} \times \ldots \times \{w_m\}) \cap \Theta^{\otimes})$ is finite.*
Proof. (1) The only-if-part is trivial.
For the if-part, assume that $(\times_{i=1}^{m} K_i) - \Theta^{\otimes}$ is infinite. Then there exists a $j \in [m]$ and an infinite set $U \subseteq (\times_{i=1}^{m} K_i) - \Theta^{\otimes}$ such that $\mathbf{proj}_j(U)$ is infinite. From the definition of $L_1, \ldots, L_m$ it follows that, for each word vector $w = (w_1, \ldots, w_m) \in (\times_{i=1}^{m} K_i)$, there exists a word vector $v_w = (v_1, \ldots, v_{j-1}, w_j, v_{j+1}, \ldots, v_m) \in (L_1 \times \ldots \times L_{j-1} \times K_j \times L_{j+1} \times \ldots \times L_m)$ such that $v_i \leq_{\mathbf{free}(i)} w_i$ for all $i \in [m] - \{j\}$. Since v_w is obtained from w by erasing free letters, it follows that $v_w \notin \Theta^{\otimes}$ whenever $w \notin \Theta^{\otimes}$. Thus the set $V = \{v_w | w \in U\}$ is an infinite subset of $(L_1 \times \ldots \times L_{j-1} \times K_j \times L_{j+1} \ldots \times L_m) - \Theta^{\otimes}$.
(2) Obvious, because each of the L_i is finite.

(3) Set $M = (\{w_1\} \times \ldots \times \{w_{j-1}\} \times \Sigma_j^* \times \{w_{j+1}\} \times \ldots \times \{w_m\})$ and set $N = (\{w_1\} \times \ldots \times \{w_{j-1}\} \times K_j \times \{w_{j+1}\} \times \ldots \times \{w_m\})$. Then $N - \Theta^{\otimes} = N - (M \cap \Theta^{\otimes})$.(Recall that $K_j \subseteq \Sigma_j^*$.) Since $M \cap \Theta^{\otimes} = (\{w_1\} \times \ldots \times \{w_{j-1}\} \times \mathbf{proj}_j(M \cap \Theta^{\otimes}) \times \{w_{j+1}\} \times \ldots \times \{w_m\}$, it follows that $N - \Theta^{\otimes} = (\{w_1\} \times \ldots \times \{w_{j-1}\} \times (K_j \text{ - } \mathbf{proj}_j(M \cap \Theta^{\otimes})) \times \{w_{j+1}\} \times \ldots \times \{w_m\})$ and hence $N - \Theta^{\otimes}$ is finite if and only if K_j - $\mathbf{proj}_j(M \cap \Theta^*)$ is finite. Since K_j is context-free and since $\mathbf{proj}_j(M \cap \Theta^{\otimes}) = \mathbf{proj}_{\Theta^\bullet,j}(\bigcap_{i=1}^{j-1} \mathbf{proj}_{\Theta^\bullet,i}^{-1}(\{w_i\}) \cap \mathbf{proj}_{\Theta^\bullet,j}^{-1}(\Sigma_j^*) \cap \bigcap_{i=j+1}^{m} \mathbf{proj}_{\Theta^\bullet,i}^{-1}(\{w_i\}) \cap \Theta^*)$ is regular, it follows that K_j - $\mathbf{proj}_j(M \cap \Theta^{\otimes})$ is (effectively) context-free. □

Since finiteness of (effectively given) context-free languages is decidable, the above lemma proves the decidability of the finiteness of $(\times_{j=1}^{m} K_j) - \Theta^{\otimes}$. Note that for the effectiveness of step (2) above the finiteness of the L_i is essential.

Corollary 4.2.11. *Let* $\mathbf{K}_1, \ldots, \mathbf{K}_n, \mathbf{K}_{n+1} \in \mathcal{F}$ *be such that* $\bigcup_{i=1}^{m} \mathbf{K}_i \subseteq \mathbf{CF}$ *and* $\bigcup_{i=m+1}^{n+1} \mathbf{K}_i = \mathbf{Mon}$. *Then the finiteness problem for* m-$\mathbf{Loss}(\mathbf{K}_1, \ldots, \mathbf{K}_n; \mathbf{K}_{n+1})$ *is decidable.* □

Summarizing Lemma 4.2.2, Lemma 4.2.4, Corollary 4.2.9, and Corollary 4.2.11 yields:

Theorem 4.2.12. *The finiteness (emptiness) problem for* m-$\mathbf{Loss}(\mathbf{K}_1, \ldots, \mathbf{K}_n; \mathbf{K}_{n+1})$, *where* $m \in [n] - [1]$, *and* $\mathbf{K}_1, \ldots, \mathbf{K}_n, \mathbf{K}_{n+1} \in \mathcal{F}$, *is decidable if and only if* $\bigcup_{i=1}^{m} \mathbf{K}_i \subseteq \mathbf{CF}$ *and* $\bigcup_{i=m+1}^{n+1} \mathbf{K}_i = \mathbf{Mon}$. □

5. COMPLETENESS

In the development of the framework of VCCSs as a model for the description and analysis of concurrent systems the completeness notion has played a prominent role. Initially developed as a (structural) property of the net-based control mechanisms of [KeeKleRoz90], the so-called Individual Token Net Controllers or ITNCs, it has (later) been characterized in [KeeKle89] as a property of vector languages. Recall that in a VCCS it is the collapse of the control language rather than the control language itself that is used to express the synchronization constraints of the control mechanism (see Definition 2.2).

The use of a control (vector) language in addition to the synchronization alphabet may induce extra "hidden" synchronizations: synchronizations that are not expressed or expressible by synchronization vectors from the synchronization alphabet. Consider, e.g., a 2-VCCS $W = (K_1, K_2; (\Theta, M))$ with $K_1 = \{\Lambda, a\}, K_2 = \{\Lambda, b, cc\}, \Theta = \{\binom{a}{\Lambda}, \binom{\Lambda}{b}\}$, and $M = \{\binom{a}{\Lambda}, \binom{\Lambda}{b}\}$. In this system the synchronization alphabet Θ does not require synchronization between the component actions a and b. However, concurrent execution of both actions is prohibited by $\mathbf{coll}(M) = M$. Intuitively completeness prescribes the absence of these hidden synchronizations: a vector language is complete if together with every pair of independent word vectors, representing independent system computations, it also contains the word vector representing their concurrent combination. In the little example above, in order to be complete, $\mathbf{coll}(M)$ should also contain $\binom{a}{b}$. In addition completeness also deals with the absence of hidden synchronizations in the case of empty computations: if every component of the system has the possibility of successfully 'doing nothing' then the system as a whole should have this possibility as well. In terms of the example, this means that **coll**(M) should contain $\binom{\Lambda}{\Lambda}$, as each of the components is allowed by M to be inactive.

Two n-dimensional word vectors w_1 and w_2 are said to be *independent* if, for all $i \in [n]$, $\mathbf{proj}_i(w_1) = \Lambda$ or $\mathbf{proj}_i(w_2) = \Lambda$. The formal definition of completeness ([KeeKle89]) is then:

Definition 5.1. An n-dimensional vector language V is *complete*, if the following two conditions are satisfied:
(1) if $w_1, w_2 \in V$ are independent, then $w_1 \odot w_2 \in V$, and
(2) if, for every $i \in [n]$, $\Lambda \in \mathbf{proj}_i(V)$, then $\bar{\Lambda} \in V$. □

In general the complete vector languages within a family of vector languages form a strict subset of this family. In [KeeKle89] the effect of the completeness property has been investigated for a number of families of vector languages associated with certain classes of control mechanisms. Also the effect of having "complete" control mechanisms on the behaviour of VCCSs has been investigated. In this section we investigate the effect of this property on (vector) residues and (vector) losses.

In order to facilitate our terminology we extend the notion of completeness to languages: a language K over a vector alphabet is said to be *complete* if the vector language **coll**(K) is complete. In this way we can speak about VCCSs with complete control languages or complete VCCSs, for short. Note that the vector language of a VCCS with complete control language is again complete (this follows directly from Definition 2.2), but that a VCCS with a complete vector language does not necessarily have a complete control language.

For language families $\mathbf{K}_1, \ldots, \mathbf{K}_n, \mathbf{K}_{n+1}$, we set $\mathbf{Res}_c(\mathbf{K}_1, \ldots, \mathbf{K}_n; \mathbf{K}_{n+1}) = \{\mathbf{res}(W)$ $|W$ is a complete n-VCCS of type $(\mathbf{K}_1, \ldots, \mathbf{K}_n; \mathbf{K}_{n+1})\}$, and similarly m-$\mathbf{Res}_c(\mathbf{K}_1, \ldots, \mathbf{K}_n;$ $\mathbf{K}_{n+1})$, $\mathbf{Loss}_c(\mathbf{K}_1, \ldots, \mathbf{K}_n; \mathbf{K}_{n+1})$, and m-$\mathbf{Loss}_c(\mathbf{K}_1, \ldots, \mathbf{K}_n; \mathbf{K}_{n+1})$ denote the families of, respectively, m-dimensional residues, losses, and m-dimensional losses of VCCS of type $(\mathbf{K}_1, \ldots, \mathbf{K}_n; \mathbf{K}_{n+1})$ with complete control languages.

Like in Sections 3 and 4 we study, for $\mathbf{K}_1, \ldots, \mathbf{K}_n, \mathbf{K}_{n+1} \in \mathcal{F}$, the language hierarchical properties of $\mathbf{Res}_c(\mathbf{K}_1, \ldots, \mathbf{K}_n; \mathbf{K}_{n+1})$ and $\mathbf{Loss}_c(\mathbf{K}_1, \ldots, \mathbf{K}_n; \mathbf{K}_{n+1})$ and the decidability of the emptiness and the finiteness problem for $\mathbf{Res}_c(\mathbf{K}_1, \ldots, \mathbf{K}_n; \mathbf{K}_{n+1})$, m-$\mathbf{Res}_c(\mathbf{K}_1, \ldots, \mathbf{K}_n; \mathbf{K}_{n+1})$, $\mathbf{Loss}_c(\mathbf{K}_1, \ldots, \mathbf{K}_n; \mathbf{K}_{n+1})$, and m-$\mathbf{Loss}_c(\mathbf{K}_1, \ldots, \mathbf{K}_n; \mathbf{K}_{n+1})$.

For one-dimensional vector languages the property of completeness is trivial: *every* one-dimensional vector language is complete. Clearly, this implies that, for $n = 1$, for the class of VCCSs and hence for the corresponding families of residues and losses having a complete control language is not a restriction. In particular we have the following versions of Corollary 3.1.(1) and Corollary 4.1.1.(1): $\mathbf{Res}_c(\mathbf{K}_1; \mathbf{K}_2) = \mathbf{K}_1 \wedge \mathbf{K}_2$ and $\mathbf{Loss}_c(\mathbf{K}_1; \mathbf{K}_2) = \mathbf{K}_1 \backslash \mathbf{K}_2$ for all families $\mathbf{K}_1, \mathbf{K}_2$ of languages. As a consequence of this all, classification results and decidability results for (1-dimensional) residues and (1-dimensional) losses can be carried over from the general case.

Completeness, however, is non-trivial for dimensions higher than 1. In the rest of this section we therefore assume that $n \geq 2$.

For the language classification of $\mathbf{Res}_c(\mathbf{K}_1, \ldots, \mathbf{K}_n; \mathbf{K}_{n+1})$ and $\mathbf{Loss}_c(\mathbf{K}_1, \ldots, \mathbf{K}_n; \mathbf{K}_{n+1})$ for $\mathbf{K}_1, \ldots, \mathbf{K}_n, \mathbf{K}_{n+1} \in \mathcal{F}$ we use the following analogue of Theorem 2.9.

Theorem 5.2. *Let* $\mathbf{K}_1, \ldots, \mathbf{K}_n$, *and* $\mathbf{K}$ *be families of languages. If there is a* $j \in [n] - [1]$ *such that* $\mathbf{K}_j$ *is closed under inverse weak codings, then*
(1) $\mathbf{Res}_c(\mathbf{K}_1, \ldots, \mathbf{K}_n; \mathbf{K}) = \mathbf{K}_1 \wedge \mathbf{WCod}(\mathbf{WCod}^{-1}(\mathbf{K}_2) \wedge \ldots \wedge \mathbf{WCod}^{-1}(\mathbf{K}_n) \wedge \mathbf{K})$ *,and*
(2) $\mathbf{Loss}_c(\mathbf{K}_1, \ldots, \mathbf{K}_n; \mathbf{K}) = \mathbf{K}_1 \backslash \mathbf{WCod}(\mathbf{WCod}^{-1}(\mathbf{K}_2) \wedge \ldots \wedge \mathbf{WCod}^{-1}(\mathbf{K}_n) \wedge \mathbf{K})$.
Proof. The inclusions from the left hand sides in the right hand sides follow directly from Theorem 2.9, because $\mathbf{Res}_c(\mathbf{K}_1, \ldots, \mathbf{K}_n; \mathbf{K}) \subseteq \mathbf{Res}(\mathbf{K}_1, \ldots, \mathbf{K}_n; \mathbf{K})$ and $\mathbf{Loss}_c(\mathbf{K}_1, \ldots, \mathbf{K}_n; \mathbf{K}) \subseteq \mathbf{Loss}(\mathbf{K}_1, \ldots, \mathbf{K}_n; \mathbf{K})$.
The converse inclusions follow from Corollary 2.8, similarly as in the proof of Theorem 2.9, because the VCCS W constructed in the statement of Corollary 2.8 always has a complete control language $\tau(K)$: from the definition of the distributed weak coding τ it follows that every non-empty word vector of $\mathbf{coll}(\tau(K))$ has a non-empty j-th component. □

And its corollary:

Corollary 5.3. *Let* $\mathbf{K}_1, \ldots, \mathbf{K}_n, \mathbf{K}_{n+1}$ *be families of languages from* $\mathcal{F}$.
(1) $\mathbf{Res}_c(\mathbf{K}_1, \ldots, \mathbf{K}_n; \mathbf{K}_{n+1}) = \mathbf{K}_1 \wedge \mathbf{WCod}(\mathbf{K}_1 \wedge \ldots \wedge \mathbf{K}_n \wedge \mathbf{K}_{n+1})$.
(2) $\mathbf{Loss}_c(\mathbf{K}_1, \ldots, \mathbf{K}_n; \mathbf{K}_{n+1}) = \mathbf{K}_1 \backslash \mathbf{WCod}(\mathbf{K}_1 \wedge \ldots \wedge \mathbf{K}_n \wedge \mathbf{K}_{n+1})$. □

Thus, by Corollary 3.1.(2) and Corollary 4.1.1.(2), for all $\mathbf{K}_1, \ldots, \mathbf{K}_n, \mathbf{K}_{n+1} \in \mathcal{F}$, we have that $\mathbf{Res}_c(\mathbf{K}_1, \ldots, \mathbf{K}_n; \mathbf{K}_{n+1}) = \mathbf{Res}(\mathbf{K}_1, \ldots, \mathbf{K}_n; \mathbf{K}_{n+1})$ and $\mathbf{Loss}_c(\mathbf{K}_1, \ldots, \mathbf{K}_n; \mathbf{K}_{n+1}) = \mathbf{Loss}(\mathbf{K}_1, \ldots, \mathbf{K}_n; \mathbf{K}_{n+1})$. Consequently the classification results of Section 3 and Section 4 carry over without any change and hence Tables 3.2 and 4.1.2 apply here as well.

Since the decidability results for $\mathbf{Res}(\mathbf{K}_1, \ldots, \mathbf{K}_n; \mathbf{K}_{n+1})$ and $\mathbf{Loss}(\mathbf{K}_1, \ldots, \mathbf{K}_n; \mathbf{K}_{n+1})$, for $\mathbf{K}_1, \ldots, \mathbf{K}_n, \mathbf{K}_{n+1} \in \mathcal{F}$, (and their one-dimensional counterparts) were directly derived from the language classification results, these results can also be carried over without change. Thus we obtain:

Theorem 5.4. (1) *The finiteness (emptiness) problem for* 1-$\mathbf{Res}_c(\mathbf{K}_1, \ldots, \mathbf{K}_n; \mathbf{K}_{n+1})$, *where* $\mathbf{K}_1, \ldots, \mathbf{K}_n, \mathbf{K}_{n+1} \in \mathcal{F}$, *is decidable if and only if there exists a* $j \in [n+1]$ *such that* $\mathbf{K}_j \subseteq \mathbf{CF}$ *and* $\bigcup_{i=1, i \neq j}^{n+1} \mathbf{K}_i \subseteq \mathbf{Reg}$.
(2) *The finiteness (emptiness) problem for* 1-$\mathbf{Loss}_c(\mathbf{K}_1, \ldots, \mathbf{K}_n; \mathbf{K}_{n+1})$, *where* $\mathbf{K}_1, \ldots, \mathbf{K}_n, \mathbf{K}_{n+1} \in \mathcal{F}$, *is decidable if and only if* $\mathbf{K}_1 \subseteq \mathbf{CF}$ *and* $\bigcup_{i=2}^{n+1} \mathbf{K}_i \subseteq \mathbf{Reg}$. □

For the higher dimensional residues and losses we proceed as follows. Assume, for the rest of this section, that $m \in [n] - [1]$.

For m-$\mathbf{Res}_c(\mathbf{K}_1, \ldots, \mathbf{K}_n; \mathbf{K}_{n+1})$, where $\mathbf{K}_1, \ldots, \mathbf{K}_n, \mathbf{K}_{n+1} \in \mathcal{F}$, we obtain the same characterization as in Section 3 for the decidability of the emptiness and the finiteness problem. For the emptiness problem this follows directly from Theorem 5.4.(1) using the same argumentation as was used in Section 3 to prove Theorem 3.4. The characterization for the finiteness problem is obtained by using the same argumentation as was used in Section 3 to prove Theorem 3.5: the result for the decidable cases follows immediately; for the undecidable cases it suffices to note that control language $\sigma(K_{n+1})$ obtained in the

reduction described in Section 3 is complete, because $\sigma = \mathbf{id}_\Sigma \otimes \ldots \otimes \mathbf{id}_\Sigma$.
Thus:

Theorem 5.5. *The finiteness (emptiness) problem for* m-$\mathbf{Res}_c(\mathbf{K}_1, \ldots, \mathbf{K}_n; \mathbf{K}_{n+1})$, *where* $\mathbf{K}_1, \ldots, \mathbf{K}_n, \mathbf{K}_{n+1} \in \mathcal{F}$, *is decidable if and only if there exists a* $j \in [n+1]$ *such that* $\mathbf{K}_j \subseteq \mathbf{CF}$ *and* $\bigcup_{i=1, i \neq j}^{n+1} \mathbf{K}_i \subseteq \mathbf{Reg}$. □

For m-$\mathbf{Loss}_c(\mathbf{K}_1, \ldots, \mathbf{K}_n; \mathbf{K}_{n+1})$, where $\mathbf{K}_1, \ldots, \mathbf{K}_n, \mathbf{K}_{n+1} \in \mathcal{F}$, we obtain a characterization which is slightly different from the one in Section 4.2 and for some of the cases we have to give fresh proofs.

Obviously, since we are dealing with a subproblem, the results of Section 4.2 for the decidable cases carry over directly.

Lemma 5.6. *Let* $\mathbf{K}_1, \ldots, \mathbf{K}_n, \mathbf{K}_{n+1} \in \mathcal{F}$ *be such that* $\bigcup_{i=1}^{m} \mathbf{K}_i \subseteq \mathbf{CF}$ *and* $\bigcup_{i=m+1}^{n+1} \mathbf{K}_i = \mathbf{Mon}$. *Then the finiteness (emptiness) problem for* m-$\mathbf{Loss}_c(\mathbf{K}_1, \ldots, \mathbf{K}_n; \mathbf{K}_{n+1})$ *is decidable.* □

For some of the undecidable cases the results of Section 4.2 can be carried over because the corresponding argumentation can be carried over. In particular this holds for Transformation 4.2.1: applying it to a VCCS W with a complete control language yields a VCCS W' which again has a complete control language. Thus, using a reasoning similar to the one in the proof of Lemma 4.2.2, we obtain from Theorem 5.4.(2):

Lemma 5.7. *Let* $\mathbf{K}_1, \ldots, \mathbf{K}_n, \mathbf{K}_{n+1} \in \mathcal{F}$ *and let* $j \in [m]$ *be such that* $\mathbf{CS} \subseteq \mathbf{K}_j$. *The finiteness (emptiness) problem for* m-$\mathbf{Loss}_c(\mathbf{K}_1, \ldots, \mathbf{K}_n; \mathbf{K}_{n+1})$ *is undecidable.* □

Since in **Mon** all languages over vector alphabets are complete, Transformation 4.2.3 can also be carried over to this section for the case that $j \in [n] - [m]$. Thus we obtain as in Lemma 4.2.4:

Lemma 5.8. *Let* $\mathbf{K}_1, \ldots, \mathbf{K}_n, \mathbf{K}_{n+1} \in \mathcal{F}$ *and let* $j \in [n] - [m]$ *be such that* $\mathbf{Reg} \subseteq \mathbf{K}_j$. *Then the finiteness (emptiness) problem for* m-$\mathbf{Loss}_c(\mathbf{K}_1, \ldots, \mathbf{K}_n; \mathbf{K}_{n+1})$ *is undecidable.*
□

It remains to determine the decidability of the emptiness and finiteness problem for m-$\mathbf{Loss}_c(\mathbf{K}_1, \ldots, \mathbf{K}_n; \mathbf{K}_{n+1})$ for the cases satisfying:
$\bigcup_{i=1}^{m} \mathbf{K}_i \subseteq \mathbf{CF}, \bigcup_{i=m+1}^{n} \mathbf{K}_i = \mathbf{Mon}$, and $\mathbf{Reg} \subseteq \mathbf{K}_{n+1}$. For this mainly new reductions and new proofs are needed.

For the case that $m < n$, we obtain the undecidability of the emptiness and finiteness problem for all the remaining cases. To prove this, a (new) reduction from the corresponding non-complete case is used (see Lemma 5.9).

For the case that $m = n$, we obtain the following:

(1) for $\mathbf{Lin} \subseteq \mathbf{K}_{n+1}$, undecidability is proved, by application of Transformation 4.2.1 (see Lemma 5.10);

(2) for $\mathbf{K}_{n+1} = \mathbf{Reg}$ and $\mathbf{Reg} \subseteq \bigcup_{i=1}^{n} \mathbf{K}_i$, undecidability is proved, by a reduction from the finiteness (emptiness) problem for (a variation of) complements of rational relations,

viz. by Lemma 1.4.(2) (see Lemma 5.11);

(3) for $\mathbf{K}_{n+1} = \mathbf{Reg}$ and $\bigcup_{i=1}^{n} \mathbf{K}_i = \mathbf{Mon}$, decidability is proved, by a direct (constructive) proof (see Lemma 5.12).

Lemma 5.9. *Let $m < n$ and let $\mathbf{K}_1, \ldots, \mathbf{K}_n, \mathbf{K}_{n+1} \in \mathcal{F}$ be such that $\mathbf{Reg} \subseteq \mathbf{K}_{n+1}$. Then the finiteness (emptiness) problem for m-$\mathbf{Loss}_c(\mathbf{K}_1, \ldots, \mathbf{K}_n; \mathbf{K}_{n+1})$ is undecidable.*

Proof. Given the m-VCCS $W = (K_1, \ldots, K_m; (\Theta, M))$ of type (**Mon**,...,**Mon**;**Reg**), let W' be the n-VCCS $W' = (K_1, \ldots, K_m, \{a\}^*, \emptyset^*, \ldots, \emptyset^*; (\epsilon(\Theta), \epsilon(M)))$ where ϵ is the homomorphism mapping each m-dimensional vector letter $(\alpha_1, \ldots, \alpha_m)$ to the n-dimensional vector letter $(\alpha_1, \ldots, \alpha_m, a, \Lambda, \ldots, \Lambda)$. Then $\epsilon(M)$ is a complete regular language over an n-dimensional vector alphabet, and hence W' is an n-VCCS of type $(\mathbf{K}_1, \ldots, \mathbf{K}_n; \mathbf{K}_{n+1})$ with a complete control language. Since m-**loss**$(W') = m$-**loss**(W) and, by Lemma 4.2.4, the finiteness (emptiness) problem for m-**Loss**(**Mon**,...,**Mon**;**Reg**) is undecidable, this proves the lemma. □

Lemma 5.10. *Let $\mathbf{K}_1, \ldots, \mathbf{K}_n, \mathbf{K}_{n+1} \in \mathcal{F}$ be such that $\mathbf{Lin} \subseteq \mathbf{K}_{n+1}$. Then the finiteness (emptiness) problem for m-$\mathbf{Loss}_c(\mathbf{K}_1, \ldots, \mathbf{K}_n; \mathbf{K}_{n+1})$ is undecidable.*

Proof. Given an $(n - m + 1)$-VCCS W of type (**Mon**,...,**Mon**;**Lin**) with a complete control language, we obtain, using Transformation 4.2.1, an n-VCCS W^1 of type $(\mathbf{K}_1, \ldots, \mathbf{K}_n; \mathbf{K}_{n+1})$ with a complete control language such that m-**loss**(W^1) is finite (empty) if and only if 1-**loss**(W) is finite (empty). This reduction proves the lemma, because, by Theorem 5.4.(2), the finiteness (emptiness) problem for 1-$\mathbf{Loss}_c$(**Mon**,...,**Mon**; **Lin**) is undecidable. □

Lemma 5.11. *Let $\mathbf{K}_1, \ldots, \mathbf{K}_n, \mathbf{K}_{n+1} \in \mathcal{F}$ be such that $\mathbf{Reg} \subseteq \mathbf{K}_{n+1}$ and $\mathbf{Reg} \subseteq \mathbf{K}_j$ for a $j \in [n]$. Then the finiteness (emptiness) problem for n-$\mathbf{Loss}_c(\mathbf{K}_1, \ldots, \mathbf{K}_n; \mathbf{K}_{n+1})$ is undecidable.*

Proof. The proof is given for $j = 1$; for $j \neq 1$, the lemma can be proved using component permutation.

Given alphabets Σ_1 and Σ_2 and a regular language R over $\Theta = \mathbf{Tot}(\Sigma_1, \Sigma_2)$, let the n-VCCS $W = (\Sigma_1^+, \Sigma_2^*, \ldots, \Sigma_2^*; (\epsilon(\Theta), R'))$ where ϵ is the homomorphism mapping each 2-dimensional vector letter (α_1, α_2) to the n-dimensional vector letter $(\alpha_1, \alpha_2, \ldots, \alpha_2)$ and where R' is the regular language over $\epsilon(\Theta)$ such that $\mathbf{coll}(R') = \mathbf{coll}(\epsilon(R)) \cap (\Sigma_1^+ \times \Sigma_2^* \times \ldots \times \Sigma_2^*)$. Since the intersection of the recognizable set $(\Sigma_1^+ \times \Sigma_2^* \times \ldots \times \Sigma_2^*)$ with the rational relation $\mathbf{coll}(\epsilon(R))$ is a rational relation again, such a regular language exists. Now R' is complete, because every non-empty word from R' has a non-empty first component. Hence W is an n-VCCS of type $(\mathbf{K}_1, \ldots, \mathbf{K}_n; \mathbf{K}_{n+1})$ with a complete control language and moreover m-**loss**(W) is finite (empty) if and only if $(\Sigma_1^+ \times \Sigma_2^*) - \mathbf{coll}(R)$ is finite (empty). By Lemma 1.4.(2), this proves the lemma. □

The use of Σ_1^+ (instead of Σ_1^*) in the proof of Lemma 5.11 is essential as is shown in the following lemma which proves that using Σ_1^* yields decidability of both the corresponding finiteness and emptiness problem.

The proof for the finiteness problem below uses induction on n. The proof for the corresponding emptiness problem does not need this induction on n, but to save writing space and reading time it has been "merged" with the other proof, thus obtaining for the emptiness problem a slightly more complicated proof than necessary.

Lemma 5.12. *Let* $\mathbf{K}_1, \ldots, \mathbf{K}_n, \mathbf{K}_{n+1} \in \mathcal{F}$ *be such that* $\mathbf{K}_{n+1} = \mathbf{Reg}$ *and such that* $\bigcup_{i=1}^{n} \mathbf{K}_i = \mathbf{Mon}$. *Then the finiteness (emptiness) problem for* n-$\mathbf{Loss}_c(\mathbf{K}_1, \ldots, \mathbf{K}_n; \mathbf{K}_{n+1})$ *is decidable.*

Proof. The statement is proved by induction on n. For $n = 1$, the problem reduces to the finiteness (emptiness) problem of the complement of a regular language, which is decidable. In this case the statement also follows from Theorem 5.4.(2).

Assume now that the above finiteness (emptiness) problem is decidable up to dimension $n-1$. We prove then that it is decidable for dimension n.

Let $W = (\Sigma_1^*, \ldots, \Sigma_n^*; (\Theta, R'))$ be an n-VCCS of type (Mon,...,Mon;Reg) such that $R = \mathbf{coll}(R')$ is complete and let $T = n\text{-}\mathbf{loss}(W) = (\times_{i=1}^{n} \Sigma_i^*) - R$. Without loss of generality we may assume that $R \subseteq \times_{i=1}^{n} \Sigma_i^*$, because the rational relations are closed under intersection with a recognizable set (such as $\times_{i=1}^{n} \Sigma_i^*$).

Set, for $i \in [n], L_i = \mathbf{proj}_i(R \cap (\{\Lambda\} \times \ldots \times \{\Lambda\} \times \Sigma_i^* \times \{\Lambda\} \times \ldots \times \{\Lambda\})$ and set $M_i = \Sigma_i^* - L_i$. By the completeness of R, it follows that $(L_1 \times \ldots \times L_n) \subseteq$ R. Denote, for all $i \in [n]$ and all $N \subseteq \Sigma_i^*$, $\Sigma_1^* \times \ldots \times \Sigma_{i-1}^* \times N \times \Sigma_{i+1}^* \times \ldots \times \Sigma_n^*$ by $[N]_i$. Then $T = \bigcup_{i=1}^{n}([M_i]_i - R)$. It is clear that $[M_i]_i - R = \bigcup_{w \in M_i}([\{w\}]_i - R_i)$ where $R_i = R \cap [\{w\}]_i$, for all $i \in [n]$. Since $[\{w\}]_i - R_i$ contains the word vector $(\Lambda, \ldots, \Lambda, w, \Lambda, \ldots, \Lambda)$ it is not empty. Hence if M_i is not finite (not empty) for at least one $i \in [n]$, then T is not finite (not empty). Since, for each $i \in [n], M_i$ is regular, this is decidable and it only remains to consider T in case M_i is finite (empty) for all $i \in [n]$.

If, for each $i \in [n], M_i$ is finite (empty), then T is finite (empty) if and only if, for all of the words w of the finite (empty) set $\bigcup_{i=1}^{n} M_i, [\{w\}]_i - R_i$ is finite (empty). Now $[\{w\}]_i - R_i$ is finite (empty) if and only if $(\Sigma_1^* \times \ldots \times \Sigma_{i-1}^* \times \Sigma_{i+1}^* \times \ldots \times \Sigma_n^*)$ - $\mathbf{proj}_{[n]-\{i\}}(R_i)$ is finite (empty); here $\mathbf{proj}_{[n]-\{i\}}(R_i) = \{(w_1, \ldots, w_{i-1}, w_{i+1}, \ldots, w_n) \mid (w_1, \ldots, w_n) \in R_i\}$. Since the latter is decidable by the induction hypothesis, the lemma follows: the finiteness (emptiness) of T is decidable. □

Summarizing Lemma 5.6, Lemma 5.7, Lemma 5.8, Lemma 5.9, Lemma 5.10, Lemma 5.11, and Lemma 5.12 we obtain:

Theorem 5.13. *The finiteness (emptiness) problem for* m-$\mathbf{Loss}_c(\mathbf{K}_1, \ldots, \mathbf{K}_n; \mathbf{K}_{n+1})$, *where* $m \in [n] - [1]$ *and* $\mathbf{K}_1, \ldots, \mathbf{K}_n, \mathbf{K}_{n+1} \in \mathcal{F}$, *is decidable if and only if*
(1) $\bigcup_{i=1}^{m} \mathbf{K}_i \subseteq \mathbf{CF}$ *and* $\bigcup_{i=m+1}^{n+1} \mathbf{K}_i = \mathbf{Mon}$, *or*
(2) $m = n, \bigcup_{i=1}^{n} \mathbf{K}_i = \mathbf{Mon}$, *and* $\mathbf{K}_{n+1} = \mathbf{Reg}$. □

6. DISCUSSION

Within the framework of the VCCS model the new notions of residue and loss have been introduced. Residues and losses (and their vector counterparts) form a natural basis for the study of the effects of vector synchronization in concurrent systems. In this paper these effects have been investigated along two different lines.

In the first place a language classification has been made of residues and losses for various VCCS submodels. For each type $\mathbf{T} = (\mathbf{K}_1, \ldots, \mathbf{K}_n; \mathbf{K}_{n+1})$, where $\mathbf{K}_1, \ldots, \mathbf{K}_n, \mathbf{K}_{n+1}$

are chosen from the extended Chomsky hierarchy $\mathcal{F} = \{\mathbf{Mon}, \mathbf{Reg}, \mathbf{Lin}, \mathbf{CF}, \mathbf{CS}, \mathbf{RE}\}$, the language families $\mathbf{Res}(\mathbf{K}_1, \ldots, \mathbf{K}_n; \mathbf{K}_{n+1})$ and $\mathbf{Loss}(\mathbf{K}_1, \ldots, \mathbf{K}_n; \mathbf{K}_{n+1})$ of, respectively, residues and losses of VCCSs of type $\mathbf{T}$ have been determined. For $\mathbf{K}_1, \ldots, \mathbf{K}_n, \mathbf{K}_{n+1}$ contained in **Reg**, there is no increase in language complexity of neither $\mathbf{Res}(\mathbf{K}_1, \ldots, \mathbf{K}_n; \mathbf{K}_{n+1})$ nor $\mathbf{Loss}(\mathbf{K}_1, \ldots, \mathbf{K}_n; \mathbf{K}_{n+1})$; both families are as complex as the largest family among $\mathbf{K}_1, \ldots, \mathbf{K}_n, \mathbf{K}_{n+1}$. In many of the cases where one of $\mathbf{K}_1, \ldots, \mathbf{K}_n, \mathbf{K}_{n+1}$ contains **Lin**, however, a considerable increase in complexity is shown. Residues can be lifted up to the level of recursively enumerable languages even when $\bigcup_{i=1}^{n+1} \mathbf{K}_i \subseteq \mathbf{Lin}$. For losses even the level of $\mathbf{RE} \wedge$ co-$\mathbf{RE}$ is reached due to the occurrence of (set) complementation. The same use of complementation makes losses in general more complex than residues and harder to classify.

The second line of research of (vector) residues and (vector) losses concerned the study of decision problems. With respect to the same language hierarchy $\mathcal{F}$ a characterization of the decidability of the emptiness and finiteness problem of (vector) residues and (vector) losses has been obtained. Many of the (un)decidability results follow directly from the earlier determined language classifications. For losses however also some results from the theory of rational relations and some new proofs have been used to complete the characterization.

It turns out that, for each of the families investigated, the results for the emptiness and finiteness problem are the same. The decidability borderline is different, however, for (vector) residues and (vector) losses.

For vector residues the characterization is independent of the dimension of the residue: decidability is obtained if and only if at most one of the languages (component languages and/or control language) is context-free and the rest is regular.

For vector losses the situation is considerably different. In the first place 1-dimensional losses and higher dimensional losses give different decidability results for certain types of VCCSs. For instance, the emptiness and finiteness problems are decidable for 1-**Loss(Reg,...,Reg;Reg)** and undecidable for m-**Loss(Reg,...,Reg;Reg)** for all $m \geq 2$. This is due to the difference in computational complexity of complements of regular languages and complements of rational relations (of dimension at least 2). Secondly, again due to the use of complementation, for m-dimensional losses there has to be made a distinction between the "lower" part $\mathbf{K}_1, \ldots, \mathbf{K}_m$ and the "upper" part $\mathbf{K}_{m+1}, \ldots, \mathbf{K}_{n+1}$. Thus, e.g., we have decidability for m-**Loss(Lin,Mon,...,Mon;Mon)** and undecidability for m-**Loss(Mon,...,Mon;Lin)** for all $m \geq 1$.

In general, as with the language classification, losses are more complex than residues: usually whenever a residue family has undecidable emptiness and finiteness problems then these problems are also undecidable for the corresponding loss families. However, in case at least two families from $\mathbf{K}_1, \ldots, \mathbf{K}_m$ equal **CF**, while $\bigcup_{i=1}^{m} \mathbf{K}_i = \mathbf{CF}$, and $\mathbf{K}_{m+1} = \ldots = \mathbf{K}_{n+1} = \mathbf{Mon}$, then m-$\mathbf{Loss}(\mathbf{K}_1, \ldots, \mathbf{K}_n; \mathbf{K}_{n+1})$ has decidable emptiness and finiteness problems, whereas for m-$\mathbf{Res}(\mathbf{K}_1, \ldots, \mathbf{K}_n; \mathbf{K}_{n+1})$ both problems are undecidable.

Many of the VCCS submodels and many of the control mechanisms studied in [KeeKleRoz91] and [KeeKle89] have been covered here. In particular, the regular Generalized Individual Token Net Controlled Systems (regular GITNCSs) occur in this paper as VCCSs of type **(Reg,...,Reg;Reg)** and their vector languages are precisely all vector languages defined by VCCSs of this type. The type **(Reg,...,Reg;Mon)** characterizes the regular Vector Synchronized Systems (regular VSSs); further, the control mechanisms of GITNCSs and VSSs— or rather their vector languages—correspond to (the vector languages of) VCCSs of type (**Mon**,...,**Mon**;**Reg**) and of type (**Mon**,...,**Mon**;**Mon**) respectively (see also [KeeKle89]). The Individual Token Net Controlled Systems are covered in this paper in Section 5 where the combination of completeness with residues and losses is investigated. Thus the vector languages of the regular ITNCSs are the same as those generated by VCCSs of type (**Reg**,...,**Reg**;**Reg**) with complete control languages and the vector languages of the Individual Token Net Controllers coincide with the vector languages of the VCCSs of type (**Mon**,...,**Mon**;**Reg**) with complete control languages.

As it turns out completeness does not affect the language classification obtained for the general case. For (vector) residues the decidability border of the emptiness and finiteness problem (w.r.t. $\mathcal{F}$) is not different either. For (vector) losses, however, there is a difference in decidability, but only in one single case: if $m = n$, then, for m-$\mathbf{Loss}_c$(**Mon**,...,**Mon**;**Reg**) the two problems are decidable, whereas they are undecidable for m-**Loss**(**Mon**,...,**Mon**;**Reg**).

Rather disappointingly—as is proved in Theorem 6.1 below—completeness itself is an undecidable property for the important family of rational relations. This means, cf. Lemma 1.3, that for the family of vector languages of VCCSs of type (**Mon**,...,**Mon**;**Reg**) completeness is undecidable. Hence, given a Generalized Individual Token Net Controller, there is no procedure to determine whether or not it can be simulated by an Individual Token Net Controller.

Theorem 6.1. *Let* $n \geq 2$ *and let* $\mathbf{Reg} \subseteq \mathbf{K}$. *Then it is undecidable, for arbitrary* $K \in \mathbf{K}$ *over an n-dimensional vector alphabet, whether* $\mathbf{coll}(K)$ *is complete or not.*

Proof. The undecidability of this problem is proved using a reduction from the emptiness problem of (a variation of) complements of collapses of regular languages, i.e. complements of rational relations.

Given arbitrary alphabets Σ_1 and Σ_2 and an arbitrary regular language R over $\mathbf{Tot}(\Sigma_1, \Sigma_2)$, let R' be a (constructible) regular language (over $\mathbf{Tot}(\Sigma_1, \Sigma_2)$) such that $\mathbf{coll}(R') = \mathbf{coll}(R) \cup (\Sigma_1^* \times \{\Lambda\}) \cup (\{\Lambda\} \times \Sigma_2^*)$. Then it is rather easy to see that R' is complete if and only if $(\Sigma_1^+ \times \Sigma_2^+) - \mathbf{coll}(R)$ is empty. Since, by Lemma 1.4.(3) the latter problem is undecidable, it follows that completeness is undecidable. □

In this paper we have expressed the effect of vector synchronization on the behaviour of sequential systems using the notions of residue and loss. A complete picture has been obtained of the language complexity and decidability properties of the emptiness and finiteness problem for families of residues and losses corresponding to various VCCS submodels. These submodels were determined by our language hierarchy $\mathcal{F}$. Naturally, in addition to the VCCS submodels obtained from this hierarchy many other submodels are worthwhile investigating. Our choice of $\mathcal{F}$ has partly been motivated by the fact that quite a lot of properties of the families from $\mathcal{F}$ are known already, making it easier to "measure" the effect of synchronization. Depending on the properties one is interested in various other VCCS submodels may be looked at.

For instance, as noted before the two decision problems studied here turn out to have identical solutions for all classes investigated. Hence, one might search for VCCS submodels for which the two problems have different decidability results (for either losses or residues). Or, conversely, one may look for various other language families for which the two problems "behave" the same. Perhaps, even a general fundamental property underlying all these families may be found.

Another natural idea would be to involve the notion of prefix closedness in the (hierarchy of) language families. In this way it becomes possible to distinguish successfully and not successfully terminating computations. Residues and losses might then be used to consider questions concerning (partial) deadlocks and starvation.

Finally we would like to remark that it may be useful, to look for other notions than residue and loss and to define, e.g., effects of the synchronization on the control (languages), in order to express and study the effects of vector synchronization in concurrent systems. As such this paper only presents a first (and hopefully useful) approach to this problem.

ACKNOWLEDGEMENTS

The authors are indebted to G. Rozenberg for suggesting the topic of this paper and for stimulating discussions. We are also grateful to H.J. Hoogeboom for his useful comments on an earlier version of this paper and his help in preparing its final TEX-version. Thanks are also due to four anonymous referees for their careful consideration of the paper and their valuable suggestions. Finally, we gratefully acknowledge the partial financial support provided by the ESPRIT BRA Project 3148, DEMON.

REFERENCES

[Arn82] Arnold, A.: Synchronized behaviours of processes and rational relations. *Acta Informatica* 17 (1982), pp. 21-29.

[BakBoo74] Baker, B.S., Book, R.V.: Reversal-bounded multipushdown machines. *Journal of Computer and System Sciences* 8 (1974), pp. 315-332.

[BeaNiv80] Beauquier, J., Nivat, M.: Application of formal language theory to problems of security and synchronization. In: Book, R. (ed.): *Formal Language Theory: Perspectives and Open Problems.* Academic Press, New York (1980), pp. 407-453.

[Ber79] Berstel, J.: *Transductions and Context-Free Languages.* Teubner, Stuttgart (1979).

[Bes87] Best, E.: COSY: its relation to nets and to CSP. Lecture Notes in Computer Science 255, Springer-Verlag (1987), pp. 416-440.

[CamHab74] Campbell, R.H., Habermann, A.N.: The specification of process synchronization by path expressions. Lecture Notes in Computer Science 16, Springer-Verlag (1974), pp. 89-102.

[Gre69] Greibach, S.: An infinite hierarchy of context-free languages, *Journal of the Association for Computing Machinery* 16 (1969), pp. 91-106.

[HopUll79] Hopcroft, J.E., Ullman, J.D.: *Introduction to Automata Theory, Languages, and Computation.* Addison-Wesley, Reading, Massachusetts (1979).

[Imm88] Immerman, N.: Nondeterministic space is closed under complementation, *SIAM Journal on Computing* 17 (1988), pp. 935-938.

[Jan85] Janicki, R.: Transforming sequential systems into concurrent systems. *Theoretical Computer Science* 36 (1985), pp. 27-58.

[JanLauKouDev86] Janicki, R., Lauer, P.E., Koutny, M., Devillers, R.: Concurrent and maximally concurrent evolution of nonsequential systems. *Theoretical Computer Science* 43 (1986), pp. 213-238.

[KeeKleRoz90] Keesmaat, N.W., Kleijn, H.C.M., Rozenberg, G.: Vector controlled concurrent systems, part I: basic classes. *Fundamenta Informaticae* 13 (1990), pp. 275-316.

[KeeKleRoz91] Keesmaat, N.W., Kleijn, H.C.M., Rozenberg, G.: Vector controlled concurrent systems, part II: comparisons. *Fundamenta Informaticae* 14 (1991), pp. 1-38.

[KeeKle89] Keesmaat, N.W., Kleijn, H.C.M.: Net-based control versus rational control in vector controlled concurrent systems. Techn. report 89-21, Department of Computer Science, Leiden University (1989). Submitted.

[LauCam75] Lauer, P.E., Campbell, R.H.: Formal semantics for a class of high level primitives for coordinating concurrent processes. *Acta Informatica* 5 (1975), pp. 297-332.

[Niv68] Nivat, M.: Transductions des langages de Chomsky. *Annales de l'Institut Fourier* 18 (1968), pp. 339-456.

[Niv82] Nivat, M.:Behaviours of processes and synchronized systems of processes. In: Broy, M., Schmidt, G. (eds.): *Theoretical Foundations of Programming Methodology.* Reidel Publishing Company, Dordrecht (1982), pp. 473-551.

[Shi79] Shields, M.W.: Adequate path expressions. Lecture Notes in Computer Science 70, Springer-Verlag (1979), pp. 249-265.

[Sze88] Szelepcsényi, R.: The method of forced enumeration for nondeterministic automata , *Acta Informatica* 26 (1988), pp. 279-284.

MODELLING SYSTEMS WITH DYNAMIC PRIORITIES

Maciej Koutny
Computing Laboratory
The University
Newcastle upon Tyne NE1 7RU, U.K.

Abstract In this paper we discuss concurrent systems with dynamic priorities, i.e. we allow the priority relation to change as the system evolves. We identify two classes of such systems, state-controlled and event-controlled priority systems. We define their non-sequential semantics (in terms of step sequences) which reflects both the priority constraints and concurrency specification. It is then shown that for a given prioritised system it is possible to construct an equivalent non-prioritised one. The systems dealt with in this paper are safe Petri nets augmented with a priority specification.

Keywords Petri nets, priorities, step sequence semantics.

CONTENTS

1 Introduction

In the design of concurrent systems it is often desirable to specify priority constraints to resolve conflicts between simultaneously enabled actions. E.g., operating systems employ priorities to control the execution of jobs waiting for processing, while programming languages provide primitives to specify the relative preferences for the execution of different parts of the program. Priority systems can be roughly divided into Static Priority Systems and Dynamic Priority Systems. In the former, all priority constraints are determined before the operation of the system or program begins, i.e., at the compile time, while in the latter, the priority relation can be changed during the execution, i.e., priorities are determined at the run time.

The meaning of static priority systems is now rather well-understood. There have been a number of papers dealing with their semantics in the context of different models of concurrency, including Petri nets [3,9], COSY [10,14], process algebras [2,4,6,7] and programming languages [1,5,13].

In this paper we will define a priority system as a pair of the form

$$\Sigma_{PR}=(\Sigma,\pi)$$

where Σ is the base non-prioritised system (Petri net) and π a priority specification. A system with static priorities is one for whom π is simply a binary relation on the actions of Σ. We will use $a<b$ to denote that b has higher priority than a, i.e. a can occur only if b is not enabled. For systems with dynamically changing priority relation, π might be defined in different ways. In this paper we will look at two intuitively appealing mechanisms for modelling dynamic priorities: the event-controlled and state-controlled priority specifications.

In the event-based approach, for each priority constraint $a<b$ there will be actions whose occurrences can activate and suspend it. In this case $\pi=\pi_{EC}=(\rho_o,\mathrm{On},\mathrm{Off})$, where ρ_o is an initial priority relation, and On, Off are two mappings such that On(a,b) and Off(a,b) are respectively the sets of actions which can activate and suspend $a<b$. As a result, at any point in the evolution of the system, the current priority relation will depend on its past history. In particular, it may happen that two executions leading to the same global state in the base system Σ have different continuations. Consider, rather informally, the system Σ in Fig. 1.1(a) together with the priority specification $\rho_o=\varnothing$ and On$(a,b)=\{c\}$. After executing c the priority constraint $a<b$ becomes active and a can no longer be executed, leading to a reachability graph (Fig.1.1(c)) which is not included in the reachability graph of the base system (Fig.1.1(b)).

In the state-based approach, $\pi=\pi_{SC}$ is a relation which, for every potential priority constraint $a<b$, specifies those local states in which it holds. The reachability graph of a state-controlled priority system is always included in the reachability graph generated by the base system. Consider again the system of Fig. 1.1(a) and a priority specification such that $a<b$ holds if place p is marked. This priority system will generate a reachability graph shown in Fig. 1.1(d).

In this paper we will discuss non-sequential semantics of priority systems expressed in terms of step sequences [17,18]. For both event- and state-controlled priority systems we will formalise their semantics and provide a translation to equivalent non-prioritised systems. As the system model we use Petri nets, and the base system Σ will always be a safe Petri net.

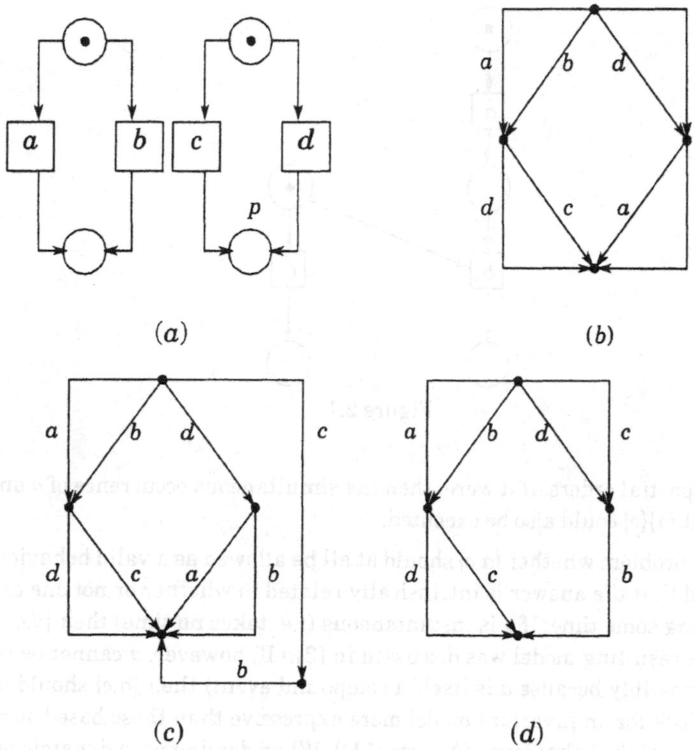

Figure 1.1: Reachability graphs (b,c,d) only show arcs labelled by single transitions.

2 Preliminaries

2.1 Priorities and Concurrency

To illustrate the problems posed by the interplay between the priority and concurrency specifications, we consider a static priority system

$$\Sigma_S = (\Sigma, \pi_S)$$

where Σ is as in Fig. 2.1, and $\pi_S = \{(c,b)\}$. (Note that Σ exhibits what is usually referred to as *confusion* situation [16].) To obtain the step sequences generated by Σ_S, we take the step sequences of Σ and delete those which are inconsistent with the priority specification. Since the step sequences of Σ are

$$\text{steps}(\Sigma) = \{\lambda, \{a\}, \{c\}, \{a,c\}, \{a\}\{c\}, \{c\}\{a\}, \{a\}\{b\}\},$$

we obtain

$$\text{steps}(\Sigma_S) = \{\lambda, \{a\}, \{c\}, \{a,c\}, \{c\}\{a\}, \{a\}\{b\}\}.$$

Note that $\{a\}\{c\} \notin \text{steps}(\Sigma_S)$ since after executing a, b becomes enabled and c cannot be executed. It is not difficult to see that $\text{steps}(\Sigma_S)$ cannot be consistent with any semantical model

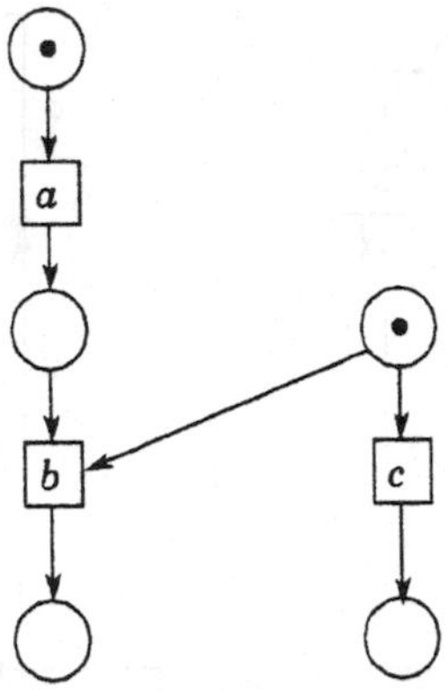

Figure 2.1

based on causal partial orders. If it were, then the simultaneous occurrence of a and c in $\{a,c\}$ would imply that $\{a\}\{c\}$ could also be executed.

We now face the problem whether $\{a,c\}$ should at all be allowed as a valid behaviour of Σ_S. In [3] it was argued that the answer is intrinsically related to whether or not one can regard a as an event taking some time: If a is instantaneous (i.e. takes no time) then $\{a,c\}$ should not be allowed. (The resulting model was discussed in [3].) If, however, a cannot be regarded as instantaneous (possibly because a is itself a compound event) then $\{a,c\}$ should be allowed, and one should look for an invariant model more expressive than those based on causal partial orders to capture the behaviour of Σ_S (see [11]). When dealing with dynamic priority systems, we also need to address the above problem (first discussed in [10]). We will adopt the same position as [3] and exclude step sequence $\{a,c\}$ from the possible behaviours of Σ_S. This decision can also be interpreted in terms of partial order behaviours (*processes* [16]). The exclusion of $\{a,c\}$ corresponds to the rejection of the process of net Σ in which a and b occurred concurrently: In such a process, there is a cut which enables b yet it is a which is actually chosen for execution.

The discussion of a dynamic priority system $\Sigma_{PR}=(\Sigma,\pi_{PR})$ will proceed along the following lines: First, we derive steps(Σ_{PR}), the step sequences of the base system which do not violate π_{PR}. Then we delete step sequences inconsistent with the partial order view of the behaviour of Σ_{PR}, like $\{a,c\}$ above, and obtain ker(Σ_{PR})$\subseteq$steps(Σ_{PR}), that is regarded as the step sequence semantics of Σ_{PR}. Finally, we construct an ordinary Petri net Π_{PR} generating ker(Σ_{PR}). (Note that the existence of such a net is not guaranteed a priori.) That is, we will adhere to the following line of development:

$$\Sigma_{PR} \rightarrow \text{steps}(\Sigma_{PR}) \rightarrow \text{ker}(\Sigma_{PR}) \rightarrow \Pi_{PR}.$$

2.2 Basic Definitions

The class of Petri nets we use are finite P/T-nets with weighted arcs [15]. Although the base systems will always be safe, the net Π_{PR} will in general be non-safe and have non-unitary arcs. (This cannot be avoided even for static priority systems [3].) The definitions of the standard notions concerning Petri nets can be found in the Appendix.

Our generic system will be a net $\Sigma=(S,T,W,M_0)$, where S are places, T are transitions, W is the arc weight function, and M_0 is the initial marking. As the semantical model we use step sequences [17,18], which are strings $\sigma=A_1...A_n$ of sets of transitions (steps) fired simultaneously. Σ generates a set of step sequences, steps(Σ). To identify step sequences like $\{a,c\}$ discussed in Section 2.1, we use the notion of a refinement (or decomposition) of a step sequence.

Definition 2.1

A refinement of a step sequence $\sigma=A_1...A_n$ is any step sequence

$$\omega=A_{11}...A_{1k_1}...A_{n1}...A_{nk_n}$$

such that for every i, the sets $A_{i1},...,A_{ik_i}$ form a partition of A_i. We will denote this by $\omega\in\mathrm{ref}(\sigma)$. □

The step sequences of a Petri net are closed w.r.t. refinement.

Proposition 2.2

steps(Σ) = ref(steps(Σ)). □

Going from steps(Σ_{PR}) to ker(Σ_{PR}) amounts to deleting those step sequences which destroy the above closure property.

Definition 2.3

Let G be a set of step sequences. Its refinement kernel, ker(G), is the maximal subset which is closed w.r.t. refinement operation, i.e.

$$\mathrm{ker(G)}=\max\{\mathrm{H}\subseteq\mathrm{G}\mid\mathrm{ref(H)=H}\}=\{\sigma\in\mathrm{G}\mid\mathrm{ref}(\sigma)\subseteq\mathrm{G}\}.\ \square$$

E.g., ker($\{c\}\{a,b,c\}$, $\{c\}\{a,b\}\{c\}$, $\{c\}\{a\}\{b\}\{c\}$, $\{c\}\{b\}\{a\}\{c\}$) = { $\{c\}\{a,b\}\{c\}$, $\{c\}\{a\}\{b\}\{c\}$, $\{c\}\{b\}\{a\}\{c\}$ }.

We will restrict the class of base systems to safe ones. Note that safeness as defined below does not constrain in any way the behaviour of the net, in contrast to the definition used, e.g., for the C/E-systems [16].

Definition 2.4

A place $s\in S$ is 1-bounded if

$$\forall t\in T\colon W(t,s)\leq 1 \wedge W(s,t)\leq 1$$
$$\forall M\in[M_0\rangle\colon M(s)\leq 1.$$

Σ is safe if every place $s\in S$ is 1-bounded. □

In the modelling of priority systems in [3] a key role was played by the notion of a generalised place complement. A generalised complement for a set P of 1-bounded places is a new place which 'counts' the number of places in P which currently are unmarked, without affecting the step sequence semantics.

For every integer n, let $\delta(n)=n$ if $n\geq 0$; and $\delta(n)=0$ otherwise.

Definition 2.5 [3]

Let P be a non-empty set of 1-bounded places of Σ. A generalised complement of P is a new place $\gamma=\gamma(P)$ such that for every $t\in T$,

$$\hat{W}(t,\gamma)=\delta(\Sigma_{p\in P}W(p,t)-W(t,p))$$
$$\hat{W}(\gamma,t)=\delta(\Sigma_{p\in P}W(t,p)-W(p,t)).$$

For every marking M of Σ, let

$$\hat{M}: S\cup\{\gamma\}\rightarrow \mathbb{N}$$

be defined by $\hat{M}(s)=M(s)$ for all $s\in S$, and

$$\hat{M}(\gamma)=|P|-\Sigma_{p\in P}M(p).$$

After adding γ to Σ we obtain a new system

$$\Sigma\blacktriangleright\gamma=(S\cup\{\gamma\},T,W\cup\hat{W},\hat{M}_o).\ \square$$

The counting property of γ is expressed as follows.

Proposition 2.6
$K(\gamma)=|P|-\Sigma_{p\in P}K(p)$ for all markings $K\in[\hat{M}_o\rangle$. $\square$

The reachable markings of Σ and $\Sigma\blacktriangleright\gamma$ are in bijection through the ˆ operation with the corresponding markings enabling the same steps. Thus, as far as the step sequence semantics is concerned, Σ and $\Sigma\blacktriangleright\gamma$ are equivalent systems.

Theorem 2.7 [3]
(1) $[\hat{M}_o\rangle=\{\hat{M}\mid M\in[M_o\rangle\}$.
(2) $M\in[M_o\rangle \Rightarrow \text{enabled}_\Sigma(M)=\text{enabled}_{\Sigma\blacktriangleright\gamma}(\hat{M})$.
(3) $\text{steps}(\Sigma)=\text{steps}(\Sigma\blacktriangleright\gamma)$. $\square$

Fig. 2.2 shows an example of generalised place complement.

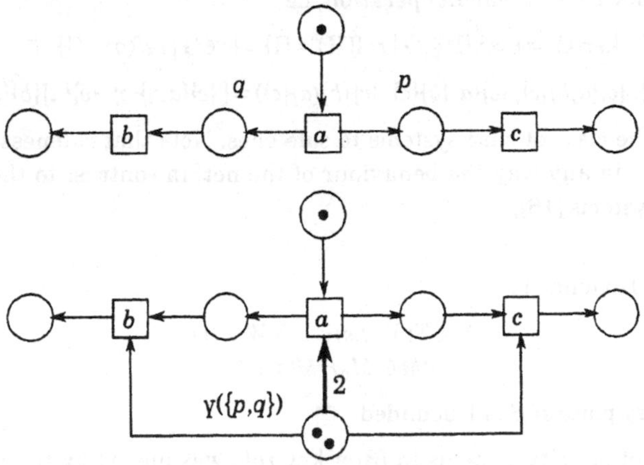

Figure 2.2

3 State-Controlled Priority Systems

Let $\Sigma=(S,T,W,M_o)$ be a safe system. A state-controlled priority system based on Σ,

$$\Sigma_{SC}=(\Sigma,\pi_{SC})$$

is characterised by a ternary relation

$$\pi_{SC} \subseteq T \times T \times 2^S.$$

Each $(a,b,Q) \in \pi_{SC}$ defines one local state Q in which a priority constraint $a<b$ holds.

We first single out those step sequences of the base system Σ which do not violate the priority specification.

Definition 3.1

Let steps(Σ_{SC}) be the maximal prefix-closed subset of steps(Σ) such that if $\sigma A \in$ steps(Σ_{SC}) and $M_0[\sigma\rangle M$ then

$$\forall (a,b,Q) \in \pi_{SC}: M(Q \cup {}^\bullet b) = \{1\} \Rightarrow a \notin A. \quad \square$$

The above definition is equivalent to saying that steps(Σ_{SC}) comprises exactly those sequences of the base system Σ, $\sigma = A_1 \ldots A_i A_{i+1} \ldots A_n$, for which there is no $i<n$ such that the following hold: (i) $\sigma_i = A_1 \ldots A_i$ leads to a marking in which a priority constraint $a<b$ holds; and (ii) a is executed in A_{i+1}. We then define

$$\text{ker}(\Sigma_{SC}) = \text{ker}(\text{steps}(\Sigma_{SC})).$$

It is possible to construct a priority-free system Π_{SC} such that

$$\text{steps}(\Pi_{SC}) = \text{ker}(\Sigma_{SC}).$$

To illustrate its construction, we consider $\Sigma_{SC} = (\Sigma, \pi_{SC})$, where Σ is shown in Fig. 3.1(a) and $\pi_{SC} = \{(a,b,\{p\})\}$. I.e. $a<b$ is the only priority constraint which holds if p is marked. The construction of Π_{SC} is carried out in two steps:

Step 1: We construct a generalised complement place $\gamma(P)$ for the set $P = \{p\} \cup {}^\bullet b$. This does not change the step sequence semantics of the system (Theorem 2.7(3)), yet enables us to find out whether both p and ${}^\bullet b$ are marked (Proposition 2.6). The resulting system is shown in Fig. 3.1(b).

Step 2: We add a loop (in fact, increment by one the arcs' weights) between a and $\gamma(P)$ to make a depend on the presence of a token in $\gamma(P)$. As a result, a can only occur if b

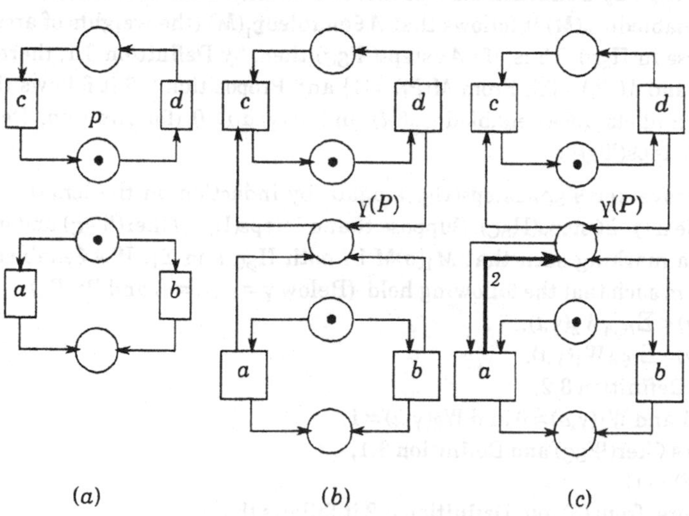

Figure 3.1

is not enabled or p is not marked (Proposition 2.6). The resulting system Π_{SC} is shown in Fig. 3.1(c).

Π_{SC} is defined in the following way.

Definition 3.2

Let $\pi_{SC}=\{(a_1,b_1,Q_1),...,(a_m,b_m,Q_m)\}$, and $P_i=Q_i\cup{}^\bullet b_i$ for $i=1,...,m$.
Let $\Sigma_1=(S_1,T,W_1,M_1)=\Sigma\blacktriangleright\gamma(P_1)\blacktriangleright...\blacktriangleright\gamma(P_m)$.

Note: We distinguish $\gamma(P_i)$ from $\gamma(P_j)$ for $i\neq j$, even if $P_i=P_j$. I.e., Σ_1 contains exactly m new places $\gamma_i=\gamma(P_i)$.

Define $\Pi_{SC}=(S_1,T,W_2,M_1)$, where W_2 is the same as W_1 with one exception: If $i\leq m$ and $W_1(\gamma_i,a_i)=0$, then

$$W_2(\gamma_i,a_i)=1$$
$$W_2(a_i,\gamma_i)=W_1(a_i,\gamma_i)+1. \square$$

Theorem 3.3

steps(Π_{SC}) = ker(Σ_{SC}).

Proof

We prove slightly stronger result (we need it in the proof of Theorem 5.4) by assuming that all places in $P_i=Q_i\cup{}^\bullet b_i$ $(i=1,...,m)$ are 1-bounded, and removing the assumption that Σ be safe.

Let $\Psi_{SC}=(\Sigma_1,\pi_{SC})$. From Theorem 2.7 it follows that ker(Σ_{SC}) = ker(Ψ_{SC}). Hence it suffices to prove that steps(Π_{SC}) = ker(Ψ_{SC}).

We will first show steps(Π_{SC})$\subseteq$ker(Ψ_{SC}). In fact, we will prove steps(Π_{SC})$\subseteq$steps(Ψ_{SC}) which suffices to show the required inclusion since ref(steps(Π_{SC})) = steps(Π_{SC}). The proof proceeds by induction on the length of the step sequence.

Clearly, $\lambda\in$steps(Ψ_{SC}). Suppose that $\sigma\in$steps(Π_{SC})$\cap$steps(Ψ_{SC}) and $\sigma A\in$steps(Π_{SC}). Let $M_1[\sigma\rangle M$ in Π_{SC}. By Definition 3.2 (the last two lines), we also have $M_1[\sigma\rangle M$ in Σ_1.
From $A\in$enabled$_{\Pi_{SC}}(M)$ it follows that $A\in$enabled$_{\Sigma_1}(M)$ (the weights of arcs in Σ_1 do not exceed those in Π_{SC}). Thus, if $\sigma A\notin$steps(Ψ_{SC}) then, by Definition 3.1, there is $i\leq m$ such that $a_i\in A$ and $M(P_i)=\{1\}$. From $M(P_i)=\{1\}$ and Proposition 2.6 it follows that $M(\gamma_i)=0$, which contradicts $a_i\in A\in$enabled$_{\Pi_{SC}}(M)$ and $W(\gamma_i,a_i)>0$ (follows from Definition 3.2). Hence $\sigma A\in$steps(Ψ_{SC}).

Next we prove ker(Ψ_{SC})$\subseteq$steps(Π_{SC}), again by induction on the length of the step sequence. Clearly, $\lambda\in$steps(Π_{SC}). Suppose that $\sigma\in$steps(Π_{SC})$\cap$ker(Ψ_{SC}) and $\sigma A\in$ker(Ψ_{SC}). Let M be a marking such that $M_1[\sigma\rangle M$ in both Π_{SC} and Σ_1. If $A\notin$enabled$_{\Pi_{SC}}(M)$ then there is $i\leq m$ such that the following hold. (Below $\gamma=\gamma_i$, $a=a_i$ and $P=P_i$.)

(1) $M(\gamma)<\Sigma_{t\in A}W_2(\gamma,t)$.
(2) $M(\gamma)\geq\Sigma_{t\in A}W_1(\gamma,t)$.

Hence, by Definition 3.2,

(3) $a\in A$ and $W_1(\gamma,a)=0$ and $W_2(\gamma,a)=1$.

Thus, by $\sigma A\in$ker(Ψ_{SC}) and Definition 3.1,

(4) $M(P)\neq\{1\}$.

Furthermore, from (3) and Definition 3.2 it follows that

(5) $\Sigma_{t\in A}W_2(\gamma,t) = 1+\Sigma_{t\in A}W_1(\gamma,t)$.

Let $C=\{t\in A \mid W_1(\gamma,t)>0\}$ and $D=\{t\in A \mid W_1(\gamma,t)=0\}$. From (3) it follows that $D\neq\emptyset$. Suppose that $C=\emptyset$. Then, by (1,2,5), $M(\gamma)=0$. Hence, by Proposition 2.6, $M(P)=\{1\}$ which produces a contradiction with (4). Thus $C\neq\emptyset$.

From $\sigma A\in\ker(\Psi_{SC})$ it follows that $\sigma CD\in\ker(\Psi_{SC})$. Let $M[C\rangle K[D\rangle L$ in Σ_1. From $a\in D$ it follows that $K(P)\neq\{1\}$. Hence, by Proposition 2.6, $K(\gamma)\geq 1$. Consequently, we have

$$1 \leq K(\gamma)=M(\gamma) + \Sigma_{t\in C}W_1(t,\gamma) - W_1(\gamma,t).$$

We also observe that (by Definition 2.5) for all $t\in A$,

$$W_1(t,\gamma)>0 \Rightarrow W_1(\gamma,t)=0 \Rightarrow t\notin C.$$

Thus

$$M(\gamma) \geq 1 + \Sigma_{t\in C}W_1(\gamma,t) = 1 + \Sigma_{t\in A}W_1(\gamma,t) =_{(5)} \Sigma_{t\in A}W_2(\gamma,t)$$

which produces a contradiction with (1). □

4 Event-Controlled Priority Systems

Let $\Sigma=(S,T,W,M_o)$ be a safe system. An event-controlled priority system based on Σ,

$$\Sigma_{EC}=(\Sigma,\pi_{EC})$$

has as its priority specification a triple $\pi_{EC}=(\rho_o,\mathrm{On},\mathrm{Off})$ such that $\rho_o\subseteq T\times T$ is an initial priority specification and

$$\mathrm{On},\mathrm{Off}: T\times T\rightarrow 2^T$$

are two mappings such that $\mathrm{On}(a,b)$ and $\mathrm{Off}(a,b)$ are disjoint, for all $a,b\in T$. As before, we first single out those step sequences of Σ which do not violate the priority specification.

Definition 4.1

Let $\rho : \mathrm{steps}(\Sigma)\rightarrow 2^{T\times T}$ be defined by $\rho(\lambda)=\rho_o$ and

$$\rho(\sigma A)=\rho(\sigma) - \mathrm{Off}^{-1}(A) \cup \mathrm{On}^{-1}(A).$$

Then $\mathrm{steps}(\Sigma_{EC})$ is the maximal prefix-closed subset of $\mathrm{steps}(\Sigma)$ such that if σA is a step sequence in $\mathrm{steps}(\Sigma_{EC})$ then

$$(a,b)\in\rho(\sigma) \wedge a\in A \Rightarrow \sigma\{b\}\notin\mathrm{steps}(\Sigma)$$
$$(a,b)\in\rho(\sigma) \Rightarrow \mathrm{On}(a,b)\cap A=\emptyset$$
$$(a,b)\notin\rho(\sigma) \Rightarrow \mathrm{Off}(a,b)\cap A=\emptyset. \ \square$$

ρ is a mapping which for every step sequence gives the current priority relation based on the initial priority relation and the transitions executed so far. The last two conditions mean that no transition in $\mathrm{On}(a,b)$ can be executed if $a<b$ holds; similarly, no transition in $\mathrm{Off}(a,b)$ can be executed if $a<b$ is suspended. We will discuss this restriction in the next section.

We then define

$$\ker(\Sigma_{EC})=\ker(\mathrm{steps}(\Sigma_{EC})).$$

As in the case of Σ_{SC}, it is possible to find a priority-free system Π_{EC} such that

$$\ker(\Sigma_{EC})=\mathrm{steps}(\Pi_{EC}).$$

The construction of Π_{EC} is based on a result which follows directly from the definition of $\ker(\Sigma_{EC})$ and Definition 4.1:

Proposition 4.2

Let $\sigma A \in \ker(\Sigma_{EC})$ and $a,b \in T$.

(1) $|\mathrm{Off}(a,b) \cap A| \leq 1$.

(2) $|\mathrm{On}(a,b) \cap A| \leq 1$. □

The problem of constructing Π_{EC} can be reduced to that discussed in the previous section. Indeed, from Definition 4.1 and Proposition 4.2 it follows that for each priority constraint $a<b$ the occurrences of the transitions of $\mathrm{On}(a,b)$ and $\mathrm{Off}(a,b)$ in the step sequences of $\ker(\Sigma_{EC})$ are totally sequentialised and strictly alternating. Thus we can augment Σ with two new places, on_{ab} and off_{ab}, and connect them with the transitions in $\mathrm{On}(a,b)$ and $\mathrm{Off}(a,b)$ in such a way that $a<b$ holds *if and only if* on_{ab} is marked. This, however, can be captured by setting a state-based priority specification

$$(a,b,\{\mathrm{on}_{ab}\}) \in \pi_{SC}.$$

Definition 4.3

Define $\Sigma_1 = (S_1, T, W_1, M_1)$ to be a safe net, where

(1) $S_1 = S \cup \{\mathrm{on}_{ab}, \mathrm{off}_{ab} \mid a,b \in T\}$.

(2) M_1 restricted to S is the same as M_o. Moreover, for all $a,b \in T$,

$$(a,b) \in \rho_o \Rightarrow M_1(\mathrm{on}_{ab}) = 1 \wedge M_1(\mathrm{off}_{ab}) = 0$$
$$(a,b) \notin \rho_o \Rightarrow M_1(\mathrm{on}_{ab}) = 0 \wedge M_1(\mathrm{off}_{ab}) = 1.$$

(3) W_1 restricted to $S \times T \cup T \times S$ is the same as W. Moreover, for all $a,b \in T$,

$$^\bullet\mathrm{on}_{ab} = \mathrm{off}_{ab}{}^\bullet = \mathrm{On}(a,b)$$
$$^\bullet\mathrm{off}_{ab} = \mathrm{on}_{ab}{}^\bullet = \mathrm{Off}(a,b).$$

Let $\Sigma_{SC} = (\Sigma_1, \pi_{SC})$ be a state-controlled priority system such that

$$\pi_{SC} = \{(a,b,\{on_{ab}\}) \mid a,b \in T\}.$$

Let $\Pi_{EC} = \Pi_{SC}$, where Π_{SC} is defined for Σ_{SC} according to Definition 3.2. □

Theorem 4.4

$\mathrm{steps}(\Pi_{EC}) = \ker(\Sigma_{EC})$.

Proof

We first show that

(1) $\sigma \in \ker(\Sigma_{SC}) \cap \ker(\Sigma_{EC}) \wedge \sigma A \in \ker(\Sigma_{EC}) \Rightarrow \sigma A \in \mathrm{steps}(\Sigma_{SC})$.

Let $M_o[\sigma\rangle K$ in Σ and $M_1[\sigma\rangle L$ in Σ_1. By Definition 4.1 and 4.3, for all $a,b \in T$,

(2) $L(\mathrm{on}_{ab}) + L(\mathrm{off}_{ab}) = 1$

(3) $(a,b) \in \rho(\sigma) \Leftrightarrow L(\mathrm{on}_{ab}) = 1$.

From Definition 4.1 and Proposition 4.2 it follows that

$$(a,b) \in \rho(\sigma) \Rightarrow \mathrm{On}(a,b) \cap A = \varnothing \wedge |\mathrm{Off}(a,b) \cap A| \leq 1$$
$$(a,b) \notin \rho(\sigma) \Rightarrow \mathrm{Off}(a,b) \cap A = \varnothing \wedge |\mathrm{On}(a,b) \cap A| \leq 1.$$

This and (2,3) means that $\sigma A \in \text{steps}(\Sigma_1)$. If $\sigma A \notin \text{steps}(\Sigma_{SC})$ then there must be $a,b \in T$ such that $a \in A$ and $L(\bullet b \cup \{\text{on}_{ab}\}) = \{1\}$. Thus, by (3), $(a,b) \in \rho(\sigma)$. This, $a \in A$ and $K(\bullet b) = L(\bullet b) = \{1\}$ produces a contradiction with Definition 4.1. Hence (1) holds.

We further observe that $\text{enabled}_{\Sigma_1}(L) \subseteq \text{enabled}_{\Sigma}(K)$ and (2,3) imply the following:

(4) $\quad \sigma \in \ker(\Sigma_{SC}) \cap \ker(\Sigma_{EC}) \wedge \sigma A \in \ker(\Sigma_{SC}) \Rightarrow \sigma A \in \text{steps}(\Sigma_{EC})$.

By (1,4) and $\lambda \in \ker(\Sigma_{SC}) \cap \ker(\Sigma_{EC})$, we obtain $\ker(\Sigma_{SC}) = \ker(\Sigma_{EC})$. Furthermore, by Theorem 3.3, $\text{steps}(\Pi_{EC}) = \text{steps}(\Pi_{SC}) = \ker(\Sigma_{SC})$ which completes the proof. □

5 Extended Event-Controlled Priority Systems

In the event-controlled priority system Σ_{EC} no transition in $\text{On}(a,b)$ could be executed when $a < b$ was active. We now want to relax this restriction. More precisely, in addition to $\text{On}(a,b)$ and $\text{Off}(a,b)$ we want to introduce two new sets of transitions, $\text{ON}(a,b)$ and $\text{OFF}(a,b)$, such that the enabling of $c \in \text{ON}(a,b) \cup \text{OFF}(a,b)$ does not depend on whether $a < b$ is currently active or not. The resulting mechanism of controlling priorities cannot be modelled within the framework of unlabelled nets. To show this we consider a priority system Σ_{PR} based on the net of Fig. 5.1 with $\rho_o = \varnothing$ and $\text{ON}(a,b) = \{c\}$.

Let $\sigma = \{a\}$ and $\sigma_i = \{c\}^i$ for $i = 1,2,\ldots$. We would expect Σ_{PR} to generate step sequences

$$\sigma, \sigma_1, \sigma_2, \sigma_3, \ldots$$

while $\omega = \{c\}\{a\}$ should not be allowed.

Suppose that $\Sigma = (S,T,W,M_o)$ is a system such that

$$\sigma, \sigma_1, \sigma_2, \sigma_3, \ldots \in \text{steps}(\Sigma) \text{ and } \omega \notin \text{steps}(\Sigma).$$

From $\sigma_1, \sigma_2, \sigma_3, \ldots \in \text{steps}(\Sigma)$ it follows that for all $s \in S$, $W(c,s) - W(s,c) \geq 0$. This, however, contradicts $\sigma \in \text{steps}(\Sigma)$ and $\omega \notin \text{steps}(\Sigma)$.

As before, let $\Sigma = (S,T,W,M_o)$ be a safe system. An extended event-controlled priority system based on Σ,

$$\Sigma_{EEC} = (\Sigma, \pi_{EEC})$$

is characterised by $\pi_{EEC} = (\rho_o, \text{On}, \text{Off}, \text{ON}, \text{OFF})$ generalising π_{EC} in the following way:

$$\text{ON}, \text{OFF} : T \times T \to 2^T$$

$\text{On}(a,b)$, $\text{Off}(a,b)$, $\text{ON}(a,b)$, $\text{OFF}(a,b)$ are disjoint sets for all $a,b \in T$.

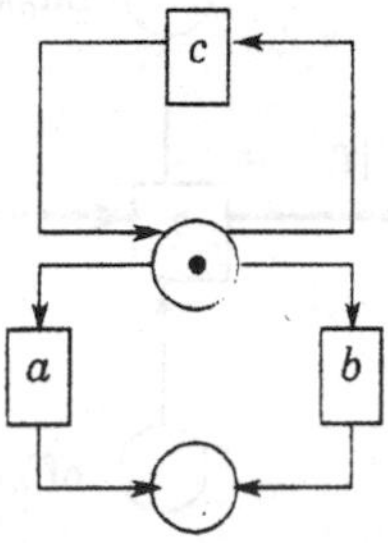

Figure 5.1

We will denote by $\underline{ON}$ and $\underline{OFF}$ two mappings defined by

$$\underline{ON}(a,b) = ON(a,b) \cup On(a,b)$$
$$\underline{OFF}(a,b) = OFF(a,b) \cup Off(a,b).$$

We first define steps(Σ_{EEC}).

Definition 5.1

Let $\rho : \text{steps}(\Sigma) \to 2^{T \times T}$ be defined by $\rho(\lambda) = \rho_0$ and

$$\rho(\sigma A) = \rho(\sigma) - \underline{OFF}^{-1}(A) \cup \underline{ON}^{-1}(A).$$

Then steps(Σ_{EEC}) is the maximal prefix-closed subset of steps(Σ) such that if σA is a step sequence in steps(Σ_{EEC}) then

$$(a,b) \in \rho(\sigma) \wedge a \in A \Rightarrow \sigma\{b\} \notin \text{steps}(\Sigma)$$
$$(a,b) \in \rho(\sigma) \Rightarrow On(a,b) \cap A = \varnothing \wedge |\underline{OFF}(a,b) \cap A| \leq 1$$
$$(a,b) \notin \rho(\sigma) \Rightarrow Off(a,b) \cap A = \varnothing \wedge |\underline{ON}(a,b) \cap A| \leq 1$$
$$\underline{ON}(a,b) \cap A = \varnothing \text{ or } \underline{OFF}(a,b) \cap A = \varnothing. \ \square$$

ρ is again a mapping which gives the current priority relation. We assumed that if a step A changes the status of a priority constraint then there is a unique transition in A which effects that. The last condition has been added to exclude a simultaneous occurrence of two transitions, one activating, the other suspending, the same priority constraint.

We then define

$$\ker(\Sigma_{EEC}) = \ker(\text{steps}(\Sigma_{EEC})).$$

As before, our aim is to construct a system which would generate the step sequences in $\ker(\Sigma_{EEC})$. As we have already seen, this cannot in general be achieved using unlabelled nets. We will have to set ourselves slightly less ambitious goal. Namely, we will construct a system Π_{EEC} and define a relabelling function on transitions, f, such that

$$f(\text{steps}(\Pi_{EEC})) = \ker(\Sigma_{EEC}).$$

The basic idea behind the construction of Π_{EEC} is to replace each $c \in ON(a,b)$ by two transitions labelled c, and to introduce four new places, on_{ab}, off_{ab}, ON_{ab} and OFF_{ab}, as shown in Fig. 5.2. The rest of the construction is essentially the same as in Section 4, however some care needs to be taken to make the application of Theorem 3.3 possible.

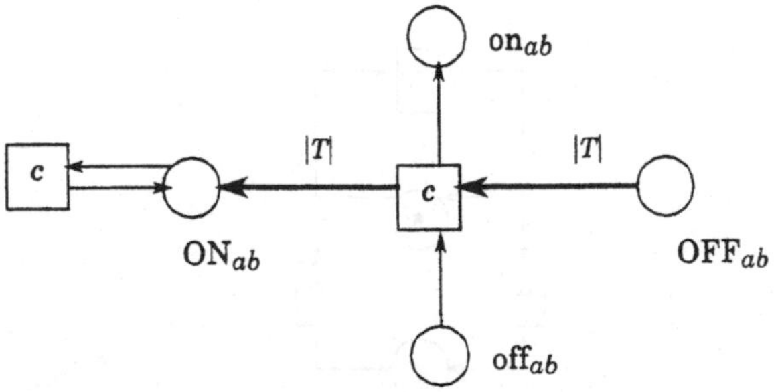

Figure 5.2

There are two points which should be mentioned. We need places ON_{ab} and OFF_{ab}, holding either 0 or $|T|$ tokens, to avoid unnecessary sequentialisation of transitions in $\mathrm{ON}(a,b)$ and $\mathrm{OFF}(a,b)$ in cases when they do not change the status of the priority constraint $a<b$. Also, we may need more than two copies of c since it may belong to several different ON and OFF sets. The definition of Π_{EEC} comes in two parts. We first formalise the construction illustrated in Fig. 5.2.

Construction 5.2

Let $\Sigma=(S,T,W,M_0)$. Then we construct a system $\Sigma_1=(S_1,T_1,W_1,M_1)$ as follows:

(1) $S_1=S\cup\{\mathrm{on}_x,\mathrm{off}_x,\mathrm{ON}_x,\mathrm{OFF}_x \mid x\in T\times T\}$.

(2) $T_1=\{t_F \mid t\in T\wedge F\subseteq\{x \mid t\in \mathrm{ON}(x)\cup\mathrm{OFF}(x)\}\}$.

(Note: $(a,b)\in F$ means that t_F always changes the status of the priority constraint $a<b$, as the right c in Fig. 5.2.)

(3) For all t_F and $s\in S$, $W_1(t_F,s)=W(t,s)$ and $W_1(s,t_F)=W(s,t)$.

(4) For all t_F and $s\in S_1\text{-}S$, $W_1(t_F,s)=W_1(s,t_F)=0$ unless one of the following holds:

(a) $t\in\mathrm{On}(x)$ or $t\in\mathrm{ON}(x)\wedge x\in F$. Then

$$W_1(t_F,\mathrm{on}_x)=W_1(\mathrm{off}_x,t_F)=1$$
$$W_1(t_F,\mathrm{ON}_x)=W_1(\mathrm{OFF}_x,t_F)=|T|.$$

(b) $t\in\mathrm{ON}(x)\wedge x\notin F$. Then

$$W_1(t_F,\mathrm{ON}_x)=W_1(\mathrm{ON}_x,t_F)=1.$$

(c,d) Similar to (a) and (b) with the roles of *on*'s and *off*'s interchanged.

(5) For $s\in S$, $M_1(s)=M_0(s)$, while for $s\in S_1\text{-}S$, if $x\in\rho_0$ then

$$M_1(\mathrm{on}_x)=1\wedge M_1(\mathrm{ON}_x)=|T|$$
$$M_1(\mathrm{off}_x)=M_1(\mathrm{OFF}_x)=0;$$

otherwise

$$M_1(\mathrm{on}_x)=M_1(\mathrm{ON}_x)=0$$
$$M_1(\mathrm{off}_x)=1\wedge M_1(\mathrm{OFF}_x)=|T|.\ \square$$

We now transform Σ_1 with the priority specification π_{EEC} into a state-controlled priority system Σ_{SC}. To be able to apply Theorem 3.3 we need to ensure that all places involved in the complement construction described in Definition 3.2 are 1-bounded. To achieve this we resort to a little trick .

Definition 5.3

Let Σ_2 be the union of Σ_1 of Construction 5.2 and the following net:

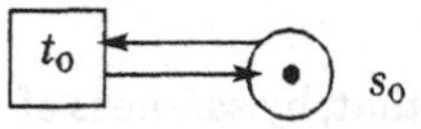

Let $\Sigma_{\mathrm{SC}}=(\Sigma_2,\pi_{\mathrm{SC}})$ be a state-controlled priority system such that

$$\pi_{\mathrm{SC}}=\{(t_o,t_o,\varnothing)\}\cup\{(t_F,t_o,{}^\bullet w\cup\{on_{tw}\}) \mid t_F\in T_1\wedge w\in T\}.$$

Let $\Pi_{\mathrm{EEC}}=\Pi_{\mathrm{SC}}$, where Π_{SC} is defined for Σ_{SC} according to Definition 3.2. $\square$

t_o is a dummy transition which is never executed in Σ_{SC} although it is always enabled in Σ_2. The original priority constraints are transformed into static priority constraints involving t_o. $(t_F,t_o,{}^\bullet w\cup\{on_{tw}\})\in\pi_{SC}$ means that $t<w$ will be properly reflected in Σ_{SC}; since t_o is always enabled in Σ_2, whenever ${}^\bullet w\cup\{on_{tw}\}$ are all marked, t_F will be disabled.

Theorem 5.4

f(steps(Π_{EEC})) = ker(Σ_{EEC}), where f(t_F) = t, for all t_F, and f(t_o) = t_o.
Note: f($A_1...A_k$) = f(A_1)...f(A_k) for every step sequence $A_1...A_k$.

Proof

(Below we use notation from Definition 5.1 and 5.3, and Construction 5.2)
From Theorem 3.3 (in its strengthened version) it follows that

$$\text{steps}(\Pi_{EEC}) = \text{ker}(\Sigma_{SC}).$$

Thus to show the result it suffices to prove that

$$\text{f}(\text{ker}(\Sigma_{SC})) = \text{ker}(\Sigma_{EEC}).$$

This in turn follows directly from $\lambda\in$ f(ker(Σ_{SC}))$\cap$ker(Σ_{EEC}) and the following two Facts.

FACT 1:

If $\sigma A\in$ steps(Σ_2) then for all $t,w\in A$

$$\text{f}(t) = \text{f}(w) \Rightarrow t = w.$$

proof of the fact: Follows from the safeness of Σ and Definition 5.2(3).

FACT 2:

Let $\sigma\in$ ker(Σ_{SC}) and f(σ)$\in$ ker(Σ_{EEC}).

(1) f(σ)$A\in$ ker(Σ_{EEC}) $\Rightarrow \exists\sigma C\in$ steps(Σ_{SC}). f(C) = A.

(2) $\sigma C\in$ ker(Σ_{SC}) $\Rightarrow$ f(σC)$\in$ steps(Σ_{EEC}).

proof of the fact:

Let M_o[f(σ)$\rangle K$ in Σ and $M_1[\sigma\rangle L$ in Σ_2. From Construction 5.2 and Definition 5.3 it follows that for all $x\in T\times T$,

(F1) $L(\text{on}_x)=1 \wedge L(\text{ON}_x)=|T| \wedge L(\text{off}_x)=L(\text{OFF}_x)=0$ or
$L(\text{off}_x)=1 \wedge L(\text{OFF}_x)=|T| \wedge L(\text{on}_x)=L(\text{ON}_x)=0$.

(F2) $x\in\rho(\text{f}(\sigma)) \Leftrightarrow L(\text{on}_x)=1$.

To show (1) we observe that from Definition 5.3, Construction 5.3 and (F1) it follows that if f(σ)$\{t\}\in$ steps(Σ) then there is t_F such that $\sigma\{t_F\}\in$ steps(Σ_2). Thus, from f(σ)$A\in$ ker(Σ_{EEC})$\subseteq$steps(Σ_{EEC}), Definition 5.1, (F1) and the safeness of Σ, it follows that there is C such that $\sigma C\in$ steps(Σ_2) and f(C) = A. Suppose that $\sigma C\notin$ steps(Σ_{SC}). Then is $t_F\in C$ and $w\in T$ such that $L({}^\bullet w\cup\{\text{on}_{tw}\})=\{1\}$. Thus, by (F2), we have: $t\in A$, $(t,w)\in\rho(\text{f}(\sigma))$ and $K({}^\bullet w)=\{1\}$, producing a contradiction with Definition 5.1. Hence (1) holds.

To show (2) we first observe that, by safeness of Σ and $(t_o,t_o,\emptyset)\in\pi_{SC}$,

$$\sigma C\in\text{ker}(\Sigma_{SC}) \Rightarrow \sigma C\in\text{steps}(\Sigma_1) \Rightarrow \text{f}(\sigma C)\in\text{steps}(\Sigma).$$

Suppose there is $(t,w)\in\rho(\text{f}(\sigma))$ such that $t\in$ f(C) and f(σ)$\{w\}\in$ steps(Σ). Then there is $t_F\in C$ and, by (F.2), $L(\text{on}_{tw})=1$. Moreover, by f(σ)$\{w\}\in$ steps(Σ), $L({}^\bullet w)=K({}^\bullet w)=\{1\}$. Hence $L({}^\bullet w\cup\{\text{on}_{tw}\})=\{1\}$, contradicting

$$\sigma C \in \text{steps}(\Sigma_{SC}) \wedge L(^\bullet t_o)=\{1\} \wedge (t_F,t_o,{}^\bullet w \cup \{on_{tw}\}) \in \pi_{SC}.$$

Hence

$$(t,w) \in \rho(\text{f}(\sigma)) \wedge t \in \text{f}(C) \Rightarrow \text{f}(\sigma)\{w\} \notin \text{steps}(\Sigma).$$

The remaining three conditions in Definition 5.1 follow directly from (F1,F2). Hence $\text{f}(\sigma C) \in \text{steps}(\Sigma_{EEC})$ and (2) holds. □

6 Final Remarks

In [12] dynamic priorities are simulated using 'ghost' events and static priority COSY path programs. The ghost events might be rendered in our framework in the following way. Suppose that $\Sigma_{SC}=(\Sigma,\pi_{SC})$ is a state-controlled priority system such that $\pi_{SC}=\{(a,b,Q)\}$. One then constructs a ghost transition gh such that ${}^\bullet gh={}^\bullet b \cup Q$ and models Σ_{SC} as a static priority system $\Sigma_S=(\Sigma',\rho)$, where $\rho=\{(gh,b),(a,gh)\}$ and Σ' is Σ after adding gh. Note that gh is never enabled in Σ_S yet it prevents a from occurring if all places in ${}^\bullet a \cup {}^\bullet b \cup Q$ are marked. The way in which ghost events are used resembles quite closely our modelling of state-controlled priorities. As far as the event-controlled priority systems are concerned, we are not aware of any published paper on these. However, it seems that within a suitably chosen process algebra it should be possible to model event-controlled priorities, extending the treatment for statically defined priorities [8].

7 Acknowledgment

This work was supported by ESPRIT BRA 3148 Project DEMON. The author would like to thank all three referees for their very helpful comments and suggestions for improvement.

References

[1] Barrett G.: The Semantics of Priority and Fairness in occam. Programming Research Group, Oxford University Computing Laboratory (1990).

[2] Beaten J.C.M., Bergstra J.A. and Klop J.W.: Ready-Trace Semantics for Concrete Process Algebra with the Priority Operator. The Computer Journal, Vol. 30(6), 498-506 (1987).

[3] Best E. and Koutny M.: Petri Net Semantics of Priority Systems. Theoretical Computer Science 94(1), 141-158 (1992).

[4] Bol R.N., Groote J.F.: The meaning of Negative Premises in Transition System Specifications. Report CS-R9054, CWI, Amsterdam (1990).

[5] Camilleri J.: An Operational semantics for occam. University of Cambridge, Computing Laboratory Technical report 144 (1988).

[6] Camilleri J. and Winskel G.: CCS with Priority Choice. Proceedings of LICS'91 Conference, IEEE Computer Society Press, 246-255 (1991).

[7] Cleaveland R. and Hennessy M.: Priorities in Process Algebras. Proceedings of LICS'89 Conference, IEEE Computer Society Press, Edinburgh (1988).

[8] Groote J.F.: Private communication (1991).

[9] Hack M.: Petri Net Languages. Technical report 159, Laboratory for Computer Science, MIT, Cambridge (1976).

[10] Janicki R.: A Formal Semantics for Concurrent Systems with a Priority Relation. Acta Informatica 24, 33-55 (1987).

[11] Janicki R. and Koutny M.: Invariants and Paradigms of Concurrency. Proceedings of PARLE'91, Lecture Notes in Computer Science 506, Springer, 59-74 (1991).

[12] Janicki R. and Lauer P.E.: Specification and Analysis of Concurrent Systems: The COSY Approach. Springer (to appear).

[13] Lamport L.: What It Means for a Concurrent Program to Satisfy a Specification: Why No One Has Specified Priority. 12th ACM Symposium on Principles of Programming Languages, New Orleans, Louisiana, 78-83 (1985).

[14] Okulicka F.: On Priority in COSY. Theoretical Computer Science 74, 199-216, (1990).

[15] Peterson J.L.: Petri Net Theory and the Modeling of Systems. Prentice Hall (1981).

[16] Reisig W.: Petri Nets: An Introduction. Springer (1985).

[17] Rozenberg G., Verraedt R.: Subset Languages of Petri Nets. Theoretical Computer Science 26, 301-323 (1983).

[18] Salwicki A., Müldner T.: On Algorithmic Properties of Concurrent Programs. Lecture Notes in Computer Science, vol. 125, Springer, 169-197 (1981).

Appendix

A net is a triple $N=(S,T,W)$ with $S\cap T=\emptyset$ and $W: S\times T\cup T\times S\to \mathbb{N}$. S is the set of places, T is the set of transitions, and W is the arc weight function. We assume that both S and T are finite sets. For $x\in S\cup T$, the pre-set of x is defined as ${}^\bullet x=\{y\in S\cup T \mid W(y,x)>0\}$ and the post-set of x is defined as $x^\bullet=\{y\in S\cup T \mid W(x,y)>0\}$. We require that for all $t\in T$, ${}^\bullet t\neq\emptyset$ and $t^\bullet\neq\emptyset$. A marking of N is defined as a function $M: S\to \mathbb{N}$. For $s\in S$, $M(s)$ denotes the number of tokens in s. A system $\Sigma=(S,T,W,M_0)$ is a net N with the initial marking M_0.

Let M be a marking of Σ and $A\neq\emptyset$ be a set of transitions of T. A is concurrently enabled at M if for all $s\in S$, $M(s)\geq\Sigma_{t\in A}W(s,t)$. We denote this by $A\in \text{enabled}_\Sigma(M)$. The marking K produced from M by the occurrence of A is defined as $K(s)=M(s)+\ \Sigma_{t\in A}W(t,s)\text{-}W(s,t)$, for all $s\in S$. We denote this by $M[A\rangle K$.

A step sequence of Σ is a sequence of sets of transitions $\sigma=A_1A_2...A_n$ $(n\geq 0)$ such that there are markings $M_1,M_2,...,M_n$ satisfying $M_{i-1}[A_i\rangle M_i$, for $i=1,...,n$. We will denote this by $M_0[\sigma\rangle M_n$. The empty step sequence will be denoted by λ. The set of the step sequences of Σ will be denoted by steps(Σ).

ON DISTRIBUTED LANGUAGES AND MODELS FOR CONCURRENCY

Brigitte ROZOY

Université de Paris XI et URA CNRS
L.R.I., Bât. 490, 91 405 Orsay Cedex, France
tel (33 1) 69 41 66 09, e_mail rozoy@lri.lri.fr

ABSTRACT.

Event Structures are a poset based model for describing the behaviour of distributed systems. They give rise to a well understood class of Scott domains. Event structures are also related to Petri nets in a fundamental way. Trace monoids are a string-based formalism for describing the behaviour of distributed systems. They have an independent theory rooted in the theory of formal languages, but are too weak to express more general nets and problems, such as the producer and consumer paradigm for example. Thus extensions of original traces have been looked at. In this paper, we describe connections between Partially Ordered Sets and Traces, using a Transition Systems, and in order to allow sound generalizations of finite traces to context-sensitive ones.
We obtain a representation of generalized trace languages in terms of labelled event structures.

KEY WORDS. Transition Systems, Event Structures, Partial Orders, Trace Languages.

CONTENTS.

This work was partially supported by the ESPRIT / BRA DEMON project and the PRC C3, CNRS.

I. INTRODUCTION

Many models are currently used to describe the running of distributed systems ; they are more or less based either on states, such as Petri Nets and Transition Systems, or on actions, such as Partially Ordered Sets and Event Structures, or on Equivalence Relations, such as Traces.

The state point of view is a basic one, even for machines that communicate by message passing along pre-defined channels. With such asynchronous systems, the trouble lies in the impossibility of having global views and therefore in the necessity of developing algorithms based on local considerations only. Here methods used for specification and validation of such communications protocols have been essentially based on ***nets, states and transitions from states to states***. It is linked with Petri Nets and is called the Transition Systems method [Hoogeb. Roze.], [Muku. Thia.], [Niel. Roze. Thia.]...

Events Based Models, the second approach to be identified, is linked with works which may be grouped under the generic heading of " Partial Order Semantic ". This method essentially involves considering that the description of the run of the system entails taking into accounts events, which are actions occurring more or less independently at various locations of a network or nodes of a graph. The Event Structure model is based on events, seen as occurrences of actions; it emphasizes relationships between these actions, and describes them by two relations, an order relation and a conflict relation. Event Structures and related semantics have been intensively studied [Bou. Cas. (1) (2) (3)], [Wins. (1) (2)], ...

Words Based Models is the last classical description for the running of distributed systems. It is well known under the denomination of " the interleaving point of view ". Given an alphabet, letters can be viewed as actions associated with a distributed system and words may be used to represent possible firing sequences, thus languages describe behaviour of the system in terms of possible sequences of actions that it can exhibit. But, in a distributed environment, the first problem lies in the fact that no one is ever able to assert either that a particular execution has really been performed or even what the real meaning of this notion is. The second problem has to be found in the feeling that words do indeed not seem to capture notions such as independence, causality or non-determinism, but other interleaving semantics like bisimulation do. Thus the interleaving models, and therefore classical tools on words and formal languages, have been under suspicions for a long time. This difficulty has been partially resolved by trace languages, which use a commutativity relation defined on the alphabet of actions and captures causal independence (concurrency) of a pair of actions as and when they occur adjacent to each other. Hence, with the help of this framework, tools and techniques of formal language theory can be applied to the study of distributed systems [Aal. Roze.], [Mazu.], [Per.],...

Several authors have developed these various approaches and *tried to connect them*. The first bridge has probably been performed by Nielsen, Plotkin and Winskel, who have established the link between Petri Nets and Domains using the event structure approach [Niel.], [Niel. Plot.

Wins.]. In a similar way, and starting with Petri Nets, Mazurkiewicz initiated the theory of traces. Then the connection between traces and other models has been studied by several authors, such as Shields, Starke, Rozoy and Thiagarajan [Muku. Thia.], [Rozo. Thia.], [Shie.], [Star.],... whereas recently Nielsen, Rozenberg and Thiagarajan started to develop a theory of transition systems in connection with Petri Nets.

Classical Mazurkiewicz traces model concurrency for a restricted subclass of Petri Nets or for transactions in a data base, but are too weak to express more general nets and problems, such as the producer and consumer paradigm for example. Thus extensions of original traces have been looked at, as for example by Arnold, Vogler, or recently by Hoogers, Kleijn and Thiagarajan [Arn.], [Hooger. Klei. Thia.], [Vog.]. The aim of this paper is to introduce a more general model of traces too, performing it in such a way that PoSet properties are still satisfied. In particular, we absolutely want to maintain the fact that the class of traces admits a representation theorem within a subclass of event structures and is therefore a finitely coherently complete prime algebraic PoSet. Thus at least two extensions may be thought out, either dealing with infinite traces in order to obtain domains, or with context dependent traces in order to get a largest class of event structures. Infinite traces and their PoSet properties have been recently studied by Diekert, Gastin, Kwiatkowska, Petit, Rozoy, Zielonka, ... [Diek. Gas. Pet.], [Gas. Pet. Ziel.], [Gas. Rozo.], [Kwia.]... We deal here with context dependent extension of finite traces. Whereas such objects have already been studied by Arnold from an algebraic point of view, we establish here connection between event structures and extended traces using transition systems. Although Winskel has reworked event structures, we deal only with the original prime event structures; moreover, there are probably some overlap with other works by previously quoted authors. It would probably be interesting now to connect all these points of views too.

II. PRIME EVENT STRUCTURES AND TRANSITION SYSTEMS

On one hand, an event structure is a partially ordered set of actions (E, $\leqslant$), together with a symmetric and irreflexive conflict relation # defined on E × E. The partial ordering is meant to capture causal dependency whereas the conflict relation models non-determinism, so that two actions that are in conflict cannot both occur in any stretch of behaviour.

On the other hand, transition systems are usually defined using two sets S, A, an element s_0 in S and a subset $\longrightarrow$ of S × A × S. The sets S and A are respectively referred to as sets of states and actions of the system, whereas $\longrightarrow$ stands for the transition relation and s_0 for the initial state. Whatever are their exact characteristics, the essential tool always hinges on the global states of the system as well as on the possible passages from one state to another.

2.1 Definition. A *conflict relation* on a partial order set (E, $\leqslant$) is any irreflexive and symmetric relation # that satisfies the inheritance property : $\forall$e, f, g $\in$ E, (e # f and e $\leqslant$ g) $\Rightarrow$ (g # f). An *Event Structure* is a 3-tuple (E, $\leqslant$, #), where (E, $\leqslant$) is a partial order set and # is a conflict relation. A *Labelled Event Structure* is a 5-tuple (E, $\leqslant$, #, ℓ, A) where (E, $\leqslant$, #) is an event structure and ℓ is a labelling function from E onto A. Elements in E are called *events*. The event structure is said to be finitary if any element admits a finite past, that is if $\forall e \in E$, $\{e' \in E \mid e' \leqslant e\}$ is of finite size. A *Transition System* is a 4-tuple (S, A, s_0, $\longrightarrow$) where S, A are sets, $\longrightarrow$ is a subset of $S \times A \times S$, and s_0 is an element of S.

Note that this definition of transition systems does not required the set A to be finite. It's necessary in order to obtain connection with event structures and will lead further to a "finite labelling problem". In order to be associated to distributed computations, those transition systems classically satisfy various axioms, depending on the considered problem. As our aim is the equivalence between event structures and transition systems, we deal with axioms technically constructed in order to come back to event structures.
The running of such a transition system is classically understood as a finite sequence σ of transitions, starting in the initial state : $\sigma = (s_0, a_1, s_1)\ (s_1, a_2, s_2)\ldots\ \ldots(s_{k-1}, a_k, s_k)$; as we study observable running of distributed systems, namely finite firing sequences only, we restrict our study to finitary prime event structures and their finite configurations. Thus, *from now on, every event structure will be assumed to be finitary and the set E to be denumerable*. The results stated here are however and clearly available for the finitary restriction of any event structure.
The connection with transition systems is done with the help of configurations ; they give an account of global states, the underlying idea being that a state is nothing simply than a structured collection of events that have been performed since the starting point.

2.2 Definition. Let ES = (E, $\leqslant$, #) be an event structure. A subset C of E is said to be *conflict-free* if $\# \cap (C \times C) = \emptyset$; it is said to be *left-closed* if $(e \in C,\ e' \leqslant e) \Rightarrow (e' \in C)$. A *configuration* is any conflict free and left-closed subset of E and the set of finite configurations is denoted $\mathscr{C}_f(ES)$. The *transition relation associated to ES* is the subset $\longrightarrow$ of $\mathscr{C}_f(ES) \times E \times \mathscr{C}_f(ES)$ defined by $(C, e, C') \in \longrightarrow$ iff $e \notin C$ and $C' = C \cup \{e\}$.

For example, let ES = (E, $\leqslant$, #) be the finitary event structure pictured in figure1, where $\longrightarrow$ stands for immediate successor relation and # for immediate conflict :

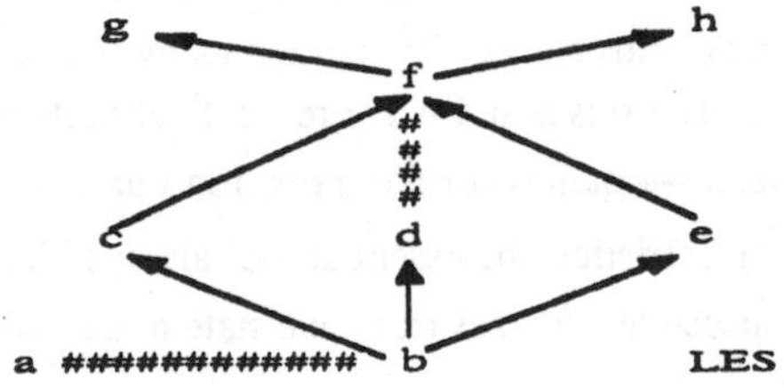

Figure 1 : Event Structure

The associated transition relation is given on the set $\mathscr{C}_f$(ES) = {∅, {a}, {b}, {b, c}, {b, d}, {b, e}, {b, c, d}, {b, d, e}, {b, c, e}, {b, d, e, c}, {b, c, e, f}, {b, c, e, f}, {b, c, e, f, g}, {b, c, e, f, h}, {b, c, e, f, g, h}} as pictured in figure 2.

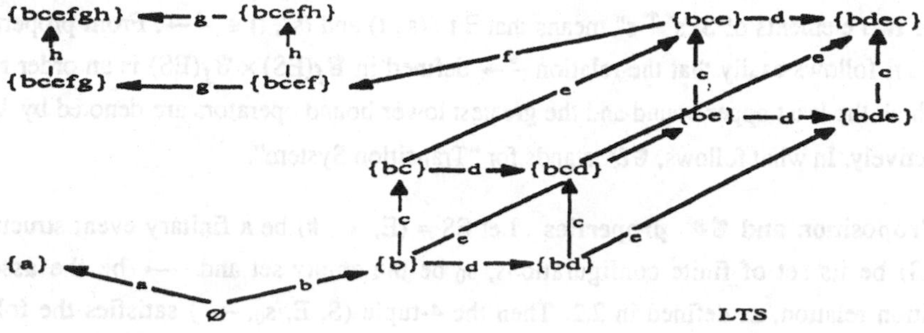

Figure 2 : Associated Transition Relation

When configurations are viewed as global states, such states carry the weight of their whole history and in consequence their number is infinite as soon as the set of events is infinite. In contrast to the complexity due to the high number of states, the running of such systems is easy to be thought of, transitions between states being simply described by the fact that a system changes its configuration to another one by adding an event.

It is well known that the set of configurations of an event structure satisfies certain important partially ordered set (PoSet) properties and that the original event structure may be recovered from its set of configurations using prime elements (see [Niel. Plot. Wins.] and [Wins. (2)]). We directly adapt this technique to transition systems : technically, previous transition relation ⟶ between configurations satisfies a family of properties that are needed in order to recover the required PoSet properties ; so they will turn out to be our axioms. Till now, we have not carefully compared them to axioms that define Elementary Transition Systems in [Niel. Roze. Thia.(1)]. However, it could be interesting to do it, both because they are clearly closed and because this could be a way to explain precisely the connection with Petri Nets.

Recall that, for any PoSet (Z, $\leqslant$) and any z in Z, ↓z denotes the set {z' ∈ Z | z' $\leqslant$ z} and is called the past of z, whereas ↑z denotes the set {z' ∈ Z | z $\leqslant$ z'} and is called the future of z. The least upper bound and the greatest lower bound operators are denoted by ⋃ and ∧ respectively. For two elements of Z, z' ↑ z" means that ∃ z : z' $\leqslant$ z and z" $\leqslant$ z. If Z' is included in Z, Z' is said to be pairwise coherent if each pair {z', z"} ⊆ Z' admits an upper bound (in Z). The PoSet (Z, $\leqslant$) is said to be *finitely coherently complete* if any finite pairwise coherent subset admits a least upper bound in Z. A prime is any element p such that, for any subset Z' of

Z, $\cup Z'$ exists and $p \leq \cup Z'$ implies $p \leq z$ for some z in Z'. Finally, (Z, $\leq$) is said to be prime algebraic if, for any z in Z, $z = \cup \{p \text{ prime} \mid p \leq z\}$.
As usually, for any sets S, A, and any relation $\longrightarrow$ defined in $S \times A \times S$, $\xrightarrow{+}$ (and $\xrightarrow{*}$) denote the non-reflexive (respectively the reflexive) transitive closure of $\longrightarrow$ viewed as a relation in $S \times S$; for two elements of S, $s' \uparrow s''$ means that $\exists\, t : (s', t)$ and $(s'', t) \in \xrightarrow{*}$. From property $\mathcal{TS}_0$ below, it follows easily that the relation $\xrightarrow{*}$ defined in $\mathcal{C}_f(ES) \times \mathcal{C}_f(ES)$ is an order relation, for which the least upper bound and the greatest lower bound operators are denoted by $\cup$ and $\wedge$ respectively. In what follows, $\mathcal{TS}$ stands for "Transition System".

2.3 Proposition and $\mathcal{TS}$ properties . Let ES = (E, $\leq$, #) be a finitary event structure, S = $\mathcal{C}_f$(ES) be its set of finite configurations, s_0 be the empty set and $\longrightarrow$ be the associated transition relation, as defined in 2.2. Then the 4-tuple (S, E, s_0, $\longrightarrow$) satisfies the following properties :

$\mathcal{TS}_0$: $\forall s', s'' \in S, (s', s'') \in \xrightarrow{+} \Rightarrow s' \neq s''$ (acyclicity).

$\mathcal{TS}_1$: $\forall s \in S, (s_0, s) \in \xrightarrow{*}$ (foundation).

$\mathcal{TS}_2$: $\forall a', a'' \in E, \forall s, s', s'' \in S, ((s, a', s'), (s, a'', s'') \in \longrightarrow) \Rightarrow (a' = a'' \Leftrightarrow s' = s'')$ (choice and causality)

$\mathcal{TS}_3$: $\forall a', a'' \in E, \forall s, s', s'' \in S, ((s, a', s'), (s, a'', s'') \in \longrightarrow, s' \uparrow s'') \Rightarrow (\exists\, t = s' \cup s''$ and $(s', a'', t), (s'', a', t) \in \longrightarrow)$ (forward diamond property).

$\mathcal{TS}_4$: $\forall a', a'' \in E, \forall t, s', s'' \in S, ((s', a'', t), (s'', a', t) \in \longrightarrow) \Rightarrow (\exists\, s = s' \wedge s''$ and $(s, a'', s''), (s, a', s') \in \longrightarrow)$ (backward diamond property).

$\mathcal{TS}_5$: $\forall n \in \mathbb{N}, \forall s, s_1, \ldots, s_n \in S, \forall a_1, \ldots, a_n \in A, (\forall k, (s, a_k, s_k) \in \longrightarrow, \forall j, k, s_j \uparrow s_k) \Rightarrow (\exists\, t : \forall k \in \{1, \ldots, n\}, (s_k, t) \in \xrightarrow{*})$ (multi coherence).

<u>Proof</u> : Let LES = (E, $\leq$, #) be a finitary event structure, S = $\mathcal{C}_f$(E) be its set of finite configurations, and the relation $\longrightarrow$ in $S \times E \times S$ be defined by :

$$(C, e, C') \in \longrightarrow \Leftrightarrow e \notin C \text{ and } C' = C \cup \{e\}$$

Note that the set S = $\mathcal{C}_f$(E) of finite configurations is partially ordered by the inclusion relation $\subseteq$, and that for any e in E, $C = \downarrow e$ and $C' = C - \{e\}$ are finite configurations such that (C', e, C) is in $\longrightarrow$. We have to verify the validity of properties $\mathcal{TS}_0 \ldots \mathcal{TS}_5$.

<u>Property $\mathcal{TS}_0$</u> : The relation $\xrightarrow{+}$ has to be acyclic in $S \times S$. Let C, C' be in S and such that $C \xrightarrow{+} C'$. Then an easy induction on the length of a path between C and C' shows that $C' = C \cup \{e_1, \ldots, e_n\}$ for some $e_1, \ldots, e_n$ not in C, and thus $C \neq C'$.

<u>Property $\mathcal{TS}_1$</u> : It asserts that the set S = $\mathcal{C}_f$(E) of finite configurations of E is the future of the empty configuration, $S = \uparrow\emptyset$, for the order relation $\xrightarrow{*}$ induced by $\longrightarrow$. Let C be in S, and n be its size. If <u>n = 0</u>, then $C = \emptyset$, and $\emptyset \xrightarrow{*} \emptyset$ is clearly true. <u>Suppose that the property is true till n-1</u> and that e is a maximal element in (C, $\leq$). Consider $C' = C - \{e\}$: C' is closed in the past, so is C and e is maximal and without conflict, so is C. Thus C' is a configuration of size n-1 and $C' \xrightarrow{e} C$. Using induction hypothesis, we get that $\emptyset \xrightarrow{*} C$.

Property $\mathscr{C}\mathscr{S}_2$

$\mathscr{C}\mathscr{S}'_2$: For C, C', C'' in S = $\mathscr{C}_f(E)$, a, b in E, suppose that (C, a, C'), (C, b, C'') ∈ ⟶ and C' ≠ C''. Then C' = C ∪ {a}, C'' = C ∪ {b}, which implies trivially a ≠ b.

$\mathscr{C}\mathscr{S}''_2$: Suppose that (C', a, C''), (C', b, C'') ∈ ⟶. Then C'' = C' ∪ {a} = C' ∪ {b}, a ∉ C', b ∉ C', which implies a = b.

Property $\mathscr{C}\mathscr{S}_3$: Suppose that C, C_1, C_2 are distinct configurations and that there exist some a_1 and a_2 in E such that $C_1 = C \cup \{a_1\}$, $C_2 = C \cup \{a_2\}$ and $(\uparrow C_1) \cap (\uparrow C_2) \neq \emptyset$. Let C' be a configuration such that $C_1 \subseteq C'$ and $C_2 \subseteq C'$: both a_1 and a_2 belong to C', thus are not in the conflict relation. This implies that $C'' = C \cup \{a_1, a_2\} = C_1 \cup C_2$ is conflict free and closed in the past, since so are C_1 and C_2, and thus is a configuration : it is clearly the least upper bound of C_1 and C_2. Since $C_1 \neq C_2$, we get $a_1 \neq a_2$ and $C_1 \xrightarrow{a_2} C''$, $C_2 \xrightarrow{a_1} C''$.

Property $\mathscr{C}\mathscr{S}_4$: Proof is rather similar and we shall omit it.

Property $\mathscr{C}\mathscr{S}_5$: Let C be a configuration, $a_1, \ldots, a_n$ be in E such that the $C_i = C \cup \{a_i\}$ are distinct pairwise coherent configurations. This implies clearly that the a_i are distinct and do not belong to the conflict relation, and thus that $C \cup \{a_i, \ldots, a_n\}$ is a configuration, which is the future of C_i for i in {1, ..., n}.

Notice that the considered transition relation is labelled with events, and that properties $\mathscr{C}\mathscr{S}_2$, $\mathscr{C}\mathscr{S}_3$, $\mathscr{C}\mathscr{S}_4$ explicitly deal with them ; it will become clear in what follows that we can not do anything without this. The last property, $\mathscr{C}\mathscr{S}_5$, allows a kind of generalisation of the diamond property to several concurrent actions : it is technically necessary to find least upper bounds for finite pairwise coherent subsets. Its semantical interpretation is the expression of concurrency through generalized interleaving ; it can be interpreted as follows : if actions $a_1, \ldots, a_m$ are possible, independent, and compatible, then it exists, somewhere in the future, some state where they all have been performed.

2.4 Definition. A *Distributed Transition System* is a transition system that satisfies $\mathscr{C}\mathscr{S}_0 \ldots \mathscr{C}\mathscr{S}_5$ properties. A *Distributed Labelled Transition System* is a 6-tuple (S, A', s_0, ⟶, ℓ, A) where (S, A', s_0, ⟶) is a distributed transition system and ℓ is a function from A' onto A.

Thus, starting with an event structure ES = (E, ≤, #) or a labelled event structure ES = (E, ≤, #, ℓ, A), above construction leads to such a distributed transition system ($\mathscr{C}_f(E)$, E, ∅, ⟶), respectively to a distributed labelled transition system ($\mathscr{C}_f(E)$, E, ∅, ⟶, ℓ, A). We set Δ((E, ≤, #)) = ($\mathscr{C}_f(E)$, E, ∅, ⟶) and Δ((E, ≤, #, ℓ, A)) = ($\mathscr{C}_f(E)$, E, ∅, ⟶, ℓ, A) too, if no confusion may arise.

Let us detail these concepts and construction on the producer and consumer example. A processor is able to produce an unbounded number of items, and then to stop, whereas another processor consumes these items. Since they act "independently", the only constraint is that an item cannot be consumed before being produced.

Event structure first. The set of events is $E = \{p_1, p_2, p_3, \ldots, s_0, s_1, s_2, s_3, \ldots, c_1, c_2, c_3, \ldots\}$ where events $p_1, p_2, p_3, \ldots$ and $c_1, c_2, c_3, \ldots$ stand respectively for the production and the consumption of the first, the second, the third item, and so on..., whereas $s_0, s_1, s_2, \ldots$ stand for stopping after producing no item, one item, two items... The alphabet of actions is $\{p, c, s\}$ with the obvious labelling function $\ell(x_i) = x$, p for "produce", c for "consume" and s for "stop". The partial order relation, shown with the help of the corresponding Hasse diagram, is the transitive and reflexive closure of $\forall i,\ p_i < p_{i+1},\ p_i < c_i,\ p_i < s_i,\ c_i < c_{i+1}$. The conflict relation is shown with the help of the closure under inheritance of the minimal conflict relation $\forall i,\ s_i \#_\mu p_{i+1}$.

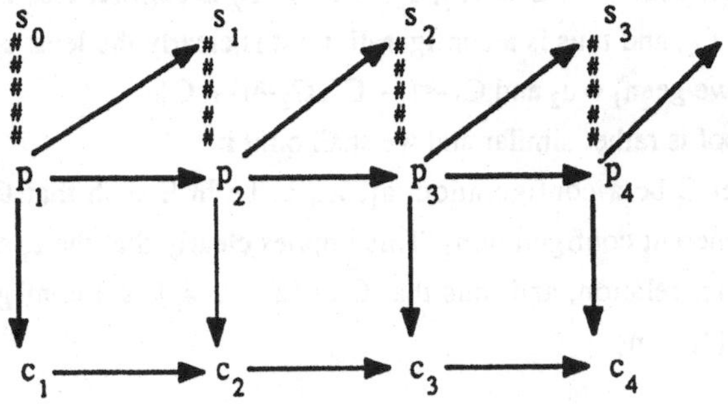

Figure 3.

In figure 3, we have shown only minimal elements for the causality relation as directed arcs, as well as for the conflict relation as #### lines. Recall that the conflict relation may be understood as the fact that two events e' and e" in conflict never occur together in the same execution of the system and note that a run of such a system is not implicitly included in its formulation : such a description has to be understood as a whole collection of occurrences of actions that may eventually arise under restrictions of causality and conflict.

Transition system now. States are configurations, that is $\emptyset$, or $\{s_0\}$, or $\{p_1, \ldots, p_j\}$, or $\{p_1, \ldots, p_j, s_j\}$ for $i \le j$, or $\{p_1, \ldots, p_j, c_1, \ldots, c_i\}$, or $\{p_1, \ldots, p_j, c_1, \ldots, c_i, s_j\}$.

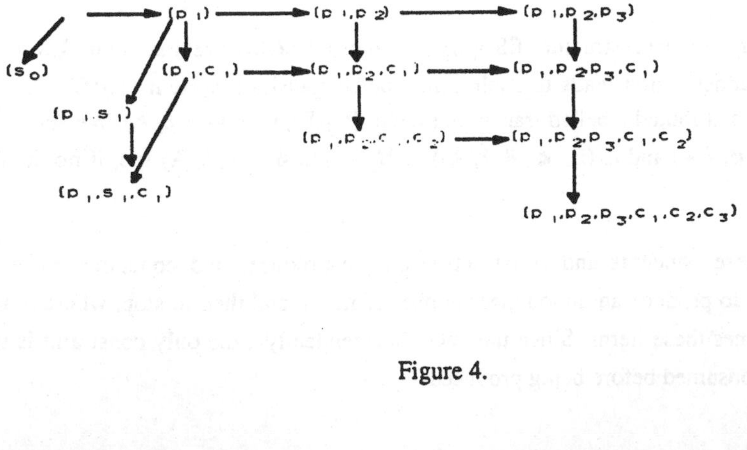

Figure 4.

The transitions are of the following forms :

$\emptyset \xrightarrow{p_1} \{p_1\}$, or $\emptyset \xrightarrow{s_0} \{s_0\}$.

$\{p_1, ..., p_j\} \xrightarrow{p_{j+1}} \{p_1, ..., p_{j+1}\}$, or $\{p_1, ..., p_j\} \xrightarrow{c_1} \{p_1, ..., p_j, c_1\}$, or $\{p_1, ..., p_j\} \xrightarrow{s_j} \{p_1, ..., p_j, s_j\}$.

$\{p_1, ..., p_j, s_j\} \xrightarrow{c_1} \{p_1, ..., p_j, s_j, c_1\}$.

$\{p_1, ..., p_j, c_1, ..., c_i\} \xrightarrow{p_{j+1}} \{p_1, ..., p_j, p_{j+1}, c_1, ..., c_i\}$, or $\{p_1, ..., p_j, c_1, ..., c_i\} \xrightarrow{s_j} \{p_1, ..., p_j, s_j, c_1, ..., c_i\}$, or $\{p_1, ..., p_j, c_1, ..., c_i\} \xrightarrow{c_{i+1}} \{p_1, ..., p_j, c_1, ..., c_i, c_{i+1}\}$ if $i < j$.

$\{p_1, ..., p_j, c_1, ..., c_i, s_j\} \xrightarrow{c_{i+1}} \{p_1, ..., p_j, c_1, ..., c_i, s_j\}$ if $i < j$.

The alphabet of actions is again $A = \{p, c, s\}$, and the labelling function ℓ is : $\forall k$, $\ell(c_k) = c$, $\ell(p_k) = p$, $\ell(s_k) = s$.

What is interesting is that $\mathcal{C}\mathcal{S}$ properties characterize exactly those transition systems that allow to recover an event structure, or equivalently transition systems such that $(S, \xrightarrow{*})$ is a finitary finitely coherently complete prime algebraic PoSet.

Similarly as it has been done when starting with configurations (see [Niel. Plot. Wins.] and [Wins. (2)]), we construct the event structure, the events of which are exactly the primes of $(S, \xrightarrow{*})$. In the following definition, an immediate predecessor of a state p is understood for the order relation $\xrightarrow{*}$, thus is a state s such that (s, a, p) belongs to $\longrightarrow$ for some a in A'.

2.5 Proposition. Let $TS = (S, A', s_0, \longrightarrow)$ be a distributed transition system. Then $\xrightarrow{*}$ is a partial order relation, the primes of which are those elements that admit exactly one immediate predecessor ; moreover, for any state s in S, if we state PR(s) for the set of primes bounded by s, ie $PR(s) = \{p \text{ prime} \mid p \leqslant s\}$, then $s = \bigcup PR(s)$. If we set E for the set PR(S) of primes, $\leqslant$ for the restriction of $\xrightarrow{*}$ to $E \times E$, # for the relation defined in $E \times E$ by p' # p" iff not(p' $\uparrow$ p"), then (E, $\leqslant$, #) is a finitary event structure.

<u>Proof</u> : By construction, $\xrightarrow{*}$ and $\xrightarrow{+}$ are transitive, $\xrightarrow{*}$ is reflexive ; by property $\mathcal{C}\mathcal{S}_0$ and transitivity, $\xrightarrow{+}$ is acyclic, thus $\xrightarrow{*}$ is a partial order relation on S.

We are now interested in the existence and the characterization of prime elements for this order. If p admits at least two immediate predecessors p' and p", then $p = p' \cup p"$, but neither $p \leqslant p'$ nor $p \leqslant p"$, so p is not a prime. Thus a prime admits at most one immediate predecessor.

The proof that any element that admits exactly one immediate predecessor is a prime is more difficult. Roughly speaking, we have to look at "events" through transitions. Imagine first that the two states s and t' admit a common bound and are immediate successors of some state t, with transition (t, a, t') between t and t' ; the diamond property $\mathcal{C}\mathcal{S}_3$ gives the least upper bounded $s' = s \cup t'$ and the transition (s, a, s') between s and s'. Thus, it suggests us some connection between the couples of states (t, t') and (s, s'). We say that they both have to be associated to the same action labelled by "a", and that this action was possibly executed starting at least in two distinct states, either t or s. This will lead to an equivalence notion between transitions, the sets of events being isomorphic to the quotient of the set of transitions by this equivalence relation.

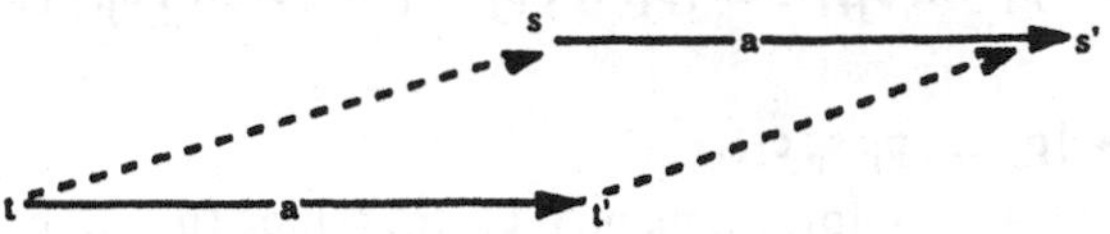

Figure 5 : Order between transitions.

Formally, first a binary relation « is defined on the set of transitions by setting (t, a, t') « (s, a, s') iff $s' = s \cup t'$ and $t = s \wedge t'$; this relation « is shown to be a partial order. Second, a binary relation ≡ is defined between transitions as the symmetric and transitive closure of (« ∪ »): two transitions (s_1, a, s'_1) and (s_n, a, s'_n) are equivalent, denoted by (s_1, a, s'_1) ≡ (s_n, a, s'_n), if there exists a chain (s_1, a, s_1') (s_2, a, s'_2), ..., (s_n, a, s'_n) such that for any k, (s_k, a, s'_k) « (s_{k+1}, a, s'_{k+1}) or (s_k, a, s'_k) » (s_{k+1}, a, s'_{k+1}) ; again, by construction, ≡ is an equivalence relation on the set of transitions. Notice that two equivalent transitions have the same name "a", which can be viewed as the name of an action : they stand for two occurrences of the same event.

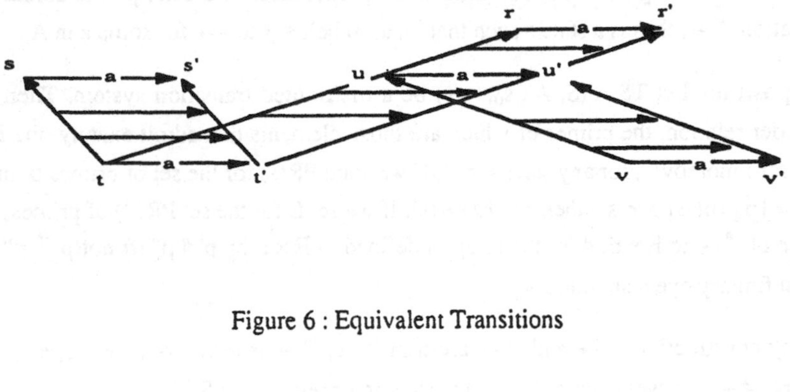

Figure 6 : Equivalent Transitions

Then it may be shown that each equivalence class of transitions admits a least element (s_k, a, s'_k) for the order relation «, and as a consequence, that s_k is the single immediate predecessor of s'_k. It is then possible to see that, for any transition (s, a, s'), there exists a single element p such that $p \leqslant s'$ and not $p \leqslant s$; we denote it p = prime(s, a, s'). Moreover, p admits exactly one predecessor.

Then, by $\mathcal{CS}_1$ and for any s in S, there exists a finite sequence of states (s_0, ..., s_m) and a finite sequence of letters (a_1, ..., a_m) such that for any k, (s_k, a_{k+1}, s_{k+1}) belongs to ⟶ and s_m = s. We note $s_0 \xrightarrow{w} s$, with w = $a_1 \ldots a_m$. As a consequence of $\mathcal{CS}_2$, $\mathcal{CS}_3$, $\mathcal{CS}_4$, if $s_0 \xrightarrow{w} s$ and $s_0 \xrightarrow{w'} s$, then w and w' have the same length, which is called the depth of s. Now, by induction on the depth of any state s and using property $\mathcal{CS}_5$, it possible to show that card({p prime | $p \leqslant s$}) = depth(s) and that $s = \cup \{p \text{ prime} \mid p \leqslant s\}$.

Finally, choose a subset S' of S such that s = $\bigcup$S' exists and set P' = {p ∈ S | p admits exactly one predecessor and ∃ s' ∈ S', p ⋖ s'}, P" = {p ∈ S | p admits exactly one predecessor and p ⋖ s}. We show that P' = P". Clearly P' ⊆ P", p' = $\bigcup$P' and p" = $\bigcup$P" exist, with p' ⋖ s, p" ⋖ s. We get that p' = $\bigcup$P' = s. Suppose now that p belongs to P" and not to P', set T = P"−{p} and t = $\bigcup$T. Since P' ⊆ T ⊆ P" and T ≠ P", we get (s $\overset{*}{\longrightarrow}$ t) and depth(s) > depth(t), which is absurd. Thus P' = P" : the set of prime elements is exactly the set of elements that admit exactly one immediate predecessor. Moreover, for any state s, s = $\bigcup$ {p prime | p ⋖ s}.

If we set E for PR(S) and ⋖ for the restriction of $\overset{*}{\longrightarrow}$ to E, (E, ⋖) is thus a PoSet and we have only to ensure that #, defined in E × E by p' # p" iff not(p' ↑ p"), is a conflict relation :

- e # e' ⇔ not (e ↑ e') ⇔ (↑e') ∩ (↑e) = ∅ ⇔ not (e' ↑ e) ⇔ e' ↑ e : it is symmetric.
- e ∈ E = PR(S) ⇒ e ∈ ↑e ⇒ (↑e) ∩ (↑e) ≠ ∅ ⇒ not (e # e) : it is irreflexive.
- e' # e" and e" ⋖ e ⇔ not (e' ↑ e") and e" ⋖ e ⇒ not (e' ↑ e) ⇔ e' # e : it is inherited.

Finally, for any e in E = PR(S), e belongs to S, thus card({p ∈ E | p ⋖ e}) = depth(e) is finite by $\mathscr{E}\mathscr{S}_1$. The event structure (E, ⋖, #) is finitary.

Therefore, what we have done is to associate with any distributed transition system TS = (S, A', s_0, ⟶) the event structure ∇(TS) = (PR(S), ⋖, #), where the order and the conflict relation have been defined above. Starting with a distributed labelled transition system (S, A', s_0, ⟶, ℓ, A), notice that any prime p admits one single immediate predecessor, s, and thus that (s, a', p) is in ⟶ for exactly one a' in A' ; set then ℓ'(p) = ℓ(a') and denote by ∇(LTS) too the event structure (PR(S), ⋖, #, ℓ', A). Note that this technique that identifies the events as the prime elements of a partial order is not new ; it as already been done in [Niel. Plot. Wins.] and [Wins. (2)]. What differs here is the formalisation of these distributed transition systems and the characterisation of primes, what will turn out to be of a real help when dealing with traces.

In the following example, (S, A, s_0, ⟶) is a distributed transition system, with S = {o, p, q, r, s, t, u, v, w, x, y, z}, A = {e, f, g, h}, and customary graphical conventions.

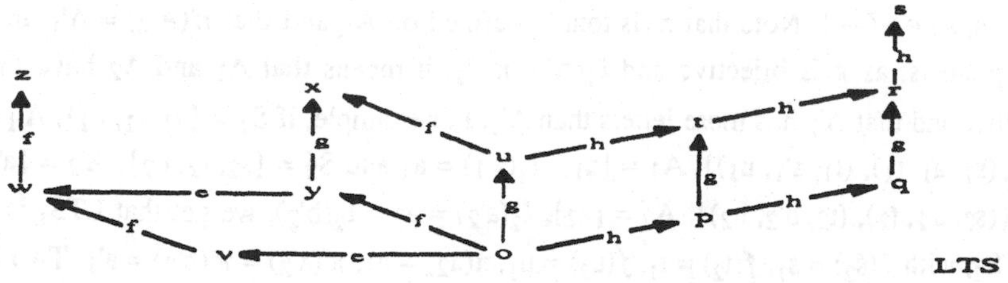

Figure 7 : A Distributed Transition System.

Its image will be the event structure (E, $\leqslant$, #), where E = {p, q, s, u, v, y, z}, the immediate order and immediate conflict relations being pictured below as usual, that is where $\longrightarrow$ stands for immediate successor relation and #### for immediate conflict.

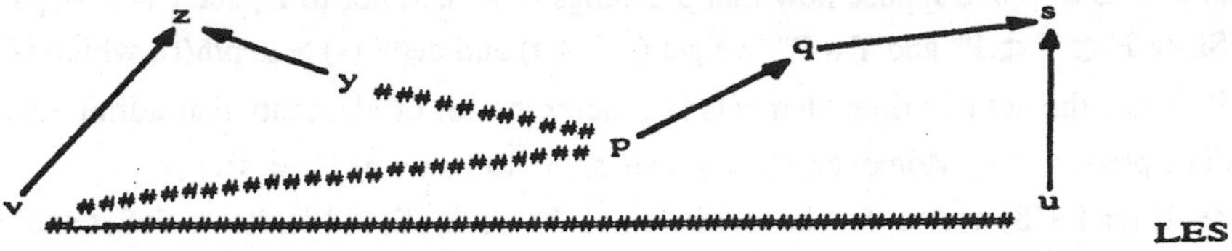

Figure 8 : The event structure associated by function ∇.

The notable result is that Δ does not destroy anything inside the set of finite configurations and that ∇ eventually creates new names for transitions but preserves the set of states, the structure of the set of transitions, and the alphabet of actions.

To prove it, we need notions of isomorphisms and order between labelled event structures and labelled transition systems, understood in a rather obvious way. Formally, two labelled event structures (E, $\leqslant$, #, ℓ, A) and (E', $\leqslant$', #', ℓ', A') are said to be *isomorphic* if there exists bijective mappings $f : E \longrightarrow E'$, $\alpha : A \longrightarrow A'$ such that $\ell' o f = \alpha o \ell$, $e \leqslant e' \Leftrightarrow f(e) \leqslant' f(e')$, $e \# e' \Leftrightarrow f(e) \#' f(e')$. Similarly, an order relation between labelled distributed transition systems is understood as isomorphism for both states and labels of actions, and embedding for actions and transitions. Formally, if $LTS_1 = (S_1, A'_1, s_1, \xrightarrow{1}, \ell_1, A_1)$ and $LTS_2 = (S_2, A'_2, s_2, \xrightarrow{2}, \ell_2, A_2)$ are two labelled distributed transition systems, we say that *LTS_1 is smaller than LTS_2*, denoted by $LTS_1 \ll LTS_2$, if there exists bijective mappings $f : S_2 \longrightarrow S_1$, $\pi : A_2 \longrightarrow A_1$, and a surjective mapping : $\pi' : A'_2 \longrightarrow A'_1$, such that : (i) $f(s_2) = s_1$ - (ii) $\ell_1 o \pi' = \pi o \ell_2$ - (iii) $\xrightarrow{1} = \{(f(s), \pi'(a), f(s')) \mid (s, a, s') \in \xrightarrow{2}\}$. Note that π' is totally defined on A'_2 and that $\pi'(A'_2) = A'_1$. In case of finite alphabets, as π is bijective and $\ell_1 o \pi' = \pi o \ell_2$, it means that A_1 and A_2 have the same cardinallity and that A'_2 has more letters than A'_1. For example, if $S_1 = \{s_1, t_1, u_1\}$, $A'_1 = \{a'_1\}$, $\xrightarrow{1} = \{(s_1, a_1, t_1), (t_1, a'_1, u_1)\}$, $A_1 = \{a_1\}$, $\ell_1(a'_1) = a_1$ and $S_2 = \{s_2, t_2, u_2\}$, $A'_2 = \{a'_2, b'_2\}$, $\xrightarrow{2} = \{(s_2, a'_2, t_2), (t_2, b'_2, u_2)\}$, $A_2 = \{a_2\}$, $\ell_2(a'_2) = a_2 = \ell_2(b'_2)$, we get that LTS_1 is smaller than LTS_2, with $f(s_2) = s_1$, $f(t_2) = t_1$, $f(u_2) = u_1$, $\pi(a_2) = a_1$, $\pi'(a'_2) = \pi'(b'_2) = a'_1$. Two labelled distributed transition systems are said to be *isomorphic* if $LTS_1 \ll LTS_2$ and $LTS_2 \ll LTS_1$. The maximallity is understood for the alphabet of transitions, and up to an isomorphism of course. We get then the following theorem :

2.6 Theorem. Let $\mathcal{LCS}$ be the family of distributed labelled transition systems and $\mathcal{LES}$ be the family of finitary labelled event structures. Then $\nabla o \Delta$ is an isomorphism on $\mathcal{LES}$, and, for any labelled transition system LTS, $\Delta o \nabla(\text{LTS})$ is the greatest element of the class of labelled transition systems for which LTS is a lower bound : LTS « LTS" ⇒ LTS" « $\Delta o \nabla(\text{LTS})$.

$$\mathcal{LES} \underset{\nabla}{\overset{\Delta}{\rightleftarrows}} \mathcal{LCS}$$

<u>Proof</u> : <u>(i)</u> Let us prove that $\nabla o \Delta$ is an isomorphism on $\mathcal{LES}$. Let $(E, \leqslant, \#, \ell, A)$ be a labelled (finitary) event structure and construct its image by $\nabla o \Delta$:

$$\nabla o \Delta : \mathcal{LES} \longrightarrow \mathcal{LCS} \longrightarrow \mathcal{LES}$$

$$(E, \leqslant, \#, \ell, A) \longrightarrow (\mathcal{C}_f(E), E, \emptyset, \longrightarrow, \ell, A) \longrightarrow (PR(\mathcal{C}_f(E)), \leqslant', \#', \ell', A)$$

The order on the set of configurations $\mathcal{C}_f(E)$ is the restriction of the inclusion among finite subsets.

• Let us first examine finite configurations, which are prime elements for this order. If C is such a prime, it admits exactly one predecessor, say C'. We get $C = C' \cup \{e\}$ and $e \notin C'$. If $C' = \emptyset$, then $C = \{e\} = \downarrow e$, where $\downarrow e$ is the past of e. If C' is not empty, let e' be one of its elements and compare it with e. Suppose that not $(e' \leqslant e)$. Since C' is finite, it contains a maximal element e" such that $e' \leqslant e''$ and thus $e'' \neq e$. This implies that $C'' = C - \{e''\}$ is a configuration, which is an immediate predecessor of C and distinct from C' : this is absurd. Being a configuration, C is closed in the past, and thus we get again that $C = \downarrow e$: any prime finite configuration admits a greatest element (for the initial order on E) and is equal to the past of that element. The converse is trivially true : since event structure $(E, \leqslant, \#, \ell, A)$ is finitary, any subset of the form $\downarrow e$ with e in E is a finite prime configuration. We get two inverse bijective mappings $\downarrow$ and γ between the sets E and $PR(\mathcal{C}_f)$, and a trivial bijective mapping Id : A ⟶ A :

$$\downarrow : E \longrightarrow PR(\mathcal{C}_f(E)) \qquad\qquad \gamma : PR(\mathcal{C}_f(E)) \longrightarrow E$$

$$e \longrightarrow \downarrow e = \{e' \mid e' \leqslant e\} \qquad\qquad C \longrightarrow \gamma(C) = e = \text{the greatest element of } C$$

This mappings are such that :

• $e \leqslant e'$ (in E) $\Leftrightarrow (\downarrow e) \subseteq (\downarrow e') \Leftrightarrow (\downarrow e) \leqslant' (\downarrow e')$ (in PR $(\mathcal{C}_f(E))$)

• $e \# e'$ (in E) $\Leftrightarrow \forall e'' >_f e, e'' \# e'$ and $\forall e'' >_f e', e \# e'' \Leftrightarrow \forall C \in \mathcal{C}_f(E), (\downarrow e) \not\longrightarrow C$ iff not $((\downarrow e') \not\longrightarrow C) \Leftrightarrow$ not $((\downarrow e) \uparrow (\downarrow e')) \Leftrightarrow (\downarrow e) \#' (\downarrow e')$ (in PR $(\mathcal{C}_f(E))$).

• $\ell' = \ell o \gamma \Rightarrow \ell' o \downarrow = \ell o \gamma o \downarrow = \ell o Id = \ell = Id o \ell$.

Thus : $(E, \leqslant, \#, \ell, A) \approx (PR(\mathcal{C}_f(E)), \leqslant', \#', \ell', A)$.

<u>(ii)</u> : We look now at $\Delta o \nabla : \mathcal{LCS} \longrightarrow \mathcal{LES} \longrightarrow \mathcal{LCS}$. Let us prove that for any labelled transition system LTS, $\Delta o \nabla(\text{LTS})$ is the greatest element of the class of labelled transition systems for which LTS is a lower bound : LTS « LTS' ⇒ LTS' « $\Delta o \nabla(\text{LTS})$. Let LTS = (S, A',

s_0, ⟶, ℓ, A) be a labelled distributed transition system ; set ∇(LTS) = (PR(S), ≤, #, ℓ', A), where ℓ' has been defined just above as ℓ' = ℓoγ ; set Δo∇(LTS) = ($\mathcal{C}_f$(PR(S)), PR(S), ∅, $\stackrel{'}{\longrightarrow}$, ℓ', A). Define a mapping PR : S ⟶ $\mathcal{C}_f$(PR(S)) by PR(s) = {p ∈ PR(S) | p ≤ s}. Thanks to proposition 2.5, ∀s ∈ S, s = ∪{p ∈ PR(S) | p ≤ s}. This implies that PR is injective.

• We have first to prove that LTS « Δo∇(LTS) ; for that, we need mappings *f*, π', π. Define *f* = PR^{-1} : $\mathcal{C}_f$(PR(S)) ⟶ S by *f*(C) = ∪C, π' = γ : PR(S) ⟶ A', and π = $Id_{|A}$; *f* and π are bijective mappings, π' is onto, *f*(∅) = s_0, ℓoπ' = ℓoγ = πo(ℓoγ). By $\mathcal{CS}_1$, for any s in S, length(s) < ∞, thus for any e ≤ s, card(↓e) < ∞. Moreover, (C, p, C') ∈ $\stackrel{'}{\longrightarrow}$ ⇔ C' = C ∪ {p} ⇒ (∪C, γ(p), (∪C) ∪ {p}) ∈ ⟶.

Now, recall that, for any transition (s, a, s'), there exists a single element p such that p ≤ s' and not p ≤ s (see proof of proposition 2.5) ; we denote it p = prime(s, a, s'). We get then that (s, a, s') ∈ ⟶ ⇒ s' = s ∪ prime(s, a, s') with γ(prime(s, a, s')) = a. We have then PR(s) = f^{-1}(s), PR(s') = f^{-1}(s') ⇒ (f^{-1}(s), prime(s, a, s'), f^{-1}(s')) ∈ $\stackrel{'}{\longrightarrow}$. Thus : LTS « Δo∇(LTS).

• Consider again LTS = (S, A', s_0, ⟶, ℓ, A), LTS' = Δo∇(LTS) = ($\mathcal{C}_f$ (PR (S)), PR(S), ∅, $\stackrel{'}{\longrightarrow}$, ℓoγ, A) and suppose that LTS is bounded by some LTS" = (S", A", s", $\stackrel{''}{\longrightarrow}$, ℓ", "A) ; set *f* : S" ⟶ S, π' : A" ⟶ A', π : "A ⟶ A, for the associated mappings. We have to prove that LTS" is bounded by LTS' and for that we shall define three mappings, "*f* : $\mathcal{C}_f$(PR(S)) ⟶ S", "π' : PR(S) ⟶ A", "π : A ⟶ "A.

– Set "*f* = f^{-1}oPR^{-1}, "π = π^{-1}. They both are bijective mappings.

– ∀s' ∈ PR(S), ∃ ! a' = γ(s'), ∃ ! s ∈ S : (s, a', s') ∈ ⟶ ⇒ ∃ ! a" ∈ A" : (f^{-1}(s), a", f^{-1}(s')) ∈ $\stackrel{''}{\longrightarrow}$. Set ∀s' ∈ PR(S), "π'(s') = a"

– (f^{-1}(s), a", f^{-1}(s')) ∈ $\stackrel{''}{\longrightarrow}$ ⇒ (s, π'(a"), s') ∈ ⟶ ⇒ π'(a") = a' = γ(s'), thus ∀s' ∈ PR(S), γ(s') = a' = π'(a") = π'o"π'(s') ⇒ π'o"π' = γ ⇒ "πo(ℓoγ) = π^{-1}oℓo π'o"π' = (π^{-1}oℓo π'o) "π' = ℓ"o"π'. Moreover "π' is onto : ∀a" ∈ A", ∃ s, s' ∈ S" : (s, a", s') ∈ $\stackrel{''}{\longrightarrow}$ ⇒ (*f*(s), π'(a"), *f*(s')) ∈ ⟶ ⇒ ∃ p ∈ γ^{-1}(π'(a")) : (PR(*f*(s)), p, PR(*f*(s'))) ∈ $\stackrel{'}{\longrightarrow}$ ⇒ ∃ p ∈ PR(S) : ("*f* (PR (*f*(s))), "π'(p), "*f* (PR (*f*(s')))) ∈ $\stackrel{''}{\longrightarrow}$. We have "*f* = f^{-1}oPR^{-1} ⇒ (s, "π'(p), s') ∈ $\stackrel{''}{\longrightarrow}$ ⇒ a" = "π'(p) : "π' is onto.

Thus LTS" « LTS'.

We have closely linked our distributed labelled transition systems and labelled event structure by representation results that express clearly the fact that they stand for the same object.

III. TRANSITION SYSTEMS AND DISTRIBUTED LANGUAGES

Our purpose now is to deal with words and equivalence relations. For Petri nets, the natural idea is to study firing sequences ; for transition systems it turns to the study of paths from one state to another. Starting with TS = (S, A', s_0, ⟶) we first look, for any word w in A'*, at the state φ(w) such that $s_0 \stackrel{w}{\longrightarrow}$ φ(w). As property $\mathcal{CS}_2$ is satisfied, φ is well defined and we may set ≈ for the associated equivalence relation, namely w' ≈ w" iff φ(w') = φ(w"). Unfortunately, the study of ≈

and φ is of some help only if the set A' is finite ! In case of infinite A', the second idea is to start with a labelled system, LTS = (S, A', s_0, $\longrightarrow$, ℓ, A) for some finite A, and to project A'^* onto A^*. The ℓ-projection of LTS = (S, A', s_0, $\longrightarrow$, ℓ, A) is defined as π_ℓ(LTS) = (S, A, s_0, $\longrightarrow^{\pi\ell}$) where (s, ℓ(a'), s') $\in \longrightarrow^{\pi\ell} \Leftrightarrow$ (s, a', s') $\in \longrightarrow$. Unfortunately again, this is suitable iff resulting projection of function φ is well defined, that is iff π_ℓ(LTS) satisfies again property $\mathcal{CS}_2$. As we have not used either ℓ or A so far, we dwell on the part held by the labelling function. Starting again with an event structure (E, $\leqslant$, #) the question is to determine wether it admits such a suitable labelling, that is wether it exists a finite alphabet A and a labelling function ℓ : E $\longrightarrow$ A such that the projection of resulting transition system satisfies property $\mathcal{CS}_2$.

3.1 Definition. An event structure is said to *admit a finite and nice labelling* if there exists a finite alphabet A and a labelling function ℓ from E onto A such that the projection of π_ℓ(Δ((E, $\leqslant$, #, ℓ, A))) = ($\mathcal{C}_f$(E), A, $\emptyset$, $\longrightarrow^{\pi\ell}$) is a distributed transition system.

For example, this is not possible for an event structure such as ES = ($\mathbb{N}$, $\emptyset$, $\mathbb{N} \times \mathbb{N}$) : Δ(ES) = ($\mathcal{C}_f$, $\mathbb{N}$, $\emptyset$, $\longrightarrow$) where $\mathcal{C}_f = \{\emptyset\} \cup \{\{p\} \mid p \in \mathbb{N}\}$ and $\longrightarrow = \{(\emptyset, p, \{p\}) \mid p \in \mathbb{N}\}$. Suppose that ℓ : E $\longrightarrow$ A is some nice labelling, thus that ($\mathcal{C}_f$, A, $\emptyset$, $\longrightarrow^{\pi\ell}$) satisfies property $\mathcal{CS}_2$. For any p in $\mathbb{N}$, ($\emptyset$, ℓ(p), {p}) is in $\longrightarrow^{\pi\ell}$, thus p' $\neq$ p" implies ℓ(p') $\neq$ ℓ(p") : the alphabet A has to be infinite. This is closely related to the fact that the number of immediate successors of the empty configurations is is not finite, what is a notion of degree.

3.2 Proposition. Let us call *the degree of the event structure* (E, $\leqslant$, #) the supremum in $\mathbb{N} \cup \{\infty\}$ of {card(E') | E' $\subseteq$ E and E' $\times$ E' $\subseteq$ co $\cup$ $\#_\mu$}, where co = E $\times$ E - ($\leqslant \cup \geqslant \cup$ #), $\#_\mu$ = # - {(e, f) | $\exists$ e' $\leqslant$ e, f' $\leqslant$ f : e $\neq$ e' or $f \neq f'$ and e' # f'}. Let us call *the degree of the transition system* (S, A, s_0, $\longrightarrow$) the greatest element in $\mathbb{N} \cup \{\infty\}$ of {card(s°) | s $\in$ S}, where s° = {s' $\in$ S | $\exists$ a : (s, a, s') $\in \longrightarrow$ }. Then the degrees of ES and Δ(ES) are equal, and, if ES admits a finite and nice labelling, then its degree is bounded by the size of the alphabet.

<u>Sketch of the proof</u> : (Complete proofs may be found in [Rozo. (2)]).
Let LES = (E, $\leqslant$, #, ℓ, A) be a labelled event structure and Δ(LES) = ($\mathcal{C}_f$(E), E, $\emptyset$, $\longrightarrow$, ℓ, A) be its associated labelled transition system.
First prove that : $\forall$ {e_1, e_2, ..., e_n} $\subseteq$ E, ($\forall$j $\neq$ k, (e_j co e_k) or (e_j $\#_\mu$ e_k) $\Leftrightarrow$ ($\exists$ s, s_1, s_2, ..., s_n in $\mathcal{C}_f$(E) : $\forall$j $\neq$ k, $s_j \neq s_k$ and (s, e_k, s_k) $\in \longrightarrow$).
Then associate a sequence (s, s_1, s_2, ...) with any chain {e_1, e_2, ...}, and conversely, which implies equality of the degrees for ES and Δ(ES). Converse derives directly from the fact that Δo∇ and ∇oΔ are isomorphisms. If ℓ : E $\longrightarrow$ A is a nice labelling on an event structure and {e_1, e_2, ...} is a chain, then, for any j $\neq$ k, (s, e_j, s_j) and (s, e_k, s_k) are in $\longrightarrow$, and $\ell(e_j) \neq \ell(e_k)$ by $\mathcal{CS}_2$; thus card(A) is greater than the degree of the event structure.

The question of course now is to determine whether an event structure of finite degree admits a finite and nice labelling. It is actually an open problem the answer to which is only known for degree two.

3.3 Theorem. If the event structure is of degree two, then there exists a finite and nice labelling of size two.

Sketch of the proof : (Complete proofs may be found in [Ass. Bou. Cha. Rozo.]).

Let (E, $\leqslant$, #) be an event structure. For two events f and g, f # g and not (f $\#_\mu$ g) is denoted by f $\#_\dagger$ g ; we say that f and g are in former conflict. Let e be in E. The subset of events that are with e in the relation $\| = \#_\mu \cup$ co is denoted Meet(e). For any event e, $\mathcal{C}$(e) denotes the configuration $\downarrow$e-{e}, and $\mathcal{D}$(e) is the depth of e, that is $\mathcal{D}$(e) = card($\mathcal{C}$(e)) ; its clear that the depth is a function compatible with the order, namely e $\leqslant$ f implies $\mathcal{D}(e) \leq \mathcal{D}(f)$, and e $\leqslant$ f, e $\neq f$ implies $\mathcal{D}(e) < \mathcal{D}(f)$. We inductively construct a nice labelling of size two, with the alphabet A = {a, b}.

— The proof relies partly on the fact that Meet(e) is a totally ordered set as long as the degree is equal to two.

— Let f and g be in Meet(e) ; $f \leqslant$ g, $f \neq$ g and f # e would imply e $\#_\dagger$ g, which is impossible since e $\|$ g. Thus we obtain that (e $\|$ f and e $\|$ g) implies (g $\leqslant$ f and e co g) or (f $\leqslant$ g and e co f) or (f = g).

— Let e be an event. Since Meet(e) is totally ordered and finitary, either it is empty or it admits a least element, denoted by inf_m(e). Moreover, the depth of this least element is bounded by the depth of e : let f = inf_m(e) be that least element, and suppose that g $\leqslant$ f, g $\neq f$. As g is not in Meet(e), g $\|$ e is impossible ; in the same way, g # e and e $\leqslant$ g are impossible, since they would imply not (f $\|$ e). We obtain g $\leqslant$ e, and thus, for any g in $\mathcal{C}(f)$, g belongs to $\mathcal{C}$(e) : $\mathcal{C}(f) \subseteq \mathcal{C}(e)$ implies $\mathcal{D}(f) \leqslant \mathcal{D}(e)$. In particular, that implies that we can decide wether Meet(e) is empty or not, and effectively compute inf_m(e).

— Set E = {e_0, e_1, ..., e_q, ...} be an enumeration of E such that k < h implies $\mathcal{D}(e_k) \leq \mathcal{D}(e_h)$; let us notice that such an enumeration is compatible with the order relation, namely $e_k \leqslant e_h$ implies $k \leq h$; for any n set E_n = {e_0, e_1, ..., e_n}. For n = 0, set $\ell(e_0)$ = a. Suppose that till n, e_0, e_1, ..., e_n have been nicely labelled with a and b, and label e = e_{n+1} by setting : if Meet(e) = $\emptyset$ or f = Inf_m(e) is not in E_n, then set ℓ(e) = a ; if f = Inf_m(e) is in E_n, then set ℓ(e) = a if $\ell(f)$ = b and ℓ(e) = b otherwise. Finally, prove that this labelling is nice, namely that f, f' in E_{n+1} and $f \| f'$ implies $\ell(f) \neq \ell(f')$.

Note : There are at most 2^{k+1} events e such that $\mathcal{D}$(e) = k. Thus, the description of every element e of E by $\mathcal{D}$(e) induces an effective description of E; hence the previous proof gives an algorithm for the nice 2-labelling.

Following this result, its seems natural to conjecture a similar one for other degrees. It is indeed not true as soon as the degree is strictly greater than 2 : a counter example due to Brochet shows that even for n =3, there exists finitary event structures of degree n such that every nice labelling needs at least (n + 1) letters. As depicted in figure 9, if E = {e, e', e", *f*, g, g', h}, with e < *f*, e < g, e' < g, e' < g', e" < g', e" < h, and e # h, then the degree is three, but every nice labelling needs at least four letters.

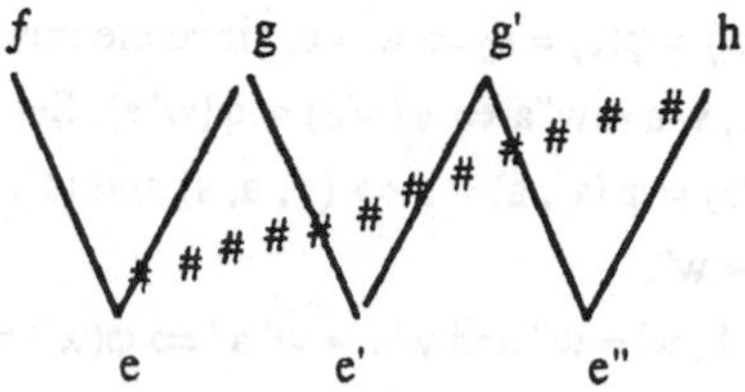

Figure 9.

Thus another conjecture is the existence of some finite nice labelling for any system of finite degree, but the question is really hard. (see [Ass. Cha.]. or [Ass. Bou. Cha. Rozo.]. In Leiden, H.J. Hoogeboom and G. Rozenberg have also considered a similar labelling problem [Hoogeb. Roze.]). Any structure associated with a "real" problem, such as the producer and consumer example, admits clearly such a finite and nice labelling, even in case of non-determinism. Thus and from now on, we restrict ourselves to event structures that admit such a labelling, and to the corresponding transition systems. Then we consider the equivalence relation defined above by means of function φ, $w' \approx w''$ iff $\varphi(w') = \varphi(w'')$, where $\varphi(w)$ is the state such that $(s_0, w, \varphi(w))$ belongs to $\xrightarrow{*}$. It satisfies a family of properties that will turn out to be our axioms for distributed equivalence. We use the quasi-prefix relation defined on $A^*/\approx$ by $s \leqslant s'$ iff $\exists$ w, w' $\in A^*$, $\exists\, a_1 \ldots a_n \in A^*$: $s = [w]$, $s' = [w']$ and $w' \approx w.a_1 \ldots a_n$. In what follows, $\mathfrak{D}$ stands for distributed.

3.4 Proposition and $\mathfrak{D}$ Properties. Let TS = $(S, A, s_0, \longrightarrow)$ be a distributed transition system and define relation $\approx$ on A^* by $w' \approx w''$ iff $\varphi(w') = \varphi(w'')$, where $\varphi(w)$ is the state such that $(s_0, w, \varphi(w))$ belongs to $\xrightarrow{*}$. Then following properties $\mathfrak{D}_0$ to $\mathfrak{D}_5$ are satisfied, $\approx$ is length preserving and the associated quasi -prefix relation $\leqslant$ is an order relation :

$\mathfrak{D}_0$: $\forall w', w'' \in A^*, \forall a \in A, w' \approx w'' \Rightarrow w'a \approx w''a$.

$\mathfrak{D}_1$: $\forall w \in A^*, w \approx \varepsilon \Rightarrow w = \varepsilon$.

$\mathfrak{D}_2$: $\forall a', a'' \in A, \forall w', w'' \in A^*, w'a' \approx w''a'' \Rightarrow (a' = a'' \Leftrightarrow w' \approx w'')$.

$\mathfrak{D}_3$: $\forall a', a'' \in A, \forall w, w', w'' \in A^*, (w' \approx wa', w'' \approx wa'' \text{ and } \exists\, u', u'' : w'u' \approx w''u'') \Rightarrow w'a'' \approx w''a'$.

$\mathfrak{D}_4$: $\forall a', a'' \in A, \forall w', w'' \in A^*, (w'a'' \approx w''a') \Rightarrow \exists\, w : w' \approx wa', w'' \approx wa'')$.

$\mathcal{D}_5$: $\forall n \in \mathbb{N}, \forall w, w_1, \ldots, w_n \in A^*, \forall a_1, \ldots, a_n \in A, (\forall k, w_k \approx w.a_k, \forall j, k, \exists t_{kj}, t_{jk} \in A^* : w_k.t_{kj} \approx w_j.t_{jk}) \Rightarrow (\exists t_1, \ldots, t_n : \forall k, w_k.t_k \approx w_1.t_1)$.

Proof : *We first prove properties* $\mathcal{D}_0$ to $\mathcal{D}_4$. We use an obvious extension of φ, defined on $S \times A^*$ by $\varphi(s, w) = s'$ iff (s, w, s') is in $\xrightarrow{*}$.

$\mathcal{D}_0$: $\forall w, w' \in A^*, \forall a \in A,\ w \approx w' \Leftrightarrow \varphi(w) = \varphi(w')$. As $(\varphi(w), a, \varphi(wa))$ and $(\varphi(w'), a, \varphi(w'a))$ both belongs to $\longrightarrow$, $\varphi(wa) = \varphi(w'a)$ by $\mathcal{CS}_2 \Leftrightarrow wa \approx w'a$.

$\mathcal{D}_1$: $\forall w \in A^*, w \approx \varepsilon \Rightarrow \varphi(w) = \varphi(\varepsilon) = s_0 \Rightarrow w = \varepsilon$, since the transition relation is acyclic.

$\mathcal{D}_2$: $\forall w', w'' \in A^*, \forall a \in A, w'a \approx w''a \Leftrightarrow \varphi(w'a) = \varphi(w''a)$. Set $s' = \varphi(w')$, $s'' = \varphi(w'')$; we get $\varphi(w'a) = \varphi'(s', a) = \varphi(w''a) = \varphi'(s'', a) = s \Leftrightarrow (s', a, s)$ and $(s'', a, s) \in \longrightarrow \Rightarrow s' = s''$ by $\mathcal{CS}_2$ $\Leftrightarrow \varphi(w') = \varphi(w'') \Leftrightarrow w' \approx w''$.

$\forall w', w'' \in A^*, \forall a', a'' \in A, w' \approx w''$ and $w'a' \approx w''a'' \Rightarrow \varphi(w') = \varphi(w'') = s'$ and $\varphi(w'a') = \varphi'(s', a') = \varphi(w''a'') = \varphi'(s', a'') = s \Rightarrow a' = a''$ by $\mathcal{CS}_2$.

$\mathcal{D}_3$: $\forall w, w', w'' \in A^*, \forall a', a'' \in A, (w' \approx wa', w'' \approx wa''$ and $\exists u', u'' \in A^* : w'u' \approx w''u'') \Rightarrow (a' = a'' \Rightarrow w' = w''$ and $w'a' = w'a'')$ and $(a' \neq a'' \Rightarrow$ if $s = \varphi(w)$, then $\varphi'(s, a') \neq \varphi'(s, a'')$ and $\exists s' = \varphi'(\varphi'(s, a'), a'') = \varphi'(\varphi'(s, a''), a')$, by $\mathcal{CS}_3 \Leftrightarrow (w'a'' \approx w''a')$.

$\mathcal{D}_4$: analogous proof using $\mathcal{CS}_4$.

We will now prove that $\approx$ *is length preserving* by induction on the length of w. If $|w| = 0$ and $w \approx w'$, then $w = \varepsilon$, which implies $w' = \varepsilon$ by $\mathcal{D}_1$. Suppose now that $\forall w$, $|w| = n$ and $w \approx w'$ implies $|w'| = n$, let w be of length $n + 1$, and w' such that $w \approx w'$. If $w' = \varepsilon$, then $w = \varepsilon$ by induction hypothesis, which is impossible. Therefore w and w' are not empty; set $w = w_1.a$ and $w' = w'_1.a'$. If $a = a'$, we get $w_1 \approx w'_1$ by $\mathcal{D}_2$, thus $|w_1| \approx |w'_1|$ by induction hypothesis, and $|w| = |w'|$. If $a' \neq a''$, we find by $\mathcal{D}_4$ some w such that $w'_1 \approx wa$ and $w_1 \approx wa'$. By induction hypothesis we obtain $|w'_1| = |wa| = |w] + 1 = |w_1|$, and thus $|w| = |w'|$. We are done.

The quasi-prefix relation is clearly reflexive. As $\approx$ is solely right compatible, it is transitive : $s \leqslant s'$ and $s' \leqslant s'' \Rightarrow \exists w, w', w'_1, w'' \in A^*, \exists a_1 \ldots a_n, b_1, \ldots, b_k \in A^* : s = [w], s' = [w'] = [w'_1]$, $s'' = [w'']$ and $w' \approx w.a_1 \ldots a_n$, $w'' \approx w'_1.b_1 \ldots b_k$. As $w' \approx w'_1$, we get $w'' \approx w'_1.b_1 \ldots b_k \approx w'.b_1 \ldots b_k \approx w.a_1 \ldots a_n.b_1 \ldots b_k$, due to the solely right compatibility. Thus $s \leqslant s''$. Let us prove it is anti-symmetric too : $s \leqslant s'$ and $s' \leqslant s$ implies $s = [w] = [w_1]$, $s' = [w'] = [w'_1]$, $w \approx w'.a_1 \ldots a_n$, $w'_1 = w_1.b_1 \ldots b_k$, which implies $|w_1| = |w| = |w'| + n$, $|w'| = |w'_1| = |w_1| + k$, thus $n = k = 0$ and $w \approx w'$, $s = s'$.

$\mathcal{D}_5$: The proof of the last property follows directly from the existence of least upper bounds for pairwise coherent subsets, which derives from proposition 2.5 and uses property $\mathcal{CS}_5$ (see also [Rozo. (2)]). Suppose that $w, w_1, \ldots, w_n$ are in A^*, $a_1, \ldots, a_n$ in A, $(\forall j \neq k, a_j \neq a_k)$ and $(\forall k, w_k \approx w.a_k)$ and $(\forall j \neq k, \exists x_{jk}$ in $A^* : w_k.x_{kj} \approx w_j.x_{jk})$. Set for any k, j , $s_k = [w_k]$, $s_{jk} = [w_k.x_{kj}] = [w_j.x_{jk}]$. Then family $\{s_k \mid k = 1 \ldots n\}$ is pairwise coherent, thus admits a least upper bound s. As property $\mathcal{CS}_1$ is satisfied, $s = [w]$ for some w in A^*.

3.5 Definition. A *Distributed Equivalence Relation* is a relation satisfying $\mathcal{D}$-properties. A *Distributed Congruence* is a distributed equivalence relation that is a congruence with respect to the usual concatenation of finite words. A *Distributed Language* is any subset of $A^*/\approx$, the quotient of A^* by a distributed equivalence relation. A *Distributed Monoid* is the quotient of a free monoid by a distributed congruence.

For example, the producer and consumer example get rise to a distributed equivalence relation on the alphabet $A = \{p, c\}$. Letters p and c commute after any prefix w that contains more p than c : ppp.pc ≈ ppp.cp but not(pcpc.pc ≈ pcpc.cp).

Notice that in general the quotient is not a monoid, which may be seen as a severe limitation as compared to classical traces. On one hand, it is not surprising, as the interpretation of concatenation is not so clear for distributed systems ; in the same way, it is well known that the resulting star operation originates difficult recognizability questions. On the other hand, it will be interesting now to look either at another operations, (generalisation of Ochmanski co-star is not obvious !) or at systems that get rise to distributed congruences. In a similar way as is the restriction of finite nice labelling, this yield probably to fact the limits of semantics based on words.

In short, a 2-tuples $(A, \approx)$ where A is an alphabet and $\approx$ a distributed equivalence relation is said to be a distributed equivalence. Now, starting with a distributed transition system, the above construction leads to such a distributed equivalence. If $TS = (S, A, s_0, \longrightarrow)$ or $LTS = (S, A', s_0, \longrightarrow, \ell, A)$ with ℓ finite and nice, we set $\Lambda(TS)$ or $\Lambda(LTS) = (A, \approx)$. Again $\mathcal{D}$-properties characterize exactly those among equivalences that allow the recovering of a distributed transition system provided with a finite and nice labelling.

3.6 Proposition. Let $\approx$ be a distributed equivalence relation on A and define the relation $\longrightarrow \subseteq (A^*/\approx) \times A \times (A^*/\approx)$ by $\longrightarrow = \{([w], a, [wa]) \mid w \in A^*, a \in A\}$. Then $V((A, \approx)) = (A^*/\approx, A, [\varepsilon], \longrightarrow)$ is a distributed transition system.

As it is clear that the labelling $Id : A \longrightarrow A$ is finite and nice, the notable result is again that " nothing has been lost ! ". Note that our purpose is not only to define languages associated to a transition system, but also to study carefully the corresponding equivalence relation on the whole set A^*. We have introduced the restriction of nice labelling in order to associate at most one state to a word. In the same way, when starting from a transition system, any word has at least to be a path leading to one state. At first glance, for any state s and any letter a, (s, a, s') has to be a transition for some state s'. If not, and without alteration of previous associated language, it is possible to make up the system, adding some fictional states : it is not a restriction. We consider only such systems, which are said to be complete. Note that there are several possible completion process that preserve the language of the considered systems, depending on the way you identify words that are outside of the language, thus impossible situations ! For the producer and consumer example, it's possible to decide either that c.ppc ≈ c.pcp or not. For sake of simplicity as this not really our matter here, we give an obvious and crude completion process, even if it generally does not get rise to congruences. Starting with TS = $(S, A, s_0, \longrightarrow)$, our completion process construct $S_0 = S$, $\longrightarrow^0 = \longrightarrow$, $S_{m+1} = S_m \cup \{(s, a) \mid s \in S, a \in A \text{ and } \forall s' \in S_m, (s, a, s') \notin \longrightarrow^m\}$, $\longrightarrow^{m+1} = \longrightarrow^m \cup \{(s, a, (s,a)) \mid s \in S_{m+1} - S_m\}$; finally $S_c = \cup S_m$ and $\longrightarrow_c = \cup \{\longrightarrow^m\}$. For example, if $S = \{s_k \mid k \in \mathbb{N}\} \cup \{u_k \mid k \in \mathbb{N}\}$, $A = \{a, b\}$, $\longrightarrow = \{(s_k, b, s_{k+1}), (u_k, b, u_{k+1}), (s_k, a, u_k) \mid k \in \mathbb{N}\}$, then $S_c \approx S \cup \{(u_k, w) \mid k \in \mathbb{N}, w \in A^+\}$, $\longrightarrow_c \approx \longrightarrow \cup \{((u_k, w), a, (u_k, wa)), ((u_k, w), b, (u_k, wb)) \mid k \in \mathbb{N}, w \in A^+\}$.

3.7 Theorem. Let $\mathcal{DJL}$ be the class of distributed equivalences and $\mathcal{LCS}_r$ be the family of distributed labelled transition systems provided with a finite and nice labelling. Then $\Lambda o V$ is equal to the identity on $\mathcal{DJL}$ and $V o \Lambda(LTS)$ is an isomorphism on $\mathcal{LCS}_r$.

$$\mathcal{LCS}_r \underset{V}{\overset{\Lambda}{\rightleftarrows}} \mathcal{DJL}$$

<u>Proof</u> : Let DL = $(A, \approx)$ be a distributed equivalence. Then $V(DL) = (A^*/\approx, A, [\varepsilon], \longrightarrow)$, where $\longrightarrow$ is the subset $\{[w], a, [wa] \mid w \in A^*\}$ and $\Lambda(V(DL)) = (A, \approx')$, the distributed equivalence $\approx'$ being $w \approx' w' \Leftrightarrow [\varepsilon]\overset{w}{\longrightarrow} s$ and $[\varepsilon]\overset{w'}{\longrightarrow} s$. We obtain $w \approx' w' \Leftrightarrow w \approx w'$, therefore DL = $\Lambda(V(DL))$.
Let now TS = $(S, A, s_0, \longrightarrow)$ be a complete distributed transition system, $\Lambda(TS) = (A, \approx)$, $V o \Lambda(TS) = (A^*/\approx, A, [\varepsilon], \overset{\prime}{\longrightarrow}) = TS'$. We have to show that TS and TS' are isomorphic. As $S = \uparrow s_0$, we define a bijective mapping from $A^*/\approx$ to S' by $f([w]) = \varphi(w)$. We get $f([\varepsilon]) = \varphi(\varepsilon) = s_0$. Finally, we have to examine transition relations. As f is a bijective mapping, $([w], a, [w']) \in \overset{\prime}{\longrightarrow} \Leftrightarrow [w'] = [wa] \Leftrightarrow f([w']) = \varphi(wa) = \varphi'(\varphi(w), a) = \varphi'(f([w]), a) \Leftrightarrow (f([w]), a, f([w'])) \in \longrightarrow \Rightarrow \longrightarrow = \{(f([w], a, f([w']) \mid ([w], a, [w']) \in \overset{\prime}{\longrightarrow}\}$: TS and TS' = $V o \Lambda(TS)$ are isomorphic.

Using transitions systems, it is thus possible to gather these results and to link closely distributed languages, distributed transition systems and labelled event structures.

3.8 Theorem. The class $\mathcal{DJL}$ of distributed equivalences admits an isomorphic representation within the classes $\mathcal{LCS}_r$ and $\mathcal{LES}_r$ of finite and nice distributed labelled transition systems, finite and nice labelled event structures respectively.

$$\mathcal{LES}_r \underset{\nabla}{\overset{\Delta}{\rightleftarrows}} \mathcal{LCS}_r \underset{V}{\overset{\Lambda}{\rightleftarrows}} \mathcal{DJL}$$

Proof : is straight forward with theorems 2.6 and 3.7.

We have achieved our aim, which was showing that objects such as nice distributed transition systems, nice labelled event structures and distributed languages are categorically equivalent. As an immediate consequence of these representation results, we obtain that the PoSet of equivalence classes of any distributed language is finitely coherently complete and prime algebraic, the set of primes being equal to the set of generalized traces that admit exactly one predecessor. Moreover, any language satisfying these properties is a distributed language !

IV. CLASSICAL MAZURKIEWICZ TRACES

First, a simple and classical example of distributed language is the language of executions of a distributed network of communicating machines, that is to say equivalence classes of firing sequences. Second, it is easy to show that classical Mazurkiewicz traces, that are defined with a distributed congruence, which is a distributed equivalence relation that does not depend on the context. On the contrary, the producer and consumer example leads to a distributed equivalence depending on the context, more exactly on the prefix. We develop the classical trace example below.

Two actions a and b that belong to a given commutativity relation, or independence relation, on an alphabet are thought as independent, which is formally expressed by the fact that sequences a.b and b.a are equivalent. Thus the equivalence relation identifies any sequences w'.ab.w" with w'.ba.w" : *we get an equivalence which is a distributed congruence and does not depend on the context..*

4.1 Definition. Let A^* denotes the free monoid generated by A, that is the set of finite sequences with the usual concatenation operation. Let I an independence relation, that is a symmetric and irreflexive relation included in $A \times A$. *The congruence relation $\approx$ generated by I on A^** is the reflexive and transitive closure of the relation $\{(x.ab.y, x.ba.y) \mid (a, b) \in I\}$. The partially commutative monoid, or trace monoid, is the quotient $A^*/\approx$.

A trace is any element of this monoid. It may be interpreted as the set of all possible sequential executions, whereas the dependence relation $D = A \times A - I$ offers in a way a characterization of the necessary dependences between these executions. Moreover the following result is available :

4.2 Theorem. The partially commutative monoid is a distributed monoid.

A direct consequence of this theorem is that results regarding distributed languages apply to classical traces languages ! This allow us to state again, but with another proof, results already given in [Rozo. Thia.]. In particular, we define the classical prefix order relation among traces by $u \leqslant u'$ iff $u' = u.u''$ for some trace u" and obtain that :

4.3 Theorem. $(A^*/\approx, \leqslant)$ is a finitely coherently complete and prime algebraic PoSet, whose set of prime elements is equal to the set of equivalence classes that admit exactly one predecessor.

Moreover, the representation theorem within event structures is of course available. This representation associates a single trace $u = \Delta(C) = \bigsqcup C$ to every configuration. Conversely, a single configuration $C = \{e \mid e \text{ is a prime and } e \leqslant u\} = PR(u) = \underline{\nabla}(u)$ is associated to every trace, where PR(u) denotes the set of prime elements bounded by u and $\bigsqcup$ is the least upper bound operator.

If the independency relation is for example $I = \{(a,c), (c, a)\}$ on the alphabet $\{a, b, c\}$, we obtain that the following dependency graph depicted below, or equivalently the following configuration, is associated to equivalence class of aaaccbacc, for the deriving congruence $\approx$.

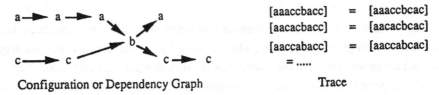

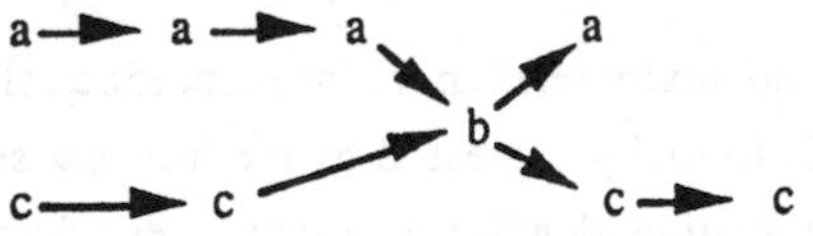

[aaaccbacc] = [aaaccbcac]
[aacacbacc] = [aacacbcac]
[aaccabacc] = [aaccabcac]
= .....

Configuration or Dependency Graph

Trace

Figure 10.

We get a new equivalent version of traces, which are identified either with configurations or with classical dependency graphs. Following this identification, events are associated to traces whose dependence graphs admit a greatest element. For example, if the independence relation is again $I = \{(a, c), (c, a)\}$ on the alphabet $A = \{a, c\}$, the set of events is $E = \{w \mid \exists n \in N : w = [a^n] \text{ or } w = [c^n]\}$, the order relation is the reflexive and transitive closure of $[a^n] \ll [a^{n+1}]$, $[c^n] \ll [c^{n+1}]$, the conflict relation is empty and the labelling function is $\ell([a^n]) = a$, $\ell([c^n]) = c$ for any n. For the same independence relation on the alphabet $A = \{a, b, c\}$, we give below a small part of the associated event structure. The order relation is the reflexive and transitive closure of the immediate predecessor relation, represented by arrows, and the conflict relation is the closure under inheritance of the minimal conflict relation, represented by grey lines.

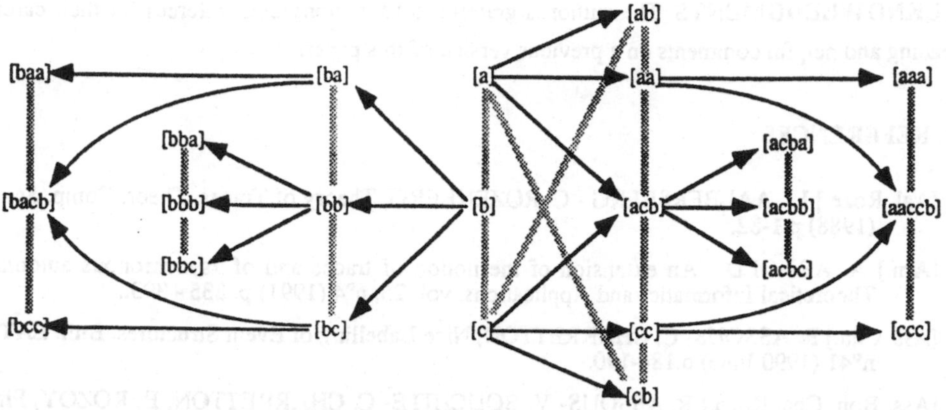

Figure 11.

If events are interpreted as primes, we get that traces such as [a], [c] and [acb] are events whereas [ac] is not. But every trace may be interpreted as a least upper bound of events, as for example [ac] = [a] $\cup$ [c]. The image under $\underline{\nabla}$ = PR of a trace t is the restriction of this event structure to a subset of the whole set E of events. For example the subsets of events associated to traces [acbac] is {[a], [b], [acb], [acba], [acbc]}. Thus the link between traces and configurations is quite clear : order among traces is nothing less than inclusion among configurations, the least upper bound operator being associated to union ; addition of an element in a configuration is the counter part of concatenation among traces.

Moreover, it is possible to characterize the subclass of event structures obtained as images of trace monoids (see also [Rozo. Thia.]). We say that an event e is enabled at a configuration C iff e is not in C and C $\cup$ {e} is a configuration ; the set of events enabled at a configuration C is denoted by $\mathcal{E}$(C) and co, $\#_\mu$, and $<\!\cdot$ denote the concurrency, immediate conflict and immediate predecessor relations respectively.

4.4 Definition. A labelled event structure is partially commutative iff it satisfies $\mathcal{M}$: $\forall a \in A$, $\forall C \in \mathcal{C}$, $\exists!\, e \in \mathcal{E}(C) : \ell(e) = a$ and $\mathcal{J} : (\ell^{-1}(a) \times \ell^{-1}(b)) \cap co \neq \emptyset \Rightarrow (\ell^{-1}(a) \times \ell^{-1}(b)) \cap <\!\cdot = \emptyset$.

Note that conditions $\mathcal{J}$ and $\mathcal{M}$ imply that $(\ell^{-1}(a) \times \ell^{-1}(b)) \cap <\!\cdot = \emptyset \Leftrightarrow (\ell^{-1}(a) \times \ell^{-1}(b)) \cap co \neq \emptyset$. These partially commutative event structures are the exact counterpart of trace monoids. We obtain that $\Lambda o \Delta$ and $\nabla o V$ are isomorphisms between partially commutative event structures and partially commutative monoids. In particular again, for any partially commutative monoid, $\nabla o V o \Lambda o \Delta(A^*/\approx) = A^*/\approx$ and $(A^*/\approx, \leqslant)$ is isomorphic to $(\mathcal{C}(\nabla o V(A^*/\approx)), \subseteq)$.

4.5 Theorem. The class $\mathcal{DIL}_{com}$ of partially commutative monoids admits an isomorphic representation within the class $\mathcal{LES}_{com}$ of partially commutative event structures.

ACKNOWLEDGMENTS. The author is grateful to four anonymous referees for their careful reading and helpful comments on a previous version of this paper.

V. REFERENCES

[Aal. Roze.] I.J. AALBERSBERG - G. ROZENBERG, Theory of Traces, Theor. Comp. Sci. 60 (1988) p.1-82.

[Arn.] A. ARNOLD - An extension of the notion of traces and of asynchronous automata, Theoretical Informatics and Applications, vol. 25, n°4 (1991) p. 335 - 393..

[Ass. Cha.] R. ASSOUS- C. CHARRETTON, Nice Labelling of Event Structures, Bull. EATCS n°41 (1990 June) p.184-190.

[Ass. Bou. Cha. Rozo.] R. ASSOUS- V. BOUCHITE- C. CHARRETTON, B. ROZOY, Finite Labelling Problem in Event Structures, (1991) to appear in Theor. Comp. Sci.

[Bou. Cas. (1)] G. BOUDOL, I. CASTELLANI, Permutations of Transitions, an Event Structure Semantic for C.C.S. and S.C.C.S., REX Workshop on Concurrency (1988) L.N.C.S. n° 354, p. 411-427.

[Bou. Cas. (2)] G. BOUDOL, I. CASTELLANI, Flow Models of Distributed Computations : Event Structure and Nets (1991) T.R. INRIA n° 1482.

[Bou. Cas. (3)] G. BOUDOL, I. CASTELLANI, Flow Models of Distributed Computations : Three equivalent Semantic for C.C.S. (1991) T.R. INRIA n° 1484.

[Diek. Gas. Pet.] V. DIEKERT, P. GASTIN, A. PETIT, Recognizable complex Trace Languages, 16th symposium on M.F.C.S., Poland (1991), L.N.C.S. n° 520, p.131-140.

[Gas. Pet. Ziel.] P. GASTIN, A. PETIT, W. ZIELONKA, A Kleene Theorem for infinite Trace Languages, 18th ICALP, Madrid (1991), L.N.C.S. n° 510, p.254-266.

[Gas. Rozo.] P. GASTIN, B. ROZOY, Infinitary Partially Commutative Monoids, (1991) Tech. Rep. 91-07, LITP, Paris 6 University, France (to appear in Theor. Comp. Sci.).

[Hoogeb. Roze.] H.J. HOOGEBOOM, G. ROZENBERG, Diamond Properties of State Spaces of Elementary Net Systems, Tech.Rep. 89-18 (1989) Leiden University, Holland.

[Hooger. Klei. Thia.] P. HOOGERS, H.C.M.. KLEIJN, P.S. THIAGARAJAN, A Trace Semantics for Petri Nets, Third Workshop on Concurrency and Compositionality (1991 March) Goslar, Germany.

[Kwia.] M. Z. KWIATKOWSKA, On the domain of traces and sequential composition, CAAP'91, Trace Languages, L.N.C.S. n° 493 (1991) p.42-56.

[Mazu.] A. MAZURKIEWICZ, Trace Theory, Advanced Course on Petri Nets, Bad Honnef, Germany (1987) L.N.C.S. n° 254, p. 269-324.

[Muku. Thia.] M. MUKUND, , P.S.. THIAGARAJAN, A Petri Net Model of Asynchronously Communicating Sequential Processes, in : A Perspective in Theor. Comp. Science, R. Narasimhan ed, World Sc. series in Comp. Science Vol. 16 (1989) p. 165-198.

[Niel.] M. NIELSEN, Models for concurrency, 16th symposium on Mathematical Foundations of Computer Science, Poland (1991) L.N.C.S. n° 520, p.43-46.

[Niel. Plot. Wins.] M. NIELSEN - G. PLOTKIN - G. WINSKEL, Petri Nets, Event Structures and Domains, Theor. Comp. Sci. 13 (1981) p. 85-108.

[Niel. Roze. Thia.(1)] M. NIELSEN, G. ROZENBERG, P.S. THIAGARAJAN, Elementary Transitions System, Tech Rep. (1990) April, Aarhus Univ., to appear in Theor. Comp. Sci.

[Niel. Roze. Thia.(2)] M. NIELSEN, G. ROZENBERG, P.S.. THIAGARAJAN, Transitions Systems, Event Structures and Unfolding, Tech Rep. 91-01, Leiden Univ., Third Workshop on Concurrency and Compositionality (1991 March) Goslar, Germany.

[Per.] D. PERRIN, Partial Commutations, ICALP 89, L.N.C.S. n° 372 (1989) p.637-651.

[Rozo. (1)] B. ROZOY, Distributed Languages, a context dependant extension of traces, Third Workshop on Concurrency and Compositionality (1991 March) Goslar, Germany.

[Rozo. (2)] B. ROZOY, Le monoïde distribué, un modèle de parallélisme, thèse d'état, université de Caen, 1987, Techn. Rep. L.I.U.C. 87-1.

[Rozo. Thia.] B. ROZOY, P.S. THIAGARAJAN, Trace Monoids and Event Structures, Theor. Comp. Sci. (1991) n°2, p.285-313.

[Shie.(1)] M.W. SHIELDS, Concurrent Machines, The Computer Journal Vol. 28 n°5 (1985) p.449-465.

[Shie.(2)] M.W. SHIELDS, Deterministic asynchronous automata (1985) in Formal Methods in Programming, North Holland.

[Shie.(3)] M.W. SHIELDS, Elements of a theory of parallelism (to be published).

[Star.] P.H. STARKE, Traces and Semi-words, L.N.C.S. n° 208 (1985) p.332-349.

[Vog.] W. VOGLER, A Generalization of Traces Theory, Tech. Rep. 9018 (1990) Technische Universität München, to appear in Theoretical Informatics and Applications.

[Wins. (1)] G. WINSKEL, Categories of Models for Concurrency, Seminar on Concurrency, Pittsburgh, U.S.A. (1984) L.N.C.S. n° 197, p. 246-267.

[Wins. (2)] G. WINSKEL, Event Structures, Advanced Course on Petri Nets, Bad Honnef, Germany (1987) L.N.C.S. n° 255, p.325-392.

Partial Words versus Processes: A Short Comparison

Walter Vogler*
Institut für Informatik
Technische Universität München
Arcisstraße 21
D-8000 München 2

ABSTRACT. In this note I want to draw attention to partial words, a less known partial order semantics of Petri nets. Partial words have recently proven to be of importance, e.g. in the study of action refinement. An important result of A. Kiehn relates partial words and Petri net processes, and a short proof of this result is given here.

Keywords. Partial order semantics, processes, partial words.

CONTENTS

0 Introduction

Petri net theory has a long tradition of studying 'true concurrency'. A 'truly concurrent' semantics describes system runs in such a way that one gets explicit information about the independence of the actions that are performed by the system. Most often, this information is given by describing a system run as a partial order of actions. In contrast to this, an interleaving semantics describes a system run by a sequence of actions; for example, the language of a Petri net is the set of its firing sequences. If actions can be performed independently, then they are arbitrarily ordered in such a sequence; thus a system run containing independent actions is described by several sequences.

*This work was partially supported by the ESPRIT Basic Research Action No. 3148 DEMON (Design Methods Based on Nets).

When speaking of partial order semantics, many people associate the partial order with the causality relation, and in the area of Petri nets they only think of Petri net processes. But other partial order semantics of nets exist as well. One example is the pomset semantics [Pra86], which is also intended to model causality. Partial order semantics that are not so closely related to the idea of causality are partial words [Gra81], semiwords [Sta81], which are a special case of partial words, and traces [Maz87]. In this note I want to draw attention to partial words, which deserve to be better known than they are.

Although processes and partial words are defined completely independently, they are actually closely related. An important result of A. Kiehn states that each least sequential partial word is the event structure of some process [Kie88]. The original proof of this result is fairly long, and the technical contribution of this note is a short proof, which is based on the marriage theorem. In the rest of this introduction, I want to collect some arguments in favour of partial words.

A partial word of a Petri net is a partial order of transition occurrences; the ordering is not the causality relation, but a precedence relation with the following property: each set C of unordered transitions can be performed concurrently provided that the precedence relation is respected, i.e. all transitions less than C are fired first. This definition sees independence of transitions as a possibility, but not as a necessity; in other words, making a partial word more sequential, i.e. increasing its precedence relation, gives a partial word again.

Partial words form a framework in which various semantics of Petri nets can be compared. Processes, see e.g. [GR83,BD87], have events and conditions; if we abstract from the conditions, we get the event structure of the process, which is a partial word. Firing sequences are partial words where the ordering is total; firing step sequences are partial words where the relation of being unordered is transitive. Semiwords are special partial words where occurrences of the same transition must be ordered. All this is pointed out in [Kie88]. We can also fit traces into this framework. A trace is built on a static dependence relation, where transitions of a net can be defined as dependent if they are adjacent to a common place. In the case of safe nets, traces correspond exactly to the event structures of processes, see [Roz87], but in general this is not true; instead they correspond to the executions of [Vog91a]. In any case, traces are partial words.

Having a general, and thus more flexible, framework of partial order semantics has been useful in the study of action refinement. Action refinement is an operation for the top-down design of concurrent systems. It allows to change the level of abstraction by replacing an action, i.e. a transition in the case of Petri nets, by a system of subactions. Recently, this operation has attracted much attention within and outside of the Petri net community, see [AH89,BDKP91,Dev90,GG89,NEL89,Vog91b,Vog91c]. Naturally, one would like a semantics to induce a congruence with respect to all operations of interest. With respect to the refinement operator, it turns out that this is not the case for interleaving based semantics. In [Pra86,CDMP87] it is suggested that partial order semantics will be helpful here. And indeed, a semantics based on processes can be shown to induce a congruence for safe labelled Petri nets [Vog91b].

Now it would be interesting to know whether partial order semantics is really needed to get a congruence for action refinement, and if so which form of partial order semantics is needed. In fact, a semantics based on partial words also gives a congruence, and it makes fewer distinctions than the one based on processes. Furthermore, the coarsest congruence for action refinement that is finer than language equivalence is determined in [Vog91b]; it is based on interval partial words. These are partial words whose partial order is an interval order. A partial order is called an interval order if its elements are in a correspondence with some closed real intervals such that an element x is less than some y if and only if the interval corresponding to x is totally 'to the left of' the interval of y; thus unordered elements correspond to overlapping intervals. The above-mentioned result answers in the framework of partial words the question to which degree partial order semantics is really necessary to get a congruence for action refinement.

In [HRT89] the authors formulate a number of quality criteria for partial order semantics of nets with capacities. They consider a parallel composition operator with synchronization that composes nets by merging transitions, and require that a semantics should be compositional w.r.t. this operator, i.e. it should be possible to determine the semantics of a composed net from the semantics of its components. Furthermore they require that a semantics should remain unchanged, if we complement a place of finite capacity or if we modify a capacity in such a way that the reachable markings and enabled transitions stay the same. If we extend event structures of processes in a natural way to a semantics for nets with capacities, then this semantics does not satisfy these quality criteria. As an alternative semantics the authors suggest the class of partial words where a transition t can be a direct predecessor of t' only if t and t' are adjacent to a common place. This research is carried on in [GV90]. Some characterization results for semantics satisfying the above-mentioned quality criteria are given, and the smallest of these semantics is determined. All these studies are carried out in the framework of partial words.

Also outside the area of Petri nets sometimes researchers do not work with causality based partial order semantics although they would like to. In [dBW90] a metric partial order semantics for a CCS-like process algebra is given. In the first part the authors give a causality based partial order semantics for a simple algebra without synchronization. In the second part they want to include a parallel composition operator with synchronization, but here there metric approach fails for the causality based semantics. In the same spirit as partial words they close there semantics under making the partial orders more sequential, and now the metric approach works fine.

1 Basic Notions

In this section a very brief introduction to Petri nets (place/transition-nets) is given. A *Petri net* $N = (S, T, W, M_N)$ (or just a *net* for short) consists of disjoint (not necessarily finite) sets S of *places* and T of *transitions*, the *weight function* $W : S \times T \cup T \times S \rightarrow \mathbb{N}_0$, and the *initial marking* $M_N : S \rightarrow \mathbb{N}_0$. In general, we will not distinguish between isomorphic nets (nor between isomorphic partial orders etc.).

We can view N as a bipartite directed graph with vertex set $S \cup T$ and arc set F, where $xy \in F$ if $W(x, y) \neq 0$. The net N has arc weight 1 if W takes values in $\{0, 1\}$; nets of arc weight 1 can be defined by giving F instead of W. For $x \in S \cup T$ the *pre-set*

$^\bullet x$ is defined as $\{y \in S \cup T \mid W(y,x) \neq 0\}$, the *post-set* $x^\bullet$ as $\{y \mid W(x,y) \neq 0\}$. We will assume that all nets are *T-restricted*, i.e. that for all transitions t we have $^\bullet t \neq \emptyset \neq t^\bullet$.

- A *multiset* over a set X is a function $\mu : X \rightarrow \mathbb{N}_0$; it is finite, if it has finite support, i.e. if $\mu(x) \neq 0$ for finitely many $x \in X$; it is empty, if $\mu(x) = 0$ for all x. The set of finite non-empty multisets over X is denoted by $\mathcal{M}(X)$. We write $x \in \mu$, if $\mu(x) \neq 0$. We identify $x \in X$ with the multiset that is 1 for x and 0 everywhere else.

- A *marking* is a multiset over S, a *step* is a finite, non-empty multiset over T. A step μ is *enabled* under a marking M, denoted by $M[\mu\rangle$, if $\sum_{t \in \mu} \mu(t) \cdot W(s,t) \leq M(s)$ for all $s \in S$.

  If $M[\mu\rangle$ and $M'(s) = M(s) + \sum_{t \in \mu} \mu(t)(W(t,s) - W(s,t))$, then we denote this by $M[\mu\rangle M'$ and say that μ can *occur* or *fire* under M yielding the *follower marking* M'. We also say that the transitions of μ can fire *concurrently.* Since transitions are special steps, this also defines $M[t\rangle$ and $M[t\rangle M'$ for $t \in T$.

- This definition of enabling and occurrence can be extended to sequences as usual. A sequence $w \in \mathcal{M}(T)^*$ is *enabled* under a marking M, denoted by $M[w\rangle$, and yields the follower marking M' if it *occurs*, denoted by $M[w\rangle M'$, if $w = \lambda$ and $M = M'$ or $w = w'\mu$, $M[w'\rangle M''$ and $M''[\mu\rangle M'$ for some marking M''. If w is enabled under the initial marking, then it is called a firing step sequence, or – in case that $w \in T^*$ – a firing sequence.

- A marking M is *reachable* if there exists some $w \in T^*$ such that $M_N[w\rangle M$. The net is *safe* if $M(s) \leq 1$ for all places s and reachable markings M.

In this note we will only deal with finite system runs, and thus we only define finite partial orders.

- A (finite) *partial order* $(E, <)$ consists of a finite set E and a transitive, irreflexive relation $<$. As usual we write $x \leq y$ for $x < y$ or $x = y$. The *downward closure* of a set $X \subseteq E$ is $\downarrow X = \{e \in E \mid \exists x \in X : e \leq x\}$. X is *downward closed* if $X = \downarrow X$.

  A *labelled partial order* (*over* some set Z) $p = (E, <, l)$ consists of a partial order $(E, <)$ and a labelling function $l : E \rightarrow Z$.

- If for some labelled partial order p elements x, y of E are unordered, i.e. we have neither $x < y$ nor $y < x$ (but possibly $x = y$), then we call x and y *concurrent*, denoted by x *co* y. A maximal set of pairwise concurrent elements is called a *cut*. The set of *minimal elements* of some set $E' \subseteq E$ is denoted by $\min E'$.

- Let $p_1 = (E_1, <_1, l_1)$, $p_2 = (E_2, <_2, l_2)$ be partial orders labelled over the same alphabet Z. Then p_1 is *less sequential* ($\preceq$) than p_2 if $E_1 = E_2$, $<_1 \subseteq <_2$ and $l_1 = l_2$. If furthermore $<_2$ is a total order, then p_2 is called a *linearization* of p_1; in this case p_2 can be identified with an element of E_2^* in an obvious way.

Figure 1 shows two labelled partial orders; the first is less sequential than the second.

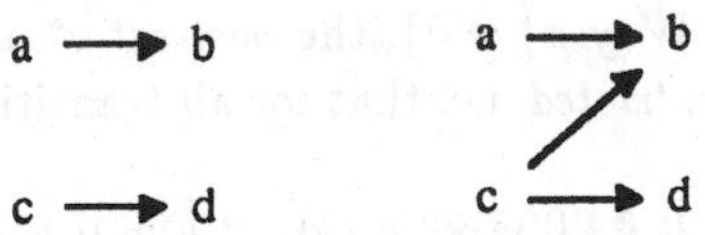

Figure 1

2 Processes and Partial Words

The purpose of studying 'true concurrency' is to distinguish the independent execution of transitions from their execution in arbitrary order. The firing sequences of a net only capture the latter view of concurrency; e.g. the nets of Figure 2 have the same

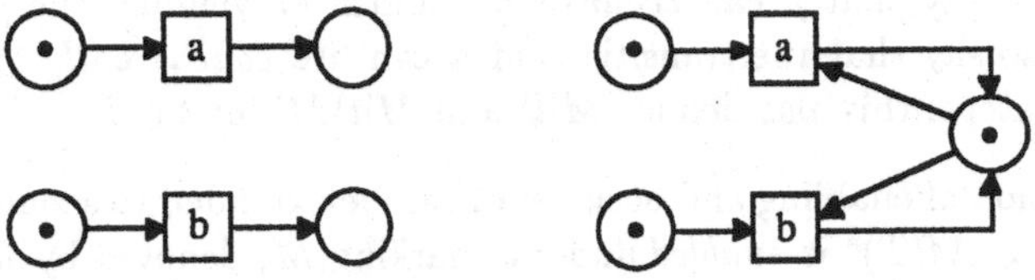

Figure 2

firing sequences, but obviously the first net can perform a and b independently of each other, while the second cannot. Petri net theory has a long tradition of studying 'true concurrency' using partial orders. Most often, a partial order semantics is given by so-called processes. In this approach the partial order models causality. Consequently, the semantics of the nets in Figure 2 are incomparable, since one can only perform sequences, while the other cannot perform any sequence. Processes are based on a special, very simple net class, the class of causal nets.

- A *causal net* is a finite net (B, E, F) of arc weight 1 without an initial marking, whose places are called *conditions*, whose transitions are called *events*, and whose arcs are given as $F \subseteq B \times E \cup E \times B$, such that
  - the net is acyclic, i.e. for all $x \in B \cup E$ we have $(x, x) \notin F^+$ (where F^+ is the transitive closure of F),
  - the conditions are not branched, i.e. $|{}^\bullet b|$, $|b^\bullet| \leq 1$ for all $b \in B$.
- A *process* $\pi = (B, E, F, l)$ of a net N consists of a causal net (B, E, F) and a labelling $l : B \cup E \to S_N \cup T_N$ such that
  - conditions correspond to places (or tokens), and events correspond to transitions, i.e. $l(B) \subseteq S_N$, $l(E) \subseteq T_N$
  - minimal conditions correspond to the initial marking M_N, i.e. for all $s \in S_N$ we have $M_N(s) = |\{b \in B \mid {}^\bullet b = \emptyset, \text{ and } l(b) = s\}|$

- the neighbourhood of transitions is respected, i.e. $W_N(s, l(e)) = |l^{-1}(s) \cap {}^\bullet e|$, $W_N(l(e), s) = |l^{-1}(s) \cap e^\bullet|$ for all $s \in S_N$ and $e \in E$.

- Processes treat places and transitions on an equal footing. Since we are mostly interested in the transitions a system can perform we define the *event structure* $ev(\pi)$ of a process π as the labelled partial order $(E, F^+|_{E\times E}, l|_E)$.

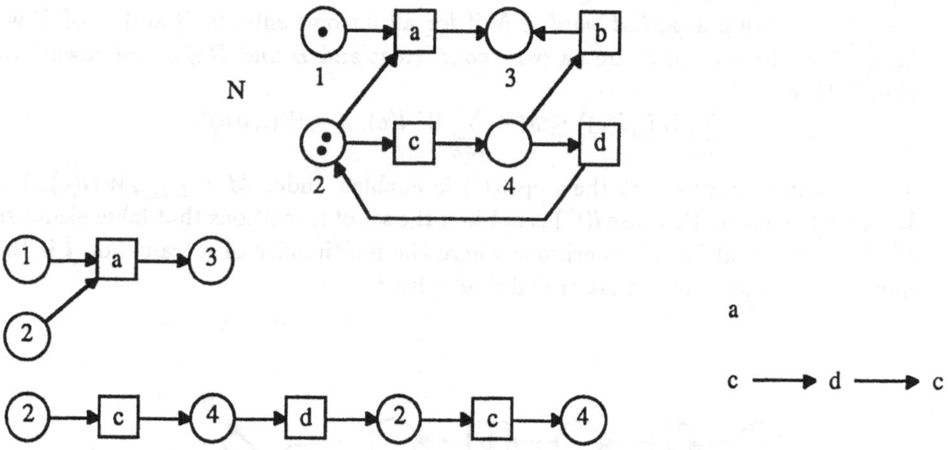

Figure 3

Figure 3 shows a net N, one of its processes, and the event structure of the process. In both, the process and its event structure we can see that a occurs independently of c and d, and that the first firing of c causes d (in the process d takes the token produced by c, in the event structure the first c is an immediate predecessor of d). Graphically, a process is an unfolding of the net where in the course of this unfolding choices are made. In the example we see that the cycle with transitions c and d is unfolded in such a way that c occurs a second time. Furthermore a choice between b and d is made; after the first c d occurs, but not b, which would also be possible.

Processes are closely related to reachable markings and firing sequences. A *slice* is a cut of $(E \cup B, F^+, l)$ that consists of conditions only. It is well known that a slice C of a process corresponds to the marking that is reached by firing the transitions that are in $\downarrow C$; more precisely, each transition t has to be fired as often as the number of events in $\downarrow C$ that are labelled t, see e.g. [BD87]. To formulate the relation between processes and firing sequences, let us call a linearization of the event structure of a process π simply a linearization of π. Then we have the following result, see e.g. [BD87].

Proposition 2.1 *Let N be a net. Then every linearization of a process of N is a firing sequence of N. Vice versa, for each firing sequence w of N there exists a process π such that w is a linearization of π. If N is safe, then w determines π uniquely.*

Another view of concurrency is that it is a possibility; thus, concurrency is more than arbitrary interleaving but includes it. From this point of view, the semantics of the first net of Figure 2 should include the semantics of the second net; the first net can perform a and b independently, but it can also perform these actions in some order. This idea is formalized in the partial word semantics of [Gra81]. A partial word of a net N is a partial order labelled with transitions of N; any set of pairwise concurrent elements of this partial order represents a step that can be fired provided the precedences prescribed by the partial order are observed.

- Let N be a net, M a marking of N, and $p = (E, <, l)$ be a partial order labelled over T. We call p a *partial word* of N if for all disjoint subsets B and C of E we have: if all elements of C are pairwise concurrent and B and $B \cup C$ are downward closed, then
$$\sum_{e \in C} W(.,l(e)) \leq M + \sum_{e \in B} W(l(e),.) - W(.,l(e)).$$
This condition means that the step $l(C)$ is enabled under $M + \sum_{e \in B} W(l(e),.) - W(.,l(e))$, where in this case $l(C)$ is not just the set of transitions that label elements of C, but the multiset of transitions where the multiplicity of a transition t is the number of elements of C that are labelled with t.

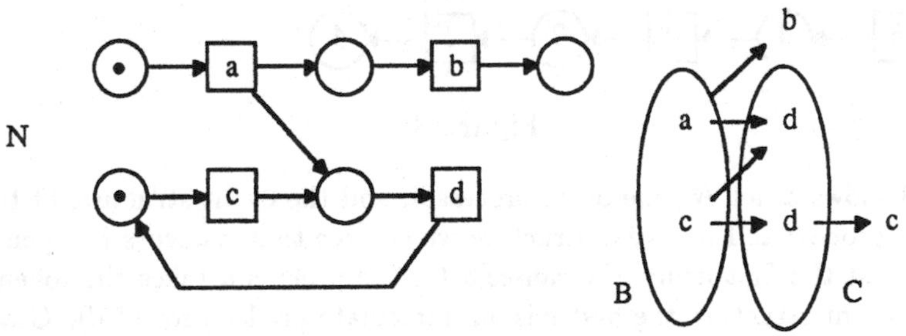

Figure 4

Figure 4 shows a net and one of its partial words; some sets B and C are indicated, and indeed, we can fire the step $2d$ if we fire a and c first. Note that the precedence relation in this partial word does not correspond to causality in the sense of processes. In this ordering relation, the first occurrence of c is an immediate predecessor of both occurrences of d, but c produces only one token; such a situation cannot occur in the event structure of a process.

It is easy to see that the set of partial words of a net is closed under making partial words more sequential.

Proposition 2.2 *Let p be a partial word of a net N, q a labelled partial order over T. If p is less sequential than q, then q is a partial word of N.*

This proposition shows that concurrency in partial words is just seen as a possibility, but concurrent actions can also be performed sequentially.

3 A Short Comparison

Now we have two ways to describe a run of a net by a partial order labelled with transitions: event structures of processes and partial words. Using the above-mentioned fact on slices of processes it is not too difficult to show the following, see [Kie88].

Proposition 3.1 *If π is a process of some net N, then $ev(\pi)$ is a partial word of N.*

Since processes are intended to model causality which in turn is thought to describe just the necessary precedences, one would expect that the labelled partial orders $ev(\pi)$ with π a process are the least sequential partial words. This is only partly true.

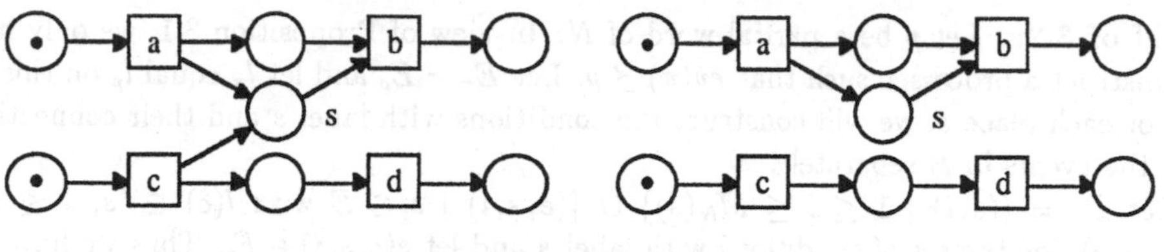

Figure 5

After firing transitions a and c in the first net of Figure 5 b has, so to speak, the choice between the token on s produced by a and the token produced by c. This choice leads to two processes that have the event structures shown in Figure 2, i.e. one process has an event structure that is strictly less sequential than the event structure of the other.

This problem is a special case of the more general problem that a firing sequence of a place/transition net does not always determine a unique process in the sense of Proposition 2.1. This problem is well known; solutions have been proposed in [BD87, Vog91a].

Although not every process gives rise to a least sequential partial word, the reverse implication does hold: every least sequential partial word is the event structure of a process, as we will show now.

Theorem 3.2 *Let N be a net. Then $\{p \mid p$ is a least sequential partial word of $N\} \subseteq \{ev(\pi) \mid \pi$ is a process of $N\}$. If N is safe, then equality holds.*

This is an important result that relates the two approaches to a semantics with 'true concurrency'. This result is obtained in [Kie88], but the proof given there is quite complicated and long. Here we give a short proof, which is based on the following version of the well-known marriage theorem (see e.g. [Bol90, III Corollary 9]).

Theorem 3.3 *Let G be a (finite) bipartite graph with vertex classes V_1 and V_2, and $f : V_2 \to \mathbb{N}_0$ be a function. Then G contains a subgraph H such that every $x \in V_2$ has degree $f(x)$ and every $y \in V_1$ has degree at most 1 if and only if for every subset U of V_2 there are at least $\sum_{x \in U} f(x)$ vertices in V_1 adjacent to a vertex in U.*

Remark: The name 'marriage theorem' stems from the following 'application' for the case that f has always the value 1: the elements of V_1 are men, the elements of V_2 are women, and an edge between v_1 and v_2 indicates that these two people know each other. Our aim is to organize a mass marriage, where each woman marries a man she knows. A corresponding scheme is described by the subgraph H: each woman marries her unique neighbour in H, and this neighbour is not married by anybody else. The theorem characterises when such a mass marriage is possible. The necessity of the characterization is obvious: a mass marriage can only be possible if each group U of women knows at least as many men as there are women in U. The sufficiency can be shown by a fairly short induction proof or by application of the maxflow-mincut-theorem.

Theorem 3.3 is a version of the marriage theorem for a polygamous society where each woman x wants to marry $f(x)$ men.

Proof of 3.2: Let p be a partial word of N. In view of Proposition 3.1, we only have to construct a process π such that $ev(\pi) \preceq p$. Let $E_\pi = E_p$ and let l_π equal l_p on this set E. For each place s, we will construct the conditions with label s and their connections with the events in E separately.

Let $B_s = \{(s,i) \mid 1 \leq i \leq M_N(s)\} \dot\cup \{(e,s,i) \mid e \in E \text{ with } l(e) \in {}^\bullet s,\ 1 \leq i \leq W(l(e),s)\}$ be the set of conditions with label s and let $e(e,s,i) \in F_s$. Thus we have the right number of conditions to represent the initial marking and the postsets of the events are correct, too.

Define a bipartite graph G_s with vertex classes B_s and E and edges $(s,i)e$ for $e \in E$, $(s,i) \in B_s$ and $(e',s,i)e$ for $e \in E$, $(e',s,i) \in B_s$ such that $e' <_p e$; let $f(e) = W(s,l(e))$. If we find a subgraph H as in 3.3 and let $ce \in F_s$ whenever ce is an edge in H, then the presets of the events have the right size, and there is a directed path of length 2 in π from some e' to some e only if $e' <_p e$. Thus, letting B_π be the union of the B_s and F_π be the union of the F_s, the resulting process π satisfies $ev(\pi) \preceq p$ (which also ensures that π is in fact acyclic, since p is a partial order).

It remains to check the condition of 3.3. Let $U \subseteq E$; we have to compare $|U|$ with the number of neighbours of U in B_s. Let U' be the downward-closure of U in p and put $C = \max U'$, $B = U' - C$. Applying the definition of a partial word gives

$$\sum_{e \in C} W(s,l(e)) \leq M_N(s) + \sum_{e' \in B} (W(l(e'),s) - W(s,l(e')))$$

or equivalently

$$\sum_{e \in B \cup C} W(s,l(e)) \leq M_N(s) + \sum_{e' \in B} W(l(e'),s).$$

Now we have

$$\begin{aligned} \Sigma_{e\in U} W(s,l(e)) &\leq \Sigma_{e\in U'} W(s,l(e)) \leq M_N(s) + \Sigma_{e'\in B} W(l(e'),s) \\ &= M_N(s) + \Sigma_{e'<e\in U} W(l(e'),s), \end{aligned}$$

and the latter is just the number of neighbours of events in U.

If for processes π, π' of a safe net we have $ev(\pi) \preceq ev(\pi')$, then every linearization of π' is also one of π. Since by Proposition 2.1 for safe nets every linearization determines the process, we have $\pi = \pi'$. Now the second part of the theorem follows from the first.

□

In view of Theorem 3.2 one can say that partial words describe the causality of a system run, but include some additional ordering information. E.g. due to some (partial) observation we know that event e really happend after e', although it was not caused by e'; this ordering information can be incorporated in a partial word.

Corollary 3.4 *If two nets have the same event structures of processes, then they have the same partial words. For safe nets the reverse implication holds, but not for nets in general.*

Proof: The partial words of a net are all labelled partial orders that are more sequential than the event structures of the processes of the net. Thus the event structures of the processes determine the partial words, and the first statement follows. For safe nets the event structures of processes are the least sequential partial words; thus the second statement follows.

As we have already seen, both labelled partial orders shown in Figure 2 are event structures of processes of the first net of Figure 5; but only the first labelled partial order is an event structure of a process of the second net. This difference vanishes for partial words by Proposition 2.2; thus the two nets have the same partial words, but different event structures of processes. □

These results show that for safe nets it does not make much of a difference whether we work with processes or partial words. This is no longer true if we work with labelled safe nets. Instead of giving precise definitions let us just remark that in such a net the transitions are labelled as shown in Figure 6; as a process semantics of labelled safe nets we can take the event structures of processes and replace each transition by its label; similarly we get a partial word semantics. With these notions the labelled partial order shown in Figure 6 is in the process semantics of the first net of Figure 6, but not in the process semantics of the second net. Intuitively, only the first net has the choice of firing b such that it depends on a or firing b such that it is independent of a. Thus the process semantics distinguishes the two nets, but the partial word semantics does not; the reason is that partial words are closed under making them more sequential and therefore firing sequences like the one shown in Figure 6 are partial words, too.

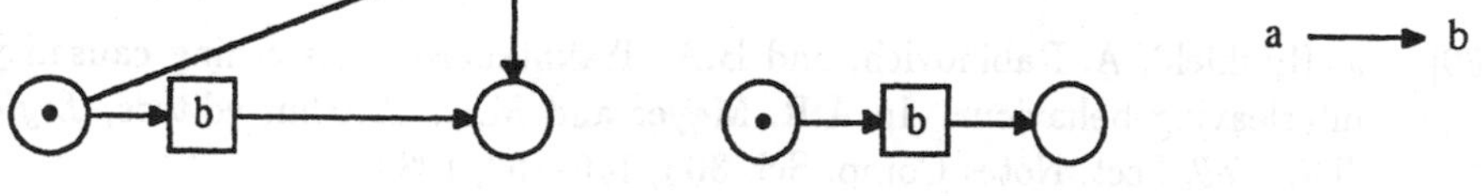

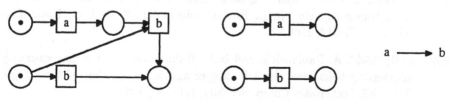

Figure 6

Acknowledgement

I thank the three anonymous referees for their helpful and encouraging comments.

References

[AH89] L. Aceto and M. Hennessy. Towards action-refinement in process algebras. In *Proc. 4th LICS*, pages 138–145. IEEE Computer Society Press, 1989. A full version has appeared as Computer Science Report 3/88, Dept. Comp. Sci. Univ. of Sussex, 1988.

[BD87] E. Best and R. Devillers. Sequential and concurrent behaviour in Petri net theory. *Theoret. Comput. Sci.*, 55:87–136, 1987.

[BDKP91] E. Best, R. Devillers, A. Kiehn, and L. Pomello. Concurrent bisimulations in Petri nets. *Acta Informatica*, 28:231–264, 1991.

[Bol90] B. Bollobàs. *Graph Theory. An Introductory Course.* Graduate Texts in Mathematics 63. Springer, 1990.

[CDMP87] L. Castellano, G. De Michelis, and L. Pomello. Concurrency vs. interleaving: An instructive example. *Bull. EATCS*, 31:12–15, 1987.

[dBW90] J.W. de Bakker and J.H.A. Warmerdam. Metric pomset semantics for a concurrent language with recursion. In I. Guessarion, editor, *Semantics of Systems of Concurrent Processes*, Lect. Notes Comp. Sci. 469, 21–49, 1990.

[Dev90] R. Devillers. Maximality preserving bisimulation. Technical Report LIT-214, Univ. Bruxelles, 1990.

[GG89] R.J. v. Glabbeek and U. Goltz. Equivalence notions for concurrent systems and refinement of actions. In A. Kreczmar and G. Mirkowska, editors, *MFCS 89*, Lect. Notes Comp. Sci. 379, 237–248, 1989.

[GR83] U. Goltz and W. Reisig. The non-sequential behaviour of Petri nets. *Information and Control*, 57:125–147, 1983.

[Gra81] J. Grabowski. On partial languages. *Fundamenta Informaticae*, IV.2:428–498, 1981.

[GV90] R. Gold and W. Vogler. Quality criteria for partial order semantics of place/transition nets. In B. Rovan, editor, *MFCS 90*, Lect. Notes Comp. Sci. 452, 306–312, 1990.

[HRT89] J. Hirshfeld, A. Rabinovich, and B.A. Trakhtenbrot. Discerning causality in interleaving behaviour. In A.R. Meyer and M.A. Taitslin, editors, *Logic at Botik '89*, Lect. Notes Comp. Sci. 363, 146–162, 1989.

[Kie88] A. Kiehn. On the interrelationship between synchronized and non-synchronized behaviour of Petri nets. *J. Inf. Process. Cybern. EIK*, 24:3–18, 1988.

[Maz87] A. Mazurkiewicz. Trace theory. In W. Brauer et al., editors, *Petri Nets: Applications and Relationships to other Models of Concurrency*, Lect. Notes Comp. Sci. 255, pages 279–324, 1987.

[NEL89] M. Nielsen, U. Engberg, and K. Larsen. Partial order semantics for concurrency. In J.W. de Bakker et al., editors, *Proc. REX School / Workshop Linear Time, Branching Time and Partial Order in Logic and Models of Concurrency. Noordwijkerhout, 1988*, Lect. Notes Comp. Sci. 354, 523–548, 1989.

[Pra86] V. Pratt. Modelling concurrency with partial orders. *Int. J. Parallel Prog.*, 15:33–71, 1986.

[Roz87] G. Rozenberg. Behaviour of elementary net-systems. In W. Brauer et al., editors, *Petri Nets: Central Models and Their Properties*, Lect. Notes Comp. Sci. 254, pages 60–94, 1987.

[Sta81] P.H. Starke. Processes in Petri nets. *J. Inf. Process. Cybern. EIK*, 17:389–416, 1981.

[Vog91a] W. Vogler. Executions: A new partial order semantics of Petri nets. *Theoret. Comput. Sci.*, 91:205–238, 1991.

[Vog91b] W. Vogler. Failures semantics based on interval semiwords is a congruence for refinement. *Distributed Computing*, 4:139–162, 1991.

[Vog91c] W. Vogler. Bisimulation and action refinement. In C. Choffrut and M. Jantzen, editors, *STACS 91*, Lect. Notes Comp. Sci. 480, 309–321, 1991.

A Survey of Basic Net Models and Modular Net Classes

Luca Bernardinello and Fiorella De Cindio

Dipartimento di Scienze dell'Informazione
Università degli Studi di Milano
via Comelico 39 - 20135 Milano (Italy)
e-mail: {bernardinello, decindio}@hermes.mc.dsi.unimi.it

ABSTRACT

The paper surveys those net classes which can be called to some extent 'modular' and the basic net models used as framework in their definition.

In particular the first part introduces Condition/Event systems, Elementary Net systems, Place/Transition systems and 1-safe systems, adhering as much as possible to the original definitions, with the few modifications consolidated in the literature. Then it discusses and compares the basic net models by considering how each one of them deals with some fundamental properties of a net model, such as simplicity, pureness, backward and forward reachability, liveness, contact-freeness.

The second part surveys the main classes of modular nets defined in the literature, showing that most of them share some basic features, since they typically refer to a common idea of building the overall net by composing the nets modelling its sequential components by means of state machines. The differences are considered from the perspective of the specific goal and field of interest of the various authors, and the technical apparatus associated with the various net classes is briefly referred to and illustrated by examples.

Table of contents

FOREWORD

Petri net theory, while recognized to be fully adequate as a theory of concurrency, is often questioned as a suitable basis for the design of non-toy distributed systems. This is due to the lack of built-in compositional constructs which are essential in this respect. Nevertheless a fair amount of work has already been done in this direction. Starting in the early '70s with the work of M. Hack at M.I.T., we can recognize a line of research aimed at developing compositional methods based on nets. In particular this research gave rise to the definition of a number of net classes which can be called to some extent 'modular'.

At first glance one realizes that most of them share some basic features, typically that they refer to a common idea of building the net model of the system by composing the net models of its sequential components modelled by means of state machines. Nevertheless the technical apparatus associated with the various net classes in some way hides the above intuition and might suggest that people are worrying about small details. The review of these classes, which constitutes the second part of this report, aims to highlight the similarities by providing a framework of reference, and suggests considering the differences from the perspective of the specific goal and field of interest of the various authors.

While carrying on this review, we encountered the need to establish a sound basis in terms of the definitions of the basic net models used as frameworks for the various modular classes. For instance, we needed to fix a definition for 1-safe nets, and to relate it, in a rigorous and meaningful way, to the oldest and newest basic models, i.e. to Condition/Event systems and to Elementary Net systems respectively, and also to Place/Transition systems, the other framework in which a number of modular net classes are characterized.

This need forced us to devote some attention to the fundamental characteristics of each one of these basic net models and their major differences. These differences are in some sense well-known, but at the same time also quite subtle and concern the way each model deals with some fundamental properties in net theory, such as simplicity, pureness, backward and forward reachability, liveness, contact-freeness. Discussing these properties, we have summarized the arguments people put forward to motivate the choice of a net model. This is the origin and the aim of the first part of this report.

Here we do not single out one model to see all the others as its specializations or extensions; instead we present the various basic net models, highlighting the specific characteristics of each one and their mutual differences. In the last paragraph of the first part we will summarize the discussion by pointing out which one of the basic net models is acquiring an ever wider audience.

We believe that this effort can turn out to be of some interest and usefulness even independently from the second part of the work, e.g. for those people who want to use nets and therefore need to choose which one of the basic net models to adopt as the framework of their work.

Let us finally remark that this survey arises within the ESPRIT Basic Research Action DEMON. One of the basic assumptions of the DEMON project [bes90a], [bes90b], [bdh90] was exactly the twofold awareness that Petri nets are recognized to be adequate as a theory of concurrency but questioned as a suitable basis for the design of non-toy distributed systems because of lack of built-in compositional constructs. We thus undertook this survey as a contribution to let DEMON start on well-founded bases.

PART I

1. Introduction

The goal of the first part of this report is to identify and mutually compare various net models which will be considered as basic in the following study of modularity in nets. They are 'basic' in the sense that there exists a large agreement on their definition and that they have been widely investigated.

This job can be done at three different levels:

1) the first level concerns net systems whose places are marked by at most one unstructured token; i.e., net systems whose places represent 'conditions';

2) the second level concerns net systems whose places are marked by several unstructured tokens; i.e., net systems whose places represent 'counters';

3) the third level concerns net systems whose places are marked by structured tokens; i.e., net systems, often denoted, in a general sense, as "high-level nets", where information is attached to tokens.

In the sequel we will use 'basic net models' to denote net systems of level one since they constitute the basis for giving the semantics of the net models of levels two ([gol87]) and three ([sr87]).

More precisely, in Section 2 we will give the definitions of the three net models of level one (Condition/Event systems, Elementary Net systems and 1-safe net systems) and of the one net model of level two (Place/Transition systems) together with the associated transition rules. This gives the syntax, in terms of the net structure, and the semantics, in terms of the net behaviour, of each model. The paragraph on Place/Transition systems sums up some of the more recent criticisms on this net model.

In Section 3 we will examine some fundamental properties which characterize the various basic net models. Namely we will consider simplicity, pureness, backward and forward reachability, liveness and contact-freeness, focusing on both theoretical aspects and system design issues.

2. Definition of the net models

We assume that the readers of this survey are quite familiar with net theory: thus, for space reasons, we just recall below the notation and terminology more frequently used in the sequel, while for other, less used, concepts, e.g. the notions of incidence matrix associated with a net, occurrence net, process, etc. we refer to the literature, namely to books and overview papers such as [gwb83], [rei85], [sil85], [bf86], [rt86], [brr87]. Other definitions, concerning the second part, are given in section 2.

A (Petri) *net* is a triple N=(S,T;F) where:

(i) $S \cap T = \emptyset$;

(ii) $S \cup T \neq \emptyset$;

(iii) $F \subseteq (S \times T) \cup (T \times S)$

(iv) $dom(F) \cup cod(F) = S \cup T$

The elements of S are called *S-elements*, the elements of T are called *T-elements*, F is the *flow_relation* and its elements are called *arcs*. The set $X = S \cup T$ is the set of *elements* of the net.

Given a net N=(S,T;F) and $x \in X$, we define

$^\bullet x = \{ y \in X \mid (y,x) \in F \}$

$^\bullet x$ is called *pre-set* of x and its elements are called *pre-elements* of x.

$x^\bullet = \{ y \in X \mid (x,y) \in F \}$

$x^\bullet$ is called *post-set* of x and its elements are called *post-elements* of x.

These definitions are generalized to a subset Y of X in the obvious way:

$^\bullet Y = \cup_{y \in Y} {}^\bullet y \qquad Y^\bullet = \cup_{y \in Y} y^\bullet$

A net N=(S,T;F) is called:

S-simple	iff	$\forall s,s' \in S$: $(^\bullet s = {}^\bullet s'$ and $s^\bullet = s'^\bullet) \Longrightarrow s=s'$
T-simple	iff	$\forall t,t' \in S$: $(^\bullet t = {}^\bullet t'$ and $t^\bullet = t'^\bullet) \Longrightarrow t=t'$
simple	iff	N is S-simple and T-simple
pure	iff	$\forall x \in X$: $^\bullet x \cap x^\bullet = \emptyset$

If $t \in T$ and $s \in {}^\bullet t \cap t^\bullet$, s is called a *side-condition* of t.

In the sequel of this section we recall the definitions of the net models to be discussed. In doing this, we aim to adhere as much as possible to the original definitions given by the authors, with the few modifications consolidated in the literature. As a consequence, some differences in the style of the following definitions can occur.

2.1 Condition/Event (C/E) systems

Condition/Event systems constitute the basic net model introduced by C.A. Petri. Here we summarize the set of definitions given in [pet79] to introduce Condition/Event systems in a single definition.

DEF. 1:

A *Condition/Event system* (C/E system) is a quadruple Σ=(B,E;F,C) where:

1) (B,E;F) is a simple net. The S-elements are called *conditions;* the T-elements are called *events;*
2) $C \subseteq \mathcal{P}(B)=K$ is the *full marking class* (or *case class*) of Σ and K is the set of *constellations* of Σ; each *case* $c \in C$ is a set of conditions;
3) $\forall e \in E\ \exists c \in C$ such that $^\bullet e \subseteq c$ and $e^\bullet \cap c = \emptyset$
   (e is said to *have concession* in c, denoted by c[e>)
4) C is an equivalence class of the *full reachability relation* R defined on the constellations K as follows:

   $R=(r \cup r^{-1})^* \subseteq K x K$

   where $r \subseteq KxK$ is the *reachability relation in one step* defined as follows:

   $(k, k') \in r \Leftrightarrow \exists\, G \subseteq E$ such that:

   (i) $\forall\, e,e' \in G$: $[e \neq e' \Rightarrow (^\bullet e \cap {}^\bullet e') = (e^\bullet \cap e'^\bullet) = \emptyset\,]$

   (ii) $k\text{-}k' = {}^\bullet G$

   (iii) $k'\text{-}k = G^\bullet$

   ($(k, k') \in r$ is usually denoted by k[G>k').

Δ

The above definition is strictly derived from the ones given by Petri, e.g. in [pet79], [bra80], recalled in [rei85], where a set of events satisfying 4.(i) is said to be *detached*. Sometimes, e.g. in [bf86] and [thi87], the definition of C/E systems is given by replacing (i) by

(i)' $\forall\, e,e' \in G$: $[e \neq e' \Rightarrow ({}^\bullet e \cup e^\bullet) \cap ({}^\bullet e' \cup e'^\bullet) = \emptyset\,]$

DEF. 2:

Let N=(B,E;F) be a net. A set of events $G \subseteq E$ satisfying (i)' above is said to be *independent*..
(Ind(G) denotes that G is independent). Δ

The relationships between the two formulations are the following:

(a) (i)' ==> (i)

proof: trivial

(b) (i) =/=> (i)'

proof: see the counter-example of Fig.1 (for the purpose of the proof, consider just the net; the marking will be used later on).

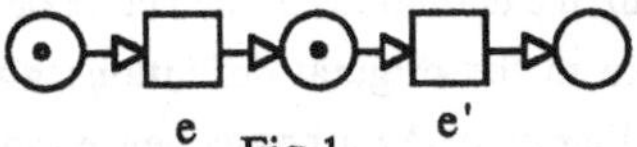

Fig.1

(c) (i) <u>and</u> (ii) <u>and</u> (iii) ==> (i)'

proof ab absurdo: let us assume (i) <u>and</u> (ii) <u>and</u> (iii) <u>and</u> <u>not</u> (i)'.

<u>not</u> (i)' holds, i.e.: $\exists e,e' \in G$:$({}^\bullet e \cup e^\bullet) \cap ({}^\bullet e' \cup e'^\bullet) \neq \emptyset$.

i.e.: $\exists e,e' \in G\ \exists x \in S$: $x \in ({}^\bullet e \cup e^\bullet) \cap ({}^\bullet e' \cup e'^\bullet)$

i.e.: $\exists e,e' \in G\ \exists x \in S$: $x \in ({}^\bullet e \cup e^\bullet)$ <u>and</u> $x \in ({}^\bullet e' \cup e'^\bullet)$. (*)

(i) holds, i.e.: $\forall\, e,e' \in G$: $[e \neq e' \Rightarrow ({}^\bullet e \cap {}^\bullet e') = (e^\bullet \cap e'^\bullet) = \emptyset\,]$. (**)

(*) <u>and</u> (**) imply that just two possibilities exist for x: either $[x \in {}^\bullet e$ <u>and</u> $x \in e'^\bullet]$ or $[x \in e^\bullet$ <u>and</u> $x \in {}^\bullet e']$. Without loss of generality, let us assume the second one, which corresponds to the counter-example above, and prove that it leads to a contradiction.

From ($x \in e^\bullet$ <u>and</u> $x \in {}^\bullet e'$) and from the definition of $G^\bullet$ and ${}^\bullet G$, it holds:

$[x \in G^\bullet$ <u>and</u> $x \in {}^\bullet G]$.

Now, let us consider (ii): $k\text{-}k' = {}^\bullet G$ ==> ${}^\bullet G \subseteq k$; since $x \in {}^\bullet G$, finally we obtain: $x \in k$,

while, by considering (iii): $k'\text{-}k = G^\bullet$ ==> $G^\bullet \subseteq k'$; since $x \in G^\bullet$, finally we obtain: $x \in k'$.

But ($x \in k$ <u>and</u> $x \in k'$) ==> ($x \notin k\text{-}k'$ <u>and</u> $x \notin k'\text{-}k$) which contradicts both (ii) and (iii), since x, while belonging to their right-hand side, would not belong to their left-hand side. (Q.E.D.)

Let us recall that C/E systems are particular transition systems which satisfy the *extensionality axiom* (or principle). It requires that "a repeatable event is fully characterized by the <u>extension of the change in conditions</u> effected by each of its occurrences. Thus, an event e may occur singly whenever its preconditions ${}^\bullet e$ are holding and its postconditions $e^\bullet$ are not holding." (from [pet79], the underlining is of the author; a more formal definition of the extensionality axiom can be found in [glt80]). According to the extensionality axiom, the definition of C/E systems imposes simplicity (point 1) and pureness (point 3) of the underlying net.

2.2 Elementary Net (EN) systems

Elementary Net systems have been introduced by Rozenberg and Thiagarajan, first in [rt86]. Here we take the definition given in [thi87].

DEF. 3:

Let N=(B,E;F) be a net, $u \subseteq E$ and $c \subseteq B$. Then u is a *step enabled* at c (denoted by $c[u>_N$) iff

- (i) Ind(u)
- (ii) $^\bullet u \subseteq c$
- (iii) $u^\bullet \cap c = \emptyset$. Δ

Let us notice that it follows from DEF. 3 that if an event e is enabled at c then $^\bullet e \cap e^\bullet = \emptyset$, i.e. events with a side-condition, which are not excluded, are never enabled (they are *dead*).

DEF. 4:

Let N=(B,E;F) be a net. Then $c[u>_N c'$ denotes the *(elementary) transition relation* in P(B)xP(E)xP(B) associated with N, defined as follows:

$$c[u>_N c' = \{ (c,u,c') \mid c[u>_N \text{ and } c'=(c - {}^\bullet u) \cup u^\bullet \}.$$ Δ

DEF. 5:

An *Elementary Net* (EN) *system* is a quadruple $\mathbf{N}=(B,E;F,c_{in})$ where (B,E;F) is a net called the *underlying net* of $\mathbf{N}$, denoted by und($\mathbf{N}$), and $c_{in} \subseteq B$ is called the *initial case* of $\mathbf{N}$. Δ

DEF. 6:

Let $\mathbf{N}=(B,E;F,c_{in})$ be an EN system. Then $C_\mathbf{N}$ denotes the *set of cases* of $\mathbf{N}$ and is the least subset of P(B) satisfying:

- (i) $c_{in} \in C_\mathbf{N}$
- (ii) if $c \in C_\mathbf{N}$, $u \subseteq E$ and $c' \subseteq B$ such that $c[u>_N c'$, then $c' \in C_\mathbf{N}$. Δ

2.3 Place/Transition (P/T) systems

Place/Transition (P/T) systems are the most widely used net model of the level two variety: their places can be marked by one or more unstructured tokens and represent counters. Places have a capacity, which expresses the maximum of tokens each place can contain; arcs have a weight, which expresses how many tokens flow through them at each occurrence of the involved transition. Although the focus of this report is on net models of level one, here we briefly consider P/T systems since 1-safe net systems, which are the third net model of level one to be introduced (in the next section), are defined as a subclass of P/T systems.

Here we take the definition given by W. Reisig in [rei87].

DEF. 7:

A sixtuple $\Sigma=(S,T;F,K,W,M_0)$ is called a *Place/Transition (P/T) system* iff:

(a) $(S,T;F)$ is a net where the S-elements are called *places* and the T-elements are called *transitions*.

(b) $K:S \text{---}> N^+ \cup \{\infty\}$ is a *capacity* function.

(c) $W:F \text{---}> N^+$ is a *weight* function.

(d) $M_0:S \text{---}> N$ is an *initial marking* function which satisfies:

$$\forall s \in S: M_0(s) \leq K(s).$$ Δ

A P/T system such that: $\forall s \in S$: $K(s)=\infty$ and $\forall f \in F$: $W(f)=1$ can be denoted simply by $\Sigma=(S,T;F,M_0)$ and is often called an *ordinary Petri Net* or simply a *Petri Net.*

DEF. 8:

Let $\Sigma=(S,T;F,K,W,M_0)$ be a P/T system.

(a) A function $M:S \text{---}> N$ is called a *marking* of Σ iff

$$\forall s \in S: M(s) \leq K(s)$$

(b) A transition $t \in T$ is *enabled* at M iff

$$\forall s \in S: \ W(s,t) \leq M(s) \leq K(s)-W(t,s)$$

(c) If $t \in T$ is a transition which is enabled at a marking M, then t may occur, yielding a new marking M' given by the equation:

$$M'(s)=M(s)-W(s,t)+W(t,s) \qquad \forall s \in S$$

(d) The occurrence of t changes the marking M into the new marking M'; we denote this fact by

$$M[t>M'$$

(e) We denote by $[M_0>$ the *(forward) reachability class* defined as the smallest set of markings of Σ such that:

(e1) $M_0 \in [M_0>$

(e2) if $M_1 \in [M_0>$ and $M_1[t>M_2$ for some $t \in T$, then $M_2 \in [M_0>$ Δ

Let us remark that the occurrence rule given in DEF.8 says when a *single transition* is enabled (point b) and what happens when it occurs (point c). On the contrary, the occurrence rules given for C/E systems in DEF.1 and for EN systems in DEF.2, 3 and 4 do the same for a *step,* i.e., for a *set of transitions* which are concurrently enabled and concurrently occur. In other words, the above definitions give the concurrent behaviour (the so-called step semantics) of C/E and EN systems and the interleaving behaviour (the interleaving semantics) of P/T systems, and thus of 1-safe systems which will be introduced in the next section as a subclass of P/T systems.

This is not only because of consistency with the overall choice done in this report of adhering as much as possible to the largest part of the literature, but also because of difficulties in the definition of the step semantics, which we will sketch below.

P/T systems have been over the years one of the more widely used net models; and, in the '70s, probably the most used and studied, both for theoretical research and for applications. The reasons for the success of this model are evident: the P/T net model allows the user to model systems in a much more compact, thus readable, way than the basic net systems. Here places no longer simply represent conditions. They

can represent 'counters'. In particular, one of the big advantages is that one can model infinite state spaces with finite nets.
Nevertheless in the last decade this model has started to be questioned. Both implicitly, by the ever more frequent restriction of the P/T model to 1-safe systems model, which will be introduced in the next section; and explicitly, by a series of papers which put in evidence some basic semantic problems of the model. Here below, we briefly survey these papers, giving a sort of annotated bibliography.

Some 'Difficulties in Interpreting Place/Transition Nets' were first drawn to people's attention by W. Brauer [bra84]. He shows that for P/T systems different token games are possible; i.e., for them different transition occurrence rules can be defined. Further and more formal studies which focus this point are [tau88], in which these differences are considered from the perspective of distributed software implementations of P/T nets, and [dev90] which contains an overview of the literature.
In particular [dev90] notices that, while the effect of transition occurrence is uniformly accepted (cfr. Def.8, point c), differences arise with respect to the definition of the enabling conditions which specify when a transition may occur in a certain marking. He compares the enabling conditions for transition occurrence in a P/T system, as given in [gs80], [rei85], [bf86], [rei87] and recalled here in Def.8 point (b), with the one given in [jv80], [win85], which is as follows:

(b') A transition $t \in T$ is *enabled* at M iff $\forall s \in S$: $W(s,t) \leq M(s) \leq K(s)-W(t,s)+W(s,t)$.

(b) and (b') differ with respect to the enabling of side-conditions (cfr. Fig.2).

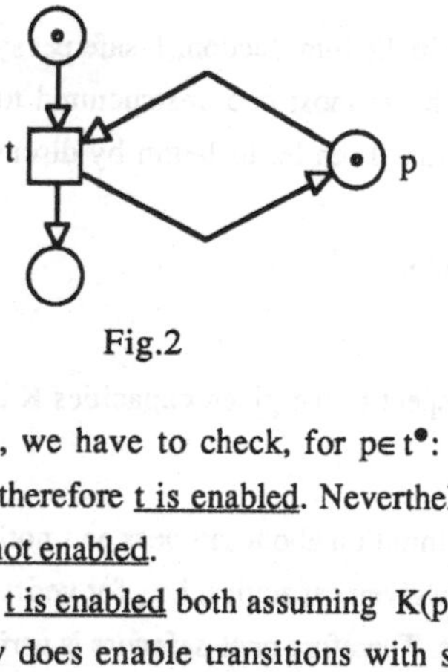

Fig.2

On the one hand, according to (b), we have to check, for $p \in t^\bullet$: $M(p) \leq K(p)-W(t,p)$. If we assume $K(p)=\infty$, we have $1 \leq \infty-1=\infty$, and therefore <u>t is enabled</u>. Nevertheless, replacing $K(p)=\infty$ by $K(p)=1$, now we find $1 \leq 1-1=0$, and thus <u>t is not enabled</u>.
On the other hand, according to (b'), <u>t is enabled</u> both assuming $K(p)=\infty$ and $K(s)=1$. We could say that (b') is more liberal since it anyhow does enable transitions with side-conditions. Let us remark that [dev90] actually introduces two further enabling rules, for completeness and symmetric reasons, but, as he claims, they do not really fit for Petri nets, so we neglect them.
[dev90] extends the two rules to define the concurrent enabling of a couple (a set, a bag) of transitions. The extension of the enabling condition (b) is straightforward, in the sense that just one extension exists: under this extension, the concurrent occurrence of a <u>set</u> of transitions corresponds to the notion of single step in [rei85b], while the concurrent occurrence of a <u>bag</u> of transitions corresponds to the notion of step in [bf86]. On the contrary, two different extensions are possible for the enabling condition (b'), which yield respectively the definition of the notion of synchronous (resp., asynchronous) concurrent enabling of a couple (a set, a bag) of transitions.

A different strand of work which highlights some essential features and problems of P/T systems concerns the relationships between P/T systems and C/E systems, which is, in net theory, one fundamental technique to give the semantics of a net model.
[gen86] introduces the notion of projection, and, by means of it, gives a basis for discussing the relationships between C/E systems, Predicate/Transition nets and P/T systems. He shows that P/T systems are a kind of 'abstraction' of the other models, where one yields a quantitative view of the system by omitting some information: namely, with respect to Pr/T nets, the omitted information concerns the identity of the tokens. The same idea of looking at P/T systems as abstractions, in this case as abstractions of C/E systems, is developed later on by J. Desel and A. Merceron [dm90] who follow a different approach, based on net topology and synchronic distances. Finally the representation of a P/T system by a corresponding C/E system is discussed in [gol87].
Unfortunately the different approaches of [gen86] and [dm90] yield different P/T systems abstracting from the same C/E system ([dm90] shows an example).
All these studies, opening new problems and proposing a multiplicity of alternative definitions for basic notions of net theory, leave the P/T model, still widely used both for practical and theoretical purposes, in some way suspended in respect to its semantic characterization. This motivates the restriction, introduced in the next section, which solves most of these problems.

2.4 1-safe systems

According to the classification given in the Introduction, 1-safe net systems belong to net systems of level one, since their places are marked by at most one unstructured token. Nevertheless they are usually defined as a subclass of P/T systems. Then let us begin by discussing the notion of safeness for P/T systems.
In [gs80] safeness is defined as follows:

DEF. 9:
A P/T system is called *safe* with respect to the given capacities K iff increasing K does not change the reachability class. Δ

This definition captures the original intuition about safeness as a notion for verifying if the behaviour of a (P/T) system is independent from the given capacities; i.e., for verifying when the given capacities do not constrain the behaviour of the system. Therefore once safeness is verified:

a) one can assume that all places have unlimited capacity (i.e., $\forall s \in S$, $K(s)=\infty$);

b) in order to check transition enabling, it is sufficient to look at the marking of the pre-conditions of the transition (to verify: $\forall s \in S$: $W(s,t) \leq M(s)$), disregarding its post-conditions (since both the conditions (b): $\forall s \in S$: $M(s) \leq K(s)-W(t,s)$ and (b'): $\forall s \in S$: $M(s) \leq K(s)-W(t,s)+W(s,t)$, discussed in the previous section, are always satisfied under the assumption: $\forall s \in S$, $K(s)=\infty$).

According to the above definition, neither the P/T system S3 of Fig.3 nor the system S4 of Fig.4 are safe, since in both cases the capacity of place b constrains the occurrence of the transition *fill*. The difference between the two systems is that in S3 *fill* can never occur, while it can in S4 (after b is emptied by the occurrence of the sequence *empty, consume, empty*). On the contrary, system S5 of Fig.5 - in which place b has unlimited capacity and the four places p1, p2, c1, c2 contain, in any reachable marking, at most one token - is safe. Let us also notice that if we define a P/T system S as in Fig.1, assigning capacity 1 to all the places, S is not safe because the capacity of the intermediate place constrains the behaviour.

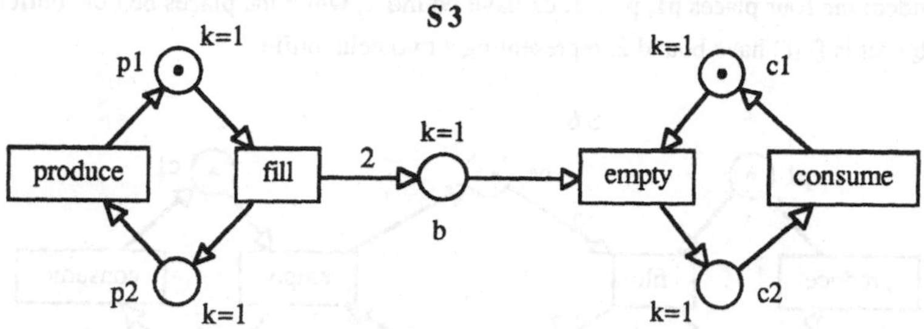

Fig.3

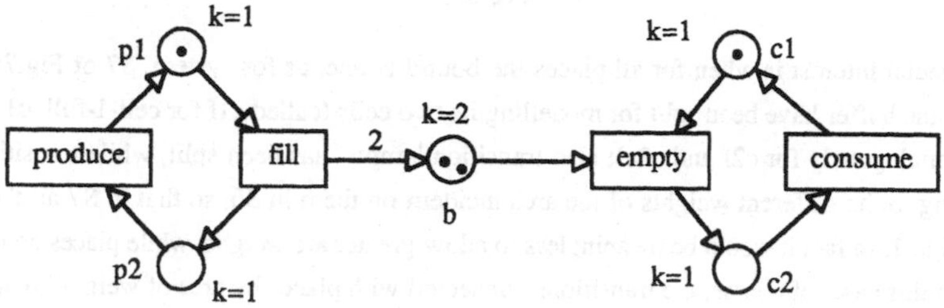

Fig.4

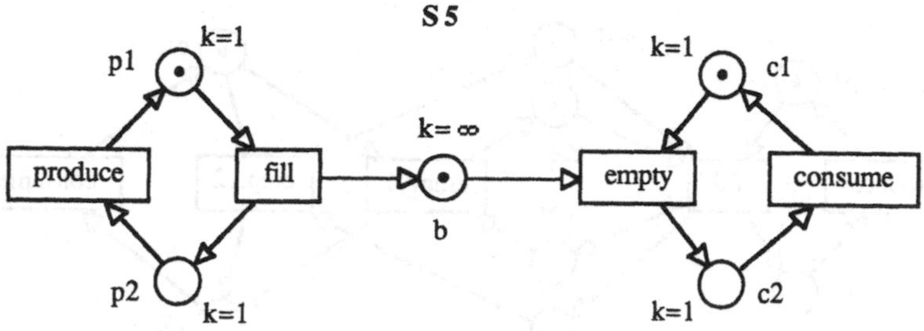

Fig.5

There is an important distinction between safe systems in which all the places contain, in any reachable marking, a limited number of tokens and safe systems with places which can contain an unlimited number of tokens. To make this distinction, the notion of boundedness is introduced, as follows:

DEF.10:
Let $\Sigma=(S,T;F,K,W,M_0)$ be a P/T system such that $\forall s\in S$: $K(s)=\infty$.
A place $s\in S$ is *bounded* iff $\exists n\in N\ \forall M\in [M_0\rangle: M(s)\leq n$

Σ is *bounded* iff $\forall s \in S$: s is bounded Δ

Once boundedness is verified, unlimited capacities can be replaced by some finite capacities without changing the marking class. P/T system S5 of Fig.5 is safe but not bounded, while the safe system S6 of Fig.6 is bounded: the four places p1, p2, c1, c2 have bound 1, while the places be ('the buffer is empty') and bf ('the buffer is full') have bound 2, representing a two cells-buffer.

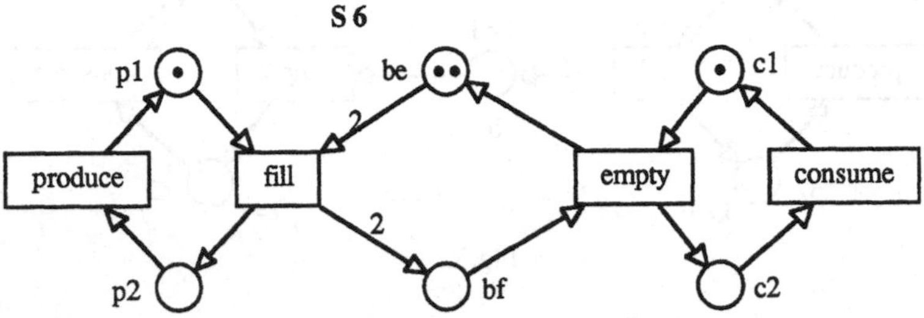

Fig.6

A case of special interest is when for all places the bound is one, as for system S7 of Fig.7: the places representing the buffer have been split for modelling its two cells (called c1f for cell-1-full, c1e for cell-1-empty, and analogously for c2f and c2e); also transition 'empty' has been split, while transition 'fill' has not, according to the different weights of the arcs incident on them in S6, so that in S7 all the arcs have weight equal to 1. In fact it would be meaningless to allow greater arc weights while places contain at most one token: in this case, of course, the transitions connected with places by arcs of weight greater than one would be destined to be dead.

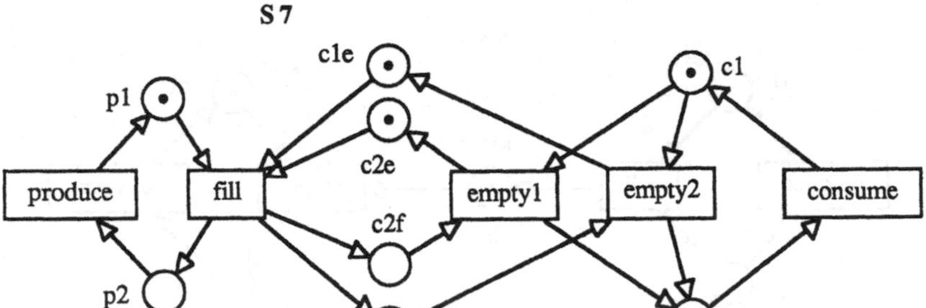

Fig.7

The class of P/T systems with these characteristics are usually called 1-safe (or simply safe) systems. They are thus defined as the bounded P/T systems with bound n=1 and all the arc weights equal to 1. These conditions are captured by the following definition:

DEF.11
A sixtuple $\Sigma=(S,T;F,K,W,M_0)$ is a *1-safe (P/T) system* iff

(i) $\forall s \in S$: $K(s)= \infty$

(ii) $\forall s \in S\ \forall M \in [M_0\rangle$: $M(s) \leq 1$

(iii) $\forall f \in F$: $W(f)=1$

If these conditions are verified, Σ can be denoted simply by $\Sigma=(S,T;F,M_0)$ in which markings of $[M_0\rangle$ can be represented as subsets of S. Δ

Very often in the literature, e.g. in [rei85] and in [rt86] among the others, safeness is used as synonymous of 1-safeness.

The conditions required by DEF.11 imply that places can be marked by at most one unstructured token. 1-safe systems can thus be properly considered a net model of level one. Nevertheless, since they are defined as subclass of the P/T systems, their behaviour is given by the P/T systems transition rule and we still have to be careful with respect to the enabling of transitions, namely with respect to the enabling of transitions with side-conditions, as for instance in the case of the net system in Fig.2 which can be viewed as a 1-safe system. Both the formalizations (b) and (b') considered in section 2.3 can be used.
Considering the first one, we still have to distinguish two cases: according to Def.11.i we can assume $K(p)=\infty$ and derive that t is enabled. Nevertheless, 1-safe systems are a particular case of bounded P/T systems, with the bound n=1. We have already pointed out that, once boundedness is verified, the unlimited capacities can be replaced by suitable finite capacities, without changing the marking class. But if we replace $K(p)=\infty$ by $K(p)=1$ we now derive that t is not enabled. On the contrary, (b') anyhow enables t.
The choice more frequently adopted in the literature is to enable transitions with side-conditions: it is sometime referred to as the safe transition rule (see e.g. [bes88]). A number of slightly different definitions by various authors ([maz77], [bes85], [ddps85], [win85], [val87] is an incomplete list) end up with 1-safe systems behaving according to the safe transition rule. Let us also remark that the opposite choice more properly fits the definition of enabledness in EN systems (cfr. Def.3).
In the following, where we consider 1-safe systems, we will assume they obey the safe transition rule.

3. About properties of basic net models

As an outcome of the previous section, one realizes that, even at the very fundamental level of nets whose places can be marked by at most one unstructured token, there are various slight differences between the models - both at the syntactic (the net structure) and at the semantic (the net behaviour) level - whose meaning is not easy to catch. While some differences, especially in the way things are formalized, might be a matter of the author's taste, there are also choices, which depend on the author's specific - in the overall framework of a theory of concurrency - target and background, rarely explicitly declared.
In this section we will examine some topics so that the differences among the basic net models whose places are marked by just one unstructured token become more evident. We will consider:

- simplicity;
- pureness;
- backward&forward reachability versus only forward reachability;
- liveness;
- contact-freeness.

The discussion will focus both on theoretical aspects and on system design issues.

3.1 Simplicity

Simplicity concerns the structure of the net underlying a net system.
Let us start by showing two fragments of nets which are not simple with respect to transitions (Fig.8a) and with respect to places (Fig.8b).

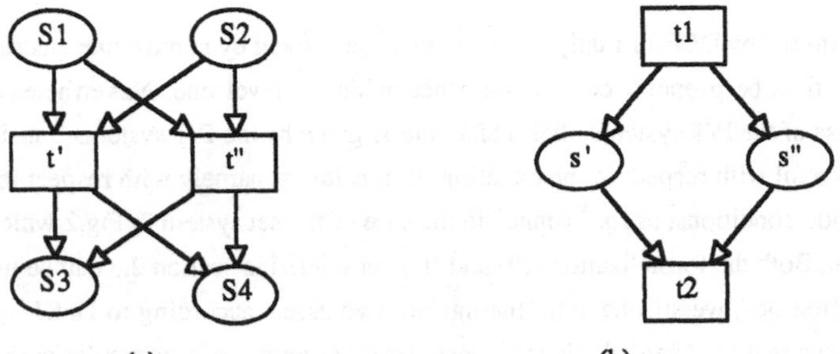

(a) Fig.8 (b)

We have seen in Section 2 that the underlying net of any C/E system has to be simple, while this is not required for EN and 1-safe systems. However, if it is not, a net system, whose underlying net is simple and which is equivalent to the source one under some equivalence notion, can be obtained in two ways, illustrated below: the first one relies on equivalences based on states, the second one on equivalences based on state/action observability (according to the terminology used in [prs92], in this volume, where one can find all the definitions mentioned in the sequel of this section).

1) The resulting net is obtained by identifying the elements of the source net which have identical pre-sets and post-sets. Fig.9 shows the result of this operation for the above examples. The source and the resulting systems are sequential case graph equivalent, i.e. their sequential case graph are isomorphic (these notions are given in [rt86] for EN systems; their formulation for 1-safe systems is straightforward), under the condition that, in situations such as (b) in Fig.8 the initial marking of s' and s" must be the same, i.e., it is not acceptable that one of them is marked while the other is not.

Let us point out that the so called *diamond property* (see [prs92]) guarantees that in the investigation of the state space of EN systems it suffices to investigate the sequential case graph only, since the usual case graph, which contains edges for steps, can be obtained from the sequential one by *diamond closure*.

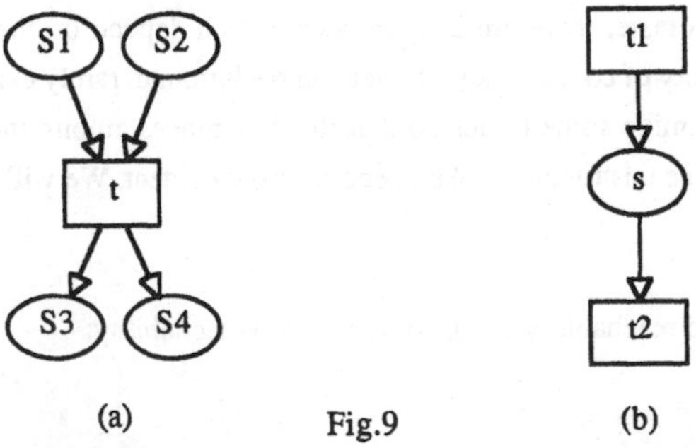

(a) Fig.9 (b)

2) The resulting net is obtained from the source one by applying some refinement which introduces more elements and making 'unobservable' some or all of them. Fig.10 shows examples of refinements applied to the two nets of Fig.8. The net of Fig.10a is equivalent to the net of Fig.8a under State-Transformation-equivalence [ps91], considering the two shaded places as unobservable. The net of Fig.10b is equivalent to the net of Fig.8b under any equivalence notion based on action observability (see again [prs92] for an overview), considering the shaded transition as unobservable and assuming for the places "consistent" initial marking (i.e.: the initial marking of s' must be preserved; if s" is marked then either s1" or s2" must be marked, but not both).

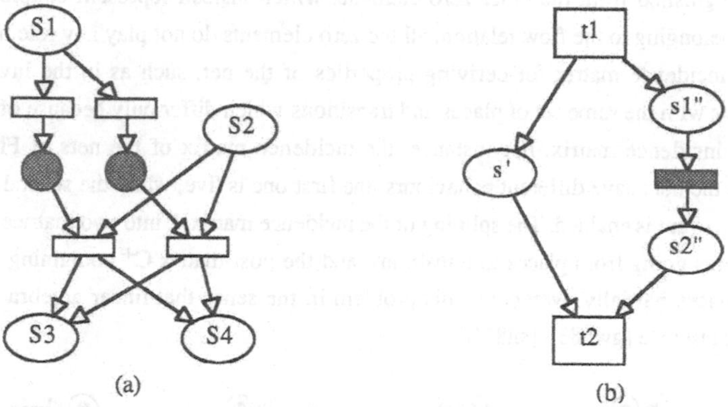

Fig.10

In the framework of system design, where the net model of the whole system is assumed to be built by successive refinements and/or abstractions and/or compositions, it seems therefore reasonable to maintain simplicity as a requirement of the net model at the broadest level of details, i.e., including all the refinements, as obtained by accomplishment of the design, whereas it doesn't matter if simplicity is violated by the intermediate net models, which, if necessary, can be studied through the corresponding simplified ones.

3.2 Pureness

As in the case of simplicity, pureness also concerns the structure of the net underlying a system. Fig.11 shows nets which are not pure since they contain one or more side-conditions, that is places which are both input and output of the same transition.

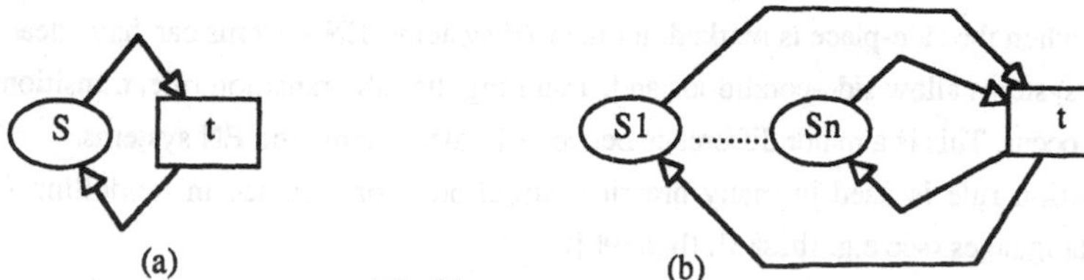

Fig.11

Once more we are dealing with a basic problem in the characterization of a net model. In fact, if we allow side-conditions, it is no longer clear, since models are in any case partial, when we have to attach zero, one or more side-conditions to a transition. Analogously, we could attach to every place one or more transitions having the place as their only input and output. Then the extensionality principle, as recalled in section 2.1, is violated[1].

These difficulties are reflected in the incidence matrix associated with the net (for a definition see, e.g., [gwb83], [rei85], [sil85], [lau87]): a side-condition s of a transition t is represented in the incidence matrix by a zero in the element (s,t), since the +1 and the -1 mutually cancel. This zero element of the matrix cannot be distinguished from the other zero elements which instead represent couples of places and transitions not belonging to the flow relation: all the zero elements do not play any role in the algorithms which use the incidence matrix for deriving properties of the net, such as in the invariant calculus. Furthermore nets with the same set of places and transitions which differ only because of side-conditions have the same incidence matrix. For instance, the incidence matrix of the nets of Fig. 12a and 12b coincide, while the nets have different behaviours: the first one is live, while the second one can reach a case in which no event is enabled. The splitting of the incidence matrix C into two matrices, the pre-matrix C^- containing arcs going from places to transitions, and the post-matrix C^+ containing arcs going from transitions to places partially overcomes this problem in the sense that linear algebra methods can be applied (see for instance [gwb83], [sil85]).

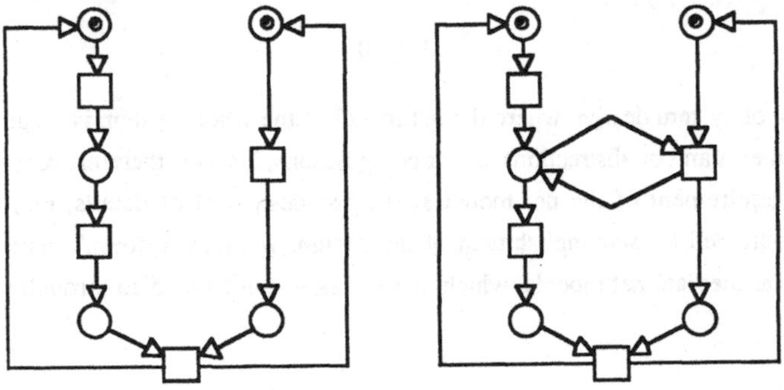

(a) (b)

Fig. 12

We have seen in Section 2 that the underlying net of every C/E system has to be pure. The definition of EN system allows side-conditions, but, according to their transition rule, transitions with side-conditions are dead, even when the side-place is marked: unlike C/E systems, EN systems can have dead transitions. Finally, 1-safe systems allow side-conditions and, assuming the safe transition rule, transitions with side-conditions can occur. This is a major difference between 1-safe systems and EN systems.

The safe transition rule is used in many practical situations, for instance in modelling (concurrent) programming languages (see e.g. [bes88], [bdhh90]).

---

[1] a less restrictive formulation of the extensionality principle which is not violated by the presence of side-conditions is presented and discussed in [val87].

For instance, the transition modelling the test of the condition of a conditional statement such as "IF x=4 THEN..." involves dependence on a place representing variable x having the particular value: this value does not change because of the execution of the test, and therefore the marking of the place does not change because of the occurrence of the transition.
The same holds in the case of modelling the assignment statement for the places representing the values of the variables occurring in the assignment right-hand side, as shown in Fig.13 for the assignment y:=x, where both x and y assume values in the integer subrange [0,1]. The shaded places represent the control flow: when p is marked, then the assignment is to be executed, i.e. one of the four transitions modelling it is enabled, depending on the current value of x and y.
Furthermore, in this framework, side-conditions are used as an explicit sequentializing device for modelling processor assignments (see [bes88]).

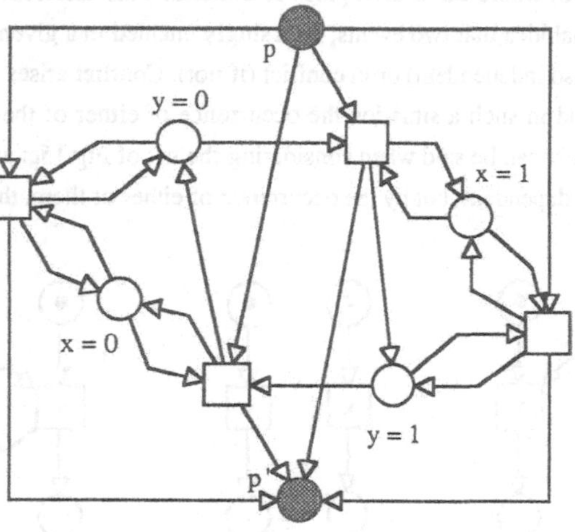

Fig. 13

Also in system design there exists a large number of situations where side-conditions are useful and used for the same reason as before, i.e. to test a condition without changing it. For instance, Fig.14 shows a fragment of a net modelling a lift: people can enter and exit from the lift at whatever floor if and only if the cabin is at that floor, but both these events do not modify the cabin state.
Furthermore, if one aims at modelling well-behaved systems (namely, live and safe systems) by some kind of well-formed nets and some associated compositional method, as for instance in [gt84] and [es89] (see also section 7.5), then one starts with the 'simplest' live and safe net, i.e. the one in Fig.11a, which should therefore belong to the class of well-formed nets.

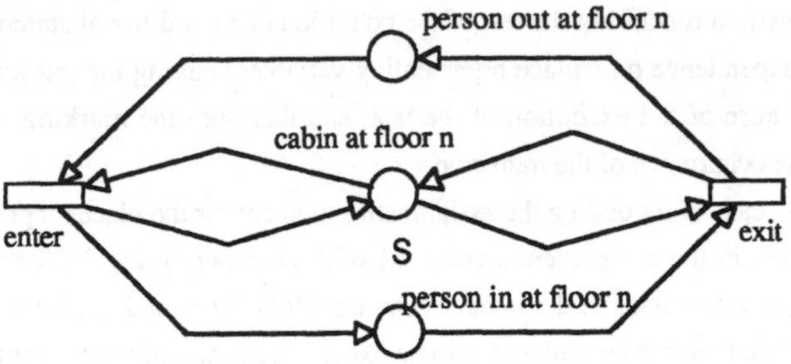

Fig.14

A major semantic difficulty with the safe transition rule concerns the notion of conflict. Let us consider the nets in Fig.15. Transitions x and y are in conflict in Fig.15a because they share one input place, while they are concurrent in Fig.15b, where the shared place is omitted. This difference between these two nets corresponds to the original idea that two events, both singly enabled in a given marking (case), are either concurrent (if they are also independent) or in conflict (if not). Conflict arises because of competition on some shared resource and in such a situation the occurrence of either of the conflicting events should disable the other one. What can be said when considering the net of Fig.15c: are x and y concurrent or in conflict ? They are not independent, but by the occurrence of either of them, the other one does not cease to be enabled.

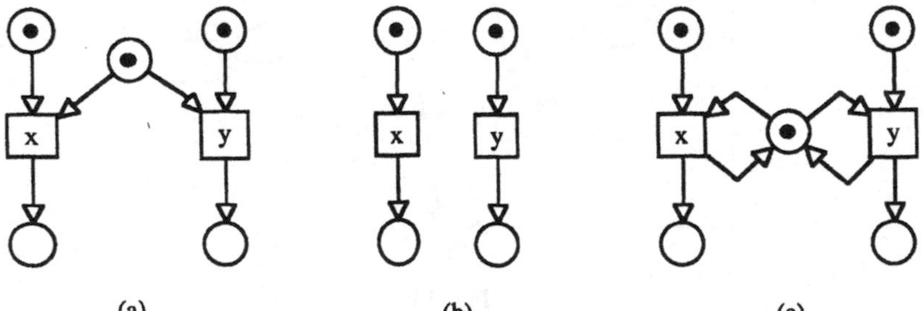

Fig. 15

There are two ways to modify a net with side-conditions into a pure one.

1) The first one consists in substituting transitions having intersecting pre- and post- conditions by a couple of transitions in sequence, as shown in Fig.16 for the nets of Fig.11. If the original transition t modelled action a, then transition t' would now model 'start a', the intermediate place 'running a', and transition t" would model 'end a'. This is the transformation suggested in [lau87] for calculating invariants for non-pure (P/T) nets.

2) The second one consists in splitting the single condition which gives rise to non-pureness into two or more conditions, so that the side-conditions can be removed. From a system design perspective, this splitting corresponds to distinguishing more states of the system, as in the case shown in Fig.14, where the place S modelling 'the cabin is at floor n' is split into a number of places: SO for 'the cabin is at floor n, with no people inside it', S1 for 'the cabin is at floor n, with one person inside it', S2 for 'the cabin is at floor n, with two persons inside it', and so on (see Fig.17).

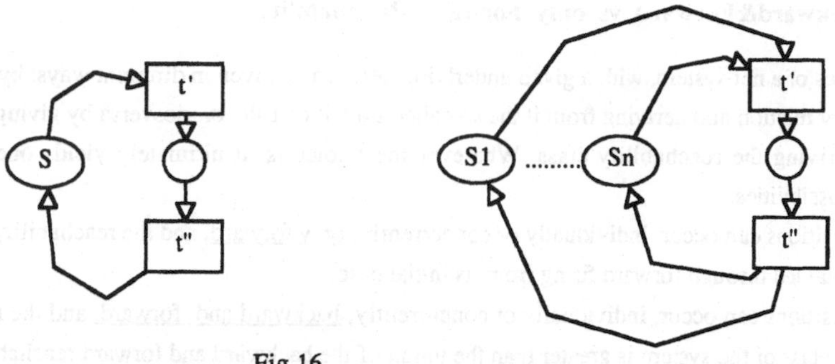

Fig.16

Nevertheless it is questionable if these transformations are actually satisfying. If we apply the first one to the case of concurrent programming languages, the splitting of the original transition into a sequence of two compromises its atomicity. Furthermore, also the possibility of modelling some special features, such as priorities, seems to rely on the possibility of using side-conditions (see [bk91]).

The second transformation usually yields a significant increase in the number of net elements, both places and transitions. Not only the effectiveness and readability of the net is somehow hampered, but, in some cases, one must face the unpleasant consequence of jumping from a finite to a infinite net model, as in the case of Fig.17.

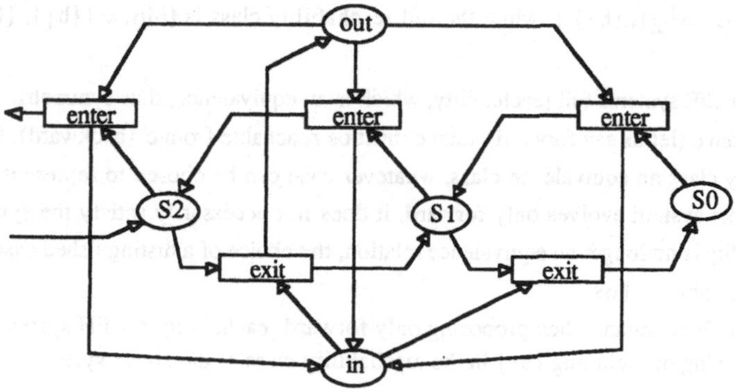

Fig. 17

These are some of the arguments people put forward in order to motivate the choice of allowing side-conditions or not, a choice which is still a matter of lively discussions. As a possible summary of the above discussion, we see stronger motivations at the theoretical/semantic level for requiring net pureness, while there are a number of modelling situations where side-conditions are very effective. This shows that the problem is still open and that more research on it is necessary, for instance for developing an (automatic) transformation of non-pure nets into pure ones, supported by a suitable equivalence notion between the two nets, which take care of the atomicity, of priorities, and so on.

3.3 Backward&Forward vs only Forward Reachability

The dynamics of a net system, with a given underlying net, can be given in different ways: by introducing a reachability relation and deriving from it the so called transition rule, or viceversa by giving a transition rule and deriving the reachability class. Whatever the choice is, it ultimately yields one of the two following possibilities:

- transitions can occur, individually or concurrently, only forward, and the reachability class of the system is obtained through forward firing from its initial case;
- transitions can occur, individually or concurrently, backward and forward, and the resulting full reachability class of the system is greater than the union of the backward and forward reachability classes, as shown by the example in Fig.18, taken from [thi87], indicating the difference between the two alternatives.

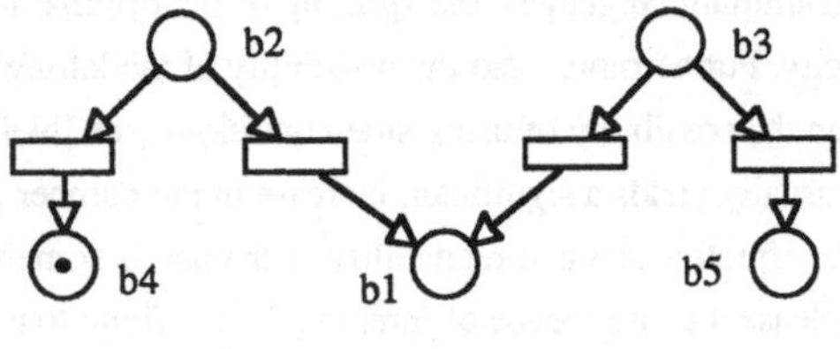

Fig.18

Let us take as initial marking M_0 with only b_4 marked. Then the forward reachability class is $\{\{b_4\}\}$, the backward one is $\{\{b_2\}, \{b_4\}\}$, while the full reachability class is $[M_0] = \{\{b_1\}, \{b_2\}, \{b_3\}, \{b_4\}, \{b_5\}\}$.

Petri adopts for C/E systems full reachability, which is an equivalence, thus symmetric relation: if case c' is reachable from c (let us say forward), then c must be reachable from c' (backward). In this case, being the reachability class an equivalence class, whatever case can be chosen to represent the class. On the contrary, if a net system evolves only forward, it does not necessarily satisfy the symmetric property. Since reachability is no longer an equivalence relation, the choice of a distinguished case as the initial one changes the reachability class.

Rozenberg and Thiagarajan, when proposing only forward reachability for EN systems, ask themselves what is the meaning of including $\{b_5\}$ in the reachability class of the above system. 1-safe systems, like P/T systems in general, also adopt forward reachability, and it is generally assumed that it suffices in system design.

This difference between C/E systems on the one hand and the other two net models on the other one may be related to the claim by Thiagarajan in [thi87]. "Wherein net theory is viewed in a larger perspective - as opposed to the narrower taken here - C/E systems are better suited to serve the role of the basic system model." How do we interpret the two perspectives evoked in this sentence? Up to now, namely in section 3.2 concerning pureness, practical considerations from system design were compared with theoretical issues, " theoretical" in the sense of a "theory of concurrency" in the context of computer science. However in this discussion about backward and forward reachability, computer science and system design jointly constitute the "narrower" perspective with respect to the larger one, adopted by Petri from the very beginning of his work, which includes arguments from other sciences, typically from physics.

Nevertheless there are areas in computer science and system design in which backward techniques are fruitfully and effectively used. Let us mention a few ones: backward reasoning in program correctness proofs according to Hoare' axiomatic approach; backward inference in logic programming and artificial intelligence; backward recovery as a standard way for handling exceptions in fault-tolerant systems; backward causality as a diagnosis technique to derive the "pre-states" which have determined an error state. These examples suggest to consider the possibility that a deeper investigation of such backward techniques in terms of nets might give hints about the usefulness of assuming backward&forward reachability, even in the computer science "narrower" perspective.

3.4 Liveness properties

Liveness properties aim at 'measuring' the possibility of transitions to occur. There are in the literature various notions about how to do this (deadlock-freeness, 1-liveness, liveness, cyclicity, home states, reproducibility of markings, etc.) and different definitions for quite the same notion. It is out of the scope of this work to review and relate all these notions. For the purpose of comparing basic net systems, it is sufficient to point out that there are two opposite needs.

On the one hand, it is quite evident that a 'good' system should not contain events which can never occur. C/E systems require by definition each event to be 1-live (an event *e* is *1-live* iff there is at least one reachable case in which *e* is enabled, i.e. if it has at least one chance of occurring; a net system is 1-live iff all its events are 1-live; *quasi-liveness* is sometimes, e.g. in [gwb83], used instead of 1-liveness). EN and 1-safe systems can contain dead transitions (a transition is *dead* iff at each reachable case it is not enabled, i.e. iff it has no chance of occurring; dead transitions can be modelled by *facts*, see e.g. [rei85] for a definition). When considering compositionality, that is when we aim at building the net model of a system starting from a certain level of abstraction and applying transformations, e.g. refinements, to it, we would like that transformations preserve (some) liveness properties, so that starting from nets satisfying some liveness property, the resulting net would also satisfy them. This was the underlying idea of Bipolar Schemes [gt84].

On the other hand it is clear that there are concrete situations where liveness, in whatever specific sense (the most frequently used definitions of liveness are recalled in section 6.1), is a property to be proved 'a posteriori' rather than a requirement to be required 'a priori'. For instance, once given the semantics of a concurrent programming language in terms of a corresponding net, one would use the net model of a program for studying if it is live or at least deadlock-free. Such reasoning requires a net model which allows dead transitions.

3.5 Contact-freeness

There is a further property which plays a major role in the foundations of net theory: contact-freeness.

In a basic net system, we say that there is a contact situation if all the pre-conditions and some of the post-conditions of an event hold simultaneously, i.e. in a case. Fig. 1 provides an example of a contact, concerning the event *e* in the given case. The event does not have concession according to the extensionality principle, recalled at the end of section 2.1, which requires an event to be completely

characterized by its extension, i.e., by the set of conditions that cease to hold (the pre-conditions) and the set of conditions that begin to hold (the post-conditions) because of its occurrence.
Accordingly, a net system is contact-free if and only if in order to check the enabling of a transition it is sufficient to look at its preconditions, disregarding its post-conditions. The formal definitions of contact-freeness are slightly different for C/E systems and EN systems because of backward&forward vs only forward occurrence.

DEF.12
A C/E system $\Sigma=(B,E;F,C)$ is *contact-free* iff

$$\forall e \in E\ \forall c \in C: [\ ({}^{\bullet}e \subseteq c \Rightarrow e^{\bullet} \cap c = \emptyset) \text{ and } (e^{\bullet} \subseteq c \Rightarrow {}^{\bullet}e \cap c = \emptyset)\ ] \qquad \Delta$$

DEF.13
An EN system $\mathcal{N}=(B,E;F,c_{in})$ is *contact-free* iff

$$\forall e \in E\ \forall c \in C_{\mathcal{N}}: ({}^{\bullet}e \subseteq c \Rightarrow e^{\bullet} \cap c = \emptyset) \qquad \Delta$$

There are a number of properties which are usually formalized for contact-free systems (e.g. [rei85] contains a lot of them), and this is why contact-freeness is often required for the various kinds of net systems. Nevertheless this is not an actual restriction, since there is a well-known construction which transforms a net system into a contact-free system which is equivalent to the original one.
The transformation is S-completion: intuitively it adds, for each place s in the original net, representing a condition c, a further place s' representing the condition $\neg c$. A net system $\mathcal{N}$ not (forward) contact-free because it contains some pattern as in Fig.19a can be transformed as shown in Fig.19b: instead of checking, for the enabling of t, that c <u>does not</u> hold (s not marked) one can check that $\neg c$ <u>does</u> hold (s' marked). If s' is not marked, then t is not enabled. Of course, the S-completion must be carried out in such a way that s and s' are suitably connected all over the net; i.e., when c ceases to hold by the occurrence of some transition in the post-set of s (e.g., t' in Fig.19), then $\neg c$ starts to hold. An analogous transformation can be defined for eliminating the situations of backward contact.
The details of the transformation are given in [rei85] for C/E systems and in [rt86] for EN systems, and it is shown that the two systems are equivalent in the sense that their case graphs are isomorphic (see, respectively: Th. (i) p. 28 in [rei85] and Th. 6.8 in [rt86]).

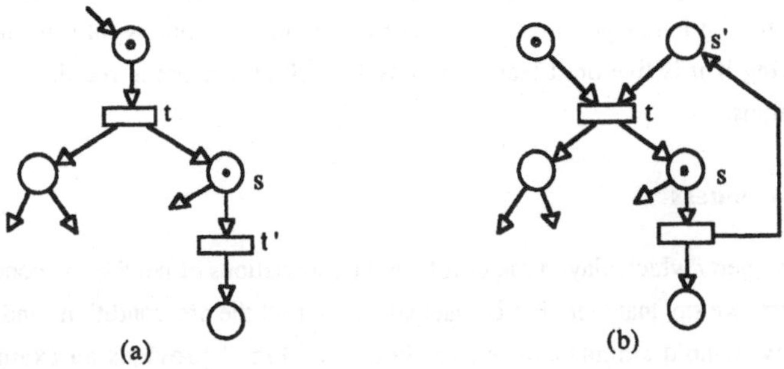

Fig.19

Let us note that contact-freeness plays, for the basic net models, the same role as safeness for P/T systems. In fact we said in Section 2.4 that the intuition behind safeness was of a notion for verifying if the behaviour of a (P/T) system is independent from the given capacities, and we saw that, once safeness is verified, for checking the enabling of a transition, it is sufficient to look at its preconditions, disregarding its post-conditions, which is the intuition behind contact-freeness. Because of this remark, when introducing contact-freeness for 1-safe systems, we have to relate it to safeness.
Let us begin by defining 1-safe contact-free systems; the definition is derived from the definition of contact-free P/T system, as given e.g. in [rei85], by considering the constraints which characterize 1-safe systems and the consequent possibility of representing markings as subsets of S.

DEF.14
A 1-safe system Σ=(S,T;F,M_0) is *contact-free* iff

$$\forall t\in T\ \forall M\in [M_0\rangle: [{}^\bullet t \subseteq M \Rightarrow t^\bullet \cap M = \emptyset\,] \qquad \Delta$$

Let us now consider, for instance, the 1-safe system S2 of Fig.2. According to the above definition, S2 is not contact-free.This shows that in general 1-safe systems may have contacts, namely because of side-conditions.
Nevertheless consider the same net in which either just one or none of the preconditions is marked. All the three net systems so obtained are contact-free, due to the fact that $\forall M\in [M_0\rangle$, ${}^\bullet t\subseteq M$ is false. This shows that in general 1-safe systems containing side-conditions may be contact-free, namely if all the transitions with side-conditions are dead.

We can summarize these considerations in the following way. Let Σ be a 1-safe system. Then it holds: Σ pure $\Rightarrow \Sigma$ contact-free. Nevertheless in general the converse: Σ contact-free $\Rightarrow \Sigma$ pure, does not hold . In fact a 1-safe system containing a side-condition which is never marked is contact-free (according to the above definition) but non pure.

Let us finally mention that, besides of the safe transition rule, some authors have introduced a different notion of contact-freeness for 1-safe systems.

DEF.15
A 1-safe (P/T) system Σ=(S,T;F,M_0) is contact-free iff

$$\forall t\in T\ \forall M\in [M_0\rangle: [{}^\bullet t \subseteq M \Rightarrow (t^\bullet - {}^\bullet t) \cap M = \emptyset] \qquad \Delta$$

According to this definition, given for instance in [bes88], a 1-safe system might be contact-free even if it contains non-dead transitions with side-conditions.

4. Emerging standard

With respect to the properties discussed in section 3., the definitions given in Section 2. can be summarized as follows.

Condition/Event systems:

i) require pureness of the underlying net;

ii) require simplicity (both for places and transitions) of the underlying net;
iii) have backward&forward occurrence and reachability;
iv) each event is 1-live

Elementary Net systems:
i) do not require pureness, but a transition with a side-condition is dead;
ii) do not require simplicity (both for places and transitions);
iii) have only forward occurrence and reachability;
iv) do not require any kind of liveness.

Both C/E systems and EN systems can be required to be contact-free without loss of generality, thanks to the result recalled in 3.5. Therefore, taking into account what we said in 3.1 about simplicity and in 3.2 about pureness, we can say that the actual differences between C/E systems and EN systems reduce to backward&forward versus only forward occurrence and reachability, and to liveness. Fig.20 shows a trivial example of an EN system which is not a C/E system. Fig.21 shows a less trivial example: the EN system is simple, pure, 1-live and contact-free, but it is not a contact-free C/E system (due to backward contact).

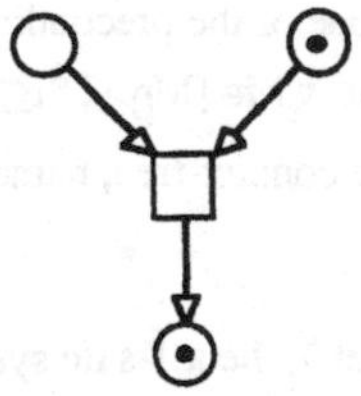

Fig.20

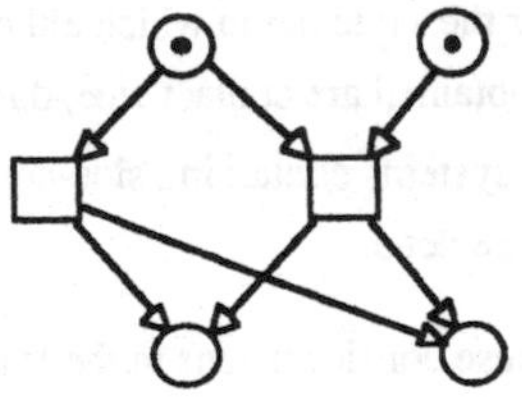

Fig.21

With respect to C/E and EN systems, 1-safe net systems:
i) have only forward occurrence and reachability;
ii) have no constraint about pureness, simplicity and 1-liveness.

We have pointed out in §3.2 that, in general, a 1-safe system may fail to be an EN system due to side-conditions (cf. Fig.2). 1-safe systems whose underlying net is pure are contact-free EN systems (cf. Th.11.3 in [rt86]).
Viceversa, an EN system may fail to be a 1-safe system due to contact situations: e.g. the net of Fig.9b is an EN system but not a 1-safe system. Nevertheless for each EN system, there exists a similar (under case graph equivalence, see [PRS92]) 1-safe system: it consists of the reduced form (in which all the events that are never enabled, and the surronding conditions, are removed; see [rt86] for a definition) of the corresponding contact-free EN system.
Let us remark that, as a consequence, contact-free (according to Def.14) 1-safe systems and contact-free EN systems coincide. In fact, contact-freeness requires, in both cases, to exclude marked side-conditions, but allows side-conditions which are never marked.
Nevertheless we have seen that 1-safe systems are quite popular exactly because of the safe transition rule: they represent a sort of compromise between the theoretical elegance of C/E and EN systems and the

practical effectiveness of P/T systems, or, in other words, they are the least extension of the above models necessary for modelling various practical situations (see discussion in Section 3.2) while avoiding the more serious troubles of P/T systems (as sketched in Section 2.3).

These considerations suggest why EN systems, in between the 'perfectness' of C/E systems and the 'concreteness' of 1-safe systems, find a wider and wider audience in the more recent literature as the target basic model. Ancient Romans would have said 'in medio stat virtus'; researchers have also to understand if and when modelling situations occur which do actually require leaving this class.

PART II

5. Introduction

One of the major drawbacks of Petri nets, particularly in a system design perspective, is the lack of "built-in" compositionality features. A line of research can be traced in the last twenty years which aims at filling this gap. This part of the survey presents problems to be faced when dealing with modularity and compositionality in the context of Petri nets and sketches various proposals along this line. It is organized as follows. The next section is an attempt to provide a unifying framework, based on the observation that, though contributions on modularity and compositionality have been carried on largely independently from one another, most of them show substantial similarities. The key notion is the idea that a system model should be obtained by composition of state machines. To this end, in section 6 we define a net model of state machine and a general notion of composition of state machine nets, whose features are briefly discussed. Some specializations of the operation are devised, in relation to several application fields. In section 7 various net classes are analyzed, pointing out for each of them specific choices in the context of the general framework and their motivations; a few exceptions to the general framework are taken into consideration at the end of the section.

6. A common framework

Historically, the first attempt to study modularity in Petri nets was undertaken at M.I.T., mainly by Hack. He introduced an idea which turned out to be fruitful and which constitutes the basis of the common framework. The idea is that the basic component in a theory of modular Petri nets is the state machine. In a state machine we can model conflict situations but not concurrency; in other words, a state machine models a sequential device whose behaviour can contain nondeterministic choices. Concurrency is introduced when a number of state machines are put together to form a compound system. Before formalizing these notions, let us point out that the idea well fits two of the most important application fields of Petri nets, i.e. concurrent programming languages and system design. In the former case state machines are an adequate model for sequential processes, while the operation of putting them together models various kinds of synchronization; in system design it is often assumed that basic components of a system can be modelled by state machines.

6.1 Basic definitions

We have collected here a number of definitions used throughout this part of the paper.

DEF. 16

An *S-graph* (or *state machine net*) is a net $N = (S, T; F)$ such that $\forall t \in T: |{}^{\bullet}t| = |t^{\bullet}| = 1$.

A *T-graph* is a net $N = (S, T; F)$ such that $\forall s \in S: |{}^{\bullet}s| = |s^{\bullet}| = 1$.

A *Free Choice net* is a net $N = (S, T; F)$ such that $\forall s \in S\ \forall t \in T$: if $(s, t) \in F$ then $s^{\bullet} = \{t\}$ or ${}^{\bullet}t = \{s\}$.

A net $N' = (S', T'; F')$ is said to be a *subnet* of $N = (S, T; F)$ iff $S' \subseteq S, T' \subseteq T$ and $F' = F \cap ((S' \times T') \cup (T' \times S'))$.

N' is said to be generated by S' iff $T' = {}^{\bullet}S' \cup S'^{\bullet}$.

N' is said to be generated by T' iff $S' = {}^{\bullet}T' \cup T'^{\bullet}$

N' is an *S-component* of N iff it is a strongly connected S-graph generated by S'.

N' is a *T-component* of N iff it is a strongly connected T-graph generated by T'.

A net $N' = (S', T'; F')$ is said to be a *partial subnet* of $N = (S, T; F)$ iff $S' \subseteq S, T' \subseteq T$ and $F' \subseteq F \cap ((S' \times T') \cup (T' \times S'))$.

A *path* of a net $N = (S, T; F)$ is an alternating sequence $(x_1, f_1, x_2, \ldots, f_{r-1}, x_r)$ of elements of $X = S \cup T$ and F such that $\forall i\ 1 \leq i \leq r-1$: $f_i = (x_i, x_{i+1})$. If all x_i are distinct, except possibly x_1 and x_r, then the path is called *elementary*. A *circuit* is a path such that $x_1 = x_r$. Δ

DEF. 17

A P/T system $\Sigma = (S,T;F,K,W,M_0)$ is said to be *live* iff $\forall M_1 \in [M_0\rangle\ \forall t \in T : \exists M_2 \in [M_1\rangle$ such that t is enabled at M_2. A net is *structurally live* iff it is live for at least one initial marking. Δ

S-graphs can be used to model the structure of a state machine. In the following they will be often called SM-nets.

6.2 The operation of SM-net synchronization

In this section we define a synchronization operation on nets. We will be interested in applying this operation to nets composed of sequential components; by imposing constraints either on the operands or on the operation itself we obtain, as particular cases, various kinds of net composition found in the literature. The idea behind the definition is that sequential components synchronize on events. This is modelled by merging transitions with the same name.

DEF. 18

Let $N_i = (S_i, T_i; F_i)$, i=1,2, be nets; then $N = N_1 \lozenge N_2$ is given by: $N = (S, T, F)$ iff:

i) $S = S_1 \cup S_2$, $T = T_1 \cup T_2$, $F = F_1 \cup F_2$,

ii) $\forall s \in S_1 \cap S_2\ \forall t \in T$: $(s,t) \in F_1 \Leftrightarrow (s,t) \in F_2$,

iii) $\forall s \in S_1 \cap S_2\ \forall t \in T$: $(t,s) \in F_1 \Leftrightarrow (t,s) \in F_2$. Δ

Conditions ii) and iii) mean that two places can be merged only if their pre-sets and post-sets are merged as well.

Let us call SSM (synchronized state machine) a net obtained by composing SM-nets in this way.

DEF. 19

A net N is said to be a *synchronized state machine net (SSM-net)* iff:

1. N is a SM-net or
2. $N = N_1 \Diamond N_2 \Diamond \ldots \Diamond N_k \Diamond \ldots$, and N_i , i = 1,..., is an SSM-net. Δ

Remark: in clause 2 of definition 19 we have omitted parentheses since the operation ◊ is commutative and associative when applied to SSM-nets.

Definition 18 is purely structural, in that it does not take markings into consideration. When we try to extend the definition to marked nets, we are faced with the problem of establishing an initial marking for the resulting net. The critical case is when two nets share a place, but that place is in the initial marking of only one of the nets. A straightforward solution could consist in imposing that the two operands agree on the initial marking of shared places.

Synchronization defined as in def.18 has an important property: if the operands are strongly connected then the resulting net is covered by S-components.

A number of meaningful restrictions can be imposed, in order, for instance, to enforce preservation of properties (e.g. structural liveness), leading to specific kinds of composition (specializations of definition 18). In the following we quickly review some of them, while in section 6.3 those restrictions are related to specific problems and application fields.

Restrictions can be classified in two categories:

1) on the operands; they can be tested separately on the nets to be composed;

2) on the operation; they involve interrelations between the nets to be composed.

The first group comprises both structural constraints (finiteness, simplicity, strong connectedness) and behavioural ones (liveness, safeness, deadlock-freeness).

The second group comprises a wide range of constraints, often depending on the intended interpretation of net elements. For instance, it can be requested that only transitions can be merged, or it can be requested that the result of the operation belongs to a certain class of nets (e.g. Free Choice nets). Conditions to be checked in order to satisfy this kind of restrictions can be either local conditions or global conditions; the former concern only the elements directly involved in the operation (e.g. the shared elements), while the latter imply tests on the whole net. Local conditions are obviously preferable in order both to maintain consistency with net theoretic notion of distributed systems and to keep complexity of the tests feasible.

Another way to limit the applicability of the operation consists in selecting a set of 'generating' nets and in requiring closure properties of the operation. In our framework, the set of generating nets is a subset of SM-nets.

6.3 Contexts and corresponding restrictions

In the next subsections we overview three contexts in which modularity and compositionality play a fundamental role, discussing for each of them how they can lead to specific specializations of the general composition operation defined above.

6.3.1 Analysis

Behavioural properties of nets are very hard to analyze in general. Working with restricted kinds or classes of nets can make that task easier. In fact, a satisfying structure theory exists only for Free Choice nets ([bes87]). Actually, necessary and sufficient conditions for liveness and 1-safeness exist only for this class of nets. It is interesting to remark that some of these conditions are related to "modularity" properties of nets, like for instance decomposability into strongly connected state machine components (see section 7.1). A great deal of effort has been done in order to extend this result to a wider class of nets, but the task has proven to be very hard.
An alternative approach to this problem involves the notion of net transformation. The idea is to apply to the net under consideration a set of transformations which are known to preserve a given property. If the transformations 'simplify' the net, then, at some stage of the process, a net can be generated which is known to possess the given property, and we can conclude that the original net also has the same property. The objective of this approach is to devise a complete set of transformation rules. In this paper we will not deal with this kind of problems. The interested reader can refer to [ber87].

6.3.2 Semantics of concurrent programming languages

In the use of Petri nets to define a semantics of a concurrent programming language, the major problem consists in faithfully modelling the particular synchronization and/or communication mechanisms specialized in the language. A distinction is generally made between modelling the control flow and modelling data. Generally, one models the basic instructions of the language (e.g. by means of nets with one transition, whose firing represents the execution of the instruction) and then one defines operations on nets corresponding to the language constructs (cf., e.g., [kot78], [bes88], [bdhh90]).The objective in defining a net semantics for a programming language is the development of formal verification methods by means of which it is possible to prove properties of a program by analyzing the correspondent net; in light of what we said in the preceding subsection, it is clear that the semantics should be compositional, in the sense that properties of a net modelling a complex program, with many components, must be deducible from properties of the components.

6.3.3 Synthesis and system design

The main objective in building a theory of compositionality for nets is to define operations such that properties of the compound system can be deduced from properties of the components. This feature is particularly important in system design, both in a top-down and in a bottom-up approach; in the former case, the fundamental operation is refinement, in which a 'module' is substituted for an element of a model; in the latter case, elementary components are designed and verified first, then put together.
We feel that modularity and compositionality in nets should be actually achieved if, together with a composition mechanism, there were also a proof rule such as the one described by the following schema (taken, with modifications, from [bes90b])

$$\frac{prop1(N1),\ prop2(N2),\ C}{prop3(N1 \boxtimes N2)}$$

where *prop i(N)* denotes a property of net N, C a condition and ¤ a composition operation on nets. Unfortunately, up to now, this is missing for the general case. Two typical ways to fill this gap have been pursued: some authors have chosen to take into consideration only a limited class of nets, typically Free Choice nets (cfr. section 7.5). This is not completely satisfactory, since in real system modelling and design Free Choice nets have too limited an expressive power. On the other hand, it is possible to leave greater freedom with respect to the structure of the components at the cost of constraining the operation itself (cfr. section 7.7). Once again, this has limitations with repect to the kind of systems we can design.

7 Modular net classes

In the following we briefly review eight classes of modular Petri nets emphasizing their relations with the general framework and their specific features.

7.1 State Machine Decomposable and State Machine Allocatable Nets

The class of State Machine Decomposable (SMD) Nets was introduced by M.Hack in [hac72] (see also [hac74c]), where he studied liveness and boundedness properties in Free Choice nets. The concept of state machine decomposability turned out to be useful even when considering ordinary Petri nets in general. State Machine Allocatable nets are a subclass of SMD nets; they were introduced in [hac74].

A net is said to be State Machine Decomposable if it is covered (in the sense of graph theory) by S-components. Thus, any SMD net is SSM, with the additional restriction that its components must be strongly connected. Figure 22 shows an SMD net. Hatched elements form an S-component.

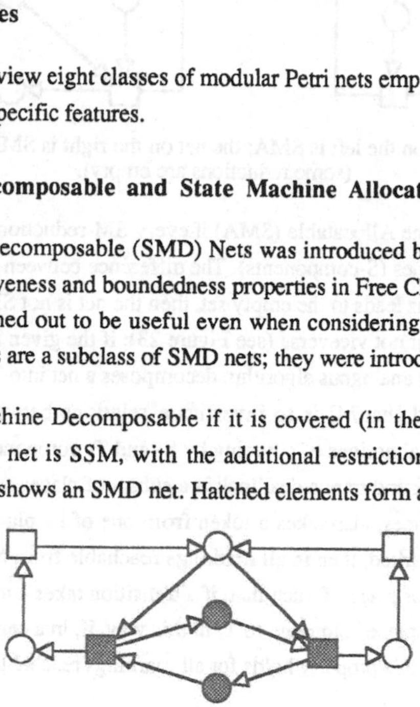

Fig 22

Given an SMD net, it is possible to find out its S-components by applying an algorithm, called SM-reduction (State Machine reduction); it is based on the notion of SM-allocation, that is a function which associates to every transition of the net one of its pre-conditions. The formal definition of the algorithm is given in [hac72].

DEF. 20

Let N = (S, T; F) be a net. An *SM-allocation* is a function *al* : $T \rightarrow S$ such that $\forall t \in T$: $al(t) \in {}^{\bullet}t$.

Let N' = (S', T'; F') be a subnet of N. N' is said to agree with *al* if:

$\forall t \in T'$: $al(t) \in S'$. Δ

The algorithm reduces the net by eliminating places and transitions which could not belong to an S-component that agrees with the given allocation function; if a net N is SMD then every reduced net is a collection of zero or more strongly connected state machines and all reduced nets cover N.

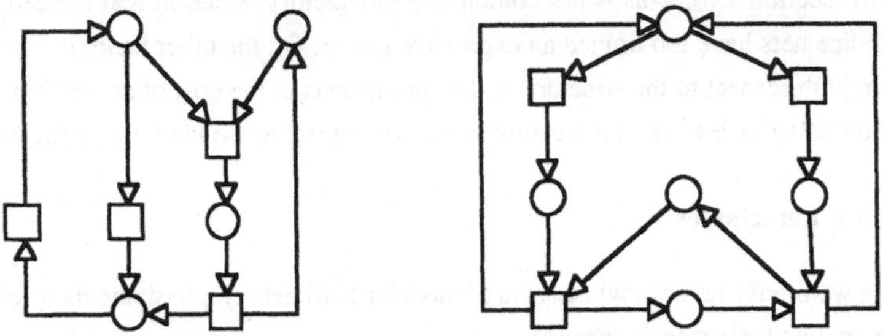

Fig. 23 The net on the left is SMA; the net on the right is SMD, but not SMA (some reductions are empty).

A net is said to be State Machine Allocatable (SMA) if every SM-reduction is a collection of one or more strongly connected state machines (S-components). The difference between SMA and SMD lies in the fact that, if one of the SM-reductions leads to the empty set, then the net is not SMA, while it can still be SMD. So, every SMA net is SMD, but not viceversa (see Figure 23); if the given net is SMA, the algorithm will generate all the components; an analogous algorithm decomposes a net into T-components.

The main aim of [hac72] and [hac74] is to investigate relations between structural and behavioral properties of nets. The structural notions of covering by S- and T- components are largely used in proofs, together with those of deadlock and trap; a deadlock is a subset of places such that every transition which puts a token into one of its places, also takes a token from one of its places; in this way, if in a certain marking M no place of D is marked, then in all markings reachable from M the same property holds. On the contrary, a trap is a subset of places T such that, if a transition takes a token from a place belonging to T, then it also puts a token in a place belonging to T; in this way, if, in a certain marking M, at least one of the places of T is marked, then this property holds for all markings reachable from M.

DEF. 21

Let N = (S, T; F) be a net.

A *deadlock* is a nonempty subset of places $D \subseteq S$ such that ${}^\bullet D \subseteq D^\bullet$.

A *minimal deadlock* is a deadlock D such that, for every $D' \subset D$, D' is not a deadlock.

A *trap* is a nonempty subset of places $Q \subseteq S$ such that $Q^\bullet \subseteq {}^\bullet Q$

A *marked trap* is a trap such that at least one of its places is marked. Δ

We now summarize some of the main results proved in the mentioned papers.

TH.1. A Free Choice net system is live if and only if every deadlock contains a trap.which is marked at the initial marking. Δ

TH.2. Every Live and Bounded Free Choice net system is State Machine Decomposable. Δ

A weaker property related to SM-reductions holds for ordinary Petri nets:

TH. 3. Every SMA net has a live and 1-safe marking. Δ

7.2 Proper Nets

The class of proper nets was introduced by R.Janicki in [jan84], in a way which slightly deviates from the standard usually adopted. In fact he introduces a notion of net which does not refer to any of the basic net models. It differs from C/E systems in that it allows transitions with side conditions to occur, and it differs from 1-safe nets in that it assumes backward&forward reachability. It imposes the structural constraint that every transition must have at least one pre-condition and one post-condition, and allows specifying a set of initial markings[2].

In order to maintain consistency with the rest of this survey we rephrase Janicki's definitions. In particular we substitute the term j-net for the term simple net (or s-net), which has a precise meaning in standard terminology.

A j-net is characterized by the fact that its places are identified by their pre- and post-sets, so that it is S-simple (see PART I, section 2):

DEF. 22

A *j-net* is a net $N = (S, T; F)$ where

i) $\forall t \in T: \exists s, s' \in S: (s \in {}^\bullet t \wedge s' \in t^\bullet)$

ii) $\forall s, s' \in S: ({}^\bullet s = {}^\bullet s' \wedge s^\bullet = s'^\bullet) \Rightarrow s = s'$. Δ

Finite j-nets may be given a lattice structure by defining a suitable ordering relation:

DEF. 23

Let $N = (S, T; F)$, $N' = (S', T'; F')$ be two finite j-nets; the relation $\lhd$ is defined by:

$N \lhd N' \Leftrightarrow [\, S \subseteq S'$ and N is a subnet of N' generated by S $]$. Δ

Every SM-net is a j-net; j-nets can be composed by means of $\Diamond$-operation; the class of proper nets is built by combining in this way SM-nets.

DEF. 24

For every j-net N, let $\text{elem}(N) = \{N' \mid N' \lhd N \wedge N' \text{ is an SM-net}\}$. Δ

That is, elem(N) contains all subnets of N generated by a set of places which are state machines (in general they are not S-components because they need not be strongly connected).

DEF. 25

A j-net N is said to be *proper* iff $N = N_1 \Diamond \ldots \Diamond N_k$, where $\{N_1, \ldots, N_k\} = \text{elem}(N)$. Δ

Example 1. The nets N_a, N_b, N_c in Figure 24 are SM-nets. Common elements are hatched. The result of their superposition is the net N_d and $\text{elem}(N_d) = \{N_a, N_b, N_c\}$.

---

[2] A similar class has been defined in [ddm88]: augmented C/E systems allow side conditions and remove the simplicity condition; transitions with side condition can occur when suitably marked.

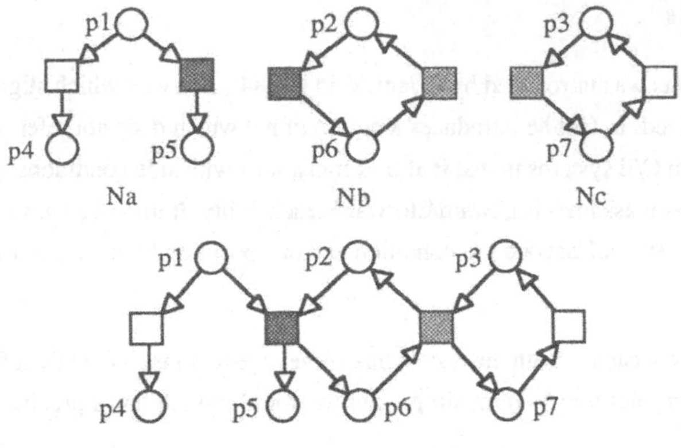

Fig 24

Some behavioural properties of proper nets are given in terms of a binary relation on the set of places. Given a covering of the places of a net, a *coexistency* relation holds between two places if and only if they never appear in the same element of the covering. The subnets generated by the elements of the covering are interpreted as sequential components of the net, while the coexistency relation can be seen as the possibility that two places belong to the same marking (two places belonging to the same sequential component model mutually exclusive local states of that component, therefore they cannot belong to the same marking).

DEF. 26

Let N=(S, T; F) be a proper net, and let C={N_1, ..., N_m} be a set of state machine j-nets, such that T = ∪ T_i and S = ∪ S_i. Then cov_C = {S_1, ..., S_m} is a covering of S.
Let $coex_C \subseteq S \times S$ be defined by:

$$(s, s') \in coex_C \Leftrightarrow [\ s \neq s' \text{ and } (\forall S_i \in cov_C: s \notin S_i \text{ or } s' \notin S_i)].$$
Δ

The behaviour of a j-net is described by giving the class of reachable markings. This must be a full reachability class (see section 2.1).

DEF. 27

A *marked j-net (mj-net)* Σ = <N, Mar> is described by its underlying j-net N = (S, T; F) and by a family of reachable markings Mar ⊆ 2^S.
Δ

If the set of reachable markings coincides with the set of maximal cliques of a coexistency relation, then the net is said to be *naturally marked.* In a naturally marked net non shared places, corresponding to 'private' states of the components are independent, in the sense that their marking does not depend upon each other.

Example 2. The net of Figure 25a is naturally marked. The full reachability class corresponding to the initial marking shown coincides with the set of maximal cliques of the coexistency relation induced by the decomposition indicated by place shadowing. The net of Figure 25b is not naturally marked. In fact, places p1 and p2 can never be simultaneously marked.

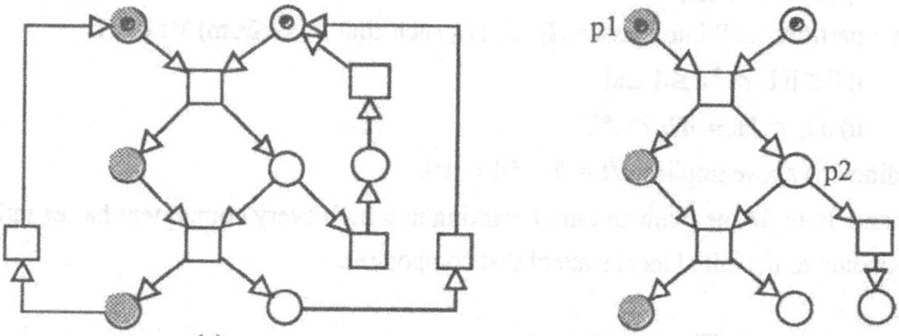

Fig 25

In [jan84] Janicki introduces a notion of safeness, taking into account backward&forward reachability, which corresponds to the notion of contact freeness, as discussed in PART I.
The main results ([jan84]) can be rephrased in this way:

TH. 4. A marked proper net with a given covering of its places is contact free if

a) it is 1-live (see section 3.4) and

b) the set of reachable markings is a subset of the set of maximal cliques of the coexistency relation. Δ

TH. 5. A naturally marked, proper net is contact free and 1-live. Δ

7.3 Superposed Automata Nets

Superposed Automata (SA) nets were introduced in [ddps82] taking inspiration from the problem of modelling CSP by means of Petri nets (see [ddps81]). They are a modular class whose basic components are state machines, and their composition is obtained by means of shared transitions superposition. This approach turned out to be fruitful also in system design and in other contexts (see [ddps87] and [dds87]).

The fundamental underlying net model is 1-safe net systems, even if, in their original definition ([ddps82]), they were introduced as a subclass of Predicate/Transition nets. In the following we use the term SA-net to denote 1-safe Superposed Automata Net

An SA-net is an SSM-net with the property that components cannot share places. This implies that transitions are *balanced*, i.e. the number of places in the pre-set of a transition is equal to the number of places in its post-set. A transition having only one incoming arc, and consequently only one outgoing arc, represents an internal action of a component, while other transitions model interactions among a number of components. The places of a component represent local states of the corresponding system component, while the global state of the system is represented by the union of all the local states.

DEF. 28

A *Superposed Automata net (SA-net)* is a pair R = <N, Π>, where:

- N = <S, T; F> is a net;
- Π is a partition of S into classes $\Pi_1, ..., \Pi_m$ such that $\forall i\ (1 \le i \le m)\ \forall t \in T$:

  i) $0 \le |\Pi_i \cap {}^\bullet t| \le 1$ and

  ii) $|\Pi_i \cap {}^\bullet t| = |\Pi_i \cap t^\bullet|$. Δ

Note that condition ii) above implies: $\forall t \in T$: $|{}^\bullet t| = |t^\bullet|$.

An SA-net system is an SA-net with an initial marking in which every component has exactly one marked place, corresponding to the initial local state of that component.

DEF. 29

An *SA-net System* is a tuple $\Sigma = (R, M_0)$ where:

- R is an SA-net.
- $M_0 \subseteq S$ is the initial marking such that : $\forall j\ (1 \le j \le m)$

  $|\Pi_j \cap M_0| = 1$. Δ

DEF. 30

A *Labelled SA-net System* is a tuple $\Sigma = (R, L, M_0)$ where:

- (R, M_0) is an SA-net.
- $L : T \rightarrow E$ is the labelling function which associates with each transition the name of the modelled action. Transitions belonging to different state-machine components may have the same name, when they specify the same action. Δ

An SA-net is built up by composing state machines by means of an operation called *T-composition*. We do not give here the formal definition of the operation since it is a particular case of the ◊-operation, in which only transitions can be merged.

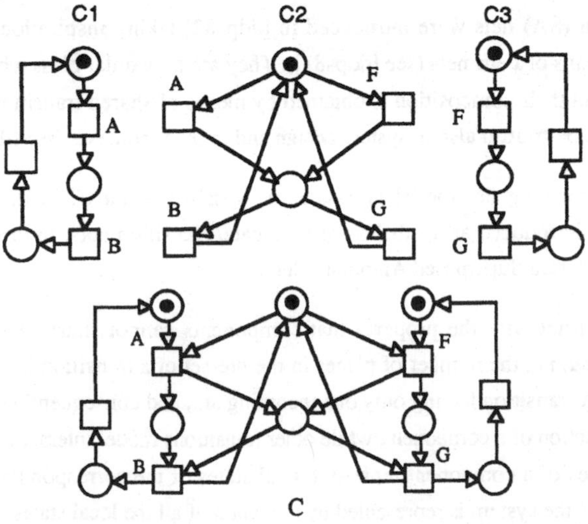

Fig. 26 - An SA system with three components modelling access to a shared resource

Example 3. In this example we model a simple system in which two processes compete for a shared resource. The two processes are modelled by, respectively, nets C1 and C3 in Fig. 26; the resource is managed by a third process, modelled by C2, which ensures mutual exclusion. Transition labels indicate which transitions model synchronous interactions among components. T-composition consists in superposing corresponding interaction transitions. The resulting net is C.

Example 4. This example illustrates the *splitting* operation which, in some cases, must precede transition superposition. Consider nets N1 and N2 of Figure 27. In composing them, we have the problem of superposing one transition labelled by a in N1 (let us call it t) with two transitions with the same label in N2. A preliminary step is necessary in which we transform N1 by splitting t in two transitions, t' and t", both labelled by a and having the same pre- and post- sets as t. We obtain a new net N1', which can be superposed to N2 producing N3. The rule can be generalized to the case in which the two nets contain, respectively, n and m transitions with the same label.

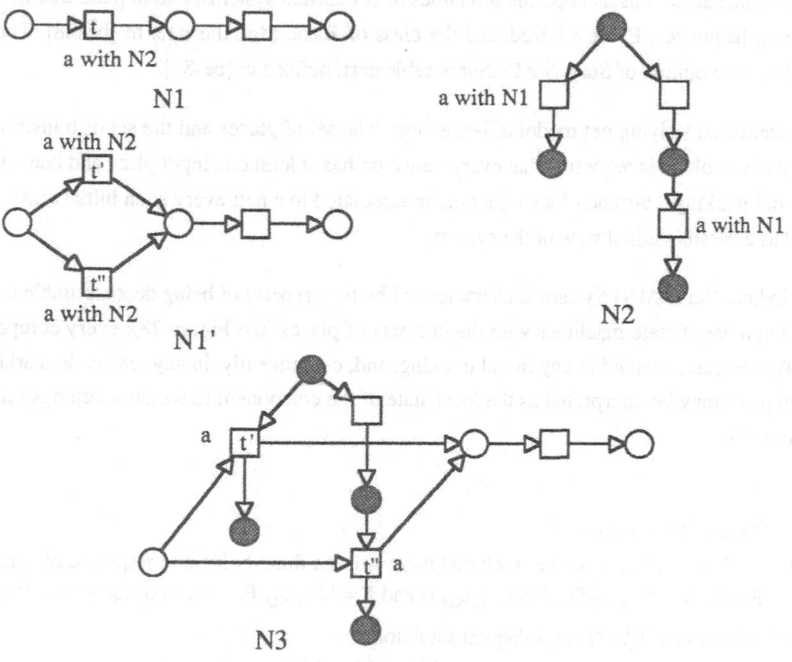

Figure 27

Refinement has been deeply studied in the context of SA systems, both theoretically and as a necessary support in system design (see, for example, [ddps87] , [dds87]).

The notion of organizational refinement allows one to specify the behaviour of a component at different levels of detail, abstracting from a number of 'internal actions', which are considered unobservable with respect to an external observer (see e.g. [ddps85]).

Functional refinement consists in refining a subnet generated by a set of transitions, while preserving the overall state transformation; intermediate states are considered unobservable; this kind of refinement allows one to enrich the system functionalities (e.g. with exception handling).
The two notions of refinement come with corresponding equivalence notions based on the notions of, respectively, (un)observable transitions and of (un)observable places. Examples illustrating both of them can be found in figures 9 and 10. For formal definitions, detailed discussion and more examples, see [ddps87], [prs92] and [ps91].

The main fields of application so far are system design ([ddps87]) and office modelling ([dds87]). In regard to the former, SA nets have been extended in such a way to combine net theory and abstract data types. The resulting model is called OBJSA Nets ([bdm88]).

7.4 Basic Modular Petri Nets

Assuming 1-safe nets as a basis to define semantics of concurrent systems, and in particular of concurrent programming languages, E. Best introduced the class of Basic Modular nets in [bes88]. They may be considered as an evolution of State Net Decomposable nets, defined in [bes85].

The fundamental underlying net model is 1-safe nets. The set of places and the set of transitions may be infinite, but countable; it is requested that every transition has at least one input place and one output place; a set of initial markings, instead of a single one, is associated to a net; every such initial marking is to be interpreted as a possible initial state of the system.

A Basic Modular Net (BMN) System is characterized by the property of being decomposable into a (finite or infinite) number of state machines with disjoint sets of places (see Figure 28); every component must have exactly one place marked in any initial marking, and, consequently, in any reachable marking, so that the marked place may be interpreted as the local state of the component to which it belongs (cfr. with SA nets, section 7.3).

DEF. 31

A pair $\langle N, \mathcal{M}\rangle$ is a *BMN system* if

i) $N = \langle S, T; F\rangle$ is a net such that there exists a finite or infinite sequence of state machines $N_i = (S_i, T_i, F_i)$ and $S = \biguplus_{1\leq i\leq\alpha} S_i$, $T = \bigcup_{1\leq i\leq\alpha} T_i$ and $F = \bigcup_{1\leq i\leq\alpha} F_i$, where α equals n if the sequence is finite and ∞ otherwise. ($\biguplus$ denotes disjoint set union);

ii) $\mathcal{M}$ is a set of subsets of S such that : $\forall M_0 \in \mathcal{M}\ \ \forall i, 1\leq i\leq \alpha$: $|M_0 \cap S_i| = 1$. Δ

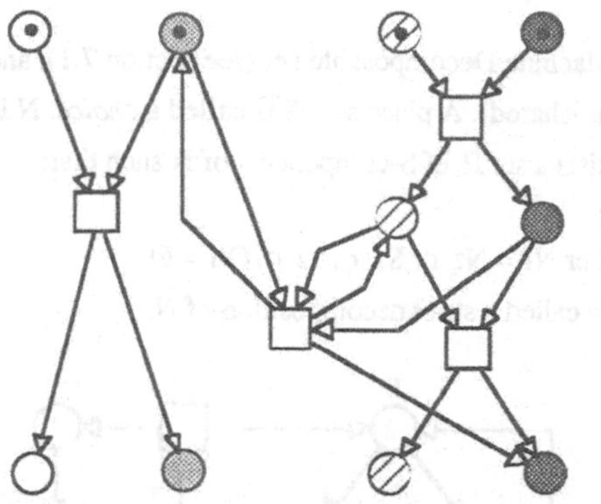

Fig 28 - A Basic Modular Net System with four components. Each component is distinguished by a different shading of its places (only one initial marking is shown).

In [bes88] "a full translation of concurrent programs (shared variable and CSP programs) into basic Petri nets" is presented; it exploits the compositional nature of BMN systems by associating a BMN system to every construct of a model of concurrent programming language and composing them by superposing transition with the same label. It is explicitly requested that every component has at most one transition with a given label; this restriction eliminates the need for splitting of transitions in the superposition operation (see section 7.3). The basic model is then "enriched to allow the formulation of quantities such as the running time and the space needed by a concurrent program". The resulting net model is called Weighted Basic Petri Nets.

7.5 Live & Bounded Free Choice Nets

Modularity in Free Choice nets has been widely studied since Hack's paper ([hac72]). While Hack's approach was analytical and gave emphasis to decomposition of a given net in order to prove behavioural properties, in [es89] and [es90] attention is focused on the synthesis of nets having desired properties. Two possibilities are considered: bottom-up synthesis, where one starts with some modules (e.g. nets modelling sequential components of a system) and composes them to obtain a model of the whole system, and top-down synthesis, where one starts with a net modelling a system at a high level of abstraction and subsequently refines it stepwise.

The fundamental underlying net model is Place/Transition nets with unbounded place capacities and weighted arcs; in particular Free Choice State Machine Decomposable Nets are considered.

The subclass of Strict Free Choice (SFC) nets, introduced in [es89], is characterized by the following property: every *choice*, that is every place having more than one post-transition, belongs to only one S-component (see Figure 29); the intuitive meaning is that, in a Strict Free Choice net , a component carries out choices with full freedom.

DEF. 32

Let N = (S, T; F) be a State Machine Decomposable net (see section 7.1), and OS = {s∈ S such that $|s^{\bullet}| > 1$} (OS stands for output-shared). A place s∈ OS is called a *choice*. N is *Strict Free Choice (SFC)* iff it is Free Choice and there exists a set $\mathfrak{R}$ of S-components of N such that:

- N is covered by $\mathfrak{R}$;
- $\forall N_1, N_2 \in \mathfrak{R}$ either $N_1 = N_2$ or $S_1 \cap S_2 \cap OS = \emptyset$;

The set $\mathfrak{R}$ of S-components is called a strict decomposition of N. Δ

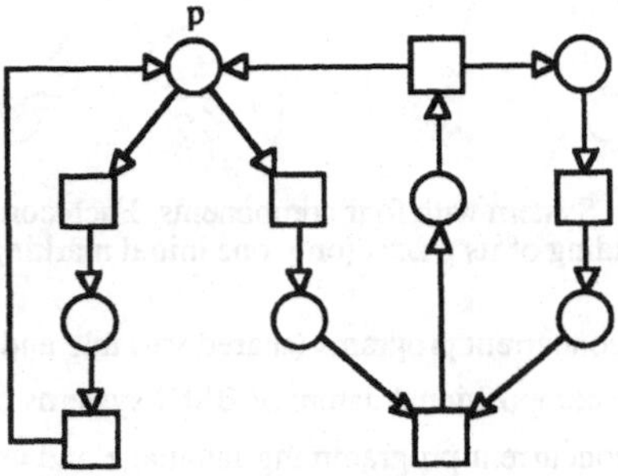

Fig 29. A Strict Free Choice net with one choice (the place p).

A particular net substructure, called *handle*, is widely used in characterizing behavioural properties of nets. We recall here its definition:

DEF. 33

Let N = (S, T; F) and N' a partial subnet of N. An elementary path $\Pi = (x_1, ..., x_M)$ is a *handle* of N' iff $\Pi \cap (S' \cup T') = \{x_1, x_M\}$. Δ

Handles are classified according to the nature of their first and last nodes into four subclasses: P(lace)T(ransition), TP, TT and PP (see Figure 30).

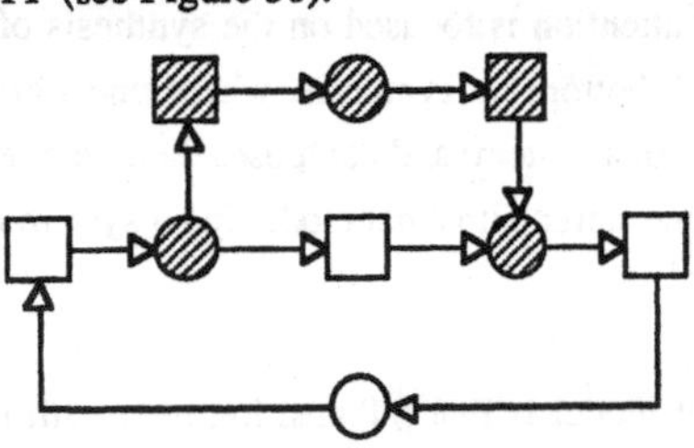

Fig 30. A handle of a circuit (a PP-handle).

A necessary and sufficient condition for structural liveness of Strict Free Choice Nets is given in terms of structural constraints:

TH. 6 . Let N = (S, T; F) be a Strict Free Choice net. N is structurally live iff no circuit of N has TP- or PT-handles. Δ

In [es90], following the top-down approach to net synthesis, two refinement rules are defined to serve as a basis for an algorithm generating all and only Live & Bounded Free Choice nets. It is possible to define their inverse as abstraction rules.

The *macroplace* rule allows us to substitute a state machine, with some structural constraints, for a place (see Example 5).

Example 5. Consider the net in Figure 31a. The hatched place is a macroplace which is refined by means of a state machine hatched in the same way giving the net in Figure 31b. Viceversa, the inverse, abstraction, operation reduces the hatched state machine subnet in 31b to a place, giving the net in 31a.

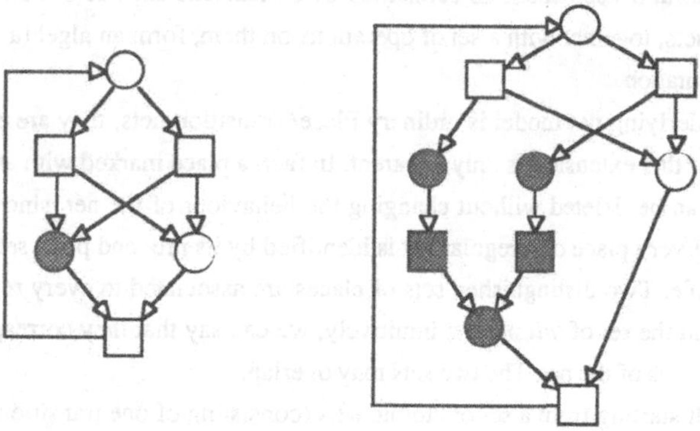

(a) (b)

Fig.31. Macroplace rule

The *marking structurally implicit place* rule allows us to add a place to a net so as to increment the concurrency degree of the net (see Example 6).

Example 6. Consider the net formed by 'white' elements in Figure 32. The hatched place is a marking structurally implicit place; refining it by means of macroplace rule application can be interpreted as adding a concurrent component to the original net.

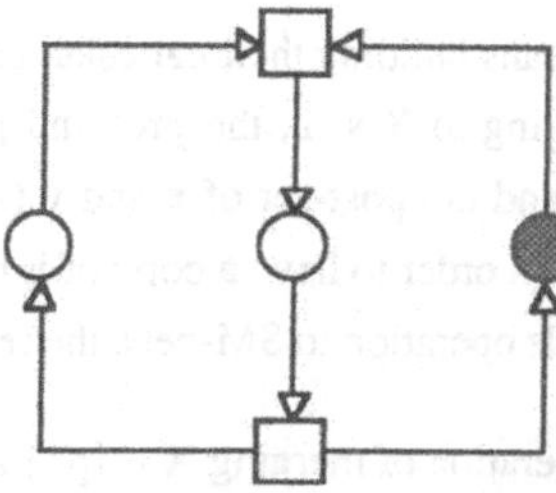

Fig 32 - Marking structurally implicit place

In [es89] an algorithm is given which generates all structurally live Strict Free Choice Nets by means of synchronisation of strongly connected state machines; at each step only the portion of the net involved in synchronisation must be considered to ensure that the resulting net is structurally live and Strict Free Choice.

The fundamental result of [es90] is that the macroplace rule and the marking structurally implicit place rule preserve liveness and boundedness, and that they are sufficient in order to generate in a top-down way all live and bounded Free Choice nets, starting from a loop composed of one transition and one place.

7.6 Regular Nets

Along the line of an algebraic approach to parallel control structures, Kotov introduced, in [kot78], the class of regular nets, and used them as semantics of concurrent control structures in programming languages. Regular nets, together with a set of operations on them, form an algebra, which provides for a linearized net representation.

The fundamental underlying net model is ordinary Place/Transition nets; they are extended by allowing infinite markings, but this extension is only apparent. In fact, a place marked with an infinity of tokens at the initial marking can be deleted without changing the behaviour of the net, since it in no way affects firing of transitions. Every place of a regular net is identified by its pre- and post- sets, so that regular nets turn out to be S-simple. Two distinguished sets of places are associated to every regular net, namely the set of *head* places and the set of *tail* places; intuitively, we can say that they correspond to, respectively, "initial" and "final" states of the net. The two sets may overlap.

Regular nets are built starting from a set of atomic nets (consisting of one transition with one input place and one output place - see Figure 33) and applying composition operations. An atomic net has exactly one head place (the input place of the transition) and exactly one tail place (the output place of the transition).

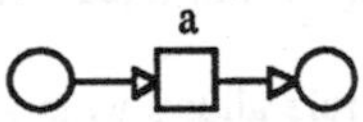

Figure 33 - An atomic net

The defined operations correspond to usual concurrent programming language constructs. In the following we informally describe them, starting with an auxiliary operation, namely merging of places, which is used in defining other operations.

Merging two sets of places X and Y means building their cartesian product X x Y and substituting it for X and Y, where, for every (x, y) belonging to X x Y, the pre- and post- sets of (x, y) are the union of, respectively, the pre-sets of x and y, and the post-set of x and y (see Example 7). In this way, a place involved in the operation must be split in order to have a copy of it matching with each place in the other set. It should be noted that, applying this operation to SM-nets, the result is still a SM-net.

Example 7. Figure 34 illustrates the operation of merging X = {p1} and Y = {p2, p3}.

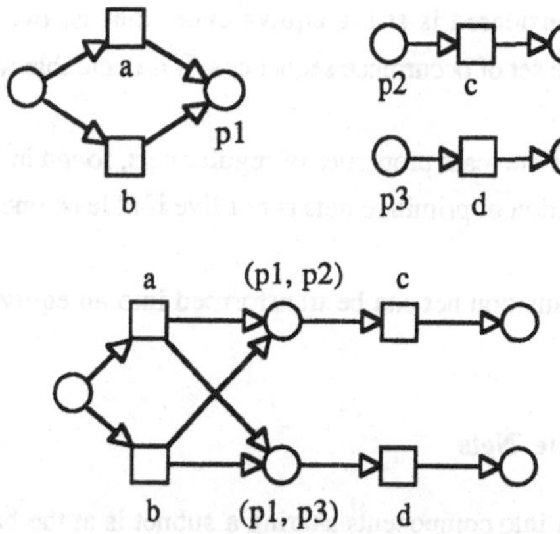

Fig. 34 - Merging of places.

The **exclusion** operation composes two nets so that the set of head places of the composed net results from merging the sets of the components head places and the set of tail places of the composed net results from merging their sets of tail places; in this way the resulting net may behave as either of the two components (see Figure 35); this operation corresponds to the usual choice operator in almost all models of concurrency.

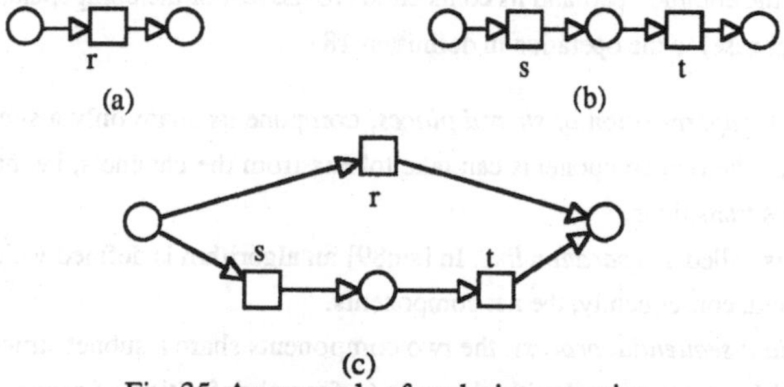

Fig. 35. An example of exclusion operation.

The **join** operation merges the tail places of the first component with the head places of the second one (Figure 34 illustrates this operation); if the first component reaches a state in which its tail places are marked, then the second one may start its computation, so that join corresponds to the usual sequence operator.
Iteration is an operation involving one net operand; it merges its head and tail places, so that it may cycle.
Superposition corresponds to ◊-operation.
The **marking** operation takes as arguments a net and an integer n (or the element ω) and puts n (or ω) tokens in the head places of the net.

A *regular net* is built starting from a set of atomic nets, applying exclusion, join, iteration, superposition and marking operations. The subclass of *primitive nets* is obtained starting from atomic nets applying all operations except superposition. Every primitive net is a SM-net, but there are SM-nets which are not primitive.

The notion of equivalence considered is string equivalence, that is, two regular nets are said to be equivalent if they have the same set of occurrence sequences. It is decidable whether two primitive nets are equivalent in this sense.
In the following we list some of the main properties of regular nets, found in [kot78].
TH. 7. A net built by superposition of primitive nets is not live if at least one of the constituent nets is not live. Δ
TH. 8. Any ordinary Place/Transition net can be transformed into an equivalent (in the sense of string-equivalence) regular net. Δ

7.7 Medium Composable Nets

The idea of decomposing a net into components sharing a subnet is at the basis of the work presented in this section. It may be traced back to [rei79], and along the same line other papers have been produced by a number of authors ([rei82], [brm83], [sb88], [sm89], [sou90]). In the following we will consider the latter two papers, in which various composition operations are defined. The fundamental underlying net model is Place/Transition nets with unbounded place capacities and weighted arcs.

In [sm89] three operations are defined, which we briefly describe in the following; in every case, components share some elements. Let us remark that, in all three cases, the only constraints imposed on the nets involve just the common part and its connections to the rest of the components, so that they are not related (in the general case) to the operation in definition 18.

1) In *composition via superposition of shared places*, components share only a subset of places, called channels; only one of the two components can take tokens from the channels, i.e. has arcs going from a channel to some of its transitions.
The set of channels is called a *separation line*. In [sm89] an algorithm is defined which, given a net, finds all separation lines and, consequently, the net components.
2) In *composition via a sequential process*, the two components share a subnet structured as a sequential process, that is, a SM-net augmented with channels (a formal definition of sequential process is given later). Composition by *rendezvous* is a particular case of this operation in which the shared subnet contains just one transition and one place connected so as to form a loop ; the only shared place does not constrain in any way firing of the shared transition, so this operation corresponds to superimposition of transitions.
3) *Composition via a well-formed block.* Intuitively, a well-formed block is a subnet in which one can distinguish two transitions, say t_{in} and t_{fin}, which mark, respectively, the beginning and the end of the subnet activity.

Let us remark that, in cases 2) and 3) composition may alternatively be seen as an operation involving three nets, one of which (namely the common subnet) plays the role of a communication medium.

In [sou90] the modular net class of Deterministic Systems of Sequential Processes is defined; they can be built in a bottom up way by means of an operation which is similar to composition via shared places. The only difference is that the constraint on arcs incoming or outgoing a shared place is released.

A Sequential Process is a SM-net augmented by a set of places called buffers.

DEF. 34

A place/transition net N = (S ∪ K, T, F, W) is a *sequential process* (SP) iff

- S ∩ K = Ø (the elements of K are called buffers)
- the subnet generated by (S, T) is a SM-net
- ∀s∈ S if |s•| > 1 then ∀t, t' ∈ s•, ∀x∈ K: W((x, t)) = W((x, t')). Δ

The last condition implies that a buffer, therefore the environment, cannot solve conflicts.

Sequential processes can be composed by superposing shared buffers provided that the following restrictions are satisfied:

- two distinct sequential processes can only have buffers in common
- a buffer can be an input (output) buffer of only one sequential process;

the resulting net is called a Deterministic System of Sequential Processes (DSSP).

Figure 36 shows a DSSP with three components. Hatched circles represent buffers.

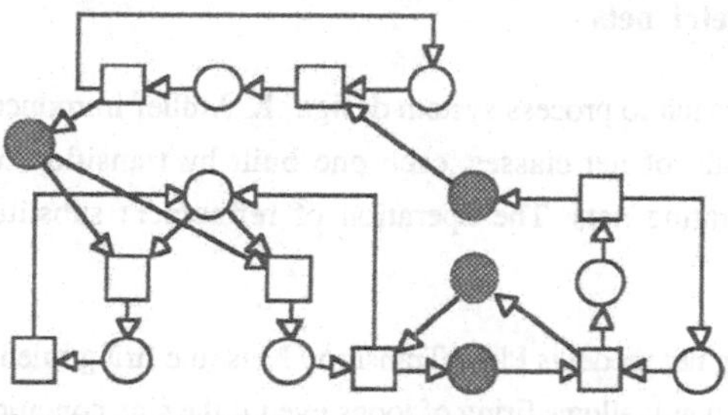

Fig. 36. A Deterministic System of three Sequential Processes.

In [sm89] some results related to liveness preservation in composition of nets are proved.

TH. 9 Liveness of the components is a necessary and sufficient condition for liveness of a net obtained via superposition of channels (recall the restriction that just one of the components can take tokens from the channels). Δ

TH. 10 Composition via a sequential process preserves both liveness and boundedness. Δ

Under suitable conditions, which, due to lack of space, are not given here, liveness of the components is a necessary and sufficient condition for liveness of a net obtained by composition via a well-formed block.

In [sou90], in order to analyze liveness and boundedness in Deterministic Systems of Sequential Processes, the notion of ring is used; intuitively, a ring is an alternating sequence of buffers and component Sequential Processes. It is possible to associate to a ring a rational number giving the ratio of production and consumption of tokens along a path in the composite net (see Example 8). If this rational number is less than 1, then the ring is said to be a small ring. The existence of a small ring in a net means that there exists a circuit formed by transitions and buffers such that more tokens are consumed than produced along that path. Therefore the presence of a small ring is a critical property with regard to liveness. More precisely, a DSSP is structurally live iff it does not contain small rings.

Example 8. The net in Figure 37 is composed of two linear processes, i.e. R1 and R2, communicating via q1 and q2. The sequence Z = q1R1q2R2 is a ring. Actually, it is a small ring, since, along the corresponding path, 5 tokens are produced and 6 are consumed.

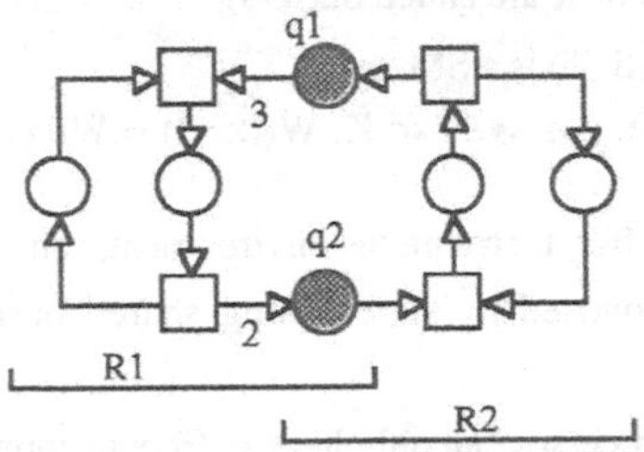

Figure 37. A small ring.

7.8 Constructable Petri nets

Following a synthesis approach to process system design, K. Müller introduced Constructable Petri nets in [mul85]. This is a family of net classes, each one built by transition refinement starting from a distinguished set of generating nets. The operation of refinement substitutes a subnet for a set of transitions.

The fundamental underlying net model is Place/Transition Nets (the firing rule is slightly different from the one given in section 2.3, in that it allows firing of loops even if the side condition capacity is one).

The classes of Constructable Petri Nets are built up starting from a set of generating nets, applying a 'refinement operation' which consists in selecting a set of transitions, called *substitution set* and in substituting for them a *refinement net.* This mechanism generalizes the classical notion of transition refinement in which a single transition, which models, at a certain level of abstraction, an atomic event, is substituted by a net.
In a refinement net there are two distinguished sets of transitions, respectively called the *entry interface* and the *exit interface*. Any transition in the substitution set is associated to one element of the entry interface and to one element of the exit interface; these two elements (which are transitions of the refinement net) are connected, respectively, to the pre-set and to the post-set of the associated transition in the original net (see Example 9). If the substitution set contains just one transition, then we obtain, as a particular case, the usual transition refinement.

Example 9. Let N be the net in Figure 38a and Nr the refinement net in Figure 38b. Then, with {t1, t2} being the substitution set, we obtain the net in Figure 38c, where t1e and t1x correspond to t1, while t2e and t2x correspond to t2.

A particular choice of a set of generating nets and of a set of refinement nets determines a particular class of constructable nets.

In [mul85], a class of so called 'specially constructable nets' is built up starting from a generating net which consists of a loop. The resulting class is a model for a concurrent programming notation.
In [mul85] equivalence issues are not explicitly addressed but proofs state, as a by product, that, under particular constraints on the refinement net, the original net and the refined one are equivalent, when considering the places of the refinement net as unobservable places (i.e. by adopting an equivalence notion similar to State-Transformation equivalence - see section 3.1).

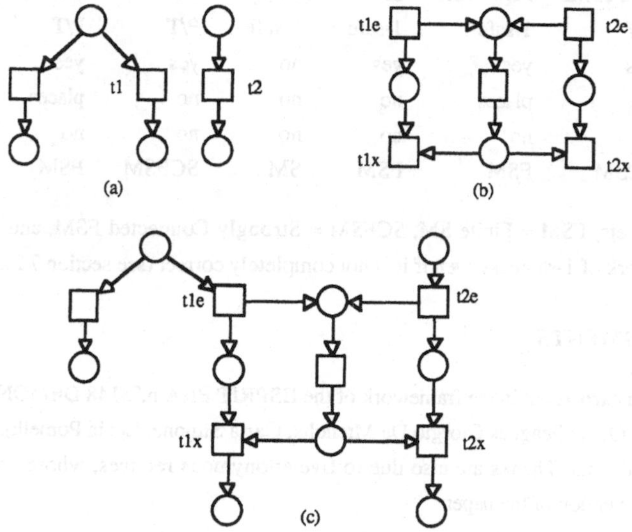

Fig. 38. A refinement operation

As we have said, the approach to system design is top-down, so there is not a composition operation between nets. However, composition by rendezvous is obtained as a special case of refinement in which the net to be refined is composed of disjoint subnets. Figure 39 shows a refinement net which can be used to obtain synchronization among three components.

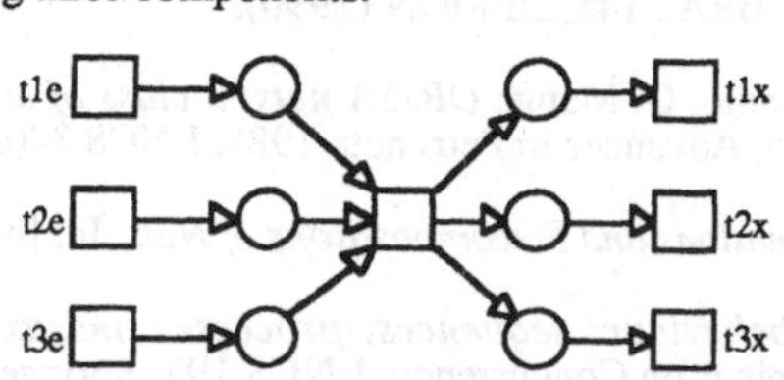

Fig. 39 - A refinement net corresponding to synchronization by rendezvous among three components

Behavioural properties of refinement nets have a counterpart in properties of the refined net. In particular, [mul85] focuses on liveness; a number of sufficient conditions to preserve liveness are given.

8. Conclusion

We have reviewed a number of classes of modular nets, trying to highlight substantial similarities. We have seen that most of them share a basic feature: a net model is composed of state machines interacting by

means of synchronization. It is interesting to note that this notion arises in widely different contexts, ranging from concurrent programming language modelling to system design and net analysis.
A comparison among the net classes analyzed above, based on some fundamental properties, is summarized in the following table. We have not included Constructable nets since their features depend on the particular choice of the generating net and of the refinement nets.

	SMA/SMD	PROPER	SA	BMN	L&BFC	REGULAR	DSSP
framework	P/T	1-safe	1-safe	1-safe	P/T	P/T	P/T
finiteness	yes	yes	yes	no	yes	yes	yes
simplicity	no	places	no	no	no	places	no
pureness	no	no	no	no	no	no	no
components	SCSM	FSM	FSM	SM	SCFSM	FSM	FSM

where SM = SM-nets, FSM = Finite SM, SCFSM = Strongly Connected FSM, and we ascribe Proper nets to the framework of 1-safeness even if it is not completely correct (see section 7.2).

ACKNOWLEDGMENTS

This work has been carried out in the framework of the ESPRIT BRA n.°3148 DEMON. The authors wish to thank their DEMON colleagues Giorgio De Michelis, Carla Simone, Lucia Pomello, Javier Esparza for their valuable comments. Thanks are also due to five anonymous referees, whose comments helped in improving an early version of the paper.

REFERENCES

[bdh90] E. Best, F. De Cindio, R. Hopkins: *DEMON, Design Methods Based On Nets: An ESPRIT Basic Research Action (#3148)*. In: The EATCS Bulletin n. 41, June 1990.

[bdhh90] O. Botti, F. De Cindio, J. Hall, R. Hopkins: *A Petri Net Semantics of Basic Occam-2*. Technical Report n.80, ESPRIT BRA 3148, DEMON (1990).

[bdm88] E. Battiston, F. De Cindio, G. Mauri: *OBJSA nets: a class of high level nets having objects as domains*. In: G. Rozenberg (ed.), Advances in Petri nets 1988, LNCS 340, Springer-Verlag (1988).

[ber87] G. Berthelot: *Transformations and Decompositions of Nets*. In: [brr87], Volume I, pp.359-376.

[bes85] E. Best: *Concurrent behaviour: sequences, processes and axioms*. In: S.D. Brookes, A.W. Roscoe, G. Winskel (eds.), Seminar on Concurrency, LNCS 197, Springer-Verlag (1985).

[bes87] E. Best: *Structure Theory of Petri Nets: the Free Choice Hiatus*. In: [brr87], Volume I, pp.168-205.

[bes88] E. Best: *Weighted Basic Petri Nets*. In: F.H. Vogt (ed.), Concurrency 88, LNCS 335, Springer-Verlag (1988).

[bes90a] E. Best (ed.): *Technical Annex of the ESPRIT BRA 3148 DEMON*. Arbeitspapiere der GMD 435 (1990).

[bes90b] E. Best: *Design Methods Based On Nets, Esprit Basic Research Action DEMON*. In: G. Rozenberg (ed.), Advances in Petri Nets 1989, LNCS 424, Springer-Verlag 1990.

[bf86] E. Best, C. Fernandez: *Notations and Terminology on Petri Net Theory*. Arbeitspapiere der GMD 195 (1986).

[bk91] E. Best, M. Koutny: *Partial Order Semantics of Priority Systems*. Hildesheimer Informatik-Berichte Nr. 6/90. (1990) To appear in: Theoretical Computer Science under the title *Petri Net Semantics of Priority Systems* (1991).

[bra80] W. Brauer (ed.): *Net Theory and Applications* . Proc. of the First Advanced Course on General Net Theory of Systems and Processes, LNCS 84, Springer-Verlag (1980).

[bra84] W. Brauer: *How to play the token game ? or Difficulties in Interpreting Place Transition Nets*. In: Petri Nets and Related System Models Newsletter, n. 16, GI, pp.3-13 (1984).

[brm83] G. Berthelot, W. Reisig, G. Memmi: *A Control Structure for Sequential Processes Synchronized by Buffers*. In: Proc. of the 4th European Workshop on Application and Theory of Petri Nets, Toulouse (1983).

[brr87] W. Brauer, W. Reisig and G. Rozenberg (eds.): *Petri Nets: Central Models and Their Properties, Proc. of 2nd Advanced Course on Petri Nets*. 2 Volumes. LNCS 254 and 255, Springer-Verlag (1987).

[ddm88] P. Degano, R. De Nicola, U. Montanari, *A Distributed Operational Semantics for CCS Based on Condition/Event Systems*. In: Acta Informatica vol.26, n.1-2, pp. 59-91 (1988)

[ddps81] F. De Cindio, G. De Michelis, L. Pomello, C. Simone: *A Petri Net Model of CSP*. Proc. CIL '81, Barcelona (1981).

[ddps82] F. De Cindio, G. De Michelis, L. Pomello, C. Simone: *Superposed Automata Nets*. IFB 52, Springer-Verlag (1982).

[ddps85] F. De Cindio, G. De Michelis, L. Pomello, C. Simone: *Exhibited-Behaviour Equivalence and Organizational Abstraction in Concurrent System Design*. In: Proc. 5th International Conference on Distributed Computing. IEEE, Denver (1985).

[ddps87] F. De Cindio, G. De Michelis, L. Pomello, C. Simone, A. Stragapede: *Le Reti di Automi Sovrapposti: una Classe Modulare di Reti di Petri*. ENEL-DSR-CRA, Milano (1987) (in Italian).

[dds87] F. De Cindio, G. De Michelis, C. Simone: *GAMERU: A language for the analysis and design of human communication pragmatics within organizational systems*. In: G. Rozenberg (ed.), Advances in Petri Nets 1987, LNCS 266, Springer-Verlag (1987).

[dev90] R. Devillers: *The Semantics of Capacities in P/T Nets*. In: G. Rozenberg (ed.), Advances in Petri Nets 1989, LNCS 424, Springer-Verlag (1990)

[dm90] J. Desel, A. Merceron: *P/T-systems as abstractions of C/E-systems*. In: G. Rozenberg (ed.), Advances in Petri Nets 1989, LNCS 424, Springer-Verlag (1990).

[es89] J. Esparza, M. Silva: *Circuits, handles, bridges and nets*. In: Proc. of the 10th International Conference on Application and Theory of Petri Nets, Bonn (1989). Also in Advances in Petri Nets 1990, LNCS 483, Springer-Verlag (1991).

[es90] J. Esparza, M. Silva: *Top-Down Synthesis of Live&Bounded Free Choice Nets*. In: Proc. of the 11th International Conference on Petri Nets, Paris (1990). Also in: G. Rozenberg (ed.), Advances in Petri Nets 1991, LNCS 524, Springer-Verlag (1991).

[gen86] H.J. Genrich: *Projections of C/E Systems*. In: G. Rozenberg (ed.) Advances in Petri Nets 1985, LNCS 222, Springer-Verlag (1986).

[glt80] H.J. Genrich, K. Lautenbach, P.S. Thiagarajan: *Elements of General Net Theory*. In: [bra80], pp.21-163 (1980).

[gol87] U. Goltz: *On Condition/Event Representations of Place/Transition Nets*. In: K.Voss, H.J. Genrich, G.Rozenberg (eds.), Concurrency and Nets, Advances in Petri Nets 1987. Springer-Verlag (1987).

[gs80] H.J. Genrich, E. Stankiewicz-Wiechno: *A Dictionary of some basic notions of net theory*. In: [bra80], pp.519-535 (1980).

[gt84] H.J. Genrich, P.S. Thiagarajan: *A Theory of Bipolar Synchronisation schemes*. In: Theoretical Computer Science, 30, pp. 241-318 (1984).

[gwb83] G.W. Brams (collective name): *Réseaux de Petri: Théorie et Pratique*. Masson (1983). (in French)

[hac72] M. Hack: *Analysis of production schemata by Petri nets*. TR-94, MIT, Boston, 1972.

[hac74c] M. Hack: *Corrections to MAC-TR 94*. MIT, Boston, 1974.

[hac74] M. Hack: *Extended State-Machine Allocatable Nets (ESMA), an extension of Free Choice Petri net results*. MIT, Boston 1974.

[jan84] R. Janicki: *Nets, sequential components and concurrency relations*. In: Theoretical Computer Science 29, pp. 87-121 (1984).

[jv80] M.Jantzen, R.Valk: *Formal Properties of Place/Transition Nets*. In: W.Brauer (ed.), Net Theory and Applications, LNCS 84, Springer-Verlag (1981).

[kot78] V.E. Kotov: *An algebra for parallelism based on Petri nets*. In: J. Winkowski (ed.), Mathematical Foundations of Computer Science 1978, LNCS 64, Springer-Verlag (1978).

[lau87] K. Lautenbach: *Linear Algebraic Techniques for Place/Transition Nets*. In: [brr87] .

[maz77] A.Mazurkiewicz: *Concurrent Program Schemes and Their Interpretations*. Århus University, Computer Science Department, DAIMI PB-78. (1977).

[mul85] K. Müller : *Constructable Petri Nets*. In: EIK 21, 4/5, pp. 171-199 (1985).

[pet79] C.A. Petri: *Concurrency as a Basis of System Thinking*. In: F.V. Jensen, B.H. Mayoh, K.K. Moller (eds.), Proc. of the 5th Scandinavian Logic Symposium, Aalborg Univ. Press (1979)

[prs92] L. Pomello, G. Rozenberg, C. Simone: *A Survey of Equivalence Notions for Net-Based Systems*. In this volume.

[ps91] L. Pomello, C. Simone: *A State Transformation Preorder over a class of EN-systems*. In: G. Rozenberg (ed.), Advances in Petri Nets 1990, LNCS 483, Springer-Verlag (1991).

[rei79] W. Reisig: *On a Class of Co-Operating Sequential Processes*. In: Proc. of the 1st European conference on parallel and distributed processing, Toulouse, 1979.

[rei82] W. Reisig: *Deterministic Buffer Synchronisation of Sequential Processes*. In: Acta Informatica 18, pp. 117-134 (1982).

[rei85] W. Reisig: *Petri Nets: an Introduction*. Springer EATCS Monograph, Vol.4 (1985).

[rei85b] W. Reisig: *On the semantics of Petri Nets* . In: Neuhold, Chroust (eds.), Formal Models in Programming. North Holland Publ. Company, IFIP, (1985).

[rei87] W. Reisig: *Place/Transition Systems*. In: [brr87], Volume I, pp. 117-141 (1987).

[rt86] G. Rozenberg, P.S. Thiagarajan: *Petri Nets: Basic Notions, Structure, Behaviour*. In: J.W. de Bakker, W.-P. de Roever, G. Rozenberg (eds.), Current Trends in Concurrency, LNCS 224, Springer-Verlag (1986).

[sb88] Y. Souissi, N. Beldiceanu: *Deterministic Systems of Sequential Processes: Theory and Tools*. In: Concurrency 88, LNCS 255, Springer-Verlag (1988).

[sil85] M. Silva: *Las Redes de Petri en la Automatica y la Informatica*. Editorial AC, Madrid (1985) (in Spanish).

[sm89] Y. Souissi, G. Memmi: *Compositions of nets via a communication medium*. In: Proc. of the 10th International Conference on Application and theory of Petri nets, Bonn (1989).

[sou90] Y. Souissi: *Deterministic Systems of Sequential Processes: a Class of Structured Petri Nets*. Private communication, 1990.

[sr87] E. Smith, W. Reisig: *The Semantics of a Net is a Net - An Exercise in General Net Theory*. In: K. Voss, H.J. Genrich, G. Rozenberg (eds.), Concurrency and Nets. Springer-Verlag (1987).

[tau88] D. Taubner: *On the Implementation of Petri Nets*. In: G. Rozenberg (ed.), Advances in Petri Nets 1988, LNCS340, Springer-Verlag (1988).

[thi87] P.S. Thiagarajan: *Elementary Net Systems*. In [brr87], Volume I, pp. 26-59 (1987).

[val87] R.Valk: *Extension and intension of actions*. In: K. Voss, H.J. Genrich, G. Rozenberg (eds.), Concurrency and Nets. Springer-Verlag (1987).

[win85] G. Winskel: *Categories of Models for Concurrency*. In: S.D. Brookes, A.W. Roscoe, G. Winskel (eds.), Seminar on Concurrency, LNCS 197, Springer-Verlag (1985).

Structural Techniques and Performance Bounds of Stochastic Petri Net Models

Javier Campos and Manuel Silva

Dpto. de Ingeniería Eléctrica e Informática
Centro Politécnico Superior
Universidad de Zaragoza
María de Luna 3
50015 Zaragoza, SPAIN

Abstract

In this paper we overview some recent results obtained by the authors and collaborators on the performance bounds analysis of some stochastic Petri net systems. The mathematical model can be seen either as a result of the addition of a particular random timing interpretation to an "autonomous" Petri net or as a generalization of classical queueing networks with the addendum of a general synchronization primitive. It constitutes an adequate tool for both the validation of logical properties and the evaluation of performance measures of concurrent and distributed systems.

Qualitative and quantitative understandings of Petri net models are stressed here making special emphasis on structural techniques for the analysis of logical and performance properties. Important aspects from the performance point of view, such as relative throughput of stations (transitions), and number of servers present at them, are related to Petri net concepts like P- or T-semiflows or liveness bounds of transitions. For the particularly interesting case of Markovian Petri net systems, some improvements of the bounds can be achieved. Marked graphs and free choice are net subclasses for which the obtained results have special quality, therefore an additional attention is focussed on them.

Keywords: graph theory, linear algebra and linear programming techniques, Markovian systems, performance evaluation, P- and T-semiflows, qualitative and quantitative analysis, stochastic Petri net systems, structural techniques, synchronized queueing networks, throughput bounds, transformation/reduction techniques.

Contents

1 Introduction

The increasing complexity of parallel and distributed systems is forcing the researchers to deeply improve the techniques for the analysis of *correctness* and *efficiency* using mathematical models. These two faces, the qualitative validation and the quantitative analysis of models, have been usually developed quasi-independently: "Stochastic Petri Nets (SPN) were initially proposed by researchers active in the applied stochastic modelling field as a convenient graphical notation for the abstract definition of Markovian models. As a consequence, the basic definitions of SPN (and of their variations as well) were originally more concerned with the characteristics of the underlying stochastic process, rather than with the structure of the underlying Petri net model" (quoted from [AM90]). Nevertheless it is easy to accept that SPN represent a meeting point for people working in Petri nets and Performance Evaluation.

Petri nets are a well known mathematical tool extensively used for the modelling and validation of parallel and distributed systems [Pet81, Sil85, Mur89]. Their success has been due not only to the graphical representation, useful in design phases, but mainly to the well-founded theory that allows to investigate a great number of logical properties of the behaviour of the system.

In the framework of Performance Evaluation, *queueing networks* (QN) are the most commonly used models for the analysis of computer systems [Kle76, LZGS84, Lav89]. Such models have the capability of naturally express *sharing of resources* and *queueing*, that are typical situations of traditional computer systems. Efficient solution algorithms, of polynomial complexity on the size of the model, have been developed for important classes of these models, contributing to their increasing success. Many proposals exist to extend the modelling power of queueing networks by adding various synchronization constraints to the basic model [SMK82, VZL87, CCS91b]. Unfortunately, the introduction of synchronization primitives usually destroys the *product form* solution, so that general parallel and distributed systems are not easily studied with this class of models.

More recently, many SPN models have been introduced as formalisms reflecting both the logical aspects, and capable of naturally represent synchronization and concurrency [TPN85, PNPM87, PNPM89, PNPM91]. One of the main problems in the actual use of SPN models for the quantitative evaluation of large systems is the explosion of the computational complexity of the analysis algorithms. In general, exact performance results are impossible to compute. Under important restrictions, enumerative techniques can be employed. For instance, assuming boundedness and exponentially distributed random variables for the transition firing times, performance indices can be computed through the numerical solution of a *continuous time Markov chain*, whose dimension is given by the size of the marking space of the model [Mol82, FN85]. Structural computation of exact performance measures has been only possible for some subclasses of nets, such as those with *state machine* topology. These nets, under certain assumptions on the stochastic interpretation are isomorphic to Gordon and Newell's networks [GN67], in queueing theory terminology. In the general case, efficient methods for the derivation of exact performance measures are still needed.

The final objective of analytical modelling is to obtain information about some performance measures of interest in the system, such as *productivity indices* (e.g., *throughput* of transitions), *responsiveness indices* (e.g., *response time* at places), and other derived *utilization* measures. Several possibilities can be explored depending upon accuracy of results and complexity of algorithms. In this paper we select *performance bounds computation* based on Petri net *structure techniques*, that usually lead to very *efficient solution algorithms*. We try to contribute to bridge the "historical" separation between qualitative and quantitative techniques in the analysis of SPN models: "It should however be stressed that the structural properties of SPN models are today used to either ease the model definition, or to compute very partial results" [AM90]. [AMBCC87] is an example for the first case. [Mol85] and [ZZ90] are examples of the second case: in [Mol85] throughput bounds are obtained under saturation conditions for the most basic SPN model [Mol82], while in [ZZ90] some transformation rules preserving throughput are suggested in a very informal way for a deterministic timing interpretation of net models. We centre our effort in the use of both structure theory of nets and transformation/reduction techniques for deriving efficient methods for performance evaluation. As in the case of qualitative analysis of "autonomous" Petri nets, more powerful results are expected for particular net subclasses (marked graphs, free choice nets...).

Several problems, preliminary to the *exact* analysis of stochastic Petri nets, can be considered that were trivially or easily solved for classical queueing networks in the past. The first of them is the meaning of an average behaviour of the model in the limit of time, i.e., the existence of a *steady-state* behaviour. The concept of *ergodicity*, classical in the framework of Markov processes, was introduced in the field of SPN by G. Florin and S. Natkin [FN85]. It allows to speak about the average behaviour estimated on the *long run* of the system, but it is valid only for very strong assumptions on the *probability distribution functions* (PDF) defining the timing of the model. For instance, deterministic duration of activities do not lead frequently to this kind of ergodic systems. *Weak ergodicity*, introduced in [CCCS89], allows the estimation of long run performances also in the case of deterministic models. Given that we will concentrate on performance bounds instead of exact performance indices, the discussion on ergodicity will not be addressed here. The reader is referred to [FN85, CCS91a, CCS91c].

The first step in the analysis of classical closed queueing networks is the computation of the *relative throughput of stations* or *visit ratios*. It is achieved by solving a system of *flow equations*, which, for each station, equates the rate of flow of customers into to the rate of flow out of the station [Kle75]. Only routing rates among stations are needed in order to do that, thus the visit ratios are the same for arbitrary service times of stations and distribution of customers in the network. The analogous problem is a bit more complicated for SPN. The computation of the relative throughput of transitions independently of the token distribution and of the service times of transitions is only possible for some net subclasses, like *FRT-nets*, a mild generalization of free choice nets [Cam90]. This computation needs the knowledge of the *routing of tokens* through the net system, based on the *deterministic routing* (fixed by the net structure) and the *conditional routing* (defining the resolution of free conflicts).

A complementary aspect to the definition of routing of tokens through the net system is the specification of the *semantics of enabling and firing* of transitions [AMBB+89]. Related concepts in the framework of queueing networks, such as the the *number of servers at each station*, can be redefined for stochastic Petri nets. If we consider *marking bounded* systems, it does not make sense to strictly speak about "infinite" number of servers at transitions. Therefore, a first goal must be to determine the real *maximum enabling degree* of transitions (or *enabling bound*), that will correspond to the number of servers used at them. The maximum number of servers available in steady state will be characterized by the *liveness bound*, a quantitative generalization of the concept of liveness of a transition.

The paper is organized as follows. In section 2, several aspects about the introduction of time in Petri net systems are considered. Relationships between stochastic Petri net systems and queueing networks with synchronizations are indicated. The computation of relative throughput of transitions is presented in section 3, while several concepts of degree of enabling of transitions are introduced and related in section 4. Sections 3 and 4 introduce concepts and results needed in the rest of the paper: the content of section 3 (section 4) is of primary importance for sections 5, 6, and 7.1 (6, 7.1, and 7.2). The computation of *insensitive* throughput bounds (bounds valid for any probability distribution of service times) is considered in sections 5 and 6. For the case of *Markovian Petri nets* some improvements of the insensitive bounds are achieved in section 7. The idea of deriving bounds for other performance indices from throughput bounds is briefly introduced in section 8. Finally, some conclusions are summarized in section 9.

2 Stochastic Petri nets and synchronized queueing networks

In the original definition, Petri nets did not include the notion of time, and tried to model only the logical behaviour of systems by describing the causal relations existing among events. Nevertheless the introduction of a timing specification is essential if we want to use this class of models for performance evaluation of distributed systems. In this section, some considerations are made about the different implications that the addition of a timing interpretation has in Petri net models. The close relations between queueing networks with synchronization primitives and stochastic Petri nets are remarked.

We assume the reader is familiar with the structure, firing rule, and basic properties of net models [Pet81, Sil85, Mur89] Let us just introduce some notations and terminology to be extensively used in the sequel. $\mathcal{N} = \langle P, T, Pre, Post\rangle$ is a net with $n = |P|$ places and $m = |T|$ transitions. We assume $\mathcal{N}$ to be strongly connected. If the *Pre* and *Post* incidence functions take values in $\{0,1\}$, $\mathcal{N}$ is said ordinary. *PRE*, *POST*, and $C = POST - PRE$ are $n \times m$ matrices representing the *Pre*, *Post*, and global incidence functions. Vectors $Y \geq 0$, $Y^T \cdot C = 0$ ($X \geq 0$, $C \cdot X = 0$) represent P-semiflows, also called conservative components (T-semiflows, also called consistent components). The support of a vector is the set of indices corresponding to non-null components, then the support $||Y||$ ($||X||$) of Y (X) is a subset of places (transitions). A semiflow is elementary if it has minimal support (in the sense of set inclusion) and the greatest common divisor of non-null elements is 1. M (M_0) is a marking (initial marking). $\langle N, M_0\rangle$ is a net system (or marked net). The symbol σ represents a firable sequence, while $\vec{\sigma}$ is the firing count vector associated to σ: $\vec{\sigma}(t_i)$ is equal to the number of times t_i appears in σ. If M is reachable from M_0 (i.e., $\exists\sigma$ such that $M_0[\sigma\rangle M$), then $M = M_0 + C \cdot \vec{\sigma} \geq 0$ and $\vec{\sigma} \geq 0$.

Among the net subclasses considered in the sequel, state machines, marked graphs, free choice nets, and simple nets are well-studied in the literature (see, for instance, [Mur89]) Finally, we call *mono-T-semiflow nets* [CCS91a] to those having a unique minimal T-semiflow.

Stochastic Petri nets are defined through a stochastic interpretation of the net model, i.e., *"SPN = PN + stochastic interpretation"*. Looking at the topological and untimed behavioural analogy of strongly connected State Machines and the networks of queues, for certain stochastic interpretations, it can be informally stated that *"SPN = QN + synchronizations"*. The modelling paradigm of SPN in our context is fixed in section 2.1, while section 2.2 consider synchronized queueing networks (SQN) and SPN.

2.1 On Stochastic Petri Nets

Time has been introduced in Petri net models in many different ways (see, for instance, references in surveys like [AM90, FFN91, Zub91]). Since Petri nets are bipartite graphs, historically there have been two ways of introducing the concept of time in them, namely, associating a time interpretation with either transitions [Ram74] or with places [Sif78]. Since transitions represent activities that change the state (marking) of the net system,

	SPNs		Synchronized QNs
places	O	waiting rooms (queues)	⊞
transitions { timed	▯	stations (servers)	O
immediate	↗↙↘	routing	⊐
	↙↓↘	splits	◁F ◁R ◁J
	↘↘↘	synchronizations	◁J △A

Informally: "SPNs = PNs + stochastic interpretation =
= QNs + general synchronization primitive"

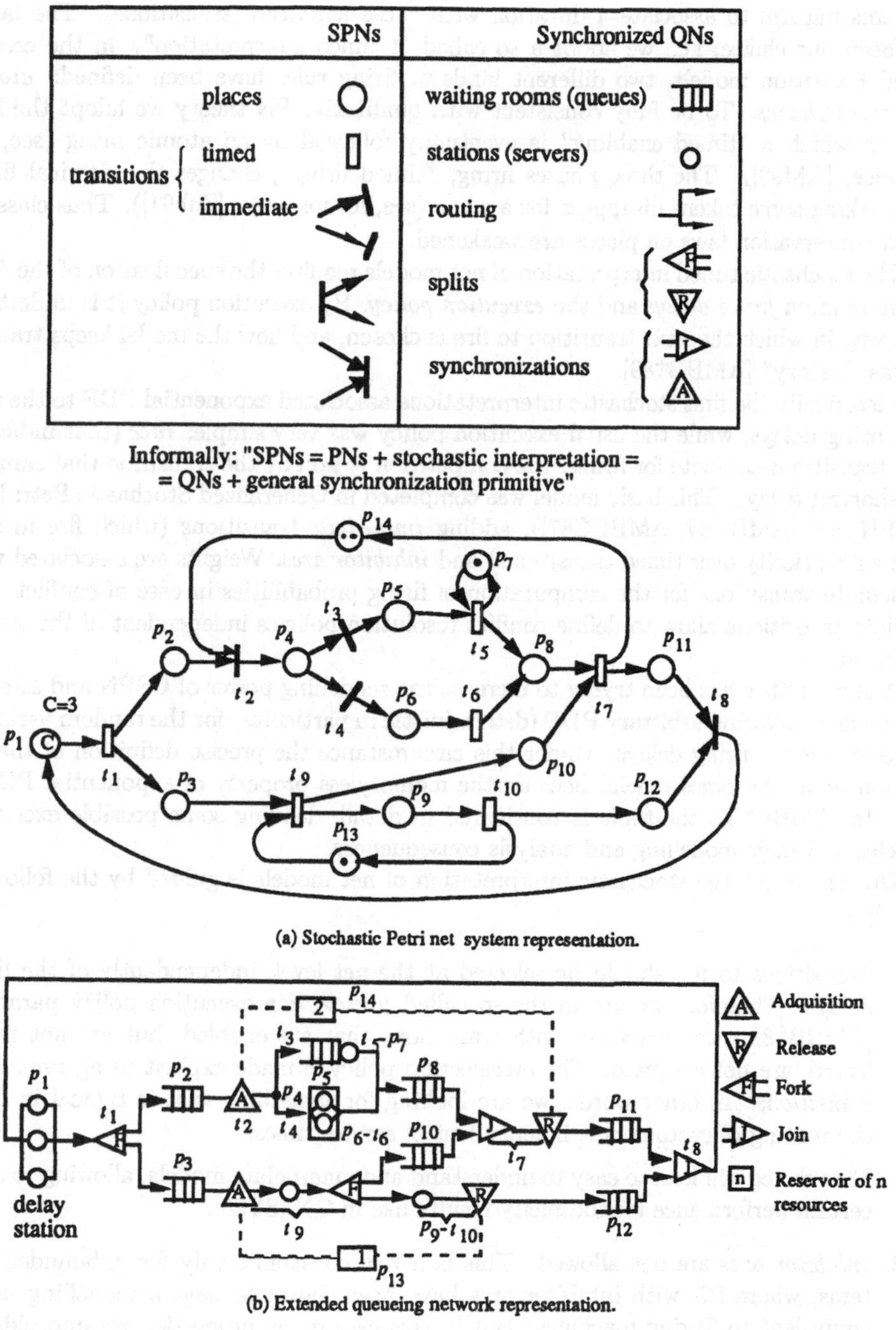

(a) Stochastic Petri net system representation.

△	Adquisition
◁R	Release
◁F	Fork
⊏▷	Join
[n]	Reservoir of n resources

(b) Extended queueing network representation.

Figure 1: A stochastic net and the corresponding synchronized queueing network.

it seems natural to associate a duration with these activities (transitions). The latter has been our choice, i.e., we adopt a so called "t-timed interpretation". In the case of timed transition models, two different kinds of firing rules have been defined: *atomic* and *three-phases*. To be fully consistent with qualitative PN theory we adopt the first one, in which a "timed enabling" is eventually followed by an atomic firing (see, for instance, [AM90]). The three phases firing, "timed firing", changes the classical firing rule making some tokens disappear for a while (see, for instance, [Zub91]). Thus classical token conservation laws on places are weakened.

The stochastic timed interpretation of net models requires the specification of the *PDF of the random firing delays* and the *execution policy*. By execution policy it is undertood "the way in which the next transition to fire is chosen, and how the model keeps track of its past history" [AMBB+89].

Historically the first stochastic interpretations associated exponential PDF to the random firing delays, while the usual execution policy was very simple: *race* (that indicates that transitions compete for firing: the competition is won by the transition that samples the shortest delay). This basic model was completed in Generalized Stochastic Petri Nets (GSPN, see [AMBC84, AMBCC87]), adding *immediate* transitions (which fire in zero time with priority over timed transitions) and *inhibitor arcs*. Weights are associated with immediate transitions for the computation of firing probabilities in case of conflict. Immediate transitions allow to define conflict resolution policies independent of the timing specification.

A step further has been trying to increase the modelling power of GSPN and alternative models, allowing arbitrary PDF (deterministic in particular) for the random variables representing the firing delays. Under this circumstance the precise definition of the execution policy becomes crucial because the memoryless property of exponential PDF is lost. In [AMBB+89] the topic is considered in detail, defining some possible execution policies and their modelling and analysis consequences.

Our choice for the stochastic interpretation of net models is guided by the following principles:

1. Transitions to fire should be selected at the net level, independently of the firing delays. Therefore we are in the so called *preselection* execution policy paradigm [AMBB+89]: the activities with transitions that are enabled, but are not preselected, are not executed. The preselection policy is made explicit using *immediate transitions*. In other words, we are looking for something that is typical in QNs: the routing of customers is independent of service times.

   This choice will lead to easy to understand and manipulate models, allowing to state certain performance monotonicity results like in QN [SY86].

2. *Inhibitor arcs* are not allowed. This is a real constraint only for unbounded systems, where PN with inhibitor arcs have been shown to have a modelling power equivalent to Turing machines. But in this case many properties are undecidable! For bounded systems, an inhibitor arc is just a modelling convenience and can be removed, expressing the constraint with normal arcs and eventually new places (see, for instance, [Sil85]).

3. *Priorities* in the firing of transitions are forbidden, except for the two levels derived from the use of *immediate* and *timed* transitions.

4. Synchronizations may be immediate, and we discard the "pathological" situation consisting of a circuit in the net including only immediate transitions.

Under the above choices our stochastic interpretation grounds in a very general framework:

1. Firing delays are random variables with arbitrary PDF. They are assumed to be time and marking independent.

2. If a transition is enabled several times, let us say q times, then q firings progress in parallel at the same time. In other words, we assume the idea that the natural interpretation of parallelism in a PN model leads to an infinite-server semantics, in QN terminology. If this is not appropiated for the system because the number of servers should be constrained to k, then a place self-loop around the transition with k tokens will guarantee the k-server semantics.

3. Any policy for conflict resolution among immediate transitions is allowed (e.g., defined through a deterministic scheduler, through a probabilistic choice...).

In practice, for computing performance bounds, only the *mean firing (service) time* of transitions and *long run routing rates* will be needed by us. More precisely, s_i, the mean firing time for transition $t_i (i = 1, \ldots, m)$ is given, and each subset of transitions $\{t_1, \ldots, t_k\} \subset T$ that are in conflict in one or several reachable markings are considered immediate, and the constants $r_1, \ldots, r_k \in \mathbb{N}^+$ are explicitly defined in the net interpretation in such a way that when $t_1, \ldots, t_k$ are enabled, transition t_i, $i = 1, \ldots, k$, fires with relative frecuency, $r_i/(\sum_{j=1}^{k} r_j)$. Note that the routing rates are assumed to be strictly positive, i.e., all possible outcomes of any conflict may fire.

In summary, we model services by means of timed transitions, routing by means of immediate transitions in conflict, and both kinds of transitions, timed and immediate, can be used as fork (split) nodes and join (synchronization) nodes.

The main price we pay for the adopted modelling paradigm is the unability to "directly" model situations like preempting scheduling disciplines, time-out mechanisms or unreliable processors which can "fail" during the processing stage. What we basically gain is the possibility of using many results from structure theory of Petri nets and queueing network theory.

A more restricted but easier to analyse stochastic interpretation, associating *time and marking independent exponential PDF* to the firing of transitions and *time and marking independent discrete probability distributions* to immediate transitions, will be called in the present framework *Markovian Petri net systems* (section 7).

2.2 Queueing networks with synchronizations

Many extensions have been proposed to introduce synchronization primitives into the queueing network formalism, in order to allow the modelling of distributed synchronous systems: *passive resources, fork and join, customer splitting*, etc. Some very restricted

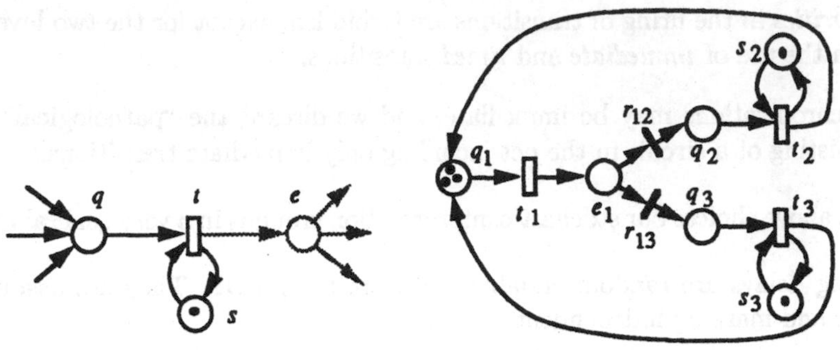

(a) (b)

Figure 2: A Petri net representation of (a) a monoclass single server queue and (b) a monoclass queueing network.

forms of synchronization, such as some special use of passive resources [AMBCD86], preserve the *local balance property* [BCMP75] that allows the use of efficient algorithms for the computation of exact *product form solutions.* In general, however, these extensions destroy the local balance property, so the extended queueing models with synchronizations are used mainly as system descriptions for simulation experiments. Even the computation of bounds for these classes of models is not yet well developed.

In [VZL87], a comparison has been proposed between synchronized queueing networks and stochastic Petri nets, showing that *the two formalisms are roughly equivalent from a modelling point of view.* Here we show how the different queueing network models with synchronizations can be uniformly represented within a Petri net formalism.

A monoclass single server station [Kle75] can be modelled by a subnet of the type depicted in figure 2.a. An infinite server queue [Kle75] (i.e., a *pure delay node*) can be represented by a place to model the number of customers in the system and a timed transition connected with the place through an input arc to model departures. *Persistent* timed transitions represent service times of the nodes, while *conflicting* immediate transitions model the routing of customers moving from one node to the other. Queueing networks containing both *delay* and *finite server* nodes are thus naturally modelled by stochastic Petri nets of the type depicted in the example of figure 2.b (t_1 is a delay, while t_2 and t_3 are single server stations). Also in this more general context conflicting immediate transitions model the routing of customers among the stations, while persistent timed transitions model the service times.

On the other hand, stochastic nets can assume forms much more complex than the one illustrated in the example of figure 2.b. Figure 1.a, taken from [CCS91b], illustrates a more general stochastic Petri net that cannot be mapped onto a product form queueing network. In fact, this net can be mapped onto a queueing network extended with synchronization primitives (figure 1.b) [SMK82], in which such constructs as fork, join, and passive resources are used to map the effect of the pairs of transitions t_2–t_7 and t_9–t_{10}, respectively. These examples show how, using a Petri net formalism, extensions of product form queueing networks are represented with an analogous level of structural complexity of Jackson networks.

As a very particular case in which the interest of making a deep bridge between PN and QN theories appears, in [DLT90] it has be pointed out the isomorphism between Fork/Join Queueing Networks with Blocking (FJQN/B) and stochastic strongly connected Marked Graphs.

Finally, let us remark that stochastic Petri nets with weighted arcs (i.e., non-ordinary nets) can be used for the modelling of *bulk arrivals* and *bulk services* [Kle75], with *deterministic size of batches* (given by the weights of arcs).

3 Relative throughput of transitions: Visit ratios

One of the most usual indices of *productivity* in performance evaluation of computer systems is the *throughput* of the different components, i.e., the number of jobs or tasks processed by each component in the unit time. In classical queueing network models, components are represented by stations, and throughput of each component is the average number of service completions of the correspondent station per unit time. For stochastic Petri nets, since actions are represented with transitions, the throughput of a component is the number of firings per unit time of the corresponding transition.

3.1 Classical queueing networks: flow of customers

In a classical monoclass queueing network, the following system can be derived by equating the rate of *flow of customers* into each station to the rate of flow out of the station [Kle75]:

$$\overline{X}(j) = X_{0j} + \sum_{i=1}^{m} \overline{X}(i)\ r_{ij}, \quad j = 1, \ldots, m \tag{1}$$

where $\overline{X}(i)$ is the limit *throughput* of station i, i.e., the average number of service completions per unit time at station i, $i = 1, \ldots, m$; r_{ij}, is the probability that a customer exiting center i goes to j $(i, j = 1, \ldots, m)$; and X_{0j} is the external arrival rate of customers to station j $(j = 1, \ldots, m)$.

If the network is open (i.e., if there exists a station j with positive external arrival rate, $X_{0j} > 0$ and also customers can leave the system), then the above m equations are linearly independent, and the exact throughputs of stations can be derived (independently of the service times, s_i, $i = 1, \ldots, m$). This is not the case for closed networks. If $X_{0j} = 0$, $j = 1, \ldots, m$, then only $m - 1$ equations are linearly independent, and thus only ratios of throughputs can be determined. These *relative throughputs* which are often called *visit ratios*, denoted as v_i for each station i, summarize all the information given by the routing that we use for the computation of the throughput bounds. The visit ratios normalized, for instance, for station j are defined as:

$$v_i^{(j)} \stackrel{\text{def}}{=} \frac{\overline{X}(i)}{\overline{X}(j)}, \quad i = 1, \ldots, m \tag{2}$$

For a restricted class of queueing networks, called *product form networks*, the exact steady-state solution can be shown to be a product of terms, one for each station, where the form of term i is derived from the visit ratio v_i and the service time s_i. The steady-state probability $\pi(\vec{n})$ of state $\vec{n} = (n_1, \ldots, n_m)^T$ (where n_i is the number of customers at center i, including those being served and those waiting) in a closed monoclass product form queueing network with m stations and N customers has the form:

$$\pi(n_1,\ldots,n_m) = \frac{1}{G(N)} \prod_{i=1}^{m} (D_i^{(j)})^{n_i} \qquad (3)$$

where $D_i^{(j)}$ is the *average service demand* of customers from station i, defined as:

$$D_i^{(j)} \stackrel{\text{def}}{=} v_i^{(j)}\, s_i, \quad i = 1,\ldots,m \qquad (4)$$

and $G(N)$ is a *normalization constant* defined so that the $\pi(\vec{n})$ sum to 1.

We remark that the knowledge of average service demands is crucial for the computation of exact measures of product form queueing networks.

3.2 Stochastic Petri nets: flow of tokens

Concerning stochastic Petri nets, we assume also that the average service times of transitions are known. Then, in order to compute the average service demand of tokens from transitions, it is necessary to compute just the visit ratios or relative throughputs of transitions.

Unfortunately, the introduction of synchronization schemes can lead to the "pathological" behaviour of models reaching a total deadlock, thus with null visit ratios for all transitions, in the limit. In other words, for these models it makes no sense to speak about steady-state behaviour. Therefore, in the rest of this paper we consider only deadlock-free Petri nets. Even more, in most subclasses in which we are interested, deadlock-freeness implies liveness of the net, in other words, the existence of an infinite activity of all the transitions is assured.

The counterpart of routing of customers in queueing networks consists both on the *net structure* $\mathcal{N}$ and the relative *routing rates at conflicts* (denoted $\mathcal{R}$) in stochastic Petri nets. Unfortunately, in the general Petri net case it is not possible to derive the visit ratios only from $\mathcal{N}$ and $\mathcal{R}$. Net systems can be constructed such that the visit ratios for transitions do depend on the net structure, on the routing rates at conflicts, but also on the initial marking (distribution of customers), and on the average service time of transitions:

$$\vec{v}^{(j)} = \vec{v}^{(j)}(\mathcal{N}, \mathcal{R}, M_0, \vec{s}) \qquad (5)$$

where $\vec{v}^{(j)}$ and $\vec{s}$ denote the vectors with components $v_i^{(j)}$ and s_i, $i = 1,\ldots,m$, respectively.

As an example, let us consider the *simple net* depicted in figure 3. Transitions t_1 and t_3 are *immediate* (i.e., they fire in zero time). The constants $r_1, r_3 \in \mathbb{N}^+$ define the conflict resolution policy, i.e., when t_1 and t_3 are simultaneously enabled, t_1 fires with relative rate $r_1/(r_1+r_3)$ and t_3 with $r_3/(r_1+r_3)$. Let s_2 and s_4 be the average service times of t_2 and t_4, respectively. If $m_5 = 1$ (initial marking of p_5) then p_1 and p_3 are *implicit* [CS91], hence they can be deleted without affecting the behaviour! Thus a closed queueing network topology is derived. A product form queueing network can be obtained and the visit ratios, normalized for transition t_1 can be computed: $\vec{v}^{(1)} = (1, 1, r_3/r_1, r_3/r_1)^T$. If $m_5 = 2$ (different initial marking for p_5) then p_5 is now implicit, hence it can be deleted; two isolated closed tandem queueing networks are obtained and $\vec{v}^{(1)\prime} = (1, 1, s_2/s_4, s_2/s_4)^T$. Obviously $\vec{v}^{(1)} \neq \vec{v}^{(1)\prime}$, in general.

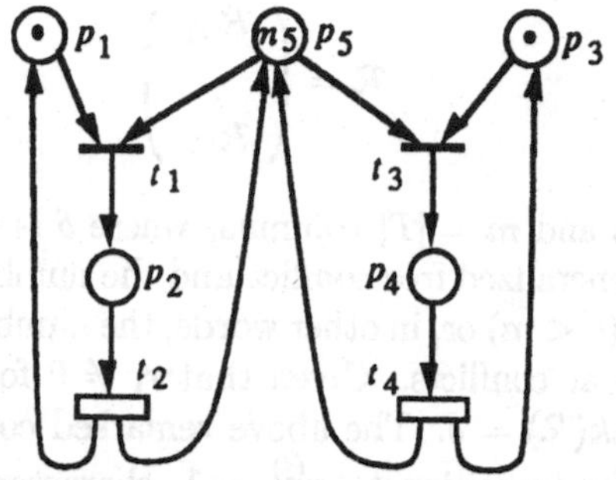

Figure 3: A simple net whose visit ratios depend on the structure, on the routing at conflicts, on the initial marking, and on the service times.

strongly connected marked graphs	$\vec{v}^{(j)} = \mathbb{1}$ {constant}
mono-T-semiflow nets	$\vec{v}^{(j)} = \vec{v}^{(j)}(\mathcal{N})$
live and bounded free choice nets	$\vec{v}^{(j)} = \vec{v}^{(j)}(\mathcal{N}, \mathcal{R})$
simple nets	$\vec{v}^{(j)} = \vec{v}^{(j)}(\mathcal{N}, \mathcal{R}, M_0, \vec{s})$

Table 1: Computability of the vector of visit ratios and net subclasses.

The computability of the vector of visit ratios on different system parameters induces a hierarchy of nets where some well-known subclasses are re-encountered (see table 1). The computation of that vector is based on the two following facts:

1. The vector of visit ratios $\vec{v}^{(j)}$ (normalized, for instance, for transition t_j) must be a non-negative right annuller of the incidence matrix:

$$C \cdot \vec{v}^{(j)} = 0 \tag{6}$$

2. The components of $\vec{v}^{(j)}$ must verify the following relations with respect to the routing rates for each subset of transitions $T_i = \{t_1, \ldots, t_k\} \subset T$ in *generalized free (or equal) conflict* (i.e., having equal pre-incidence function: $PRE[t_1] = \ldots = PRE[t_k]$):

$$\begin{aligned} r_2\vec{v}^{(j)}(t_1) - r_1\vec{v}^{(j)}(t_2) &= 0 \\ r_3\vec{v}^{(j)}(t_2) - r_2\vec{v}^{(j)}(t_3) &= 0 \\ &\cdots \\ r_k\vec{v}^{(j)}(t_{k-1}) - r_{k-1}\vec{v}^{(j)}(t_k) &= 0 \end{aligned} \tag{7}$$

Expressing the former homogeneous system of equations in matrix form: $\mathcal{R}_{T_i} \cdot \vec{v}^{(j)} = 0$, where $\mathcal{R}_{T_i}$ is a $(k-1) \times m$ matrix. Now, by considering all generalized free conflicts $T_1, \ldots, T_r$: $\mathcal{R} \cdot \vec{v}^{(j)} = 0$, where $\mathcal{R}$ is a matrix:

$$\mathcal{R} = \begin{pmatrix} \mathcal{R}_{T_1} \\ \vdots \\ \mathcal{R}_{T_r} \end{pmatrix} \tag{8}$$

$\mathcal{R}$ is a matrix with δ rows and $m = |T|$ columns, where δ is the difference between the number of transitions in generalized free conflict and the number of subsets of transitions in generalized free conflict ($\delta < m$) or, in other words, the number of independent relations fixed by the routing rates at conflicts. Given that $r_i \neq 0$ for all i, it can be observed that, by construction, $rank(\mathcal{R}) = \delta$. The above remarked conditions together with the normalization constraint for transition t_j, $v_j^{(j)} = 1$, characterize a unique vector if and only if the number of independent rows of the matrix

$$\begin{pmatrix} C \\ \mathcal{R} \end{pmatrix} \tag{9}$$

is $m - 1$. Particularly interesting subclasses verifying this condition are structurally live and structurally bounded *mono-T-semiflow* nets [CCS91a] and structurally live and structurally bounded *free choice* nets [CCS91b]. We introduce now a more general class of structurally live and structurally bounded nets verifying the previous condition. In order to do that, we define an equivalence relation on the set of T-semiflows of the net. After that, the class of *FRT-nets* will be defined as nets having only one equivalence class for this relation.

Definition 3.1 *Let $\mathcal{N}$ be a Petri net and X_a, X_b two different T-semiflows of $\mathcal{N}$. X_a and X_b are said to be freely connected by places $P' \subset P$, denoted as $X_a \overset{P'}{\wedge} X_b$, iff $\exists t_a \in ||X_a||$, $t_b \in ||X_b||$ such that: $PRE[t_a] = PRE[t_b]$ and $^\bullet t_a = {}^\bullet t_b = P'$.*

Definition 3.2 *Let $\mathcal{N}$ be a Petri net and X_a, X_b two T-semiflows of $\mathcal{N}$. X_a and X_b are said to be freely related, denoted as $(X_a, X_b) \in FR$, iff one of the following conditions holds:*

1. *$X_a = X_b$,*
2. *$\exists P' \subset P$ such that $X_a \overset{P'}{\wedge} X_b$, or*
3. *$\exists X_1, \ldots, X_k$ T-semiflows of $\mathcal{N}$ and $P_1, \ldots, P_{k+1} \subset P$, $k \geq 1$, such that $X_a \overset{P_1}{\wedge} X_1 \overset{P_2}{\wedge} \ldots \overset{P_k}{\wedge} X_k \overset{P_{k+1}}{\wedge} X_b$.*

From the above definition the next property trivially follows:

Property 3.1 *FR is an equivalence relation on the set of T-semiflows of a net.*

The introduction of this equivalence relation on the set of T-semiflows induces a partition into equivalence classes. FRT-nets are defined as follows:

Definition 3.3 [Cam90] *$\mathcal{N}$ is a net with freely related T-semiflows (FRT-net, for short) iff the introduction of the freely relation on the set of its T-semiflows induces only one equivalence class.*

The next result gives a *polynomial time* method for the computation of the vector of visit ratios for transitions of a live and structurally bounded FRT-net, from the knowledge of the net structure and the routing rates at conflicts.

Theorem 3.1 [Cam90] *Let $\langle \mathcal{N}, M_0 \rangle$ be a live and structurally bounded FRT-net system. Let C be the incidence matrix of $\mathcal{N}$ and $\mathcal{R}$ the previously introduced matrix. Then, the vector of visit ratios $\vec{v}^{(j)}$ normalized for transition t_j can be computed from C and $\mathcal{R}$ by solving the following linear system of equations:*

$$\begin{pmatrix} C \\ \mathcal{R} \end{pmatrix} \cdot \vec{v}^{(j)} = 0, \quad v_j^{(j)} = 1 \qquad (10)$$

The reader can notice that a *rank condition* over the incidence matrix C exists underlying theorem 3.1: the system of equations (10) has a unique solution $\vec{v}^{(j)}$ if and only if $rank(C) = m - \delta - 1$, where δ is the rank of $\mathcal{R}$. For the particular case of free choice nets, a stronger result about the rank of the incidence matrix (that first appeared in [CCS91b]) can be formulated as:

Theorem 3.2 [ES91] *Let $\mathcal{N}$ be a free choice net. $\mathcal{N}$ is structurally live and structurally bounded iff it is conservative, consistent, and $rank(C) = m - 1 - (a - n)$, with $a = \sum_{p \in P, t \in T} PRE[p, t]$ (i.e., the number of input arcs to transitions).*

An important fact about this qualitative property suggested by the performance evaluation analysis is that many of Hack's classical results [Hac72] can be derived from it or the proof process (see [CCS91b] or [ES91]). On the other hand, theorem 3.2 gives a *polynomial* (on the net size) *time* method to decide if a given free choice net is structurally live and structurally bounded.

4 Number of servers at transitions: Enabling and liveness bounds

In a classical product-form QN, the number of servers at each station is explicitly given as a modelling choice (e.g., it can be said that a certain station has two servers). Stations may vary between *single* server and *delay* node (infinite server). In the second case, the maximum number of servers that can be working at such delay node is exactly the number of customers in the whole net system.

In section 2.1 we explicitly adopted the convention that several instances of a same transition can work in parallel at a given marking. How many of them? The answer is given by the *degree of enabling of a transition, t, at a given marking, M*:

$$E(t, M) \stackrel{\text{def}}{=} \max\{\, k \mid M \geq k\, PRE[t] \}$$

Therefore it can be said that at M, in transition t, $E(t, M)$ servers work in parallel. This value can be eventually reduced by a design choice adding a self-loop place around t with q tokens: it is obvious that in this case $E(t, M) \leq q$.

The maximum number of servers working in parallel clearly influences the performance of the system. This value, in net systems terms, has been called the *enabling bound* of a transition.

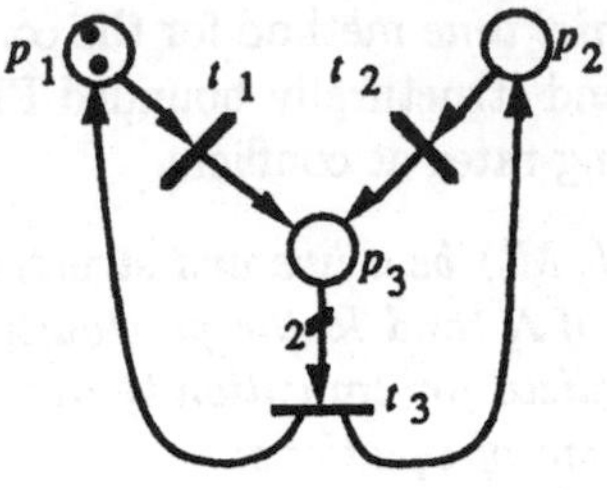

Figure 4: $E(t_1) = 2$, while $L(t_1) = 1$ (i.e., $L(t_1) < E(t_1)$).

Definition 4.1 [CCCS89] *Let $\langle \mathcal{N}, M_0 \rangle$ be a net system. The enabling bound of a given transition t of $\mathcal{N}$ is*

$$E(t) \stackrel{\text{def}}{=} \max \{ \; k \mid \exists \sigma, M_0[\sigma\rangle M : \; M \geq k \; PRE[t] \; \} \tag{11}$$

The enabling bound is a quantitative generalization of the basic concept of enabling, and is closely related to the concept of *marking bound of a place.*

Definition 4.2 *Let $\langle \mathcal{N}, M_0 \rangle$ be a net system. The marking bound of a given place p of $\mathcal{N}$ is*

$$B(p) \stackrel{\text{def}}{=} \max \{ \; M(p) \mid M_0[\sigma\rangle M \; \} \tag{12}$$

Since we are interested in the steady-state performance of a model, one can ask the following question: how many servers can be available in transitions in any possible steady-state condition? The answer is given by the definition of the *liveness bound* concept.

Definition 4.3 [CCS91a] *Let $\langle \mathcal{N}, M_0 \rangle$ be a net system. The liveness bound of a given transition t of $\mathcal{N}$ is*

$$L(t) \stackrel{\text{def}}{=} \max \{ \; k \mid \forall M' : M_0[\sigma\rangle M', \exists M : M'[\sigma'\rangle M \wedge M \geq k \; PRE[t] \; \} \tag{13}$$

The above definition generalizes the classical concept of liveness of a transition. In particular, a transition t is live if and only if $L(t) > 0$, i.e., if there is at least one working server associated with it in any steady-state condition. The following is also obvious from the definitions.

Property 4.1 [CCS91a] *Let $\langle \mathcal{N}, M_0 \rangle$ be a net system. For any transition t in $\mathcal{N}$, $E(t) \geq L(t)$ (see figure 4).*

Since for any *reversible* net system (i.e., such that M_0 can be recovered from any reachable marking: M_0 is a *home state*) the reachability graph is strongly connected, the following can be stated:

Property 4.2 [CCS91a] *Let $\langle \mathcal{N}, M_0 \rangle$ be a reversible net system. For any transition t in $\mathcal{N}$, $E(t) = L(t)$.*

The definition of enabling bound refers to a behavioural property. Since we are looking for computational techniques at the structural level, we define also the structural counterpart of the enabling bound concept. Structural net theory has been developed from two complementary points of view: graph theory [Bes87] and mathematical programming (or more specifically linear programming and linear algebra) [SC88]. Let us recall our structural definition from the mathematical programming point of view; essentially in this case the reachability condition is substituted by the (in general) weaker (linear) constraint that markings satisfy the net state equation: $M = M_0 + C \cdot \vec{\sigma}$, with $M, \vec{\sigma} \geq 0$.

Definition 4.4 [CCCS89] *Let $\langle \mathcal{N}, M_0 \rangle$ be a net system. The structural enabling bound of a given transition t of $\mathcal{N}$ is*

$$SE(t) \stackrel{\text{def}}{=} \max \ \{k \mid M = M_0 + C \cdot \vec{\sigma} \geq 0, \vec{\sigma} \geq 0 : M \geq kPRE[t]\} \qquad \text{(LPP1)}$$

Note that the definition of structural enabling bound reduces to the formulation of a *linear programming problem*, that can be solved in polynomial time [NRKT89].

Now let us remark the relation between behavioural and structural enabling bound concepts that follows from the implication "$M_0[\sigma\rangle M \;\Rightarrow\; M = M_0 + C \cdot \vec{\sigma} \wedge \vec{\sigma} \geq 0$".

Property 4.3 [CCS91a] *Let $\langle \mathcal{N}, M_0 \rangle$ be a net system. For any transition t in $\mathcal{N}$, $SE(t) \geq E(t)$.*

As we remarked before, the concept of enabling bound of transitions is closely related to the marking bound of places. In an analogous way, the structural enabling bound is closely related to the *structural marking bound* of places.

Definition 4.5 [SC88] *Let $\langle \mathcal{N}, M_0 \rangle$ be a net system. The structural marking bound of a given place p of $\mathcal{N}$ is*

$$SB(p) \stackrel{\text{def}}{=} \max \ \{ M(p) \mid M = M_0 + C \cdot \vec{\sigma} \geq 0 \ , \ \vec{\sigma} \geq 0 \} \qquad \text{(LPP2)}$$

It is well-known that the structural marking bound of a place is, in general, greater than or equal to the marking bound of the same place (for instance, for the net in figure 4, the marking bound of p_2 is 1 while its structural marking bound is 2). For the particular case of live and bounded free choice systems, both the marking bound and the structural marking bound of a place are always the same [Esp90]. A similar result can be shown for the enabling bound, the structural enabling bound, and the liveness bound of transitions of such net subclass.

Theorem 4.1 [CCS91b] *Let $\langle \mathcal{N}, M_0 \rangle$ be a live and bounded free choice system. For any transition t in $\mathcal{N}$, $SE(t) = E(t) = L(t)$.*

Now, from the previous theorem and taking into account that for any transition t the computation of the structural enabling bound $SE(t)$ can be formulated in terms of the problem (LPP1), the following monotonicity property of the liveness bound of a transition with respect to the initial marking is obtained.

Corollary 4.1 [CCS91b] *If $\langle \mathcal{N}, M_0 \rangle$ is a live and bounded free choice system and $M_0' \geq M_0$ then the liveness bound of t in $\langle \mathcal{N}, M_0' \rangle$ is greater than or equal to the liveness bound of t in $\langle \mathcal{N}, M_0 \rangle$.*

The previous result appears to be a generalization (stated for the particular case of bounded nets) of the classical liveness monotonicity property for free choice systems (see, e.g., [Bes87]).

Once the computability of visit ratios and enabling/liveness bounds have been addressed using concepts and techniques from linear (algebra/programming) structure theory, bounds on throughput are presented in the following sections.

5 Insensitive upper bounds on throughput

In this section we present the computation of upper bounds for the throughput of transitions for stochastic Petri nets with general distribution of service times. The obtained bounds are called *insensitive* because they are valid for arbitrary forms of the probability distribution functions of service (including deterministic timing), since only mean values of random variables are used.

Let us just precise for stochastic Petri net systems the weak ergodicity notions for the marking and firing processes:

Definition 5.1 [CCS91b] *The marking process M_τ, where $\tau \geq 0$ represents the time, of a stochastic marked net is weakly ergodic iff the following limit exists:*

$$\lim_{\tau \to \infty} \frac{1}{\tau} \int_0^\tau M_u \, du = \overline{M} < \vec{\infty}, \;\; a.s. \tag{14}$$

and the constant vector $\overline{M}$ is called the limit average marking.

The firing process $\vec{\sigma}_\tau$, where $\tau \geq 0$ represents the time, of a stochastic marked net is weakly ergodic iff the following limit exists:

$$\lim_{\tau \to \infty} \frac{\vec{\sigma}_\tau}{\tau} = \vec{\Sigma} < \vec{\infty}, \;\; a.s. \tag{15}$$

and the constant vector $\vec{\Sigma}$ is the limit of transition throughputs (or limit firing flow vector).

For bounded net systems, the existence of a home state (i.e., a marking reachable from any other) is a sufficient condition for weak marking ergodicity [Cam90].

5.1 Little's law and P-semiflows

Three of the most significant performance measures for a closed region of a network in the analysis of queueing systems are related by Little's formula [Lit61], which holds under very general (i.e., weak) conditions. This result can be applied to each place of a weakly ergodic net system. Denoting $\overline{M}(p_i)$ the limit average number of tokens at place p_i, $\vec{\Sigma}$ the limit vector of transition throughputs, and $\overline{R}(p_i)$ the average time spent by a token within the place p_i (average residence time at place p_i), the above mentioned relationship is stated as follows (see [FN85]):

$$\overline{M}(p_i) = (PRE[p_i] \cdot \vec{\Sigma})\ \overline{R}(p_i) \tag{16}$$

where $PRE[p_i]$ is the ith row of the pre-incidence matrix of the underlying Petri net, thus $PRE[p_i] \cdot \vec{\Sigma}$ is the output rate of place p_i.

In the study of computer systems, Little's law is frequently used when two of the related quantities are known and the third one is needed. This is not exactly the case here. In the equation (16), $\vec{\Sigma}$ can be computed except for a scaling factor for important net system subclasses (see section 3):

$$\vec{\Sigma} = \frac{1}{\Gamma^{(j)}}\ \vec{v}^{(j)} \tag{17}$$

where $\vec{v}^{(j)}$ is the vector of visit ratios normalized for t_j and $\Gamma^{(j)}$ is the inverse of the limit throughput of transition t_j, that we call the *mean interfiring time* of that transition, i.e., the mean time between two consecutive firings of t_j.

The average residence time $\overline{R}(p_i)$ at places with more than one output transition is null because such transitions are considered immediate. For the places p_i with only one output transition, the average response time can be expressed as sum of the average waiting time due to a possible synchronization in the output transition and the mean service time associated with that transition. Thus the average residence times can be lowerly bounded from the knowledge of the mean service times of transitions, s_i, $i = 1, \ldots, m$, and the following system of inequalities can be derived from (16) and (17):

$$\Gamma^{(j)}\ \overline{M} \geq PRE \cdot \vec{D}^{(j)} \tag{18}$$

where $\vec{D}^{(j)}$ is the vector of average service demands, introduced in section 3.1: $D_k^{(j)} = v_k^{(j)} s_k$.

The limit average marking $\overline{M}$ is unknown. However, taking the product with a P-semiflow Y (i.e., $Y \geq 0$, $Y^T \cdot C = 0$, thus $Y^T \cdot M_0 = Y^T \cdot M = Y^T \cdot \overline{M}$ for all reachable marking M), the following inequality can be derived:

$$\Gamma^{(j)} \geq \max \left\{ \frac{Y^T \cdot PRE \cdot \vec{D}^{(j)}}{Y^T \cdot M_0} \mid Y^T \cdot C = 0\ ,\ Y \geq 0 \right\} \tag{19}$$

The previous lower bound for the mean interfiring time (or its inverse, an upper bound for the throughput) can be formulated in terms of a *fractional programming problem* [NRKT89] and later, after some considerations, transformed into a linear programming problem.

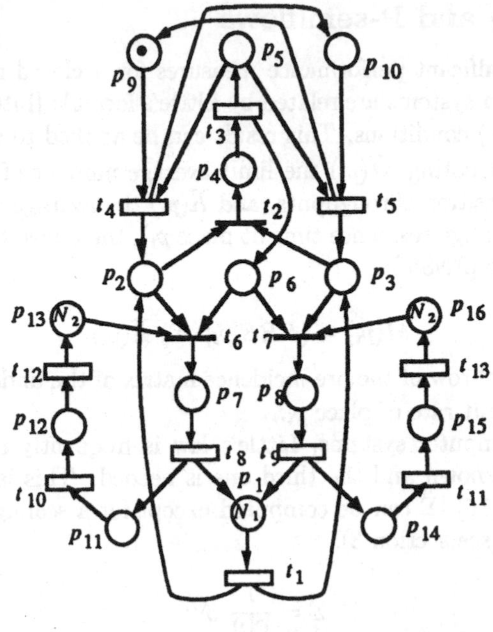

Figure 5: A live and bounded stochastic Petri net.

Theorem 5.1 [CCS91b] *For any net system, a lower bound for the mean interfiring time* $\Gamma^{(j)}$ *of transition* t_j *can be computed by solving the following linear programming problem:*

$$\Gamma^{(j)} \geq \max \ \{Y^T \cdot PRE \cdot \vec{D}^{(j)} | Y^T \cdot C = 0 \ , \ Y^T \cdot M_0 = 1 \ , \ Y \geq 0\} \qquad \text{(LPP3)}$$

The basic advantage of the previous theorem lies in the fact that the *simplex* method for the solution of a linear programming problem has almost linear complexity in practice, even if it has exponential worst case complexity. In any case, algorithms of polynomial worst case complexity can be found in [NRKT89]. Since for live and bounded free choice systems the computation of vector $\vec{v}^{(j)}$ (hence of $\vec{D}^{(j)}$) can be done by solving a linear system of equations (cf. theorem 3.1), the computation of a lower bound for the mean interfiring time (thus, of the upper bound on throughput) of a transition has worst case polynomial complexity on the net size.

In order to interpret theorem 5.1, let us consider the *mono-T-semiflow net* [CCS91a] depicted in figure 5. The unique minimal T-semiflow of the net is:

$$X = (2, 2, 2, 1, 1, 1, 1, 1, 1, 1, 1, 1, 1)^T \qquad (20)$$

Therefore, according to (4), the vector of average service demands for transitions (if the visit ratios are normalized, for instance, for t_3) is

$$\vec{D}^{(3)} = (2s_1, 0, 2s_3, s_4, s_5, 0, 0, s_8, s_9, s_{10}, s_{11}, s_{12}, s_{13})^T \qquad (21)$$

because the vector of visit ratios is $\vec{v}^{(3)} = X$ (see section 3) and transitions t_2, t_6, and t_7 are assumed to be immediate ($s_2 = s_6 = s_7 = 0$).

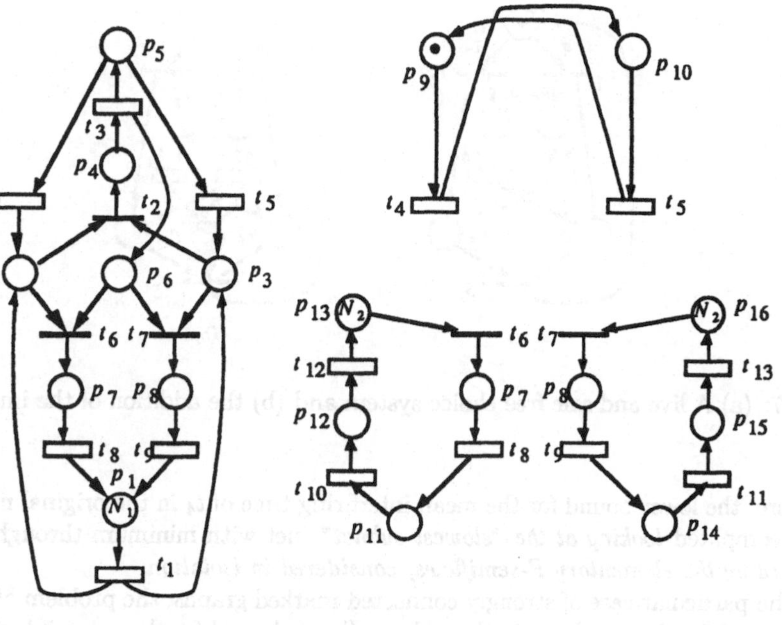

Figure 6: Subsystems of the net system in figure 5 generated by minimal P-semiflows.

The minimal P-semiflows (minimal support solutions of $Y^T \cdot C = 0, Y \geq 0$) of this net are:

$$\begin{aligned}
Y_1 &= (2,1,1,2,1,1,2,2,0,0,0,0,0,0,0,0)^T \\
Y_2 &= (0,0,0,0,0,0,0,0,1,1,0,0,0,0,0,0)^T \\
Y_3 &= (0,0,0,0,0,0,1,0,0,0,1,1,1,0,0,0)^T \\
Y_4 &= (0,0,0,0,0,0,0,1,0,0,0,0,0,1,1,1)^T
\end{aligned} \tag{22}$$

Then, the application of (LPP3) gives:

$$\begin{aligned}
\Gamma^{(3)} \;\geq\; \max\{\; & (4s_1 + 2s_3 + 2s_4 + s_5 + 2s_8 + 2s_9)/2N_1, \\
& s_4 + s_5, \\
& (s_8 + s_{10} + s_{12})/N_2, \\
& (s_9 + s_{11} + s_{13})/N_2 \}
\end{aligned} \tag{23}$$

where $N_1 > 0$ is the initial marking of place p_1, and $N_2 > 0$ is the initial marking of p_{13} and p_{16}. Now, let us consider the *P-semiflow decomposed view* of the net: the four subnets generated by Y_1, Y_2, Y_3, and Y_4 are depicted in isolation in figure 6.

The exact mean interfiring times of (all the transitions of) the second, third, and forth subnets are $s_4 + s_5$, $(s_8 + s_{10} + s_{12})/N_2$, and $(s_9 + s_{11} + s_{13})/N_2$, respectively (remember that infinite-server semantics is assumed). The exact mean interfiring time of t_3 in the first subnet (generated by Y_1) cannot be computed in a compact way (like the others), because it includes synchronizations (it has not queueing network topology). In any case, its mean interfiring time is greater than $(4s_1+2s_3+2s_4+s_5+2s_8+2s_9)/2N_1$, because this would be the cycle time of a queueing network (without delays due to synchronizations) of infinite-server stations with the same average service demands and number of customers.

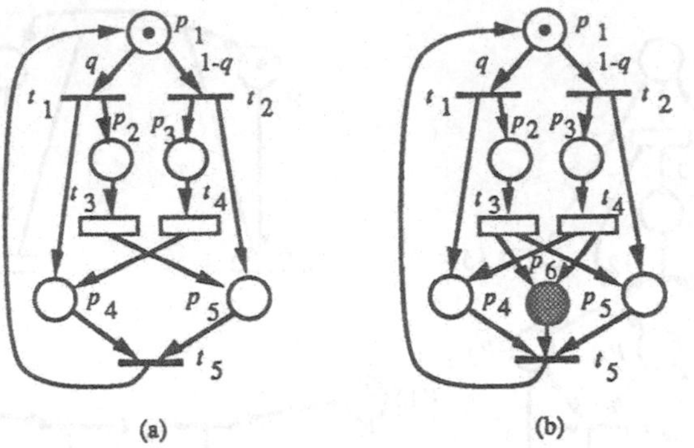

Figure 7: (a) A live and safe free choice system and (b) the addition of the implicit place p_6.

Therefore, the lower bound for the mean interfiring time of t_4 in the original net given by (23) is computed *looking at the "slowest subnet"* (net with minimum throughput for t_4) *generated by the elementary P-semiflows, considered in isolation.*

In the particular case of strongly connected marked graphs, the problem of finding an upper bound for the steady-state throughput (lower bound for the mean interfiring time) can be solved looking at the *mean interfiring time* associated with each elementary circuit (minimal P-semiflows for marked graphs) of the net, considered in isolation. These times can be computed making the summation of the mean service times of all the transitions involved in the P-semiflow (service time of the whole circuit), and dividing by the number of tokens present in it (customers in the circuit).

5.2 About the reachability of the bound

The above bound, that holds for any probability distribution function of service times of transitions, happens to be the same that has been obtained for strongly connected deterministically timed marked graphs by other authors (see for example [Ram74, Sif78, RH80]), but here it is considered in a practical linear programming form. For deterministically timed marked graphs, the reachability of this bound has been shown [Ram74, RH80]. Even more, it has been shown [CCCS89, CCCS90] that the previous bound cannot be improved, for the case of strongly connected marked graphs, only on the base of the knowledge of the coefficients of variation for the transition service times.

We remark that the importance of a tightness result for performance bounds lies in the fact that the bounds cannot be improved without increasing the information about the model (in particular, the moments of order greater than two of the associated random variables).

For the more general case of live and bounded free choice systems, the bound given by theorem 5.1 cannot be reached for some models, for any probability distribution function of service times. Let us consider, for instance, the live and safe free choice system in figure 7.a.

Let s_3 and s_4 be the mean service times associated with t_3 and t_4, respectively. Let t_1, t_2, and t_5 be *immediate* transitions (i.e., they fire in zero time). Let $q, 1-q \in (0,1)$ be the probabilities defining the resolution of conflict at place p_1. The vector of visit ratios (normalized for t_5) is

$$\vec{v}^{(5)} = (q, 1-q, q, 1-q, 1)^T \tag{24}$$

The elementary P-semiflows are

$$\begin{aligned} Y_1 &= (1,1,0,0,1)^T \\ Y_2 &= (1,0,1,1,0)^T \end{aligned} \tag{25}$$

Applying (LPP3) the following lower bound for the mean interfiring time of transition t_5 is obtained:

$$\Gamma^{(5)} \geq \max \{ \, qs_3, (1-q)s_4 \, \} \tag{26}$$

while the actual mean interfiring time for this transition is

$$\Gamma^{(5)} = qs_3 + (1-q)s_4 \tag{27}$$

independently of the higher moments of the probability distribution functions associated with transitions t_3 and t_4. Therefore the bound given by theorem 5.1 is non-reachable for the net system in figure 7.a.

Methods for the improvement of this bound have been presented in [CCS91c] and [CC91]. We just summarize here some ideas about them. The first one concerns the addition of *implicit places* to the net system. From a pure qualitative point of view, in [CS91] it is shown that the addition of "judicious" implicit places eliminates some of the *spurious* solutions of the linear relaxation of a net system (i.e., those integer solutions of $M = M_0 + C \cdot \vec{\sigma} \geq 0, \vec{\sigma} \geq 0$ that are non reachable). In [CCS91b], an analogous improvement is shown to hold at the performance level. Let us explain here this improvement by using again the example depicted in figure 7.a: consider the net in figure 7.b, where the implicit place p_6 has been added to the original net. The addition of implicit places can generate more elementary P-semiflows. In this case:

$$Y_3 = (1,1,1,0,0,1)^T \tag{28}$$

Then, the application of (LPP3) can eventually lead to an improvement of the previous bound. For this net system:

$$\Gamma^{(5)} \geq \max \{ \, qs_3, (1-q)s_4, qs_3 + (1-q)s_4 \, \} = qs_3 + (1-q)s_4 \tag{29}$$

which is exactly the actual mean interfiring time of t_5.

Details on this technique can be found in [CCS91c]. Moreover, it should be pointed out that the addition of implicit places does not guarantee the bound to be reachable. As an example, look at the net in figure 8.a. The exact mean interfiring time of t_7 for deterministic timing is:

$$\Gamma^{(7)} = \max \{ \, qs_3+s_6, (1-q)s_4+s_5, qs_3+(1-q)s_4+(1-q)s_5+qs_6, qs_5+(1-q)s_6 \, \}+s_7 \tag{30}$$

and its clearly greater than the bound obtained after the addition of the implicit place p_8 (figure 8.b):

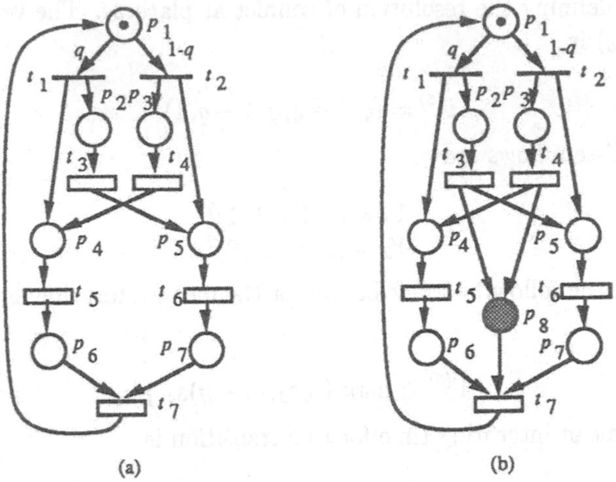

Figure 8: (a) A live and safe free choice system and (b) the addition of the implicit place p_8.

$$\Gamma^{(7)} \geq \max \{ qs_3 + s_6, (1-q)s_4 + s_5, qs_3 + (1-q)s_4 \} + s_7 \tag{31}$$

The reader can check that addition of any set of implicit places to the system in figure 8.a does not allow to reach the value in (30).

Another approach for improving the throughput upper bound of theorem 5.1 is presented in [CC91], for the case of live and safe free choice systems. It is based on the consideration of some specific *multisets of circuits* of the net in which elementary circuits appear a number of times according to the visit ratios of the involved transitions. Basically, it is a generalization (in the *graph theory* sense) of the application of theorem 5.1 for the case of marked graphs, because circuits (P-semiflows) of the marked graph are substituted now by multisets of circuits. The improvement is based on the application of a linear programming problem to a net obtained from the original one after a *transformation* of linear size increasing. The transformation, that is a modification of the *Lautenbach transformation for the computation of minimal traps in a net* [Lau87], will not be presented here (interested readers are referred to [CC91]). The application of this method to the net in figure 8.a gives exactly the mean interfiring time of t_7, given by (30), for deterministic service times of transitions.

5.3 Some derived results

Linear programming problems give an easy way to derive results and interpret them. Looking at (LPP3), the following *monotonicity property* can be obtained: the lower bound for the mean interfiring time of a transition does not increase if $\vec{s}$ (the mean service times vector) decreases or if M_0 increases.

Property 5.1 [CCCS89] *Let $\langle \mathcal{N}, M_0 \rangle$ be a net system and $\vec{s}$ the vector of mean service times of transitions.*

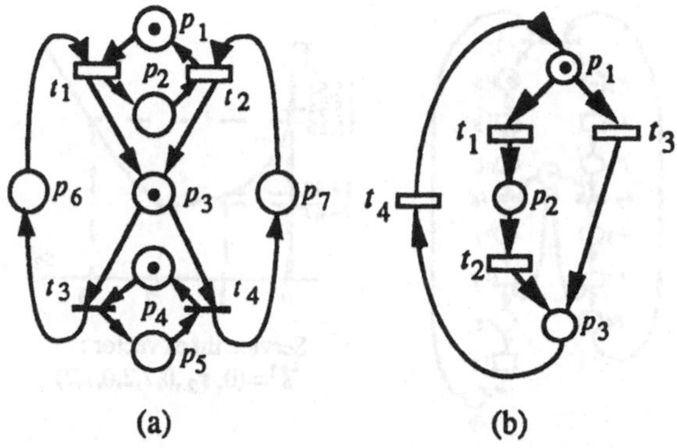

Figure 9: "Apparent improvements" lead to worse results: (a) The addition of a token to p_5 kills the net system (the sequence $\sigma = t_4$ leads to a deadlock); (b) Decreasing s_1 (mean service time of t_1), the mean interfiring time of t_4 increases if $s_2 \gg s_i$, $i = 1,3$, and if exponential services and race policy are assumed.

1. *For a fixed $\vec{s}$, if $M_0' \geq M_0$ (i.e., more resources) then the lower bound for the mean interfiring time of any transition of $\langle \mathcal{N}, M_0', \vec{s} \rangle$ computed through (LPP3) is less than or equal to the one of $\langle \mathcal{N}, M_0, \vec{s} \rangle$.*

2. *For a fixed M_0, if $\vec{s}' \leq \vec{s}$ (i.e., faster resources) then the lower bound for the mean interfiring time of any transition of $\langle \mathcal{N}, M_0, \vec{s}' \rangle$ computed through (LPP3) is less than or equal to the one of $\langle \mathcal{N}, M_0, \vec{s} \rangle$.*

For the case of live and bounded free choice systems, the above *monotonicity* properties for the bound hold also for the *exact* throughput. We recall that live and bounded free choice net systems can be decomposed into several strongly connected state machines (*P-components*) connected by means of synchronization transitions [Bes87]. Moreover, from the definition of free choice nets, if p_a and p_b are input places to a synchronization transition t, then t is the unique output transition of p_a and p_b. In other words, once a synchronization transition has been enabled in a free choice system, its firing is unavoidable. Then, because we assume (section 2.1) that all choices are among immediate transitions, if the service time of a transition decreases or the number of tokens at some place increases, the mean interfiring time of transitions can never increase: it is possible to increase for certain tokens the pure waiting time at some synchronizations (i.e., the time elapsed from the time instant in which the tokens arrive until the transition becomes enabled).

Property 5.2 *Let $\langle \mathcal{N}, M_0 \rangle$ be a live and bounded free choice system and $\vec{s}$ the vector of mean service times of transitions.*

1. *For a fixed $\vec{s}$, if $M_0' \geq M_0$ (i.e., more resources) then the mean interfiring time of any transition of $\langle \mathcal{N}, M_0', \vec{s} \rangle$ is less than or equal to the one of $\langle \mathcal{N}, M_0, \vec{s} \rangle$ (i.e., $\Gamma^{(j)\prime} \leq \Gamma^{(j)}$).*

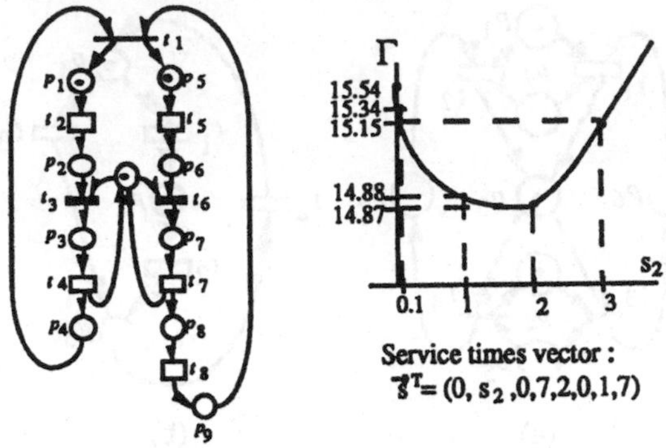

Figure 10: Increasing the mean service time s_2 of t_2 on the Markovian net system leads to better overall throughput (i.e., the mean interfiring time Γ of every transition decreases).

2. *For a fixed M_0, if $\vec{s}' \leq \vec{s}$ (i.e., faster resources) then the mean interfiring time of any transition of $\langle \mathcal{N}, M_0, \vec{s}' \rangle$ is less than or equal to the one of $\langle \mathcal{N}, M_0, \vec{s} \rangle$ (i.e., $\Gamma^{(j)'} \leq \Gamma^{(j)}$).*

The result stated in the above property does not hold for other net subclasses. For instance, increasing the number of initial resources (by adding one token to p_5) in the net system of figure 9.a, the obtained system reaches a *total deadlock*, therefore the throughput of the derived system is null.

On the other hand, the intuitive idea that decreasing the service time of a transition leads to a slower system is paradoxically wrong in general! Figure 10 shows a *Markovian Petri net system* (exponentially distributed service times of transitions) where increasing the mean service time s_2 of t_2, while $s_2 \in (0,2)$, the throughput increases. Moreover, the statement 2 in the property 5.2 does not hold even for state machine topology using the basic stochastic interpretation in [Mol82] or [FN85]: all transitions are timed with exponential PDF and conflicts are solved with race policy. This "anomaly", illustrated in the extremely simple case of figure 9.b, appears because the routing and timing are *coupled* in this class of models.

Finally, an interesting interpretation of the problem (LPP3), that provides another example of possible interleaving between qualitative and quantitative analysis for stochastic net systems, is the following characterization of liveness for structurally live and structurally bounded free choice nets.

Corollary 5.1 *Assuming that $\vec{v}^{(j)} > 0$ and that there do not exist circuits containing only immediate transitions, liveness of structurally live and structurally bounded free choice nets can be decided in polynomial time, checking the boundedness of the problem (LPP3).*

This result is nothing more than deciding liveness by checking if all P-semiflows are marked (the linear programming problem is bounded if and only if for all $Y \geq 0$ such that $Y^T \cdot C = 0$, then $Y^T \cdot M_0 > 0$).

For more general net subclasses, if the solution of (LPP3) is unbounded (i.e., there exists an unmarked P-semiflow), since $\Gamma^{(j)}$ it is a lower bound for the mean interfiring time of transition t_j, the non-liveness can be assured (infinite interfiring time). Nevertheless, a net system can be non-live and the obtained lower bound for the mean interfiring time be finite (e.g., the mono-T-semiflow net in figure 9.a with the addition of a token in place p_5).

6 Insensitive lower bounds on throughput

In this section, lower bounds on throughput are presented, independent of the higher moments of the service time probability distribution functions, based on the computation of the vector of visit ratios for transitions as introduced in section 3 and on the transition liveness bounds, defined in section 4.

A "trivial" lower bound in steady-state performance for a live net system with a given vector of visit ratios for transitions is of course given by the inverse of the sum of the services times of all the transitions weighted by the vector of visit ratios. Since the net system is live, all transitions must be firable, and the sum of all service times multiplied by the number of occurrences of each transition in the average cycle of the model corresponds to any *complete sequentialization* of all the transition firings. This *pessimistic* behaviour is always reached in a marked graph consisting on a single loop of transitions and containing a single token in one of the places, independently of the higher moments of the probability distribution functions (this observation can be trivially confirmed by the computation of the upper bound, which in this case gives the same value).

This trivial lower bound has been improved in [CCS91b] for the case of live and bounded free choice systems based on the knowledge of the liveness bound $L(t)$ for all transitions t of the net system.

Theorem 6.1 [CCS91b] *For any live and bounded free choice system, an upper bound for the mean interfiring time* $\Gamma^{(j)}$ *of transition* t_j *can be computed as follows:*

$$\Gamma^{(j)} \leq \sum_{i=1}^{m} \frac{D_i^{(j)}}{L(t_i)} = \sum_{i=1}^{m} \frac{v_i^{(j)} s_i}{L(t_i)} \qquad (32)$$

We recall (cf. theorem 4.1) that in the case of live and bounded free choice systems:

1. The liveness bound equals the structural enabling bound for each transition (Theorem 4.1) and this one can be computed by solving (LPP1).

2. The vector of visit ratios for transitions is obtained by solving the linear system of equations (10).

Therefore, the lower bound for the throughput of live and bounded free choice systems can be computed efficiently. Its worst case complexity is *polynomial time* on the net size.

The lower bound in performance given by the computation of theorem 6.1 can be shown [CCCS89] to be reachable for any marked graph topology and for some assignment of PDF to the service time of transitions. Therefore, if nothing but the average value is known about the PDF of the service time of transitions, the bound provided by Theorem 6.1 is *tight*.

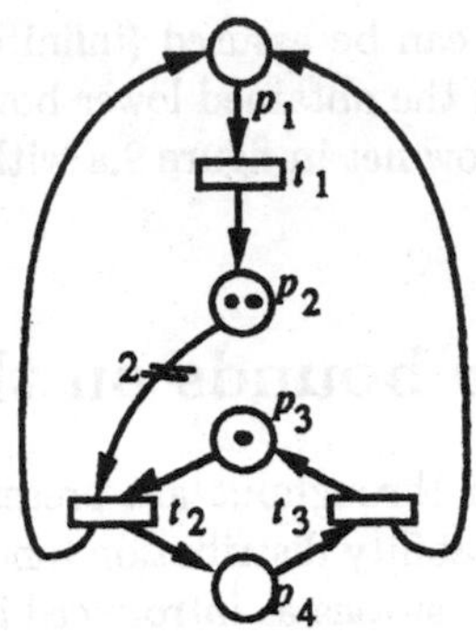

Figure 11: "Non-trivial" upper bound for the mean interfiring time cannot be applied.

Concerning non-free choice net systems, only the trivial bound, given by the sum of the mean service times of all transitions weighted by the vector of visit ratios, can be computed.

An example showing that the bound presented in theorem 6.1 is not valid for non-free choice net systems is depicted in figure 11, where s_1, s_2, s_3 are the mean service times of transitions t_1, t_2, t_3, respectively. For this net, the vector of visit ratios normalized for transition t_2 is

$$\vec{v}^{(2)} = (2, 1, 1)^T \tag{33}$$

and the liveness bounds of transitions are given by $L(t_1) = 2$, $L(t_2) = 1$, and $L(t_3) = 1$. Thus, the theorem 6.1 would give the bound:

$$\Gamma^{(2)} \leq s_1 + s_2 + s_3 \tag{34}$$

If exponentially distributed random variables (with means s_1, s_2, s_3; $s_1 \neq s_3$) are associated with transitions, the steady-state mean interfiring time for transition t_2 is

$$\Gamma^{(2)} = s_1 + s_2 + s_3 + \frac{s_1^2}{2(s_1 + s_3)} \tag{35}$$

which is greater than the value obtained from the theorem 6.1, thus the "non-trivial" bound does not hold in general.

7 Throughput bounds for Markovian Petri net systems

In sections 5 and 6, insensitive bounds (valid for any probability distribution function of service times and for any conflict resolution policy) on throughput have been presented. The quality of the bounds is poor in some cases due to the fact that only mean values of the involved random variables have been used for the computation. In order to improve the bounds, it will be necessary to take into account more information from the form of the probability distribution functions.

Exponential distribution of service times is one of the most usual in performance modelling of systems. The main reason is that the *memoryless property* greatly simplifies the analysis of models. Therefore, in this section we assume that timed transitions represent exponentially distributed services, the maximum number of servers being defined by the liveness of the transitions. Marking independent discrete probability distributions are used for defining the solution of conflicts among immediate transitions. The general techniques in the literature for the analysis of this particular case of stochastic Petri net models are, in general, *enumerative* since they are based on the solution of an embedded *continuous time Markov chain* whose state space is the set of reachable markings of the net system [AMBC84].

In summary, in this section we present better bounds for stochastic Petri net systems with exponentially distributed timed transitions, $L(t)$-server semantics, and marking independent discrete probability distributions for the resolution of conflicts, that we already call (section 2.1) *Markovian Petri net systems*, for short.

7.1 Embedded queueing networks

Insensitive lower bounds for the mean interfiring time of transitions were introduced in section 5 looking for the maximum of the mean interfiring time of transitions of isolated subnets generated by elementary P-semiflows. A more realistic computation of the mean interfiring time of transitions of these subsystems than that obtained from the analysis in complete isolation is considered now using, once more, the concept of liveness bound of transitions (section 4). The number of servers at each transition t of a given net in steady state is limited by its corresponding liveness bound $L(t)$ (or by its structural enabling bound which can always be computed in an efficient manner), because this bound is the *maximum reentrance* (or maximum self-concurrency) that the net structure and the marking allow for the transition.

The technique we are going to briefly present (a more detailed discussion can be found in [CS92]) is based on a *decomposition* of the original model in subsystems. In particular, we look for *embedded product-form closed monoclass queueing networks*. Well-known efficient algorithms exist for the computation of exact values or bounds for the throughput of such models [RL80, ZSEG82, ES83].

Therefore, let us concentrate in the search of such subsystems. How are they structurally characterized? From a topological point of view, they are *P-components*: strongly connected state machines. Timing of transitions must be done with exponentially distributed services. Moreover, conditional routing is modelled with decisions among immediate transitions, corresponding to generalized free conflicts in the whole system. In other words, if t_1 and t_2 are in conflict in the considered P-component, they should be in generalized free conflict in the original net: $PRE[t_1] = PRE[t_2]$. The reason for this constraint is that since we are going to consider P-components as product-form closed monoclass queueing networks with limited number of servers at stations (transitions), the throughput of these systems is *sensitive to the conflict resolution policy*, even if the relative firing rates are preserved. Therefore, conflicts in the P-component must be solved with exactly the same marking independent discrete probability distributions as in the whole net system, in order to obtain an optimistic bound for the throughput of the original net system. We call *RP-components* the subnets verifying the previous constraints.

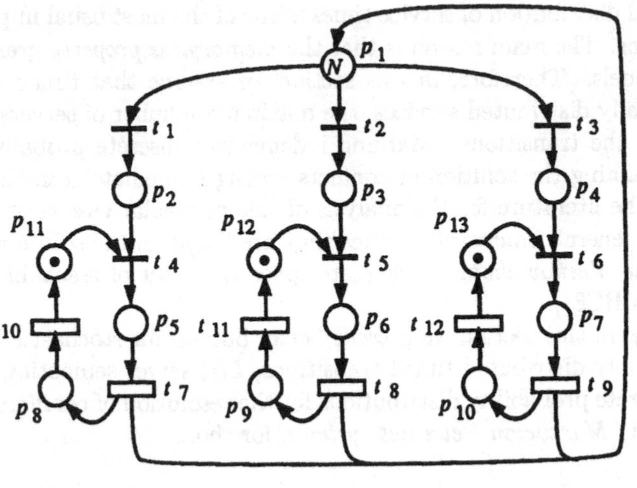

Figure 12: A live and bounded free choice system.

Definition 7.1 *Let $\mathcal{N}$ be a net and $\mathcal{N}_i$ a P-component of $\mathcal{N}$ (strongly connected state machine subnet). $\mathcal{N}_i$ is a routing preserving P-component, RP-component, iff for any pair of transitions, t_j and t_k, in conflict in $\mathcal{N}_i$, they are in generalized free (equal) conflict in the whole net $\mathcal{N}$: $PRE[t_j] = PRE[t_k]$.*

An improvement of the insensitive lower bound for the mean interfiring time of a transition t_j computed in theorem 5.1 can be eventually obtained computing the exact mean interfiring time of that transition in the RP-component generated by a minimal P-semiflow Y, with $L(t)$–server semantics for each involved transition t (in fact, it is not necessary that t_j belongs to the P-component; the bound for other transition can be computed and then weighted according to the visit ratios in order to compute a bound for t_j). The P-semiflow Y can be selected among the optimal solutions of (LPP3) or it can be just a feasible *near-optimal* solution.

As an example, let us consider the net system depicted in figure 12. Assume that routing probabilities are equal to 1/3 for t_1, t_2, and t_3, and that t_7, t_8, t_9, t_{10}, t_{11}, t_{12} have exponentially distributed service times with mean values $s_7 = s_8 = s_9 = 10$, $s_{10} = s_{11} = s_{12} = 1$. The elementary P-semiflows of the net are:

$$\begin{aligned} Y_1 &= (1,1,1,1,1,1,1,0,0,0,0,0,0)^T \\ Y_2 &= (0,0,0,0,1,0,0,1,0,0,1,0,0)^T \\ Y_3 &= (0,0,0,0,0,1,0,0,1,0,0,1,0)^T \\ Y_4 &= (0,0,0,0,0,0,1,0,0,1,0,0,1)^T \end{aligned} \tag{36}$$

Then, if the initial marking of p_{11}, p_{12}, and p_{13} is 1 token, and the initial marking of p_1 is N tokens, the lower bound for the mean interfiring time derived from (LPP3) is

$$\Gamma^{(1)}_{(\text{LPP3})} = \max\{30/N, 11, 11, 11\} \tag{37}$$

For $N = 1$, the previous bound, obtained from Y_1, gives the value 30, while the exact mean interfiring time is 31.06. For $N = 2$, the bound is 15 and it is derived also from Y_1 (mean

N	$\Gamma^{(1)}$	$\Gamma^{(1)}_{(Y_1)_L}$	$\Gamma^{(1)}_{(\text{LPP3})}$
1	31.06	30	30
2	21.05	20	15
3	17.71	16.67	11
4	16.03	15	11
5	15.03	14	11
10	13.02	12	11
15	12.35	11.34	11

Table 2: Exact mean interfiring time of t_1, bounds obtained using (LPP3), and the improvements presented in this section, for different initial markings of p_1 in the net system of figure 12.

interfiring time of the P-component generated by Y_1, considered in isolation with infinite server semantics for transitions). This bound does not take into account the queueing time at places due to synchronizations (t_4, t_5, and t_6), and the exact mean interfiring time of t_1 is $\Gamma^{(1)} = 21.05$. For larger values of N, the bound obtained from (LPP3) is equal to 11 (and is given by P-semiflows Y_2, Y_3 and Y_4). This bound can be improved if the P-component generated by Y_1 is considered with liveness bounds of transitions t_7, t_8, and t_9 reduced to 1 (which is the liveness bound of these transitions in the whole net).

The results obtained for different values of N are collected in table 2. Exact values of mean interfiring times for the P-component generated by Y_1 were computed using the *mean value analysis* algorithm [RL80]. This algorithm has $O(A^2B)$ worst case time complexity, where $A = Y^T \cdot M_0$ is the number of tokens at the P-component and $B = Y^T \cdot PRE \cdot \mathbb{1}$ is the number of involved transitions ($\mathbb{1}$ is a vector with all entries equal to 1). Exact computation on the original system takes several minutes in a *Sun SPARC Workstation* while bounds computation takes only a few seconds.

We also remark that other techniques for the computation of throughput upper bounds (instead of exact values) of closed product-form monoclass queueing networks could be used, such as, for instance, *balanced throughput upper bounds* [ZSEG82] or *throughput upper bounds hierarchies* [ES83]. Hierarchies of bounds guarantee different levels of accuracy (including the exact solution), by investing the necessary computational effort. This provides also a hierarchy of bounds for the mean interfiring time of transitions of Markovian Petri net systems.

Finally, the technique sketched in this section can be applied to the more general case of *Coxian* distributions (instead of exponential) for the service time of those transitions having either liveness bound equal to one (i.e., single-server stations) or liveness bound equal to the number of tokens in the RP-component (i.e., delay stations). The reason is that in these cases the embedded queueing network has also product-form solution, according to a classical theorem of queueing theory: the *BCMP theorem* [BCMP75].

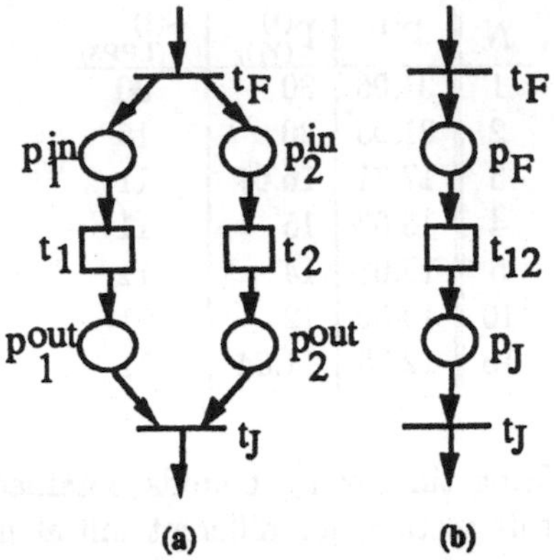

Figure 13: (a) Elementary fork-join and (b) its reduction.

7.2 Transformation techniques

The lower bounds for the throughput of transitions presented in section 6 are valid for any probability distribution function of service times but can be very pessimistic in some cases. In this section, an improvement of such results is briefly explained for the case of those net systems in which the following *performance monotonicity* property holds: *a local pessimistic transformation leads to a slower transformed net system* (i.e., a pessimistic local transformation guarantees a pessimistic global behaviour). This property is not always true as already mentionned (see, for instance, figure 10). Using the concept of *stochastic ordering* [Ros83], a pessimistic transformation is, for example, to substitute the PDF of a service (or token-subnet traversing) time by a *stochastically greater* PDF. Live and bounded free choice is a class of systems for which the above performance monotonicity property holds (property 5.2 is a particular case). Details about the techniques presented here can be found in [CSS91]. The basic ideas are:

1. To use local pessimistic transformation rules to obtain a net system "simpler" than the original (e.g., with smaller state space) and with equal or less performance.
2. To evaluate the performance for the derived net system, using insensitive bounds presented in section 6, exact analysis, or any other applicable technique.

In order to obtain better bounds (after these two steps) than the values computed in section 6, at least one of the transformation rules of item 1 must be less pessimistic than a total sequentialization of the involved transitions. We present first a rule whose application allows such *strict* improvement: the *fork-join rule*. Secondly, a rule that does not change at all the performance (*deletion of multistep preserving places*) is presented. Finally, a rule that does not follow the above ideas is also presented: the goal of this rule (*split of a transition*) is to make reapplicable the other transformation rules.

The most simple case of fork-join subnet that can be considered is depicted in figure 13.a. In this case, if transitions t_1 and t_2 have exponential services X_1 and X_2 with means s_1 and s_2, they are reduced to a single transition (figure 13.b) with exponential service time and mean:

$$s_{12} = E[\max\{X_1, X_2\}] = s_1 + s_2 - \left(\frac{1}{s_1} + \frac{1}{s_2}\right)^{-1} \tag{38}$$

Therefore, even if the *mean traversing time* of the reduced subnet by a single token has been preserved, it has been substituted by a stochastically greater variable. A trivial extension can be applied if the fork-join subnet includes more than two transitions in parallel.

Other transformation rules that have been presented in [CSS91] are:

Deletion of a multistep preserving place: allows to remove some places without changing the *exact* performance indices of the stochastic net system. In fact the places that can be deleted are those whose elimination preserves the multisets of transitions simultaneously firable in all reachable markings (e.g., place p_{14} in figure 14.a). The size of the state space of the model is preserved and also the exact throughput of transitions of the system.

Reduction of transitions in sequence: reduces a series of exponential services to a single exponential service with the same mean. Intuitively, this transformation makes indivisible the service time of two or more transitions representing elementary actions which always occur one after the other and lead to no side condition (e.g., transitions t_6 and t_9 in figure 14.a). Therefore, the state space of the model is reduced. The throughput of transitions is, in general, reduced.

Split of a transition: this is not a state space reduction rule since it increases the state space of the transformed net system. The advantage of the rule is that it allows to proceed further in the reduction process using again the previous rules (e.g., transition t_3 in figure 14.c).

An example of application of all above transformation rules is depicted in figure 14 for a strongly connected marked graph with exponential timing. Let us assume that mean service times of transitions are: $s_i = 1$, $i = 1, 2, 3, 7, 8, 12, 13, 14$ and $s_i = 10$ otherwise.

In order to compute firstly the insensitive lower bounds on throughput introduced in section 6, it is necessary to derive the liveness bounds of transitions (section 4). In this case it is easy to see that $L(t_j) = 2$ for every transition t_j.

The vector of visit ratios of a marked graph is the unique minimal T-semiflow of the net: $\vec{v}^{(j)} = \mathbb{1}$, for all transitions t_j. Therefore, the insensitive upper bound (valid for any probability distribution function of service times) of the mean interfiring time of any transition of the net system is $\Gamma \leq 34$. This value can be reached for some distributions of service times (see comment on tightness on section 6). Nevertheless, if services are exponential the exact mean interfiring time of transitions is $\Gamma = 14.15$.

The quantitative results of the transformation process illustrated in figure 14 are shown in table 3. We remark that the bound has been improved in polynomial time from 34 to 19.2.

8 Bounds for other performance indices

Up to this point we just concentrated on throughput bounds. The purpose of this section is to bring the idea that given some throughput bounds, bounds for other performance

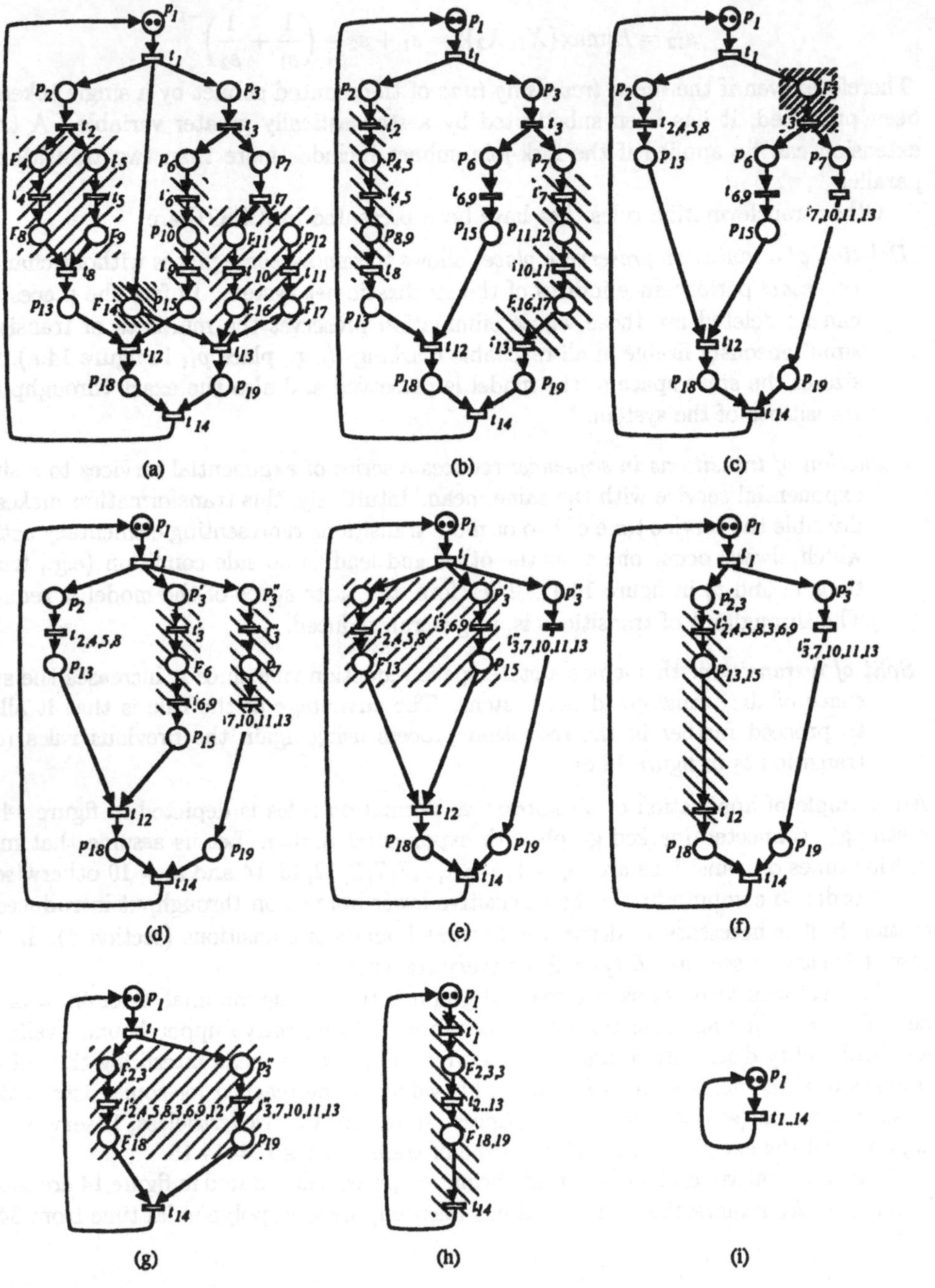

Figure 14: A complete reduction process. The relative error between insensitive bound and exact value diminishes from 140% to 35%.

System	Γ^{ub}	Relative error
Fig. 14.a	34	140 %
Fig. 14.b	29	105 %
Fig. 14.c	29	105 %
Fig. 14.d	29.5	108 %
Fig. 14.e	29.5	108 %
Fig. 14.f	24.8	75 %
Fig. 14.g	24.8	75 %
Fig. 14.h	19.2	35 %
Fig. 14.i	19.2	35 %

Table 3: Successive improvements of the upper bound for the mean interfiring time of transitions of the net in figure 14 and relative errors with respect to the exact value $\Gamma = 14.15$.

indices can be computed using classical formulas in QN theory such as Little's formula.

The number of tokens in a place defines the lenght of the represented queue (including the customers in service!). Thus it may be important to known bounds on average marking of places.

As an example, in [CCS91b] it has been shown that the following are lower and upper bounds for the average marking, $\overline{M}$:

$$\overline{M}^{lb} = PRE \cdot S \cdot \vec{\Sigma}^{lb} \tag{39}$$

$$\overline{M}^{ub}(p) = \max \{ M(p) \mid B^T \cdot M = B^T \cdot M_0 \ , \ M \geq \overline{M}^{lb} \} \tag{LPP4}$$

where $S = \text{diag}(s_i)$ and the rows of B^T are the basis of left annullers of C (the incidence matrix of the net).

As an interesting remark, the reader can check that a structural absolute bound for the marking of a place is given for conservative nets (i.e., $\exists Y > 0$, $Y^T \cdot C = 0$) by the following expression:

$$SB(p) = \max \{ M(p) \mid B^T \cdot M = B^T \cdot M_0 \ , \ M \geq 0 \} \tag{LPP5}$$

The constraint in (LPP5) being weaker than that in (LPP4) ($M \geq \overline{M}^{lb}$ is transformed into $M \geq 0$), it is obvious that $\overline{M}^{ub} \leq SB(p)$.

9 Conclusions

The main motivation to write this paper has been to show how the qualitative theory (and in particular the structural analysis techniques) of net systems can be useful in performance bounds computation for stochastic Petri net models. Several interesting questions that were easily answered in the past for classical queueing networks turn into non-trivial problems (ergodicity, visit ratios, number of servers at stations, performance bounds) in the case of stochastic Petri net systems. However, structural techniques can be used in order to solve those problems in an efficient way, at least for important subclasses of net systems. Moreover, the benefits of this approach have been not only for the quantitative understanding of the models but also for the qualitative point of view: some fundamental new results have appeared as by-products of the performance perspective. We remark the following points among those presented in this survey:

1. The (quoted) equation "SPNs = PNs + time = QNs + synchronization" must be always in mind in performance evaluation of stochastic Petri nets, since both qualitative theory of Petri nets and results from queueing theory are needed in order to solve the stated problems.

2. The computability of the vector of visit ratios from the different system parameters (structure, routing policy, initial marking, and service times) induces a new hierarchy of nets, being re-encountered well-known subclasses (e.g., marked graphs, free choice nets). Specially important appear those nets as FRT and subclasses (free choice, marked graphs...), whose vector of visit ratios does not depend neither on the initial marking nor in the service times (i.e., the vector of visit ratios can be computed using only structural and routing information).

3. The rank theorem [CCS91b, ES91], suggested by the performance approach, has important consequences in the qualitative theory of nets. Some extensions of that theorem appear in [CCS90b] for the characterization of structural liveness in general nets.

4. The enabling bound is a quantitative generalization of the basic concept of enabling, and is closely related to the concept of marking bound of a place.

5. The liveness bound is also a quantitative generalization of the classical concept of liveness.

6. Performance bounds can be derived from structural components and properties: P-semiflows, T-semiflows, multisets of circuits, structural enabling bounds...

7. An step to extend the classical theory of qualitative transformation/reduction of nets has been achieved, including quantitative aspects, for deriving throughput bounds of Markovian Petri net system.

8. As in the case of (qualitative) structural theory of net systems, the derived performance-oriented results are specially powerful for some well-known subclasses (e.g., live and bounded free choice net systems).

Additional results to those presented here can be found in [CS90], related with exact performance analysis of a net subclass. In particular, for ***totally open deterministic systems of Markovian sequential processes***, exact computation of limit throughput can be done in polynomial time, assuming ***consistency*** of the net and some ***synchronic distance relations*** among transitions.

In sections 5, 6, and 7, we focused on the computation of throughput bounds. From these results and using classical laws from queueing theory, bounds can be derived for other interesting performance indices (section 8), such as the *mean queue lengths* (or mean marking of places), or *mean response times* (or mean residence times of tokens at places).

In this paper, we have tried to clearly state concepts and results, illustrating them by means of examples and omitting the proofs (for more technical presentations the readers should consult the references). The net based examples have been choosed to illustrate the theory. Applications of some of the presented results in the manufacturing domain are considered in [CCS90a].

We are far from solving many of the problems related with performance analysis of Petri net systems. However, what is clear now is that such problems must be attacked by deeply bridging qualitative and quantitative aspects of the model and making use of several active fields like Petri net theory, graph theory, linear algebra, convex geometry, queueing networks, and applied stochastic processes.

Acknowledgements

This work was partially supported by the DEMON Esprit Basic Research Action 3148 and the Spanish Plan Nacional de Investigación, Grant PRONTIC-0358/89. The authors are indebted to G. Chiola of the Università di Torino and J. M. Colom of the Universidad de Zaragoza, co-authors of many of the results surveyed in this work. The comments and suggestions of three referees helped us for the improvement of the submitted draft.

References

[AM90] M. Ajmone Marsan. Stochastic Petri nets: An elementary introduction. In G. Rozenberg, editor, *Advances in Petri Nets 1989*, volume 424 of *LNCS*, pages 1–29. Springer-Verlag, Berlin, 1990.

[AMBB+89] M. Ajmone Marsan, G. Balbo, A. Bobbio, G. Chiola, G. Conte, and A. Cumani. The effect of execution policies on the semantics and analysis of stochastic Petri nets. *IEEE Transactions on Software Engineering*, 15(7):832–846, July 1989.

[AMBC84] M. Ajmone Marsan, G. Balbo, and G. Conte. A class of generalized stochastic Petri nets for the performance evaluation of multiprocessor systems. *ACM Transactions on Computer Systems*, 2(2):93–122, May 1984.

[AMBCC87] M. Ajmone Marsan, G. Balbo, G. Chiola, and G. Conte. Generalized stochastic Petri nets revisited: Random switches and priorities. In *Proceedings of the International Workshop on Petri Nets and Performance Models*, pages 44–53, Madison, WI, USA, August 1987. IEEE-Computer Society Press.

[AMBCD86] M. Ajmone Marsan, G. Balbo, G. Chiola, and S. Donatelli. On the product-form solution of a class of multiple-bus multiprocessor system models. *Journal of Systems and Software*, 6(1,2):117–124, May 1986.

[BCMP75] F. Baskett, K. M. Chandy, R. R. Muntz, and F. Palacios. Open, closed, and mixed networks of queues with different classes of customers. *Journal of the ACM*, 22(2):248–260, April 1975.

[Bes87] E. Best. Structure theory of Petri nets: The free choice hiatus. In W. Brauer, W. Reisig, and G. Rozenberg, editors, *Advances in Petri Nets 1986 - Part I*, volume 254 of *LNCS*, pages 168–205. Springer-Verlag, Berlin, 1987.

[Cam90] J. Campos. *Performance Bounds for Synchronized Queueing Networks*. PhD thesis, Departamento de Ingeniería Eléctrica e Informática, Universidad de Zaragoza, Spain, October 1990. Research Report GISI-RR-90-20.

[CC91] J. Campos and J. M. Colom. A reachable throughput upper bound for live and safe free choice nets. In *Proceedings of the Twelfth International Conference on Application and Theory of Petri Nets*, pages 237–256, Gjern, Denmark, June 1991.

[CCCS89] J. Campos, G. Chiola, J. M. Colom, and M. Silva. Tight polynomial bounds for steady-state performance of marked graphs. In *Proceedings of the 3rd International Workshop on Petri Nets and Performance Models*, pages 200–209, Kyoto, Japan, December 1989. IEEE-Computer Society Press.

[CCCS90] J. Campos, G. Chiola, J. M. Colom, and M. Silva. Properties and performance bounds for timed marked graphs. Research Report GISI-RR-90-17, Departamento de Ingeniería Eléctrica e Informática, Universidad de Zaragoza, Spain, July 1990. To appear in *IEEE Transactions on Circuit and Systems*.

[CCS90a] J. Campos, J. M. Colom, and M. Silva. Performance evaluation of repetitive automated manufacturing systems. In *Proceedings of the Rensselaer's Second International Conference on Computer Integrated Manufacturing*, pages 74–81, Rensselaer Polytechnic Institute, Troy, NY, USA, May 1990. IEEE-Computer Society Press.

[CCS90b] J. M. Colom, J. Campos, and M. Silva. On liveness analysis through linear algebraic techniques. In *Proceedings of the Annual General Meeting of ESPRIT Basic Research Action 3148 Design Methods Based on Nets (DEMON)*, Paris, France, June 1990.

[CCS91a] J. Campos, G. Chiola, and M. Silva. Ergodicity and throughput bounds of Petri nets with unique consistent firing count vector. *IEEE Transactions on Software Engineering*, 17(2):117–125, February 1991.

[CCS91b] J. Campos, G. Chiola, and M. Silva. Properties and performance bounds for closed free choice synchronized monoclass queueing networks. *IEEE Transactions on Automatic Control*, 36(12):1368–1382, December 1991.

[CCS91c] J. Campos, J. M. Colom, and M. Silva. Improving throughput upper bounds for net based models. In *Proceedings of the IMACS-IFAC SYMPOSIUM Modelling and Control of Technological Systems*, pages 573–582, Lille, France, May 1991. To appear in the *IMACS Transactions*.

[CS90] J. Campos and M. Silva. Steady-state performance evaluation of totally open systems of Markovian sequential processes. In M. Cosnard and C. Girault, editors, *Decentralized Systems*, pages 427–438. Elsevier Science Publishers B.V. (North-Holland), Amsterdam, The Netherlands, 1990.

[CS91] J. M. Colom and M. Silva. Improving the linearly based characterization of P/T nets. In G. Rozenberg, editor, *Advances in Petri Nets 1990*, volume 483 of *LNCS*, pages 113–145. Springer-Verlag, Berlin, 1991.

[CS92] J. Campos and M. Silva. Embedded queueing networks and the improvement of insensitive performance bounds for Markovian Petri net systems. Research Report GISI-RR-92-10, Departamento de Ingeniería Eléctrica e Informática, Universidad de Zaragoza, Spain, February 1992.

[CSS91] J. Campos, B. Sánchez, and M. Silva. Throughput lower bounds for Markovian Petri nets: Transformation techniques. In *Proceedings of the 4th International Workshop on Petri Nets and Performance Models*, pages 322–331, Melbourne, Australia, December 1991. IEEE-Computer Society Press.

[DLT90] Y. Dallery, Z. Liu, and D. Towsley. Equivalence, reversibility and symmetry properties in fork/join queueing networks with blocking. Technical report, MASI 90-32, University Paris 6, 4 Place Jussieu, Paris, France, June 1990.

[ES83] D. L. Eager and K. C. Sevcik. Performance bound hierarchies for queueing networks. *ACM Transactions on Computer Systems*, 1(2):99–115, May 1983.

[ES91] J. Esparza and M. Silva. On the analysis and synthesis of free choice systems. In G. Rozenberg, editor, *Advances in Petri Nets 1990*, volume 483 of *LNCS*, pages 243–286. Springer-Verlag, Berlin, 1991.

[Esp90] J. Esparza. *Structure Theory of Free Choice Nets*. PhD thesis, Departamento de Ingeniería Eléctrica e Informática, Universidad de Zaragoza, Spain, June 1990. Research Report GISI-RR-90-03.

[FFN91] G. Florin, C. Fraize, and S. Natkin. Stochastic Petri nets: Properties, applications and tools. *Microelectronics and Reliability*, 31(4):669–698, 1991.

[FN85] G. Florin and S. Natkin. Les réseaux de Petri stochastiques. *Technique et Science Informatiques*, 4(1):143–160, February 1985. In French.

[GN67] W. J. Gordon and G. F. Newell. Closed queueing systems with exponential servers. *Operations Research*, 15:254–265, 1967.

[Hac72] M. H. T. Hack. Analysis of production schemata by Petri nets. M. S. Thesis, TR-94, M.I.T., Boston, USA, 1972.

[Kle75] L. Kleinrock. *Queueing Systems Volume I: Theory.* John Wiley & Sons, New York, NY, USA, 1975.

[Kle76] L. Kleinrock. *Queueing Systems Volume II: Computer Applications.* John Wiley & Sons, New York, NY, USA, 1976.

[Lau87] K. Lautenbach. Linear algebraic calculation of deadlocks and traps. In K. Voss, H. Genrich, and G. Rozenberg, editors, *Concurrency and Nets*, pages 315–336. Springer-Verlag, Berlin, 1987.

[Lav89] S. S. Lavenberg. A perspective on queueing models of computer performance. *Performance Evaluation*, 10:53–76, 1989.

[Lit61] J. D. C. Little. A proof of the queueing formula $L = \lambda W$. *Operations Research*, 9:383–387, 1961.

[LZGS84] E. D. Lazowska, J. Zahorjan, G. S. Graham, and K. C. Sevcik. *Quantitative System Performance.* Prentice-Hall, Inc., Englewood Cliffs, NJ, USA, 1984.

[Mol82] M. K. Molloy. Performance analysis using stochastic Petri nets. *IEEE Transaction on Computers*, 31(9):913–917, September 1982.

[Mol85] M.K. Molloy. Fast bounds for stochastic Petri nets. In *Proceedings of the International Workshop on Timed Petri Nets*, pages 244–249, Torino, Italy, July 1985. IEEE-Computer Society Press.

[Mur89] T. Murata. Petri nets: Properties, analysis, and applications. *Proceedings of the IEEE*, 77(4):541–580, April 1989.

[NRKT89] G. L. Nemhauser, A. H. G. Rinnooy Kan, and M. J. Todd, editors. *Optimization*, volume 1 of *Handbooks in Operations Research and Management Science.* North-Holland, Amsterdam, The Netherlands, 1989.

[Pet81] J.L. Peterson. *Petri Net Theory and the Modeling of Systems.* Prentice-Hall, Englewood Cliffs, NJ, USA, 1981.

[PNPM87] *Proceedings of the International Workshop on Petri Nets and Performance Models*, Madison, WI, USA, August 1987. IEEE-Computer Society Press.

[PNPM89] *Proceedings of the 3rd International Workshop on Petri Nets and Performance Models*, Kyoto, Japan, December 1989. IEEE-Computer Society Press.

[PNPM91] *Proceedings of the 4th International Workshop on Petri Nets and Performance Models*, Melbourne, Australia, December 1991. IEEE-Computer Society Press.

[Ram74] C. Ramchandani. *Analysis of Asynchronous Concurrent Systems by Petri Nets.* PhD thesis, MIT, Cambridge, MA, USA, February 1974.

[RH80] C. V. Ramamoorthy and G. S. Ho. Performance evaluation of asynchronous concurrent systems using Petri nets. *IEEE Transactions on Software Engineering*, 6(5):440–449, September 1980.

[RL80] M. Reiser and S. S. Lavenberg. Mean value analysis of closed multichain queueing networks. *Journal of the ACM*, 27(2):313–322, April 1980.

[Ros83] S. M. Ross. *Stochastic Processes.* John Wiley & Sons, New York, NY, USA, 1983.

[SC88] M. Silva and J. M. Colom. On the computation of structural synchronic invariants in P/T nets. In G. Rozenberg, editor, *Advances in Petri Nets 1988*, volume 340 of *LNCS*, pages 386–417. Springer-Verlag, Berlin, 1988.

[Sif78] J. Sifakis. Use of Petri nets for performance evaluation. *Acta Cybernetica*, 4(2):185–202, 1978.

[Sil85] M. Silva. *Las Redes de Petri en la Automática y la Informática.* Editorial AC, Madrid, 1985. In Spanish.

[SMK82] C. H. Sauer, E. A. MacNair, and J. F. Kurose. The research queueing package: past, present, and future. In *Proceedings of the 1982 National Computer Conference.* AFIPS, 1982.

[SY86] J. G. Shanthikumar and D. D. Yao. The effect of increasing service rates in a closed queueing network. *Journal of Applied Probability*, 23:474–483, 1986.

[TPN85] *Proceedings of the International Workshop on Timed Petri Nets*, Torino, Italy, July 1985. IEEE-Computer Society Press.

[VZL87] M. Vernon, J. Zahorjan, and E. D. Lazowska. A comparison of performance Petri nets and queueing network models. In *Proceedings of the 3rd International Workshop on Modelling Techniques and Performance Evaluation*, pages 181–192, Paris, France, March 1987. AFCET.

[ZSEG82] J. Zahorjan, K. C. Sevcik, D. L. Eager, and B. Galler. Balanced job bound analysis of queueing networks. *Communications of the ACM*, 25(2):134–141, February 1982.

[Zub91] W. M. Zuberek. Timed Petri nets: Definitions, properties and applications. *Microelectronics and Reliability*, 31(4):627–644, 1991.

[ZZ90] W. M. Zuberek and M. S. Zuberek. Transformations of timed Petri nets and performance analysis. In *Proceedings of the Midwest Simposium on Circuits and Systems'90 (Special Session on Petri Net Models)*, pages 1–5, 1990.

A SURVEY OF RECOGNIZABLE LANGUAGES OF INFINITE TRACES*

Paul GASTIN
Université PARIS 6
LITP, Institut Blaise Pascal
4, place Jussieu
75 252 PARIS CEDEX 05
FRANCE
gastin@litp.ibp.fr

Antoine PETIT
Université PARIS SUD
LRI, URA CNRS 410
Bât. 490
91 405 ORSAY CEDEX
FRANCE
petit@lri.lri.fr

ABSTRACT: A. Mazurkiewicz [Maz77] defined traces in order to represent non-sequential processes. In order to describe non-sequential processes which never terminate, e.g. distributed operating systems, the notion of infinite traces is needed. The aim of this survey is to present in a uniform way the results on recognizable infinite trace languages stated in [Gas91], [GPZ91] and [DGP91]. The proofs of the presented results are not proposed here but can be found in the original papers.

Keywords: Semantics of concurrent processes, Infinite traces, Recognizable languages.

CONTENTS

1. Introduction

The concept of traces has been introduced by A. Mazurkiewicz [Maz77] as a suitable semantics for non-sequential processes. There are at least two equivalent ways to see a trace. A trace can be considered as the set of all possible sequential observations of a concurrent process. Each sequential observation is described, in a classical way, by a finite word. Hence, a trace is an equivalence class of words. An equivalent point of view is to see a trace as a finite labelled acyclic graph where edges represent dependence between actions. Such a graph is called a dependence graph and the intuitive meaning is that an execution has to respect the induced partial order. Whatever the approach chosen, the definition of the concatenation of two traces is easy and natural and traces form a monoid. Originally, this monoid has been introduced and studied by combinatorists [CF69] for other purposes. But it has particularly been investigated

---

* This work has been partly supported by the ESPRIT Basic Research Action N° 3148 (DEMON).

as a model for concurrent systems since the pioneering work of Mazurkiewicz. Let us refer, for instance, to surveys [Maz86, AR88, Per89] or to the monograph [Die90] where also extensive bibliographies on the subject are given.

In order to describe non-sequential processes which never terminate, e.g. distributed operating systems, the notion of infinite traces is needed. An infinite (real) trace is an infinite dependence graph where every vertex has only a finite past. This notion has been introduced and studied in distinct frameworks by many authors: Flé and Roucairol [FR85] for problems of infinite serialisabilities, Best and Devillers [BD87] in relation with Petri Nets, Mazurkiewicz [Maz86], Gastin [Gas90a] and Kwiatkowska [Kwi90] to generalize the notion of finite traces. They have all proposed definitions which turn out to be equivalent. Then, the theory of infinite real traces has been developed in several papers. Topological properties of infinite traces [BMP89, Gas90b], PoSet properties [Kwi90, GR91] and links with event structures [GR91] have in particular been studied.

The concatenation of two infinite dependence graphs can naturally be defined. Unfortunately, the restriction of the graph concatenation to real traces is not an internal operation since the concatenation of two real traces may contain vertices with an infinite past. A first obvious solution to this problem is to consider only a partial concatenation on real traces. Another possibility, proposed by Kwiatkowska [Kwi91], is to erase vertices with an infinite past. Acting this way, she obtained a non associative total concatenation on real traces. Independently, and in order to define an associative total operation, Gastin [Gas90a] added a new element, the error, used as a result for all non real concatenations. Hence, he obtained a monoid which is in fact the Rees quotient of the monoid of infinite dependence graphs by an appropriate ideal (the set of infinite dependence graphs which have vertices with infinite past). One of the main drawbacks of this concatenation is that when all actions are pairwise dependent, the trace monoid is not isomorphic to the free monoid of (finite and infinite) words. Diekert [Die91] proposed a new solution to the problem of concatenation. He defined the notion of complex traces using a suitable quotient of the set of dependence graphs and studied their topological properties. A complex trace is simply a real trace together with a second component which is some alphabetic information. Acting this way, a concatenation between complex traces is defined, which combines both the free case and the pure concurrent one.

Recognizable languages describe the behaviour of finite state systems and hence form one of the basic families of a monoid. The family of recognizable real trace languages has been introduced in [Gas90] and studied in [Gas91, GPZ91, GP92, Ebi92], whereas recognizable complex trace languages have been investigated in [DGP91]. The aim of this survey is to give a uniform presentation of the results on recognizable infinite trace languages.
We will now recall some aspects of the theory of recognizable languages of finite traces and infinite words. Next we present the results of recognizable infinite trace languages.
For finite and infinite words, there exist several equivalent characterizations of the family of recognizable languages. The principal ones are: recognizability by a morphism in a finite monoid, acceptance by a finite automaton, definition by a rational expression (Kleene's theorem) or by a monadic second order logic formula. The reader is referred to [Eil74, Tho90, PP91] for surveys on recognizable (infinite) word languages.

For finite traces, the recognizable languages are defined as the languages recognized by morphisms in finite monoids (as usual in a finitary monoid). These languages are exactly those recognized by "diamond finite automata" or by the more specific asynchronous (cellular) automata introduced by Zielonka [Zie87, Zie89, CMZ89]. A lot of papers are devoted to the study of closure properties of the family of recognizable languages of finite traces. This family is closed under boolean operations and concatenation [Fli74, CP85, Och85] but it turns out that a trace language T may be recognizable whereas T^* is not. Therefore the family of recognizable trace languages is strictly included in the family of rational trace languages i.e. the smallest family of trace languages containing the finite languages and closed under union, concatenation and star iteration. In order to generalize Kleene's theorem to trace languages it was then necessary to find new operations instead of the star iteration. To this purpose, several papers discussed sufficient conditions ensuring the recognizability of T^* [CM85, FR85, Sak87, Och90, Roz90, MR91]. But the most interesting sufficient condition has been found independently by Métivier [Mét86] and Ochmanski [Och85]. They showed that if a recognizable language T is connected then the language T^* is recognizable too. Moreover Ochmanski defined a concurrent version of the star iteration, the concurrent iteration, and proved the equality of the families of recognizable trace languages and co-rational trace languages. This latter family is obtained as the rational one by simply replacing the star iteration by the concurrent one.
The family of recognizable infinite trace languages is defined using recognizing morphisms in finite monoids. This family is a boolean algebra which is closed under concatenation, left and right quotients. But similarly to the finite case, this family is neither closed under Kleene's iteration nor under infinite iteration. Therefore the same problems as in the finite case arise: find sufficient conditions ensuring the recognizability of T^* and T^ω and new operations to obtain a generalization of Kleene's and Ochmanski's theorems. In fact, as long as the Kleene's iteration of a language of finite traces is recognizable, then so is its infinite iteration. Hence, any sufficient condition ensuring the recognizability of T^* holds also for T^ω. Then, we generalize the notion of connectivity to infinite traces. We show that if a language T containing connected (infinite) traces only is recognizable then so are T^* and T^ω. Then we propose a canonical representation for recognizable trace languages. We define concurrent iterations on trace languages and the family of co-rational trace languages is introduced. This family is equal to the family of recognizable trace languages. Hence we obtain a generalization of Kleene's and Ochmanski's theorems to languages of infinite traces.

Instead of presenting formal proofs, we choose in this survey to illustrate definitions and results by numerous examples. The detailed proofs can be found in the original papers [Gas91, GPZ91, DGP91].

2. Preliminaries

In this section, we recall definitions and results on traces which are relevant in this paper. For more detailed discussions, the reader is referred to [Maz86, AR88, Per89, Die90] as concerns finite traces, to [Gas90b] as concerns real traces and to [Die91] for complex traces.

2.1. Dependence graphs

In the following (X,D) denotes a finite dependence alphabet, i.e., X is a finite alphabet together with a reflexive and symmetric dependence relation $D \subseteq X \times X$. We denote by $I = X \times X \setminus D$ the independence relation which is the complement of D. For a subset $A \subseteq X$, define $D(A) = \{b \in X / \exists\, a \in A, (a,b) \in D\}$ and $I(A) = X \setminus D(A) = \{b \in X / \forall\, a \in A, (a,b) \in I\}$. **A dependence graph** over (X,D) is (an isomorphism class of) a labelled acyclic graph $[V,E,\lambda]$ where V is the (at most) countable set of vertices, $E \subseteq V \times V$ is the set of arcs, $\lambda: V \rightarrow X$ is the labelling and which satisfies:

i) the induced partial order $(V, \leq)$ is well-founded: there does not exist an infinite descending chain i.e. an infinite sequence (x_i) such that $(x_{i+1}, x_i) \in E$ for all i.

ii) edges are between dependent vertices:

$$\forall\, x,y \in V,\ ((\lambda(x),\lambda(y)) \in D \Leftrightarrow x = y \text{ or } (x,y) \in E \text{ or } (y,x) \in E$$

Then, for any a in X, the restriction to the set of vertices with label a is well-ordered. This allows us to think of dependence graphs by standard representations where the vertices are pairs (a,i) with $a \in A$ and i is a countable ordinal.

For instance, let (X,D) = a — b — c, a dependence graph is presented in Figure 2.1(a). Since we are only interested in the isomorphism class of the graph, we only write the labelling of vertices. Moreover, in order to simplify the pictures, we will not draw the edges which can be obtained by composition of other edges. Using these remarks, the dependence graph of Figure 2.1(a) can be simply presented as in Figure 2.1(b). As another example, an infinite dependence graph is presented in Figure 2.2.

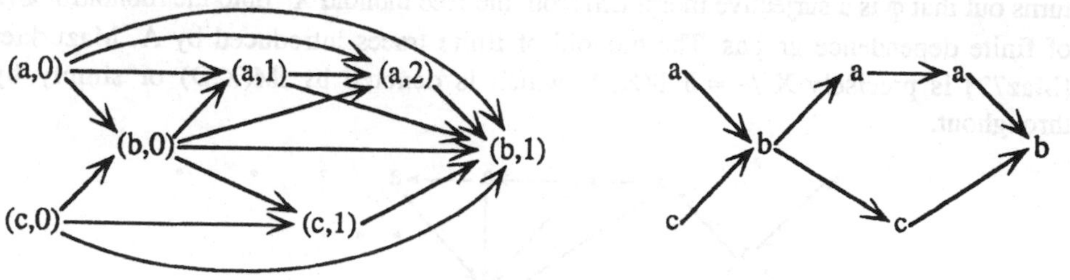

(a) Figure 2.1 (b)

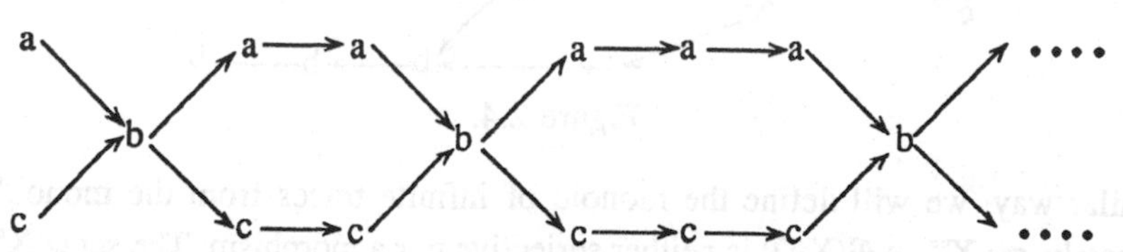

Figure 2.2.

The set of dependence graphs over the dependence alphabet (X,D) is denoted by $\mathbb{G}(X,D)$ or simply by $\mathbb{G}$ when there is no risk of confusion. It is a monoid by the operation $[V_1,E_1,\lambda_1][V_2,E_2,\lambda_2] = [V,E,\lambda]$ where $[V,E,\lambda]$ is the disjoint union of $[V_1,E_1,\lambda_1]$ and

$[V_2,E_2,\lambda_2]$ together with new arcs (p_1,p_2) for all vertices $p_1 \in V_1$, $p_2 \in V_2$ such that $(\lambda_1(p_1),\lambda_2(p_2)) \in D$ (see Figure 2.3). The neutral element is the empty graph $1 = [\emptyset,\emptyset,\emptyset]$.

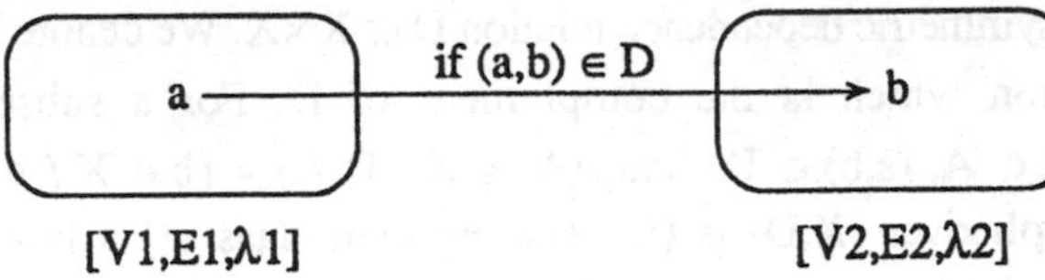

Figure 2.3.

The concatenation is generalized to an infinite product as follows. Let (g_i) be any finite or infinite sequence of dependence graphs. Then $g = g_1g_2\dots g_i\dots \in \mathbb{G}$ is defined as the disjoint union of the g_i with the obvious new arcs from g_i to g_j for $i<j$ whenever the vertices have dependent labels. Note that concatenation and infinite product are associative operations.

2.2. Traces

Using these operations, we relate words and dependence graphs. We recall that X^ω denotes the set of infinite words whereas $X^\infty = X^\omega \cup X^*$ denotes the set of all finite and infinite words. We define the mapping $\varphi : X^\infty \to \mathbb{G}(X,D)$ by $\varphi(a) = [\{x\},\emptyset,x \mapsto a]$ for each a in X and $\varphi(a_1a_2\dots) = \varphi(a_1)\varphi(a_2)\dots$ for each word $a_1a_2\dots$ in X^∞. For instance, if (X,D) = a — b — c then, φ(cabacab) and φ(acbaaccbaaacccb...) are the graphs presented in Figures 2.1 and 2.2. Note that φ is not injective, for instance φ(ab) = φ(ba) iff (a,b) ∈ I. We define an equivalence $\sim_I$ (or simply $\sim$ when there is no confusion) on X^∞ by, for u,v in X^∞, $u \sim v$ if $\varphi(u) = \varphi(v)$. It turns out that φ is a surjective morphism from the free monoid X^* onto the monoid $\mathbb{FG}(X,D)$ of finite dependence graphs. The monoid of finite traces introduced by A. Mazurkiewicz [Maz77] is precisely $X^*/\sim = \mathbb{FG}(X,D)$ which is denoted by $\mathbb{M}(X,D)$ or simply by $\mathbb{M}$ throughout.

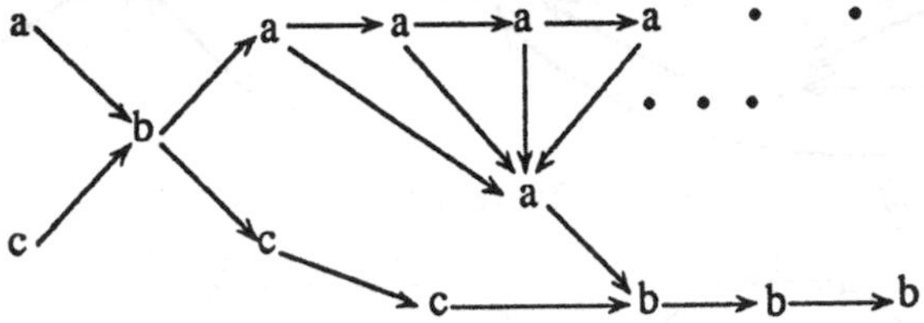

Figure 2.4.

In a similar way, we will define the monoid of infinite traces from the monoid $\mathbb{G}(X,D)$. Unfortunately, $\varphi : X^\infty \to \mathbb{G}(X,D)$ is neither surjective nor a morphism. The set $\varphi(X^\infty) = X^\infty/\sim$ of dependence graphs which can be represented by words is denoted by $\mathbb{R}(X,D)$ or simply by $\mathbb{R}$ when there is no confusion. Its elements are called real dependence graphs or **real traces.** $\mathbb{R}$ is characterized as follows: a dependence graph $[V,E,\lambda]$ is real if the past $p{\downarrow} = \{q \in V \,/\, q \le p\}$ is finite for every vertex p of V. For instance, the dependence graphs of Figure 2.1 and 2.2 are real whereas, with the same dependence alphabet, the graph of Figure 2.4 is not a real dependence graph although it can be obtained as the concatenation of the two real dependence graphs $\varphi(acba^{\omega})$ and $\varphi(ccab^3)$. Note that, apart from the first one, all occurrences of b have an infinite past (this is not in contradiction with the well-foundedness: there is no infinite descending chain).

More generally, each element $g = [V,E,\lambda] \in \mathbb{G}$ splits into its real part Re(g) and its transfinite part Tr(g) which are the restrictions of the dependence graph g to $\{p \in V / p\!\downarrow \text{ is finite}\}$ and $\{p \in V / p\!\downarrow \text{ is infinite}\}$ respectively. For instance, let g be the dependence graph of Figure 2.4, we have $\mathrm{Re}(g) = \varphi(acbcca^{\omega})$ and $\mathrm{Tr}(g) = \varphi(ab^3)$. Obviously, Re(g) and Tr(g) are dependence graphs and, in $\mathbb{G}$, we have the equation: $g = \mathrm{Re}(g)\mathrm{Tr}(g)$. In fact, $\mathbb{R}$ is the set of dependence graphs with an empty transfinite part.

Two dependence graphs $g,h \in \mathbb{G}$ are said to be **practically distinguishable** if there exists a (finite) real trace s such that gs and hs have different real parts, i.e., if $\mathrm{Re}(gs) \neq \mathrm{Re}(hs)$. In particular, two traces with different real parts are practically distinguishable. It turns out [Die91] that **practical-indistinguishability** is the coarsest congruence of $\mathbb{G}$ which respects real parts. The quotient of $\mathbb{G}(X,D)$ by this congruence yields the monoid of **complex traces** $\mathbb{C}(X,D)$ (denoted also by $\mathbb{C}$ when there is no risk of confusion). Note that the infinite product is well-defined in $\mathbb{C}$ since practical-indistinguishability is also a "congruence" with respect to the infinite product in $\mathbb{G}$.

2.3. Calculus in the monoid of complex traces

In order to give an explicit characterization of the congruence "practical-indistinguishability", we introduce the following notations. For a dependence graph $g = [V,E,\lambda]$, let $\mathrm{alph}(g) = \lambda(V)$ be the set of letters which occur in g at least once and let $\mathrm{alphinf}(g) = \{a \in X / |\lambda^{-1}(a)| \text{ is infinite}\} \cup \mathrm{alph}(\mathrm{Tr}(g))$ be the alphabet at infinity of g. Finally, let $\mathrm{Im}(g) = D(\mathrm{alphinf}(g))$ be the imaginary part of g. For instance, let g be the dependence graph of Figure 2.4, we have $\mathrm{alph}(g) = \{a,b,c\}$, $\mathrm{alphinf}(g) = \{a,b\}$ and $\mathrm{Im}(g) = \{a,b,c\}$.
Two dependence graphs $g,h \in \mathbb{G}$ are practically indistinguishable if and only if $\mathrm{Re}(g) = \mathrm{Re}(h)$ and $\mathrm{Im}(g) = \mathrm{Im}(h)$ [Die91]. Hence a complex trace is a pair $(r,D(A)) = (\mathrm{Re}(g),\mathrm{Im}(g))$ for some $g \in \mathbb{G}$.

For instance, let $(X,D) = a — b — c — d$. The dependence graphs $g = \varphi((ac)^{\omega})$ and $h = \varphi((ac)^{\omega})\cdot\varphi(b)$ are practically indistinguishable since $\mathrm{Re}(g) = \mathrm{Re}(h) = g$ and $\mathrm{alphinf}(g) = \{a,c\}$, $\mathrm{alphinf}(h) = \{a,b,c\}$ whence $\mathrm{Im}(g) = \mathrm{Im}(h) = \{a,b,c,d\}$. They represent the complex trace $((ac)^{\omega},D(a,c)) = ((ac)^{\omega},D(a,b,c)) = ((ac)^{\omega},\{a,b,c,d\})$.

For a complex trace x, define $D(x) = D(\mathrm{alph}(g))$ and $\mathrm{Im}(x) = \mathrm{Im}(g)$ for some dependence graph g representing x. Note that, for a complex trace $x = (r,D(A))$, there may exist dependence graphs g and h representing x such that $\mathrm{alph}(g) \neq \mathrm{alph}(h)$ and $\mathrm{alphinf}(g) \neq \mathrm{alphinf}(h)$. Hence neither the set A nor the alphabet of x are well-defined. Nevertheless we have $\mathrm{Im}(x) = D(A)$ and $D(x) = D(r) \cup D(A)$. For instance, with the practically indistinguishable graphs g and h defined above, we have $\mathrm{alph}(g) = \mathrm{alphinf}(g) = \{a,c\}$ whereas $\mathrm{alph}(h) = \mathrm{alphinf}(h) = \{a,b,c\}$ but $D(g) = D(h) = \{a,b,c,d\}$.

Note that two real traces are practically indistinguishable if and only if they are equal. Thus, $\mathbb{R}(X,D)$ is embedded in $\mathbb{C}(X,D)$. More precisely, a real trace $r \in \mathbb{R}(X,D)$ is identified with its image $(r,\mathrm{Im}(r))$ in $\mathbb{C}(X,D)$.

Even if the concatenation in $\mathbb{C}$ is of course defined through the practical-indistinguishability congruence, it will be convenient to have a direct formula of the concatenation of two complex traces $(r,D(A))$ and $(s,D(B))$. To this purpose we extract from the real part s, the maximal real prefix $\mu_A(s)$ of s containing letters from I(A) only. Formally for any element $g = [V,E,\lambda]$ of $\mathbb{G}$, $\mu_A(g)$ is the restriction to $\{p \in V \,/\, p\!\downarrow \text{ is finite } \& \ \mathrm{alph}(p\!\downarrow) \subseteq I(A)\}$ of the dependence graph g. Since $\mathbb{G}$ is left-cancellative [Die91], there is a unique dependence graph $\mathrm{suff}_A(g)$ such that $g = \mu_A(g)\mathrm{suff}_A(g)$. With these notations, the concatenation in $\mathbb{C}$ is simply given by [Die91]:

$$(r,D(A))\cdot(s,D(B)) = \big(r\mu_A(s),D(A) \cup D(B) \cup D(\mathrm{alph}(\mathrm{suff}_A(s)))\big).$$

This formula is of first importance when dealing with complex traces and will be used extensively throughout this paper. For instance, let $(X,D) = a — b — c — d — e$ and consider the complex traces $x = (e^\omega,D(d,e))$ and $y = (b^2c^2da^\omega,D(a))$. Then, $\mu_{\{d,e\}}(b^2c^2da^\omega) = b^2a^\omega$, $\mathrm{suff}_{\{d,e\}}(b^2c^2da^\omega) = c^2d$ and $x\cdot y = (b^2(ae)^\omega, D(d,e) \cup D(a) \cup D(c,d))$.

In order to link real and complex trace languages, we define, for a real trace language R and a subset A of X, the language $\mathrm{inf}_A(R) = \{r \in R \,/\, \mathrm{alphinf}(r) = A\}$. For a complex trace language L and a subset B of X, we define $L_B = \{x \in L \,/\, \mathrm{Im}(x) = D(B)\}$. A couple (A,B) of subsets of X is said to be **consistent** if $\mathrm{inf}_A(\mathrm{Re}(\mathbb{C}_B))$ is not empty i.e. there exists a real trace r such that $\mathrm{alphinf}(r) = A$ and $(r,D(B))$ is a complex trace. Consistent couples admit the following decidable characterization: (A,B) is consistent if and only if there exists a sequence of letters $a_1,\ldots,a_k$ such that $a_{i+1} \in D(A \cup \{a_1,\ldots,a_i\})$ for all $i < k$ and $D(B) = D(A \cup \{a_1,\ldots,a_k\})$. Moreover, for every consistent couple (A,B), there exists a finite trace $s_{A,B}$ of length at most $|X|$ (for instance $s_{A,B} = a_1\ldots a_k$) such that $r\cdot s_{A,B} = (r,D(B))$ for all real traces r in $\mathrm{inf}_A(\mathbb{R})$.

For instance, let (X,D) = 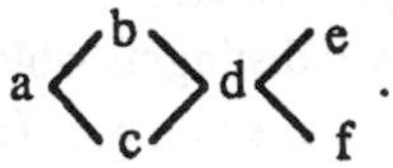 . The couple $(\{a\},\{a,d\})$ is consistent since

$b \in D(a)$, $d \in D(a,b)$ and $D(a,b,d) = D(a,d)$. On the contrary, one can verify that the couple $(\{a\},\{a,e\})$ is not consistent.

Real trace languages and complex trace languages are closely related. For any complex trace language, it holds:

$$L = \bigcup_{(A,B)\ \text{consistent}} \mathrm{inf}_A(\mathrm{Re}(L_B))\cdot s_{A,B}$$

This formula will be mainly used to infer results on complex trace languages from results on real trace languages.

3. Recognizable languages

Recognizable languages describe the behaviour of finite state systems and hence form one of the basic families of a monoid. For finite traces and finite and infinite words, there exist several equivalent characterizations of the family of recognizable languages. These languages are those which are recognized by some morphism in a finite monoid. Kleene's, Büchi's and Ochmanski's theorems provide characterizations of recognizable languages by means of rational or co-rational expressions. Finite automata which provide the most intuitive idea of finite state machines can also be used to define recognizable languages. Finally the languages defined by some monadic second order logic formula are again the recognizable ones.

In this section, we introduce recognizable languages of complex traces using the first characterization above (recognizing morphisms). In Section 7, we prove that these languages are exactly the languages defined by some co-rational expression which asserts the robustness of our definition. A characterization by means of finite asynchronous (cellular) automata has also been proposed recently in [GP92]. Ebinger [Ebi92] obtained another characterization of these languages using monadic second order formulae

First of all, let us recall the definition of a recognizable word language: a language $U \subseteq X^{\infty}$ is recognizable if there exists a morphism η from X^* into a finite monoid S such that for any (finite or infinite) sequence $u_1,u_2,u_3\ldots$ of finite words we have:

$$u_1 \cdot u_2 \cdot u_3 \ldots \in U \Rightarrow \eta^{-1}\eta(u_1)\cdot\eta^{-1}\eta(u_2)\cdot\eta^{-1}\eta(u_3)\ldots \subseteq U$$

The family of recognizable word languages is denoted by Rec X^{∞}.
We can extend this definition to languages of infinite traces by considering a morphism from the monoid of finite traces IM into a finite monoid. But a finite or infinite product of finite traces is always a real trace. Therefore this generalization can be used for real trace languages only.

Definition 3.1. A real trace language R is recognized by a morphism η from IM into a finite monoid S if for any (finite or infinite) sequence $r_1,r_2,r_3\ldots$ of finite traces, we have:

$$r_1 \cdot r_2 \cdot r_3 \ldots \in R \Rightarrow \eta^{-1}\eta(r_1)\cdot\eta^{-1}\eta(r_2)\cdot\eta^{-1}\eta(r_3)\ldots \subseteq R$$

A real trace language is recognizable if it is recognized by some morphism. The family of recognizable real trace languages is denoted by Rec IR.

Several characterizations of recognizable real trace languages have been proposed in [Gas91]. In particular a notion of syntactic congruence has been defined and studied. But in this survey we only need the two properties below. The first one, along the lines of [Arn85] and [PP91], gives an extension of the known algebraic formulation of Büchi recognizability for ω-languages. This result will be used in a crucial way in Section 7.

Proposition 3.2 [Gas91]. Let R be a real trace language recognized by some morphism η from IM into a finite monoid S. Then:

$$R = \bigcup_{(s,e)\in P} \eta^{-1}(s).(\eta^{-1}(e))^{\omega} \text{ with } P = \{(s,e) \in S^2 \,/\, se=s,\ e^2=e \text{ and } \eta^{-1}(s).(\eta^{-1}(e))^{\omega} \subseteq R\}.$$

For instance, for any subset A of X, the real trace language $\inf_A(\mathbb{R}) = \{t \in \mathbb{R} \,/\, \text{alphinf}(t) = A\}$ is recognized by the morphism $\eta : \mathbb{M} \to \mathcal{P}(X)$ defined by $\eta(r) = \text{alph}(r)$ for all r in IM. Moreover, the set P associated with $\inf_A(\mathbb{R})$ is simply $P = \{(B,A) \,/\, A \subseteq B\}$.
The second property shows that the families of recognizable real trace languages and of recognizable word languages are closely related (recall that φ is the canonical surjection from X^{∞} onto IR).

Proposition 3.3 [Gas91]. Let R be a real trace language. Then:

$$R \in \text{Rec}\,\mathbb{R} \Leftrightarrow \varphi^{-1}(R) \in \text{Rec}\,X^{\infty}$$

From this characterization, we can easily deduce that the family Rec $\mathbb{R}$ is closed under finite union, intersection and complement.

It is possible to define the recognizability of a complex trace language by a morphism using an $(\omega + 1)$-product of finite traces. Here we use the following (equivalent) definition.

Definition 3.4. Let L be a complex trace language. The language L is recognizable if, for every $A \subseteq X$, the set of real traces $\text{Re}(L_A) = \{r \in \mathbb{R} \,/\, (r,D(A)) \in L\}$ is recognizable. The set of recognizable complex trace languages is denoted by Rec $\mathbb{C}$.

For instance, for any subset B of X, the complex trace language $\mathbb{C}_B = \{x \in \mathbb{C} \,/\, \text{Im}(x) = D(B)\}$ is recognizable since for any subset A of X, $(\mathbb{C}_B)_A$ is either empty if $D(A) \neq D(B)$ or the whole set $\mathbb{C}_B$ and $\text{Re}(\mathbb{C}_B) = \bigcup_{(A,B) \text{ consistent}} \inf_A(\mathbb{R})$.

Although this definition may seem artificial, we will prove its soundness throughout this paper. More precisely we will show that Rec $\mathbb{C}$ is a boolean algebra which is closed under concatenation and quotients (Section 4). In fact it is the unique family of complex trace languages which satisfies 1) and 2) below and which is closed under union, intersection and concatenation (with a finite trace). Moreover, the family of recognizable trace languages so-defined is exactly the family of co-rational trace languages (Section 7).

Remarks

1) Let $L \in \text{Rec}\,\mathbb{C}$, then $\text{Re}(L) = \bigcup_{A \subseteq X} \text{Re}(L_A) \in \text{Rec}\,\mathbb{R}$.
2) Let R be a real trace language, then R is recognizable if and only if its image as complex trace language $L = \{(r,\text{Im}(r)) \,/\, r \in R\} \subseteq \mathbb{C}$ is recognizable since, for all subsets B of X, $\text{Re}(L_B) = \bigcup_{D(A)=D(B)} R \cap \inf_A(\mathbb{R})$

Let us point out that it is not possible to define recognizability via the projection Re: $\mathbb{C} \to \mathbb{R}$ saying that $L \in \text{Rec}\,\mathbb{C}$ if and only if $\text{Re}(L) \in \text{Rec}\,\mathbb{R}$. Namely if $(X,D) = a — b — c — d$ and $L = \varphi((ac)^*b^{\omega})\cdot\varphi(c) \cup \varphi((a+c)^*b^{\omega})$, $\text{Re}(L) = \varphi((a+c)^*b^{\omega})$ is a recognizable real trace language whereas $L_{\{b,c\}} = L \cap \mathbb{C}_{\{b,c\}}$ is not recognizable since $\text{Re}(L_{\{b,c\}}) = \varphi((ac)^*b^{\omega})$. Therefore we would obtain a class of languages which were not closed under intersection.

Proposition 3.5 [DGP91]. Rec $\mathbb{C}$ is a boolean algebra, i.e., it is closed under union, intersection and complementation.

4. Concatenation

In this section, we investigate the closure of the family of recognizable complex trace languages under concatenation, left and right quotients. To this purpose, we have to study the family Rec $\mathbb{R}$ and to introduce new operators on complex trace languages.

First, the family Rec $\mathbb{R}$ is closed under concatenation, left and right quotients.

Proposition 4.1 [Gas91, DGP91]. Let R and S be recognizable real trace languages. It holds:

i) $R\cdot S \in \text{Rec}\,\mathbb{R}$ if $\text{alphinf}(R)\times\text{alph}(S)\subseteq I$

ii) $R\cdot S^{-1} = \{r\in \mathbb{R} \,/\, rs \in R \text{ for some } s\in S \text{ s.t. } \text{alphinf}(r)\times\text{alph}(s)\subseteq I\} \in \text{Rec}\,\mathbb{R}$

iii) $R^{-1}\cdot S = \{s\in \mathbb{R} \,/\, rs \in S \text{ for some } r\in R \text{ s.t. } \text{alphinf}(r)\times\text{alph}(s)\subseteq I\} \in \text{Rec}\,\mathbb{R}$

Note that the alphabetic conditions ensure that the concatenations remain real traces.

The proof of these results follows from the two following lemmas and the characterization of recognizable real trace languages by means of the canonical morphism φ (Proposition 3.3). First, we introduce the following operators on word languages. Recall that two words $u,v \in X^\infty$ are independent, denoted by $(u,v)\in I$, if $\text{alph}(u)\times\text{alph}(v)\subseteq I$. Let $U,V\subseteq X^\infty$, we define

$$U \sqcup\!\sqcup_I V = \{u_1v_1u_2v_2\ldots \in X^\infty \,/\, u_i, v_i \in X^* \text{ for all } i,\; u_1u_2\ldots \in U,\; v_1v_2\ldots \in V \text{ and } (v_i,u_j)\in I \text{ for all } i<j\}$$

$$U \sqcup\!\sqcup_I V^{-1} = \{u\in X^\infty \,/\, (u \sqcup\!\sqcup_I v)\cap U \neq \emptyset \text{ for some } v\in V\}$$

$$U^{-1} \sqcup\!\sqcup_I V = \{v\in X^\infty \,/\, (u \sqcup\!\sqcup_I v)\cap V \neq \emptyset \text{ for some } u\in U\}$$

As the following lemma shows, these operators are the word counterparts of the concatenation, left and right quotients in $\mathbb{R}$.

Lemma 4.2. Let R,S be real trace languages. Then

$$\varphi^{-1}(R\cdot S) = \varphi^{-1}(R) \sqcup\!\sqcup_I \varphi^{-1}(S)$$

$$\varphi^{-1}(R\cdot S^{-1}) = \varphi^{-1}(R) \sqcup\!\sqcup_I \varphi^{-1}(S)^{-1}$$

$$\varphi^{-1}(R^{-1}\cdot S) = \varphi^{-1}(R)^{-1} \sqcup\!\sqcup_I \varphi^{-1}(S)$$

Moreover, using classical closure properties of recognizable word languages, it can be proved that these operators preserve the recognizability of word languages:

Lemma 4.3. Let U, V be recognizable word languages. Then, $U \sqcup\!\sqcup_I V$, $U \sqcup\!\sqcup_I V^{-1}$ and $U^{-1} \sqcup\!\sqcup_I V$ are recognizable.

In order to extend these results to complex traces, we introduce the following operators. Let A,B be subsets of X and let L be a complex trace language. Define

$$\text{Shift}_{A,B}(L) = \{y\in L \,/\, xy \in \mathbb{C}_B \text{ for some } x\in \mathbb{C}_A\}$$

$$\mu_{A,B}(L) = \mu_A(\text{Re}(\text{Shift}_{A,B}(L)))$$

Intuitively, a trace is in $\text{Shift}_{A,B}$ if it shifts the imaginary part from D(A) to D(B) by right concatenation. Note that, in the definition of $\text{Shift}_{A,B}$, the statement "for some $x\in\mathbb{C}_A$" can be replaced by "for all $x\in\mathbb{C}_A$" since the imaginary part of a product xy depends on Im(x) and y only.

For instance, let (X,D) = a — b — c — d, then we have :

$$\text{Shift}_{\{a\},\{a,b\}}(\mathbb{C}) = \{(r,\emptyset) \,/\, r\in \{a,c,d\}^*b\{a,b\}^*\} \cup \{(r,D(a)) \,/\, r\in \{a,c,d\}^*b\{a,b\}^*a^\omega\} \cup \{(r,D(a,b)) \,/\, r\in \{a,c,d\}^*b\{a,b\}^\omega\}$$

Therefore, $\mu_{\{a\},\{a,b\}}(\mathbb{C}) = \{c,d\}^*$.

The following lemma states that these operators preserve the recognizability.

Lemma 4.4 [DGP91]. Let A,B be subsets of X and let L be a recognizable complex trace language. Then

i) $\mathrm{Shift}_{A,B}(L) \in \mathrm{Rec}\,\mathbb{C}$

ii) $\mu_A(\mathrm{Re}(L)) \in \mathrm{Rec}\,\mathbb{R}$

iii) $\mu_{A,B}(L) \in \mathrm{Rec}\,\mathbb{R}$.

With these operators, it can be checked that the real part of the concatenation (resp. of the left and right quotients) of two complex trace languages is expressed in the following way.

Lemma 4.5. Let K and L be complex trace languages. The following formulae hold.

$$\mathrm{Re}((K\cdot L)_B) = \bigcup_{A\subseteq X} \mathrm{Re}(K_A)\cdot\mu_{A,B}(L)$$

$$\mathrm{Re}((K\cdot L^{-1})_A) = \bigcup_{B\subseteq X} (\mathrm{Re}(K_B)\cdot\mu_{A,B}(L)^{-1}) \cap \mathrm{Re}(\mathbb{C}_A)$$

$$\mathrm{Re}((K^{-1}\cdot L)_C) = \bigcup_{A,B\subseteq X\ \&\ F\subseteq I(E)} \left((\mathrm{Re}(K_A)^{-1}\cdot\mathrm{Re}(L_B) \cap R_{A,E})\cdot S_{A,F}\right) \cap \mathrm{Re}(\mathrm{Shift}_{A,B}(\mathbb{C}_C))$$

where, $R_{A,E} = \{r \in \mathbb{R} \,/\, \mathrm{alph}(r) \subseteq I(A)\ \&\ \mathrm{alphinf}(r) = E\}$ and $S_{A,F} = \overline{\bigcup_{a\in I(A)} a.\mathbb{R}} \cap \mathrm{alph}_F(\mathbb{R})$ is the set of real traces with no minimal vertex in I(A) and with alphabet F.

Using Proposition 4.1 and Lemmas 4.4 and 4.5, we can generalize Proposition 4.1 to complex traces.

Theorem 4.6 [DGP91]. The family Rec $\mathbb{C}$ of recognizable complex trace languages is closed under concatenation, left and right quotients.

5. Connected traces

The next problem, as regards the family Rec $\mathbb{C}$, concerns its closure under iterations. It is not a surprise that, as for finite traces, the family Rec $\mathbb{C}$ is not closed under iterations. For instance, let (X,D) = a — b — c. The languages $\{\varphi(ac)\}^*$ and $\{\varphi(ac),\varphi(b)\}^\omega$ are not recognizable since $\varphi^{-1}(\{\varphi(ac)\}^*) = \{u \in \{a,c\}^* \,/\, |u|_a = |u|_c\}$ and $\varphi^{-1}(\{\varphi(ac),\varphi(b)\}^\omega) \cap \{\varphi(a),\varphi(c)\}^*\varphi(b)^\omega = \{u \in \{a,c\}^* \,/\, |u|_a = |u|_c\}b^\omega$ which are not recognizable word languages.

The most widely known condition which ensures the recognizability of the iteration of a recognizable language of finite traces T is the connectivity of the traces in T [Mét86, Och85]. In order to generalize this result to complex traces, we define now the notion of connectivity for complex traces.

Intuitively, a trace is connected if it cannot be split into two non-empty independent traces. Thus we have first to introduce notions of independence. This is clear in $\mathbb{G}$: two graphs f and g are independent, denoted by (f,g) ∈ I, if $\mathrm{alph}(f) \times \mathrm{alph}(g) \subseteq I$. Unfortunately, we cannot use this definition in $\mathbb{C}$ since the alphabet of a complex trace is not well-defined (see Section 2.3). Nevertheless, it is easy to verify that the independence relation in $\mathbb{G}$ factorizes through the congruence "practically indistinguishable". Hence the independence relation in $\mathbb{C}$ is well-defined and it can be characterized as follows. Two complex traces $(r,D(A))$ and $(s,D(B))$ are independent if and only if $(\mathrm{alph}(r) \cup A) \times (\mathrm{alph}(s) \cup B) \subseteq I$.

For example, let (X,D) = 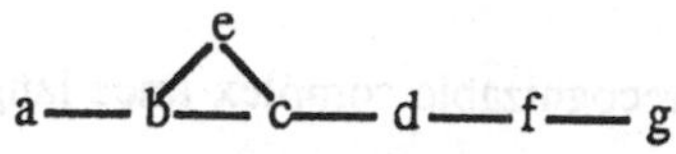 , the complex traces $(gga^\omega, D(a))$ and $(d^\omega,D(c,d))$ are independent whereas the traces $(gga^\omega, D(a,b))$ and $(d^\omega,D(c,d))$ are not. We define now connected traces and connected components of a trace.

Definition 5.1. A complex trace z is said to be connected if $z = xy$ with $(x,y) \in I$ implies $x = 1$ or $y = 1$. A trace x is called a connected component of z if either $x = z = 1$ or x is a connected non-empty trace such that $z = xy$ for some complex trace y with $(x,y) \in I$. The set of connected components of z is denoted by C(z).

For instance, with the dependence alphabet defined above, the trace $x = (gg(ad)^\omega, X\backslash\{g\})$ is not a connected trace since $x = (gga^\omega, D(a))\cdot(d^\omega,D(c,d))$ is the product of two independent traces. The connected components of x are $y = (gg,\emptyset)$, $y_1 = (a^\omega,D(a))$, $z_1 = (d^\omega,D(c,d)\})$, $y_2 = (a^\omega,D(a,b))$ and $z_2 = (d^\omega,D(d))$.

Note that using a direct translation of Definition 5.1 we can define the connectivity notions on dependence graphs as well. The following remarks explain why we chose these formulations for the definitions of connectivity although they may seem different from the usual ones. First, one can check that a finite trace t is connected if and only if the graph (X,D) restricted to alph(t) is connected. But, this *usual* characterization of connectivity for finite traces cannot be used to define the connectivity in $\mathbb{C}$ since the alphabet of a complex trace is not well-defined. Second, one can verify that a dependence graph is connected if and only if so is its underlying undirected graph. Again, this *usual* definition of connected dependence graphs cannot either be used to define connectivity on $\mathbb{C}$ since a complex trace may have connected and non-connected representatives. For instance, let (X,D) = a — b — c. The complex trace $((ac)^\omega,X)$ is represented by the non-connected dependence graph $\varphi((ac)^\omega)$ and by the connected one $\varphi((ac)^\omega)\cdot\varphi(b)$.

Every dependence graph in $\mathbb{G}$ is the disjoint union of its connected components. It follows that every graph g in $\mathbb{G}$ (in particular any real trace) can uniquely be written as a product of independent connected components (called a decomposition of g). Moreover, if $g = g_1 \cdots g_k$ is such a decomposition then $\{g_1,\ldots,g_k\}$ is exactly the set C(g) of connected components of g. This is not true for traces in $\mathbb{C}$. A complex trace may have several decompositions and some of its connected components may not be independent. Nevertheless, every complex trace admits at least one decomposition.

For instance, the trace x defined above admits two decompositions $x = yy_1z_1 = yy_2z_2$ but neither (y_1,y_2) nor (z_1,z_2) nor (z_1,y_2) are independent. Note that, $\{y,y_1,z_2\}$ is a maximal set of pairwise independent components of x but $yy_1z_2 = (gg(ad)^\omega, X\backslash\{e,g\}) \neq x$.

The notation C is extended to complex trace languages in the obvious way. A trace language L is said to be connected if L = C(L). The following inclusions hold: $L^* \subseteq C(L)^*$, $L^\omega \subseteq C(L)^\omega$. We will see in the next section that if L is recognizable then so are $C(L)^*$ and $C(L)^\omega$. For this, we need the following lemma.

Lemma 5.2 [DGP91]. Let L be a recognizable complex trace language. Then the language C(L) is recognizable too.

6. Iterations

The aim of this section is to find sufficient conditions on a recognizable complex trace language L which ensure that L^* and L^ω are recognizable too. We prove that connectivity is such a condition. Again in this section, results on real traces are basic. Hence we first study the infinite iterations of a language of finite traces. As a first step, we will restrict ourselves to languages where all elements have the same connected alphabet. Recall that a subset A of X is connected if the restriction of (X,D) to A is connected.

Proposition 6.1 [GPZ91]. Let A be a connected subset of X and let T be a recognizable language of finite traces such that alph(t) = A for any t in T. Then T^ω is a recognizable real trace language.

It is already known that under the hypotheses of Proposition 6.1, T^* is a recognizable language of finite traces [Mét86, Och85]. In order to extend this result to the infinite iteration, we first reduce to the case where all the traces of T have the same alphabet. For any subset $A \subseteq X$, we denote $\text{alph}_A(T) = \{t \in T \,/\, \text{alph}(t) = A\}$.

Lemma 6.2 [GPZ91]. Let T be a language of finite traces such that $T^* = T$. Then,

$$T^\omega = \bigcup_{A \subseteq X} T \cdot (\text{alph}_A(T))^\omega$$

In order to use Proposition 6.1, we reduce once more to the case where all traces in T have the same *connected* alphabet.

Lemma 6.3 [GPZ91]. Let A be a subset of X, let $A_1,\ldots,A_k$ be the connected components of A and let T be a language of finite traces such that T^* is recognizable and alph(t) = A for all t in T. Then T^ω is a finite union of sets of the form $RS_1{}^\omega \ldots S_k{}^\omega$ where $R, S_1, \ldots, S_k$ are in Rec IM and alph(t) = A_i for all t in S_i.

We are now ready to give the main result on the infinite iteration of languages of finite traces. It claims that any sufficient condition ensuring the recognizability of T^* holds also for T^ω.

Theorem 6.4 [GPZ91]. Let T be a language of finite traces such that T^* is recognizable. Then T^ω is a recognizable real trace language.

From this theorem and the result of Métivier and Ochmanski [Mét86, Och85], we deduce immediately:

Corollary 6.5 [GPZ91]. Let T be a recognizable language of connected finite traces. Then T^{ω} is a recognizable real trace language.

Now we come back to complex traces. As announced, we will show that L^* and L^{ω} are recognizable provided L is a recognizable language of connected complex traces.
For a complex trace language L, define $\nu_A(L) = \mu_{A,A}(L)$. Note that each trace in $\nu_A(L)$ is finite since for any real trace r, we have $alph(r) \subseteq I(A)$ and $Im(r) \subseteq D(A)$ imply $alphinf(r) = \emptyset$.

Lemma 6.6 [DGP91]. Let L be a complex trace language, then $L^{\dagger}$ (with $\dagger = *$ or ω) is a finite union of languages $\nu_{B_0}(L)^*Shift_{B_0,B_1}(L)\nu_{B_1}(L)^*\ldots Shift_{B_{k-1},B_k}(L)\nu_{B_k}(L)^{\dagger}$ where B_0, $B_1,\ldots, B_k$ is a sequence of subalphabets such that $\emptyset = D(B_0) \subsetneq D(B_1) \subsetneq \ldots \subsetneq D(B_k) \subseteq X$.

Hence, from Lemma 4.4, Theorem 6.4 and the closure properties of Rec $\mathbb{C}$, we obtain:

Theorem 6.7 [DGP91]. Let L be a recognizable complex trace language such that $\nu_A(L)^*$ is recognizable for all $A \subseteq X$. Then L^* and L^{ω} are both recognizable.

In order to generalize Corollary 6.5 to complex trace languages, we need the following lemma:

Lemma 6.8 [DGP91]. Let L be a connected complex trace language, then $\nu_A(L)$ is connected for any subset A of X.

Now using this lemma, the result of Métivier and Ochmanski and Theorem 6.7, we get:

Theorem 6.9 [DGP91]. Let L be a recognizable complex trace language. If L contains connected traces only then L^* and L^{ω} are recognizable too. In particular, $C(L)^*$ and $C(L)^{\omega}$ are recognizable for all recognizable complex trace language L.

As shown in the first example of Section 5, the finite iteration of a single trace is not necessarily recognizable. For instance, let (X,D) = a — b — c, the trace language $\{ac\}^*$ is not recognizable (see Section 5). However the real trace language $\{ac\}^{\omega}$ is recognized by the morphism $\eta : \mathbb{M} \to \mathcal{P}(X)$ defined by $\eta(r) = alph(r)$ for all r in $\mathbb{M}$. The set P associated with $\{ac\}^{\omega}$ (see Proposition 3.2) is simply the singleton $P = \{(\{a,c\},\{a,c\})\}$. This surprising result can be generalized to any complex trace, as stated in the following proposition.

Proposition 6.10 [DGP91]. Let x be a complex trace such that the language $L = \{x\}$ is recognizable. Then the language $L^{\omega} = \{x^{\omega}\}$ is recognizable too.

This result fails as soon as the language L contains at least two traces. For instance, if (X,D) = a — b — c, the language $\{ac,b\}^{\omega}$ is not recognizable (see Section 5).

7. Canonical form and co-rational languages

In this section, we first propose a characterization of recognizable languages of infinite traces in terms of appropriate "rational operations". It extends to traces the Büchi characterization of recognizable word languages by means of a finite union of sets of the form UV^{ω} where

$U, V \in \text{Rec } X^*$. This charaterization provides a "canonical" form for recognizable languages of infinite traces.

Theorem 7.1 [GPZ91, DGP91]. A complex trace language L is recognizable if and only if L is a finite union of languages $RS_1^{\omega}\ldots S_k^{\omega}.s$ where s is a finite trace, R, $S_i \in \text{Rec } \mathbb{M}$ are such that all traces in S_i have the same connected alphabet A_i and $A_i \times A_j \subseteq I$ for all $i \neq j$. Moreover, if $L \subseteq \mathbb{R}$ then we may assume that the finite trace s is empty.

Apart from the family of recognizable sets, the family of rational sets is also a basic family in a monoid since it collects languages which can be generated in a modular way starting from actions and using rational operators. Therefore, the study of the relationships between the recognizable and the rational families is of first importance.
Kleene's theorem states the equality of these families in the free monoid X^*. It has been generalized to infinite words by Büchi and to finite traces by Ochmanski (using co-rationals instead of rationals). Our aim is to suppress the question mark in the diagram below.

	Words	Traces
Finite	Kleene	Ochmanski
Infinite	Büchi	?

As for finite traces [Och85], define the concurrent iterations co-* and co-ω of a trace language L by $L^{\text{co-}*} = C(L)^*$ and $L^{\text{co-}\omega} = C(L)^{\omega}$.
Let the co-rational family Co-Rat $\mathbb{C}$ be the smallest family of trace languages containing finite sets of finite traces and closed under union, concatenation, co-star and co-omega.
From Proposition 3.5 and Theorems 4.6 and 6.9 for one inclusion and from Theorem 7.1 using Ochmanski's result $\text{Rec } \mathbb{M} \subseteq \text{co-Rat } \mathbb{M}$ [Och85] for the converse, we obtain:

Theorem 7.2 [DGP91]. $\text{Rec } \mathbb{C} = \text{co-Rat } \mathbb{C}$.

Finally, note that the family Rec $\mathbb{C}$ is the smallest family of complex trace languages which contains finite sets of finite traces and which is closed under finite union, concatenation and iterations $*$ and ω restricted to languages of finite connected traces.

8. Conclusion

Recognizable languages describe the behaviour of finite state systems and hence form one of the basic families. For infinite traces, we defined this family using morphisms into finite monoids. Its closure properties under rational operations have been investigated. Then we gave a characterization of this family by means of co-rational expressions.
But, the characterization of recognizable languages which provides the most intuitive idea of finite state machines uses finite automata (see [Eil74, Tho90, PP91] for automata on infinite words and [Zie87, Zie89, CMZ89] for asynchronous automata on finite traces). For infinite traces, such a characterization has been recently proposed by means of (non-deterministic) Büchi asynchronous (cellular) automata [GP92]. On the other hand, Ebinger [Ebi92] obtained a

characterization of these languages using monadic second order formulae (see also [Tho89] for finite traces and [Tho90] for words).

Acknowledgement: *We thank the four anonymous referees for many comments and suggestions about the presentation of this survey.*

9. References

[Arn85] A. ARNOLD, "A syntactic congruence for rational ω-languages", Theoretical Computer Science 39, p. 333-335, 1985.

[AR88] I.J. AALBERSBERG and G. ROZENBERG, "Theory of traces", Theoretical Computer Science 60, p. 1-82, 1988.

[BD87] E. BEST and R. DEVILLERS, "Sequential and concurrent behaviour in Petri Net theory", Theoretical Computer Science 55, p. 87-136, 1987.

[BMP89] P. BONIZZONI, G. MAURI and G. PIGHIZZINI, "About infinite traces", Proceedings of the ASMICS Workshop on Partially Commutative Monoids, Tech. Rep. TUM-I 9002, Technische Universität München, p. 1-10, 1989.

[CF69] P. CARTIER and D. FOATA, "Problèmes combinatoires de commutation et réarrangements", Lecture Notes in Mathematics 85, 1969.

[CM85] R. CORI and Y. METIVIER, "Recognizable subsets of some partially abelian monoids", Theoretical Computer Science 35, p. 179-189, 1985.

[CMZ89] R. CORI, Y. METIVIER and W. ZIELONKA, "Asynchronous mappings and asynchronous cellular automata", Tech. Rep. 89-97, LaBRI, Université de Bordeaux, France, 1989.

[CP85] R. CORI and D. PERRIN, "Automates et commutations partielles", RAIRO Theoretical Informatics and Applications 19, p. 21-32, 1985.

[DGP91] V. DIEKERT, P. GASTIN, A. PETIT, "Recognizable complex trace languages", MFCS'91, Lecture Notes in Computer Science 520, p. 131-140, 1991. Also available as Technical Report , LRI, Université de Paris-Sud, France.

[Die90] V. DIEKERT, "Combinatorics on traces", Lecture Notes in Computer Science 454, 1990.

[Die91] V. DIEKERT, "On the concatenation of infinite traces", STACS'91, Lecture Notes in Computer Science 480, p. 105-117, 1991.

[Ebi92] W. EBINGER, "On logical definability of infinite trace languages", Proceedings of the ASMICS Workshop on Infinite Traces, to appear as Tech. Rep., Universität Stuttgart, 1992.

[Eil74] S. EILENBERG, "Automata, Languages and Machines", Academic Press, New York, 1974.

[Fli74] M. FLIESS, "Matrices de Hankel", J. Math. pures et appl. 53, p. 197-224, 1974.

[FR85] M.P. FLE and G. ROUCAIROL, "Maximal serializability of iterated transactions", Theoretical Computer Science 38, p. 1-16, 1985.

[Gas90a] P. GASTIN, "Un modèle asynchrone pour les systèmes distribués", Theoretical Computer Science 74, p. 121-162, 1990.

[Gas90b] P. GASTIN, "Infinite traces", Proceedings of the Spring School of Theoretical Computer Science on "Semantics of concurrency", Lecture Notes in Computer Science 469, 1990.

[Gas91] P. GASTIN, "Recognizable and rational languages of finite and infinite traces", STACS'91, Lecture Notes in Computer Science 480, p. 89-104, 1991.

[GPZ91] P. GASTIN, A. PETIT, W. ZIELONKA, "A Kleene theorem for infinite trace languages", ICALP'91, Lecture Notes in Computer Science 510, p. 254-266,1991. Also available as Technical Report , LRI, Université de Paris-Sud, France.

[GP92] P. GASTIN and A. PETIT, "Asynchronous cellular automata for infinite traces", ICALP'92, Proceedings to appear in Lecture Notes in Computer Science. Also available as Tech. Rep. 91-68, LITP, Université Paris 6, France, 1991.

[Gra81] R. L. GRAHAM, "Rudiments of Ramsey theory ", Regional conference series in mathematics 45, 1981.

[GR91] P. GASTIN and B.ROZOY, "The Poset of infinitary traces", to appear in Theoretical Computer Science, also available as Technical Report 91-07, LITP, Université Paris 6, France, 1991.

[Kwi90] M.Z. KWIATKOWSKA, "A metric for traces", Information and Processing Letters 35, p. 129-135, 1990.

[Kwi91] M.Z. KWIATKOWSKA, "On the domain of traces and sequential composition", CAAP'91, Lecture Notes in Computer Science 493, p. 42-56,1991.

[Maz77] A. MAZURKIEWICZ, "Concurrent program Schemes and their interpretations", Aarhus University, DAIMI Rep. PB 78, 1977.

[Maz86] A. MAZURKIEWICZ, "Trace theory", Advanced Course on Petri Nets, Lecture Notes in Computer Science 255, p. 279-324, 1986.

[Mét86] Y. METIVIER, "On recognizable subsets in free partially commutative monoids", ICALP'86, Lecture Notes in Computer Science 226, p. 254-264, 1986.

[MR91] Y. METIVIER and B. ROZOY, "On the star operation in free partially commutative monoid", to appear in International Journal of Foundations of Computer Science, also available as Technical Report, Université de Paris-Sud, France, January 1991.

[Och85] E. OCHMANSKI, "Regular behaviour of concurrent systems", Bulletin of EATCS 27, p. 56-67, October 1985.

[Och90] E. OCHMANSKI, "Notes on a star mystery", Bulletin of EATCS 40, p. 252-257, February 1990.

[Per89] D. PERRIN, "Partial commutations", ICALP'89, Lecture Notes in Computer Science 372, p. 637-651, 1989.

[PP91] D.PERRIN and J.E. PIN, "Mots Infinis", Tech. Rep. 91-06, LITP, Université Paris 6, France, 1991. Book to appear.

[Roz90] B. ROZOY, "On Traces, Partial Order Sets and Recognizability", Proceedings of ISCIS V, Cappadocia, Turkey, 1990.

[Sak87] J. SAKAROVITCH, "On regular trace languages", Theoretical Computer Science 52, p. 59-75, 1987.

[Tho89] W. THOMAS, "On logical definability of trace languages", Proceedings of the ASMICS Workshop on Partially Commutative Monoids, Tech. Rep. TUM-I 9002, Technische Universität München, p. 172-182, 1989.

[Tho90] W. THOMAS, "Automata on infinite objects", Handbook of Theoretical Computer Science (J.V. Leeuwen, Ed.), Elsevier, Amsterdam, Vol. B, p. 135-191, 1990.

[Zie87] W. ZIELONKA, "Notes on finite asynchronous automata and trace languages", RAIRO Theoretical Informatics and Applications 21, p. 99-135, 1987.

[Zie89] W. ZIELONKA, "Safe execution of recognizable trace languages by asynchronous automata", Lecture Notes in Computer Science 363, p. 278-289, 1989.

A Survey of Equivalence Notions for Net Based Systems

L. Pomello*, G. Rozenberg+, C. Simone*

* Dipartimento di Scienze dell'Informazione, Univesita' di Milano, via Comelico 39, 20135 Milano, Italy

+ Department of Computer Science, Leiden University
P.O. Box 9512, 2300 RA Leiden, The Netherlands

ABSTRACT This paper surveys various notions of equivalence for concurrent systems in the framework of Elementary Net Systems, a fundamental class in the family of Petri Net models. Two types of equivalences are considered: equivalences based on observations of actions defined in the framework of interleaving, step and partial order semantics; and equivalences based on state spaces and state observability.

Keywords: elementary net systems, action observability, state observability, interleaving semantics, step semantics, partial order semantics, action based equivalence, state based equivalence, morphism, abstraction, refinement.

CONTENTS

This work has been carried on within the framework of the ESPRIT BRA project DEMON N.3148

1. INTRODUCTION

The notion of equivalence is central to any theory of systems. It allows one to compare systems and, in particular, it is needed whenever one wants to replace a subsystem by another subsystem without changing the behaviour of the system. In this case, the equivalence should be a congruence w.r.t. the replacement.

In the theory of sequential systems various notions of behaviour were introduced by considering a system as a realization of an input-output transformation. However, this point of view does not work for concurrent systems, where the interaction of a system with an environment, rather than its input-output function is essential - as has been pointed out for the first time by R. Milner [Mil80].

In the approach due to Milner the environment in which the system is embedded is formalized through the notion of an observer. This allows one to distinguish operationally between internal, i.e., not observable, system behaviour, and external, i.e., observable, system behaviour. Then two systems are equivalent if one cannot distinguish between the patterns of their interactions with all possible environments (i.e., all possible observers). Roughly speaking, system behaviour is visible to its observer either in terms of the actions it performs or in terms of the states the system goes through.

When the interactions happen through actions, the interface between the system and its observer consists of synchronous communications. When interactions happen through states, the interface between the system and its observer consists of (local) states they reach - independently of the type of communication that takes place. These two observation modalities allow for the abstraction of two classes of unwanted details: unobservable actions and all states, in the first case; unobservable states and all actions, in the second one.

Accordingly one obtains two types of equivalences of systems.

1) Equivalences based on observation of actions. They support refinement, allowing one
(i) to consider a system on a particular level of abstraction as the parallel composition of a number of interacting components, and
(ii) to refine a component of the system as the parallel composition of a number of interacting subcomponents - hence going to a more structured model.

2) Equivalences based on observation of states. They also support refinement allowing one
(i) to consider an action as an atomic state transformation on a particular level of abstraction, and
(ii) to refine an action as a composition of more elementary state transformations - hence going to a more specified model.

It is worthwile to note that some equivalences based on observation of actions are suitable to support this second type of refinement. However this aspect will be marginally considered in this paper, since it has been handled in detail elsewhere, (e.g., in [BGV90]).
In all cases, the refinement is correct if and only if the patterns of the interactions with any possible environment are preserved - in this way one can check a specification against an implementation.

One of the characteristic features of the net based models of concurrent systems, referred to generically as Petri Nets (see e.g., [Pet73], [Rei85a] and [BRR87]), is that states and transitions (transformations of states) are treated on an equal footing. Here, global states (cases) are collections of local states (conditions), and global transitions (steps) are collections of local ones (events). Hence, both types of equivalences discussed above arise in a natural way in the framework of net based systems since one can get directly action observability through a labelling of events, and one can get state observability through observability of conditions.

In this paper we survey these two types of equivalences, and we do this in the framework of a specific subclass of Petri Nets called Elementary Net systems, (EN systems), which are fundamental in the family of Petri net models (see e.g., [RT86], [Roz87] and [Thi87]).

The paper is organized as follows.

Basic notions and notations concerning EN systems are recalled in Section 2.

Section 3 discusses a number of preorders and equivalences based on observation of actions for EN systems equipped with an event labelling function. These notions are given in the framework of interleaving semantics, step semantics and partial order semantics, and they are compared w.r.t. their discerning power; also various conditions on the labelling functions are considered.

Section 4 presents equivalences based on state spaces, and an equivalence based on state observability.

Section 5 compares the main features of the various equivalence notions presented before.

2. BASIC DEFINITIONS

In Section 2.1. we establish the basic mathematical notations and terminology used throughout this survey, and in Section 2.2. we recall some basic notions concerning Elementary Net Systems.

2.1. Preliminaries

For a set Z, $|Z|$ denotes the <u>cardinality</u> of Z and 2^Z is the set of subsets of Z; $\emptyset$ is the empty set. $[\![n]\!]$ denotes the set $\{1, ..., n\}$. Z^* is the free monoid generated by Z and Z^+ the monoid without the empty word. Moreover, id_Z denotes the <u>identity function</u> on Z. For $Z' \subseteq Z$ and a function $f : Z \text{--->} Z$, $f_{/Z'}$ denotes the <u>restriction of f</u> to Z'.

Let $f: X \text{--->} Y$ and $g : X' \text{--->} Y'$, where $X \subseteq X'$ and $Y \subseteq Y'$, be total functions; then $f \subseteq g$ iff $\forall x \in X \;\; f(x) = g(x)$.

$\exists! \, x \in Z$ means that there is a unique x in Z (with a given property), and $\nexists \, x \in Z$ means that there is no x in Z (with a given property).

For a relation $R \subseteq Y \times Z$, <u>dom</u>$(R) = \{x : (x,y) \in R\}$ and <u>ran</u>$(R) = \{y : (x,y) \in R\}$.

For a relation $R \subseteq Z \times Z$, $R^0 = id_Z$, $R^{n+1} = R \circ R^n$, $R^+ = \bigcup_{n>0} R^n$ and $R^* = \bigcup_{n \geq 0} R^n$; R^+ is referred to as the <u>transitive closure</u> of R and R^* as the <u>reflexive and transitive closure</u> of R; moreover, $R^{-1} = \{(x,y) \in Z \times Z : (y,x) \in R\}$ is referred to as the <u>inverse</u> of R.

Let A be a set and $\leq$ a binary relation on it. The pair $(A, \leq)$ is a partially ordered set (abbreviated <u>poset</u>) if the relation $\leq$ is reflexive, antisymmetric and transitive.

Given a poset $(A, \leq)$, we derive the following relations: $< = (\leq - id_A)$; $\geq = \leq^{-1}$; <u>li</u> $= (\leq \cup \geq)$; <u>co</u> $= (A \times A - $ <u>li</u>$) \cup id_A$. On the basis of <u>li</u> and <u>co</u> the notions of chain and antichain are defined as follows: $l \subseteq A$ is a <u>li-set</u> (chain) iff $\forall x, y \in l \;\; (x,y) \in$ <u>li</u>; $c \subseteq A$ is a <u>co-set</u> (antichain) iff $\forall x, y \in c \;\; (x,y) \in$ <u>co</u>; a maximal li-set w.r.t. set inclusion is called a <u>line</u>; a maximal co-set w.r.t. set inclusion is called a <u>cut</u>. For $X \subseteq A$, a cut c is an <u>X-cut</u> iff $c \subseteq X$.

For a cut c of a poset $(A, \leq)$, $\downarrow c = \{x \in A : \exists y \in c\ x \leq y\}$; $\downarrow c$ is referred to as the downset of c.

An element x of a poset $(A, \leq)$ is called minimal (maximal) iff
$\forall y \in A\ [y \leq x \Rightarrow x = y]$ $(\forall y \in A\ [x \leq y \Rightarrow x = y])$.

A transition system is a 4-tuple $h = (V, \Delta, A, v_{in})$, where V is a nonempty finite set of states, Δ is a finite alphabet of actions, or labels, $A \subseteq V \times \Delta \times V$ is the set of labelled edges or transitions, and $v_{in} \in V$ is the initial state.
Hence, a transition system is an edge-labelled graph with a distinguished initial node.

For $v \in V$ and $\sigma \in \Delta$ we write $v \xrightarrow{\sigma}$ (whenever h is understood) iff there exists $v' \in V$ such that $(v, \sigma, v') \in A$.

A path in a transition system $h = (V, \Delta, A, v_{in})$ is a sequence of transitions (v_1, σ_1, v'_1) $(v_2, \sigma_2, v'_2) \ldots (v_n, \sigma_n, v'_n)$, such that $n \geq 1$, and $v'_i = v_{i+1}$ for all $1 \leq i \leq n-1$; this path leads from v_1 to v'_n. We use path(h) to denote the set of paths of h. A state $v \in V$ is reachable in h iff $v = v_{in}$ or there exists a path leading from v_{in} to v.

2.2. Elementary Net Systems and their behaviour

In the following we recall some basic notions concerning Elementary Net Systems (see, e.g., [BRR87], [RT86], [Roz87], [Thi87]).

Definition 2.2.1. *(net)*
A net is a triple $N = (S,T,F)$, where
(1) S and T are finite sets such that: $S \cap T = \emptyset$ and $S \cup T \neq \emptyset$.
(2) $F \subseteq (S \times T) \cup (T \times S)$ is such that: $dom(F) \cup ran(F) = S \cup T$. ♦

S is the set of S-elements, T is the set of T-elements, and F is the flow relation. Also, $X = S \cup T$ is the set of elements of N. Condition (1) means that S, T form a partition of X and that X, and thus the net, cannot be empty. Condition (2) means that the net has no isolated elements.

For $x \in X$, $\bullet x = \{y \in X : (y,x) \in F\}$ is the set of pre-elements of x, and $x\bullet = \{y \in X : (x,y) \in F\}$ is the set of post-elements of x. Then, for $Y \subseteq X$, $\bullet Y = \bigcup_{y \in Y} \bullet y$ and $Y\bullet = \bigcup_{y \in Y} y\bullet$.

Definition 2.2.2. *(static properties)*
Let $N = (S,T,F)$ be a net:
(1) N is T-restricted iff $T \subseteq dom(F) \cap ran(F)$.
(2) N is connected iff $\forall x, y \in X\ (x,y) \in (F \cup F^{-1})^*$.
(3) N is pure iff $\forall x \in X\ \bullet x \cap x\bullet = \emptyset$.
(4) N is simple w.r.t. the T-elements iff $\forall t_1, t_2 \in T\ [(\bullet t_1 = \bullet t_2 \text{ and } t_1\bullet = t_2\bullet) \Rightarrow t_1 = t_2]$.
(5) N is simple w.r.t. the S-elements iff $\forall s_1, s_2 \in S\ [(\bullet s_1 = \bullet s_2 \text{ and } s_1\bullet = s_2\bullet) \Rightarrow s_1 = s_2]$.
(6) N is simple iff N is simple both w.r.t. the S-elements and the T-elements.
(7) If $T' \subseteq T$, then the subnet of N generated by T' is the net (S',T',F'), where:
$S' = \bullet T' \cup T'\bullet$, and $F' = F \cap ((S' \times T') \cup (T' \times S'))$.
(8) If $S' \subseteq S$, then the subnet of N generated by S' is the net (S',T',F'), where:
$T' = \bullet S' \cup S'\bullet$, and $F' = F \cap ((S' \times T') \cup (T' \times S'))$. ♦

Definition 2.2.3. *(elementary net system)*
An elementary net system, abbreviated EN system, is a 4-tuple $\Sigma = (B,E,F,c_{in})$, where (B,E,F) is a net and $c_{in} \subseteq B$. ♦

Elements of B are called conditions, elements of E are called events, (B,E,F) is called the underlying net of Σ, denoted und(Σ), and c_{in} is called the initial case of Σ, denoted inc(Σ). One may also specify Σ as a pair (und(Σ), inc(Σ)). To avoid unnecessary complications we assume that inc(Σ) is nonempty.

The underlying net captures the structure of the system modelled by Σ. The evolution of the system, hence its behaviour, is defined through the transition rule which specifies the conditions under which an event can occur, and how the event occurrences modify the holding of conditions. Unless clear otherwise, we shall consider finite behaviours only.

Definition 2.2.4. *(transition rule)*
Let N = (B,E,F) be a net, $e \in E$ and $c \subseteq B$.

(1) e is said to be enabled at c, denoted $c[e>_N$, iff $\bullet e \subseteq c$ and $e\bullet \cap c = \emptyset$.

(2) If e is enabled at c, then the occurrence of e leads from c to c', denoted $c\ [e>_N c'$, iff $c' = (c - \bullet e) \cup e\bullet$. ♦

Definition 2.2.5. *(steps)*
Let N = (B, E, F) be a net and $\emptyset \neq U \subseteq E$.

(1) U is independent iff $\forall e_1, e_2 \in U\ [\, e_1 \neq e_2 \Rightarrow (\bullet e_1 \cup e_1\bullet) \cap (\bullet e_2 \cup e_2\bullet) = \emptyset\,]$.

(2) Let $c \subseteq B$. Then U is a step enabled at c, denoted $c[U>_N$, iff U is independent and $\forall e \in U\ c[e>_N$.

(3) Let $c_1, c_2 \subseteq B$. Then U is a step leading from c_1 to c_2, denoted $c_1\ [U>_N c_2$, iff $c_1\ [U>_N$ and $c_2 = (c_1 - \bullet U) \cup U\bullet$. ♦

Obviously, when a step U is a singleton {e}, then $c_1\ [U>_N c_2$ corresponds to the previously introduced enabling and occurrence of the single event e.

In the following, we will also write "... [U> ... in N" rather than "... $[U>_N$...".

Definition 2.2.6. *(Set of cases, set of steps)*
Let $\Sigma = (B, E, F, c_{in})$ be an EN system and N = und(Σ).
The set of cases of Σ, denoted C_Σ, is the smallest subset of 2^B such that:

(1) $c_{in} \in C_\Sigma$.

(2) $\forall c \in C_\Sigma, \forall c' \subseteq B, \forall e \in E\ [\ c\ [e>_N c' \Rightarrow c' \in C_\Sigma\ ]$.

The set of steps of Σ, denoted U_Σ, is the set $\{U \subseteq E : \exists c \in C_\Sigma\ c\ [U>_N \}$. ♦

If Σ is such that each step in U_Σ is a singleton, then Σ is a sequential EN system.

Definition 2.2.7. *(step sequence transition rule)*
Let Σ be an EN system, N = und(Σ) = (B,E,F), SE = 2^E - {$\emptyset$}, $W \in SE^*$ and $c \subseteq B$.

(1) If $W = U_1 ... U_n$ where $U_1, ..., U_n \in U_\Sigma$, then W is enabled at c, denoted $c[W>_N$, iff $\exists c_1, ..., c_{n-1} \in C_\Sigma$ $c[U_1> c_1 ... c_{n-1}[U_n>$.

(2) If W is enabled at c, then the occurrence of W leads from c to c', denoted $c\ [W>_N c'$, iff $c_{n-1}\ [U_n> c'$, where c_{n-1} is as in (1).

(3) If W is the empty word in SE* then $c\ [W>_N c$ for all $c \subseteq B$. ♦

Definition 2.2.8. *(dynamic properties)*

Let $\Sigma = (B,E,F, c_{in})$ be an EN-system with $SCG(\Sigma) = (C_\Sigma, E, A, c_{in})$.

(1) Σ is contact-free iff $\forall e \in E, \forall c \in C_\Sigma$ [$\bullet e \subseteq c \Rightarrow e\bullet \cap c = \emptyset$].

(2) An event e is dead in Σ iff $\nexists c \in C_\Sigma$ $c[e>$.

(3) Σ is reduced iff $\forall e \in E\ \exists c, c' \in C_\Sigma$ $(c, e, c') \in A$.

(4) Σ is deadlock-free iff $\forall c \in C_\Sigma\ \exists e \in E$ $c[e>$. ♦

Definition 2.2.9. *(case graph)*

Let $\Sigma = (B,E,F, c_{in})$ be an EN-system, N = und(Σ) and $E' \subseteq E$ the set of non-dead events of Σ.

(1) The Case Graph of Σ, denoted CG(Σ), is the transition system (C_Σ, U_Σ, A, c_{in}), where $A = \{ (c, U, c') :\ c, c' \in C_\Sigma, U \in U_\Sigma$, and $c[U>_N c' \}$.

(2) The Sequential Case Graph of Σ, denoted SCG(Σ), is the transition system (C_Σ, E', A, c_{in}), where $A = \{ (c, e, c') : c, c' \in C_\Sigma, e \in E'$, and $c\ [e>_N c' \}$. ♦

Whenever N or Σ is clear from the context the subscript N or Σ may be dropped; moreover all notations introduced for the net N = und(Σ) apply also to Σ.

The most popular partial order semantics of an EN system is given by the non sequential processes (called simply "processes") [Pet77b] which describe the system behaviour in terms of partial orders of event occurrences and of condition holding. (For step semantics and partial order semantics based on processes see [BF88] and the included references, while for alternative approaches to partial order semantics of nets see [Maz77], [Gra81], [Kie87], [Rei85b], [Sta81].) Processes will be introduced for contact-free EN systems whose underlying nets are T-restricted [Roz87].

These restrictions are not severe. In fact, there is an algorithm - based on complementation of conditions [Thi87] - that transforms a non-contact-free EN system into a contact-free one establishing the same behaviour. In case of contact-free systems T-restrictedness can be easily obtained by adding post-conditions to the events that violate the requirement. Also this transformation does not affect system behaviour.

Processes of EN systems are represented by a special kind of nets called occurrence nets.

Definition 2.2.10. *(occurrence net)*

An occurrence net is a triple N = (B, E, F), where B is a finite nonempty set of conditions, E is a finite set of events and $F \subseteq (B \times E) \cup (E \times B)$ is a flow relation such that :

(1) $B \cap E = \emptyset$.

(2) $\forall b \in B$ [$|\bullet b| \leq 1$ and $|b\bullet| \leq 1$].

(3) F* is antisymmetric. ♦

Since the occurrence net N = (B, E, F) is an acyclic graph, one can associate with it the poset (X, ≤), where $X = B \cup E$ and $\leq\; = F^*$. In the following Min(N) and Max(N) will denote the set of minimal and maximal elements of (X, ≤) respectively, and B-cut(N) the set of B-cuts of (X, ≤).

Remark
Unlike nets, occurrence nets can have isolated B-elements: in particular, the triple (B, Ø, Ø) is an occurence net.

We are now ready to give the definition of a process of an EN system. A process is defined as an occurrence net together with a labelling of its elements satisfying properties that allows one to interpret the process as a "record" of a concurrent run of the system.

Definition 2.2.11. *(process)*
Let $\Sigma = (B, E, F, c_{in})$ be a contact-free EN system whose underlying net is T-restricted, N'= (B', E', F') an occurrence net, and let $p' : B' \cup E' \rightarrow B \cup E$.
The pair (N', p') is a <u>process</u> of Σ iff
(1) $p'(B') \subseteq B$ and $p'(E') \subseteq E$.
(2) $\forall a,b \in B'$ [$p'(a) = p'(b) \Rightarrow a$ <u>li</u> b].
(3) $\forall e' \in E'$ [$p'(\bullet e') = \bullet p'(e')$ and $p'(e'\bullet) = p'(e')\bullet$].
(4) $p'(Min(N')) = c_{in}$.
The set of <u>maximal events</u> of a process $\pi = (B', E', F', p')$ is the set $\{e \in E' : (e\bullet)\bullet = \emptyset\}$. ♦

P(Σ) denotes the class of processes of the EN system Σ.

Definition 2.2.12. *(isomorphism of processes)*
Let Σ be a contact-free EN system whose underlying net is T-restricted, and let $\pi' = (N', p')$, $\pi'' = (N'', p'') \in P(\Sigma)$. Then π' and π'' are isomorphic iff there is a bijection $\beta : B' \cup E' \dashrightarrow B'' \cup E''$ such that:
(1) $\forall x \in B' \cup E'$ [$p'(x) = p''(\beta(x))$].
(2) $\forall x, y \in B' \cup E'$ [$x \leq y \Leftrightarrow \beta(x) \leq \beta(y)$]. ♦

Definition 2.2.13. *(inclusion of processes)*
Let Σ be a contact-free EN system whose underlying net is T-restricted, and let $\pi' = (N', p')$, $\pi'' = (N'', p'') \in P(\Sigma)$. Then
<u>π'' is contained in π'</u>, denoted $\pi'' \leq \pi'$, iff

$$\exists c \in \text{B-cut}(N') \quad \pi'' = ((B' \cap \downarrow c, E' \cap \downarrow c, F' \cap (\downarrow c \times \downarrow c)), p'/_{\downarrow c}).$$

<u>π'' is properly contained in π'</u>, denoted $\pi'' < \pi'$, iff $\pi'' \leq \pi'$ and $\pi'' \neq \pi'$.

If $\pi'' \leq \pi'$ ($\pi'' < \pi'$) we say that π' is an <u>extension</u> (a proper extension) of π'', or that π'' is a <u>prefix</u> (a proper prefix) of π'. ♦

Remark
≤ is a partial order relation on P(Σ).
Let **P**(Σ) denote the poset (P(Σ), ≤) of processes of $\Sigma = (B, E, F, c_{in})$. **P**(Σ) has a <u>least</u> element (up to isomorphism) $\pi^\circ = (c_{in}, \emptyset, \emptyset, id_{c_{in}})$, called the <u>initial process</u> of Σ.

Definition 2.2.14. *(difference of processes)*
Let $\pi' = (B', E', F', p')$ and $\pi'' = (B'', E'', F'', p'')$ be processes of the EN system $\Sigma = (B, E, F, c_{in})$ such that: $\pi'' < \pi'$. Then $\pi' - \pi''$ denotes the labelled net $\underline{\pi} = (\underline{B}, \underline{E}, \underline{F}, \underline{p})$ where $(\underline{B}, \underline{E}, \underline{F})$ is the subnet of (B', E', F') generated by the set of events $\underline{E} = E' - E''$, and $\underline{p} = p'_{/\underline{B} \cup \underline{E}}$ ♦

3. EQUIVALENCES BASED ON ACTION OBSERVATION

Following the approach proposed by Milner [Mil80], a number of equivalences based on action observation have been proposed for different models of concurrent systems. The examples include [Abr87], [BHR84], [BBK87b], [CH87], [DK83], [DDM87], [DDPS85], [DeN87], [Dev90], [DH84], [Hen88], [GW89a,b], [HO86], [Mil89], [Par81], [Lar87], [PW86], [TRH88], [TV89], [Vog89], [Vos87]. Some of these notions, e.g., observation equivalence [Mil80], bisimulation [Par81],testing-equivalence [DH84], [Hen88], failure-equivalence [BHR84], string-equivalence (trace equivalence) [Hoa81], which have been introduced for CCS and TCSP, have been redefined for net systems [Pom84], [NT84]. Moreover, other notions have been introduced for net based systems, for example: behaviour equivalence [And82a,b], exhibited behaviour equivalence [DDPS85], maximality preserving bisimulation [Dev90], interface equivalence [Vos87].

Roughly speaking, the behaviour of a net based system is defined either through an interleaving semantics, or through a step semantics, or through a partial order semantics. Accordingly, the above mentioned notions of equivalence among net systems have been considered in these three frameworks; for example, in: [BDKP89], [Dev90], [GG89], [GG90b], [GV87], [Pom88], [Vog90a], [Vos87].

In this section we consider EN systems whose events are labelled with action names and we discuss the definitions based on interleaving (Section 3.1), step (Section 3.2) and partial order (Section 3.3) semantics. Moreover, in this section we compare various kinds of equivalences w.r.t. their power of identifying EN systems. An analogous comparison of equivalence notions has been done also in [DeN87], [Gla90b] in the framework of transition systems.

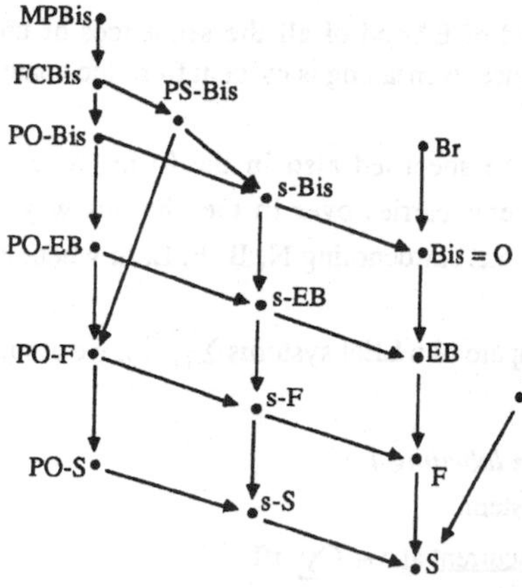

Table A

The relationships between various equivalences are given in Table A, in which the equivalences based on interleaving semantics are placed in the right column. In particular, we consider string equivalence (S), observation equivalence (O), bisimulation (Bis), branching bisimulation (Br), exhibited behaviour equivalence (EB), failure equivalence (F), and testing equivalence (T). The central column describes the relationships among the various notions in the framework of step semantics: by convention, we use the same abbreviations as before with the prefix s- for step semantics. The left column lists the notions based on partial order semantics, here the prefix PO- means 'partial order semantics'. In this framework we also discuss maximality preserving bisimulation (MPBis) , fully concurrent-bisimulation (FCBis) and pomset-bisimulation (PS-Bis). In the diagram, whenever a directed edge (or a directed path) exists from an equivalence X to an equivalence Y, then X is stronger than Y; otherwise X and Y are incomparable.

In Section 3.4 we consider the effect made by the various restrictions of the event labelling on the discerning power of the equivalences.

In this section we consider event labelled EN systems. Labelling events of EN systems will allow us to define observability of actions.

Definition 3.1. *(labelled EN system)*
A labelled EN system, abbreviated LEN system, is a 5-tuple $\Sigma = (B, E, F, c_{in}, h)$, where (B,E,F,c_{in}) is a contact-free EN system whose underlying net is T-restricted, and $h : E \rightarrow L \cup \{ \tau \}$, where L is the alphabet of observable actions and $\tau \notin L$ denotes the "unobservable" action. [1]
Let ε denote the empty word of E* and λ denote the empty word of L*.
h is extended to a homomorphism $h^*: E^* \rightarrow L^*$ in the following way:

$h^*(\varepsilon) = \lambda$;

$\forall e \in E,\ \forall w \in E^* [\ h(e) \neq \tau \ \Rightarrow h^*(ew) = h(e)\, h^*(w)$ and
$h(e) = \tau \ \Rightarrow h^*(ew) = h^*(w)\ ]$.

LEN denotes the class of LEN systems. ♦

Remark
λ is the image of the empty word of E* and of all the sequences of unobservable events. In what follows h denotes both h and h* since its meaning is evident from the context.

A LEN system Σ may be specified also in the form (N, c_{in}, h). All the notations and terminology concerning EN systems carries over in the obvious way to LEN systems. We use the notation $N_\Sigma, B_\Sigma, E_\Sigma, L_\Sigma, h_\Sigma$, etc. for denoting N, B, E, L, h; whenever Σ is clear from the context the subscript Σ may be dropped.
In this section, whenever we compare two LEN systems Σ_1, Σ_2, we assume that $L_{\Sigma_1} = L_{\Sigma_2} = L$.

Definition 3.2. *(restrictions on labelling)*
Let $\Sigma = (N, c_{in}, h)$ be a LEN system.
(1) A label $a \in L$ is autoconcurrent at $c \in C_\Sigma$ iff

[1] Unlike case graphs (Definition 2.2.9.) and transition systems (Section 2.1.), in the definition of LEN systems the labelling function h is explicitly specified since in what follows h is widely referred to.

$\exists\, e_1, e_2 \in E$ [$e_1 \neq e_2$, $c[\{e_1, e_2\}>$, and $h(e_1) = h(e_2) = a$].

(2) Σ is autoconcurrency-free iff $\forall\, a \in L$, $\nexists\, c \in C_\Sigma$ a is autoconcurrent at c.

(3) Σ is τ-free iff $h(E) \subseteq L$.

(4) Σ is an identity LEN system iff $h = id_{/E}$. ♦

Any EN system can be seen as an identity LEN system.

When discussing equivalences we will often consider systems composed of two systems interacting by means of synchronous actions, i.e., events labelled by the same observable action (like in TCSP [BHR84]). This kind of system composition is formalized in the following definition where actions of the two systems are made synchronous by joining them into pairs whose pre-sets and post-sets are the union of the pre-sets and post-sets of the source events.

Definition 3.3. *(parallel composition)*
Let $\Sigma_1 = (B_1, E_1, F_1, c_{in1}, h_1)$ and $\Sigma_2 = (B_2, E_2, F_2, c_{in2}, h_2)$ be LEN systems with $B_1 \cap B_2 = \emptyset$ and $E_1 \cap E_2 = \emptyset$. Let $E'_1 = \{ e_1 \in E_1 : \exists\, e' \in E_2\ \ h_1(e_1) = h_2(e') \neq \tau \}$, $E'_2 = \{ e_2 \in E_2 : \exists\, e' \in E_1\ \ h_2(e_2) = h_1(e') \neq \tau\}$, $E''_1 = E_1 - E'_1$ and $E''_2 = E_2 - E'_2$.
Let $E_{<>} = \{ (e_1, e_2) : e_1 \in E'_1, e_2 \in E'_2, \text{ and } h_1(e_1) = h_2(e_2) \neq \tau\}$.
The parallel composition of Σ_1 and Σ_2, denoted $\Sigma_1 \parallel \Sigma_2$, is the LEN $\Sigma = (B,E,F, c_{in}, h)$, where:

$B = B_1 \cup B_2$;

$E = E''_1 \cup E''_2 \cup E_{<>}$;

$F = (F_1 \cap ((B_1 \times E''_1) \cup (E''_1 \times B_1))) \cup (F_2 \cap ((B_2 \times E''_2) \cup (E''_2 \times B_2))) \cup$
$\quad \{ (s, (e_1,e_2)) : (e_1,e_2) \in E_{<>} \text{ and } (s \in {}^\bullet e_1 \text{ or } s \in {}^\bullet e_2) \} \cup$
$\quad \{ ((e_1,e_2), s) : (e_1,e_2) \in E_{<>} \text{ and } (s \in e_1{}^\bullet \text{ or } s \in e_2{}^\bullet) \}$;

$c_{in} = c_{in1} \cup c_{in2}$;

$h : E \dashrightarrow L \cup \{\tau\}$ is defined as follows:

$$h(e) = \begin{cases} h_1(e) & \text{if } e \in E''_1 \\ h_2(e) & \text{if } e \in E''_2 \\ h_1(e) = h_2(e) & \text{if } e = (e_1,e_2) \in E_{<>}. \end{cases}$$

♦

3.1. INTERLEAVING SEMANTICS

In this section we consider equivalence notions which are based on the observability of sequences of events. In order to capture the behaviour that can be obtained through system observation, it is necessary to define a new transition rule which takes into account only the images of observable events. This transition rule corresponds to the transition relation that is the basis of weak bisimulation and weak observation equivalence [Mil89b].

Definition 3.1.1. *(image transition rule : $c(v>$)*
Let $\Sigma = (B,E,F, c_{in}, h)$ be a LEN system, $v \in L^*$ and $c, c' \in C_\Sigma$.

(1) v is enabled at c, denoted $c(v>$, iff $\exists\ w \in E^*$ [$h(w) = v$ and $c[w>$].

(2) If v is enabled at c, then the occurrence of v can lead from c to c', denoted $c(v>c'$, iff

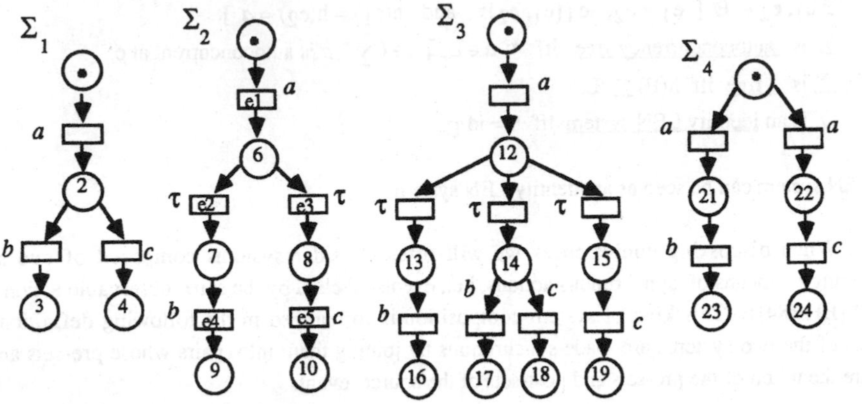

Figure 3.1.1

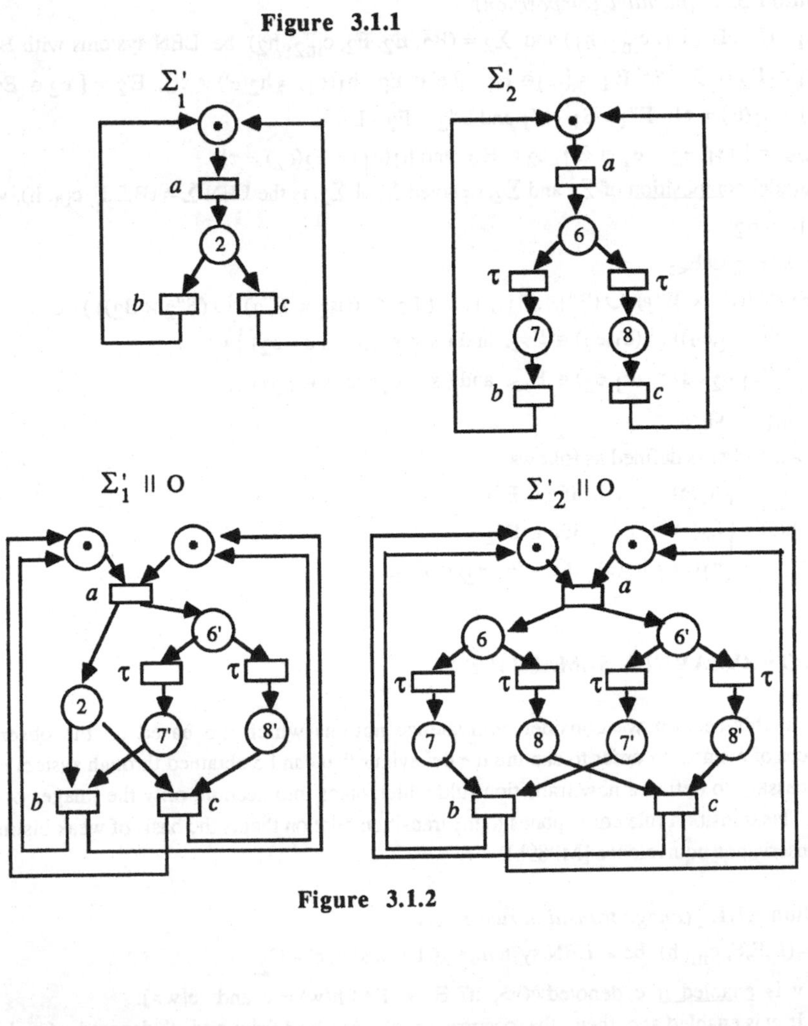

Figure 3.1.2

$\exists w \in E^*$ [$h(w) = v$ and c [w> c']. ♦

Example 3.1.
Let us consider the LEN system Σ_2 from Figure 3.1.1 The observable action *a* is enabled at inc(Σ_2) and can lead to the case {6}, because inc(Σ_2) [e_1> {6} and $h_2(e_1) = a$; it also can lead to the case {7}, because inc(Σ_2) [e_1e_2> {7} and $h_2(e_1e_2) = a$; and to the case {8} for similar reasons. It is easy to see that inc(Σ_2) also enables sequences *ab* and *ac*. ♦

3.1.1. String-equivalence

This is the least discriminating equivalence notion among those proposed in the literature. Two systems are string equivalent if they can perform the same sequences of observable actions. No attention is paid to the possible unobservable actions which represent the internal system behaviour and it does not matter when choices between alternative behaviours are made. This notion corresponds to the notion of strong equivalence for sequential programming and to the equivalence notion used in the automata and languages theory (see, e.g., [Sal85], [Jan87] and [Pete81]). String equivalence is the basis of the first semantical model [Hoa81] of Hoare's CSP [Hoa78]; in this context it is called Trace equivalence.

Definition 3.1.2. *(S-equivalence)*
Let Σ_1 and Σ_2 be LEN systems. Then Σ_1 and Σ_2 are string equivalent, abbreviated S-equivalent and denoted $\Sigma_1 \approx^S \Sigma_2$, iff $\forall v \in L^*$ [inc(Σ_1) (v> $\Leftrightarrow$ inc(Σ_2) (v>]. ♦

Example 3.1.1.
All the LEN systems of Figure 3.1.1 are S-equivalent since they generate the same sequences of observable actions, namely: *ab* and *ac* together with their prefixes. ♦

S-equivalence is not suitable when considering systems which interact with other systems. In particular, S-equivalent systems may exhibit different behaviours when composed with other systems, as shown by the following example.

Example 3.1.2.
Let us consider the LEN systems $\Sigma'_1 \| O$ and $\Sigma'_2 \| O$ of Figure 3.1.2, where the observer O is a LEN system isomorphic to Σ'_2 (this observer was used by Milner [Mil80] in order to criticize S-equivalence). They show different behaviour: in fact, if after executing *a*, Σ'_2 resolves the local conflict among τ events in favour of *b* and reaches the case {7}, while O decides for *c*, then $\Sigma'_2 \| O$ enters a deadlock, whereas such a situation cannot happen in the behaviour of $\Sigma'_1 \| O$.
In Σ'_1 the conflict between *b* and *c* can be solved by an observer which autonomously decides which action is to be chosen, whereas in Σ'_2 this choice cannot be influenced by an observer, but rather it is the result of an internal conflict resolution. In spite of this difference Σ'_1 and Σ'_2 are S-equivalent. ♦

An equivalence (called behaviour equivalence or B-equivalence) based on S-equivalence was defined by Andre' for a subclass of Place/Transition systems with the aim of applying it in hardware implementation of industrial processes [And82a,b]. This application domain motivates the decision to compare systems that have a deterministic behaviour only [AAB79], i.e., systems in which "equivalent sequences of events" (sequences of events whose observable images coincide) are "able to be prolonged by equivalent sequences of events". This property is formalized in the following definition.

Definition 3.1.3. *(B-condition)*
A LEN system $\Sigma = (N, c_{in}, h)$ satisfies the B-condition iff
$\forall v \in L^*, \forall a \in L \; [c_{in}(va> \;\Rightarrow\; \forall c \in C_\Sigma \; [c_{in}(v>c \Rightarrow c(a>] \,]$. ♦

Then two systems which satisfy the B-condition are behavioural equivalent if and only if they are S-equivalent. B-condition is a very strong one; in fact in the case of systems satisfying the B-condition all the equivalences considered here collapse.

Example 3.1.3.
The LEN system Σ_2 of Figure 3.1.1 does not satisfy the B-condition: different occurrences of a can enable two different observable event images, namely e_1e_2 enables only b, while e_1e_3 enables only c. ♦

B-equivalence can be established by means of some elementary transformations preserving the equivalencee given in [And82b]. These transformations are mainly based on the net structure.

3.1.2. Bisimulation and Observation equivalence

The first proposal of an equivalence notion based on an observer and on observable/unobservable actions is due to Milner, who defined in his Calculus of Communicating Systems [Mil80] the notion of observation equivalence. Milner [Mil83], [Mil84], [Mil89a,b] has considered several variations of observation equivalence, in particular bisimulation, as proposed in [Par81]. bisimulation is stronger than observation equivalence but these two notions coincide if the compared systems are "image finite" (i.e., $\forall c \in C_\Sigma \; | \{ c' : c\,(a > c' \text{ and } a \in L \} | < \infty$) [HM80]. This is trivially true for LEN systems since they are finite.

Two systems are observation equivalent if they provide the observer with the same sets of possibilities at each intermediate state of the observation. The definition is given as the intersection of a sequence of equivalence relations $\approx_n^O$ ($n \geq 0$), where $\approx_0^O$ is the universal relation and, for each $n > 0$, the relation $\approx_n^O$ is defined in terms of $\approx_{n-1}^O$.

Definition 3.1.4. *(O-equivalence)*
Let $\Sigma_1 = (N_1, c_{in,1}, h_1)$ and $\Sigma_2 = (N_2, c_{in,2}, h_2)$ be LEN systems. Then Σ_1 and Σ_2 are observation equivalent, abbreviated O-equivalent and denoted $\Sigma_1 \approx^O \Sigma_2$, iff
$\forall n \geq 0 \;\; \Sigma_1 \approx_n^O \Sigma_2$, where:

(1) $\Sigma_1 \approx_0^O \Sigma_2$ is always true.

(2) $\Sigma_1 \approx_{n+1}^O \Sigma_2$ iff $\forall v \in L^*$
$[\forall c_1 \, [\,\underline{inc}(\Sigma_1)\,(v > c_1 \Rightarrow \exists c_2 \, [\,\underline{inc}(\Sigma_2)\,(v > c_2 \text{ and } (N_1,c_1,h_1) \approx_n^O (N_2,c_2,h_2)\,]]$
and (vice versa)
$[\forall c_2 \, [\,\underline{inc}(\Sigma_2)\,(v > c_2 \Rightarrow \exists c_1 \, [\,\underline{inc}(\Sigma_1)\,(v > c_1 \text{ and } (N_1,c_1,h_1) \approx_n^O (N_2,c_2,h_2)]]]$. ♦

Remark

O-equivalence implies S-equivalence; in particular, it follows from the definitions that: $\approx_1^O \equiv \approx^S$, but $\approx_2^O \subset \approx^S$, and thus $\approx^O \subset \approx^S$, as shown in Example 3.1.4. (1).

We give now the definition of bisimulation.

Definition 3.1.5. *(bisimulation)*
Let Σ_1 and Σ_2 be LEN systems. Then Σ_1 and Σ_2 are Bisimilar, denoted $\Sigma_1 \approx^{Bis} \Sigma_2$, iff $\exists\, r \subseteq C_{\Sigma_1} \times C_{\Sigma_2}$ such that :

1) $(\underline{inc}(\Sigma_1), \underline{inc}(\Sigma_2)) \in r$.
2) $\forall\ (c_1, c_2) \in r, \forall\, \nu \in L^*$

$[\ \forall c'_1\ [\ c_1\ (\nu > c'_1 \Rightarrow \exists\, c'_2\ [c_2\ (\nu > c'_2$ and $(c'_1, c'_2) \in r\ ]]]$
and (vice versa)
$[\ \forall c'_2\ [\ c_2\ (\nu > c'_2 \Rightarrow \exists\, c'_1\ [c_1\ (\nu > c'_1$ and $(c'_1, c'_2) \in r\ ]]]$.

Such a relation r is called bisimulation. ♦

Example 3.1.4.
Let us consider again the LEN systems of Figure 3.1.1.

(1) $\underline{not}(\Sigma_1 \approx^O \Sigma_2)$, since $\underline{not}(\Sigma_1 \approx_2^O \Sigma_2)$. In fact, $\underline{inc}(\Sigma_2)\ (a > \{7\}$ and for all c_1 such that $\underline{inc}(\Sigma_1)\ (a > c_1$ we have: $\underline{not}\ ((N_1, c_1, h_1) \approx_1^O (N_2, \{7\}, h_2))$.
If we consider Σ'_1 and Σ'_2 of Figure 3.1.2, then $\underline{not}(\Sigma'_1 \approx^O \Sigma'_2)$ holds for similar reasons.

(2) $\underline{not}\ (\Sigma_2 \approx^O \Sigma_3)$, since $\underline{not}\ (\Sigma_2 \approx_3^O \Sigma_3)$, while $\Sigma_2 \approx_2^O \Sigma_3$. For example, for each observable sequence in Σ_3 leading from $\underline{inc}(\Sigma_3)$ to c_3, it is always possible to find a corresponding observable sequence in Σ_2 leading from $\underline{inc}(\Sigma_2)$ to c_2 such that $(N_2,c_2,h_2) \approx^S (N_3,c_3,h_3)$, and vice versa; but if for example we choose $c_3=\{14\}$ then there is no c such that $\underline{inc}(\Sigma_2)\ (a > c$ and $(N_2,c,h_2) \approx_2^O (N_3,c_3,h_3)$. The difference between the two LEN systems is that, after the interaction *a*, in Σ_2 the choice between *b* and *c* is always due to an internal conflict resolution, while in Σ_3 the internal conflict resolution can result in *b* and *c* being in a conflict, which can be resolved externally.

This example shows that O-equivalence distinguishes two systems not only w.r.t. the possibility of generating deadlocks (as shown in (1), see also Example 3.1.2) but also w.r.t. the type of conflict resolution (either purely local to the system or not).

(3) $\underline{not}\ (\Sigma_2 \approx^O \Sigma_4)$, since in Σ_2 *a* can lead from $\underline{inc}(\Sigma_2)$ to $\{6\}$ where both *b* and *c* are enabled, whereas in Σ_4, after *a*, either *b* or *c* is enabled but never both.

This example shows that O-equivalence distinguishes two systems also w.r.t. the point at which the choice between two events is resolved: in Σ_4 the non-deterministic choice between *b* and *c* is made at the occurrence of *a*, while in Σ_2 it is delayed until after the occurrence of *a*.

(4) The LEN systems Σ_1 and Σ_2 of Figure 3.1.3 are O-equivalent and so are the LEN systems Σ_1 and Σ_2 of Figure 3.1.4. ♦

Darondeau [Dar82] presented an interesting critique of O-equivalence by noting that an "effective observer" is not able to distinguish, e.g., between the systems Σ_2 and Σ_4 of Figure 3.1.1. In fact, O-

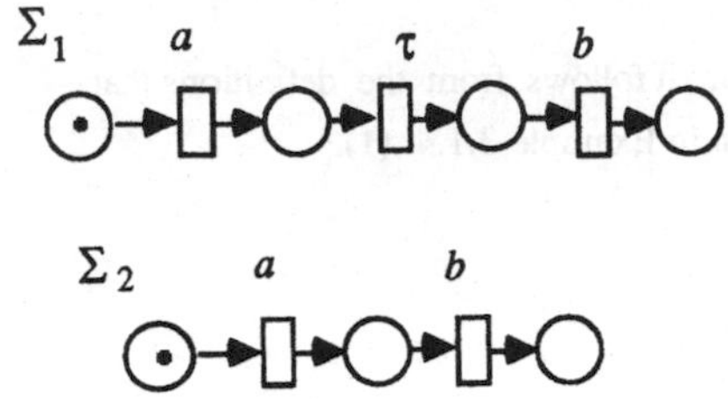

Figure 3.1.3

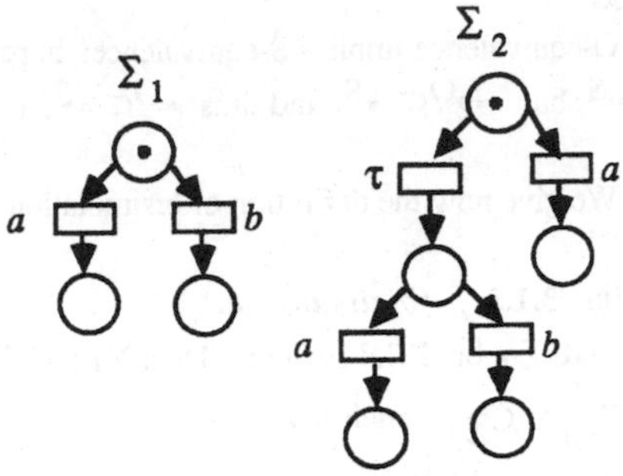

Figure 3.1.4

equivalence implicitly assumes that, at each move, an observer is able to make copies of the observed system and then to test them separately. Abramsky [Abr87] defined a notion of equivalence based on a generalization of the notion of tests (tests will be presented in section 3.1.7) which is equivalent to O-equivalence; he pointed out that for establishing O-equivalence "we need some idea of performing separate tests on the copies, and then combining the information from the outcomes of the subtests in some way to obtain an outcome of the overall test".

O-equivalence and bisimulation have been widely studied by many authors (e.g., see: [BBK87a], [BK85], [Bro83], [DK83]). Moreover, Hennessy and Milner defined and characterized O-equivalence through algebraic axioms and in terms of a modal logic [HM80], [HM85].

For Place/Transition systems, a notion of simulation [Bes87] related to bisimulation has been introduced; it preserves some behavioural properties (e.g., safeness and liveness [Rei85a]).

From the very beginning Milner was concerned with the definition of an equivalence notion which would be a congruence w.r.t. the operation of parallel and alternative composition. O-equivalence does not satisfy this requirement and the notion of O-congruence had to be introduced in [Mil80].

Milner also faced the problem of a complete axiomatization of his calculus. In [Mil80] various equational laws were proved for observation congruence and in [HM80] a set of such laws was shown to be complete for behaviours without recursion. A complete axiomatization of O-congruence in the presence of recursion is given in [Mil89a].

3.1.3. Branching Bisimulation

This is one of the more recently proposed notions of equivalence between concurrent systems. The motivations given by van Glabbeek and Weijland [GW89a,b], [Gla90] are twofold: finding a notion of equivalence preserved under refinement of actions and preserving the branching structure of processes. In fact, in the presence of τ -actions an important feature of bisimulation (as proposed by Park [Par81]) is missing, namely the property that any computation in one system corresponds to a computation in the other in such a way that if from two corresponding cases c_1 and c_2 we reach two corresponding cases c'_1 and c'_2 , the first by means of a single observable event and the second by means of a sequence of events

that are all unobservable except for the last one, then all cases between c_2 and c'_2 have to correspond to c_1. Actually it is sufficient to require that only the case enabling the observable event in the second system corresponds to c_1 [GW89b], as formalized in the following definition.

Definition 3.1.6. ***(Br-equivalence)***

Let Σ_1 and Σ_2 be LEN systems. Then Σ_1 and Σ_2 are Branching equivalent, abbreviated Br-equivalent and denoted $\Sigma_1 \approx^{Br} \Sigma_2$, iff there is a relation $R \subseteq C_{\Sigma_1} \times C_{\Sigma_2}$ such that:

1) $(\underline{inc}(\Sigma_1), \underline{inc}(\Sigma_2)) \in R$.

2) $\forall (c_1, c_2) \in R$

$$[\forall e_1 \in E_1, \forall c'_1 \in C_{\Sigma_1} [c_1 [e_1> c'_1 \Rightarrow [[h_1(e_1) = \tau \text{ and } (c'_1, c_2) \in R] \text{ or }$$
$$[\exists c'_2, c''_2 \in C_{\Sigma_2}, \exists w \in E_2^*, \exists e_2 \in E_2 [h_2(w) = \lambda, h_2(e_2) = h_1(e_1),$$
$$c_2 [w> c''_2 [e_2> c'_2, (c_1, c''_2) \in R, \text{ and } (c'_1, c'_2) \in R]]]]]$$

and (vice versa)

$$[\forall e_2 \in E_2, \forall c'_2 \in C_{\Sigma_2} [c_2 [e_2> c'_2 \Rightarrow [[h_2(e_2) = \tau \text{ and } (c_1, c'_2) \in R] \text{ or }$$
$$[\exists c'_1, c''_1 \in C_{\Sigma_1}, \exists w \in E_1^*, \exists e_1 \in E_1 [h_1(w) = \lambda, h_1(e_1) = h_2(e_2),$$
$$c_1 [w> c''_1 [e_1> c'_1, (c''_1, c_2) \in R, \text{ and } (c'_1, c'_2) \in R]]]]]. \quad \blacklozenge$$

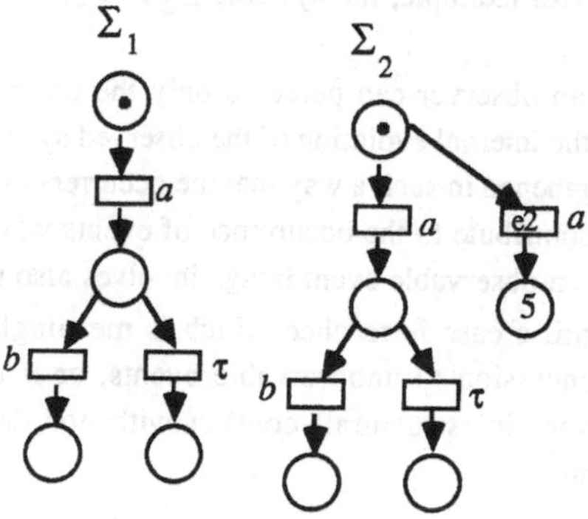

Figure 3.1.5

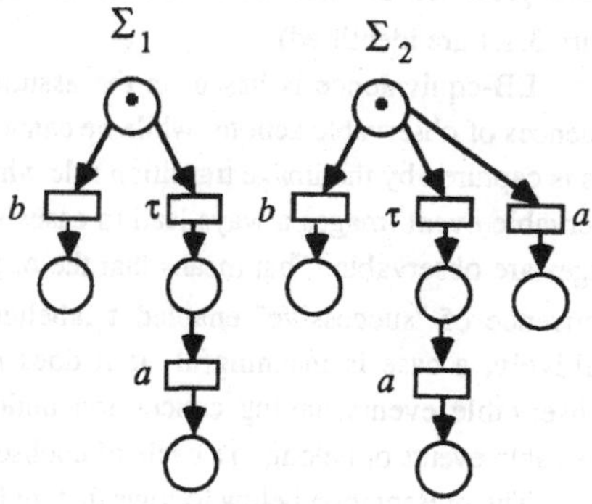

Figure 3.1.6

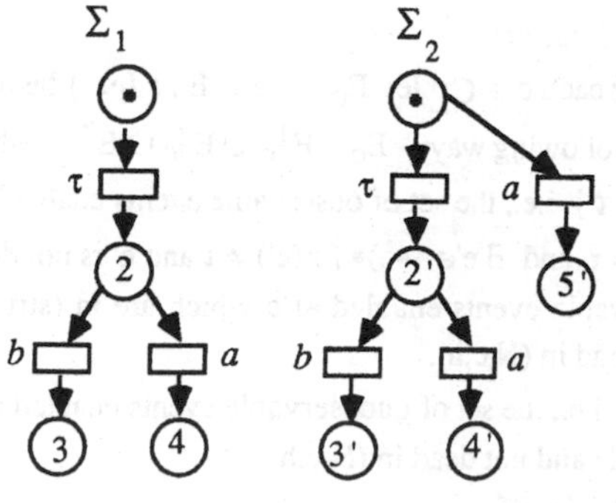

Figure 3.1.7

Example 3.1.5.

Let us consider the systems Σ_1 and Σ_2 of Figure 3.1.5. They are not Br-equivalent since the latter contains a computation leading to case {5} which has no corresponding computation according to Definition 3.1.6. For similar reasons the systems of Figure 3.1.6 are not Br-equivalent. The systems Σ_1 and Σ_2 of Figure 3.1.7. are Br-equivalent with the following being the pairs of equivalent cases: ({1},{1'}), ({2},{1'}), ({2},{2'}), ({3},{3'}), ({4},{4'}), ({4},{5'}). ♦

The notion of Br-congruence has been defined in [GW89a] and in [Gla90a] where its complete axiomatization has also been given.

3.1.4. Exhibited Behaviour-equivalence

Exhibited behaviour equivalence, abbreviated EB-equivalence, has been introduced in [DP83], [DDPS85] and it has been proposed as a notion suitable for modeling organizational systems [DDS87].

EB-equivalence distinguishes systems not only w.r.t. deadlocks in the interactions with the environment, but also w.r.t. the possible choices in their behaviours and then w.r.t. the type of conflict resolution (for example, the systems Σ_2 and Σ_3 from Figure 3.1.1 are distinguished). In addition, unlike O-equivalence, it abstracts from the "when the choices are made" property. The conflict among multiple occurrences of the same observable action *a* is considered equivalent to the conflict among unobservable actions preceded or followed by the observable action *a* (for example, the systems Σ_2 and Σ_4 from Figure 3.1.1 are identified).

EB-equivalence is based on the assumption that an observer can perceive only the possible sequences of observable actions, while he cannot perceive the internal evolution of the observed system. This is captured by the image transition rule which is strengthened in such a way that the occurrences of observable event images always lead to cases which can contribute to the occurrence of events whose images are observable. That means that the occurrence of an observable event image involves also the occurrence of "successive" enabled τ-labelled events until a case is reached which is meaningful. Intuitively, a case is meaningful if it does not give concession to unobservable events, or if the unobservable events having concession under it are either in (structural) conflict with non-dead observable events or belong to a cycle of unobservable events.

The presentation below follows that in [Pom88].

Definition 3.1.7. *(meaningful cases)*

Let Σ be a LEN system and for each $c \in C_\Sigma$ let $E_c = \{ e \in E : c\,[e> \}$ be the set of events enabled at c. E_c can be partitioned in the following way: $E_c = E^1{}_c \cup E^2{}_c \cup E^3{}_c$, where

(1) $E^1{}_c = \{ e \in E_c : h(e) \neq \tau \}$, i.e., the set of observable events enabled at c.

(2) $E^2{}_c = \{ e \in E_c : h(e) = \tau$ and $\exists\, e' \in (\bullet e)\bullet\ [\, h(e') \neq \tau$ and e' is not dead in (N,c,h)$] \}$, i.e., the set of unobservable events enabled at c which are in (structural) conflict with events which are observable and not dead in (N,c,h).

(3) $E^3{}_c = E_c - (E^1{}_c \cup E^2{}_c)$, i.e., the set of unobservable events enabled at c which are not in conflict with events which are observable and not dead in (N,c,h).

A case $c \in C_\Sigma$ is a <u>meaningful case</u> iff

$$\forall\, v \in (E - (E^1{}_c \cup E^2{}_c))^*\ [\, c\,[v> \Rightarrow h(v) = \lambda \text{ and } \exists\, v' \in E^* [h(v') = \lambda \text{ and } c\,[vv'> c\,]\,]. \ \blacklozenge$$

Remark

From the previous definition it follows that the first element of each nonempty sequence of $(E - (E^1_c \cup E^2_c))^*$ belongs to E^3_c. Moreover, if E^3_c is empty, then the only sequence belonging to $(E - (E^1_c \cup E^2_c))^*$ is the empty sequence, and therefore c is meaningful.

Example 3.1.6.

Let us consider the LEN system Σ of Figure 3.1.8.

(1) The case $c = \{2,3\}$ is meaningful since $E^3_c = \emptyset$; note that the τ-labelled event e_3 enabled at $\{2,3\}$ is in conflict with the observable events e_4; therefore e_3 belongs to E^2_c and not to E^3_c.

(2) The case $c = \{5,9,11,12\}$ is meaningful since the τ-labelled event enabled at $\{5,9,11,12\}$ is e_9 which lies on a cycle of τ-labelled events.

(3) The case $c = \{3,4\}$ is not meaningful since the unobservable event e_5 is enabled at $\{3,4\}$, and it is neither in conflict with an observable event nor on a cycle of τ-labelled events. ♦

Remark

Let Σ be a LEN system. Then the following holds (see [Pom88]).

(1) $\forall c \in C_\Sigma \ \exists w \in E^* [\ c[w> c',\ h(w) = \lambda$ and c' is meaningful].

(2) $\forall c \in C_\Sigma \ \forall e \in E\ [[\ c\,[e>$ and $h(e) \neq \tau\ ] \Rightarrow$

$\exists w \in E^* [\ c\,[w> c',\ h(w) = \lambda,\ c'[e>,$ and c' is meaningful]].

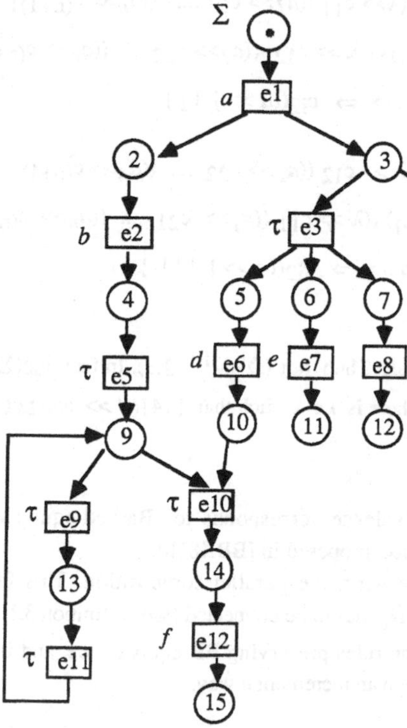

Figure 3.1.8

We now give the transition rule on which EB-equivalence is based.

Definition 3.1.8. *(EB-transition rule: c ((a>>c')*

Let Σ be a LEN system, c, c' $\in C_\Sigma$ and, for every w $\in$ E*, let N_w denote the subnet generated by the set of events appearing in w.

(1) c ((λ >> c' iff $\exists$ w $\in$ E* [c [w> c', h(w) = λ, and c' is meaningful].

(2) c ((a >> c' iff

$\exists$ w $\in$ E* [c [w> c', h(w) = a, c' is meaningful, and N_w is connected]. ♦

Remark

For τ-free EN systems the EB-transition rule coincides with the image transition rule.

Two LEN systems Σ_1 and Σ_2 are EB-equivalent if and only if for each occurrence of a sequence of observable event images with intermediate meaningful cases in one system, there is a sequence with the same image and with intermediate meaningful cases which correspond to the previous ones in the other system. Two cases correspond to each other if and only if they give concession to the same set of observable event images.

Definition 3.1.9. *(EB-equivalence)*

Let Σ_1 and Σ_2 be LEN systems. Then Σ_1 and Σ_2 are <u>exhibited behaviour-equivalent</u>, abbreviated EB-equivalent and denoted $\Sigma_1 \approx^{EB} \Sigma_2$, iff $\forall$ $a_1, \ldots, a_n \in$ L

[[$\forall$ $c_{11}, \ldots, c_{(n+1)1} \in C_{\Sigma_1}$ [<u>inc</u>(Σ_1) ((λ>> c_{11} ((a_1>> c_{21} .... ((a_n>> $c_{(n+1)1}$ $\Rightarrow$

$\exists$ $c_{12}, \ldots, c_{(n+1)2} \in C_{\Sigma_2}$ [<u>inc</u>(Σ_2) ((λ >> c_{12} ((a_1>> c_{22} .... ((a_n>> $c_{(n+1)2}$

and $\forall$ i $\in$ [[n+1]], $\forall$ $a \in$ L [c_{i1}((a >> $\Leftrightarrow$ c_{i2}((a >>]]]]

and (vice versa)

[$\forall$ $c_{12}, \ldots, c_{(n+1)2} \in C_{\Sigma_2}$ [<u>inc</u>(Σ_2) ((λ >> c_{12} ((a_1>> c_{22} .... ((a_n>> $c_{(n+1)2}$ $\Rightarrow$

$\exists$ $c_{11}, \ldots, c_{(n+1)1} \in C_{\Sigma_1}$ [<u>inc</u>(Σ_1) ((λ >> c_{11} ((a_1>> c_{21} .... ((a_n>> $c_{(n+1)1}$

and $\forall$ i $\in$ [[n+1]], $\forall$ $a \in$ L [c_{i1}((a >> $\Leftrightarrow$ c_{i2}((a >>]]]]]. ♦

Example 3.1.7.

Let us consider the systems of Figure 3.1.1. Then <u>not</u> ($\Sigma_2 \approx^{EB} \Sigma_3$). In fact, <u>inc</u>($\Sigma_3$) (($a$>> {14} and for all cases c such that <u>inc</u>(Σ_2) ((a>> c there is $l \in$ L such that {14}((l >> and <u>not</u> (c ((l >>).

On the other hand, $\Sigma_2 \approx^{EB} \Sigma_4$. ♦

For τ-free EN systems EB-equivalence corresponds to Barbed-equivalence introduced in [Pnu85] and to the Ready Trace equivalence proposed in [BBK87b].

EB-equivalence is a congruence w.r.t. the parallel composition. This fact depends on the requirement that in the EB-transition rule N_w has to be connected (see Definition 3.1.8).

[Mar87] considers some reduction rules preserving EB-equivalence, and it gives some results which allow one to prove EB-equivalence in an incremental way.

3.1.5. Failure equivalence

In the "failure set semantics" of CSP given in [BHR84] the behaviour of a system is described in terms of "failures", i.e., pairs (w, X) in which w is a possible sequence of observable actions the system may perform, and X is a set of observable actions the system may refuse to perform after the sequence w. Failures capture the possibilities of generating deadlocks in the interactions between the system and its environment; in fact, a deadlock may occur when (w, X) is a system failure and the environment can perform actions in X only, after the execution of w.

In this approach the behaviour of a system is determined by its failure set. This leads to a failure equivalence relation: two systems are failure equivalent if and only if their failure sets coincide. In [Bro83] S.D. Brookes defined failure equivalence through a preorder on CSP terms. Here we give the failure equivalence definition for LEN systems in the same way.

Definition 3.1.10. *(F-equivalence)*
Let Σ_1 and Σ_2 be LEN systems. Then

(1) Σ_1 <u>is less than</u> Σ_2 <u>w.r.t. failures</u>, denoted $\Sigma_1 \subseteq^F \Sigma_2$, iff
$\forall w \in L^*, \forall X \subseteq L\ [\exists c_2\ [\underline{inc}(\Sigma_2)\ (w\rangle\ c_2$ and $\forall a \in X\ \underline{not}(c_2\ (a\rangle)\ ] \Rightarrow$
$\exists c_1\ [\ \underline{inc}(\Sigma_1)\ (w\rangle\ c_1$ and $\forall a \in X\ \underline{not}\ (\ c_1\ (a\rangle)\ ]].$

(2) Σ_1 and Σ_2 are <u>failure equivalent</u>, abbreviated F-equivalent and denoted $\Sigma_1 \approx^F \Sigma_2$, iff $\Sigma_1 \subseteq^F \Sigma_2$ and $\Sigma_2 \subseteq^F \Sigma_1$. ♦

Example 3.1.8.
Consider the LEN systems from Figure 3.1.1: $\Sigma_2 \subseteq^F \Sigma_1$ and <u>not</u> ($\Sigma_1 \approx^F \Sigma_2$).
Note that $\underline{inc}(\Sigma_2)\ (a\rangle\{7\}$ and <u>not</u> $(\{7\}\ (c\rangle)$, while for all c_1 such that $\underline{inc}(\Sigma_1)\ (a\rangle\ c_1$, it holds: $c_1\ (c\rangle$. On the other hand, $\Sigma_2 \approx^F \Sigma_3$ and $\Sigma_3 \approx^F \Sigma_4$. ♦

[Bro83] contains a complete axiomatization of F-equivalence for finite CSP terms.

In [Bro84] the failures model of CSP [Bro83], [BHR84] is extended by adding divergence sets and requiring a kind of "consistency" between failures and divergences in such a way that divergence is catastrophic. The new equivalence has been called failure&divergence-equivalence. The concept of divergence is introduced in the next section, where failure&Divergence-equivalence is also discussed and compared with testing equivalence. [Bro84] gives a complete proof system for failure&divergence-equivalence of CSP terms with recursion.

It is shown in [Vog89] that F-equivalence is the coarsest congruence w.r.t. the parallel composition which preserves deadlock-freeness.

3.1.6. Testing equivalence

Let us consider the two LEN systems Σ_1 and Σ_2 represented in Figure 3.1.9. All the previous equivalence notions do not distinguish between them, even though their behaviours show a difference. In fact, after the interaction *a*, Σ_2 can always be involved in the interaction *b*, whereas Σ_1 may diverge, i.e., it may continuously perform unobservable actions and never again interact with the environment.

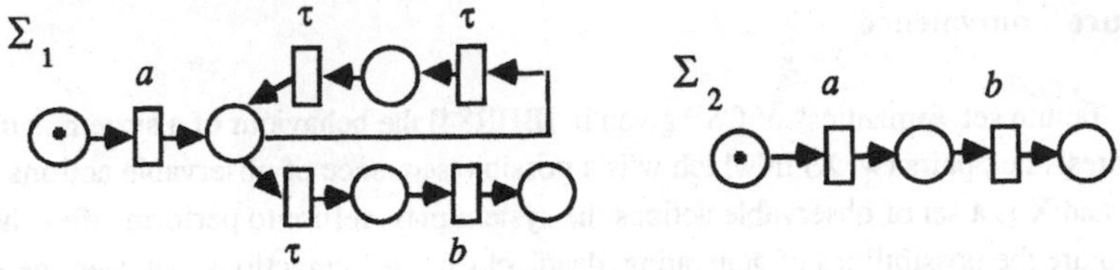

Figure 3.1.9

In [DH84] R. De Nicola and M. Hennessy introduced testing equivalence within a rather general approach which compares the behaviour of concurrent systems by tabulating the possible effects of the interactions between the observers and the systems. Observers are thought of as agents that perform tests, and therefore systems are distinguished w.r.t. their ability to pass tests and their inability not to fail tests. testing equivalence distinguishes systems not only w.r.t. the possibility to generate deadlocks but also w.r.t. the possibility to diverge (see also [DeN87], [Hen88]).

In the following we formulate the testing-equivalence for LEN systems in the same way as in [DH84], i.e., on the basis of three preorders. Let Σ and O be LEN systems, with O playing the role of the observer of Σ, and let $C_{SO} \subseteq C_O$ be an arbitrary subset of the reachable cases of O representing its "successful case set". Let $\mathbb{S} = \Sigma \parallel O$ be the parallel composition of Σ and O. In this composition we use the following convention: the events obtained through the fusion of events labelled, say, with a, are labelled with $\underline{a}$ (where $\underline{a} \in \underline{L} = \{\underline{x} : x \in L\}$); the remaining ones keep the same label as in Σ or in O.

A system Σ passes a test performed by O if and only if a sequence of interactions "observer-observed system" (possibly interleaved with unobservable actions) leads O to a succesful case. In order to formalize this notion in terms of the compound system $\mathbb{S}$, we need to consider only the cases of $\mathbb{S}$ reachable through an element of $\underline{L}^*$ (these are the kind of interactions that are considered in the following), and, among them, the cases which contain a successful case of O as a subset. These notions are expressed in the following definition.

Definition 3.1.11. *(case set and successful case set of* $\mathbb{S}$ *)*
Let Σ, O and $\mathbb{S} = \Sigma \parallel O = \langle B_{\mathbb{S}}, E_{\mathbb{S}}, F_{\mathbb{S}}, \underline{inc}(\mathbb{S}), h_{\mathbb{S}} \rangle$ be LEN systems and let C_{SO} be the successful cases of O.

(1) The case set of $\mathbb{S}$ is the set $\underline{C}_{\mathbb{S}} = \{ c \subseteq B_{\mathbb{S}} : \exists\, \underline{w} \in \underline{L}^*\ \underline{inc}(\mathbb{S})\ (\underline{w}> c \}$.

(2) The successful case set of $\mathbb{S}$ is the set $\underline{C}^S{}_{\mathbb{S}} = \{ c \in \underline{C}_{\mathbb{S}} : c \cap B_O \in C_{SO} \}$. ♦

A behaviour of $\mathbb{S}$ is considered successful if and only if the corresponding sequence leads to a successful case; it is considered unsuccessful otherwise.

Definition 3.1.12. *(result set)*
Let $\mathbb{S} = \Sigma \parallel O$ be a LEN system, $\{\mathsf{T}, \perp\}$ be the simple two point lattice where $\mathsf{T} \geq \perp$. The result set of $\mathbb{S}$, denoted $RS(O,\Sigma)$, is a subset of $\{\mathsf{T}, \perp\}$ defined as follows :

(1) $\mathsf{T} \in RS(O,\Sigma)$ iff $\underline{C}^S{}_{\mathbb{S}} \neq \emptyset$.

(2) $\perp \in RS(O,\Sigma)$ iff $\underline{inc}(\mathbb{S}) \notin \underline{C}^S{}_{\mathbb{S}}$ and

$[\,[\forall\, \underline{l} \in \underline{L}\ \ \underline{not}\,(\,\underline{inc}(\mathbb{S})(\underline{l}>)]$ or $\underline{inc}(\mathbb{S}) \rightarrow \tau^{\omega}$ or

$[\ \exists\, \underline{a}_1, \dots, \underline{a}_n \in \underline{L},\ \exists\, c_{1\mathbb{S}}, \dots, c_{n\mathbb{S}} \in \underline{C}_{\mathbb{S}}\ \ [\ \underline{inc}(\mathbb{S})\ (\underline{a}_1> c_{1\mathbb{S}} \dots (\underline{a}_n> c_{n\mathbb{S}}$ and

$[\forall j \in [\![n]\!]\ c_{j\mathbf{S}} \notin \mathbf{C}^{s}_{\mathbf{S}}$ and

$[[\forall l \in \mathbf{L}$ $\underline{\text{not}}\,(c_{n\mathbf{S}}\ (l>)]$ or

$[\exists\ a_{n+1}, a_{n+2}, \ldots \in \mathbf{L},\ \exists\ c_{n+1\mathbf{S}}, c_{n+2\mathbf{S}}, \ldots \in \mathbf{C_S}\ [c_{n\mathbf{S}}\ (a_{n+1}>c_{n+1\mathbf{S}} \ldots$

and $\forall i > 0\ c_{n+i\mathbf{S}} \notin \mathbf{C}^{s}_{\mathbf{S}}]\ ]$ or $c_{n\mathbf{S}} \to \tau^{\omega}\ ]]]]\ ]$

(where $c \to \tau^{\omega}$ iff there is an infinite sequence of events $e_1e_2 \ldots e_k \ldots$ such that:

$\forall i > 0\ [\ h(e_1 \ldots e_i) = \lambda$ and $c\ [e_1 \ldots e_i>]$,

i.e., c may give a concession to an infinite sequence of τ-labelled events). ♦

Remark

The previous definition states that:

1) **T** belongs to the result set if and only if there exists in **S** a sequence of interactions leading to a successful case;

2) ⊥ belongs to the result set if and only if the initial case in **S** is not a successful case, and either no interaction between Σ and O are enabled at it, or it enables an infinite sequence of τ-labelled events, or in **S** there exists an interaction sequence leading to a case not preceded by a successful one, which

i) is a deadlock (i.e., no interaction between Σ and O is enabled at it), or

ii) enables an infinite sequence of interactions between Σ and O not leading to a successful case ("divergence" - **S** diverges), or

iii) enables an infinite sequence of τ-labelled events (i.e., either Σ or O diverges).

Note that both deadlocks and divergences contribute ⊥ to the result set.

On the basis of the previous definition it is possible to distinguish systems that *must* pass a test performed by O ($RS(O,\Sigma)=\{\mathbf{T}\}$) and systems that *may* pass a test performed by O ($RS(O,\Sigma) = \{\mathbf{T},\bot\}$), obtaining the following definition:

Definition 3.1.13. *(testing-equivalence)*

Let Σ_1 and Σ_2 be LEN systems.

(1) Σ_1 is <u>less than</u> Σ_2 <u>w.r.t. must-test</u>, denoted $\Sigma_1 \subseteq_{must} \Sigma_2$, iff
$\forall O \in \mathbf{LEN}\ [\ RS(O,\Sigma_1) = \{\mathbf{T}\} \Rightarrow RS(O,\Sigma_2) = \{\mathbf{T}\}]$.

(2) Σ_1 is <u>less than</u> Σ_2 <u>w.r.t. may-test</u>, denoted $\Sigma_1 \subseteq_{may} \Sigma_2$, iff
$\forall O \in \mathbf{LEN}\ [\ \mathbf{T} \in RS(O,\Sigma_1) \Rightarrow \mathbf{T} \in RS(O,\Sigma_2)\ ]$.

(3) Σ_1 and Σ_2 are <u>must-equivalent</u>, denoted $\Sigma_1 \approx_{must} \Sigma_2$, iff
$\Sigma_1 \subseteq_{must} \Sigma_2$ and $\Sigma_2 \subseteq_{must} \Sigma_1$.

(4) Σ_1 and Σ_2 are <u>may-equivalent</u>, denoted $\Sigma_1 \approx_{may} \Sigma_2$, iff
$\Sigma_1 \subseteq_{may} \Sigma_2$ and $\Sigma_2 \subseteq_{may} \Sigma_1$.

(5) Σ_1 is <u>less than</u> Σ_2 <u>w.r.t. testing</u>, denoted $\Sigma_1 \subseteq^{T} \Sigma_2$, iff
$\Sigma_1 \subseteq_{must} \Sigma_2$ and $\Sigma_1 \subseteq_{may} \Sigma_2$.

(6) Σ_1 and Σ_2 are <u>testing-equivalent</u>, abbreviated T-equivalent and denoted $\Sigma_1 \approx^{T} \Sigma_2$,
iff $\Sigma_1 \approx_{must} \Sigma_2$ and $\Sigma_1 \approx_{may} \Sigma_2$. ♦

Remark

It is easily proved that $\approx_{may}$ corresponds to S-equivalence.

In addition $\approx_{must}$ and $\approx_{may}$ are incomparable; in fact, by considering the systems Σ_1, Σ_2 and Σ_3 from Figure 3.1.10, one can see that:

- $\Sigma_1 \approx_{may} \Sigma_2$ and not ($\Sigma_1 \approx_{must} \Sigma_2$); not ($\Sigma_1 \approx_{may} \Sigma_3$) and $\Sigma_1 \approx_{must} \Sigma_3$.

T-equivalence and F-equivalence are incomparable; in fact, by considering the systems Σ_1 and Σ_2 from Figure 3.1.9 one can see that: $\Sigma_1 \approx^F \Sigma_2$ while not ($\Sigma_1 \approx_{must} \Sigma_2$) and then not ($\Sigma_1 \approx^T \Sigma_2$), and for the systems Σ_1 and Σ_2 from Figure 3.1.11 it holds: $\Sigma_1 \approx^T \Sigma_2$ while not ($\Sigma_1 \approx^F \Sigma_2$).

Moreover, in the case of systems without divergence, T-equivalence coincides [DeN85], [DeN87] with F-equivalence and with fully observational equivalence introduced by Darondeau in [Dar82].

Example 3.1.9.

(1) Let us consider the LEN systems of Figure 3.1.9.

We observe that not ($\Sigma_1 \approx^T \Sigma_2$); in fact, $\Sigma_1 \approx_{may} \Sigma_2$ and not ($\Sigma_1 \approx_{must} \Sigma_2$).

(2) Let us consider the systems of Figure 3.1.1. Then not ($\Sigma_1 \approx^T \Sigma_2$); in fact, there is an observer O isomorphic to Σ_2 with the successful case set {{9}, {10}}, which can distinguish between their behaviours, since RS(O,Σ_1)={T} while RS(O,Σ_2)={T,⊥}.

Hence, not ($\Sigma_1 \approx_{must} \Sigma_2$), while $\Sigma_1 \approx_{may} \Sigma_2$. It is easy to verify that $\Sigma_2 \approx^T \Sigma_3 \approx^T \Sigma_4$. ♦

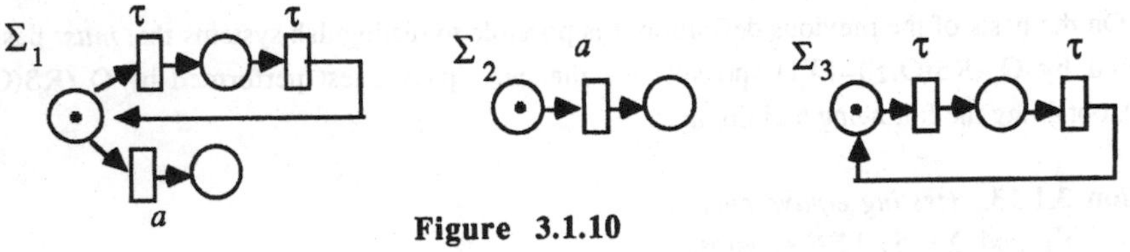

Figure 3.1.10

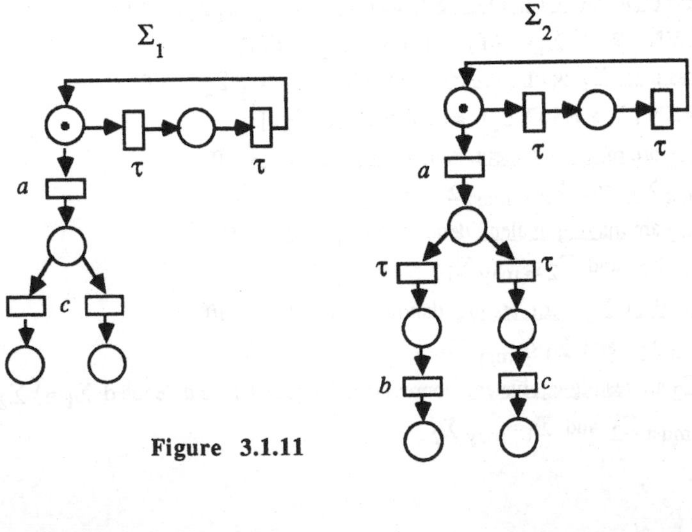

Figure 3.1.11

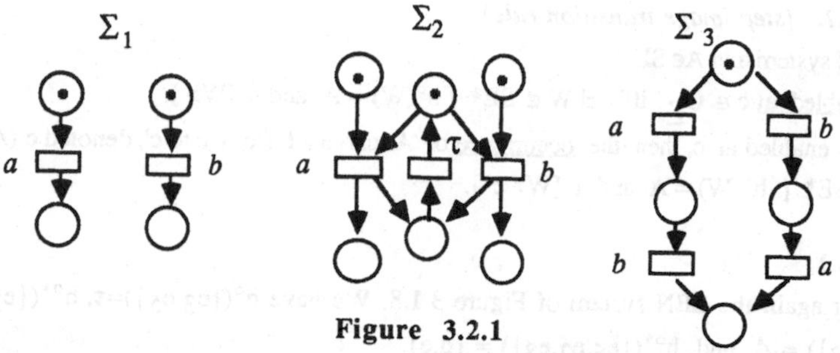

Figure 3.2.1

De Nicola and Hennessy give in [DH84] a complete proof system for the above three preorders for CCS. The topic of defining complete proof systems in a more general context is discussed in [Hen88].

The $\approx_{must}$ relation coincides with failure&divergence-equivalence [Bro84] [DeN85] since like failure&divergence-equivalence it distinguishes systems w.r.t. the possibility to generate deadlocks and divergence, and it regards divergence as catastrophic (e.g., it does not distinguish between the systems Σ_1 and Σ_3 of Figure 3.1.10).

3.2. STEP SEMANTICS

The equivalence notions introduced in the previous section would consider all the LEN systems of Figure 3.2.1 as equivalent. However, their behaviours are different if we consider actions that can occur concurrently. In fact, while in Σ_1 the actions *a* and *b* are concurrent, this is not true in the other systems where *a* and *b* can occur in any order but never concurrently. To be able to capture this difference, the equivalence notions have to be reformulated by considering the images of steps instead of the images of single events. To this end it is necessary to extend the labelling function and the transition rule to multisets of events.

Definition 3.2.1. *(step labelling function)*

Let $\Sigma = (B, E, F, c_{in}, h)$ be a LEN system, $SE = 2^E - \{ \emptyset \}$ and SL be the set of non-empty multisets over the set of labels L.

Then $h^\circ : SE \rightarrow SL \cup \{ \tau \}$ is defined for every $X \in SE$ by

$$\begin{cases} h^\circ(X) = \tau & \text{if } \forall e \in X \;\; h(e) = \tau, \\ h^\circ(X) = \sum_{a \in L} n_a a & \text{otherwise,} \end{cases}$$

where $n_a = | h^{-1}(a) \cap X |$.

Let us denote by Λ the empty word in SE* and by $\mathit{\Lambda}$ the empty word in SL*.

h° can be extended to a homomorphism $h^{\circ *}: SE^* \rightarrow SL^*$ such that:

$h^{\circ *}(\Lambda) = \mathit{\Lambda}$;

$\forall X \in SE, \forall W \in SE^* [\, [\, h^\circ(X) \neq \tau \;\Rightarrow\; h^{\circ *}(XW) = h^\circ(X)\, h^{\circ *}(W)\,]$ and

$[\, h^\circ(X) = \tau \;\Rightarrow\; h^{\circ *}(XW) = h^{\circ *}(W)\,]\,]$. ♦

As in Sections 3 and 3.1, in what follows h° denotes both h° and $h^{\circ *}$ since its meaning is evident from the context.

Definition 3.2.2. *(step image transition rule)*
Let Σ be a LEN system and $A \in SL$.

(1) A is enabled at $c \in C_{\Sigma}$ iff $\exists W \in SE^* \; [h°(W) = A$ and $c\,[W>]$.

(2) If A is enabled at c, then the occurrence of A can lead from c to c', denoted $c\,(A> c'$, iff $\exists W \in SE^* \; [\; h°(W) = A$ and $c\,[W> c'\,]$. ♦

Example 3.2.1.
Let us consider again the LEN system of Figure 3.1.8. We have $h°(\{e_3,e_5\})=\tau$, $h°^*(\{e_3,e_5\}) = \Lambda$; $h°^*(\{e_3,e_5\}\{e_8\}) = \Lambda$ and $h°^*(\{e_6,e_7,e_8\}) = \{d,e\}$.
Moreover, $\{2,3\}\;(\;\{d,e\}> \{2,10,11,12\}$. ♦

The equivalences for the step semantics are based on the above transition rule and the equivalences introduced in the previous section. The new equivalences deal with sequences of multisets of observable actions instead of sequences of observable actions; in addition, they consider sets of observable action multisets, or sequences of observable action multisets having a concession in the reached cases instead of sets of single observable actions, or sequences of observable actions. Moreover, when a multiset A of observable actions has concession in a given case, the new equivalences consider not only the effect of its occurrence but also the effects of the occurrences of all the multisets contained in A.

As an example of the new equivalence notions, we present the string equivalence based on step semantics, called step-string-equivalence and abbreviated s-S-equivalence, and bisimulation based on step semantics, called step-bisimulation and abbreviated s-bisimulation.

Note that the same notational convention is used for the equivalence notions defined in the framework of step semantics troughout the paper and, in particular, in the diagram presented at the beginning of Section 3.

Definition 3.2.3. *(s-S-equivalence)*
Let Σ_1 and Σ_2 be LEN systems.
Then Σ_1 and Σ_2 are s-S-equivalent, denoted $\Sigma_1 \approx^{s\text{-}S} \Sigma_2$, iff

$\forall Z \in SL^* \; [\; \underline{inc}(\Sigma_1)\,(\,Z> \;\Leftrightarrow\; \underline{inc}(\Sigma_2)\,(\,Z>\,]$. ♦

Definition 3.2.4. *(s-bisimulation)*
Let Σ_1 and Σ_2 be LEN systems.
Then Σ_1 and Σ_2 are s-bisimilar, denoted $\Sigma_1 \approx^{s\text{-}Bis} \Sigma_2$, iff there is $R \subseteq C_{\Sigma_1} \times C_{\Sigma_2}$ such that:

1) $(\underline{inc}(\Sigma_1)\,,\,\underline{inc}(\Sigma_2)) \in R$.

2) $\forall\,(c_1, c_2) \in R,\; \forall\, Z \in SL^*$
$[\;\; \forall c'_1\,[\; c_1\,(Z> c'_1 \;\Rightarrow\; \exists c'_2\;[\,c_2\,(Z> c'_2$ and $(c'_1, c'_2) \in R\,]]]$
and (vice versa)
$[\;\; \forall c'_2\,[\; c_2\,(Z> c'_2 \;\Rightarrow\; \exists c'_1\,[\,c_1\,(Z> c'_1$ and $(c'_1, c'_2) \in R\,]]]$.

Such a relation R is called s-bisimulation. ♦

Example 3.2.2.
Let us consider the LEN system of Figure 3.2.1.
$\Sigma_2 \approx^{s\text{-}S} \Sigma_3$ and not ($\Sigma_1 \approx^{s\text{-}S} \Sigma_2$): in fact, inc($\Sigma_1$) ({a,b}> and not (inc($\Sigma_2$) ({a,b}>).
Similarly, $\Sigma_2 \approx^{s\text{-}Bis} \Sigma_3$ and not ($\Sigma_1 \approx^{s\text{-}Bis} \Sigma_2$).
Let us consider the LEN systems of Figure 3.3.1. One can see that: $\Sigma_1 \approx^{s\text{-}S} \Sigma_2$ and $\Sigma_1 \approx^{s\text{-}Bis} \Sigma_2$. ♦

Bisimulation based on steps has been also introduced in [NT84]. Furtheremore, a notion related to bisimulation and based on the step semantics has been introduced in [Vos87] under the name of "interface equivalence". Interface equivalence is defined for the class of strictly labelled contact-free Condition Event systems in which not only observable events, but also observable places are considered. The class of Condition Event systems [Pet77a] corresponds to the class of reduced, simple, contact-free EN systems in which the class of the cases both forward and backward reachable is considered as the system state space. This makes interface equivalence incomparable with the equivalences presented here.

The definitions of the remaining equivalences in the framework of the step semantics are given and discussed in [Pom84], where sets of labels instead of multisets are considered.
Failure equivalence based on steps has been also studied in [TV89].

Remark
In the case when multisets are singletons, the definitions of the equivalences based on step semantics yield the notions based on interleaving semantics. Therefore, for sequential systems, each equivalence based on step semantics and the corresponding one based on interleaving semantics coincide.

3.3. PARTIAL ORDER SEMANTICS

Going into the framework of partial order semantics leads to new equivalences. One of the central issues motivating particular choice of equivalences is the issues of refinement (we refer the reader to [BGV90] which discusses the relationships between the choice of equivalences and refinements).

Let us consider the LEN systems Σ_1 and Σ_2 of Figure 3.3.1. They are equivalent w.r.t. all the equivalences introduced so far; for example, it is easy to verify that they are s-bisimilar (see Example 3.2.2). However, the observable actions *a* and *b* are causally independent in Σ_1, while they are both causally independent and causally dependent in Σ_2.

If we want to distinguish concurrent systems w.r.t. the level of concurrency they exhibit, i.e., w.r.t. the relations of causal independence and causal dependence between observable actions, it is necessary to formulate the equivalences presented in Sections 3.1 and 3.2 in the framework of a partial order semantics. To this end we will consider system processes instead of occurrence sequences or step sequences; more exactly we will consider equivalence classes of processes defined up to process isomorphism (see Definition 2.2.12.).

The new notions do not identify the systems Σ_1 and Σ_2 of Figure 3.3.1. Let us consider the processes π = (N, p) ∈ P(Σ_1) and π'= (N', p') ∈ P(Σ_2) shown in Figure 3.3.2. There is no process in P(Σ_1) corresponding to π' and having the same causality relation between the observable actions. In fact, the only process in P(Σ_1) containing both *a* and *b* is the process π where *a* and *b* are causally independent, while they are causally dependent in π'.

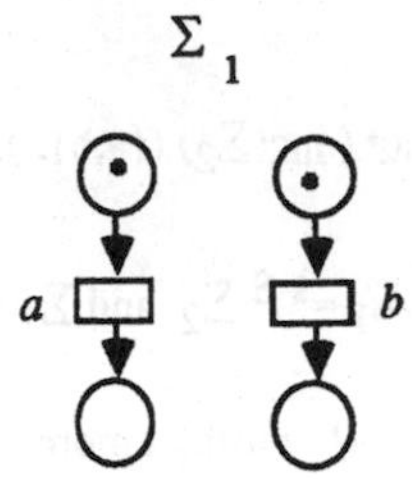

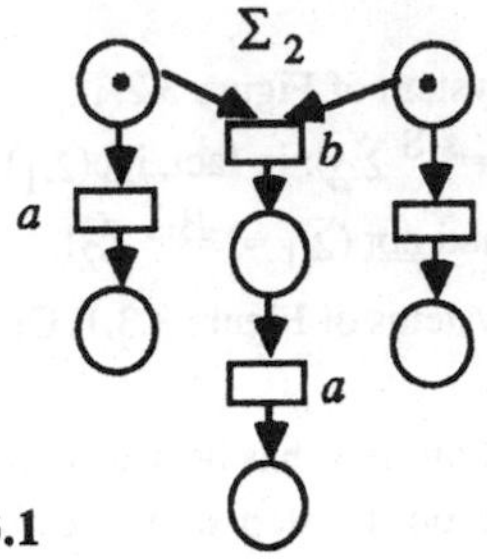

Figure 3.3.1

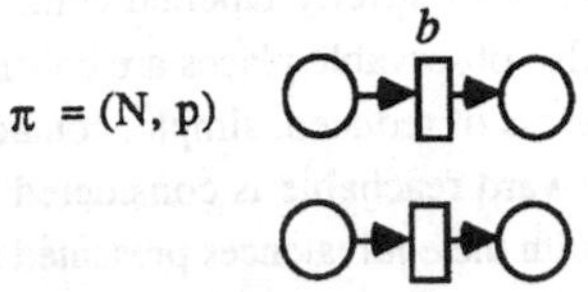

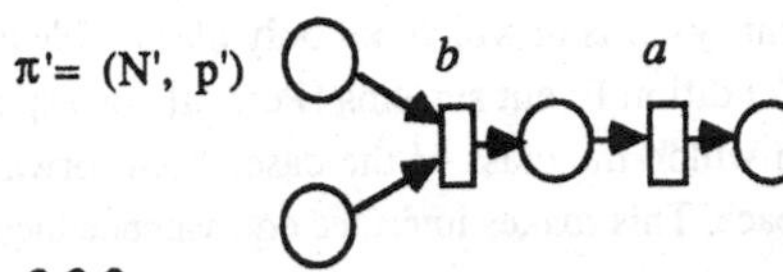

Figure 3.3.2

In order to deal with the equivalence notions in the framework of partial order semantics we need three auxiliary definitions. The first one associates to a process of a LEN system its abstraction, i.e., the labelled poset of the events modelling observable action occurrences. The second allows one to identify different abstractions if they are order-isomorphic. The third considers the possibility of extending a process by a multiset of observable actions, i.e., of extending a process π to a process π' which contains, in addition to π, a multiset of independent observable actions.

Definition 3.3.1. *(process abstraction)*
Let $\Sigma = (N, c_{in}, h)$ be a LEN system and $\pi = (N', p')$ be a process of Σ where $N'=(B',E',F')$.
The abstraction of π with respect to h is the labelled poset (with labels in the action set L) $abs_h(\pi) = (E'', \leq, h'')$ where:

(1) $E''=\{e \in E' : h(p'(e)) \neq \tau\}$.

(2) $\leq = (F')^* \cap (E'' \times E'')$.

(3) $h'' : E'' \to L$ is such that : $\forall e \in E''\ h''(e) = h(p'(e))$. ♦

Clearly, the notion of process abstraction can be applied also to labelled subnets of processes; e.g., in the next section we will consider the abstraction of the labelled subnet $\pi' - \pi$, where π' and π are two processes of a LEN system such that $\pi < \pi'$.

Definition 3.3.2. *(order-isomorphism of abstractions)*
Let Σ_1 and Σ_2 be LEN systems, $\pi_1 \in P(\Sigma_1)$, $\pi_2 \in P(\Sigma_2)$, and $abs_{h1}(\pi_1) = (E''_1, \leq_1, h''_1)$ and $abs_{h2}(\pi_2) = (E''_2, \leq_2, h''_2)$ be the abstractions of π_1 and π_2, respectively.

(1) $f : abs_{h1}(\pi_1) \to abs_{h2}(\pi_2)$ is an order-isomorphism iff
f is a bijective mapping of events such that :
(i) $\forall e \in E''_1\ h''_1(e) = h''_2(f(e))$.
(ii) $\forall e_1, e_2 \in E''_1\ [e_1 \leq_1 e_2 \Leftrightarrow f(e_1) \leq_2 f(e_2)]$.

(2) $abs_{h1}(\pi_1)$ and $abs_{h2}(\pi_2)$ are called order-isomorphic, denoted $abs_{h1}(\pi_1) \cong abs_{h2}(\pi_2)$, iff there exists an order isomorphism between them. ♦

Definition 3.3.3. *(process extension by multiset, $\pi <_A \pi'$)*
Let $\pi = (B,E,F,p)$ be a process of a LEN system Σ, and A be a multiset of observable actions. π can be extended by A to a process π', denoted $\pi <_A \pi'$, iff $\pi' = (B',E',F',p') \in P(\Sigma)$ is a process such that

$[\ \pi < \pi',\ h^{\circ}(p'(E' - E)) = A,$ and

$\forall e_1, e_2 \in E' - E\ [\ [\ h(p'(e_1)) \neq \tau$ and $h(p'(e_2)) \neq \tau\ ] \Rightarrow e_1\ \underline{co}\ e_2\ ]\ ].$ ♦

In what follows S-equivalence, bisimulation, EB-equivalence and F-equivalence will be considered in the framework of the partial order semantics given in terms of processes. In discussing these notions we will not consider the property of an equivalence being preserved by action refinement, which has been one of the basic motivations for their introduction.

To improve the readability of the examples we introduce the following notational convention:
$\forall$ w, w' $\in L^*$

ww' means that w and w' are in sequence,

w || w' means that w and w' are concurrent/independent, i.e., let v , v' $\in E^+$, where $v = e_1...e_n$ and $v' = e'_1...e'_k$, are such that h(v) = w and h(v') = w'; then for all $i \in [\![n]\!]$ and for all $j \in [\![k]\!]$ it holds that e_i and e'_j are independent (see Definition 2.2.5).

3.3.1. Partial Order-String equivalence

The notion of process equivalence corresponding to the notion of string equivalence is straightforward: two LEN systems are process equivalent if and only if for each process π_1 in one LEN system there is a process π_2 in the other LEN system such that their abstractions are order-isomorphic. The acronym for this equivalence is PO-S-equivalence which stands for "partial order version of string equivalence".

Definition 3.3.4. *(PO-S-equivalence)*
Let Σ_1 and Σ_2 be two LEN systems and $P(\Sigma_1)$, $P(\Sigma_2)$ be their posets of processes. Then Σ_1 and Σ_2 are PO-S-equivalent, denoted $\Sigma_1 \approx_{PO\text{-}S} \Sigma_2$, iff

$\forall \pi_1 \in P(\Sigma_1), \exists \pi_2 \in P(\Sigma_2)\ \ abs_{h_1}(\pi_1) \cong abs_{h_2}(\pi_2)$

and (vice versa)

$\forall \pi_2 \in P(\Sigma_2), \exists \pi_1 \in P(\Sigma_1)\ \ abs_{h_1}(\pi_1) \cong abs_{h_2}(\pi_2).$ ♦

Example 3.3.1.
(1) The systems Σ_1 and Σ_2 in Figure 3.3.1 are not PO-S-equivalent (see the discussion in the introduction of Section 3.3).
(2) The sequential systems Σ_1 and Σ_2 in Figure 3.1.1 are not only S-equivalent but also PO-S-equivalent.
(3) The systems Σ'_1 and Σ'_2 in Figure 3.3.3. are PO-S-equivalent; in particular, in both cases the maximal processes (i.e., the processes such that there are no proper extensions of them) are such that a_1a_2b or $(a_1a_2)||b$. ♦

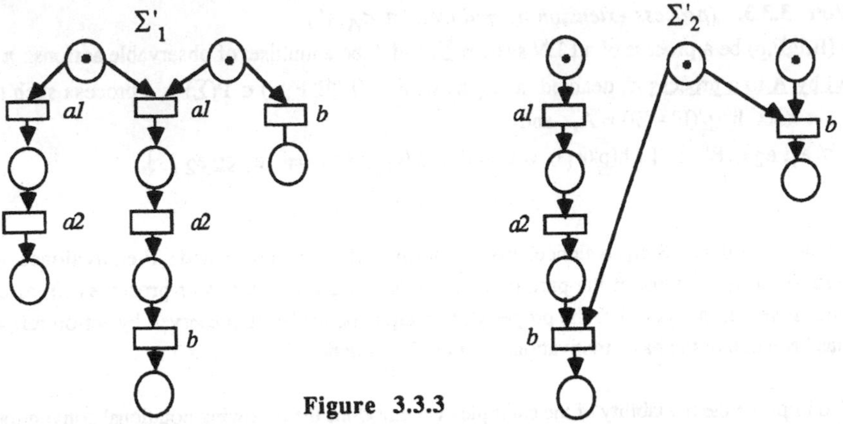

Figure 3.3.3

3.3.2. Bisimulations and Observational Equivalences on Processes

Various generalizations of bisimulation or observational equivalence for the partial order semantics have been proposed in the literature. In particular, O-equivalence has been defined for trace languages (a concurrency model proposed in [Maz77]) in [DDPS83], and for labelled event structures in [CFM83].

In [BC87] bisimulation has been defined for transition systems whose transitions are labelled by pomsets (pomsets are a concurrency model proposed in [Pra86]); this notion was considered for partial order semantics of net based systems in [Pom88] and in [BDKP89]. In the following we call it pomset-bisimulation, abbreviated PS-bisimulation.

Various definitions of bisimulation based on pomsets have also been studied in [GV87].

Another definition of bisimulation on partial orders, which is incomparable with PS-bisimulation, has been proposed for nondeterministic measurement systems in [DDM87]. A similar notion was proposed also in [Dev88], where it was called true concurrency bisimulation, for partial order semantics of P/T systems and in [GG89] where it was called weak history preserving bisimulation, for event structures (a concurrency model proposed in [Win80]). This notion will be presented here for LEN systems under the name of partial order-bisimulation, abbreviated PO-bisimulation.

A more restrictive definition of bisimulation for partial orders, called Behaviour Structures bisimulation, has been given in terms of behaviour structures in [TRH88], [RT88]; the same notion, under the name of history preserving bisimulation, has been studied in [GG89] for the event structures and in [GG90b] for the flow event structures (a concurrency model proposed in [BC89]). This notion was also introduced for P/T systems in [BDKP89] under the name of fully concurrent bisimulation, abbreviated FC-bisimulation.

Fully concurrent bisimulation gave rise to a stronger equivalence notion introduced for P/T systems in [Dev90], and called maximality preserving bisimulation, or MP-bisimulation (the same name will be used here); and for an equivalence for the labelled event structures in [Vog90b] under the name of history-preserving ST-bisimulation, which is based on the ST-semantics (a concurrency model introduced in [GV87]) .

Other generalizations of bisimulation based on non-interleaving semantics, including partial words and semi words, can be found in [AH89], [Cas87], [CH87], [DD90], [DDM89], [Gla90a], [Vog90b] and [Wink89].

In the following we give the definitions of PS-bisimulation, PO-bisimulation, FC-bisimulation and MP-bisimulation. Figure 3.3.4 shows the relationships among these equivalences.

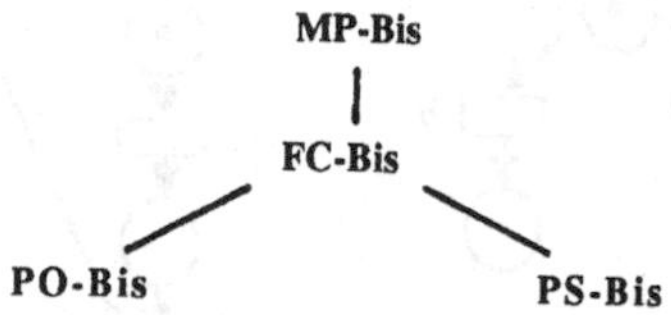

Figure 3.3.4

1) Pomset-bisimulation

PS-bisimulation requires that the processes of two LEN systems are related in such a way that the initial ones correspond to each other, and the corresponding processes may be extended to corresponding processes such that the abstractions of the extended parts are order isomorphic.

Definition 3.3.5. *(PS-bisimulation)*
Let Σ_1 and Σ_2 be two LEN systems. Then Σ_1 and Σ_2 are PS-bisimilar, denoted $\Sigma_1 \approx_{\text{PS-Bis}} \Sigma_2$, iff there is $\rho \subseteq P(\Sigma_1) \times P(\Sigma_2)$ such that:

(1) $(\pi^\circ_1, \pi^\circ_2) \in \rho$.

(2) $\forall (\pi_1, \pi_2) \in \rho$.

$[\ \forall \pi'_1 \in P(\Sigma_1)\ [\ \pi_1 \leq \pi'_1 \Rightarrow \exists \pi'_2 \in P(\Sigma_2)\ [\ \pi_2 \leq \pi'_2,\ (\pi'_1, \pi'_2) \in \rho$, and $\text{absh}_1(\pi'_1 - \pi_1) \cong \text{absh}_2(\pi'_2 - \pi_2)\ ]\ ]$,

and (vice versa)

$\forall \pi'_2 \in P(\Sigma_2)\ [\ \pi_2 \leq \pi'_2 \Rightarrow \exists \pi'_1 \in P(\Sigma_1)\ [\ \pi_1 \leq \pi'_1,\ (\pi'_1, \pi'_2) \in \rho$, and $\text{absh}_1(\pi'_1 - \pi_1) \cong \text{absh}_2(\pi'_2 - \pi_2)\ ]\ ]\ ]$. ♦

Example 3.3.2.

(1) Let us consider the LEN systems Σ_1 and Σ_2 of Figure 3.3.5. In both systems either $a||b$, or ab can be executed. However, in Σ_1 the choice between these two options is made at the beginning, while in Σ_2 the choice can be made after the execution of a. In spite of this difference, Σ_1 and Σ_2 are PS-bisimilar; in both cases the process whose abstraction is b can be "extended by a", and the process whose abstraction is a can be "extended by b".

(2) The LEN systems Σ'_1 and Σ'_2 of Figure 3.3.3 are not PS-bisimilar; the process of Σ'_2 whose abstraction is a_1 can be "extended by b", while this is not always possible for the two processes of Σ'_1 whose abstraction is a_1. It is worth observing, note that Σ'_1 and Σ'_2 have been obtained from Σ_1 and Σ_2 of Figure 3.3.5, respectively, by refining action a with the sequence a_1a_2: thus PS-bisimulation is not a congruence w.r.t. refinement.

(3) Consider the LEN systems Σ_1 and Σ_2 of Figure 3.3.6. In both systems the sequence ab is executed concurrently with a. However, in Σ_2 the choice between the two different events modelling the action b can be made at the beginning, while in Σ_1 this choice can be postponed until the execution of the two actions a has been completed. Σ_1 and Σ_2 are not PS-bisimilar since in Σ_1 a process with abstraction a can always be extended in such a way that the extended part is the sequence ab, while this is not true in Σ_2. ♦

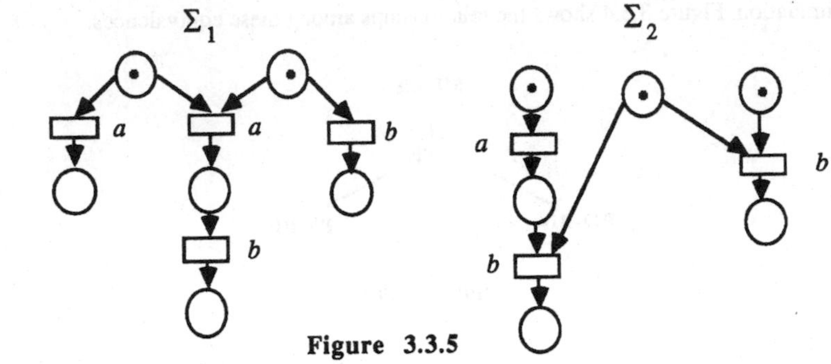

Figure 3.3.5

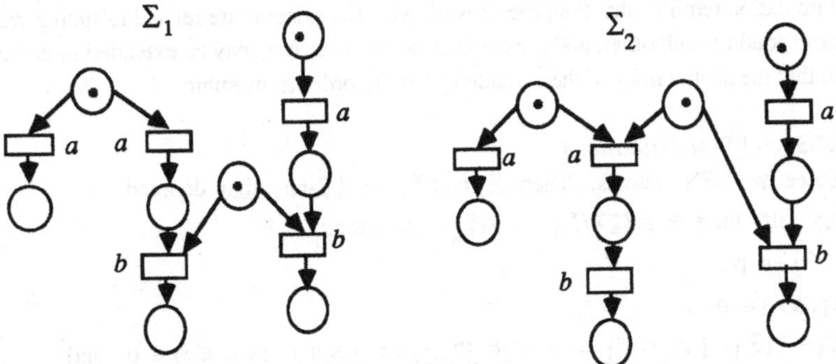

Figure 3.3.6

2) Partial order-bisimulation

The discussion in Example 3.3.2.(1) suggests an alternative definition of bisimulation based on partial orders which takes into account how processes and their extended parts are concatenated. This intuition is the basis of partial order-bisimulation, which requires a relation between processes such that: the initial processes are related, the related processes have order-isomorphic abstractions, and if two processes π_1 and π_2 are related and π'_1 is an extension of π_1 then there is an extension of π_2, let say π'_2, which is related to π'_1.

Definition 3.3.6. *(PO-bisimulation)*
Let Σ_1 and Σ_2 be two LEN systems. Then Σ_1 and Σ_2 are PO-bisimilar , denoted $\Sigma_1 \approx$PO-Bis Σ_2, iff there is $\rho \subseteq P(\Sigma_1) \times P(\Sigma_2)$ such that :

(1) $(\pi^\circ_1, \pi^\circ_2) \in \rho$.

(2) $\forall (\pi_1, \pi_2) \in \rho \;\; abs_{h1}(\pi_1) \cong abs_{h2}(\pi_2)$.

(3) $\forall (\pi_1, \pi_2) \in \rho$

$[\forall \pi'_1 \in P(\Sigma_1) \, [\, \pi_1 \leq \pi'_1 \Rightarrow \exists \, \pi'_2 \in P(\Sigma_2) \, [\, \pi_2 \leq \pi'_2$ and $(\pi'_1, \pi'_2) \in \rho \,]\,]$,

and (vice versa)

$\forall \pi'_2 \in P(\Sigma_2) \, [\, \pi_2 \leq \pi'_2 \Rightarrow \exists \, \pi'_1 \in P(\Sigma_1) \, [\, \pi_1 \leq \pi'_1$ and $(\pi'_1, \pi'_2) \in \rho \,]\,]\,]$. ♦

Remark
PO-bisimulation and PS-bisimulation are incomparable, as shown in the following example.

Example 3.3.3.

(1) The systems Σ_1 and Σ_2 in Figure 3.3.5 are not PO-bisimilar. The process π of Σ_2 whose abstraction is *a* can be extended both by a process whose abstraction is *ab*, and by a process whose abstraction is *a* || *b*. π does not correspond to any process of Σ_1; in fact, the two processes whose abstraction is *a* can be extended only either by a process whose abstraction is *ab*, or by a process whose abstraction is *a* || *b*. Recall that Σ_1 and Σ_2 are PS-bisimilar, as shown in Example 3.3.2.(1).

(2) The systems Σ_1 and Σ_2 in Figure 3.3.6 are PO-bisimilar [GG89]: in both systems, a process whose abstraction is *a* can be extended by a process whose abstraction is *a* || *a*, or by a process whose abstraction is *a* || *ab*; a process whose abstraction is *a* || *a* can be extended by a process whose abstraction is *a* || *ab*; and a process whose abstraction is *ab* can be extended by a process whose abstraction is *a*|| *ab*. Recall that, Σ_1 and Σ_2 are not PS-bisimilar, as shown in Example 3.3.2.(3). ♦

3) <u>FC-bisimulation</u>

In order to be able to distinguish not only between the systems in Figure 3.3.5, but also between those in Figure 3.3.6, PO-bisimulation has to be strengthened by specifying that the "extension property" concerns not only processes but also the isomorphisms of their abstractions. The resulting notion is FC-bisimulation.

Definition 3.3.7. *(FC-bisimulation)*

Let Σ_1 and Σ_2 be two LEN systems. Then Σ_1 and Σ_2 are <u>FC-bisimilar</u>, denoted $\Sigma_1 \approx_{\text{FC-Bis}} \Sigma_2$, iff there is a set

$\mathbf{B} \subseteq \{ (\pi_1, \pi_2, \beta) : \pi_1 \in P(\Sigma_1), \pi_2 \in P(\Sigma_2)$, and $\beta : abs_{h_1}(\pi_1) \text{ -> } abs_{h_2}(\pi_2)$ is an order-isomorphism $\}$ with the following properties:

(1) $(\pi^\circ_1, \pi^\circ_2, \emptyset) \in \mathbf{B}$.

(2) $\forall (\pi_1, \pi_2, \beta) \in \mathbf{B}$

$[\ \forall\ \pi'_1 \in P(\Sigma_1)\ [\ \pi_1 \leq \pi'_1 \Rightarrow \exists\ (\pi'_1, \pi'_2, \beta') \in \mathbf{B}\ [\ \pi_2 \leq \pi'_2$ and $\beta \subseteq \beta'\ ]\ ]$,

and (vice versa)

$\forall\ \pi'_2 \in P(\Sigma_2)\ [\ \pi_2 \leq \pi'_2 \Rightarrow \exists\ (\pi'_1, \pi'_2, \beta') \in \mathbf{B}\ [\ \pi_1 \leq \pi'_1$ and $\beta \subseteq \beta'\ ]\ ]\ ]$. ♦

Remark

The discerning power of FC-bisimulation does not change if the extensions involve only single events, i.e., if FC-bisimulation definition is formulated in such a way that processes π'_i have only one event more than π_i [BDKP89].

From the definitions of FC-bisimulation and PO-bisimulation it is immediate to see that in general FC-bisimulation is strictly stronger than PO-bisimulation; PO-bisimulation can be regarded as FC-bisimulation without the requirement that $\beta \subseteq \beta'$ (see Example 3.3.4.(2)).

For LEN systems free of autoconcurrency FC-bisimulation and PO-bisimulation coincide.

Example 3.3.4.

(1) The systems Σ_1 and Σ_2 given in Figure 3.3.5 are not PO-bisimilar and they are also not FC-bisimilar, while they are PS-bisimilar as shown in Example 3.3.2.(1).

(2) The systems Σ_1 and Σ_2 given in Figure 3.3.6 are not FC-bisimilar, while they are PO-bisimilar as shown in Example 3.3.3.(2).

In both systems, a process whose abstraction is $a||a$ can be extended by a process whose abstraction is $a||ab$, but while in Σ_1 the event modelling the action b can be concurrent with any of the two events modelling action a, in Σ_2 the event modelling the action b has to be concurrent with a specific event modelling action a.

(3) The systems Σ_1 and Σ_2 given in Figure 3.1.5 are FC-bisimilar. This example, already discussed to show that systems Σ_1 and Σ_2 are not branching bisimilar, can be used also for proving that for sequential systems branching bisimulation is strictly stronger than FC-bisimulation. ♦

4) MP-bisimulation

FC-bisimulation can be further strenghten by requiring the preservation of maximality of observable events. The equivalence obtained is called MP-bisimulation [Dev90]. It has been introduced mainly because it is preserved by action refinement even in the presence of unobservable events [Dev90]; [Vog90b] also connected this notion to bisimulations based on ST-configurations.

The definition of MP-bisimulation requires the following auxiliary notion.

Definition 3.3.8 *(MP-bisimulation for a visible action set)*

Let Σ_1 and Σ_2 be two LEN systems and $A \subseteq L$ be a subset of visible actions. Then Σ_1 and Σ_2 are maximality preserving bisimilar for the actions in A, abbreviated A MP-bisimilar, and denoted $\Sigma_1 \approx_{A\text{MP-Bis}} \Sigma_2$, iff there is a set $\mathbf{B} \subseteq \{ (\pi_1,\pi_2,\beta)$: $\pi_1 = (B_1,E_1,F_1,p_1) \in P(\Sigma_1)$, $\pi_2 = (B_2,E_2,F_2,p_2) \in P(\Sigma_2)$, and $\beta : abs_{h_1}(\pi_1) \to abs_{h_2}(\pi_2)$ is an order-isomorphism$\}$ with the following properties:

(1) $(\pi^\circ_1, \pi^\circ_2, \emptyset) \in \mathbf{B}$.

(2) $\forall (\pi_1, \pi_2, \beta) \in \mathbf{B}$

$[[\forall \pi'_1 = (B'_1,E'_1,F'_1,p'_1) \in P(\Sigma_1)\ [\ [\pi_1 \leq \pi'_1$ and $E'_1 - E_1 = \{e'_1\}] \Rightarrow$

$\exists (\pi'_1, \pi'_2, \beta') \in \mathbf{B}\ [\pi_2 \leq \pi'_2,\ \beta \subseteq \beta'$,

$[h_1(p'_1(e'_1)) \in A \Rightarrow \beta'(e'_1)$ is a maximal event of π'_2], and

$[\forall e_1 \in E_1\ [\ [h_1(p_1(e_1)) \in A$, e_1 is a maximal event of π'_1, and

$\beta(e_1)$ is a maximal event of π_2] $\Rightarrow \beta(e_1)$ is a maximal event of π'_2]]]]],

and (vice versa)

$[\ \forall \pi'_2 = (B'_2,E'_2,F'_2,p'_2) \in P(\Sigma_2)\ [\ [\pi_2 \leq \pi'_2$ and $E'_2 - E_2 = \{e'_2\}] \Rightarrow$

$\exists (\pi'_1, \pi'_2, \beta') \in \mathbf{B}\ [\pi_1 \leq \pi'_1,\ \beta \subseteq \beta'$,

$[h_2(p'_2(e'_2)) \in A \Rightarrow \beta'^{-1}(e'_2)$ is a maximal event of π'_1], and

$[\forall e_2 \in E_2\ [\ [h_2(p_2(e_2)) \in A$, e_2 is a maximal event of π'_2, and

$\beta^{-1}(e_2)$ is a maximal event of π_1] $\Rightarrow \beta^{-1}(e_2)$ is a maximal event of π'_1]]]]]].♦

Definition 3.3.9. *(MP-bisimulation)*

Σ_1 and Σ_2 are maximality preserving bisimilar, abbreviated MP-bisimilar and denoted $\Sigma_1 \approx_{\text{MP-Bis}} \Sigma_2$, iff they are maximality preserving bisimilar for all the visible actions, i.e.;

$\Sigma_1 \approx_{\text{MP-Bis}} \Sigma_2 \Leftrightarrow \Sigma_1 \approx_{L\text{ MP-Bis}} \Sigma_2$, where L is the set of observable action names. ♦

Remark

As shown in [Dev90], $\Sigma_1 \approx_{\text{FC-Bis}} \Sigma_2$ iff $\Sigma_1 \approx_{\emptyset\text{ MP-Bis}} \Sigma_2$, i.e., FC-bisimulation is a sort of maximality preserving bisimulation. This is based on the fact that AMP-bisimulation requires additional conditions on A-labelled events. These conditions essentially say that "the maximality of A-

labelled events should be preserved: if a new A-labelled event is added on one side (it is then maximal), then it is possible to extend the other side in such a way that the corresponding event (with the same label) is also maximal; and if an A-labelled event is maximal on one side before and after the extension while on the other side the corresponding event is also maximal before the extension, then this event remains maximal also after the extension" [Dev90].

In Section 3.4. it is shown that in the case of τ-free LEN systems FC-bisimulation and MP-bisimulation coincide.

Example 3.3.5.
(1) The systems Σ_1 and Σ_2 given in Figure 3.1.5. are not MP-bisimilar. If we consider, as an extension of π°_2, the process π_2 with only one event e_2 corresponding to the execution of the action a which is not followed by b or τ, then there is no extension π_1 of π°_1 such that $(\pi_1,\pi_2,\beta) \in \mathbf{B}$ (see Definition 3.3.8.) and $\beta^{-1}(e_2)$ is a maximal event of π_1. Therefore this example shows that MP-bisimulation is strictly stronger than FC-bisimulation (see Example 3.3.4.(3)).
(2) The systems Σ_1 and Σ_2 given in Figure 3.1.6. are MP-bisimilar; the process π_1 of Σ_1 modelling the sequence τa corresponds to the process π_2 of Σ_2 with only one event modelling action a; in π_1 as well as in π_2 the event modelling a is maximal.
Notice that Σ_1 and Σ_2 are not branching bisimilar as shown in Example 3.1.5. For sequential systems branching bisimulation is therefore strictly stronger than MP-bisimulation. ♦

3.3.3. Exhibited-Behaviour Equivalence on Processes

By generalising EB-equivalence (see Section 3.1.5) we obtain PO-EB-equivalence which takes into consideration those processes whose final cuts correspond to cases which are meaningful in the sense of Definition 3.1.7; these processes are called EB-observable.

Definition 3.3.10. *(EB-observable processes)*
Let Σ be a LEN system and let $\pi = (N, p) \in P(\Sigma)$. Then π is an <u>EB-observable process</u> of Σ iff $p(Max(N))$ is a meaningful case of Σ. $P^{obs}(\Sigma)$ denotes the set of EB-observable processes of Σ. ♦

When comparing systems by means of PO-EB-equivalence we consider chains of EB-observable processes such that each process π approximates its successor π' in the chain, denoted $\pi \lhd \pi'$, in the sense that if π' is obtained by extending π with a connected labelled subnet in which there is exactly one event modelling an observable action.

Definition 3.3.11. *($\pi \lhd \pi'$)*
Let Σ be a LEN system and $\pi=(B, E, F, p)$, $\pi'=(B', E', F', p')$ be EB-observable processes of Σ. Then π' <u>immediately EB-follows</u> π, denoted $\pi \lhd \pi'$, iff

a) $\pi < \pi'$;

b) the net $\underline{N}=(\underline{B}, \underline{E}, \underline{F})$ generated by $\underline{E}=(E'-E)$ is connected, and $\exists!\, e \in \underline{E} : h(p'(e)) \neq \tau$. ♦

Remark
The relation $\lhd^*$ is a partial order relation.

Definition 3.3.12. *(chain of EB-observable processes)*
Let Σ be a LEN system and $\pi^1, \pi^2, ..., \pi^n$ be EB-observable processes of Σ such that:
$\forall i \in [\![n-1]\!]\ \pi^i \lhd \pi^{i+1}$. Then $\pi^1 \lhd \pi^2 \lhd \dots \lhd \pi^n$ is a chain in $P_{obs}(\Sigma)$ iff
$abs_h(\pi^1) = (\emptyset, \emptyset, \emptyset)$
(or, equivalently, iff $\pi^1 = (B^1, E^1, F^1, p^1)$ is such that: $E^1 = \emptyset$ or $\forall e \in E^1\ h(p^1(e)) = \tau$).
ch-$P_{obs}(\Sigma)$ denotes the set of chains in $P_{obs}(\Sigma)$. ♦

Definition 3.3.13. *(PO-EB-equivalence)*
Let Σ_1 and Σ_2 be two LEN systems. Then Σ_1 and Σ_2 are partial order-EB-equivalent, abbreviated PO-EB-equivalent and denoted $\Sigma_1 \approx^{PO\text{-}EB} \Sigma_2$, iff

$\forall\ \pi_1^1 \lhd \pi_1^2 \lhd \dots \lhd \pi_1^n \in$ ch-$P_{obs}(\Sigma_1)\ \ \exists\ \pi_2^1 \lhd \pi_2^2 \lhd \dots \lhd \pi_2^n \in$ ch-$P_{obs}(\Sigma_2)$

$[\forall i \in [\![n]\!]\ [abs_{h_1}(\pi_1^i) \cong abs_{h_2}(\pi_2^i)$ and $\forall A \in SL,$

$\forall\ \pi_1' \in P_{obs}(\Sigma_1)\ [\pi_1^i <_A \pi_1' \Rightarrow \exists\ \pi_2'\ [\pi_2^i <_A \pi_2'$ and $abs_{h_1}(\pi_1') \cong abs_{h_2}(\pi_2')]\,]$

and (viceversa)

$\forall\ \pi_2' \in P_{obs}(\Sigma_2)\ [\pi_2^i <_A \pi_2' \Rightarrow \exists\ \pi_1'\ [\pi_1^i <_A \pi_1'$ and $abs_{h_1}(\pi_1') \cong abs_{h_2}(\pi_2')]\,]\,]]$

and (vice versa)

$\forall\ \pi_2^1 \lhd \pi_2^2 \lhd \dots \lhd \pi_2^n \in$ ch-$P_{obs}(\Sigma_2)\ \ \exists\ \pi_1^1 \lhd \pi_1^2 \lhd \dots \lhd \pi_1^n \in$ ch-$P_{obs}(\Sigma_1)$

$[\forall i \in [\![n]\!]\ [abs_{h_1}(\pi_1^i) \cong abs_{h_2}(\pi_2^i)$ and $\forall A \in SL,$

$\forall\ \pi_2' \in P_{obs}(\Sigma_2)\ [\pi_2^i <_A \pi_2' \Rightarrow \exists\ \pi_1'\ [\pi_1^i <_A \pi_1'$ and $abs_{h_1}(\pi_1') \cong abs_{h_2}(\pi_2')]\,]$

and (viceversa)

$\forall\ \pi_1' \in P_{obs}(\Sigma_1)\ [\pi_1^i <_A \pi_1' \Rightarrow \exists\ \pi_2'\ [\pi_2^i <_A \pi_2'$ and $abs_{h_1}(\pi_1') \cong abs_{h_2}(\pi_2')]]\ ]].$ ♦

Remark
PO-EB-equivalence and PS-bisimulation are incomparable. This is shown in the next example (see also Example 3.3.2.)
It can be proved that PO-EB-equivalence is weaker than PO-bisimulation; Example 3.3.6.(3) shows that it is strictly weaker.

Example 3.3.6.
(1) The systems Σ_1 and Σ_2 in Figure 3.3.5. are not PO-EB-equivalent; in Σ_2, the process whose abstraction is *a* can be extended by {b} by means of both the process whose abstraction is *ab* and the process whose abstraction is *a*||*b*; on the contrary, in Σ_1 there are two different processes whose abstraction is *a*: one of them can be extended by {b} by means of a process whose abstraction is *ab*, while the other one can be extended by {b}by a process whose abstraction is *a*||*b*.
It has been shown in Example 3.3.2.(1) that the two systems are PS-bisimilar.
(2) The systems Σ_1 and Σ_2 in Figure 3.3.6. are PO-EB-equivalent. In particular, if we consider in one system the chain of the two processes whose abstractions are *a* and *ab*, respectively (note that this chain contains the processes crucial for proving other equivalences such as PS-bisimulation and FC-bisimulation); then in the other system there is a corresponding chain and, in both chains, the process whose abstraction is *a* can be extended either by a process whose abstraction is *a*||*a*, or by a process whose abstraction is *ab*; and the process whose abstraction is *ab* can be extended by a process whose abstraction is *a*||*ab*.
It has been shown in Example 3.3.2.(3) that the two systems are not PS-bisimilar.

(3) The systems Σ_2 and Σ_4 in Figure 3.1.1 are PO-EB-equivalent, while they are not PO-bisimilar, and not even bisimilar as shown in Example 3.1.4.(3). ♦

3.3.4. Failure Equivalence on Processes

In the following we give the definition of failure equivalence on processes, called partial order-F-equivalence and abbreviated PO-F-equivalence.

In this case the failures of a LEN system Σ are pairs (ϕ, X) where:

(1) ϕ is a labelled partial order of observable events for which there is a process of Σ with abstraction order-isomorphic to ϕ.

(2) X is a (possibly empty) set of multisets over L ($X \subseteq SL$).

If (ϕ, X) is a failure of Σ, then Σ may perform the partial order of observable actions ϕ, i.e., it has a process π such that $abs_h(\pi) \cong \phi$, and afterwards refuse to perform any multiset of observable actions belonging to X.

We say that a process cannot be extended by a multiset A iff $\nexists \pi' \; \pi <_A \pi'$ (see Definition 3.3.3.).

Definition 3.3.14. *(PO-F-equivalence)*
Let Σ_1 and Σ_2 be two LEN systems. Then

(1) Σ_1 is less than Σ_2 w.r.t. partial order-failures, denoted $\Sigma_1 \subseteq_{PO-F} \Sigma_2$,
iff $\forall X \subseteq SL$
$[\exists \pi_1 \in P(\Sigma_1)\; [\forall A \in X \;\; \pi_1$ cannot be extended by A $] \Rightarrow$
$\exists \pi_2 \in P(\Sigma_2)\; [\forall A \in X \;\; \pi_2$ cannot be extended by A and $abs_{h1}(\pi_1) \cong abs_{h2}(\pi_2)]\,]$;

(2) Σ_1 and Σ_2 are partial order-failure-equivalent, abbreviated PO-F-equivalent, and denoted $\Sigma_1 \approx_{PO-F} \Sigma_2$, iff $\Sigma_1 \subseteq_{PO-F} \Sigma_2$ and $\Sigma_2 \subseteq_{PO-F} \Sigma_1$.

Remark
PO-F-equivalence is weaker than both PO-EB-equivalence and PS-bisimulation, and it is stronger than PO-S-equivalence [Pom88]. The following example shows that these relationships are strict.

Example 3.3.7.

(1) The systems Σ_1 and Σ_2 in Figure 3.3.5 are PO-F-equivalent, while they are not PO-EB-equivalent (see Example 3.3.6).

(2) The systems Σ_1 and Σ_2 in Figure 3.3.6 are PO-F-equivalent, while they are not PS-bisimilar (see Example 3.3.2).

(3) The systems Σ'_1 and Σ'_2 in Figure 3.3.3 are not PO-F-equivalent: system Σ'_1 has a process constituted of only one event labelled by a_1, which cannot be extended by {b}, while the only process of Σ'_2 constituted by an event labelled by a_1 can be extended by {b}. It has been shown in Example 3.3.1 that Σ'_1 and Σ'_2 are PO-S-equivalent. ♦

In [ADF87] Testing equivalence has been redefined for labelled event structures. In this formulation divergent processes have not been considered, and the obtained notion is related to PO-F-equivalence.

In [Vog90a] another notion of failure equivalence is introduced; it is based on interval semiwords, a semantics in between step and partial order semantics, and it is related to ST-semantics [Gla90a].

Remark

In the case of sequential systems, processes are just labelled occurrence nets in which the events are all in sequence; in this case the relation ≤ between actions is a total order and process abstractions are sets of totally ordered and τ-free labelled events. Therefore, in the case of sequential systems each equivalence based on partial order semantics concides with the corresponding one based on interleaving semantics.

3.4. RESTRICTIONS ON LABELLING

In the previous sections we have introduced various equivalences, and discussed their relationships. These relationships have been sumarized in Table A.

In this section we discuss how restrictions on event labelling weaken the discerning power of the considered equivalences. In particular we consider identity LEN systems and τ-free LEN systems (see Definition 3.2), comparing them between themselves or with general LEN systems.
Most of the results of this section can be found in [Pom87], [Pom88], [Vos87], where the meaning of such restrictions are discussed in relation to the 'extensionality principle' of net theory [Pet 73].

The diagram given in Table B summarizes the results we are going to present. The first column shows the relationships among the equivalences when comparing identity LEN systems (here abbreviated EN, since EN systems can be seen as identity LEN systems), the second column concerns the comparison of identity LEN systems with LEN systems, while the third column gives the comparison of τ-free LEN systems.

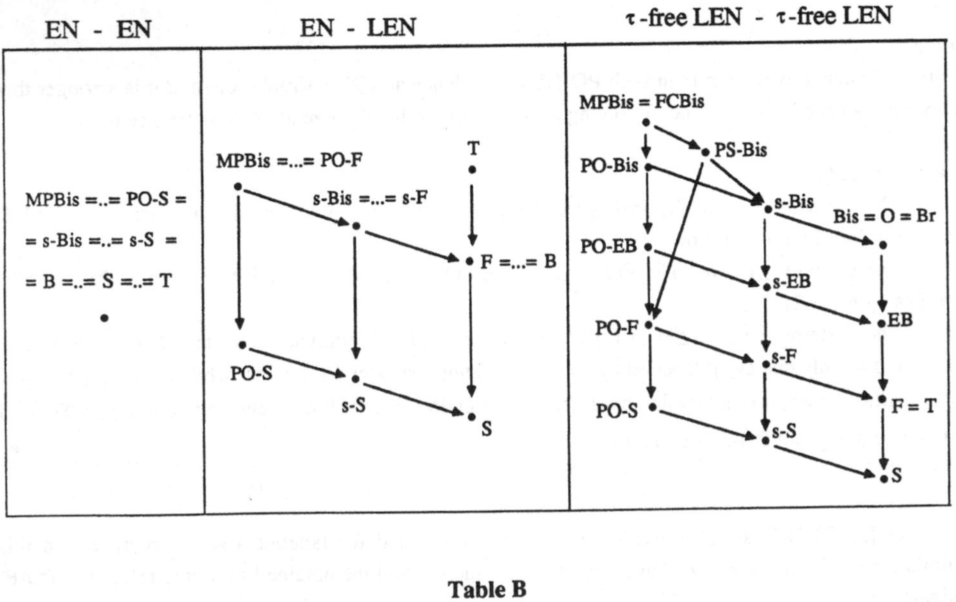

Table B

Theorem 3.4.1.
All the equivalences introduced in Sections 3.1, 3.2 and 3.3 coincide in the case of identity LEN systems. ♦

Remark

This theorem has been proved, for interleaving and step semantics in [Pom87], and for partial order semantics in [Pom88], without considering branching bisimulation and FC-bisimulation, but the proofs can be extended also to them.

In [Pom88] it is proved that s-S-equivalence and simulation similarity (see Section 4.1) coincide in the case of identity LEN systems. Hence, for the theorems given in Section 4.1, in the case of identity LEN systems all the equivalences considered so far and all the equivalences considered in Section 4.1 coincide.

Note that if one of the compared system is not an identity LEN system but an identity labelled safe system [Rei85a], [BD90], i.e., a system in which events with not necessarily disjoint pre-conditions and post-conditions may occur, then the above theorem is no more valid. In this case the equivalences defined in the framework of interleaving semantics coincide, while they are weaker than those defined in the framework of step and partial order semantics which still coincide.

Theorem 3.4.2.
When comparing identity LEN systems with LEN systems, the following relations hold:

(1) for $X \in \{S, F, EB, Bis\}$ $\approx^{X} \supset \approx^{s\text{-}X} \supset \approx^{PO\text{-}X}$.

(2) $\approx^{F} \equiv \approx^{EB} \equiv \approx^{Bis} \equiv \approx^{Br}$ and $\approx^{Br} \supset \approx^{T}$ and $\approx^{s\text{-}F} \equiv \approx^{s\text{-}EB} \equiv \approx^{s\text{-}Bis}$ and $\approx^{PO\text{-}F} \equiv \approx^{PO\text{-}EB} \equiv \approx^{PS\text{-}Bis} \equiv \approx^{PO\text{-}Bis} \equiv \approx^{FCBis} \equiv \approx^{MPBis}$.

(3) $\approx^{S} \supset \approx^{F}$ and $\approx^{s\text{-}S} \supset \approx^{s\text{-}F}$ and $\approx^{PO\text{-}S} \supset \approx^{PO\text{-}F}$. ♦

Remark

This theorem has been proved in [Pom88] without considering branching bisimulation, FC-bisimulation and MP-bisimulation. The equalities $\approx^{Bis} \equiv \approx^{Br}$ and $\approx^{PS\text{-}Bis} \equiv \approx^{PO\text{-}Bis} \equiv \approx^{FCBis} \equiv \approx^{MPBis}$ can be proved using the same techniques.

Theorem 3.4.3.
The following holds for τ-free LEN systems:

(1) T-equivalence and F-equivalence coincide [DeN87].

(2) branching bisimulation and bisimulation coincide.

(3) MP-bisimulation and FC-bisimulation coincide. ♦

Moreover, if the compared systems are LEN systems free of autoconcurrency, then the following theorem holds.

Theorem 3.4.4
For LEN systems free of autoconcurrency FC-bisimulation and PO-bisimulation coincide. ♦

Remark

Proof of Theorem 3.4.4 has been given for labelled event structures in [GG89]; a similar proof can be given also for LEN systems.

4. EQUIVALENCES BASED ON STATES

A natural way to describe the behaviour of an EN system is through its state space - i.e., the collection of all the global states together with the transitions between them. The state space is formalized through the notion of case graph, and the sequential state space through the notion of sequential case graph. A characteristic feature of SCG(Σ) for a simple EN system Σ is that if v_1, v_2 are nodes of it (hence cases of Σ) such that (v_1, e, v_2) is a transition, then e is uniquely determined by the pair (v_1, v_2), viz., e is the event of Σ such that $\bullet e = v_1 - v_2$ and $e\bullet = v_2 - v_1$. Hence, the states of the system identify the labels of transitions between them. This simple observation lies behind many considerations and techniques concerning state spaces of EN systems; for this reason we have decided to place equivalences based on case graphs in this section.

This section presents two approaches to the investigation of the behaviour of EN systems through their state spaces.

In Section 4.1 the equivalence of two EN systems is formalized as an isomorphism between case graphs. In the second approach (Section 4.2) the state space of an EN system is represented through a relational algebra generated by a suitable subset of reachable cases (viz., the observable cases). Here homomorphisms are introduced to compare the behaviour of systems at various levels of observability; the preorder induced in this way generates (in the usual way) an equivalence relation. In both approaches one obtains a canonical representative for an equivalence class of EN systems.

4.1 EQUIVALENCES BASED ON STATE SPACES

Now we will investigate the equivalence of EN systems with respect to their state spaces. In this section we will consider a restricted class of EN systems, viz. we will assume that an EN system is both reduced and simple. Clearly, if an EN system Σ is reduced, then it is also pure. Also, by definition, CG (Σ) and SCG (Σ) are reachable in the sense that each node of CG (Σ) and of SCG (Σ) is reachable by a path from the initial node.

In this section we will assume that each transition system $h = (V, \Delta, A, v_{in})$ satisfies the following axioms:

(A1) $\forall\ (v_1, \sigma, v_2) \in A\ [\, v_1 \neq v_2 \,]$.

(A2) $\forall\ (v, \sigma_1, v_1), (v, \sigma_2, v_2) \in A\ [v_1 = v_2 \Rightarrow \sigma_1 = \sigma_2]$.

(A3) $\forall \sigma \in \Delta\ \exists\ v_1, v_2 \in V\ [\, (v_1, \sigma, v_2) \in A \,]$.

(A4) $\forall v \in V$ [v is reachable in h].

Hence a transition system h cannot have loops (A1), and it cannot have multiple edges between a pair of states (A2). On the other hand, each action must have an occurrence in h (A3), and each state must be reachable from the initial state (A4).

In order to compare transition systems we need the notion of an isomorphism between them.

Definition 4.1.1. *(isomorphism of transition systems)*

Let $h_1 = (V_1, \Delta_1, A_1, v_{in,1})$ and $h_2 = (V_2, \Delta_2, A_2, v_{in,2})$ be transition systems.

(1) An <u>isomorphism of</u> h_1 <u>onto</u> h_2 is a pair of bijections (φ, ψ) such that:

$\varphi : V_1 \rightarrow V_2,\ \psi : \Delta_1 \rightarrow \Delta_2,\ \varphi(v_{in,1}) = v_{in,2}$, and $\forall\ v_1, v_2 \in V_1, \forall\ \sigma \in \Delta_1$

$[(v_1, \sigma, v_2) \in A_1$ iff $(\varphi(v_1), \psi(\sigma), \varphi(v_2)) \in A_2]$.

(2) h_1, h_2 are <u>isomorphic</u>, denoted $h_1 \cong h_2$, iff there exists an isomorphism of h_1 onto h_2. ♦

Definition 4.1.2. *(case graph equivalence)*

(1) EN systems Σ_1, Σ_2 are <u>case graph equivalent</u>, denoted $\Sigma_1 \cong \Sigma_2$, iff $CG(\Sigma_1) \cong CG(\Sigma_2)$.

(2) EN systems Σ_1, Σ_2 are <u>sequential case graph equivalent</u>, denoted $\Sigma_1 \simeq \Sigma_2$, iff $SCG(\Sigma_1) \cong SCG(\Sigma_2)$. ♦

Example 4.1.1.

Let Σ_1 be the EN system of Figure 4.1.1 and Σ_2 be the EN system of Figure 4.1.2

Then, $SCG(\Sigma_1)$ and $SCG(\Sigma_2)$ are as in Figure 4.1.3 and Figure 4.1.4, respectively.

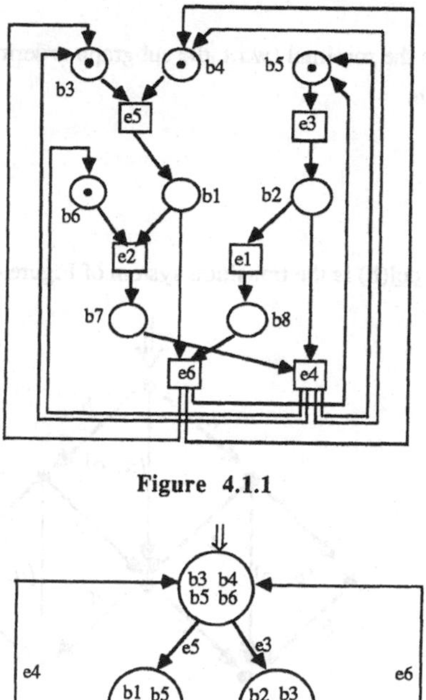

Figure 4.1.1

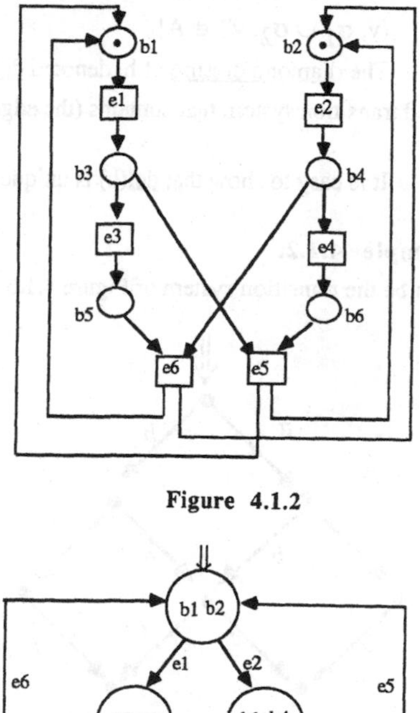

Figure 4.1.2

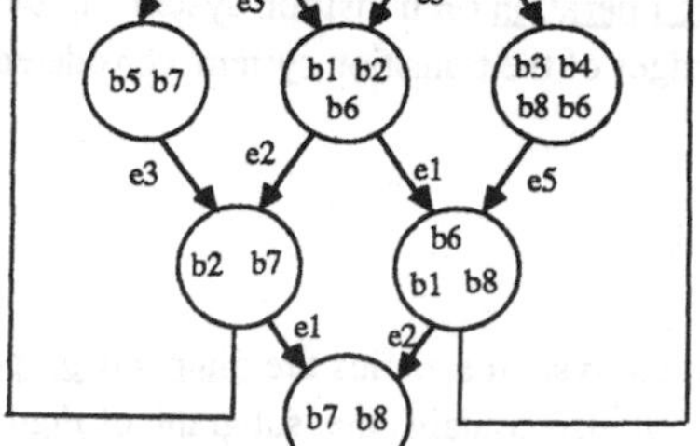

Figure 4.1.3

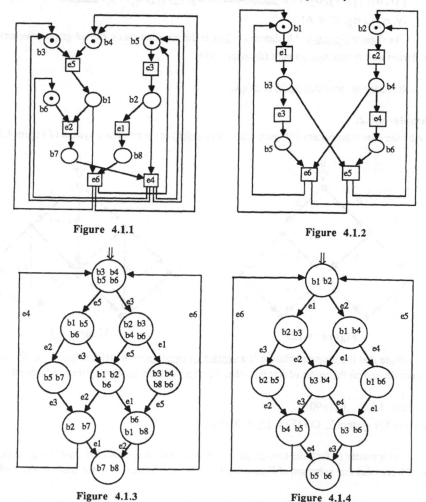

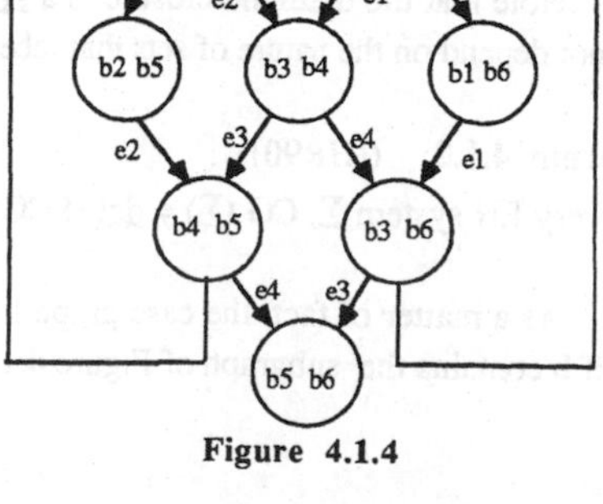

Figure 4.1.4

It is easy to see that SCG(Σ_1) and SCG(Σ_2) are isomorphic, and so $\Sigma_1 \simeq \Sigma_2$. (As usual, in the diagrams we follow the notational convention that a singleton set is identified with its element). ♦

The following is a fundamental result of the theory of EN systems.

Theorem 4.1.1. ([HR90])
For all EN systems Σ_1, Σ_2, $\Sigma_1 \equiv \Sigma_2$ iff $\Sigma_1 \simeq \Sigma_2$. ♦

As a matter of fact, given an EN system Σ, one can obtain CG(Σ) from SCG(Σ) as follows.

Definition 4.1.3. *(diamond closure)*
Let $h_1 = (V, \Delta, A, v_{in})$ be a transition system such that labels in Δ are sets.

(1) h is diamond closed iff $\forall\ v, v_1, v_2, v' \in V\ \ \forall\ \sigma_1, \sigma_2 \in \Delta$

$[\ (v, \sigma_1, v_1)\ (v_1, \sigma_2, v') \in$ path(h) and $(v, \sigma_2, v_2)\ (v_2, \sigma_1, v') \in$ path (h) $\Rightarrow$

$(v, \sigma_1 \cup \sigma_2, v') \in A]$.

(2) The diamond closure of h, denoted dcl(h), is the minimal (w.r.t. the subgraph ordering) diamond closed transition system that contains (the edges of) h. ♦

It is easy to show that dcl(h) is unique.

Example 4.1.2.
Let h be the transition system of Figure 4.1.5. Then dcl(h) is the transition system of Figure 4.1.6. ♦

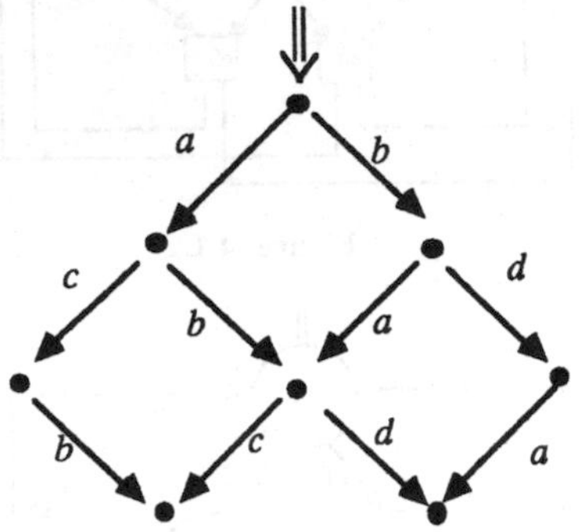

Figure 4.1.5

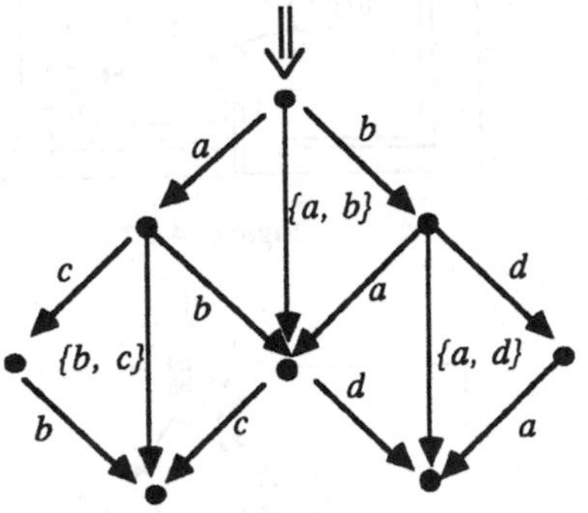

Figure 4.1.6

Note that the diamond closure is a syntactic operation on transition systems in the sense that it does not depend on the nature of sets that label the edges of the transition system considered.

Theorem 4.1.2. ([HR90])
For every EN system Σ, CG (Σ) = dcl (SCG(Σ)). ♦

As a matter of fact, the case graph h of an EN system satisfies the diamond property meaning that, if h contains the subgraph of Figure 4.1.7, then it also contains the subgraph of Figure 4.1.8.

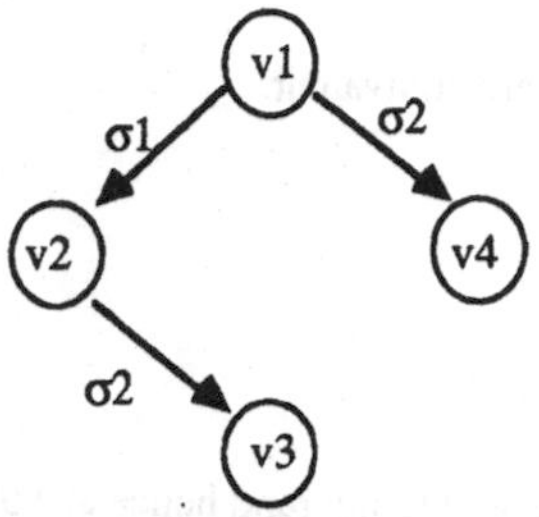

Figure 4.1.7

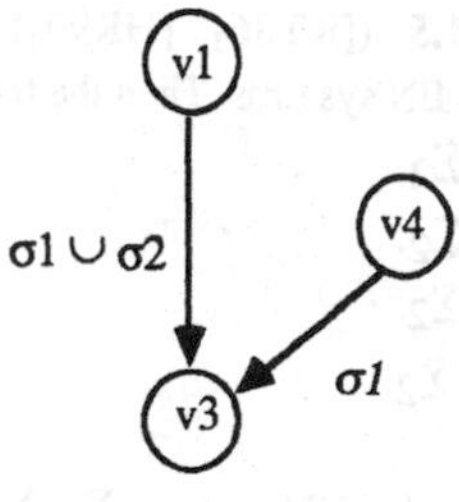

Figure 4.1.8

By Theorem 4.1.1 and Theorem 4.1.2, in the investigation of the state spaces of EN systems it suffices to investigate sequential case graphs only.

Yet another way to compare EN systems is through mutual simulation. This leads to the following notions.

Definition 4.1.4. *(simulation similarity)*
Let $\Sigma_1 = (B_1, E_1, F_1, c_{in,1})$ and $\Sigma_2 = (B_2, E_2, F_2, c_{in,2})$ be EN systems.

(1) Σ_1, Σ_2 are <u>simulation similar</u>, denoted $\Sigma_1 \approx \Sigma_2$, iff there exist bijections
$\alpha : C_{\Sigma_1} \longrightarrow C_{\Sigma_2}$ and $\beta : E_1 \longrightarrow E_2$ such that: $\alpha(c_{in,1}) = c_{in,2}$ and
$\forall c, c' \in C_{\Sigma_1}, \forall U \in 2^{E_1}$ $[c\,[U\rangle\, c'$ in $\Sigma_1 \Leftrightarrow \alpha(c)\,[\beta(U)\rangle\, \alpha(c')$ in $\Sigma_2]$.

(2) Σ_1, Σ_2 <u>are sequential simulation similar,</u> denoted $\Sigma_1 \sim \Sigma_2$, iff there exists bijections
$\alpha : C_{\Sigma_1} \longrightarrow C_{\Sigma_2}$ and $\beta : E_1 \longrightarrow E_2$ such that: $\alpha(c_{in,1}) = c_{in,2}$ and
$\forall c, c' \in C_{\Sigma_1}, \forall e \in E_1$ $[c\,[e\rangle\, c'$ in $\Sigma_1 \Leftrightarrow \alpha(c)\,[\beta(e)\rangle\, \alpha(c')$ in Σ_2]. ♦

Note that there is a subtle but important difference between a pair of bijections (α,β) establishing simulation similarity (as above) and a pair of bijections (φ,ψ) establishing isomorphism between case graphs (as in Definition 4.1.1). ψ is a bijection between steps independent of their cardinality (i.e., ψ does not have to preserve the cardinality of steps), while β is a bijection between steps mapping events in one step into events in the other - hence β is a bijection that preserves cardinality.

Once again, it turns out that it suffices to consider the sequential case only.

Theorem 4.1.3 ([RT86])
Let Σ_1, Σ_2 be EN systems. Then $\Sigma_1 \approx \Sigma_2$ iff $\Sigma_1 \sim \Sigma_2$. ♦

It is easily seen that the notion of an isomorphism of sequential case graphs and the notion of sequential simulation similarity coincide.

Theorem 4.1.4 ([RT86], [HR90])
Let Σ_1, Σ_2 be EN systems. Then $\Sigma_1 \sim \Sigma_2$ iff $\Sigma_1 \simeq \Sigma_2$. ♦

By combining the above results one obtains the following corollary.

Corollary 4.1.5 ([RT86], [HR90])

Let Σ_1, Σ_2 be EN systems. Then the following statements are equivalent:

(1) $\Sigma_1 \sim \Sigma_2$.

(2) $\Sigma_1 \approx \Sigma_2$.

(3) $\Sigma_1 \simeq \Sigma_2$.

(4) $\Sigma_1 \cong \Sigma_2$.   ◆

We say that EN systems Σ_1, Σ_2 are <u>similar</u> if and only if any (and hence all) of the relationships from the statement of the above result holds.

In the theory of EN systems one often deals only with contact-free systems. The following result justifies such a restriction.

Theorem 4.1.6   ([Rei85a],[RT86])

For every EN system there exists a similar contact-free EN system.   ◆

An EN system Σ can be considered to be a realization (an implementation) of <u>any</u> transition system h such that $SCG(\Sigma) \cong$ h. However it is not true that for each transition system h there exists an EN system that realizes it; those transition systems that have an EN system realization are called <u>abstract state spaces of EN systems</u>. Note that even if h is an abstract state space of an EN system, then its nodes do not have to be sets (they can be any objects) and its edge labels do not have to be events (they can be any objects).

In order to identify those transition systems that are abstract state spaces of EN systems we need the notion of a region.

Definition 4.1.5. *(region)*

Let $h = (V, \Delta, A, v_{in})$ be a transition system, and let $Z \subseteq V$. Then Z is a <u>region of</u> h iff

$\forall \; \sigma \in \Delta \, [\; (v_1, \sigma, v'_1), (v_2, \sigma, v'_2) \in A \; \Rightarrow$

$[\; (v_1 \in Z \text{ and } v'_1 \notin Z) \; \Leftrightarrow \; (v_2 \in Z \text{ and } v'_2 \notin Z) \,] \text{ and}$

$[\; (v_1 \notin Z \text{ and } v'_1 \in Z) \; \Leftrightarrow \; (v_2 \notin Z \text{ and } v'_2 \in Z) \,] \;].$ ◆

Thus if Z is a region of h, and σ is a label of h, then either all edges labeled by σ are "entering" Z, or all edges labeled by σ are "leaving" Z , or all edges labeled by σ are not "crossing" (the boundary of) Z at all : they are either "inside" Z or "outside" Z.

We will use R_h to denote the set of all <u>nontrivial</u> regions of h, i.e., the set of all regions of h excluding V and $\emptyset$. For each $v \in V$, $R_h (v) = \{ Z \in R_h : v \in Z \}$. For each $\sigma \in \Sigma$ the set of all <u>pre-regions of σ</u>, denoted $°\sigma$, is the set

$\{ Z \in R_h : \exists \, (v, \sigma, v') \in A \, [\, v \in Z \text{ and } v' \notin Z] \},$

and the set of all <u>post-regions of σ</u>, denoted $\sigma°$, is the set

$\{ Z \in R_h : \exists \, (v, \sigma, v') \in A \, [\, v \notin Z \text{ and } v' \in Z] \}.$

Example 4.1.3

Let h be the transition system of Figure 4.1.9.

Then $Z_1 = \{3,4,5\}$ is a region of h: a is entering Z_1, d is leaving Z_1, and b, c are not crossing Z_1 at

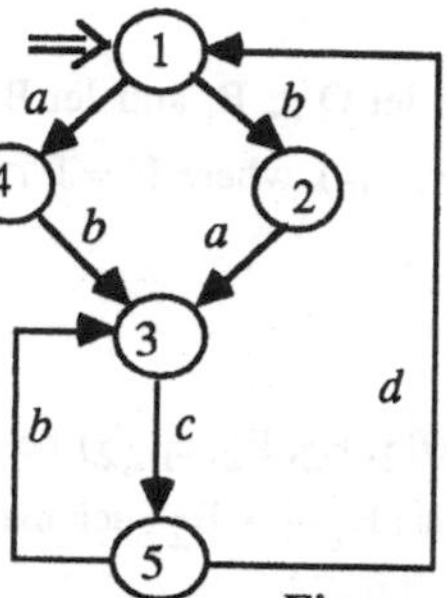

Figure 4.1.9

all. On the other hand, Z_2 = {3,4} is not a region of h: there is (an edge labelled by) *b* entering Z_1, and there is (an edge labelled by) *b* inside Z_1! Also, °*b* ={{1,4,5}}, *a*° ={{3,4,5}}, $\underline{R}_h$ (1) = {{1,4,5},{1,2}}, and $\underline{R}_h$ (3) = {{3,4,5}}. ♦

We are now ready to identify precisely those transition systems that can be realized by EN systems.

Definition 4.1.6 *(Elementary transition system)*
A transition system h = (V, Δ, A, v_{in}) is elementary iff it satisfies (in addition to the axioms (A1) through (A4)) the following two conditions:

(1) $\forall$ v, v' $\in$ V [$\underline{R}_h$ (v) = $\underline{R}_h$ (v') $\Rightarrow$ v = v'].

(2) $\forall$ v $\in$ V,$\forall$ σ $\in$ Δ [°σ $\subseteq$ $\underline{R}_h$ (v) $\Rightarrow$ v $\xrightarrow{\sigma}$>]. ♦

Theorem 4.1.7 ([ER90b], [NRT90b])
A transition system h is an abstract state space of an EN system iff it is elementary. ♦

Now for a given elementary transition system h one can consider the class **ENR**(h) of all EN systems that realize h (i.e., Σ $\in$ **ENR** (h) if and only if SCG(Σ) ≅ h). It turns out that all the information about this class of state space equivalent EN systems is "encoded" in a single EN system constructed from h on the basis of its regions; this EN system is defined as follows.

Definition 4.1.7 *(EN system of h)*
Let h = (V, Δ, A, v_{in}) be an elementary transition system.The EN system of h, denoted Σ_h, is the EN system ($\underline{R}_h$, Δ, F_h, $\underline{R}_h$ (v_{in})), where
F_h = {(Z, σ) : Z $\in \underline{R}_h$, σ $\in$ Δ, and Z $\in$ °σ} $\cup$ { (σ, Z) : Z $\in$ $\underline{R}_h$, σ $\in$ Δ, and Z $\in$ σ°}. ♦

For an elementary transition system h, Σ_h is a maximal EN system in **ENR** (h) in the sense that every Σ $\in$ **ENR** (h) can be obtained from Σ_h by removing some conditions, and then renaming the remaining conditions (and events). Hence for the equivalence class **ENR** (h) we have a canonical maximal representative, viz. Σ_h.

This is formalized in the next theorem; however we need two definitions first - one formalizing the removal of conditions, and the other formalizing the renaming of conditions (and events). In what follows we will identify an event e of an EN system with its characteristic pair (•e, e•); since we consider only simple EN systems we can make such an identification without loss of generality.

Definition 4.1.8 *(Q-removal)*
Let $\Sigma = (B, E, F, c_{in})$ be an EN system, let $Q \subseteq B$, and let $B' = B - Q$. Then the Q-removal of Σ, denoted Σ/Q, is the EN system (B', E', F', c'_{in}), where $F' = F \cap (B' \times E \cup E \times B')$, $E' = E \cap (\underline{dom}(F') \cup \underline{ran}(F'))$, and $c'_{in} = c_{in} \cap B'$. ♦

Definition 4.1.9 *(condition-renaming)*
Let $\Sigma_1 = (B_1, E_1, F_1, c_{in,1})$ and $\Sigma_2 = (B_2, E_2, F_2, c_{in,2})$ be EN systems. Then Σ_2 is a condition-renaming of Σ_1 iff there exists a bijection $\varphi : B_1 \longrightarrow B_2$ such that

(1) $c_{in,2} = \varphi(c_{in,1})$.

(2) the function $\varphi' : E_1 \longrightarrow E_2$ defined by: $\forall e_1 \in E_1, \forall e_2 \in E_2$
$[\varphi'(e_1) = e_2 \Leftrightarrow (\varphi(\bullet e_1), \varphi(e_1\bullet))$ is the characteristic pair of e_2]
is a bijection.

(3) $\forall b \in B_1, \forall e \in E_1$
$[((b, e) \in F_1 \Leftrightarrow (\varphi(b), \varphi'(e)) \in F_2]$ and $[(e, b) \in F_1 \Leftrightarrow (\varphi'(e), \varphi(b)) \in F_2)]$. ♦

Theorem 4.1.8 ([ER90b], [NRT90b])
Let h be an elementary transition system, and let $\Sigma_h = (B, E, F, c_{in})$.

(1) $h \cong SCG(\Sigma_h)$.

(2) $\Sigma \in ENR(h) \Rightarrow \exists Q \subseteq B [\ \Sigma$ is a condition-renaming of Σ_h/Q]. ♦

Example 4.1.4
Let h be the following elementary transition system:

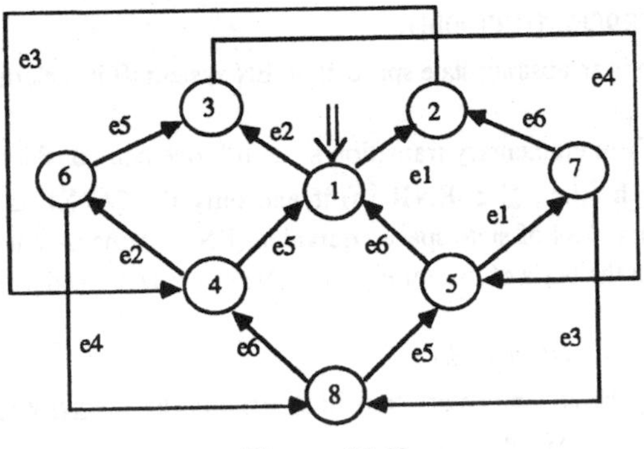

Figure 4.1.10

Then Σ_h is the EN system of Figure 4.1.11, where (note that Z'_i is the complement of Z_i):

$Z_1 = \{1,4,5,8\}$ $Z'_1 = \{2,3,6,7\}$
$Z_2 = \{1,3,5\}$ $Z'_2 = \{2,4,6,7,8\}$
$Z_3 = \{1,2,3,5,7\}$ $Z'_3 = \{4,6,8\}$
$Z_4 = \{1,3,4,5,6,8\}$ $Z'_4 = \{2,7\}$
$Z_5 = \{1,2,4\}$ $Z'_5 = \{3,5,6,7,8\}$
$Z_6 = \{1,2,3,4,6\}$ $Z'_6 = \{5,7,8\}$
$Z_7 = \{1,2,4,5,7,8\}$ $Z'_7 = \{3,6\}$.

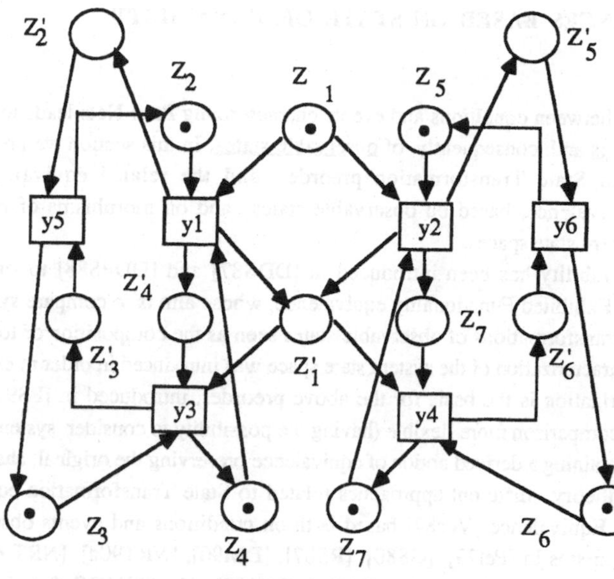

Figure 4.1.11

It can be easily seen that for the following EN system Σ_1:

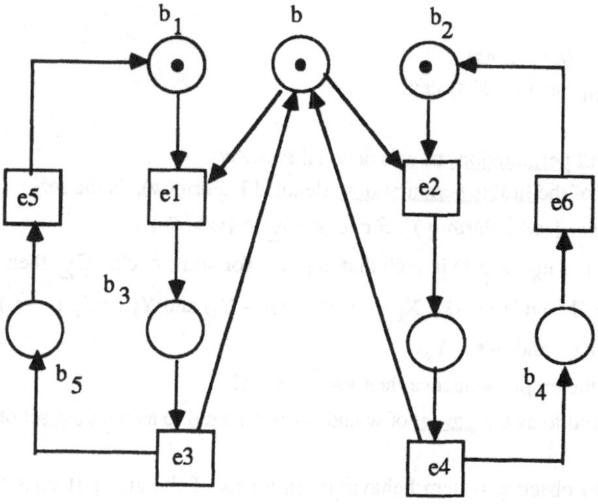

Figure 4.1.12

we have $SCG(\Sigma_1) \cong h$.
Indeed, Σ_1 is a condition-renaming of Σ_h/Q where $Q = \{Z'_1, Z'_2, Z'_5, Z_3, Z_4, Z_6, Z_7\}$. ♦

In the above example Σ_h results from Σ_1 by adding complementary conditions to all conditions of Σ_1. It must be said here that in general when one starts with an EN system Σ and considers an elementary transition system h such that $h \cong SGG(\Sigma)$ then Σ_h will contain more additional conditions than the complemets of the conditions of Σ only.

4.2. EQUIVALENCES BASED ON STATE OBSERVABILITY

The duality between conditions and events characterizing Petri Nets leads to the definitions of observable conditions and, consequently, of observable states. In this section we present a preorder of EN systems, called State Transformation preorder, and the related equivalence, called State Transformation equivalence, based on observable states and on morphisms of relational algebras representing the system state spaces.

Place observability has been introduced in [DDS87] and [DDPS88] to support a notion of equivalence, called Exhibited Functionality equivalence, whose aim is to compare system functionality expressed through transformations of observable states seen as the composition of local states. To this aim an algebraic characterization of the system state space was introduced in order to express this locality. The same characterization is the basis for the above preorder, introduced in [PS90] with the aim of making the system comparison more flexible (having the possibility to consider systems at different level of details), and of obtaining a derived notion of equivalence preserving the original characteristics.

Within net theory, different approaches related to State Transformation equivalence are: the notion of Interface Equivalence [Vos87] based both on conditions and events observability; various notions of net morphisms in [Pet73], [GS80], [RS87], [DM90], [NRT90a], [NRT90b], [Win87]; the notions of refinement as defined in [Val79], [SM83], [Mul85], [Vog87], [GG90a]; finally, the reduction rules preserving system behaviour defined in [Ber87].

In this section we introduce the main results on state observability introduced in [DDPS88], [PS90] and [PS91]. To this aim some additional notations are needed.

Definition 4.2.1. *(notations)*
Let $\Sigma = (B, E, F, c_{in})$ be an EN system.
For all $w \in E^*$:

(1) The set of all permutations of w is denoted Perm(w).

(2) The subset of the firable permutations, denoted F-Perm(w), is the set
$\text{F-Perm}(w) = \{ w' \in \text{Perm}(w) : \exists\, c, c' \in C_\Sigma \;\; c\,[w'> c' \}$.

(3) (i) If $w = e_1 \dots e_k$ $(k \geq 1)$ is such that $c\,[w>c'$ for some $c, c' \in C_\Sigma$ then let us define
$X_0 = X_y = \emptyset$ and $\forall\, i \in [k]$ $X_i = X_{i-1} \cup ({}^\bullet e_i - Y_i)$ and $Y_i = (Y_{i-1} - {}^\bullet e_i) \cup e_i{}^\bullet$;
then ${}^\bullet w = X_k$ and $w^\bullet = Y_k$.
(ii) If w is the empty sequence then ${}^\bullet w = w^\bullet = \emptyset$.
${}^\bullet w$ is referred to as the pre-set of w and $w^\bullet$ is referred to as the post-set of w. ♦

In order to observe system behaviour in terms of the states it goes through, we define the notions of observable conditions and of systems having observable cases (S-labelled systems) [DDPS88], [PS90]. In particular, this requires that each observable condition belongs to at least one observable case (this guarantees that system behaviour is observed only when each component is in an observable local state).

Definition 4.2.2. *(S-labelled system)*
A pair (Σ, O) (Σ for short) is an S-labelled system iff:

(1) $\Sigma = (B, E, F, c_{in})$ is an EN system.

(2) $O \subseteq B$ is such that $\forall s \in O\ \exists c \in C_\Sigma\ [\, s \in c$ and $c \subseteq O\,]$. O is called the set of observable conditions of Σ.

(3) $c_{in} \subseteq O$.

$C_{obs}(\Sigma) = \{\, c \in C_\Sigma : c \subseteq O\}$ is the set of observable cases of Σ. ♦

Example 4.2.1.

From now on observable conditions are represented by shaded circles.

The EN system Σ_1 in Figure 4.2.1 is an S-labelled system. The EN system Σ_2 in Figure 4.2.4 is an S-labelled system; if q_5 was not an observable condition then Σ_2 could not be an S-labelled system since neither q_4 nor q_6 would belong to an observable case.

Having defined the observable states, we now define that an occurrence sequence is minimal w.r.t. this kind of observation if all its firable permutations lead from one observable case to another one without passing through intermediate observable cases.

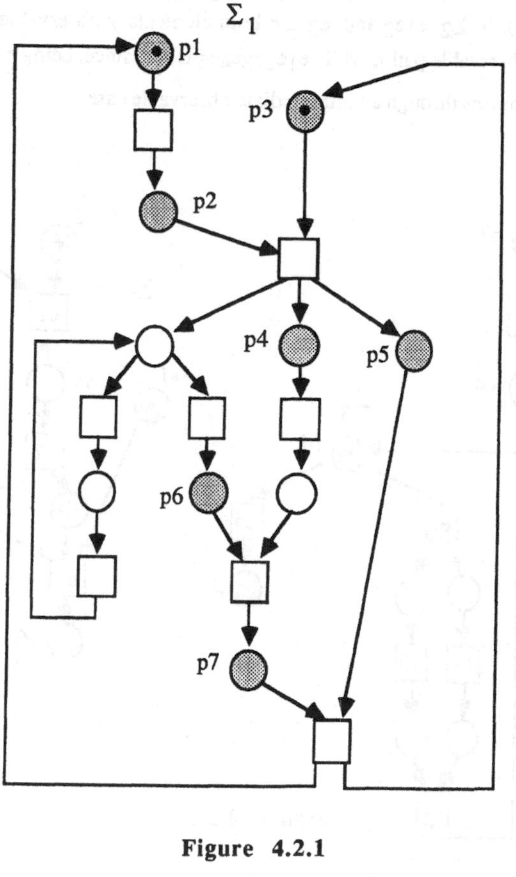

Figure 4.2.1

Definition 4.2.3. *(elementary observable path)*

Let $\Sigma = (B, E, F, c_{in})$ be an S-labelled system, $w \in E^+$ and $c, c' \in C_{obs}(\Sigma)$ be such that $c\ [w\!>\ c'$.
Then w is an <u>elementary observable path</u> from c to c' of Σ iff

$$\forall\ u_1, ..., u_k \in E\ [\ u_1 ... u_k \in \text{F-Perm}(w) \text{ and } c\ [u_1\!>\ c_1\ ...\ c_{k-1}\ [u_k\!>\ c'\ ] \Rightarrow$$
$$\forall\ i \in [\![k-1]\!]\ c_i \notin C_{obs}(\Sigma).$$

$c\ [(w\!>\!>\ c'$ denotes the occurrence of an elementary observable path w leading from c to c'.
W_Σ denotes the set of elementary observable paths of Σ. ♦

Remark

The empty word is not an elementary observable path.
All the firable permutations of w are considered in order to be sure that, no matter what is the order in which the events of w are executed, an intermediate observable case cannot be reached.

Example 4.2.2.

Let us consider the systems of Figure 4.2.2. In Σ_1 e_1, e_2 and e_3 are all elementary observable paths, while e_1e_2 is not an elementary observable path since $\{p_1, p_2\}\ [e_1\!>\ \{p_2, p_3\}\ [e_2\!>\ \{p_3, p_4\}$, and $\{p_2, p_3\}$ belongs to $C_{obs}(\Sigma_1)$. In Σ_2 e_1e_2 and e_3 are both elementary observable paths. In Σ_3 e_5 and $e_1e_2e_3e_4$ are elementary observable paths, while $e_1e_2e_3e_4e_5$ is not, since, being a prolongation of an elementary observable path, it passes through an intermediate observable case. ♦

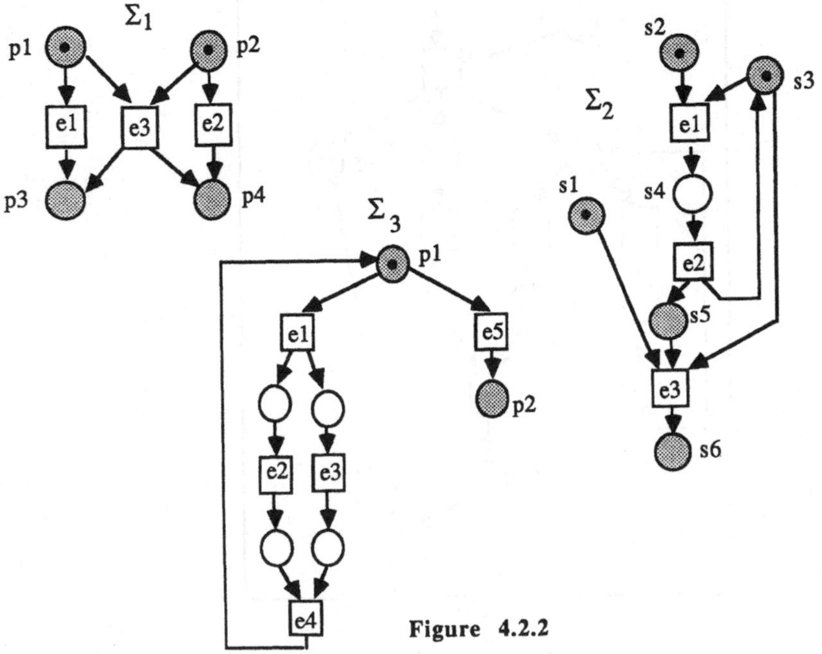

Figure 4.2.2

The system behaviour can be characterized in terms of state transformations within the system state space by using the notions of observable local states and of elementary observable paths. To this end the state space is structured in terms of a relational algebra generated by the set of observable reachable cases and the operations of set difference and intersection, in which the relation between local states represents the existence of an elementary observable path connecting them. The operations of set difference and intersection represent the part of the local state which is modified and remains unchanged, respectively, during the local state transformation.

Definition 4.2.4. *(OLST algebra)*
Let (Σ,O) be an S-labelled system. Its observable local state transformation algebra, abbreviated OLST algebra and denoted **I**, is the 6-tuple $<I, -, \cap, \cup, c_{in}, \rightarrow>$, where

(1) $<I, -, \cap, \cup>$ is the observable local state algebra of Σ, abbreviated OLS algebra, in which: I is the minimal set of subsets of O that contains $C_{obs}(\Sigma)$ and is closed under the binary operation of set difference (-);
$\cap$ is set intersection and $\cup$ is the set union.

(2) c_{in} is the initial case of Σ.

(3) $\rightarrow \subseteq I \times I$ is an irreflexive relation which is called local state transformation relation and is defined as follows:

$$\forall x,y \in I \quad x \rightarrow y \quad \Leftrightarrow \quad \exists w \in W_{\Sigma} \quad [\bullet w \subseteq x \text{ and } y = (x - \bullet w) \cup w\bullet].$$

Elements of $C_{obs}(\Sigma)$ are called generators of I.

$I_{min} = \{x \in I: x \neq \emptyset \text{ and } \nexists\, y \in I\ [y \neq \emptyset \text{ and } y \subset x]\}$. I_{min} is referred to as the set of the minimal elements of $I - \{\emptyset\}$ w.r.t. set inclusion. ♦

Remark
One may check that $\forall\, x, y \in I\ [x \cap y \in I \text{ and } x \cup y \in I] \Leftrightarrow \exists\, z \in I\ \ x \cup y \subseteq z$.
Moreover, $\forall\, x \in C_{obs}(\Sigma), \forall\, y \in I\ \ x \rightarrow y \Rightarrow y \in C_{obs}(\Sigma)$.
The elements of I_{min} are maximal sets of observable conditions such that they are all together either marked or not marked in each observable case. That is why the empty set is excluded as an element of I_{min}.

Example 4.2.3.
Figure 4.2.1 contains an S-labelled system Σ_1. Its OLST algebra $\mathbf{I}_1 = <I_1, -, \cap, \cup, c_{in,1}, \rightarrow_1>$ is such that: $I_1 = \{\{p_1,p_3\}, \{p_2,p_3\}, \{p_4,p_5,p_6\}, \{p_5,p_7\}, \{p_4,p_6\}, \{p_7\}, \{p_1\}, \{p_2\}, \{p_3\}, \{p_5\}, \emptyset\}$; $c_{in,1} = \{p_1,p_3\}$; $\rightarrow_1 = \{ <\{p_1\},\{p_2\}>, <\{p_1,p_3\},\{p_2,p_3\}>, <\{p_2,p_3\},\{p_4,p_5,p_6\}>, <\{p_4,p_5,p_6\},\{p_5,p_7\}>, <\{p_5,p_7\},\{p_1,p_3\}>, <\{p_4,p_6\},\{p_7\}>$. The observable local state $\{p_5\}$ is obtained from the intersection of $\{p_5, p_7\}$ and $\{p_4, p_5, p_6\}$, while the observable local state $\{p_4, p_6\}$ is obtained from the difference between $\{p_4, p_5, p_6\}$ and $\{p_5, p_7\}$. ♦

A preorder is defined on the class of S-labelled systems [PS90], i.e., a reflexive and transitive relation, with the following intuition behind it. A system Σ_1 precedes a system Σ_2 in the preorder if and only if 1) the OLST algebra of Σ_1 is a substructure of the OLST algebra of Σ_2; 2) for each elementary observable path producing a local state transformation in Σ_1 there is a (sequence of) elementary observable path(s) in Σ_2 producing a corresponding local state transformation.

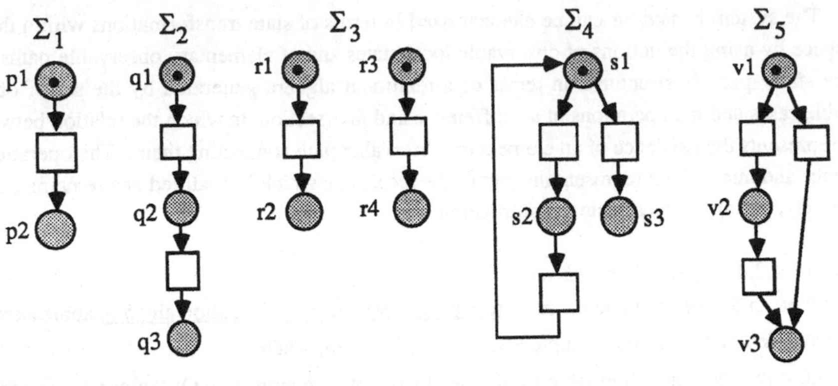

Figure 4.2.3

Definition 4.2.5. *($\Sigma_1 \subseteq^{ST} \Sigma_2$)*

Let Σ_1 and Σ_2 be S-labelled systems, and $\mathbf{I_1} = <I_1, -, \cap, \cup, c_{in,1}, \rightarrow_1>$ and $\mathbf{I_2} = <I_2, -, \cap, \cup, c_{in,2}, \rightarrow_2>$ be their OLST algebras. Σ_1 is <u>less or equal</u> to Σ_2 <u>w.r.t. state transformation</u>, denoted $\Sigma_1 \subseteq^{ST} \Sigma_2$, iff there is an injective morphism $h : <I_1, -, \cap, \cup> \dashrightarrow <I_2, -, \cap, \cup>$, i.e., an injective mapping between I_1 and I_2 which preserves $-, \cap, \cup$, such that :

(1) $h(c_{in,1}) \subseteq c_{in,2}$.

(2) $\forall x, y \in I_1$ [$x \rightarrow_1 y \Rightarrow$ [$h(x) \rightarrow_2 h(y)$ or $\exists n \geq 1, \exists i_1, i_2, ..., i_n \in (I_2 - h(I_1))$ $h(x) \rightarrow_2 i_1 \rightarrow_2 ... i_n \rightarrow_2 h(y)$]]. ♦

Example 4.2.4.

Let us consider the systems Σ_i of Figure 4.2.3 and their OLST algebras $\mathbf{I_i}$ ($i = 1, ..., 5$).

(1) $\Sigma_1 \subseteq^{ST} \Sigma_2$: in fact, considering $I_1 = \{\{p_1\}, \{p_2\}, \emptyset\}$, $I_2 = \{\{q_1\}, \{q_2\}, \{q_3\}, \emptyset\}$, $\rightarrow_1 = \{<\{p_1\}, \{p_2\}>\}$, $\rightarrow_2 = \{<\{q_1\}, \{q_2\}>, <\{q_2\}, \{q_3\}>\}$, there are two possible injective morphisms $h, k : <I_1, -, \cap, \cup> \dashrightarrow <I_2, -, \cap, \cup>$ defined respectively by: $h(\{p_1\}) = \{q_1\}$ and $h(\{p_2\}) = \{q_3\}$; $k(\{p_1\}) = \{q_1\}$ and $k(\{p_2\}) = \{q_2\}$, such that : $c_{in,2} = h(c_{in,1})$ and $h(\{p_1\}) \rightarrow_2 \{q_2\} \rightarrow_2 h(\{p_2\})$; $c_{in,2} = k(c_{in,1})$ and $k(\{p_1\}) \rightarrow_2 k(\{p_2\})$.

On the basis of the morphism h, $\Sigma_1 \subseteq^{ST} \Sigma_2$ means that Σ_2 is an <u>expansion</u> of Σ_1, i.e., Σ_2 refines the observable state transformations performed by Σ_1 into a sequence of more elementary transformations of observable states. On the basis of the morphism k, $\Sigma_1 \subseteq^{ST} \Sigma_2$ means that Σ_2 is an <u>extension</u> of Σ_1, i.e., in addition to the observable state transformations performed by Σ_1, Σ_2 performs other observable state transformations.

(2) $\Sigma_1 \subseteq^{ST} \Sigma_3$: in fact, considering $I_3 = \{\{r_1,r_3\}, \{r_2,r_4\}, \{r_2,r_3\}, \{r_1,r_4\} \{r_1\}, \{r_2\}, \{r_3\}, \{r_4\}, \emptyset\}$, $\rightarrow_3 = \{ <\{r_1,r_3\},\{r_2,r_3\}>, <\{r_1,r_4\},\{r_2,r_4\}>, <\{r_1,r_3\},\{r_1,r_4\}>, <\{r_2,r_3\},\{r_2,r_4\}>, <\{r_1\},\{r_2\}>, <\{r_3\},\{r_4\}> \}$, there is for example the injective morphism $h: <I_1, -, \cap, \cup> \dashrightarrow <I_3, -, \cap, \cup>$ defined by: $h(\{p_1\}) = \{r_1\}$ and $h(\{p_2\}) = \{r_2\}$.

Σ_3 is an extension of Σ_1 obtained by adding a concurrent component to it.

(3) $\Sigma_1 \subseteq^{ST} \Sigma_4$: in fact, considering $I_4 = \{\{s_1\}, \{s_2\}, \{s_3\}, \emptyset\}$ and $\rightarrow_4 = \{<\{s_1\},\{s_2\}>, <\{s_1\},\{s_3\}>, <\{s_2\},\{s_1\}>\}$, there are the injective morphisms

h, k : $< I_1, -, \cap, \cup >$ --> $< I_4, -, \cap, \cup >$ defined respectively by: $h(p_1) = s_1$ and $h(p_2) = s_2$; $k(p_1) = s_1$ and $k(p_2) = s_3$. In both cases Σ_4 is an extension of Σ_1.

(4) $\Sigma_1 \subseteq^{ST} \Sigma_5$: in fact, considering $I_5 = \{\{v_1\}, \{v_2\}, \{v_3\}, \emptyset\}$ and $\rightarrow_5 = \{<\{v_1\},\{v_2\}>, <\{v_1\},\{v_3\}>, <\{v_2\},\{v_3\}>\}$, there is an injective morphism
h: $< I_1, -, \cap, \cup >$ --> $< I_4, -, \cap, \cup >$ defined by: $h(\{p_1\}) = \{v_1\}$ and $h(\{p_2\}) = \{v_3\}$.
In this case Σ_5 is both an extension and an expansion of Σ_1. ♦

An isomorphism $h : \mathbf{I_1}$ --> $\mathbf{I_2}$ between two OLST algebras is an isomorphism
$h : < I_1, -, \cap, \cup >$ --> $< I_2, -, \cap, \cup >$ such that:

(1) $h(c_{in,1}) = c_{in,2}$.

(2) $\forall x,y \in I_1 \; [\, x \rightarrow_1 y \Leftrightarrow h(x) \rightarrow_2 h(y) \,]$.

If Σ_1 and Σ_2 are S-labelled systems and $h : \mathbf{I_1}$ --> $\mathbf{I_2}$ is an isomorphism between their OLST algebras. Then $x \in I_{1min} \Leftrightarrow h(x) \in I_{2min}$ and $x \in C_{obs}(\Sigma_1) \Leftrightarrow h(x) \in C_{obs}(\Sigma_2)$.

The following theorem states a fundamental property of the ST-preorder, that is the basis of a definition of an equivalence notion based on $\subseteq$ ST.

Theorem 4.2.1. [PS90]
Let Σ_1 and Σ_2 be S-labelled systems and $\mathbf{I_1}$, $\mathbf{I_2}$ be their OLST algebras.
Then $\Sigma_1 \subseteq^{ST} \Sigma_2$ and $\Sigma_2 \subseteq^{ST} \Sigma_1 \Leftrightarrow \mathbf{I_1}$ and $\mathbf{I_2}$ are isomorphic. ♦

Definition 4.2.6. *($\Sigma_1 \approx^{ST} \Sigma_2$)*
Let Σ_1 and Σ_2 be S-labelled systems and $\mathbf{I_1}, \mathbf{I_2}$ be their OLST algebras. Then Σ_1 and Σ_2 are equivalent with respect to state transformations, abbreviated ST-equivalent, and denoted $\Sigma_1 \approx^{ST} \Sigma_2$, iff $\Sigma_1 \subseteq^{ST} \Sigma_2$ and $\Sigma_2 \subseteq^{ST} \Sigma_1$ (or equivalently, iff $\mathbf{I_1}$ and $\mathbf{I_2}$ are isomorphic). ♦

Remark
The only other equivalence notion which considers observability of conditions is the notion of Interface equivalence [Voss87]. For the reasons discussed in Section 3.2 it is incomparable with ST-equivalence, even when restricted to observability of conditions ([PS90]).

Example 4.2.5.
Let us consider the S-labelled systems Σ_1 and Σ_2 of Figure 4.2.4. They are not ST-equivalent. In fact, there exists no isomorphism between their OLST algebras since the cardinality of the sets $I_1 = \{\{p_1\}, \{p_2\}, \{p_3\}, \{p_4\}, \emptyset\}$, and $I_2 = \{\{q_1,q_3\}, \{q_2,q_3\}, \{q_4,q_5\}, \{q_5,q_6\}, \{q_3\}, \{q_4\}, \{q_1\}, \{q_2\}, \{q_5\}, \{q_6\}, \emptyset\}$ are different.
Notice that Σ_1 and Σ_2 are equivalent for any of the equivalence notions presented up to now, since there is an isomorphism between the events of the two systems and between global states transformations. On the contrary, ST-equivalence distinguishes Σ_1 from Σ_2, since in Σ_1 the events e_1 and e_3 transform global states only, while the corresponding ones in Σ_2 transform local states too.
Moreover $\Sigma_1 \not\subseteq^{ST} \Sigma_2$; in fact it is possible to show that any possible injective morphism between I_1 and I_2 does not preserve local state transformations. For example, if we consider the morphism
$h : < I_1, -, \cap, \cup >$ --> $< I_2, -, \cap, \cup >$ defined by $h(\{p_1\}) = \{q_1\}$, $h(\{p_2\}) = \{q_2\}$, $h(\{p_3\}) =$

{q_4}, h({p_4}) = {q_6}, then we have {p_2} $\rightarrow_1$ {p_3} , while not (h({p_2}) $\rightarrow_2$ h({p_3})), and also there are no intermediate states such that h({p_2}) $\rightarrow_2$ ...$\rightarrow_2$ h({p_3}).
Let us remark that the mapping h defined as follows: h(p_1) = {q_1}, h(p_2) = {q_2,q_3}, h(p_3) = {q_4,q_5}and h(p_4) = {q_5,q_6} is not an injective morphim since the images of two disjoint elements, namely p_3 and p_4 , are not disjoint.
The S-labelled system Σ_1 of Figure 4.2.1 is ST-equivalent to the S-labelled system Σ_2 of figure 4.2.4. Let us exhibit the bijection between I_{min1} and I_{min2}, from which the bijection between I_1 and I_2 can be easily derived since it preserves set union: {p_1} $\leftrightarrow$ {q_1}; {p_2} $\leftrightarrow$ {q_2}; {p_3} $\leftrightarrow$ {q_3}; {p_4, p_6} $\leftrightarrow$ {q_4}; {p_5} $\leftrightarrow$ {q_5}; {p_7} $\leftrightarrow$ {q_6}. ♦

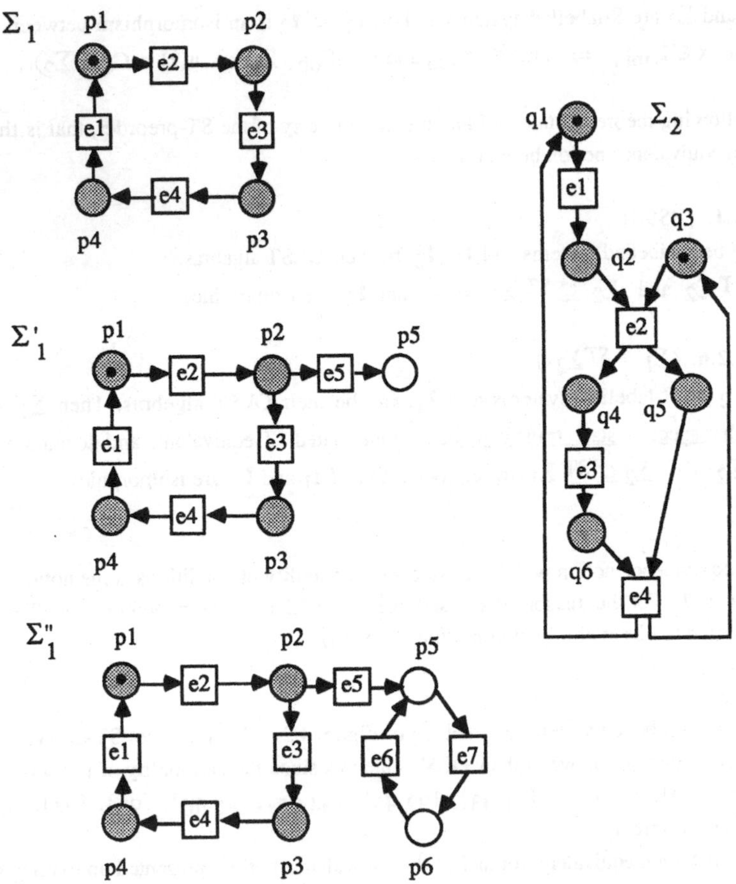

Figure 4.2.4

ST-equivalence between S-labelled systems does not preserve deadlock-freedom. In fact, an S-labelled system can reach a case at which no event is enabled (a case in which the system is blocked) and which is unobservable.

Example 4.2.6.

The S-labelled system Σ_1 and Σ'_1 given in Figure 4.2.4 are ST-equivalent. While Σ_1 is deadlock-free, Σ'_1 can reach an (unobservable) case at which no event is enabled. ♦

In order to preserve deadlock-freedom without modifying the notion of ST-equivalence, we have to consider systems satisfying the requirement that any reachable case enables a finite sequence leading to an observable case, or an infinite sequence which does not reach any observable case. In fact the following theorem holds.

Theorem 4.2.2. [PS90]

Let Σ_1 and Σ_2 be S-observable systems such that $\Sigma_1 \approx^{ST} \Sigma_2$ and Σ_1 is deadlock-free.
Then Σ_2 is deadlock-free if and only if Σ_2 is such that:

(*) $\forall c_2 \in C_{\Sigma_2}$ [[$\exists c'_2 \in C_{obs}(\Sigma_2)$, $\exists w \in E^*$ $c_2[w> c'_2$] or

[$\exists e_1, e_2, \ldots \in E_2$, $\exists c^1{}_2, c^2{}_2, \ldots \notin C_{obs\Sigma_2}$ $c_2 [e_1> c^1{}_2 [e_2> c^2{}_2 \ldots$]]. ♦

Example 4.2.7.

Let us consider the systems of Figure 4.2.4 The S-labelled system Σ_1 and Σ''_1 are ST-equivalent and deadlock-free. It is immediate to verify that they both satisfy the condition (*) of Theorem 4.2.2, while Σ'_1 does not. ♦

The notion of ST-equivalence originated from the attempt to define a preorder whose related equivalence coincides with the notion of EF equivalence presented in [DDPS88]. Let us now give the original definition of the latter and state the correspondence between the two equivalence notions.

Definition 4.2.7. *($\Sigma_1 \approx^{EF} \Sigma_2$)*

Let Σ_1 and Σ_2 be two S-labelled systems and $< I_1, -, \cap, \cup >$ and $< I_2, -, \cap, \cup >$ their OLS algebras. Then Σ_1 and Σ_2 are <u>equivalent with respect to exhibited functionality</u>, abbreviated EF-equivalent and denoted $\Sigma_1 \approx^{EF} \Sigma_2$, iff there is an isomorphism

$h : < I_1, -, \cap, \cup > \;\text{-->}\; < I_2, -, \cap, \cup >$ such that:

$\forall w_1,\ldots,w_n \in W_{\Sigma_1}$ [$\underline{inc}(\Sigma_1)$ [$(w_1\gg c_{11} \ldots$ [$(w_n\gg c_{1n}$ $\Rightarrow$

$\exists v_1,\ldots,v_n \in W_{\Sigma_1}$ $\underline{inc}(\Sigma_2) = h(\underline{inc}(\Sigma_1))$ [$(v_1\gg h(c_{11}) \ldots$ [$(v_n\gg h(c_{1n})$]

and (vice versa)

$\forall w_1,\ldots,w_n \in W_{\Sigma_2}$ [$\underline{inc}(\Sigma_2)$ [$(w_1\gg c_{21} \ldots$ [$(w_n\gg c_{2n}$ $\Rightarrow$

$\exists v_1,\ldots,v_n \in W_{\Sigma_2}$ $\underline{inc}(\Sigma_1) = h(\underline{inc}(\Sigma_2))$ [$(v_1\gg h(c_{21}) \ldots$ [$(v_n\gg h(c_{2n})$]. ♦

EF-equivalence could be formulated in a way similar to ST-equivalence by requiring an isomorphis between the OLST algebras in which the relation $\rightarrow$ is contained in $C_{obs}(\Sigma) \times C_{obs}(\Sigma)$.

It can be proved that ST-equivalence is stronger than EF-equivalence [PS90]. This fact is supported by the following counter-example: the two S-labelled systems Σ_1 and Σ_2 from Figure 4.2.5 are EF-equivalent and not ST-equivalent. In fact, if we consider the only possible isomorphism between their OLS algebras, in Σ_1 we have $p_2 \rightarrow_1 p_3$ while in Σ_2 $q_2 = h(p_2)$ and $q_3 = h(p_3)$ are not related by $\rightarrow_2$.

It easy to see that, although EF-equivalence is weaker than ST-equivalence, Theorem 4.2.2 holds also for EF-equivalent systems.

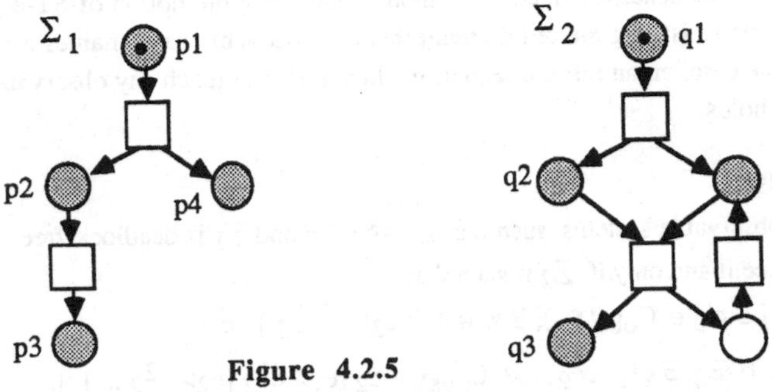

Figure 4.2.5

On the other hand, ST- and EF-equivalences coincide for a subclass of S-labelled systems, called S-observable systems [DDPS88]. Intuitively, S-observable systems are S-labelled systems which cannot contain "observable side conditions" on elementary observable paths.

Definition 4.2.8. *(S-observable systems)*
Let Σ be an S-labelled system.Then Σ is S-observable iff $\forall\, w \in W_\Sigma$ $\bullet w \cap w\bullet = \emptyset$. ♦

Remark
The previous definition implies that for each $c, c' \in C_{obs}(\Sigma)$ and for each $w \in W_\Sigma$ it holds: c $[(w\gg c'$ if and only if $c - c' = \bullet w$ and $c' - c = w\bullet$.
Theorem 4.2.2 concerning deadlock-freedom holds a fortiori for S-observable systems.

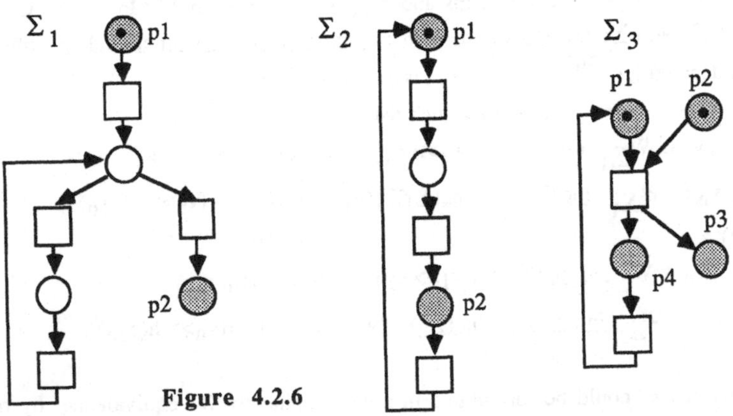

Figure 4.2.6

Example 4.2.8.
The S-labelled system Σ_2 in Figure 4.2.2 is not S-observable since condition s_3 belongs to both $\bullet w$ and $w\bullet$, with $w = e_1e_2$. On the other hand, the S-labelled systems Σ_1, Σ_2, Σ_3, in Figure 4.2.6, are all S-observable.
♦

A basic property of any S-observable systems Σ is that, being $< I, -, \cap, \cup >$ its OLS algebra, for each $w \in W_\Sigma$ $\bullet w, w\bullet \in I$. This does not hold in the case of S-labelled systems. For example, the S-labelled system Σ_2 of Figure 4.2.2 is not S-observable since the elementary path e_1e_2 is such that $\bullet w = \{s_2, s_3\}$ and $w\bullet = \{s_3, s_5\}$ and $\bullet w \cap w\bullet \neq \emptyset$. In addition, both $\bullet w$ and $w\bullet$ do not belong to I_2.

Theorem 4.2.3. [DDPS88]
Each equivalence class generated by the ST (EF)-equivalence over the class of S-observable systems contains a unique (up to isomorphism) canonical representative that is minimal w.r.t. the elements of the underlying net, i.e., it is a simple and reduced S-observable systems in which every condition is observable.
♦

The proof is based on the following construction. Given an S-observable system and its OLST algebra, the canonical representative of the equivalence class to which it belongs is constructed:

(1) By associating a condition to each element of I_{min}.

(2) By associating an event to each equivalence class of local state transformations, where two local state transformations $x \to y$ and $v \to z$ are equivalent if and only if $x - y = v - z$ and $y - x = z - v$, i.e.: they transform the same local states.

(3) By connecting a condition c to an event e if c corresponds to an element of I_{min} contained in the precondition of a local state transformation corresponding to e, and an event to a condition in a similar way.

(4) The initial case is the set of conditions corresponding to the elements of I_{min} constituting the initial case of the given system.

Note that, this construction could also be applied to S-labelled systems but in this case the underlying net of the resulting system can be not pure - and then the system can contain dead transitions. In this case, it cannot be considered as the canonical representative of the equivalence class to which the source system belongs.

Example 4.2.9.
The canonical representative of the class to which Σ_1 of figure 4.2.1. belongs is the EN system Σ_2 of figure 4.2.4. Point (1) of the construction is illustrated in the last two lines of example 4.2.5. ♦

The degree of concurrency of an S-observable system can be defined in terms of the maximal number of distinguishable observable conditions that concurrently hold and in terms of the elementary observable paths that can be concurrently activated.

Definition 4.2.9. *(degree of concurrency)*
Let Σ be an S-observable system and CR the canonical representative of the equivalence class to which it belongs. Then the degree of concurrency of Σ is the pair $<m_{CR}, n_{CR}>$, where $m_{CR} = \max_{c \in C_{CR}} |c|$ and $n_{CR} = \max_{U \in U_{CR}} |U|$.
♦

The ST preorder preserves the degree of concurrency in the sense of the following theorem.

Theorem 4.2.4. [PS90]
Let Σ_1 and Σ_2 be S-observable systems having $<m_1, n_1>$ and $<m_2, n_2>$ as the degree of concurrency. Then $\Sigma_1 \subseteq^{ST} \Sigma_2 \Rightarrow (m_1 \leq m_2 \text{ and } n_1 \leq n_2)$ and $\Sigma_1 \approx^{ST} \Sigma_2 \Rightarrow (m_1 = m_2 \text{ and } n_1 = n_2)$. ♦

Example 4.2.10.
The S-observable systems Σ_1 and Σ_3 of Figure 4.2.3 are in canonical form, they are not isomorphic and thus not ST-equivalent, while $\Sigma_1 \subseteq^{ST} \Sigma_3$ and Σ_3 has a higher degree of concurrency.
If we consider the S-observable systems Σ_3 of Figure 4.2.2 and Σ_1 of Figure 4.2.6, they are ST-equivalent and show the same degree of concurrency. Notice that in Σ_3 the concurrency within the unobservable part of the system does not influence the degree of concurrency. ♦

In the case of S-observable systems in which all conditions are observable, i.e., such that O = B and $C_{obs}(\Sigma) = C_\Sigma$, then OLST algebras, ST-preorder and ST-equivalence characterize the system behaviour in an exhaustive way. More specifically, systems belonging to the same equivalence class may only differ from the related canonical representative in that they can contain dead events, and can be not simple both w.r.t. conditions and events. [PS91] gives the conditions under which a relational algebra is the Local State Transformation algebra of an EN system. In [DeM90] operations of local state transformation algebras are related to operations between EN systems based on fusion of conditions.

The notion of observable places has been recently used [Cha91] to introduce the concept of interface for P/T nets.This is the basis of a notion of preorder that compares systems by considering their evolution in terms of both interface markings and some internal markings. These latter are called stable as they allow only evolutions involving the interface.The kernel of the preorder is an equivalnce relation called stable functionality bisimulation. This equivalence is strengthened to obtain a congruence with respect to the operation of subnet substitution, called statble state transformation equivalence.

5. CONCLUSIONS

In this paper we have surveyed different equivalence notions for the models of concurrent systems based on EN systems. We have divided the equivalence notions into two groups:
(i) those based on observing the actions carried out by the system, and
(ii) those based on observing state transformations that system goes through.
In both cases, some parts of the system behaviour may be internal, i.e. not observable.

There is a number of conclusions which could be drawn from the discussion presented in this paper.

(1) The equivalence notions based on action observation compare system behaviour by considering either occurrence sequences or nonsequential processes, together with their "continuations" ("prolongations"). This family of notions (and results concerning them) is historically older and (perhaps also for this reason) really rich.

(2) The equivalence notions based on the state space are quite typical for net theory. They are mainly based on the notion of morphisms between state based representations of system behaviour. The two approaches we present cover the main developments from the literature. In the first approach the equivalence notions correspond to case graph isomorphisms. Within this approach the 'synthesis' theory has been also developped. The second approach can also be seen as based on morphisms between system state spaces from which the notion of state observation can be derived [PS91]. Here the equivalence notion is finer than the one based on case graph isomorphisms because the isomorphism of algebra of local state transformations requires the preservation of "locality" in the change of condition holding.

(3) Both approaches have yet to deal with problems like refinement and congruence w.r.t. different operators, and synthesis of systems from a representation of their behaviour. At this point it is possible to make the following remarks.

(3.1) The two families of equivalence notions support the notion of refinement in different ways. An interesting and open problem (area) is to obtain a characterization of refinement in both approaches, and to understand how they could be used together in the system modeling process. Representative papers for efforts in this direction are [BGV90] and [NRT90b].

(3.2) In the action based framework the notion of congruence with respect to various operations - allowing system composition while preserving behavioural properties - has been considered from the very beginning, starting with Milner's calculus. Here Petri nets are "weaker" than other concurrency models, since up to now they do not have an algebraic/compositional definition (except for some attempts of defining modular net classes- see, e.g., [BD90]). However, there exist two notions of compositions of net systems, one based on transition fusion (given in Definition 3.3) and the other one based on place fusion (a sort of alternative composition); since places and transitions are basic units of nets these notions seem to arise naturally in the framework of net based systems. Hence the problem of congruence w.r.t. parallel and alternative composition has been faced for the equivalence notions based on action observability (the case of parallel composition was briefly reported here). For the state based equivalence notions the problem has still to be tackled.

(3.3) The problem of synthesising systems from a description of their behaviour has been considered for state based framework (yielding for each of the two approaches presented here the construction of a canonical representative). For the action based approach the problem of system synthesis has not been handled yet.

ACKNOWLEDGEMENTS

This survey has been one of the goals of the ESPRIT Basic Research Action DEMON. In our work on it we have benefited from the comments of our DEMON collegues (Eike Best, Fiorella De Cindio, Giorgio De Michelis, Raymond Devillers, Rob van Glabbeek, Ursula Goltz, Walter Vogler), and from the comments of Ugo Moscato. We are also very indebted to six anonymous referees for very valuable suggestions and criticisms, and to Roberto Gorrieri for his careful reading of an early version of the paper.

6. REFERENCES

Acta Inf. Acta Informatica, Springer Verlag, Berlin
APN Advances in Petri Nets, Springer Verlag, Berlin
IFB Informatik Fachberichte, Springer Verlag, Berlin
LNCS Lecture Notes in Computer Science, Springer Verlag, Berlin
TCS Theoretical Computer Science, North Holland, Amsterdam
JCSS Journal of Computer and System Sciences, Academic Press, San Diego

[AAB79] C. Andre', P.Armand, F.Boeri, Synchronic Relations and Applications in Parallel Computation, Digital Processes 5, Georgi Pub. Comp., 1979.

[Abr87] S. Abramsky, Observation Equivalence as a Testing Equivalence, TCS 53, pp. 225-241, 1987.

[ADF87] L. Aceto, R. De Nicola, A. Fantechi, Testing Equivalences for Event Structures, in M.V. Zilli (ed.), "Mathematical Models for the Semantics of Parallelism", LNCS 280, pp. 1-20, 1987.

[AH89] L. Aceto, M. Hennessy, Towards Action - Refinement in Process Algebras, in Proc. LICS'89, Asilomar, California, IEEE Computer Society Press, Washington, pp. 138-145, 1989.

[And82a] C. Andre', Behaviour of a Place-Transition Net on a Subset of Transitions, and Use of The Behaviour Equivalence in Place-Transition Net Analysis, in C. Girault, W. Reisig (eds.), "Applications and Theory of Petri Nets", IFB 52, pp. 131-135 and pp.241-250, 1982.

[And82b] C. Andre', Structural Transformations giving B-equivalent PT-Nets, in A. Pagnoni, G. Rozenberg (eds.), "Applications and Theory of Petri Nets", IFB 66, pp. 14-28, 1982.

[BBK87a] Baeten, J. A. Bergstra, J. W. Klop, Decidability of Bisimulation Equivalence for Processes generating Context-free Languages, in J.W. de Bakker, A.J. Nijman, P.C. Treleaven (eds.), "PARLE 87, Vol.II: Parallel Languages", LNCS 259, pp.94-113, 1987.

[BBK87b] Baeten, J. A. Bergstra, J. W. Klop, Ready-trace Semantics for Concrete Process Algebra with the Priority Operator, The Computer Journal 30(6), pp.498-506, 1987.

[BC87] G. Boudol, I. Castellani, On the Semantics of Concurrency: Partial Orders and Transition Systems, in H. Ehrig, R. Kowalski, G. Levi, U. Montanari (eds.), "TAPSOFT 87", LNCS 249, pp. 123-137, 1987.

[BC89] G. Boudol, I. Castellani, Permutation of Transitions: An Event Structure Semantics for CCS and SCCS, in J.W. de Bakker, W. P. de Roever, G. Rozenberg (eds.) "Linear Time, Branching Time and Partial Order in Logics and Models for Concurrency", LNCS 354, pp 411-427, 1989.

[BD90] L. Bernardinello, F. De Cindio, A Survey of Basic Net Models and Modular Net Classes, DEMON Esprit BRA 3148 Deliverables, June 1990 (the revised version is in this special issue).

[BDKP89] E. Best, R. Devillers, A. Kiehn, L. Pomello, Fully Concurrent Bisimulation, Université Libre de Bruxelles, LIT-202, July 1989. An improved version appeared under the title: Concurrent Bisimulations in Petri Nets, Acta Inf. 28, pp 231-264, 1991

[Ber87] G. Berthelot, Transformations and Decompositions of Nets, in [BRR87], pp. 359-376, 1987.

[Bes87] E. Best, Structure Theory of Petri Nets: the Free Choice Hiatus, in [BRR87], pp.168-206,1987.

[BF88] E. Best, C. Fernandez, Nonsequential Processes, a Petri Net View, EATCS Monographs on Theoretical Computer Science n.13, Springer Verlag, 1988.

[BGV90] W. Brauer, R. Gold, W. Vogler, Behaviour and Equivalences Preserving Refinements of Petri Nets, in G. Rozenberg (ed.) APN'90, LNCS 483, pp.1-46, 1991.

[BHR84] S.D. Brookes, C.A.R. Hoare, A.W. Roscoe, A Theory of Communicating Sequential Processes, Journal of the ACM 31 N.3, 1984.

[BK85] J. A. Bergstra, J. W. Klop, Algebra of Communicating Processes with Abstraction, TCS 37 1, pp.77-121, 1985.

[Bro83] S.D. Brookes, On the Relationship of CCS and CSP, in J. Diaz (ed.), "Automata Languages and Programming 83", LNCS 154, pp. 83-96, 1983.

[Bro84] S.D. Brookes, A Semantics and Proof System for Communicating Processes, in E. Clarke and D. Kozen (eds.), "Logics of Programs", LNCS 164, pp. 68-85, 1984.

[BRR87] W. Brauer, W. Reisig, G. Rozenberg (eds.), Petri Nets: Central Models and Their Properties, LNCS 254, 1987.

[Cas87] I. Castellani, Bisimulations for Concurrency, Ph.D. Thesis, University of Edinburgh, 1987.

[CFM83] I. Castellani, P. Franceschi, U. Montanari, Labeled Event Structures: A Model for Observable Concurrency, in D.Bjorner (ed.), "Formal Description of Programming Concepts II", pp. 383-400, North-Holland, 1983.

[CH87] I. Castellani, M. Hennessy, Distributed Bisimulations, Report N. 4/87, University of Sussex, July 1987.

[Cha91] G. Chehaibar, Replacement of Open Interface Subnets and Stable State Transformation Equivalence, Proc. XII International Conference on Applicatons and Theory of Petri Nets, Gjern (DK), pp 490-509,.1991.

[Dar82] P. Darondeau, An enlarged Definition and complete Axiomatization of Observational Congruence of Finite Processes, in M. Dezani-Ciancaglini, U. Montanari (eds.), "International Symposium on Programming", LNCS 137, pp. 47-62, 1982.

[DD90] P. Darondeau, P.Degano, Event Structures, Causal Trees, and Refinements, in B. Rovan (ed.), "Mathematical Foundations of Computer Science", LNCS 452, 1990.

[DDM87] P. Degano, R. De Nicola, U. Montanari, Observational Equivalences for Concurrency Models, in M. Wirsing (ed.), "Formal Description of Programming Concepts III", North Holland, pp 105-132, 1987.

[DDM89] P. Degano, R. De Nicola, U. Montanari, Partial Ordering Description of Nondeterministic Concurrent Systems, in Proc. REX School/Workshop on Linear, Branching Time and Partial Order in Logics and Models of Concurrency, LNCS 354, pp.438-466, 1989.

[DDPS83] F. De Cindio, G. De Michelis, L. Pomello, C. Simone, Equivalence Notions For Concurrent Systems, in A. Pagnoni, G. Rozenberg (eds.), "Applications and Theory of Petri Nets", IFB 66, pp. 29-39, 1983.

[DDPS85] F. De Cindio, G. De Michelis, L. Pomello, C. Simone, Exhibited-Behaviour Equivalence and Organizational Abstraction in Concurrent System Design, Proc. 5th International Conference on Distributed Computing, IEEE, Denver Co., pp. 486-495, 1985.

[DDPS88] F. De Cindio, G. De Michelis, L. Pomello, C. Simone, A State Transformation Equivalence for Concurent Systems: Exhibited Functionality Equivalence, in F.H. Vogt (ed.),"CONCURRENCY 88", LNCS 335, pp. 222-236, 1988.

[DDS87] F. De Cindio, G. De Michelis, C. Simone, GAMERU: a Language for the Analysis and Design of human Communication Pragmatics, in G.Rozenberg (ed.), APN' 86, LNCS 266, pp. 21-44, 1987.

[DeM90] G. De Michelis, Domains of EN systems (extended abstract), 2nd Workshop on Concurrency and Compositionality, San Miniato, February-March 1990.

[DeN85] R. De Nicola, Two Complete Sets of Axioms for a Theory of Communicating Sequential Processes, Information and Computation 64, 1,3, pp.136-176, 1985.

[DeN87] R. De Nicola, Extensional Equivalences for Transition Systems, Acta Inf. 24, Springer Verlag, pp 211-237, 1987.

[Dev88] R. Devillers, On the Definition of a Bisimulation Notion Based on Partial Words, Petri Net Newsletter 29, pp. 16-19, April 1988.

[Dev 90] R. Devillers, Maximality Preserving Bisimulation, Université Libre de Bruxelles, LIT-214,

March 1990 (to appear in TCS).

[DH84] R. De Nicola, M. Hennessy, Testing Equivalences for Processes, TCS 34, pp. 83-134, 1984.

[DK83] P. Darondeau, L. Kott, On the Observational Semantics of Fair Parallelism, LNCS 154, pp. 147-159, 1983.

[DM90] J. Desel, A. Merceron, Vicinity Respecting Morphisms, in G. Rozenberg (ed.) APN'90, LNCS 483, pp.165-185, 1991.

[DP83] G. De Michelis, L. Pomello, A Less Restrictive Observational Equivalence Notion, Proc.IV Workshop on Application ad Theory of Petri Nets, Toulose, pp. 364-381, 1983.

[ER90a] A. Ehrenfeucht, G. Rozenberg, Partial (Set) 2-Structures - Part I: Basic Notion and the Representation Problem, Acta Inf., vol. 26, pp. 315-342, 1990.

[ER90b] A. Ehrenfeucht, G. Rozenberg, Partial (Set) 2-Structures- Part II: State Spaces of Concurrent Systems, Acta Inf., vol. 26, pp.343-368, 1990.

[GG89] R. van Glabbeek, U. Goltz, Equivalence Notions for Concurrent Systems and Refinement of Actions, in A. Kreczmar and G. Mirkowska (eds.), "Mathematical Foundations of Computer Science 1989", LNCS 379, pp. 237-248, 1989.

[GG90a] R. van Glabbeek, U. Goltz, Refinement of Actions in Causality based Models, in J.W. de Bakker, W. P. de Roever, G.Rozenberg (eds.), "Stepwise Refinement of Distributed Systems: models, formalism, correctness", LNCS 430, pp. 267-300, 1990.

[GG90b] R. van Glabbeek, U. Goltz, Equivalence Notions and Refinement of Actions for Flow Event Structures, DEMON Esprit BRA 3148 Deliverables, June 1990.

[Gla90a] R. van Glabbeek, Comparative Concurrency Semantics and Refinement of Actions, PhD. Thesis, Centrum voor Wiskunde en Informatica, Amsterdam, 1990.

[Gla90b] R. van Glabbeek, The Linear Time - Branching Time Spectrum, in J.C.M. Baeten and J.W. Klop (eds) CONCUR'90, LNCS 458, pp. 278-297, 1990.

[Gra81] J. Grabowski, On Partial languages, Fundamenta Informaticae, Vol. IV.2, North Holland, Amsterdam, pp. 428-498, 1981.

[GS80] H.J. Genrich, E. Stankiewicz-Wiechno, A Dictionary of Some Basic Notations of Net Theory, in W. Brauer (ed.), "Net Theory and Applications", LNCS 84, pp. 519-535, 1980.

[GV87] R. van Glabbeek, F. Vandraager, Petri Net Models for Algebraic Theories of Concurrency, in J.W. de Bakker, A.J. Nijman, P.C. Treleaven (eds.), "Parallel Languages", LNCS 259, pp. 224-242, 1987.

[GW89a] R. van Glabbeek, W.P. Weijland, Branching Time and Abstraction in Bisimulation Semantics, (extended abstract), in G.X. Ritter (ed.), "Information Processing 89", North Holland, pp. 613-618, 1989.

[GW89b] R. van Glabbeek, W. Weijland, Refinement in Branching Time Semantics, in Proc. of the Int. Conf. on Algebraic Methodology and Software Technology, Iowa City, USA, pp. 197-201, 1989.

[Jan87] M. Jantzen, Language Theory of Petri Nets, in [BRR87], pp. 397-412, 1987.

[Hen88] M. Hennessy, Algebraic Theory of Processes, The MIT Press, 1988.

[Hoa78] C.A.R. Hoare, Communicating Sequential Processes, Communication of the ACM 21, Vol.8, pp. 666-677, 1978.

[Hoa81] C.A.R. Hoare, A Model for Communicating Sequential Processes, Technical Monograph, Prg 22, Comp. Lab., Univ. of Oxford, 1981.

[HM80] M. Hennessy, R. Milner, On Observing Non-Determinism and Concurrency, in J.W. de Bakker, J. van Leeuwen (eds.), "Automata Languages and Programming", LNCS 85, pp.299-309, 1980.

[HM85] M. Hennessy, R. Milner, Algebraic Laws for Nondeterminism and Concurrency, Journal of ACM 32, pp. 136-161, 1985.

[HO86] C.A.R. Hoare, E. R. Olderog Specification-oriented Semantics for Communicating Processes,

Acta Inf. 23, pp. 9-66, 1986.

[HR90] H.J. Hoogeboom, G. Rozenberg, Diamond Properties of State Spaces of Elementary Net Systems, Fundamenta Informaticae, North Holland, Amsterdam, 1990.

[Kie87] A. Kiehn, Infinitary partial Petri net languages and their relationship to other Petri net semantics, TUM Report - I8705, 1987.

[Lar87] K. G. Larsen, A Context-Dependent Bisimulation between Processes, TCS 49, 1987.

[Mar87] G. Marcon, TEBE: Tools for Exhibited-Behaviour Equivalence, DSI Technical Report, University of Milano, June1987.

[Maz77] A. Mazurkiewicz, Concurrent Program Schemes and Their Interpretation, DAIMI PB-78, Comp. Science Depart., Aarhus University, July 1977.

[Mil80] R. Milner, A Calculus of Communicating Systems, LNCS 92, 1980.

[Mil83] R. Milner, Calculi for Synchrony and Asynchrony, TCS 25, pp. 276 - 310, 1983.

[Mil84] R. Milner, A Complete Inference System for a Class of Regular Behaviours, JCSS Vol. 28 N. 3, pp. 439-466, 1984.

[Mil89a] R. Milner, A complete Axiomatization for Observational Congruence of Finite-State Behaviours, Information and Computation 81, pp. 227-247, 1989.

[Mil89b] R. Milner, Communication and Concurrency, Prentice Hall, 1989.

[Mul85] K. Mueller, Constructable Petri nets, Elektr. Informationverarbeitung und Kybernetik EIK 21,4/5, pp. 171-199, 1985.

[NRT90a] M. Nielsen, G. Rozenberg, P.S. Thiagarajan, Elementary Transition Systems, Tech. Report, Dept. of Computer Science, University of Leiden, 1990.

[NRT90b] M. Nielsen, G. Rozenberg, P.S. Thiagarajan, Elementary Transition Systems and Refinement, Tech. Report, Dept. of Computer Science, University of Leiden, 1990. (to appear in TCS)

[NT84] M. Nielsen, P.S. Thiagarajan, Degrees of Non-Determinism and Concurrency : a Petri Net view, in Mathai Josef, Rudrapatna Shyamasundar (eds.),"Foundations of Software Technology and Theoretical Computer Science", LNCS 181, pp. 89-117, 1984.

[Par81] D. Park, Concurrency and Automata on Infinite Sequences, Proc. 5th GI Conference, in P. Deusseu (ed.), "Theoretical Computer Science", LNCS 104, pp. 167-183, 1981.

[Pet73] C.A. Petri, Concepts in Net Theory, Mathematical Foundations of Computer Science: Proc. of Symposium and Summer School, High Tatras, sept. 1973, Math. Inst. of the Slovak Acad. of Sciences, pp. 137-146, 1973.

[Pet77a] C.A. Petri, General Net Theory, in B. Shaw (ed.), "Computing Systems Design", Proc. of the Joint IBM - University of Newcastle upon Tyne Seminar, Univ. Newcastle upon Tyne, 1977.

[Pet77b] C.A. Petri, Non-sequential Processes, ISF-Bericht ISF -77-5,.1977.

[Pete81] J. L. Peterson, Petri Nets Theory and Modelling of Systems, Englewood Cliffs, NJ, Prentice Hall, 1981

[Pnu85] A. Pnueli, Linear and Branching Structures in the Semantics and Logics of Reactive Systems, in W. Brauer (ed.), Proc. ICALP 85, LNCS 194, pp. 15-32, 1985.

[Pom84] L. Pomello, Some Equivalence Notions for Concurrent Systems: An Overview, GMD Report Nr.103, (1984); also in G.Rozenberg (ed.), APN'85, LNCS 222, pp. 381-400, 1986.

[Pom87] L. Pomello, Observing Net Behaviour, in K. Voss, H.J. Genrich, G. Rozenberg (eds.), "Concurrency and Nets", Springer Verlag, pp.403-421, 1987

[Pom88] L. Pomello, Osservatore, Reti di Petri, Processi, PhD Thesis Univ. of Milano and Torino, 1988.

[Pra86] V. Pratt, Modelling Concurrency with Partial Orders, Int. Journal of Parallel Programming Vol. 15 N.1, pp. 33-71, 1986.

[PS90] L. Pomello and C. Simone, A State Transformation Preorder over a Class of EN Systems, in G.

Rozenberg (ed.) APN'90, LNCS 483, pp.436-456, 1991.

[PS91] L. Pomello, C. Simone, An algebraic Characterization of EN System (observable) State Space, DSI Technical Report, University of Milano, January 1991 (to appear in Formal Aspects of Computing).

[PW86] L. Priese, U. Willecke-Klemmme, On State Equivalence Relations in Nondeterministic or Concurrent Systems, Univ. Paderborn, Reihe Theoretische Informatik, Bericht Nr. 34, December 1986.

[Rei85a] W. Reisig, Petri Nets: an Introduction, Springer Verlag, Berlin, 1985.

[Rei85b] W. Reisig, On the Semantics of Petri Nets, Formal Models in Programming, IFIP, 1985.

[Roz87] G. Rozenberg, Behaviour of Elementary Net Systems, in [BRR87], pp. 60 94, 1987.

[RS87] W. Reisig, E. Smith, The Semantics of a Net is a Net -An Exercise in General Net Theory, in K. Voss, H.J. Genrich, G. Rozenberg (eds.), "Concurrency and Nets", Springer Verlag, pp.461-480, 1987.

[RT88] A. Rabinovich, B.A.Trakhtenbrot, Behaviour Structures and Nets, Fundamenta Informaticae, Vol XI, N. 4, pp. 357-404, 1988.

[RT86] G. Rozenberg, P.S. Thiagarajan, Petri Nets: basic notions, structure, behaviour, in J.W. de Bakker, W.P. de Rover and G. Rozenberg (eds.), "Current Trends in Concurrency", LNCS 224, pp. 585-668, 1986.

[Sal85] A. Salomaa, Computation and Automata, Encyclopedia of Mathematics and its Applications Vol. 25, Cambridge Univ. Press, 1985.

[Sta81] P.H. Starke, Processes in Petri nets, Journal Inf. Process. Cybern. EIK, 17, pp. 389-416, 1981.

[SM83] I. Suzuki, T. Murata, A Method for Stepwise Refinement and Abstraction of Petri Nets, JCSS Vol. 27, pp. 51-76, 1983.

[Thi87] P.S. Thiagarajan, Elementary Net Systems, in [BRR87], pp. 26-59, 1987.

[TRH88] B.A. Trakhtenbrot, A. Rabinovich, J. Hirshfeld, Nets of Processes, Tech/Rep 97/88, Tel Aviv Univ., 1988.

[TV89] D. Taubner, W. Vogler, The Step Failure Semantics and Complete Proof System, Acta Inf. 27, pp. 125-156, 1989.

[Val79] R. Valette, Analysis of Petri Nets by Stepwise Refinements, JCSS Vol.18 , pp. 35-46, 1979.

[Vog87] W. Vogler, Behaviour preserving Refinements of Petri Nets, in Proc. 12th Int. Workshop on Graph Theoretic Concepts in Computer Science, LNCS 246, pp.82-93, 1987.

[Vog89] W. Vogler, Failures Semantics and Deadlocking of Modular Petri Nets, Acta Inf. 26, pp. 333-348, 1989.

[Vog90a] W. Vogler, Failures Semantics based on Interval Semiwords is a Congruence for Refinements, in C. Choffrut, T. Lengauer (eds.), Proc. STACS 90, LNCS 415, pp.285-297, 1990

[Vog90b] W. Vogler, Bisimulation and Action refinement, SFB-Bericht Nr. 342/10/90 A, TUM Munchen, May 1990.

[Vos87] K. Voss, Interface as a Basic Concept for Systems Specification and Verification, in K. Voss, H.J. Genrich, G. Rozenberg (eds.), "Concurrency and Nets", Springer Verlag, pp.585-604, 1987.

[Win80] G. Winskel, Events in Computation, Ph.D. Thesis, University of Edinburgh, Great Britain, 1980.

[Win87] G. Winskel, Event Structures, LNCS 235, pp. 325-392,1987.

[Wink89] J. Winkowski, An Equivalence of Communicating Processes in Distributed Environments, Fundamenta Informaticae XII, North Holland, Amsterdam, pp. 97-128, 1989.

Lecture Notes in Computer Science

For information about Vols. 1–529
please contact your bookseller or Springer-Verlag

Vol. 530: D. H. Pitt, P.-L. Curien, S. Abramsky, A. M. Pitts, A. Poigné, D. E. Rydeheard (Eds.), Category Theory and Computer Science. Proceedings, 1991. VII, 301 pages. 1991.

Vol. 531: E. M. Clarke, R. P. Kurshan (Eds.), Computer-Aided Verification. Proceedings, 1990. XIII, 372 pages. 1991.

Vol. 532: H. Ehrig, H.-J. Kreowski, G. Rozenberg (Eds.), Graph Grammars and Their Application to Computer Science. Proceedings, 1990. X, 703 pages. 1991.

Vol. 533: E. Börger, H. Kleine Büning, M. M. Richter, W. Schönfeld (Eds.), Computer Science Logic. Proceedings, 1990. VIII, 399 pages. 1991.

Vol. 534: H. Ehrig, K. P. Jantke, F. Orejas, H. Reichel (Eds.), Recent Trends in Data Type Specification. Proceedings, 1990. VIII, 379 pages. 1991.

Vol. 535: P. Jorrand, J. Kelemen (Eds.), Fundamentals of Artificial Intelligence Research. Proceedings, 1991. VIII, 255 pages. 1991. (Subseries LNAI).

Vol. 536: J. E. Tomayko, Software Engineering Education. Proceedings, 1991. VIII, 296 pages. 1991.

Vol. 537: A. J. Menezes, S. A. Vanstone (Eds.), Advances in Cryptology – CRYPTO '90. Proceedings. XIII, 644 pages. 1991.

Vol. 538: M. Kojima, N. Megiddo, T. Noma, A. Yoshise, A Unified Approach to Interior Point Algorithms for Linear Complementarity Problems. VIII, 108 pages. 1991.

Vol. 539: H. F. Mattson, T. Mora, T. R. N. Rao (Eds.), Applied Algebra, Algebraic Algorithms and Error-Correcting Codes. Proceedings, 1991. XI, 489 pages. 1991.

Vol. 540: A. Prieto (Ed.), Artificial Neural Networks. Proceedings, 1991. XIII, 476 pages. 1991.

Vol. 541: P. Barahona, L. Moniz Pereira, A. Porto (Eds.), EPIA '91. Proceedings, 1991. VIII, 292 pages. 1991. (Subseries LNAI).

Vol. 542: Z. W. Ras, M. Zemankova (Eds.), Methodologies for Intelligent Systems. Proceedings, 1991. X, 644 pages. 1991. (Subseries LNAI).

Vol. 543: J. Dix, K. P. Jantke, P. H. Schmitt (Eds.), Nonmonotonic and Inductive Logic. Proceedings, 1990. X, 243 pages. 1991. (Subseries LNAI).

Vol. 544: M. Broy, M. Wirsing (Eds.), Methods of Programming. XII, 268 pages. 1991.

Vol. 545: H. Alblas, B. Melichar (Eds.), Attribute Grammars , Applications and Systems. Proceedings, 1991. IX, 513 pages. 1991.

Vol. 546: O. Herzog, C.-R. Rollinger (Eds.), Text Understanding in LILOG. XI, 738 pages. 1991. (Subseries LNAI).

Vol. 547: D. W. Davies (Ed.), Advances in Cryptology – EUROCRYPT '91. Proceedings, 1991. XII, 556 pages. 1991.

Vol. 548: R. Kruse, P. Siegel (Eds.), Symbolic and Quantitative Approaches to Uncertainty. Proceedings, 1991. XI, 362 pages. 1991.

Vol. 549: E. Ardizzone, S. Gaglio, F. Sorbello (Eds.), Trends in Artificial Intelligence. Proceedings, 1991. XIV, 479 pages. 1991. (Subseries LNAI).

Vol. 550: A. van Lamsweerde, A. Fugetta (Eds.), ESEC '91. Proceedings, 1991. XII, 515 pages. 1991.

Vol. 551:S. Prehn, W. J. Toetenel (Eds.), VDM '91. Formal Software Development Methods. Volume 1. Proceedings, 1991. XIII, 699 pages. 1991.

Vol. 552: S. Prehn, W. J. Toetenel (Eds.), VDM '91. Formal Software Development Methods. Volume 2. Proceedings, 1991. XIV, 430 pages. 1991.

Vol. 553: H. Bieri, H. Noltemeier (Eds.), Computational Geometry - Methods, Algorithms and Applications '91. Proceedings, 1991. VIII, 320 pages. 1991.

Vol. 554: G. Grahne, The Problem of Incomplete Information in Relational Databases. VIII, 156 pages. 1991.

Vol. 555: H. Maurer (Ed.), New Results and New Trends in Computer Science. Proceedings, 1991. VIII, 403 pages. 1991.

Vol. 556: J.-M. Jacquet, Conclog: A Methodological Approach to Concurrent Logic Programming. XII, 781 pages. 1991.

Vol. 557: W. L. Hsu, R. C. T. Lee (Eds.), ISA '91 Algorithms. Proceedings, 1991. X, 396 pages. 1991.

Vol. 558: J. Hooman, Specification and Compositional Verification of Real-Time Systems. VIII, 235 pages. 1991.

Vol. 559: G. Butler, Fundamental Algorithms for Permutation Groups. XII, 238 pages. 1991.

Vol. 560: S. Biswas, K. V. Nori (Eds.), Foundations of Software Technology and Theoretical Computer Science. Proceedings, 1991. X, 420 pages. 1991.

Vol. 561: C. Ding, G. Xiao, W. Shan, The Stability Theory of Stream Ciphers. IX, 187 pages. 1991.

Vol. 562: R. Breu, Algebraic Specification Techniques in Object Oriented Programming Environments. XI, 228 pages. 1991.

Vol. 563: A. Karshmer, J. Nehmer (Eds.), Operating Systems of the 90s and Beyond. Proceedings, 1991. X, 285 pages. 1991.

Vol. 564: I. Herman, The Use of Projective Geometry in Computer Graphics. VIII, 146 pages. 1992.

Vol. 565: J. D. Becker, I. Eisele, F. W. Mündemann (Eds.), Parallelism, Learning, Evolution. Proceedings, 1989. VIII, 525 pages. 1991. (Subseries LNAI).

Vol. 566: C. Delobel, M. Kifer, Y. Masunaga (Eds.), Deductive and Object-Oriented Databases. Proceedings, 1991. XV, 581 pages. 1991.

Vol. 567: H. Boley, M. M. Richter (Eds.), Processing Declarative Kowledge. Proceedings, 1991. XII, 427 pages. 1991. (Subseries LNAI).

Vol. 568: H.-J. Bürckert, A Resolution Principle for a Logic with Restricted Quantifiers. X, 116 pages. 1991. (Subseries LNAI).

Vol. 569: A. Beaumont, G. Gupta (Eds.), Parallel Execution of Logic Programs. Proceedings, 1991. VII, 195 pages. 1991.

Vol. 570: R. Berghammer, G. Schmidt (Eds.), Graph-Theoretic Concepts in Computer Science. Proceedings, 1991. VIII, 253 pages. 1992.

Vol. 571: J. Vytopil (Ed.), Formal Techniques in Real-Time and Fault-Tolerant Systems. Proceedings, 1992. IX, 620 pages. 1991.

Vol. 572: K. U. Schulz (Ed.), Word Equations and Related Topics. Proceedings, 1990. VII, 256 pages. 1992.

Vol. 573: G. Cohen, S. N. Litsyn, A. Lobstein, G. Zémor (Eds.), Algebraic Coding. Proceedings, 1991. X, 158 pages. 1992.

Vol. 574: J. P. Banâtre, D. Le Métayer (Eds.), Research Directions in High-Level Parallel Programming Languages. Proceedings, 1991. VIII, 387 pages. 1992.

Vol. 575: K. G. Larsen, A. Skou (Eds.), Computer Aided Verification. Proceedings, 1991. X, 487 pages. 1992.

Vol. 576: J. Feigenbaum (Ed.), Advances in Cryptology - CRYPTO '91. Proceedings. X, 485 pages. 1992.

Vol. 577: A. Finkel, M. Jantzen (Eds.), STACS 92. Proceedings, 1992. XIV, 621 pages. 1992.

Vol. 578: Th. Beth, M. Frisch, G. J. Simmons (Eds.), Public-Key Cryptography: State of the Art and Future Directions. XI, 97 pages. 1992.

Vol. 579: S. Toueg, P. G. Spirakis, L. Kirousis (Eds.), Distributed Algorithms. Proceedings, 1991. X, 319 pages. 1992.

Vol. 580: A. Pirotte, C. Delobel, G. Gottlob (Eds.), Advances in Database Technology – EDBT '92. Proceedings. XII, 551 pages. 1992.

Vol. 581: J.-C. Raoult (Ed.), CAAP '92. Proceedings. VIII, 361 pages. 1992.

Vol. 582: B. Krieg-Brückner (Ed.), ESOP '92. Proceedings. VIII, 491 pages. 1992.

Vol. 583: I. Simon (Ed.), LATIN '92. Proceedings. IX, 545 pages. 1992.

Vol. 584: R. E. Zippel (Ed.), Computer Algebra and Parallelism. Proceedings, 1990. IX, 114 pages. 1992.

Vol. 585: F. Pichler, R. Moreno Díaz (Eds.), Computer Aided System Theory – EUROCAST '91. Proceedings. X, 761 pages. 1992.

Vol. 586: A. Cheese, Parallel Execution of Parlog. IX, 184 pages. 1992.

Vol. 587: R. Dale, E. Hovy, D. Rösner, O. Stock (Eds.), Aspects of Automated Natural Language Generation. Proceedings, 1992. VIII, 311 pages. 1992. (Subseries LNAI).

Vol. 588: G. Sandini (Ed.), Computer Vision – ECCV '92. Proceedings. XV, 909 pages. 1992.

Vol. 589: U. Banerjee, D. Gelernter, A. Nicolau, D. Padua (Eds.), Languages and Compilers for Parallel Computing. Proceedings, 1991. IX, 419 pages. 1992.

Vol. 590: B. Fronhöfer, G. Wrightson (Eds.), Parallelization in Inference Systems. Proceedings, 1990. VIII, 372 pages. 1992. (Subseries LNAI).

Vol. 591: H. P. Zima (Ed.), Parallel Computation. Proceedings, 1991. IX, 451 pages. 1992.

Vol. 592: A. Voronkov (Ed.), Logic Programming. Proceedings, 1991. IX, 514 pages. 1992. (Subseries LNAI).

Vol. 593: P. Loucopoulos (Ed.), Advanced Information Systems Engineering. Proceedings. XI, 650 pages. 1992.

Vol. 594: B. Monien, Th. Ottmann (Eds.), Data Structures and Efficient Algorithms. VIII, 389 pages. 1992.

Vol. 595: M. Levene, The Nested Universal Relation Database Model. X, 177 pages. 1992.

Vol. 596: L.-H. Eriksson, L. Hallnäs, P. Schroeder-Heister (Eds.), Extensions of Logic Programming. Proceedings, 1991. VII, 369 pages. 1992. (Subseries LNAI).

Vol. 597: H. W. Guesgen, J. Hertzberg, A Perspective of Constraint-Based Reasoning. VIII, 123 pages. 1992. (Subseries LNAI).

Vol. 598: S. Brookes, M. Main, A. Melton, M. Mislove, D. Schmidt (Eds.), Mathematical Foundations of Programming Semantics. Proceedings, 1991. VIII, 506 pages. 1992.

Vol. 599: Th. Wetter, K.-D. Althoff, J. Boose, B. R. Gaines, M. Linster, F. Schmalhofer (Eds.), Current Developments in Knowledge Acquisition - EKAW '92. Proceedings. XIII, 444 pages. 1992. (Subseries LNAI).

Vol. 600: J. W. de Bakker, K. Huizing, W. P. de Roever, G. Rozenberg (Eds.), Real-Time: Theory in Practice. Proceedings, 1991. VIII, 723 pages. 1992.

Vol. 601: D. Dolev, Z. Galil, M. Rodeh (Eds.), Theory of Computing and Systems. Proceedings, 1992. VIII, 220 pages. 1992.

Vol. 602: I. Tomek (Ed.), Computer Assisted Learning. Proceedigs, 1992. X, 615 pages. 1992.

Vol. 603: J. van Katwijk (Ed.), Ada: Moving Towards 2000. Proceedings, 1992. VIII, 324 pages. 1992.

Vol. 604: F. Belli, F.-J. Radermacher (Eds.), Industrial and Engineering Applications of Artificial Intelligence and Expert Systems. Proceedings, 1992. XV, 702 pages. 1992. (Subseries LNAI).

Vol. 605: D. Etiemble, J.-C. Syre (Eds.), PARLE '92. Parallel Architectures and Languages Europe. Proceedings, 1992. XVII, 984 pages. 1992.

Vol. 606: D. E. Knuth, Axioms and Hulls. IX, 109 pages. 1992.

Vol. 607: D. Kapur (Ed.), Automated Deduction – CADE-11. Proceedings, 1992. XV, 793 pages. 1992. (Subseries LNAI).

Vol. 608: C. Frasson, G. Gauthier, G. I. McCalla (Eds.), Intelligent Tutoring Systems. Proceedings, 1992. XIV, 686 pages. 1992.

Vol. 609: G. Rozenberg (Ed.), Advances in Petri Nets 1992. VIII, 472 pages. 1992.

Vol. 610: F. von Martial, Coordinating Plans of Autonomous Agents. XII, 246 pages. 1992. (Subseries LNAI).

Vol. 612: M. Tokoro, O. Nierstrasz, P. Wegner (Eds.), Object-Based Concurrent Computing. Proceedings, 1991. X, 265 pages. 1992.

Vol. 613: J. P. Myers, Jr., M. J. O'Donnell (Eds.), Constructivity in Computer Science. Proceedings, 1991. X, 247 pages. 1992.